EDITION
5

Psychology
Applied to Work

An Introduction to Industrial and Organizational Psychology

PAUL M. MUCHINSKY
University of North Carolina

Brooks/Cole Publishing Company
I**T**P® *An International Thomson Publishing Company*

Pacific Grove • Albany • Belmont • Bonn • Boston • Cincinnati • Detroit • Johannesburg • London
Madrid • Melbourne • Mexico City • New York • Paris • Singapore • Tokyo • Toronto • Washington

Sponsoring Editor: *Marianne Taflinger*
Marketing Team: *Gay Meixel, Deborah Petit*
Editorial Assistant: *Laura Donahue*
Production Editor: *Nancy L. Shammas*
Production Assistant: *Dorothy Bell*
Manuscript Editor: *Kay Mikel*
Permissions Editor: *Lillian Campobasso*
Interior Design: *Sharon Kinghan*

Interior Illustration: *LM Graphics*
Cover Design and Illustration: *Susan Horovitz*
Art Editor: *Kathy Joneson*
Photo Editor: *Robert Western*
Indexer: *DoMi Stauber*
Typesetting: *Weimer Graphics*
Cover Printing: *Phoenix Color Corporation, Inc.*
Printing and Binding: *Courier Westford, Inc.*

For more information, contact:

BROOKS/COLE PUBLISHING COMPANY
511 Forest Lodge Road
Pacific Grove, CA 93950
USA

International Thomson Publishing Europe
Berkshire House 168-173
High Holborn
London WC1V 7AA
England

Thomas Nelson Australia
102 Dodds Street
South Melbourne, 3205
Victoria, Australia

Nelson Canada
1120 Birchmount Road
Scarborough, Ontario
Canada M1K 5G4

International Thomson Editores
Seneca 53
Col. Polanco
México, D. F., México
C.P. 11560

International Thomson Publishing GmbH
Königswinterer Strasse 418
53227 Bonn
Germany

International Thomson Publishing Asia
221 Henderson Road
#05-10 Henderson Building
Singapore 0315

International Thomson Publishing Japan
Hirakawacho Kyowa Building, 3F
2-2-1 Hirakawacho
Chiyoda-ku, Tokyo 102
Japan

Printed in the United States of America

10   9   8   7   6   5   4   3   2

Library of Congress Cataloging-in-Publication Data

Muchinsky, Paul M.
    Psychology applied to work / by Paul M. Muchinsky. — 5th ed.
      p.   cm.
    Includes bibliographical references and index.
    ISBN 0-534-33876-3 (hardcover)
    1. Psychology, Industrial.   2. Organizational behavior.
  I. Title
  HF5548.8.M756   1996
  158.7—dc20   96-20143
                                                              CIP

Photo credits: pp. 1, 243, PhotoDisc, Inc.; p. 59, © Tony Freeman/PhotoEdit; p. 385, PhotoDisc, Inc. and Gazelle Technologies, Inc. "People in Business" photo CD collection.

To Noël

Life

RELATED TITLES

- *A Lifetime of Relationships* by Nelly Vanzetti and Steve Duck
- *Our Social World* by Donelson R. Forsyth
- *Psychological Testing* (3rd ed.) by Robert Kaplan and Dennis Saccuzzo
- *Psychology and the Legal System* (3rd ed.) by Larry Wrightsman, Michael Nietzel, and William Fortune
- *Training in Organizations* (3rd ed.) by Irwin L. Goldstein

ADVANCED SOCIAL PSYCHOLOGY TITLES

- *Group Process, Group Decision, Group Action* by Robert S. Baron, Norbert Kerr, and Norman Miller
- *Human Aggression* by Russell Geen
- *Negotiation in Social Conflict* by Dean G. Pruitt and Peter J. Carnevale
- *Social Psychology and Health* by Wolfgang Stroebe and Margaret S. Stroebe
- *Social Influence* by John Turner
- *Social Perception* by Leslie A. Zebrowitz
- *Relating to Others* by Steve Duck

PAUL M. MUCHINSKY

About the Author

Paul M. Muchinsky was born and raised in Connecticut. He received his B.A. degree in psychology from Gettysburg College, his M.S. degree in industrial/organizational psychology from Kansas State University, and his Ph.D. from Purdue University. He was a faculty member of Iowa State University for twenty years. In 1993 he was appointed the Joseph M. Bryan Distinguished Professor of Business at the University of North Carolina at Greensboro. Throughout his career, Dr. Muchinsky has been very active in a wide range of professional activities within the field of industrial/organizational psychology. Many of the cases and examples of concepts presented in this book come directly from his professional experiences. When not engaged as an I/O psychologist, Dr. Muchinsky fantasizes about playing baseball for the New York Yankees.

Brief
Contents

Contents

Preface

This is the 5th edition of *Psychology Applied to Work: An Introduction to Industrial and Organizational Psychology*. Some editions call for minor surgery and fine tuning, while others require a major revision. This edition represents great changes in the book, commensurate with the great changes occurring in the field of I/O psychology as well as in the world of work. Four totally new chapters were written. There were substantial revisions in a few chapters and major revisions in most chapters. Two chapters from the previous edition were dropped, reflecting the changing focus of the field. For the first time this edition also contains a final chapter that offers a glimpse into the future of work and how it will change the substance of I/O psychology. In addition to the reorganization of content throughout this book, sections of new material are as follows:

Chapter 1: Historical Background of I/O Psychology
• Cross-cultural I/O psychology

Chapter 2: Research Methods in I/O Psychology
• Discussion of observation, questionnaire, and computer simulation as research methods
• Making causal inferences in research
• Expanded discussion of meta-analysis

Chapter 3: Criteria: Standards for Decision Making
• Use of subject matter experts (SMEs) as sources of job information
• Discussion of dynamic criteria
• Advances in criterion conceptualization

Chapter 4: Predictors: Psychological Assessments
• Updated sources of information about tests
• Current research on the predictive efficiency of *g*

- Recent advances in personality inventories, integrity tests, and biographical inventories
- Physical ability testing
- Drug testing

Chapter 5: Personnel Decisions
- Legal foundation of personnel decisions including ADA and the Civil Rights Act of 1991
- Recent advances in validity generalization
- Issues in the determination of the cut-off score
- Banding of test scores
- Social validity in assessment
- Recent advances in placement and classification

Chapter 6: Training and Development
- Recent advances on the relationship between learning and task performance
- Strategic organizational value of training and development
- Recent advances in organizational analysis and KSA analysis
- Advances in simulation as a training method
- Managerial development
- Cultural diversity training
- Sexual harassment
- 360-degree feedback
- Mentoring
- Importance of the posttraining environment

Chapter 7: Performance Appraisal
- Recent advances in halo error and rater training
- Rater motivation
- Contextual performance

Chapter 8: Organizations and Teams (new chapter)
- Mintzberg's theory of organization
- Reorganizing and downsizing
- Work teams
- Decision making in teams
- Principles of teamwork
- Personnel selection for teams

Chapter 9: Organizational Behavior (new chapter)
- Organizational justice
- Organizational citizenship behavior
- The psychological contract
- Individual responses to downsizing
- Psychology of mergers and acquisitions
- Violence in the workplace

Chapter 10: Stress and Well-Being at Work (new chapter)
- Environmental influences on mental health
- The concept of mental health

- Dispositional factors in mental health
- Work stress
- Sick building syndrome
- Work/family conflict
- Dual-career families
- Psychological effects of unemployment

Chapter 11: Work Motivation
- Five critical concepts to work motivation
- Recent advances in motivational theories
- Kanfer's integration of motivational theories

Chapter 12: Leadership
- Recent advances in major theoretical approaches to leadership
- Points of convergence and divergence among leadership issues
- Cross-cultural leadership
- Diversity issues in leadership

Chapter 13: Job Design and Organizational Development
- Organizational implications of job redesign
- Organizational culture change
- Total quality management

Chapter 14: Union/Management Relations
- Socialization processes in unions
- Union influence on employee involvement
- Recent advances in union commitment

Chapter 15: Ergonomics and Work Conditions
- Recent advances in psychological approaches to accident reduction
- Recent advances in shift work
- Alcoholism and drug abuse in the workplace

Chapter 16: The Changing Nature of Work (new chapter)
- How the changing nature of work affects individuals, work, and society

I felt it advisable to make such comprehensive changes in *Psychology Applied to Work* to remain congruent with the evolution of the field of I/O psychology. More than 300 new studies representing the most recent findings and issues were referenced in this edition. I do hope you find that the changes enhance the value of the book. However, the book also retains many of the standard features found in previous editions, such as field notes, case studies, figures, and cartoons. Chapter objectives now appear in the front of the chapter to prepare the student for what is to come. Highly relevant field notes have again been strategically placed in the text to animate the relevance of I/O psychology to the world of work. Case studies are presented at the end of each chapter, illustrating and illuminating concepts discussed in the text. Responding to the questions accompanying each case compels the reader to understand the complexity of workplace issues. Five new case studies were written for this edition.

Acknowledgments

The revisions were guided by many insightful comments provided by the reviewers. I would like to express my sincere gratitude to them for their time and effort. They were: Terry Beehr, Central Michigan University; John Binning, Illinois State University; Kim Buch, University of North Carolina; Leslie Hammer, Portland State University; Bruce H. Johnson, Gustavus Adolphus College; Howard J. Klein, Ohio State University; Michael McCall, Ithaca College; Tom Mitchell, University of Baltimore; Craig D. Parks, Washington State University; Steven G. Rogelberg, Bowling Green State University; and Howard Tokunaga, San Jose State University. Finally, if you are lucky in life you will have the pleasure of working with an artisan of his or her craft. Not just an expert, but a craftmaster. I have been fortunate enough to have such a secretary for this edition. My secretary, Lynn Baird, elevated the process of manuscript development to new heights. Because she was so good at what she does, I could concentrate my efforts exclusively on writing, Thank you, Lynn.

Available Supplements

Two supplemental aids have been developed for *Psychology Applied to Work*. One is a *Student Workbook*, which contains many features designed to enhance learning for the student through problem exercises, case studies, definitions of terms, and practical applications. The *Workbook* brings greater life to the material presented in the text. Second, an *Instructor's Manual* has been developed that presents chapter objectives, diagrams that can be used as overhead transparencies, essay test questions, and other instructional aids. Also included is a computerized test bank of multiple choice test questions. I am very indebted to two of my friends and former students, Dr. Marc Marchese and Dr. Connie Wanberg, for developing these supplements. Their high professional standards for quality continue to manifest themselves in these works. Collectively, the textbook, student workbook, and instructor's manual offer a comprehensive pedagogical approach for learning and teaching I/O psychology. Marc, Connie, and I would welcome any feedback you care to offer on our efforts.

Obesa interum cantavit!

Paul M. Muchinsky

THE FOUNDATIONS OF INDUSTRIAL/ ORGANIZATIONAL (I/O) PSYCHOLOGY

CHAPTER 1

The Historical Background of I/O Psychology

Major Chapter Objectives

- Understand how I/O psychology relates to the profession of psychology as a whole.

- Be able to identify the major fields of I/O psychology.

- Understand how and why psychologists are licensed and certified.

- Learn the history of I/O psychology, including major people, events, and eras.

- Understand why cross-cultural interests are important in I/O psychology.

MISS PEACH   SOURCE: By permission of Mell Lazarus and Creators Syndicate.

Psychology is defined as the scientific study of behavior. It is a complex discipline examining the behavior of both animals and humans. It is a science because psychologists use the same rigorous methods of research found in other areas of scientific investigation. Some psychological research is more biological in nature (such as the effects of brain lesions on a rat's food consumption). Other research is more social in nature (such as identifying the factors that lead to bystander apathy). Because psychology covers such a broad spectrum of content areas, it is difficult to have a clear and accurate image of what a psychologist does. Many people think that every psychologist "is a shrink," "has a black couch," "likes to discover what makes people tick," and so on. In fact, these statements usually refer to the specialty of clinical psychology—the diagnosis and treatment of mental illness or abnormal behavior. Most psychologists do not treat mental disorders, nor do they practice psychotherapy. In reality, psychologists are a very diversified lot with many specialized interests.

Many psychologists are united professionally through membership in the American Psychological Association (APA), founded in 1892. As of 1996, there were more than 72,000 members, 58% men and 42% women. The diversification of interest among psychologists is reflected in the 49 divisions of the APA, each representing a special-interest subgroup. Matarazzo (1987) notes there are not really 49 different specialty areas of psychology, just many fields in which the same basic psychological principles are applied. Some members have no divisional affiliation, but others belong to more than one. The APA publishes several journals—vehicles through which psychologists can communicate their research findings to other scholars. The APA also holds regional and national conventions, sets standards for graduate training in certain areas of psychology (that is, clinical, counseling, and school), develops and enforces a code of professional ethics, and helps psychologists find employment.

In 1988 the American Psychological Society (APS) was founded, in part because the membership and emphasis of the APA had shifted significantly toward the health care practice areas of psychology. The purpose of the APS is to advance the discipline of psychology primarily from a scientific perspective. As of 1993 the APS had approximately 15,000 members.

Both the APA and the APS have three classes of membership. An associate has a minimum of either two years of graduate work in psychology or a master's degree in psychology. A member has a Ph.D. degree based in part on a psychological dissertation. A fellow has a Ph.D. degree, a minimum of five years' subsequent professional experience, and is judged to have made exceptional scientific contributions in his or her area of expertise. Colleges and universities employ the greatest number of psychologists, followed by those who work in independent practice. Most psychologists who specialize in basic areas (for example, experimental, social, developmental) are employed in colleges or universities. Many applied psychologists (those with training in clinical, counseling, industrial/organizational, school) work in nonacademic settings. In summary, psychology is a complex and varied profession whose members work in a wide variety of jobs.

Industrial/Organizational Psychology

One of the specialty areas of psychology is industrial/organizational (I/O) psychology (represented by Division 14 of the APA, the Society for Industrial-Organizational Psychology). In 1996 there were about 2,500 members of Division 14, 71% male and 29% female. However, the percentage of women entering the field has accelerated in recent years. For example, in 1989 almost half (46%) of those receiving doctorates in I/O psychology were women (Howard, 1990). All members of the Society for Industrial-Organizational Psychology (SIOP), the primary professional organization for I/O psychologists in this nation, must be members of either the APA or the APS.

I wish I could say that becoming an I/O psychologist was my childhood ambition, but such was not the case. I originally wanted to be a chemist, but in college it soon became apparent that I lacked the skills and talents needed for that discipline. By accident I took an introductory psychology course taught by an I/O psychologist. I was so impressed by his teaching that I wanted to emulate him and soon embarked on a new career. My happenstance entry into the field places me in some distinguished company. Stagner (1981) reported that industrial psychology was the second career choice of many past presidents of Division 14 of the APA. Like me, they gave circumstance or luck as the reason for "finding" I/O psychology. Perhaps this book will serve as a catalyst for some students to select a career in I/O psychology rationally rather than depending on fate.

A master's degree is necessary to qualify as an I/O psychologist (and for membership in Division 14 of the APA). However, many obtain a Ph.D. degree, which gives them more expertise and professional mobility. Approximately 3% of all psychologists are in the I/O area. Our relatively small representation in the total population of psychologists probably contributes to why some people are unaware of industrial/organizational psychology. Unlike some areas of psychology, job opportunities are extremely good for I/O psychologists.

As a specialty area, I/O psychology has a more restricted definition than psychology as a whole. Guion (1965) defines industrial/organizational psychology as "the scientific study of the relationship between man and the world at work: the study of the adjustment people make to the places they go, the people they meet, and the things they do in the process of making a living" (p. 817). Blum and Naylor (1968) define it as "simply the application or extension of psychological facts and principles to the problems concerning human beings operating within

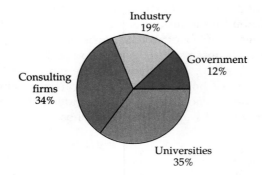

Figure 1–1   *Principal work settings of I/O psychologists*
SOURCE: APA, "Profile of Division 14 Members: 1993." Reprinted by permission of the author.

the context of business and industry" (p. 4). Broadly speaking, the I/O psychologist is concerned with behavior in work situations. There are two sides of I/O psychology: science and practice. I/O psychology is a legitimate field of scientific inquiry, concerned with advancing knowledge about people at work. As in any area of science, questions are posed by I/O psychologists to guide their investigations, and scientific methods are used to obtain answers. They try to form the results of studies into meaningful patterns that will be useful in explaining behavior and to replicate findings to make generalizations about behavior. In this respect, I/O psychology is an academic discipline.

The other side of I/O psychology—the professional side—is concerned with applying knowledge to solve real problems in the world of work. I/O psychological research findings can be used to hire better employees, reduce absenteeism, improve communication, increase job satisfaction, and solve countless other problems. Most I/O psychologists feel a sense of kinship with both sides, science and practice.

As an I/O psychologist, I am pleased that the results of my research can be put to some practical use. But by the same token, I am more than a technician—someone who goes through the motions of solving problems without knowing why they "work" and what their consequences will be. I/O psychology is more than just a tool for business leaders to use to make their companies more efficient. So the I/O psychologist has a dual existence. The well-trained I/O psychologist realizes that effective applications can come only from a sound knowledge base. I/O psychologists contribute both to knowledge and to the application of that knowledge.

Figure 1–1 shows the main work settings of I/O psychologists. They are represented across four areas, with universities and consulting firms being the primary employers, although industry employment has declined in recent years as many corporations have downsized their professional staffs. But across these four areas, I/O psychologists are unevenly split as to their scientist/practitioner orientation. Universities employ more scientists; consulting firms employ more practitioners; industry and government have a good mix of both.

This orientation difference has caused many problems in deciding the best way to train I/O psychologists. Should graduate programs train students as scientists or as practitioners? This question is important because practitioners need certain skills to be successful that scientists do not, and vice versa (Mayfield, 1975). Such I/O psychologists as Meyer (1972), Naylor (1970), and Muchinsky (1973) have discussed the consequences of poorly trained students, the product of unintelligent handling of this dualism issue. Although many "solutions" to the problem have been proposed (Task Force on the Practice of Psychology in Industry, 1971), no final blueprint has yet been devised. Some psychologists recommend adopting a strict "scientist" model of graduate training for all students. Others have proposed the separation of academic and professional training. I prefer the scientist end of the continuum for graduate training, but students who wish to become practitioners should have a chance to serve as interns in business or industry during this period (Muchinsky, 1976). Although training to become an I/O psychologist is an arduous process, the rewards in terms of challenging work, intellectual stimulation, and feelings of accomplishment are great.

(*Fields of I/O Psychology*)

#1

Like psychology in general, I/O psychology is a diversified science containing several subspecialties. Personnel psychology and organizational behavior dominate the field, but the other subspecialty areas are also relevant. Let's take a closer look at this diversity.

Personnel Psychology. The word *personnel* means people. So personnel psychology is concerned with all aspects of applied individual differences. Among other things, personnel psychologists determine what human skills and talents are needed for certain jobs, how to assess potential employees, how to grade employee job performance, and how to train workers to improve job performance. Personnel psychology is one of the oldest and most traditional activities of I/O psychologists. In fact, for many years personnel psychology and I/O psychology were synonymous. It was only after other topics caught the interest of I/O psychologists that personnel psychology became just one subspecialty of the total profession.

Organizational Behavior. We know that organizations can influence the attitudes and behaviors of people associated with them, and almost all employees work within some organizational context. Work in this area focuses on such factors as role-related behavior, pressures that groups can impose on individuals, personal feelings of commitment to an organization, and patterns of communication within an organization. There is a strong social influence in organizational behavior research because organizations are social collectivities. At the risk of overgeneralizing, personnel psychology is more concerned with individual-level issues (for example, who gets hired and who doesn't); organizational behavior is more concerned with social and group influences.

✳ *Ergonomics.* Ergonomics concerns the understanding of human performance in person-machine systems, including the design of equipment and machinery to enhance worker productivity and safety. Most tools, equipment, and machines are designed for a human to operate. However, humans have limitations of strength, reaction time, coordination, sensory acuity, and so on. No one benefits if a machine's demands exceed the limits of human capabilities. Ergonomics tries to modify the work environment to be compatible with human skills and talents. *Human factors psychology* and *engineering psychology* are also names for this specialized field.

✳ *Vocational and Career Counseling.* This subspecialty is a cross between counseling and I/O psychology; the counseling applies to people's problems at work. Industrial-oriented counselors help employees choose a rewarding and satisfying career path, resolve conflicts between work and nonwork interests, adjust to changing career interests, and prepare for retirement. I/O psychologists in this area may research these issues, or they may work for large organizations as in-house staff counselors.

✳ *Organization Development.* I/O psychologists in this area are concerned with improving or changing (that is, "developing") organizations to make them more efficient. The I/O psychologist must be able to diagnose an organization's problems, recommend or enact changes, and then assess the effectiveness of the changes. Organization development involves the planned, deliberate change of an organization to resolve a particular problem; the change may involve people, work procedures, or technology. Organization development provides an exciting opportunity for some I/O psychologists to help organizations resolve or adapt to their problems.

✳ *Industrial Relations.* The final specialty area of I/O psychology is industrial relations. Industrial relations deals with problems between employers and employees and usually involves a labor union. I/O psychologists interested in industrial relations address such issues as cooperation and conflict between work parties, resolution of disputes in the work force, and bargaining or negotiation of agreements between various segments of the work force. I/O psychologists in this area have close contact with specialists in labor relations—that is, people with knowledge of federal and state laws on employee rights, collective bargaining, and dispute settlement. Industrial relations is heavily legislated, and a person who works in this area must have knowledge of these laws.

In summary, psychology as a discipline is composed of many specialty areas, one of which is I/O psychology. And I/O psychology consists of several subspecialties. Although some of these subspecialties overlap, many are quite distinct from one another. Thus, I/O psychology is not really a single discipline. It is a mix of subspecialties bonded together by a concern for people at work. Each of the subspecialties of I/O psychology will be explored to various degrees in this book.

Licensing and Certification of Psychologists

What makes a psychologist a psychologist? What prevents people with no psychological training from passing themselves off as psychologists? One way professions offer high-quality service to the public is by regulating their own membership. Selective admission into the profession helps protect the public against quacks and charlatans who risk great damage not only to their clients but also to the profession they allegedly represent.

The practice of professional psychology is regulated by law in every state. When both the title and practice of psychology are regulated, the law is called a *licensing law.* When only the title of psychologist is regulated, the law is called a *certification law* (Hess, 1977). Laws limit licensure to those qualified to practice psychology as defined by state law. Each state has its own standards for licensure, and these are governed by regulatory boards. The major functions of any professional board are to determine the standards for admission into the profession and to conduct disciplinary actions involving violations of professional standards.

Typically, licensure involves educational, experience, examination, and administrative requirements. A doctoral degree in psychology from an approved program is usually required, as well as one or two years of supervised experience. Applicants must also pass an objective, written examination covering all areas of psychology. Specialty examinations (for example, in I/O psychology) usually are not given. Currently, psychologists must pass a uniform national examination to obtain a license (Hoffman, 1980). Finally, the applicant must meet citizenship and residency requirements and be of good moral character.

Licensing and certification are intended to ensure that clients receive services from qualified practitioners (Fretz & Mills, 1980). However, scrupulous I/O psychologists can never guarantee results, and they should never try. Companies have been duped by consulting firms and individuals into believing a wide range of claims that simply cannot be substantiated. The problems the I/O psychologist faces are too complex for guarantees. Reasonable expectations on the part of both the I/O psychologists and the company are the best way to avoid such difficulties.

There is currently a controversy regarding the licensure of I/O psychologists. The original purpose of licensure was to protect the public in the health care areas of psychology, such as clinical and counseling. Because I/O psychologists are not health care providers, there is not as pressing a need for licensure to protect the public (Howard & Lowman, 1985). Most states regard I/O psychologists as they do other types of applied psychologists who offer services to the public and thus require them to be licensed. However, some states regard I/O psychologists as having a sufficiently different mandate to prohibit them from obtaining licensure.

The History of I/O Psychology

It is always difficult to write *the* history of anything—there are different perspectives with different emphases. It is also a challenge to divide the historical evolution of a discipline into units of time. In some cases, time itself is a convenient watershed (decades or centuries); in others, major events serve as landmarks. In the case of I/O psychology, the two world wars were major catalysts for changing the discipline. This historical overview will show how the field of I/O psychology came to be what it is and how some key individuals and events helped shape it.[1]

The Early Years (1900–1916)

In its beginnings, what we know today as I/O psychology didn't even have a name—it was a merging of two forces that gathered momentum before 1900. One force was the pragmatic nature of some basic psychological research. Most psychologists at this time were strictly scientific and deliberately avoided studying problems that strayed outside the boundaries of pure research. However, a psychologist named W. L. Bryan published a paper (Bryan & Harter, 1897) about how professional telegraphers develop skill in sending and receiving Morse code. A few years later in 1903, Bryan's presidential address to the American Psychological Association (Bryan, 1904) touched on having psychologists study "concrete activities and functions as they appear in everyday life" (p. 80). Bryan did not advocate studying problems found in industry per se; rather, he stressed examining real skills as a base upon which to develop scientific psychology. Bryan is not considered the father of I/O psychology but rather is considered a precursor.[2]

The second major force in the evolution of the discipline came from the desire of industrial engineers to improve efficiency. They were concerned mainly with the economics of manufacturing and thus the productivity of industrial employees. A husband and wife team, Frank and Lillian Gilbreth, contributed pioneering knowledge about time and motion in industrial production. They are perhaps best known for their research on the elements of human motion, which they called "therbligs" (Gilbreth spelled backwards, almost). Thus, merging psychology with applied interests and a concern for increasing industrial efficiency was the principal ingredient in the emergence of I/O psychology. By 1910, "industrial psychology" (the "organizational" appendage did not become official until 1970) was a legitimate specialty area of psychology.

Three individuals stand out as the founding fathers of I/O psychology. They worked independently; in fact, their work barely overlapped. The major contributions of these individuals deserve a brief review.

Walter Dill Scott.   Scott, a psychologist, was persuaded to give a talk to some Chicago business leaders on the need for applying psychology to advertising. His talk was well received and led to the publication of two books, *The Theory of Advertising* (1903) and *The Psychology of Advertising* (1908). The first book dealt

---

[1] A more detailed treatment of the history of I/O psychology can be found in the excellent books by Ferguson (1962) and Napoli (1981), and the article by Katzell and Austin (1992).

[2] The term *industrial psychology* was apparently used for the first time in Bryan's 1904 article. Ironically, it appeared in print only as a typographical error. Bryan was quoting a sentence he had written five years earlier (Bryan & Harter, 1899) in which he spoke of the need for more research in individual psychology. Instead, Bryan wrote industrial psychology and did not catch his mistake.

Walter Dill Scott
SOURCE: Archives of the History of American Psychology

with suggestion and argument as means of influencing people. The second book was aimed at improving human efficiency with such tactics as imitation, competition, loyalty, and concentration. By 1911, he had increased his areas of interest and published two more books, *Influencing Men in Business* and *Increasing Human Efficiency in Business.* During World War I, Scott was instrumental in the application of personnel procedures within the army.

Frederick W. Taylor.   Taylor was an engineer by profession. His formal schooling was limited, but through experience and self-training in engineering he went on to obtain many patents. As he worked himself up through one company, from worker, to supervisor, and finally to plant manager, Taylor realized the value of redesigning the work situation to achieve both higher output for the company and a higher wage for the worker. His best-known work is *The Principles of Scientific Management* (1911). These principles were (1) scientifically designing work methods for efficiency; (2) selecting the best workers and training them in new methods; (3) developing a cooperative spirit between managers and workers; and (4) sharing the responsibility of the design and conduct of work between management and worker. In perhaps the most famous example of his methods, Taylor showed that workers who handled heavy iron ingots (pig iron) could be more productive through the use of work rests. Training employees when to work and when to rest increased average worker productivity from 12.5 to 47.0 tons moved per day (with less reported fatigue), which resulted in increased wages for them. The company also drastically increased efficiency by reducing costs from 9.2 cents per ton to 3.9 cents per ton.

As a consequence of this method, it was charged that Taylor inhumanely

Frederick W. Taylor
SOURCE: Stevens Institute of Technology

exploited workers for a higher wage and that great numbers of workers would be unemployed because fewer were needed. Because unemployment was rampant at this time, the attacks on Taylor were virulent. His methods were eventually investigated by the Interstate Commerce Commission (ICC) and the U.S. House of Representatives. Taylor replied that increased efficiency led to greater, not less, prosperity, and that workers not hired for one job would be placed in another that would better use their potential. The arguments were never really resolved—World War I broke out, and the controversy faded.

Hugo Münsterberg.   Münsterberg was a German psychologist with traditional academic training. The noted American psychologist William James invited Münsterberg to Harvard University, where he applied his experimental methods to a variety of problems, including perception and attention. He was a popular figure in American education, a gifted public speaker, and a personal friend of President Theodore Roosevelt. Münsterberg was interested in applying traditional psychological methods to practical industrial problems. His book *Psychology and Industrial Efficiency* (1913) was divided into three parts: selecting workers, designing work situations, and using psychology in sales. One of Münsterberg's most renowned studies involved determining what makes a safe trolley car operator. He systematically studied all aspects of the job, developed an ingenious laboratory simulation of a trolley car, and concluded that a good operator could comprehend simultaneously all of the influences that bear on the car's progress. Some writers consider Münsterberg the father of industrial psychology. Landy (1992) reported that many prominent I/O psychologists throughout the course of the 20th century can trace their professional roots back to Münsterberg. Münsterberg's influence

Hugo Münsterberg

throughout the history of the field is well evidenced by the coterie of I/O psychologists who were guided by his teachings.

When World War I broke out in Europe, Münsterberg supported the German cause. He was ostracized for his allegiance, and the emotional strain probably contributed to his death in 1916. Münsterberg's sudden departure from the field of industrial psychology created a scientific vacuum, as he left no colleagues behind to continue his work. Only the U.S. involvement in the war gave some unity to the profession. The primary emphasis of the early work in I/O psychology was on the economic gains that could be accrued by applying the ideas and methods of psychology to problems in business and industry. Business leaders began to employ psychologists, and some psychologists entered applied research. However, World War I caused a shift in the direction of industrial psychological research.

World War I (1917–1918)

World War I was a potent impetus to psychology's rise to respectability. Psychologists believed they could provide a valuable service to the nation, and some saw the war as a means of accelerating the profession's progress. Robert Yerkes was the psychologist most instrumental in getting psychology into the war. As president of the APA, he maneuvered the profession into assignments in the war effort. The APA suggested many proposals, including ways of screening recruits for mental deficiency and of assigning selected recruits to jobs within the army. Committees of psychologists investigated soldier motivation, morale, psychological problems of physical incapacity, and discipline. Yerkes continued to press his point that psychology could be of great help to our nation in wartime.

The army, in turn, was somewhat skeptical of the psychologists' claims. It eventually approved only a modest number of proposals, mostly involving assessment of recruits. Yerkes and other psychologists reviewed a series of general intelligence tests and eventually developed one that they called the Army Alpha. When they discovered that 30% of the recruits were illiterate, they developed the Army Beta, a special test for those who couldn't read English. Meanwhile, Walter Scott was doing research on the best placement of soldiers in the army. He classified and placed enlisted soldiers, conducted performance ratings of officers, and developed and prepared job duties and qualifications for more than 500 jobs.

Plans for testing recruits proceeded at a slow pace. The army instructed its camps to build special testing sites and ordered all existing officers, officer candidates, and newly drafted recruits to be tested. Both the Army Alpha and Beta group intelligence tests were used, as were a few individual tests. The final order authorizing the testing program came from the adjutant general's office in August 1918. However, the Armistice was signed only three months later, and World War I was over. Testing was terminated just as it was finally organized and authorized. As a result, the intelligence testing program didn't contribute as much to the war as Yerkes would have liked. Even though 1,726,000 individuals were ultimately tested in the program, actual use of the results was minimal.

Although psychology's impact on the war effort was not substantial, the very process of giving psychologists so much recognition and authority was a great impetus to the profession. Psychologists were regarded as capable of making valuable contributions to society and of adding to a company's (and in war, a nation's) prosperity. Also in 1917, the oldest and most representative journal in the field of I/O psychology, the *Journal of Applied Psychology*, began publication. Some of the articles in the first volume included "Practical Relations Between Psychology and the War" by Hall, "Mentality Testing of College Students" by Bingham, and "The Moron as a War Problem" by Mateer. The first article published in the *Journal of Applied Psychology* not only summarized the prevailing state of industrial psychology at the time but also addressed the science-versus-practice issue that still faces I/O psychologists today.

> The past few years have witnessed an unprecedented interest in the extension of the application of psychology to various fields of human activity. . . . But perhaps the most strikingly original endeavor to utilize the methods and the results of psychological investigation has been in the realm of business. This movement began with the psychology of advertising. . . . Thence the attention of the applied psychologist turned to the more comprehensive and fundamental problem of vocational selection—the question, namely, of making a detailed inventory of the equipment of mental qualities possessed by a given individual, of discovering what qualities are essential to successful achievement in a given vocation, and thus of directing the individual to the vocational niche which he is best fitted to fill. . . . Every psychologist who besides being a "pure scientist" also cherishes the hope that in addition to throwing light upon the problems of his science, his findings may also contribute their quota to the sum-total of human happiness; and it must appeal to every human being who is interested in increasing human efficiency and human happiness by the more direct method of decreasing the number of cases where a square peg is condemned to a life of fruitless endeavor to fit itself comfortably into a round hole. (Hall, Baird, & Geissler, 1917, pp. 5–6)

After the war, there was a boom in the number of psychological consulting firms and research bureaus. The birth of these agencies ushered in the next era in I/O psychology.

Between the Wars (1919–1940)

Applied psychology emerged from the war as a recognized discipline. Society was beginning to realize that industrial psychology could solve practical problems. Following the war, several psychological research bureaus came into full bloom. The Bureau of Salesmanship Research was developed by Walter Bingham at the Carnegie Institute of Technology. There was little precedent for this kind of cooperation between college and industry. The bureau intended to solve problems with psychological research techniques, problems that had never been examined scientifically. Twenty-seven companies cooperated with Bingham, each contributing $500 annually to finance applied psychological research. One of the early products of the bureau was a book, *Aids in Selecting Salesmen*. For several years, the bureau concentrated on selection, classification, and development of clerical and executive personnel as well as salespeople. When the Carnegie Institute stopped offering graduate work in psychology, the bureau was disbanded.

Another influential company during the period was the Psychological Corporation, founded by James Cattell in 1921. Cattell formed it as a business corporation and asked psychologists to buy stock in it. Its purpose was to advance psychology and promote its usefulness to industry. The corporation also served as a clearinghouse for information. As protection against quacks and charlatans, who were becoming increasingly prevalent, it provided companies with reference checks on any prospective psychologists. Unlike many agencies at the time, the Psychological Corporation remained in business. Over the years it changed its early mission, and today it is one of the country's largest publishers of psychological tests.

During the 1920s, the emphasis of industrial psychology was on testing, but the focus switched from mental testing of people in a laboratory setting to employment testing of industrial workers in field settings. The *Journal of Personnel Research* (later renamed *Personnel Journal*) began in this era and has remained useful, especially for practitioners. Also the term *industrial psychology* achieved its own identity, as evidenced by the book by Viteles (1932).

In 1924 a series of experiments began at the Hawthorne Works of the Western Electric Company. Although they seemed to be initially of minor scientific significance, they became classics in industrial psychology. In the opinion of many writers, the Hawthorne studies "represent the most significant research program undertaken to show the enormous complexity of the problem of production in relation to efficiency" (Blum & Naylor, 1968, p. 306).

The Hawthorne studies were a joint venture between Western Electric and several researchers from Harvard University (none of whom were industrial psychologists by training). The original study attempted to find the relationship between lighting and efficiency. The researchers installed various sets of lights in workrooms where electrical equipment was being produced. In some cases, the light was intense; in other cases, it was reduced to the equivalent of moonlight.

Much to the researchers' surprise, productivity seemed to have no relationship to the level of illumination. The workers' productivity increased or remained at a satisfactory level whether the illumination was decreased, increased, or held constant. The results of the study were so bizarre that the researchers hypothesized some other factors as being responsible for productivity.

The results of the first study initiated four other major studies over a 12-year period: (1) relay assembly test room, (2) mass interviewing program, (3) bank wiring observation room, and (4) personnel counseling. (For more information on these studies, see the original text by Roethlisberger and Dickson, 1939.) In essence, the Hawthorne studies revealed many previously unrecognized aspects of human behavior in a workplace. Researchers hypothesized that the study's results were caused by the employees' desire to please them. Flattered at having distinguished investigators from Harvard University take the time to study them, the workers had gone out of their way to do what they thought would impress them—namely, to be highly productive. They therefore had produced a lot whether the room was too light or too dark. The researchers learned that factors other than purely technical ones (like illumination) influence productivity.

One of the major findings from the studies was a phenomenon labeled the *Hawthorne effect.* The workers' job performance began to improve following the start of the researchers' intervention and continued to do so because of the novelty of the situation; that is, the employees responded positively to the novel treatment they were getting from the researchers. Eventually, however, the novelty began to wear off, and productivity returned to earlier levels. This phenomenon of a change in behavior following the onset of novel treatment that culminates in a gradual return to the previous level of behavior as the effect of novelty dissipates is an example of the Hawthorne effect. However, as Adair (1984) observed, the precise reason for the change in behavior (for example, the novelty of the situation, special attention, prestige from being selected for study) is not always clear.

A Hawthorne effect is represented graphically in Figure 1–2. Its significance is that sometimes behavior change is due just to a change in the environment (for example, the presence of the researchers) and not to the effect of some experimentally manipulated variable (for example, the amount of illumination). The psychological literature indicates that Hawthorne effects may last anywhere from a few days to two years, depending on the situation. Throughout this book, research findings that appear to be attributable to Hawthorne effects will be noted.

The Hawthorne studies also revealed the existence of informal employee work groups and their controls on production, as well as the importance of employee attitudes, the value of having a sympathetic and understanding supervisor, and the need to treat workers as people instead of merely as human capital. Their revelation of the complexity of human behavior opened up new vistas for industrial psychology, which for nearly 40 years had been dominated by the desire to improve company efficiency. Today the Hawthorne studies, while regarded by some contemporary psychologists as having been based on flawed research methods (e.g., Bramel & Friend, 1981), are regarded as the greatest single episode in the formation of industrial psychology. They also showed that researchers sometimes obtain totally unexpected results. Because the investigators were not

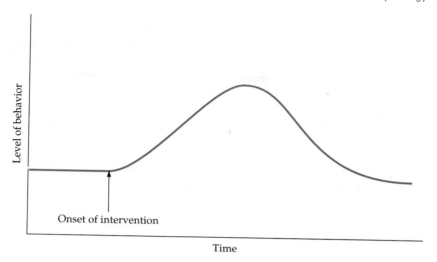

Figure 1–2   *Graphic portrayal of a Hawthorne effect*

tied to any one explanation, their studies took them into areas never before studied by industrial psychology and raised questions that otherwise might never have been asked. Industrial psychology was never the same again.

This era in industrial psychology ended with the coincidental conclusion of the Hawthorne studies and the outbreak of World War II. Industrial psychologists were now faced with an immense task: helping mobilize a nation for a two-continent war.

World War II (1941–1945)

When the United States entered World War II, industrial psychologists were more prepared for their role in the war effort than they had been in 1917. By this time psychologists had studied the problems of employee selection and placement and had refined their techniques considerably.

Walter Bingham chaired the advisory committee on classification of military personnel that had been formed in response to the army's need for classification and training. Unlike World War I, this time the army approached the psychologists first. One of the committee's earliest assignments was to develop a test that could sort new recruits into five categories based on their ability to learn the duties and responsibilities of a soldier. The test that was finally developed was the Army General Classification Test (AGCT), a benchmark in the history of group testing. Harrell (1992), in reflecting on his own involvement in developing the AGCT 50 years earlier, reported that 12 million soldiers were classified into military jobs on the basis of the test. The committee also worked on other projects, such as methods of selecting people for officer training, trade proficiency tests, and supplemental aptitude tests.

Psychologists also worked on the development and use of situational stress tests, a project undertaken by the United States Office of Strategic Services (OSS) (Murray & MacKinnon, 1946). The purpose of this testing program was to assess candidates for assignment to military intelligence units. During a 3-day session of extremely intensive testing and observation, the candidates lived together in small groups under almost continual observation by the assessment staff. Specially constructed situational tests, many modeled after techniques developed in the German and British armies, were used to assess candidates in nontraditional ways. One test, for example, involved constructing a 5-foot cube from a collection of wooden poles, pegs, and blocks. It was impossible for one person to assemble the cube in the allotted time, so two "helpers" were provided. These were actually psychologists who played prearranged roles. One helper acted very passive and contributed little; the other obstructed work by making impractical suggestions and ridiculing and criticizing the candidate. Of course, no candidate could complete the project with this kind of "help." The real purpose of the test was not to see if the candidates could construct the cube but to assess their emotional and interpersonal reactions to stress and frustration. In general, the OSS assessment program was judged to be quite successful.

Another area of work was in the selection and training of pilots to fly warplanes. The committee formed for this purpose consisted of psychologists, military personnel, and civilian pilots. The committee's policy was to move the traditional experimental test setting from the laboratory to the cockpit. Airplanes were outfitted with recording and monitoring devices to assess the problems and reactions of student pilots. The product of this research was twofold. First, good candidates were selected and trained as pilots (the traditional domain of personnel psychology). Second, equipment was designed to make the pilot's job easier and safer (a contribution of the new field of engineering psychology).

Throughout the war, industrial psychology was also being used in civilian life. There was great increase in the use of employment tests in industry. Because the nation needed a productive work force, psychologists were also called on to help reduce employee absenteeism (Pickard, 1945). Industry discovered that many of the techniques of industrial psychologists were useful, especially in the areas of selection, training, and machine design, and industrial leaders were particularly interested in the applications of social psychology. New methods of measuring soldier attitude and morale could also be applied to industry. In short, the techniques developed during the war could be applied to business and industry in peacetime. World War II was a springboard for refining industrial psychological techniques and honing the skills of applied psychologists.

Each of the two world wars had a major effect on industrial psychology but in somewhat different ways. World War I helped form the profession and give it social acceptance. World War II helped develop and refine it. The next era in the history of I/O psychology saw the discipline evolve into subspecialties and attain higher levels of academic and scientific rigor.

Toward Specialization (1946–1963)

In this era industrial psychology evolved into a legitimate field of scientific inquiry, having already established itself as an acceptable professional practice. More colleges and universities began to offer courses in industrial psychology, and graduate degrees (both M.S. and Ph.D.) were soon given.

As with any evolving discipline, subspecialties of interest began to crystallize, and industrial psychology experienced a splintering effect. New journals emerged along with new professional associations. Engineering psychology, born during World War II, was recognized as a separate area, in part due to such seminal books as *Applied Experimental Psychology* (Chapanis, Garner, & Morgan, 1949) and the *Handbook of Human Engineering Data* (1949). Engineering psychology entered an explosive period of growth from 1950 to 1960. This was due mainly to research done in affiliation with the defense industries (Grether, 1968). Engineering psychology's heritage was a mixture of both experimental and industrial psychology, as seen in its early label, "applied experimental psychology." That part of industrial psychology specializing in personnel selection, classification, and training also got its own identity, "personnel psychology." Sometime in the 1950s, interest grew in the study of organizations. Long the province of sociologists, this area caught the interest of psychologists. In the 1960s there was a stronger organizational flavor to industrial psychology research. Investigators gave more attention to social influences that impinge on behavior in organizations. Terms such as *organizational change* and *organization development* appeared in the literature regularly. Industrial psychology addressed a broader range of topics. Classic textbooks of the 1950s such as *Personnel and Industrial Psychology* by Ghiselli and Brown (1955) gave way (in title as well as in substance) to books with more of an organizational thrust. Traditional academic boundaries between disciplines began to blur in this postwar period. Engineering psychology was a fusion of experimental and industrial psychology; organizational behavior was a mix of industrial psychology, social psychology, and sociology. This melding of disciplines was healthy because it decreased the probability of narrow, parochial attempts to address complex areas of research.

Government Intervention (1964–Present)

In the late 1950s and early 1960s the nation was swept up in what became known as the "civil rights movement." As a nation, we became more sensitized to the plight of minorities who had systematically been denied equal opportunities to various sectors of life, including housing, education, and employment. In 1964 Congress passed the Civil Rights Act, a far-reaching piece of legislation designed to reduce unfair discrimination against minorities. One component of the Civil Rights Act, Title VII, addressed the issue of discrimination in employment. This law had a significant impact on I/O psychology. For years I/O psychologists had been given a relatively free rein to use a wide variety of psychological assessment devices (that is, tests, interviews, and so on) to make employment decisions. The product of these employment decisions was the disproportionately small representation of minorities (most notably blacks and women) in the workplace, particularly above lower level jobs. Therefore, since I/O psychologists contributed to making employment decisions, and since (historically) these decisions seemingly resulted in discrimination against minorities, the government would now enter the picture to monitor (and if necessary, remedy) employers' personnel practices.

In essence, the profession of I/O psychology was placed "on trial" to demonstrate the appropriateness of its personnel selection methods. By 1978 the government had drafted a uniform set of employment guidelines to which employers were bound. Companies were legally mandated to demonstrate that their employment tests did not uniformly discriminate against any minority group. In addition, the new government standards were not limited to just paper-and-pencil tests or the personnel function of selection—they addressed all devices (interviews, tests, application blanks) used to make all types of personnel decisions (selection, placement, promotion, discharge, and so on).

The discipline of I/O psychology now had to direct itself to serving two ultimate authorities. The first authority is what all disciplines must serve—namely, that of performing high-quality work, be it in scientific research or in providing services to clients. However, the second authority was government scrutiny and evaluation. We now had to accept the consequences of being legally accountable for our actions. As a profession we would continue to evaluate ourselves, but government policies and agencies would also be used to judge our actions. In 1990 President George Bush signed into law the Americans with Disabilities Act, and in 1991 an updated version of the Civil Rights Act. Both acts are designed to remedy further inequities in the workplace.

Much has been discussed about the overall effect of government intervention in the profession of I/O psychology. Some people believe it has been an impetus to our profession, compelling us to address issues and develop solutions that we might otherwise have ignored. Others believe that our profession has been compromised by the intrusion of political and legal influences that serve to deflect our activities into areas beyond our traditional domain. Some of the greatest advances in our profession have been made in the past 15 to 20 years, and I attribute these advances, in part, to our being accountable to forces beyond our own profession. Legal oversight has, in my opinion, prompted I/O psychologists to broaden their horizons in terms of the problems they address and the solutions they propose. In any case, the reality of being an I/O psychologist in the 1990s involves attentiveness to legal standards, parameters that our professional predecessors never had to deal with.

I/O psychology also made a major contribution to the military during this era of our history. Campbell (1990) described the efforts of I/O psychologists to develop a test used for the selection and classification of military personnel. This project involved many psychologists and took almost 10 years to complete. Called Project A, it consisted of developing the Armed Services Vocational Aptitude Battery (ASVAB). Every year the ASVAB is administered to 300,000 to 400,000 people; of that number, 120,000 to 140,000 individuals are selected. I/O psychologists are now assisting the military in another large research project, Project B, which involves the families of military personnel.

In retrospect, the history of I/O psychology is rich and diverse. We were born at the confluence of several forces, developed and grew through global conflict, and were woven into the societal fabric of which we are a part. Our history is relatively brief and our members are not great in number, but I believe I/O psychologists have contributed strongly to the domains of both economic and personal welfare. In 1992, the 100th anniversary of the American Psychological Association, Katzell and Austin (1992) wrote a major review of the history of I/O psychology in celebration of our centennial. They noted that our history is marked by a continual interweaving of scientific and professional contributions. At certain points in our history, the practice of I/O psychology has been at the vanguard of our professional efforts (particularly during wars). At other times our scientific advances have been more noteworthy, as in the past decade when we have witnessed what some scholars refer to as the "cognitive revolution" in psychology, which reflects an emphasis on cognitive processes in understanding human behavior. However, as stated previously in this chapter, the science and practice of I/O psychology can never be too far apart from each other. Katzell and Austin quoted a memorable statement by Morris Viteles, one of the early pioneers of our field, who aptly summarized the two interlocking domains of I/O psychology: "If it isn't scientific, it's not good practice, and if it isn't practical, it's not good science" (p. 826). In 1990 the *Handbook of Industrial and Organizational Psychology* was published (Dunnette & Hough), the first of a four-volume set that documents some of our profession's finest scientific achievements. Today, I/O psychology is multidisciplinary with regard to both its content and its methods of inquiry. On reflection, it was the same at the turn of the century—a confluence of interest in advertising research, industrial efficiency, and mental testing. In a sense, the evolution of I/O psychology is the chronicle of mushrooming interests along certain common dimensions as molded by a few seismic events.

Cross-Cultural I/O Psychology

Cross-cultural psychology studies "similarities and differences in individual psychological and social functioning in various cultures and ethnic groups" (Kagiticibasi & Berry, 1989, p. 494). Given the central role that work plays in our lives, it is not surprising that I/O psychologists are being compelled to examine cross-cultural factors in work behavior. Erez (1994) described the significant changes in world conditions that affect our work lives. Among them are the following:

• *Cultural diversity of the labor force.* Demographic trends in the United States suggest that by the year 2000 about one-third of the labor force will be black or Latino. The unification of Europe as well as the political changes in the former Soviet republics have resulted in waves of immigrants across cultural boundaries.

• *Scope of the work environment.* In the United States more than 100,000 American companies do business overseas. It is estimated that one-third of the profit of U.S. companies is derived from international business, along with one-sixth of the nation's jobs. The competitive global market requires greater knowledge of cultures, values, and business practices other than our own. The fall of communism, for example, provides many opportunities for I/O psychologists to apply their knowledge to enhance economic productivity in Eastern Europe (Roe, 1995). Yet Westerners are not very knowledgeable about the cultural values and business practices that have long been dominant in these countries.

• *Mergers and acquisitions.* In recent years a substantial number of companies have gone through mergers, acquisitions, and downsizing. There were more foreign acquisitions of U.S. companies than vice versa. These mergers and acquisitions have resulted in organizational downsizing and massive layoffs. From 1985 to 1988, approximately 15 million workers were affected by mergers and acquisitions. Very often a confrontation between organizational cultures results when two or more companies are merged.

• *Emergence of high technology and telecommunication systems.* The revolution in telecommunication systems introduced electronic mail, fax machines, cellular phones, and teleconferences. New technology has facilitated communication across geographic boundaries and reduced the time needed for communication. Such changes have accelerated cross-cultural communication and exposure to different systems of values, norms, and behaviors.

Erez sounded a warning note about why I/O psychologists must be aware of cultural differences in proposing solutions to problems of work behavior. "The successful implementation of managerial techniques depends on their congruence with cultural values. Cultural values serve as criteria for evaluating the contributions of various managerial practices to employee well-being" (p. 601). Triandis (1994) described several practical examples of work-related problems arising from being insensitive to cultural differences. For example, 25 to 40% of U.S. managers selected for overseas assignments have failed because of "culture shock" associated with their new assignments. Values and customs prevalent in our society do not necessarily generalize to other cultures. Additionally, what constitutes satisfying work differs across cultures. Jobs that provide a sense of challenge appeal more to people in Western cultures, whereas jobs that provide opportunities for affiliation are more appealing to people in some other cultures.

It is abundantly clear that the very meaning and nature of work is not universal. I/O psychologists are called upon to assist in the process of developing work procedures that span diverse cultural groups to produce a uniformly desired outcome—our economic and personal well-being.

The Mandate of I/O Psychology

I/O psychology is confronted with a daunting task—to increase the fit between the work force and the workplace at a time when the composition of both is rapidly changing. Today's work force is unlike any other in our history. More people are seeking employment than ever before, and they have higher levels of education. Many more women are entering the work force seeking full-time careers, and more dual-income couples and individuals whose native language is not English are part of the work force today.

Likewise, the nature of work is changing. There are an increasing number of jobs in service industries, jobs that require computer literacy, and part-time jobs. Rapid economic changes are forcing large-scale layoffs, often requiring individuals to learn new job skills at midlife. Societal changes also influence employment, as is evidenced by the growing problem of drugs in the workplace.

Another feature of the changing employment picture is the rate or speed of change. Although there has always been a sense of urgency to our work, time pressures are seemingly becoming more acute. Rapid large-scale changes in automation and computerization are changing the skill levels needed by employees. Life expectancy is increasing, and many once-retired people are returning to the work force. Medical costs are escalating at a severe rate, and employers are being compelled to find ways to curb their liability for employee health-related expenses. Business mergers and acquisitions are at an all-time high, and the affected employees must find ways to accommodate the trauma of job loss, transfers, and reassignments. Factors and conditions such as these add to the pressures of designing work that is both economically efficient and personally satisfying. The year 2000 was once held out as a futuristic date and symbolized an era when life would be very different than it is today. Whether I/O psychology is ready for it or not, we are now painfully close to the year 2000.

There is also the growing realization among I/O psychologists that our work lives are intimately tied to our personal lives. It is just not realistic to try to segment our work and personal lives. We take our work problems home with us, and our personal problems can and sometimes do affect our work lives. We are now witnessing more of an integrated, holistic approach to the psychology of work and its associated impact on our total well-being. I/O psychologists are currently studying such topics as leisure, emotional support provided by family members, and how job stress is dealt with at home. We have learned that our scope of concern as I/O psychologists extends beyond the traditional 8:00 A.M. to 5:00 P.M. hours of employment.

I/O psychology is concerned with the work lives of people, and because the work lives of people are changing, so too is I/O psychology. As a profession, we find ourselves on the threshold of some areas where we have little prior experience. We would be remiss if we did not venture into these new territories, for they are legitimate and important concerns within the world of work. I find the mandate of I/O psychology to be very challenging, with the continual variety of issues we address being a great source of stimulation. While some disciplines rarely change their content, I/O psychology most certainly is not the "same old stuff."

I can think of few other fields of work that are as critical to human welfare as I/O psychology. We spend more of our lifetimes engaged in working than in any other activity. Thus, I/O psychology is devoted to understanding our major mission in life. As our nation faces increasing problems of economic productivity, the field of I/O psychology continues to contribute to making our world a better place in which to live. Indeed, Katzell and Guzzo (1983) reported that 87% of the psychological approaches to improving employee productivity have been successful. Additionally, the scientific contributions that I/O psychologists have made are regarded as sufficiently noteworthy to occasion revision of federal laws governing fair employment practices.

In general, we as professionals are striving to gain a complete understanding of the problems and issues associated with the world of work, embracing both its quantitative and its humanistic dimensions (Stagner, 1982). When you have finished reading this book, you should have a much better understanding of human behavior in the workplace. Perhaps some of you will be stimulated enough to continue work in I/O psychology. It is a most challenging, rewarding, and useful profession.

Research Methods in I/O Psychology

Major Chapter Objectives

- *Understand the empirical research cycle.*

- *Understand the relative advantages and disadvantages of laboratory experiments, field experiments, questionnaires, observations, and computer simulations.*

- *Understand the statistical concepts of central tendency and variability.*

- *Understand the concept of correlation and its interpretation.*

- *Be aware of and appreciate the ethical issues associated with research.*

We all have hunches or beliefs about the nature of human behavior. Some of us believe that red-haired people are temperamental, dynamic leaders are big and tall, blue-collar workers prefer beer to wine, the only reason people work is to make money, and the like. The list is endless. Which of these beliefs are true? The only way to find out is to conduct research—the systematic study of phenomena according to scientific principles. Much of this chapter is devoted to research methods used in I/O psychology. Understanding the research process helps people solve practical problems, apply the results of studies reported by others, and assess the accuracy of claims made about new practices, equipment, and so on.

I/O psychologists are continually faced with a host of practical problems. Knowledge of research methods gives us a better opportunity to find useful solutions to problems rather than merely stumbling across them by chance. An understanding of research methods also helps us apply the results of studies reported by others. Some factors promote the generalizability of research findings; others retard it. Finally, people often assert the superiority of some new technique or method; a knowledge of research methods will help you determine which ones are merely cheap gimmicks.

Kaplan (1964) suggests that science has three goals: description, prediction, and explanation. The descriptive function is like taking a photograph—a picture of a state of events. Researchers may describe levels of productivity, number of employees who quit during the year, average level of job satisfaction, and so on. The second function is prediction. Researchers try to predict which employees will be productive, which ones are likely to quit, and which ones will be dissatisfied. This information is then used to select applicants who would be better employees. The explanatory function is perhaps the most difficult to unravel; it is a statement of why events occur as they do. It tries to find causes: Why is production at a certain level, why do employees quit, why are they dissatisfied? This chapter will give you some insight into the research process in I/O psychology and should help you become a knowledgeable consumer of I/O psychological research.

The research process is a five-step procedure with an important feedback factor—that is, the results of the fifth step influence the first step in future research studies. Figure 2–1 shows the five steps that are followed in conducting empirical research. The research process begins with a statement of the problem: What question or problem needs to be answered? Second, how do you design a study to answer the question? Third, how do you measure the variables and collect the necessary data? Fourth, how do you apply statistical procedures to analyze the data? (In other words, how do you make some sense out of all the information collected?) Finally, how do you draw conclusions from analyzing the data? Let's look at each of these steps in more detail.

Statement of the Problem

Questions that initiate research don't arise out of thin air. They are based on existing knowledge—your own and others' experiences with the problem, personal intuition or insight, or some formal theory. Most research begins with per-

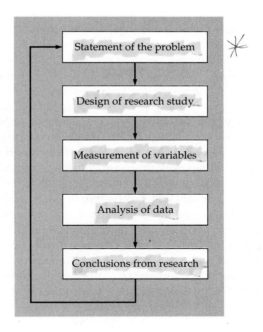

Figure 2–1   *The empirical research cycle*

sonal insight or intuition. As researchers conduct their studies, they become more familiar with the problem and may expand the scope of their questions. One person's research may stimulate similar research by someone else; thus, researchers often benefit from their colleagues' studies. After conducting much research on a topic, researchers may propose a theory about why the behavior occurs. The sequence that starts with data and culminates in theory is the *inductive* method of science. The opposite sequence is the *deductive* method. In the deductive method, a researcher first forms a theory (perhaps by intuition or by studying previous research) and then tests the theory by collecting data. If the theory is accurate, the data will support it; if it is inaccurate, they will not.

The value of theory in science is that it integrates and summarizes large amounts of information and provides a framework for the research. Campbell (1990) notes, however, that as a scientific discipline psychology is much more difficult to investigate than physics or chemistry. People are far too variable, both across individuals and from day to day within one person to be defined by a singular structure. The situation is not the same in physics or chemistry. A molecule of water has the same structure no matter where in the world it might be. There is no equivalent in psychology to universal natural laws such as Newton's three laws of motion. Accordingly, the role of theory in psychology as a method for guiding research is somewhat more controversial than in other disciplines. The following quotes illustrate three different yet equally valid views on theory:

- "There is nothing quite so practical as a good theory."
  —*Kurt Lewin, noted social psychologist*
- "Research designed with respect to theory is likely to be wasteful."
  —*B. F. Skinner, noted experimental psychologist*
- "Theory, like mist on eyeglasses, obscures facts."
  —*Charlie Chan, noted fictional detective*

Lewin's statement is often cited in psychology. Its essence is that a theory is useful for conducting research. A theory synthesizes information, organizes it into logical components, and directs the researcher's efforts in future studies. But Skinner believes that too much effort is spent on "proving" theories; that is, the theory is master of the research. Skinner feels that most theories eventually fall out of favor and that productive research does not require a theory. His position is an extreme case of empiricism. Charlie Chan thinks that researchers become too committed to proving their theories and become blinded to information that doesn't conform to what they want to believe. A good researcher doesn't let the theory obscure the facts. Rather than thinking of theories as "right" or "wrong," try to think of them in terms of their usefulness. A useful theory helps give meaning to the problem. It helps the subject matter make more sense.

Campbell (1990) believes that theories are only a means to an end and thus have no inherent value. He states that theories should "help us develop better research questions, provide more useful interpretation of data, or guide the future investment of research resources" (pp. 66–67). Webster and Starbuck (1988) noted that scientists would be better off with no theories at all than with theories that lead them nowhere or in incompatible directions. Theory is only one way to formulate a research problem; other methods can also result in high-quality research. This is especially true in a pragmatic area like I/O psychology where some research problems come from everyday experiences in industry. If 50% of a company's work force quits every year, you don't need a theory to realize that this is a serious problem. Developing a carefully thought-out research problem is far more important than determining which source (experience, theory, intuition) it came from. I believe the value of theory in I/O psychology is to provide a useful explanation for work-related behaviors as opposed to being the sole source of a research idea.

Design of the Research Study

A research design is a plan for conducting a study. There are a number of strategies a researcher can use; the choice of method depends on the nature of the problem being studied, as well as matters of cost and feasibility. The strategies can be compared along several dimensions, but the two most important dimensions are (1) the naturalness of the research setting and (2) the investigator's degree of control over the study. No one strategy is best under all conditions; there are always trade-offs.

Naturalness of the research setting. In some research strategies, the problem can be studied in the environment in which it naturally occurs. This method is desirable because we don't want the research strategy to destroy or distort the phenomenon under study. Some research strategies appear phony because the problem is studied in unnatural ways. For example, the Hawthorne studies were conducted right in the plant with actual employees performing their normal jobs. However, some studies do not need to be conducted in a natural environment because the behavior under investigation is assumed to be independent of the setting. For example, an engineering psychology study testing whether people react faster to red or to green lights could be conducted as appropriately in a laboratory as in a natural field setting.

Degree of control. In some research strategies, the researcher has a high degree of control over the conduct of the study. In others, very little control is possible. In the Hawthorne studies, the researchers could control the exact amount of lighting in the work area by installing (or removing) lights, although it turned out that factors other than lighting affected the workers' performance. But suppose you want to study the relationship between people's ages and their attitude toward I/O psychology. You are particularly interested in comparing the attitudes of people over 40 with those under 40. You develop a questionnaire that asks their opinions about I/O psychology (is it interesting, difficult to understand, and so on) and distribute it to your classmates. But it turns out that every person in the class is under 40. You have no information on the over-40 group, so you can't answer your research question. This is an example of a low degree of control (you cannot control the age of the people in the study). Low control is particularly endemic to the questionnaire research method.

The next section discusses five research methods used in I/O psychology. No one method is perfect—that is, none offers a high degree of both naturalism and control. Each method will be described and illustrated with an example.

Major Research Methods

Laboratory Experiment

Laboratory experiments are conducted in contrived settings as opposed to naturally occurring organizational settings. In a laboratory, the researcher has a high degree of control over the conduct of the study, especially over those conditions associated with the observations of behavior. The experimenter designs the study to test how certain aspects of an actual environment affect behavior. The laboratory setting must mirror certain dimensions of the natural environment where the behavior normally occurs. A well-designed laboratory experiment will have some of the conditions found in the natural environment but will omit those that would never be present (Fromkin & Streufert, 1976).

Streufert et al. (1992) conducted a laboratory experiment on the effects of alcohol intoxication on visual-motor performance. A sample of adult men participated for two days, one day when they consumed alcohol and the other when they consumed mineral water (disguised with a mild ethanol spray to provide the odor of alcohol). The alcohol dosage was designed to produce breath alcohol levels of .05 and .10 (the conventional legal standard for alcohol intoxication). Visual-motor performance was measured on a task similar to the PacMan video game. The researchers studied several aspects of performance including risk taking and errors. Performance under alcohol intoxication was compared to performance under the control conditions for each person. The results showed that error rates were dramatically higher under conditions of alcohol consumption. Serious performance deterioration was found to occur even at the lower (.05) intoxication level. Under the effects of alcohol some individuals exhibited greater cautiousness (that is, slower reaction time) to the visual-motor task, trading off speed of response for fewer errors. The researchers regarded errors in the task to be equivalent to an air traffic controller's failure to guide aircraft that have come too close to each other toward safer paths. Additionally, while reduced speed of response may reduce errors, it also may prevent engaging in needed defensive maneuvers.

In evaluating this study, the defining characteristics of a laboratory experiment can be clearly noted. By controlling for other factors, the researchers were able to determine the causal link between alcohol consumption and performance in a visual-motor task. They could also control the dosage of alcohol to produce precise breath alcohol levels of .05 and .10, typical levels of alcohol intoxication associated with drinking alcohol in natural settings. Nevertheless, one can question the generalizability of the skills needed to perform the selected visual-motor task to real jobs. Some jobs (surgeon, for example) would require even greater degrees of concentration and coordination. In such a case the magnitude of the "errors" caused by alcohol intoxication would be greater. Other jobs (laborer) have fewer visual-motor skill requirements, in which case the errors would be fewer. In short, the findings from the study pertain to the effects of alcohol on visual-motor performance, not to the total spectrum of skills needed for performance across many jobs. Nevertheless, the laboratory experiment is a classic research method for addressing highly specific research questions, and the results from such experiments can often be interpreted with a high degree of conviction.

Field Experiment

A field experiment is a research strategy in which manipulation of independent variables occurs in a natural setting (that is, the people in the study do not perceive the setting as having been created to conduct the research). As in a laboratory experiment, the researcher tests the effects of a few variables on the subjects' behavior. But there is also less control. In a laboratory experiment, all the variables are manipulated at the researcher's discretion and can be included or excluded according to the design of the study. However, in a field experiment, variables that occur in the natural setting are also part of the experiment. Though they add to the richness and realism of the field experiment, they also lessen the researcher's control.

Latham and Kinne (1974) reported a study that used the field experiment as a research method. It examined how a one-day training program on goal setting affected the job performance of pulpwood workers. The subjects in the study were 20 pulpwood logging crews. Their behavior was observed as they performed their normal job duties harvesting lumber in a forest. The experimenters split the subjects into two groups of 10 crews each. They matched the two groups on a number of factors so that they would be equal in terms of ability and experience. One group was given a one-day course in how to set production goals—that is, how many cords of wood to harvest per hour. The other group was not given any special instructions and worked in the usual way. The experimenters then monitored the job performance of the wood crews over the next three months. Results showed that the crews who were trained to set production goals for themselves harvested significantly more wood than the other crews. This study supported the use of goal setting in an industrial context.

The major strength of this study in terms of demonstrating the field experiment method was that the context was very real. Actual workers were used in the context of their everyday jobs. The setting was a forest, not a laboratory where the subjects would have been pretending to be in a forest. Although the study's design was not complex enough to rule out competing explanations for the observed behavior, it did allow the researchers to conclude that the goal-setting technique probably caused the increase in job performance. This study also illustrates some weaknesses of the field experiment method. Some workers who were supposed to participate in the goal-setting group decided not to. This forced the researchers to redesign part of the study. Also, few I/O psychologists would be able to influence a company to change its work operations for research purposes. (In fact, one of the authors of this study was employed by the lumber company, which undoubtedly had some effect on the company's willingness to participate.)

Questionnaire

Questionnaires rely on individuals' self-reports as the basis for obtaining information. They can be constructed to match the reading ability level of the individuals being surveyed. They represent a means of maintaining respondent anonymity if the subject matter being covered is sensitive. Furthermore, questionnaires are a highly effective means of data collection.

Murphy, Thornton, and Prue (1991) used the questionnaire method to ascertain the acceptability of employee drug testing. The authors asked two samples of individuals (college-aged students and nontraditional students) to indicate the degree to which testing for illicit drug use was viewed as justified in each of 35 jobs (such as salesperson, surgeon, mechanic, and airline pilot). Each job was rated on a 7-point scale ranging from low to high acceptance of drug testing. The jobs were carefully selected to represent different types of skills and temperaments needed for their successful conduct, as well as the physical conditions under which the jobs were performed. The results indicated that the degree to which different jobs involved danger to the worker, co-workers, or the public was most strongly related to the acceptability of employee drug testing. The authors concluded that it would be relatively easy to justify drug testing for some jobs, whereas substantial efforts may be necessary to overcome resistance to drug testing for other jobs. Furthermore, the responses by both sets of respondents were virtually the same. That is, the attitudes of college-aged students generalized to individuals who were older (average age of 35). However, the results also revealed a high degree of variability in attitudes toward drug testing among members of both groups. Some individuals were in favor of drug testing across all jobs, whereas other individuals were opposed to drug testing for any job.

Questionnaires are a very popular method of research in I/O psychology. However, they do suffer from several practical limitations. Some people are not willing to complete a questionnaire and return it to the researcher. The return rate of mailed questionnaires is often less than 50%. For example, in the Murphy et al. (1991) study the return rate of questionnaires mailed to the homes of the nontraditional students was 31%. Such a low response rate raises the question of how representative or unbiased the responses are of the group as a whole. Rising postal rates are also a concern for mail surveys. Researchers usually pay the postage both ways. At a conceptual level there is also some debate as to how accurate self-report measures are. The tendency to slant responses in socially desirable directions can be an issue for some topics. Despite these limitations, questionnaires are used extensively in I/O psychology to address a broad range of research questions.

Observation

Observation is a method that can be used when the research is directed to overt behaviors. Observation occurs in natural field settings where behavior is observed over prolonged periods of time and is recorded and categorized. As a research method it is not used very frequently in I/O psychology, primarily because it requires substantial amounts of time and energy.

Komaki (1986) sought to identify the behaviors that differentiate effective from ineffective work supervisors. She had observers record the behaviors of 24 managers: 12 had been previously judged as effective in motivating others, and 12 judged as relatively ineffective. Approximately twenty 30-minute observations were made of each manager's behavior over a 7-month period (232 hours of observation in total). The managers were observed as they conducted their normal day-to-day duties. The observer would stand out of sight but within hearing distance of the manager. A specially designed observation form was provided for recording and coding the observations. Komaki found the primary behavior differentiating the effective and ineffective managers was the frequency with which they monitored their employees' performance. Compared to ineffective managers, effective managers spent more time sampling their employees' work. The findings were interpreted as underscoring the importance of monitoring critical behaviors in producing effective supervisors. However, such a conclusion would require corroborating empirical evidence, as the two groups of managers were merely observed without attempting to control for other variables that might account for the results.

Observation is often a fruitful method for generating ideas that can be further tested with other research methods. The observation method is rich in providing data from environments where the behavior in question occurs. However, how successful can observers be in acting as "flies on the wall," observing behavior but not influencing it? In this study the managers were highly aware that they were being observed. Given that, to what degree did the managers modify their conduct to project socially desirable behaviors (for example, monitoring their subordinates)? Perhaps effective managers are more sensitive to social cues than ineffective managers and are better able to be perceived in a positive fashion. Note we are dealing with interpretations of the behavior (the "why"), not merely the behavior itself (the "what"). It has been suggested that the acceptance and trust of the observers by the study participants is critical to the success of this research method.

Computer Simulation

Computer simulation is a method for modeling various aspects of an environment to assess their effect on behavior in a comprehensive manner. The closer the simulation is to real life, the more accurate are the conclusions drawn from the method.

Computer simulation is increasing in use as a research method, but to date it is not used as frequently in I/O psychology as are other methods. Seymour, Stahl, Levine, Ingram, and Smith (1994) described several computer-controlled simulations used by law enforcement and military personnel being trained in how to employ good judgment in the use of firearms under situations of threat. The simulations use computer-controlled, life-sized, projected video images of scenarios that may or may not present a threat. The trainee is required to shoot or not shoot a firearm in each scenario. Actual firearms are used, either with real ammunition or with a laser or infrared-light-emitting device. For realism, the laser and infrared-light systems have been developed with the balance, weight, and feel of firearms loaded with live ammunition. Some simulators are portable, whereas those using live ammunition requiring a bullet trap are not. The trainee responds to a sequence of "shoot/no-shoot" judgment scenarios, resulting in data on three factors: judgment, reaction time, and accuracy. Most simulations can be modified to alter the parameters selected for presentation, such as the speed of the threat.

As Lewandowsky (1993) has noted, the value of a simulation is to vary the levels of the parameters selected for study and to assess their corresponding effect on behavior. However, the parameters themselves are explicit and can be modified only by creating a different simulation. The degree to which the simulation parameters (for example, degree of threat in the scenario) model the critical factors in real-life situations affects the generalizability of the conclusions drawn from the research. Some factors can be simulated faithfully whereas others cannot. For example, while the video images of people may appear very lifelike, those images will not return "live fire" in the simulation. In general, computer simulation offers the opportunity to study issues that do not readily or safely lend themselves to investigation in real life. Findings from simulations should be com-

Table 2–1 Comparison of empirical research strategies

	Laboratory Experiment	Field Experiment	Questionnaire	Observation	Computer Simulation
Control (potential for testing causal relationships)	High	Moderate	Low	Low	High
Realism (naturalness of setting)	Low	High	High	High	Moderate

pared with results from other research methods. As Sackett and Larson (1990) observed, "Getting caught up in making one's simulation more and more elaborate without turning to nonhypothetical data for some reality-testing is a serious mistake" (p. 466).

Table 2–1 compares the five research methods on two major dimensions: researcher control and realism. No method is high on both factors; there is always a trade-off. A researcher may sacrifice realism for control or vice versa, depending on the study's objectives. Choice of strategy should be guided by the purpose of the research and the resources available. A well-trained I/O psychologist knows the advantages and disadvantages of each method.

Measurement of Variables

After developing a study design, the researcher must next enact it and measure the variables of interest. A variable is a symbol that can assume a range of numerical values. Quantitative variables (age, time, and so on) are inherently numerical (21 years or 16 minutes). Qualitative variables (sex, race, and the like) are not inherently numerical, but they can be "coded" to give them numerical meaning: female 0, male 1, or white 0, black 1, Latino 2, Asian 3, and so forth. For research purposes, it doesn't matter what numerical values are given to the qualitative variables, because they merely identify these variables for measurement purposes.

Variables of Interest in I/O Psychological Research

The term *variable* is often used in conjunction with other terms in I/O psychological research. Four such terms that will be used throughout this book are *independent, dependent, predictor,* and *criterion.*

Independent and *dependent* variables are associated in particular with experimental (laboratory or field) research strategies. Independent variables are manipulated or controlled by the researcher. They are chosen by the experimenter, set or manipulated to occur at a certain level, and then examined to assess their effect on

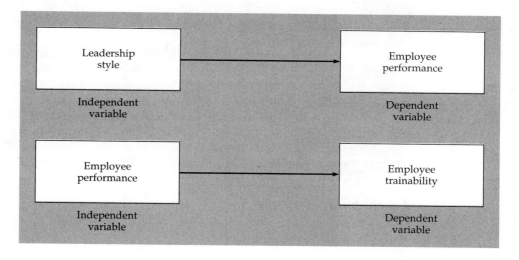

Figure 2–2 *Employee performance used as either a dependent or an independent variable*

some other variable. In the laboratory experiment by Streufert et al. (1992), the independent variable was the level of alcohol intoxication. In the field experiment by Latham and Kinne (1974), the independent variable was the effect of a one-day training program on goal setting.

Experiments assess the effects of independent variables on the dependent variable. The dependent variable is most often the object of the researcher's interest. It is usually some aspect of behavior (or, in some cases, attitudes). In the Streufert et al. study, the dependent variable was the subjects' performance in a visual-motor task. In the Latham and Kinne study, the dependent variable was the number of cords of wood harvested by the lumber crews. The same variable can be selected as the dependent or independent variable depending on the goals of the study. Figure 2–2 shows how a variable (employee performance) can be used as either one. In the former case, the researcher wants to study the effect of various leadership styles (independent variable) on employee performance (dependent variable). The researcher might select two types of leadership styles (a stern taskmaster approach versus a relaxed, easygoing one) and then assess their effects on job performance. In the latter case, the researcher might want to know what effect performance (independent variable) has on the ability to be trained (dependent variable). The employees are divided into "high-performer" and "low-performer" groups. Both groups then attend a training program to assess whether the high performers learn faster than the low performers. Note that variables are never inherently independent or dependent. Whether they are one or the other is up to the researcher's discretion.

Predictor and *criterion* variables are often used in I/O psychology. When scores on one variable are used to predict scores on a second, the variables are called predictor and criterion variables, respectively. For example, a student's high school grade point average might be used to predict his or her college grade point average. High school grades are the predictor variable; college grades are the criterion variable.

As a rule, criterion variables are the focal point of the study. Predictor variables may or may not be successful in predicting what we want to know (the criterion). Predictor variables are similar to independent variables; criterion variables are similar to dependent variables. The distinction between the two is a function of the research strategy. Independent and dependent variables are used in the context of experimentation. Predictor and criterion variables are used in any research strategy where the goal is to determine the status of subjects on one variable (the criterion) as a function of their status on another variable (the predictor).

Levels of Measurement

Variables must be measured as accurately as possible. Some variables can be measured precisely, but others can be measured only in a coarse way. A scale is a measuring device to assess a person's score or status on some variable. Although there are many scales, there are only four basic types: nominal, ordinal, interval, and ratio (Stevens, 1958).

Nominal Scale.   A nominal scale, the crudest type, classifies objects or people into categories. It simply shows that a person (or object) is a member of one of these categories. For example, a nominal scale could classify people by sex into one of two categories (male or female). Racial groups (Caucasian, Asian, and the like) can also be categorized on a nominal scale. Note that a nominal scale does not arrange people or objects in some order or sequence.

Ordinal Scale.   An ordinal scale orders objects along some dimension. The most common type of ordinal scale is a rank order. If you were asked to rank order three foods—pizza, chicken, and steak—along a dimension of taste preference, you might rank them steak, pizza, and chicken. We know you like pizza better than chicken and steak better than both pizza and chicken. But we don't know how much you like these foods. You may like all three or despise all three, or you may like only one. So an ordinal scale shows how things are ranked along a dimension but not the distance between the ranked items.

Interval Scale.   An interval scale measures how much of a variable is present (using equal distances between scale units). A thermometer represents an interval scale. The distance between 10° and 15° (5°) is the same as the distance between 87° and 92° (5°). An interval scale is more precise than an ordinal scale, because it shows not only relative preference (that is, rank order) but also how much the objects are preferred. Suppose you rated the three foods on a 10-point scale (where a rating of 10 is high and 1 is low) and the results were steak 9, pizza 2, and chicken 1. The scale shows that you like steak a lot but not pizza or chicken. A person who had the same rank order but rated the foods as steak 10, pizza 9, and chicken 8 would obviously feel differently.

Ratio Scale.   A ratio scale is the most precise type of scale. It has all the properties of the other three scales and one more: a true zero-point. Measures such as length, weight, and age are all ratio scales. The true zero-point in the scale means that nothing can be shorter than 0 inches (or centimeters), lighter than 0 ounces (or grams), or younger than 0 seconds. A Fahrenheit or Celsius thermometer is not a ratio scale because it has no true zero-point (minus 25° is a negative temperature).[1] The term *ratio* means that a ratio can be formed between two objects; for example, a 20-year-old is twice as old as a 10-year-old. But we cannot say that 20° is twice as warm as 10°.

Analysis of Data

After the data have been collected, the researcher has to make some sense out of them. Here's where statistics come in. Many students get anxious over the topic of statistics. Although some statistical analytic methods are quite complex, most are reasonably straightforward. I like to think of statistical methods as golf clubs—tools that help us do a job better. Just as some golf shots call for different clubs, different research problems require different statistical analyses. Knowing a full range of statistical methods will help you better understand the research problem. It's also impossible to understand the research process without some knowledge of statistics.

Descriptive statistics simply describe data. They are the starting point in the data analysis process; they give the researcher a general idea of what the data are like. Descriptive statistics can show the shape of a distribution of numbers, measure the central tendency of the distribution, and measure the spread or variability in the numbers.

Distributions and Their Shape

Suppose a researcher measures the intelligence of 100 people with a traditional IQ test. Table 2–2 shows those 100 scores. To make some sense out of all these num-

FRANK AND ERNEST   SOURCE: Reprinted by permission of Newspaper Enterprise Association, Inc.

[1] Temperature recorded on a Kelvin thermometer would be a ratio scale.

Table 2–2   *One hundred IQ scores*

133	141	108	124	117
110	92	88	110	79
143	101	120	104	94
117	128	102	126	84
105	143	114	70	103
151	114	87	134	81
87	120	145	98	95
97	157	99	79	107
108	107	147	156	144
118	127	96	138	102
141	113	112	94	114
133	122	89	128	112
119	99	110	118	142
123	67	120	89	118
90	114	121	146	94
128	125	114	91	124
121	125	83	99	76
120	102	129	108	98
110	144	89	122	119
117	127	134	127	112

bers, the researcher arranges the numbers according to size and then plots them in a scatter diagram. Figure 2–3 shows what those 100 test scores would look like. This is called a *frequency distribution*. Because so many scores are involved, they are grouped into categories of equal size with each interval containing ten possible scores.

The figure tells something about the IQ data. We can see that the most frequently occurring scores are in the middle of the distribution; extreme scores (both high and low) taper off as we move away from that point. The general shape of the distribution in Figure 2–3 is called a *normal* or *bell-shaped* distribution. Many variables in psychological research are distributed normally—that is, with the most frequently occurring scores in the middle of the distribution and progressively fewer scores at the extreme ends. Figure 2–4a shows a classic normal distribution. The smoothness of the curve in Figure 2–4a compared to that in Figure 2–3 is due to the fact that the occurrence of many test scores would take the "kinks" out of the distribution.

Not all distributions of scores are normal in shape—some are lopsided or pointed. If a professor gives an easy test, there will be a larger proportion of high scores, resulting in a pointed or *skewed* distribution. Figure 2–4b shows a *negatively skewed* distribution (the tail of the distribution is in the negative direction). The opposite would occur if the professor gives a difficult test; the result would be a *positively skewed* distribution (the tail points in the positive direction), as in Figure 2–4c.

Thus, plotting the distribution of data is one way to understand it. We can make inferences based on the shape of the distribution. (In the case of the negatively skewed distribution of test scores, we infer that the test was easy.)

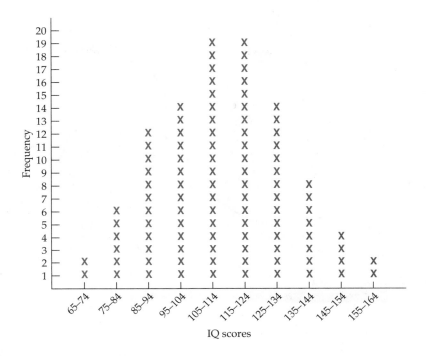

Figure 2–3   *Frequency distribution of 100 IQ scores (grouped data)*

Measures of Central Tendency

After we learn the shape of the distribution, the next step is to find the typical score. One of three measures of *central tendency* is usually used for this, depending on the shape of the distribution. The *mean* is the most common measure of central tendency. The mean is the arithmetic average score in the distribution. It is computed by adding all of the individual scores and dividing by the total number of scores in the distribution. The formula for computing the mean is:

$$\bar{X} = \frac{\Sigma X}{N}$$

[Formula 2–1]

where $\bar{X}$ is the symbol for the mean, Σ is the symbol for summation, X is the symbol for each individual score, and N is the total number of scores in the distribution. The mean for the data in Table 2–2 is as follows:

$$\bar{X} = \frac{11,322}{100} = 113.22$$

[Formula 2–2]

The average IQ in the sample of people tested is 113.22 (or 113 rounded off). The entire distribution of 100 scores can be described by one number: the mean. The

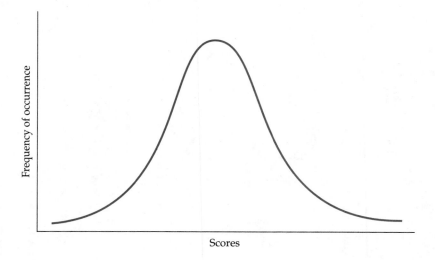

Figure 2–4a   A normal or bell-shaped distribution of scores

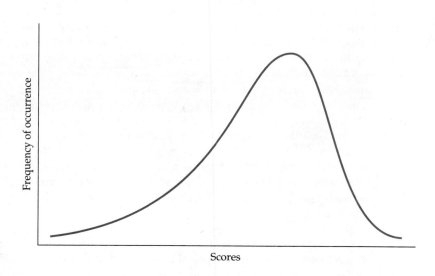

Figure 2–4b   A negatively skewed distribution of scores

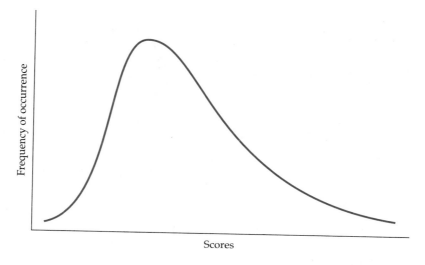

Figure 2–4c *A positively skewed distribution of scores*

mean is a useful measure of central tendency and is most appropriately used with normally distributed variables.

The *median* is the midpoint of all the scores in the distribution. So 50% of all scores are above the median and 50% are below. If we have a distribution of four scores and they are 1, 2, 3, and 4, the median would be 2.5; that is, half the scores (3 and 4) will be above this point, and half (1 and 2) will be below it. (The statistical procedure used to compute the median for graphed data is quite lengthy and will not be presented here. For information purposes, the median for the data presented in Table 2–2 is 112.9.) Because skewed distributions always contain some extreme scores, the median is the best measure of central tendency for them because the median would be relatively insensitive to these scores. In contrast, the mean would be affected by these extremes.

The *mode*, the least common measure of central tendency, is the most frequently occurring score in a distribution. The mode is not used for many statistical analyses, but it may have a practical purpose. Some concepts are best understood in whole numbers (that is, integers), not in fractions or decimals. For example, it makes more sense to say "The modal number of children in a family is 3" rather than "The mean number of children in a family is 2.75." It is difficult to imagine what three-fourths of a child would be. In cases such as this, the mode is the preferred measure of central tendency. Although the mean would be more appropriate than the mode for describing the data in Table 2–2, the mode is 114.

In the normal distribution, the mean ($\overline{X}$), median (*Md*), and mode (*Mo*) are equal to each other, as shown in Figure 2–5a. In a skewed distribution, the mean is pulled out the farthest toward the tail of the distribution, as shown in Figure 2–5b.

Thus, one of the three measures of central tendency can be used to describe a typical score in a distribution.

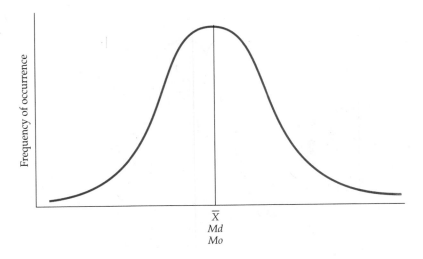

Figure 2–5a   *Position of the mean, median, and mode in a normal distribution*

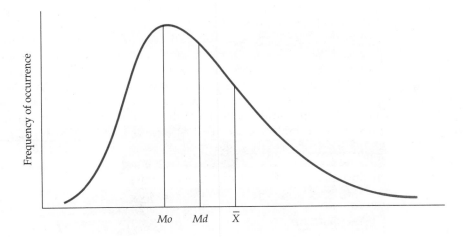

Figure 2–5b   *Position of the mean, median, and mode in a skewed distribution*

Measures of Variability

In addition to describing a set of scores by the shape of their distribution and central tendency, we can also talk about the spread of the scores or their variability. The scores' variability is an indication of how representative the mean is as a measure of central tendency. There are several numerical indices to describe variability in scores. The simplest index is called the range, which is obtained by

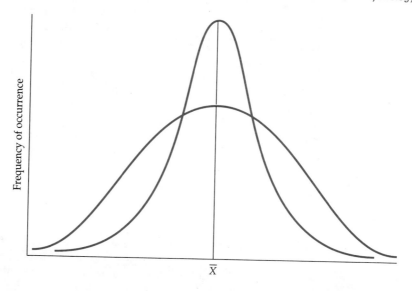

Figure 2–6 *Two distributions with the same mean but different variability*

subtracting the lowest score from the highest. The range of the data in Table 2–2 would be 157 – 67 = 90.

Consider Figure 2–6. Here there are two normal distributions with equal means but unequal variability. One distribution is very peaked with a small range; the other is quite flat with a big range. In addition to having different ranges, these distributions also differ with regard to another measure of variability, the *standard deviation*. The standard deviation is a measure of the spread of scores around the mean. The formula for the standard deviation is as follows:

$$s = \sqrt{\frac{\Sigma(X - \overline{X})^2}{N}}$$

[Formula 2–3]

where s is the standard deviation, X is each individual score, Σ is the symbol for summation, $\overline{X}$ is the mean of the distribution, and N is the total number of scores in the distribution. To compute the standard deviation, subtract the mean $(\overline{X})$ from each individual score (X) in the distribution, square that number, add up all the numbers, divide that total by the number of scores in the distribution, and then take the square root of the figure. By applying this formula to the data in Table 2–2, the standard deviation for that distribution is 19.96 (or 20 rounded off).

The standard deviation is particularly important in conjunction with the normal distribution. Given the mathematical properties of the normal curve, we know that theoretically 68% of all scores fall within ±1 standard deviation of the mean. So from the data in Table 2–2 (which has a mean of 113 and a standard deviation of 20), we know that theoretically 68% of all the scores should fall between 93 (113 – 20) and 133 (113 + 20). Furthermore, the mathematical derivation of the normal curve indicates that theoretically 95% of all the scores should fall within ±2 standard deviations from the mean; that is, between 73 (113 − 40) and 153 (113 + 40). Finally, theoretically 99% of all the scores should fall within ±3 standard deviations from the mean, between 53 (113 − 60) and 173 (113 + 60). The actual percentage of scores from the data in Table 2–2 is very close to the theoretical values; 69% of the scores fell within 1 standard deviation, 96% fell within 2 standard deviations, and 100% fell within 3 standard deviations. Although other measures of variability besides the range and standard deviation are also used, these two measures will suffice for the purposes of this book. Variability is important because it tells about the spread of scores in a distribution. This can be just as important as knowing the most typical score in a distribution.

The Concept of Correlation

So far we have been concerned with the statistical analysis of only one variable: its shape, typical score, and dispersion. But in most I/O psychological research, we are concerned with the relationship between two (or more) variables. In particular, we are usually interested in the extent that we can understand one variable (the criterion or dependent variable) on the basis of our knowledge about another (the predictor or independent variable). A statistical procedure useful in determining this relationship is called the *correlation coefficient*. A correlation coefficient reflects the degree of linear relationship between two variables, which we shall refer to as X and Y. The symbol for a correlation is r, and its range is from −1.00 to +1.00. A correlation coefficient tells two things about the relationship between two variables: the direction of the relationship and its magnitude.

The *direction* of the relationship is either positive or negative. A positive relationship means that as one variable increases in magnitude, so does the other. An example of a positive correlation would be that between height and weight. As a rule, the taller a person is, the more he or she weighs; increasing height is associated with increasing weight. A negative relationship means that as one variable increases in magnitude, the other gets smaller. An example of a negative correlation would be the correlation between production workers' efficiency and scrap rate. The more efficient workers are, the less scrap is left. The less efficient they are, the more scrap is left.

The *magnitude* of the correlation is an index of the strength of the relationship. Large correlations indicate greater strength than small correlations. A correlation of .80 indicates a very strong relationship between the variables, whereas a correlation of .10 indicates a very weak relationship. Also, magnitude and direction are independent. A correlation of −.80 is just as strong as one of +.80.

The four parts of Figure 2–7 show graphic portrayals of correlation coefficients. The first step in illustrating a correlation is to plot all pairs of variables in the study. For a sample of 100 people, record the height and weight of each person. Then plot the pairs of data points (height and weight) for each person. The stronger the relationship between the two variables, the tighter is the spread of data points around the line of best fit that runs through the scatterplot. Figure 2–7a shows a scatterplot for two variables that have a *high positive*

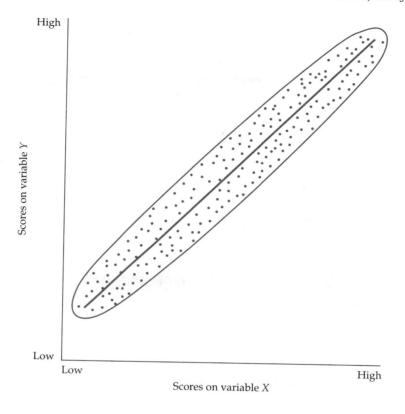

High

Scores on variable Y

Low

Low

High

Scores on variable X

Figure 2–7a   *Scatterplot of two variables having a high positive correlation*

correlation. Notice that the slope of the line through the data points slants in the positive direction, and most of the data points are packed tightly around the line.

Figure 2–7b shows a scatterplot for two variables that have a *high negative* correlation. Again, notice the data points are packed tightly around the line. But in this case, the line slants in the negative direction.

Figure 2–7c shows a scatterplot between two variables that have a *low positive* correlation. Although the line slants in the positive direction, the data points are spread quite widely throughout the scatterplot.

Finally, Figure 2–7d shows a scatterplot between two variables that have a *low negative* correlation. The line of best fit slants in the negative direction, and the data points are not packed tightly around the line.

The stronger the correlation between two variables (either positive or negative), the more accurately we can predict one variable from the other. The statistical formula used to compute a correlation will not be presented in this book as it isn't necessary for you to compute any correlations. However, it is important to know what a correlation is and how to interpret one. The only way to derive the

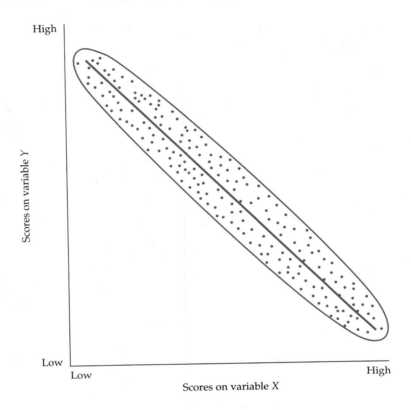

Figure 2–7b   *Scatterplot of two variables having a high negative correlation*

exact numerical value of a correlation is to apply the statistical formula. Although the eyeball-inspection method of looking at a scatterplot will yield some idea of what the correlation is, research has shown that people are generally not very good at inferring the magnitude of correlations by using this method (Bobko & Karren, 1979).

Calculation of a correlation coefficient does not permit any inferences about causality—that is, whether one variable caused the other to occur. Even though a causal relationship may exist between two variables, just computing a correlation will not reveal this fact.

Suppose you wish to compute the correlation between (1) the amount of alcohol consumed in a town and (2) the number of people who attend church there. You collect data on each of these variables in many towns in your area. The correlation turns out to be .85. On the basis of this high correlation, you conclude that because people drink all week, they go to church to repent (alcohol consumption causes church attendance). Your friends take the opposite point of view. They say that because people have to sit cramped together on hard wooden pews, after church they "unwind" by drinking (church attendance causes alcohol consump-

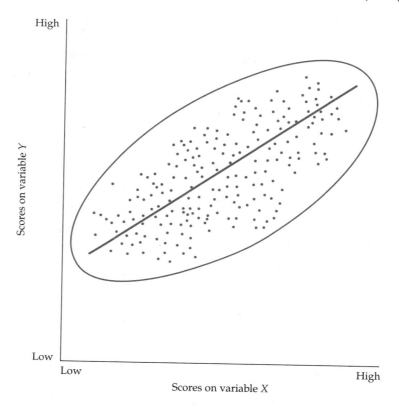

Figure 2–7c   *Scatterplot of two variables having a low positive correlation*

tion). Who is correct? On the basis of the existing data, no correct answer is possible, because causality cannot be inferred from a single correlation coefficient. One opinion may be correct, but proof of causality must await experimental research. In point of fact, the causal basis of this correlation is undoubtedly neither of the above opinions but is due to the fact that the various towns in the study have different populations, which produces a systematic relationship between these two variables along with many others, such as the number of people who eat out in restaurants or attend movies. Computing the correlation in this example will not even determine if the church-goers are the drinkers. The effect of a third variable on the two variables being correlated can serve to retard our ability to understand the relationship among the variables in purely correlational research.

To what degree can we determine causality in I/O research? Making a clear determination of causality in research is never easy, but two basic approaches have been developed. Both involve the critical factor of control—to control for other explanations for the obtained results. The classic approach is the laboratory experiment. In this case a small number of factors are selected for study, the experiment is carefully designed to control other variables, and the causal-based con-

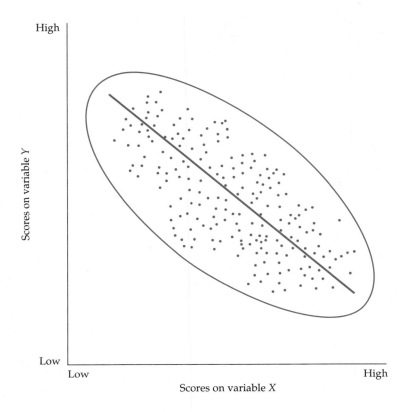

Figure 2–7d   *Scatterplot of two variables having a low negative correlation*

clusions are limited to the variables examined in the study. The Streufert et al. (1992) study on the effects of alcohol intoxication on visual-motor performance is one such example. The second approach to assessing causality is more recent (and somewhat more controversial). It is based on advances in mathematical techniques for abstracting causal information from nonexperimental data. However, these mathematical approaches require restrictive assumptions—the availability of well-developed theoretical formulations, measurement of all critical variables, and a high precision of measurement. Under these conditions, assessments of causality are permissible. For the most part, however, given the complexity of work behavior and the interrelatedness of our concepts, I/O psychologists seldom have the opportunity to make unequivocal assessments of causality. But our findings and our methods permit conclusions suggestive of causality, which in itself can be highly informative to the researcher.

Because correlation is a common analytical technique in I/O psychological research, many of the empirical findings in this book will be expressed in those terms. However, the concept of correlation will not magically yield accurate inferences in I/O psychological research. As Mitchell (1985) notes, a poorly designed research study cannot be "saved" by the use of correlation to draw valid conclusions. Researchers must carefully plan studies, use sound methodological procedures, and use appropriate statistical analyses to arrive at meaningful conclusions.

Meta-Analysis

A relatively new method of statistical analysis called *meta-analysis* (Hunter & Schmidt, 1990; Rosenthal, 1991) is being used with increasing frequency in I/O psychology. Meta-analysis is a statistical procedure designed to combine the results of many individual, independently conducted empirical studies into a single result or outcome. The logic behind meta-analysis is that we can arrive at a more accurate conclusion regarding a particular research topic if we combine or aggregate the results of many studies that address the topic instead of relying on the findings of a single study. The result of a meta-analysis study is often referred to as an "estimate of the true relationship" among the variables examined, because we believe such a result is a better approximation of the "truth" than would be found in any one study. A typical meta-analysis study might combine the results from 25 individual empirical studies. As such, meta-analysis investigations are sometimes referred to as "a study of studies." Although the nature of the statistical equations performed in meta-analysis exceed the scope of this book, they often entail adjusting for characteristics of a research study (for example, the quality of the measurements used in the study and the sample size) that are known to influence the study's results.

Despite the apparent objectivity of this method, the researcher must make a number of subjective decisions in conducting a meta-analysis. For example, one decision involves determining which empirical studies will be included in a meta-analysis. Every known study ever conducted on the topic could be included or only those studies that meet some criteria of empirical quality or rigor. The latter approach can be justified on the grounds that the results of a meta-analysis are only as good as the quality of the original studies used. The indiscriminate inclusion of low-quality empirical studies would lower the quality of the conclusion reached. Another issue is referred to as the "file drawer effect." Research studies that yield negative or nonsupportive results are not published (and thus are not widely available to other researchers) as often as studies that yield positive findings. The nonpublished studies are "filed away" by researchers, resulting in published studies being biased in the direction of positive outcomes. Thus, a meta-analysis of published studies could lead to a distorted conclusion caused by the relative absence of (unpublished) studies reporting negative results. These are two issues that must be addressed in conducting a meta-analysis (Wanous, Sullivan, & Malinak, 1989).

Despite the difficulty in making some of these decisions, meta-analysis is a popular research procedure in I/O psychology. Recent refinements and theoretical extensions in meta-analytic techniques (Raju, Burke, Normand, & Langlois,

1991) attest to the sustained interest in this method across the areas of psychology. For example, many companies have sponsored smoking cessation programs for their employees to promote health and reduce medical costs. Viswesvaran and Schmidt (1992) meta-analyzed the results from 633 studies of smoking cessation involving more than 70,000 individual smokers. The findings showed that 18.6% of smokers quit after participation in a cessation program, but the results differed by type of program. Instructional programs were found to be twice as effective as drug-based programs. The results of this meta-analysis can be of considerable practical value in assisting organizations to develop effective smoking cessation programs for their employees. Schmidt (1992) is particularly positive about the benefits of meta-analysis to cumulate scientific knowledge and to transform the way psychologists view the general research process. It is clear that meta-analysis has become a prominent data-analytic method for researchers and will undoubtedly continue to be so in the future.

Conclusions from Research

After the data have been analyzed, the researcher draws conclusions. A conclusion may be that alcohol intoxication impairs certain skills more than others. Jobs that require skills more adversely impaired by alcohol might impose more restrictive standards than other jobs. Latham and Kinne's study (1974) concluded that goal setting increased the rate of wood harvesting. So a company might decide to implement the goal-setting procedure throughout the firm. Generally, it is unwise to implement any major changes based on the results of only one study. As a rule, we prefer to know the results from several studies. We want to be as certain as possible that any organizational changes are grounded in repeatable, generalizable results.

Sometimes the conclusions drawn from a study modify beliefs about a problem. In Figure 2–1 a feedback loop extends from "conclusions from research" to "statement of the problem." The findings from one study influence research problems in future studies. Theories may be altered if empirical research fails to confirm some of the hypotheses put forth. One of the critical issues in conducting research is the quality of the generalizations that can be drawn from the conclusions. A number of factors determine the boundary conditions for generalizing the conclusions from a research study to a broader population or setting. One factor is the individuals who serve as the research subjects. The generalizability of conclusions drawn from research on college students has been questioned on the grounds that college-aged students are not representative of the general population. It is advisable to explicitly assess the generalizability of findings across groups, as was done in the Murphy et al. (1991) study on attitudes toward drug testing. A second factor is the degree of fit between the subjects and the research task. Studying what college students believe is important in finding a job is a reasonable fit between subjects and the task. Studying what leisure activities college students will engage in after they retire from the work force is not. A third factor addresses the generalizability of conclusions as a function of the research method. Dipboye (1990) argues that research topics are studied in either laboratory or field settings. He feels that laboratory and field research strategies should be used in coordination with each other rather than in competition. Dipboye believes that each basic strategy has something to offer and that researchers can gain understanding by studying the problem with both methods. Laboratory research has traditionally been regarded as more scientifically rigorous, whereas field research is seen as more representative of real-world conditions. Locke (1985) reached the conclusion that most findings from laboratory experiments can be generalized beyond the lab, but other individuals (for example, Mook, 1983) are more skeptical.

Research is a cumulative process. Researchers build on one another's work in formulating new research questions. They communicate their results by publishing articles in journals. A competent researcher must keep up to date in his or her area of expertise to avoid repeating someone else's study. The conclusions drawn from research can affect many aspects of our lives. Research is a vital part of industry; it is the basis for changes in products and services. Research can truly be an exciting activity. It is only tedious if you approach it from the perspective of testing stuffy theories, using sterile statistics, and inevitably reaching dry conclusions. Daft (1983) has suggested that research is a craft and that a researcher, like an artist or craftsperson, has to pull together a wide variety of human experiences to produce a superior product. Being a researcher is more like unraveling a mystery than following a cookbook (see Field Note 1). However, research is not flash-in-the-pan thrill seeking; it involves perseverance, mental discipline, and patience. There is also no substitute for hard work. I can recall many times when I anxiously anticipated seeing computer analyses that would foretell the results of a lengthy research study. This sense of anticipation is the fun of doing research—

FIELD NOTE 1

Being a good researcher is a lot like being a good detective. You have to use all of your senses to buttress information collected by traditional research methods. I often administer and interpret attitude surveys for my industrial clients. The results of these surveys reveal a wealth of information about the companies. However, if judged only in statistical terms, this information can often seem somewhat dry and bland. Therefore, I decided to experience the organizations in person to better understand and appreciate the statistical results. I have smelled acid fumes in a metal fabricating company that burned my nose and eyes after only a few minutes' exposure. I have tasted a rancid bologna sandwich from a vending machine situated by a big window in the company cafeteria (the sun shining through the window heated the machine and spoiled the food). I have walked (and slipped) across a company parking lot that was a solid 2- to 3-inch sheet of ice during the months of January and February. I have been in a "sound-sensitive" room that was so quiet I could hear my heartbeat. And in the president's office of one status-conscious organization, I have seen a white llama-wool carpet thick enough to swallow most of my shoes as I walked across it. In and of themselves, these events have little meaning, but when considered as part of the total organizational fabric, they provide a rich texture to I/O research findings.

and research, in the spirit of Daft's view of researchers being craftspersons, is a craft I try to pass on to my students.

McCall and Bobko (1990) also note the importance of *serendipity* in scientific research. Serendipity refers to a chance occurrence or happening that influences the research process. The history of science is filled with chance discoveries. For example, a contaminated culture eventually led Fleming to learn about and recognize the properties of penicillin. Rather than discarding the culture because it was contaminated, Fleming sought to understand how it had become so. We should always allow room for lucky accidents and unexpected observations and be prepared to pursue them.

Ethical Problems in Research

Research subjects have certain legal rights (Kelman, 1972) pertaining to physical treatment during a study, confidentiality of information, privacy, and voluntary consent (no one can be forced to take part in a study). Researchers who violate these rights, particularly in studies that involve physical or psychological risk, can be subject to professional censure and possible litigation. The American Psychological Association (1992) has a code of ethics that must be honored by all APA members who conduct research. Among the researcher responsibilities covered by the code of ethics are the accurate advertising of psychological services, confidentiality of information collected during the research, and the rights of human subjects participating in it. The code of ethics was created to protect the rights of subjects and to avoid the possibility of having research conducted by unqualified people.

The researcher is faced with additional problems with employees of companies. Argyris (1968) reports that although managers generally favor research, it can cause its own share of problems in an industrial context. Employees who are naive about the purpose of research are often suspicious when asked to participate. They wonder how they were "picked" for inclusion in the study and if they will be asked difficult questions. Some people even think a psychologist can read their minds and thus discover all sorts of private thoughts. Research projects that arouse emotional responses place managers in an uncomfortable interpersonal situation.

Mirvis and Seashore (1979) have described some of the problems facing those who conduct research with employees. Most problems involve role conflict, the dilemma of being trained to be a good researcher yet having to comply with both company and professional standards (London & Bray, 1980). For example, consider a role-conflict problem I faced doing research with industrial employees. I used a questionnaire to assess the employees' opinions and morale.

Management had commissioned the study. As part of the research design, all employees were told that their responses would be confidential. One response revealed the existence of employee theft. Although I did not know the identity of the employee, with the information given and a little help from management, that person could have been identified. Was I to violate my promise and turn over the information to management? Should I tell management that some theft had occurred but I had no way to find out who had done it (which would not have been true)? Or was I to ignore what I knew and fail to tell management about a serious problem in the company? In this case I informed the company of the occurrence of theft, but I refused to supply any information regarding the personal identity of the thief. This was an uneasy compromise between serving the needs of my client and maintaining the confidentiality of the information source. These types of problems are not unique to my study (Williams, Seybolt, & Pinder, 1975).

Lowman (1985) has presented a series of cases on ethical problems for I/O psychologists taken from real-life experiences. The book reveals a multitude of ethical dilemmas covering such issues as conflict of interest, plagiarizing, and "overselling" research results. The pressures to conduct high-quality research, the need to be ethical, and the reality of organizational life sometimes place the researcher in a difficult situation (see Field Note 2). These demands place constraints on the I/O psychologist that researchers in other areas do not always face. Freeman (1990) notes a trend of increasing concern for ethics in all facets of I/O psychological research including drug testing and the moral rights of employees.

Research in Industry

Although the empirical research process shown in Figure 2–1 portrays the conduct of most I/O psychological research, research conducted in industry (as opposed to universities or research centers) often has some additional distinguishing features. Boehm (1980) has observed that in industry, research questions inevitably arise from organizational problems. For example, problems of excessive employee absenteeism, turnover, job dissatisfaction, and so on may be the genesis for a research study designed to reduce their severity. Rarely will research questions be posed just to "test a theory." In fact, a study by Flanagan and Dipboye (1981) revealed that psychologists who view organizations simply as laboratories to test theories are not looked on favorably.

A second major difference involves how the results will be used. In industry, if the results of the study turn out to be positive and useful, the research unit of the organization will then try to "sell" (that is, gain acceptance of) the findings throughout the rest of the organization. For example, if providing job applicants with a very candid and realistic preview of the organization reduces turnover, the researchers will try to persuade the rest of the organization to use such procedures in recruiting new employees. If the results of a study turn out negative, the organization will look for side products or secondary ideas that will be of value. In research outside industry, less attention is given to implementing the findings and convincing other people of their utility.

Third, industry has different motives for conducting research. Industrial research is conducted to enhance the organization's efficiency. Among private-sector employers this usually translates into greater profitability. For example, research can be of vital importance in discovering consumer responses to new products and services, identifying ways to reduce waste, and making better use of employees. In university settings research may not have such an instrumental purpose. The research questions have relevance to industry, but the link between the findings and their implementation may not be as direct (see Field Note 3).

I am reminded of a student who approached an organization with a research idea. The student needed a sample of managers to test a particular hypothesis. After patiently listening to the student's request, the organizational representative asked: "Why should we participate in this study? How can this study help us?"

FIELD NOTE 2

Most ethical problems do not have clear-cut solutions. Here is one I ran into. I was trying to identify some psychological tests that would be useful in selecting future salespeople for a company. As part of my research, I administered the tests in question to all the employees in the sales department. With the company's consent, I assured the employees that the test results would be confidential. I explained that my purpose in giving the tests was to test the tests—that is, to assess the value of the tests—and no one in the company would ever use the test results to evaluate the employees. In fact, no one in the company would even know the test scores. The results of my research were highly successful. I was able to identify the tests that were useful in selecting potentially successful salespeople.

A few weeks later the same company's management approached me and said they now wanted to look into the value of using psychological tests to promote salespeople to the next highest job in the department, that of sales manager. In fact, they were so impressed with the test results for selecting new salespeople, they wanted to assess the value of these very same tests for identifying good sales managers. And since I had already given the tests to their salespeople and had the scores, all I would have to do is turn over the scores to the company, and they would determine if there was any relationship between the scores and promotability to sales manager. I said I couldn't turn over the test results, because that would violate my statement that the results were confidential and that no one in the company would ever know how well the employees did on the tests. I offered two alternatives. One

would be to readminister the same tests to the employees under a different set of test conditions; namely, that the company *would* see the test results, and in fact the results could be used to make promotion decisions. The second alternative would be for me (not the company) to determine the value of these tests to make promotion decisions. In that way I would maintain the confidentiality of the test scores.

Management totally rejected the first alternative, saying it made no sense to readminister the same tests to the same people. I already had the test results, so why go back and get them a second time? The second alternative was also not approved. They said I was deliberately creating a need for the company to pay me for a second consulting project when they were perfectly capable of doing the work with no outside help and at no extra cost. They said, in effect, I was holding the test results "hostage" and would not release them. In my opinion the company's management was asking me to compromise my professional integrity by using the test results in a way that violated the principles under which the tests were originally administered.

The issue was never really resolved. The company soon faced some major sales problems caused by competitors and lost interest in the idea of using psychological tests to identify sales managers. The management is still angered by my decision, asserting I am assuming ownership of "their" test results. I have not been asked to do any more consulting work for them, but it is also quite possible they would no longer have needed my services even if I had turned the test results over.

Industries that sponsor and participate in research do so for a reason: to enhance their welfare. Universities also conduct research for a reason, but it may be nothing more than intellectual curiosity. Some recent studies have examined the extent to which research influences policy makers; that is, how much do the results of research studies influence important decisions. Ruback and Innes (1988) concluded that to have the greatest impact we need to study dependent variables that are important to decision makers—such as human lives and dollars saved. They also believe we should focus our attention on independent variables that policy makers have the power to change.

While academic and industrial research may be guided by somewhat different factors, both have contributed substantially to the I/O psychological literature. The infusion of research from both sectors has in fact been very healthy and stimulating for the profession. Jahoda (1981) has commented that more psychological research needs to be done in anticipation of future work problems as opposed to a reaction to current problems. Industrial researchers seem to be in the best position to forecast future organizational concerns. Thus, they may be able to find answers to problems before they become crises.

What *should* I/O psychologists study? Strasser and Bateman (1984) surveyed both managers and nonmanagers, and the predominant answer from both groups

FIELD NOTE 3

Industrial research is always embedded in a larger context; that is, it is conducted for a specific reason. Sometimes the research is successful, sometimes it isn't, and sometimes you can win the battle but lose the war. A client of mine gave promotional tests—tests that current employees would take to be advanced to higher positions in the company at higher rates of pay. These tests were important to the employees, for only through the tests could they be promoted. The company gave an attitude survey and discovered that many employees did not like the tests. The employees said that many test questions were outdated, there were no correct answers to some questions, and that most questions were poorly worded. As a result of all these "bad" questions, employees were failing the tests and not getting promoted.

I was hired to update and improve the promotional tests (there were 75 of them). Using the full complement of psychological research procedures, I analyzed every question on every test, eliminated the poor questions, had new questions developed, and in general "cleaned up"

each of the tests. By every known standard the tests were now of very high quality. Both the company's management and I felt confident that the employees would be delighted with these revised tests. We were wrong. In the next attitude survey given by the company, the employees continued to think poorly of the (new) tests, but their reasons were different from before. Now they complained that the tests were too hard, too technical, and required too much expertise to pass. The employees failed the new tests with the same frequency as they had failed the old tests, and they were just as unhappy. In fact, they may have been even more unhappy since their expectations about the tests had been elevated because the company had hired me to revise them. I felt I had done as good a job in revising the tests as I possibly could have, but in the final analysis I didn't really solve the company's problem. I was hired to revise the tests, but what the management really wanted was to have the employees be satisfied with the tests, which didn't occur.

related to how people can learn to get along with one another in a work context. As one respondent in their survey said, "People all have different personalities and some people we just can't get along with. How can we avoid personality conflicts and still have a good working relationship?" (p. 87). The second most pressing research need was better communication among people.

Thomas and Tymon (1982) believe there is an unhealthy split between academicians who research topics ("knowledge producers") and practitioners who want to implement research findings ("knowledge users"). They feel that individuals tend to fall into one of the camps and that we need closer interplay between producing knowledge and using it. More recently, other researchers have echoed these same thoughts (for example, Harmon, 1991). Although it may be tempting to say that researchers should tackle big, socially important problems, such problems are usually very complex and difficult to research. However, the contributions I/O psychologists have made to such areas are among our profession's proudest achievements. I/O psychological research has been instrumental in enhancing our nation's productivity (Guzzo, Jette, & Katzell, 1985) and the quality of our work life (Lawler, 1982).

CASE STUDY   *How Should I Study This?*

Robin Mosier had just returned from her psychology class and was anxious to tell her roommate about an idea she had. Julie Hansen had taken the same class the previous semester, so Robin was hopeful that Julie could help her out. The psychology professor gave the class an assignment to come up with a research design to test some hypothesis. The basis for Robin's idea stemmed from the job she had held the past summer.

Robin began to describe her idea. "Last summer I worked as a clerk in the bookkeeping department of a bank. Sometimes it wasn't always clear how we should fill out certain reports and forms. I was always pretty reluctant to go to my supervisor, Mr. Kast, and ask for help. So were the other female workers. But I noticed the guys didn't seem to be reluctant at all to ask him for help. So I got this idea, see, I think females are more reluctant than males to ask a male superior for help."

"Okay," replied Julie. "So now you have to come up with a way to test that idea."

"Right," said Robin. "I was thinking maybe I could make up a questionnaire and ask students in my class about it. I think people would know if they felt that way or not."

"Maybe so," Julie said, "but maybe they wouldn't want to admit it. You know, it could be one of those things that you either don't realize about yourself, or if you do, you just don't want to say so."

"Well, if I can't just ask people about it, maybe I could do some sort of experiment," Robin commented. "What if I gave students some tasks to do but the instructions weren't too clear? If I'm right, more males than females will ask a male experimenter for help."

"Do you think you'd get the opposite effect with a female experimenter?" asked Julie.

"You mean, would more females than males ask a female experimenter for help? I don't know. Maybe," answered Robin.

"If that's the case," said Julie, "you might want to test both male and female experimenters with both male and female subjects."

Robin scratched some notes on a pad. Then she said, "Do you think an experimenter in a study is the same thing as a boss on a job? You see your boss every day, but you may only be in an experiment for about an hour. Maybe that would make a difference in whether you sought help."

"I'm sure it could," replied Julie. "I know I would act differently toward someone I might not see again than toward someone I'd have to work with a long time."

"I know what I'll do," Robin responded. "I won't do the experiment in a lab setting, but I'll go back to the company where I worked last summer. I'll ask the male and female office workers how they feel about asking Mr. Kast for help. I saw the way they acted last summer, and I'd bet they tell me the truth."

"Wait a minute," cautioned Julie. "Just because some females may be intimidated by Mr. Kast doesn't mean that effect holds for all male supervisors. Mr. Kast is just one man. How do you know it holds for men in general? That's what you want to test, right?"

Robin looked disconsolate. "There's got to be a good way to test this, although I guess it's more complicated than I thought."

Questions

1. What research method should Robin use to test her idea? How would you design the study?
2. What other variables might explain the employees' attitude toward Mr. Kast?
3. If this idea were tested in a laboratory or field experiment, what variables should be eliminated or controlled for in the research design?
4. If this idea were tested with a questionnaire, what questions should be asked?
5. If this idea were tested with the observation method, what behaviors would you look for?

PERSONNEL PSYCHOLOGY

Criteria: Standards for Decision Making

Major Chapter Objectives

- Understand the distinction between conceptual and actual criteria.

- Understand the meaning of criterion deficiency, relevance, and contamination.

- Understand the purpose of a job analysis and know the various methods of conducting one.

- Understand the purpose of a job evaluation and the related issues associated with determining the worth of a job.

- Identify the major types of criteria examined by I/O psychologists.

Each time you evaluate someone or something, you use criteria. *Criteria* (the plural of *criterion*) are best defined as evaluative standards; they are used as reference points in making judgments. We may not be consciously aware of the criteria that affect our judgments, but they do exist. We use different criteria to evaluate different kinds of objects or people. That is, we use different standards to determine what makes a good (or bad) movie, dinner, ball game, friend, spouse, or teacher. In the context of I/O psychology, criteria are most important for defining the "goodness" of employees, programs, and units in the organization, as well as the organization itself.

Disagreement among People in Making Evaluations

When you and some of your associates disagree in your evaluation of something, what is the cause? Chances are good the disagreement is caused by one of two types of criterion-related problems. For example, take the case of rating Professor Jones as a teacher. One student thinks he is a good teacher; another disagrees. The first student defines "goodness in teaching" as (1) preparedness, (2) course relevance, and (3) clarity of instruction. In the eyes of the first student, Jones scores very high on these criteria and receives a positive evaluation. The second student defines goodness as (1) enthusiasm, (2) capacity to inspire students, and (3) ability to relate to students on a personal basis. This student scores Jones low on these criteria and thus gives him a negative evaluation. Why the disagreement? Because the two students have different criteria for defining teaching effectiveness.

Disagreements over the proper criteria in decision making are quite common. Values and tastes often dictate people's choice of criteria. For someone with limited funds, a good car may be one that gets high gas mileage. But for a wealthy person, the main criterion may be physical comfort. Dyer, Schwab, and Theriault (1976) describe how managers and their bosses disagree on the criteria used in giving raises. Managers feel their performance is not given enough weight and that budgets are given too much weight. Such disagreements over the right criteria can adversely affect employee motivation and satisfaction.

Not all disagreements are caused by using different criteria, however. Suppose that both students in our teaching example define teaching effectiveness as preparedness, course relevance, and clarity of instruction. The first student thinks Professor Jones is ill prepared, teaches an irrelevant course, and gives unclear instruction. But the second student thinks he is well prepared, teaches a relevant course, and gives clear instruction. Both students are using the same evaluative standards, but they do not reach the same judgment. The difference of opinion in this case is due to discrepancies in the meaning attached to Professor Jones's behavior. These discrepancies may be due to perceptual biases, differential expectations, or different interpretations of the operational definitions associated with the criteria. Thus, people who use the same standards in making judgments do not always reach the same conclusion.

The profession of I/O psychology does not have a monopoly on criterion-related issues and problems. They occur in all walks of life, ranging from criteria used to judge interpersonal relationships (for example, communication, trust, respect) to criteria used to judge the welfare of nations (for example, literacy rates, per capita income, infant mortality rates). Differences of opinion about criteria even extend to how national industries evaluate themselves. Garvin (1986) reported that in Japanese companies issues of product quality are the primary concern, but in U.S. companies meeting production schedules is the primary goal. Since many important decisions are made on the basis of criteria, it would be difficult to overstate their significance in the decision-making process. Because criteria are used to render a wide range of judgments, I define them as the "evaluative standards by which objects, individuals, procedures, or collectivities are assessed for the purpose of ascertaining their quality." Criterion issues have major significance in the field of I/O psychology.

Conceptual versus Actual Criteria

Psychologists have not always felt that criteria are of prime importance. Before World War II, they were inclined to believe that "criteria were either given of God or just to be found lying about" (Jenkins, 1946, p. 93). Unfortunately, this is not so. We must carefully consider what is meant by a "successful" worker, student, parent, and so forth. We cannot plunge headlong into measuring success, goodness, or quality until we have a fairly good idea as to what (in theory, at least) we should be looking for.

A good beginning point is the notion of a conceptual criterion. The *conceptual criterion* is a theoretical construct, an abstract idea that can never actually be measured. It is an ideal set of factors that constitute a successful person (or object or collectivity) as conceived in the psychologist's mind. Let's say we want to define a successful college student. We might start off with *intellectual growth;* that is, capable students should experience more intellectual growth than less capable students. Another dimension might be *emotional growth.* A college education should help students clarify their own values and beliefs, and this should aid in emotional development and stability. Finally, we might say that a good college student should want to have some voice in civic activities, to be a "good citizen" and contribute to the well-being of his or her community. As an educated person, the good college student will assume an active role in helping to make society a better place in which to live. We might call this dimension a *citizenship* factor.

Thus, these three factors become the conceptual criteria for defining a "good college student." We could apply this same type of process to defining a "good worker," "good parent," or "good organization." However, because conceptual criteria are theoretical abstractions, we have to find some way to turn them into measurable, real factors. That is, we have to obtain *actual criteria* to serve as measures of the conceptual criteria that we would prefer to (but cannot) assess. The decision then becomes which variables to select as the actual criteria.

A psychologist might choose grade point average as a measure of intellectual growth. Of course, a grade point average is not equivalent to intellectual growth, but it probably reflects some degree of growth. To measure emotional growth, a

Table 3–1 *Conceptual and actual criteria for a successful college student*

Conceptual Criteria	Actual Criteria
1. Intellectual growth	Grade point average
2. Emotional growth	Adviser rating of emotional maturity
3. Citizenship	Number of volunteer organizations joined in college

psychologist might ask the student's adviser to judge how much the student has matured over his or her college career. Again, maturation is not exactly the same as emotional growth, but it is probably an easier concept to grasp and evaluate than the more abstract notion of emotional growth. Finally, as a measure of citizenship, a psychologist might count the number of volunteer organizations (student government, charitable clubs, and so on) the student has joined over his or her college career. It could again be argued that the sheer number (quantity) of joined organizations is not equivalent to the quality of participation in these activities and that "good citizenship" is more appropriately defined by quality rather than quantity of participation. Nevertheless, because of the difficulties inherent in measuring quality of participation, plus the fact that one cannot speak of quality unless there is some quantity, the psychologist decides to use this measure. Table 3–1 shows the relationship between the conceptual criteria and actual criteria of success as a college student.

How do we define a "good" college student in theory? Using the conceptual criteria as the evaluative standard, a good college student should display a high degree of intellectual and emotional growth and should be a responsible citizen in the community. How do we operationalize a good college student in practice? Using the actual criteria as the evaluative standard, we say a good college student has earned high grades, is judged by an academic adviser to be emotionally mature, and has joined many volunteer organizations throughout his or her college career. In reviewing the relationship between the two sets of criteria (conceptual and actual), remember "the goal is to obtain an approximate estimate of the (conceptual) criterion by selecting one or more actual criteria which we think are appropriate" (Blum & Naylor, 1968, p. 176).

Criterion Deficiency, Relevance, and Contamination

The relationship between conceptual and actual criteria can be expressed in terms of three concepts: deficiency, relevance, and contamination. Figure 3–1 shows the degree of overlap between conceptual and actual criteria. The circle represents the content of each type of criterion. Because the conceptual criterion is a theoretical abstraction, we can never know exactly how much overlap occurs. The actual criteria selected are never totally equivalent to the conceptual criteria we have in mind, so there will always be a certain amount (although unspecified) of deficiency, relevance, and contamination.

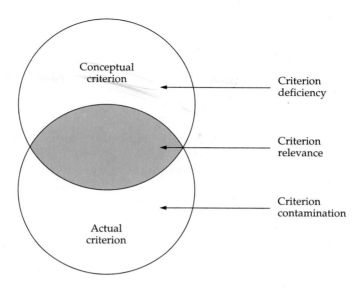

Figure 3–1 *Criterion deficiency, relevance, and contamination*

Criterion Deficiency. Criterion deficiency is the degree to which the actual criteria fail to overlap the conceptual criteria; that is, how deficient the actual criteria are in representing the conceptual ones. There is always some degree of deficiency in the actual criteria. By careful selection of the actual criteria, we can reduce (but never eliminate) criterion deficiency. Conversely, criteria that are selected because they are simply expedient, without much thought given to their match to conceptual criteria, will be grossly deficient.

Criterion Relevance. Criterion relevance is the degree to which the actual criteria and conceptual criteria coincide. The greater the match between the conceptual and actual criteria, the greater is the criterion relevance. Again, because the conceptual criteria are theoretical abstractions, we cannot know the exact amount of relevance.

Criterion Contamination. Criterion contamination is that part of the actual criteria that is unrelated to the conceptual criteria. It is the extent to which the actual criteria measure something other than the conceptual criteria. Contamination consists of two parts. One part, called *bias*, is the extent to which the actual criteria systematically or consistently measure something other than the conceptual criteria. The second part, called *error*, is the extent to which the actual criteria are not related to anything at all. Both contamination and deficiency are undesirable in the actual criterion, and together they distort the conceptual criterion. This prompted Brogden and Taylor (1950) to refer to them as *criterion distortion*. Criterion contamination distorts the actual criterion because certain factors are included that don't belong (that is, they are not present in the conceptual criterion). Criterion deficiency distorts the actual criterion because certain important dimensions of the conceptual criterion are not included in the actual criterion.

Let us consider criterion deficiency and contamination in the example of setting criteria for a good college student. How might the actual criteria we chose be deficient in representing the conceptual criteria?

Students typically begin a class with differing degrees of prior knowledge of the subject matter. One student may know nothing of the material, while another student may be very familiar with it. At the end of the term, the former student might have grown more intellectually than the latter student, but the latter student might get a higher grade in the course. However, by using the grade point average as our criterion, we would (falsely) conclude that the latter student grew more intellectually. So the relationship between grades and intellectual growth is not perfect (that is, it is deficient). A rating of emotional maturity by an academic adviser might be deficient because the adviser is not an ideal judge. He or she might have only a limited perspective of the student. Finally, it is not enough to just count how many volunteer groups a student belongs to. Quality of participation is as important (if not more so) than quantity.

How might these actual criteria be contaminated? If some academic majors are more difficult than others, grades will be a contaminated measure of intellectual growth; students in "easy" majors will be judged to have experienced more intellectual growth than students in difficult majors. This is a bias between earned grade point average and the difficulty of the student's academic major. The source of the bias affects the actual criterion (grades) but not the conceptual criterion (intellectual growth). A rating of emotional maturity by the student's adviser could be contaminated by the student's grades. The adviser might believe that students with higher grades have greater emotional maturity than students with low grades. Thus, the grade point average might bias an adviser's rating even though it probably has no relationship to the conceptual criterion of emotional growth. Finally, counting the number of organizations a student joins might be contaminated by the student's popularity. Students who join many organizations may simply be more popular rather than better citizens (which is what we wanted to measure).

If we know that these criterion measures are contaminated, why would we use them? In fact, when a researcher knows a certain form of contamination is present, its influence can be controlled through experimental or statistical procedures. The real problem lies in anticipating the occurrence of contaminating factors.

As Wallace (1965) has observed, psychologists have spent a great deal of time trying to discover new and better ways to measure actual criteria. They have used various analytical and computational procedures to get more precise assessments. Wallace has recommended that rather than dwelling on finding new ways to measure actual criteria, psychologists should spend more time choosing actual criteria that will be adequate measures of the conceptual criteria that they really seek to understand. The adequacy of the actual criterion as a measure of the conceptual criterion is always a matter of professional judgment—no equation or formula will determine it. As Wherry (1957) has said, "If we are measuring the wrong thing, it will not help us to measure it better" (p. 5).

Criterion Development

I/O psychologists use several different means to identify or develop criteria because it is vital to determine the appropriate evaluative standards for making judgments. The adequacy and appropriateness of criteria set the limits for the quality of the judgments. Poor criteria beget poor judgments. But the issue of appropriate criteria is made more difficult by a time dimension. Short-term criteria for defining the goodness or quality of something may not be the same as long-term criteria. In deciding to buy a car, a short-term criterion may be initial cost, and a long-term standard may be its resale value. Standards used to make short-term decisions about quality are called *proximal criteria*. Standards used to make long-term decisions about quality are called *distal criteria*. The following two studies of criterion development show different approaches to this topic.

Criteria may be developed *deductively* (from theory to data) or *inductively* (from data to theory). An example of the deductive approach was reported by Freeberg (1976), who wanted to define relevant criteria for judging the quality of a youth work-training program. The program's purpose was to train hard-to-employ teenagers in certain skills so they could get full-time jobs. Freeberg carefully examined the existing literature on training programs and arrived at 32 variables indicative of performance in the training program (proximal criteria) and 40 variables for postprogram job performance (distal criteria). Trainees rated themselves on the 32 program-completion variables (for example, their degree of vocational awareness and confidence, personal adjustment, and motivation). Former trainees who now held jobs rated themselves on the 40 postprogram variables (for example, their level of job performance, extent and level of employment, and vocational planning). Freeberg used a statistical procedure called *factor analysis* to identify the major dimensions of training and posttraining success based on these ratings. The results showed that the 32 program-completion variables could be reduced to four major criteria of success in the training program: work motivation and social attitudes, social-community adjustment, training-program adjustment, and competence in vocational planning. The 40 postprogram variables were reduced to five major criteria of success on the job: overall social and vocational adjustment, on-the-job success and satisfaction, job search motivation, competence in job planning, and short-range job orientation. This study is a good example of the deductive approach to criterion development. It starts with a careful and rational identification of possible criterion variables, followed by an empirical assessment of their value.

One of my own studies (Muchinsky, 1975b) provides an example of the inductive approach to criterion development. I was interested in establishing the criteria of consumer credit risk. I wanted to learn how people were judged to be good or poor credit risks. Unlike the author of the previous study, I had no prior theoretical notions as to what constitutes credit risk. I used the inductive approach—starting with data and culminating with some conceptual ideas—to establish the criteria of credit risk. I obtained the financial records of many people who had borrowed money from loan companies. Half of them were judged poor credit risks on the basis of how they repaid their loans and had been denied further credit. The other half were judged good credit risks and would be granted another loan by the company. I wanted to find out which aspects of loan repayment affect people's credit ratings. After comparing the two groups on several variables associated with loan repayment, I found two critical dimensions: how delinquent the people were in making their monthly loan payments and whether they missed payments. The poor credit risks either missed several payments or were often late making them. So I determined the concept of credit risk is defined by two criteria: missed payments and delinquency of payments. Working inductively, I then proposed an explanation of consumer credit risk (Muchinsky, 1975a).

What do we "do" with criteria once we have established them? They serve many purposes, both theoretical and applied. From a theoretical viewpoint, criteria are the basis for understanding a concept. In fact, the concept is best defined by the interrelationships among the criteria used to assess it. I was able to define the concept of credit risk after identifying its criterion dimensions. This procedure, called *construct validation*, will be discussed in more detail in a later chapter.

From a practical standpoint, the identification of criteria provides a rational basis for "treating" people, programs, or social collectivities. For example, as a loan company official, you would not give a loan to someone who has a history of missing payments or of being delinquent. As a training program director, you would want the program to enhance trainee motivation and increase competence in vocational planning. As the director of a welfare agency, you would want to extend financial or medical aid to communities at certain poverty or illness levels. Identifying criteria is the first step in initiating action (for example, selecting, training, assisting), which is part of an organization's goals.

Job Analysis

I/O psychologists must often identify the criteria of effective job performance. These criteria then become the basis for hiring people (choosing them on the basis of ability to meet the criteria of job performance), training them (to perform those aspects of the job that are important), paying them (high levels of performance should warrant higher pay), and classifying jobs (jobs with similar performance criteria would be grouped together). A procedure useful in identifying the criteria or performance dimensions of a job is called *job analysis;* it is conducted by a job analyst. Harvey (1991) defines job analysis as "the collection of data describing (a) observable (or otherwise verifiable) job behaviors performed by workers, including both *what is accomplished* as well as *what technologies are employed* to accomplish the end results and (b) verifiable characteristics of the job environment with which workers interact, including physical, mechanical, social, and informational elements" (p. 71). A thorough job analysis will document the tasks performed on the job, the situation in which the work is performed (for example, tools and equipment present, working conditions), and the human qualities needed to perform the work. These data then provide the basic building blocks needed for many personnel decisions.

Sources of Job Information

A critical issue in job analysis is the accuracy and completeness of the information about the job. Three major sources of job information are often relied upon; their common ingredient is a "subject matter expert" (SME). The qualifications for being termed an SME are not precise, but a minimum condition is that the person has direct, up-to-date experience with the job for a long enough time to be familiar with all of its tasks (Thompson & Thompson, 1982).

The most common source of information is the *job incumbent*; that is, the holder of the job. The use of job incumbents as SMEs is predicated on their implicit understanding of their own jobs. Landy and Vasey (1991) believe the sampling method by which SMEs are selected is very important. They found that experienced job incumbents provided the most valuable job information. Other individual characteristics such as verbal ability, having a good memory, and cooperativeness also contributed to the effectiveness of job incumbents as SMEs. Also, if incumbents are suspicious of the motives behind conducting a job analysis, they are inclined to magnify the importance or difficulty of their abilities as a self-protective tactic (see Field Note 1).

A second source of SMEs is the *supervisors* of the job incumbent. Supervisors play a major role in determining what job incumbents do on their jobs and thus are a credible source of information. While supervisors may describe jobs somewhat more objectively than incumbents, there can be legitimate differences of opinion between incumbents and supervisors. It has been my experience that most differences occur over not what is accomplished in a job but the critical abilities actually needed to perform the job.

The third source of job information is a trained *job analyst*. Job analysts are used as SMEs when comparisons are needed across many jobs. Because of their familiarity with job analysis methods, analysts often provide the most consistent across-job ratings. Job analyst expertise lies not in the subject matter of various jobs per se but in their ability to understand similarities and differences across jobs in terms of tasks performed and abilities needed.

In general, incumbents and supervisors are the best sources of job descriptive information, while job analysts are best qualified to comprehend the relationships among a set of jobs. The most desirable strategy in understanding a job is to collect information from as many qualified sources as possible, as opposed to exclusive reliance on just one source.

Methods of Job Analysis

There are four major methods for analyzing jobs. The first is a variation of the *interview.* Employees are asked questions about the nature of their work. They may be interviewed individually, in small groups, or through a series of panel discussions. A trained interviewer questions the employees to get an understanding of the activities performed on the job and the skills needed to perform them. The interview method is probably the most commonly used job analysis method because it is adaptable to a wide variety of jobs.

FIELD NOTE 1

When interviewing employees about their jobs, job analysts should explain what they are doing (and why they are doing it). If they do not fully explain their role, employees may feel threatened, fearing the analysts may somehow jeopardize their positions by giving a negative evaluation of their performance, lowering their wages, firing them, and so on. While job analysts do not have the power to do these things, some employees assume the worst. When employees feel threatened, they usually magnify the importance or difficulty of their contributions to the organization in an attempt to protect themselves. Therefore, to ensure accurate and honest responses, all job analysts should go out of their way to disarm any possible suspicions or fears.

I learned the importance of this point early in my career. One of my first job analyses focused on the job of a sewer cleaner. I had arranged to interview three sewer cleaners about their work. However, I had neglected to provide much advance notice about myself—why I would be talking to them, or what I was trying to do. I simply arrived at the work site, introduced myself, and told the sewer cleaners that I wanted to talk to them about their jobs. Smelling trouble, the sewer cleaners proceeded to give me a memorable lesson on the importance of first establishing a nonthreatening atmosphere. One sewer cleaner turned to me and said:

"Let me tell you what happens if we don't do our job. If we don't clean out the sewers of stuff like tree limbs, rusted hubcaps, and old tires, the sewers get clogged up. If they get clogged up, the sewage won't flow. If the sewage won't flow, it backs up. People will have sewage backed up into the basements of their homes. Manhole covers will pop open, flooding the streets with sewage. Sewage will eventually cover the highways, airport runways, and train tracks. People will be trapped in their homes surrounded by sewage. The entire city will be covered with sewage, with nobody being able to get in or out of the city. And that's what happens if we don't do our job of cleaning the sewers."

Sadder but wiser, I learned the importance of not giving employees any reason to overstate their case.

The second method of job analysis uses structured *questionnaires* or *inventories*. The typical questionnaire would list many activities that could be performed on a job (several hundred questions would not be unusual). The employee would rate these activities on several scales, such as how often they are performed, how important they are, and so on. The answers would then be statistically analyzed to arrive at an understanding of job content. The questionnaire method is most useful for drawing comparisons among different jobs.

The third method is called *direct observation*. In this method employees are observed as they perform their jobs. Observers try to be unobtrusive, observing the jobs but not getting in the employees' way (see Field Note 2). Observers do not talk to the employees because it interferes with the conduct of work. Sometimes cameras or videotape equipment are used to facilitate the observation. Direct observation is an excellent method for appreciating and understanding the adverse conditions (such as noise or heat) under which some jobs are performed; however, it is a poor method for understanding "why" certain behaviors occur on the job.

Answers about why the job behavior occurs should be ascertained with another method, such as the interview.

In the final method of job analysis, the analyst asks workers to record their own activities in *logbooks* or *work diaries*. The analyst then studies these books to infer the nature of the work performed. This is the least common and least desirable method of job analysis, primarily because individuals differ markedly in their written communication skills. Some people can clearly and concisely describe in writing what they do on the job. Other people have a difficult time writing a simple sentence. Consequently, the quality of information gleaned from this method can be questionable.

In practice, a job analyst may use more than one method to study a job. I often use three methods in my job analysis work. First, I observe the people at the work site to get a general feel for the jobs. Next, I interview the workers, asking questions about what I've observed. Finally, I follow up with the questionnaire, which I have found to be the most thorough method of job analysis. Although all four methods differ somewhat in the type of job-related information they provide, each method can be useful in establishing the criteria of job performance.

Job-Oriented and Worker-Oriented Procedures

It is also possible to differentiate job analysis questionnaires into "job-oriented" versus "worker-oriented" procedures. *Job-oriented* procedures are geared to the work that gets performed on the job. The emphasis is on the nature of the work activities conducted. Some job-oriented procedures break down a job into all the tasks that are performed, and the list may include as many as 400 to 500 tasks. Such analyses are sometimes called *task analyses*. Jobs are expressed in terms of the

FIELD NOTE 2

Although logically it may not seem so, it takes talent to watch people at work. Observation is one of the methods job analysts use to study jobs. The object is to unobtrusively observe the employee at work. The analyst doesn't need to hide; he or she simply needs to blend in. In attempts to avoid interfering with employees, I have inadvertently positioned myself too far away to really see what was happening. I have also learned to bring earplugs and goggles to work sites, because when watching people at work the analyst is exposed to the same environmental conditions they are. Although you can be "too far" from a worker to make accurate observations, you can also get "too close." Cascio (1982) describes this true story:

While riding along in a police patrol car as part of a job analysis of police officers, an analyst and an officer were chatting away when a call came over the radio regarding a robbery in progress. Upon arriving at the scene the analyst and the officer both jumped out of the patrol car, but in the process the overzealous analyst managed to position himself between the robbers and the police. Although the robbers were later apprehended, they used the analyst as a decoy to make their getaway from the scene of the crime. (p. 56)

Listed below is a duty and the tasks which it includes. Check all tasks which you perform. Add any tasks you do which are not listed. Then rate the tasks you have checked.		Time Spent	Importance
		1. Very much below average	1. Extremely unimportant
		2. Below average	2. Very unimportant
		3. Slightly below average	3. Unimportant
A. Installing and removing aerial cable systems.		4. About average	4. About medium importance
	Check ✔ if done	5. Slightly above average	5. Important
		6. Above average	6. Very important
		7. Very much above average	7. Extremely important
1. Attach suspension strand to pole.			
2 Change and splice lasher wire.			
3. Deliver materials to lineman with snatch block and handline.			
4. Drill through-bolt holes and secure suspension clamps on poles.			
5. Install cable pressurization systems.			
6. Install distribution terminals.			
7. Install pulling-in line through cable rings.			
8. Load and unload cable reels.			
9. Load lashing machine with lashing wire.			

Figure 3–2 Portion of a task analysis inventory for the Air Force

SOURCE: From *Procedural Guide for Conducting Occupational Surveys in the United States Air Force* by J. E. Morsh and W. B. Archer, 1967 (September). (Lackland Air Force Base, TX: Personnel Research Laboratory, Aerospace Medical Division.)

tasks performed through the use of such job terminology as inspecting, repairing, hammering, and so forth. Figure 3–2 shows part of a task analysis inventory used in the U.S. Air Force.

In contrast, a *worker-oriented* procedure is geared to the human talents needed to perform the job, and jobs are typically expressed in terms of knowledge, skill, ability, and personal characteristics. A worker-oriented job analysis would express the job in terms of the required human characteristics, such as visual acuity, intelligence, depth perception, physical stamina, and so forth. An example of a worker-oriented procedure is the Position Analysis Questionnaire (PAQ) (McCormick, Jeanneret, & Mecham, 1972). The PAQ consists of 194 statements used to describe the human attributes needed to perform a job. The statements are orga-

Relationships with Other Persons

This section deals with different aspects of interaction between people involved in various kinds of work.

Code	Importance to this job
DNA	Does not apply
1	Very minor
2	Low
3	Average
4	High
5	Extreme

4.1 Communications

Rate the following in terms of how *important* the activity is to the completion of the job. Some jobs may involve several or all of the items in this section.

4.1.1 Oral (communicating by speaking)

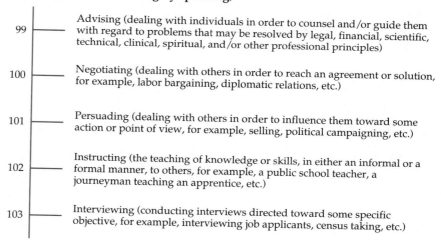

99 ——— Advising (dealing with individuals in order to counsel and/or guide them with regard to problems that may be resolved by legal, financial, scientific, technical, clinical, spiritual, and/or other professional principles)

100 ——— Negotiating (dealing with others in order to reach an agreement or solution, for example, labor bargaining, diplomatic relations, etc.)

101 ——— Persuading (dealing with others in order to influence them toward some action or point of view, for example, selling, political campaigning, etc.)

102 ——— Instructing (the teaching of knowledge or skills, in either an informal or a formal manner, to others, for example, a public school teacher, a journeyman teaching an apprentice, etc.)

103 ——— Interviewing (conducting interviews directed toward some specific objective, for example, interviewing job applicants, census taking, etc.)

Figure 3–3   *Sample items from the PAQ*

SOURCE: From Position Analysis Questionnaire. Copyright 1969 by Purdue Research Foundation. All rights reserved. Reprinted by permission.

nized into six major categories: information input, mental processes, work output, relationships with other persons, job context, and other job requirements. Some sample statements from the relationships with other persons category are shown in Figure 3–3. The statements shown here reflect the emphasis the PAQ places on the importance of human attributes needed to perform the job.

Both the job-oriented and worker-oriented procedures can be used to develop criteria. Job-oriented procedures define job success in terms of tasks performed; worker-oriented procedures define job success in terms of human characteristics. Most job-oriented procedures have to be handmade for each job to be analyzed because of the wide variation in jobs (McCormick, 1976). Worker-oriented procedures are more likely to be standardized and thus applicable across a broad array of jobs.

Problem Solving			
The job functions include		**The incumbent must**	
processing information to reach specific conclusions, answers to problems, to adapt and assess ideas of others, to revise into workable form.		analyze information and, by inductive reasoning, arrive at a specific conclusion or solution. (This trait is also referred to as *convergent thinking, reasoning*.)	
This level means	That the job activities require solving . . .	At this level	The incumbent must solve . . .
0	very minor problems with fairly simple solutions (running out of supplies or giving directions).	0	very minor problems with fairly simple solutions.
1	problems with known and limited variables (diagnosing mechanical disorders or customer complaints).	1	problems with known and limited variables.
2	more complex problems with many known variables (programming or investment analysis).	2	problems with many known and complex variables.
3	very complex and abstract problems with many unknown variables (advanced systems design or research).	3	very complex and abstract problems with many unknown variables.

Figure 3–4   *Sample item from the threshold traits analysis method of job analysis*
SOURCE: From "An Empirical Test of a Trait-Oriented Job Analysis Technique" by F. M. Lopez, G. A. Kesselman, and F. E. Lopez, 1981, *Personnel Psychology, 34*, p. 485. Reprinted by permission.

It is also possible to have a "hybrid" job analysis procedure that looks at both the job functions performed and the human attributes required. An example is the Threshold Traits Analysis developed by Lopez, Kesselman, and Lopez (1981). Lopez and associates identified 33 human traits (for example, strength, problem solving, oral expression) that represent the domain of traits used in performing jobs. They further studied jobs in terms of the tasks and activities performed. Knowing what jobs consisted of in terms of tasks or functions performed, they then sought to identify the human traits needed to perform them. Figure 3–4 illustrates their strategy for addressing a job from both the work-function and human attribute perspectives. The figure identifies one human attribute, problem solving, presented in the context of a job demand and human trait. The object is to get a "fit" between task requirements and human attributes as a means of understanding job content.

Evaluating Job Analysis Methods

It should be evident that there are multiple ways of analyzing jobs. Are some methods better than others? Most of what we know about the relative merits of job analysis methods is limited to the questionnaire procedure. For example, Arvey, Passino, and Lounsbury (1977) showed that the PAQ gave job analysis information that was not strongly biased either by the sex of the employee or of the analyst. Conley and Sackett (1987) demonstrated that high-performing and low-performing job incumbents gave equivalent descriptions of their jobs. That is, job analytic information is not biased by the performance level of the incumbent. Cornelius, DeNisi, and Blencoe (1984) reported differences in using the PAQ between the conclusions reached by expert job analysts and those of college students. As with most sophisticated measuring instruments, the PAQ's conclusions are influenced by the qualifications of the user. The PAQ does have some general and a few specific limitations that apply to many job analysis questionnaires, mostly involving user reactions. Ash and Edgell (1975) reported the PAQ requires reading ability between high school and college graduate level. This limits the type of people who could accurately use the procedure. Harvey, Friedman, Hakel, and Cornelius (1988) developed a worker-oriented job analysis inventory that has a much lower reading level than the PAQ but conceptualizes job structures in much the same way.

The PAQ has aided our understanding of jobs more than any other single job analysis method. The results of a study by Levine, Ash, Hall, and Sistrunk (1983) comparing seven major questionnaire methods of job analysis reflect what the I/O profession as a whole has come to understand about job analysis methods. The authors found that different methods are regarded as differentially effective and practical depending on the purposes for which they may be used. No one method consistently surfaces as the best across the board. I believe that a well-trained job analyst could draw accurate inferences and conclusions using any one of several questionnaire methods. However, the converse is also true. No method can ensure accurate results when used by someone who is inexperienced with job analysis. A related opinion was reached by Harvey and Lozada-Larsen (1988), who concluded that the most accurate job analysis ratings are provided by raters who are highly knowledgeable about the job. Finally, Spector, Brannick, and Coovert (1989) described using computers to develop an artificial intelligence system to perform a job analysis. If successful, the computer would model the human judgment process in assembling information about jobs, and thereby remove the human job analyst from the process of analyzing jobs.

Figure 3–5 reveals the relationship among four job-related concepts. At the lowest level of aggregation we have *tasks*. *Tasks* are the basic units of work that are directed toward specific job objectives. A *position* is defined by a set of tasks performed by a single employee. There are usually as many positions in an organization as there are employees. However, many positions may be similar to each

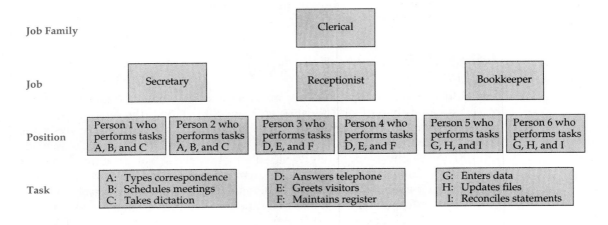

Figure 3–5   *Relationships among tasks, positions, jobs, and job family*

other. In such a case similar positions are grouped or aggregated to form a *job*. An example would be the job of secretary. Another job might be that of bookkeeper. Similar jobs may be further aggregated based on general similarity of content to form a *job family*, in this case, the clerical job family.

One of the many uses of job analysis results is the capacity to compare and contrast different jobs and to group jobs into similar job families. Having families of like jobs helps determine wage rates, training needs, and other administrative functions. Indeed, Taylor (1978) reported that the PAQ helped reduce 76 insurance company jobs into six families based on similar performance criteria.

Another illustration of the value of job analysis results was reported by Arvey and Begalla (1975). On the surface it may appear that two jobs are very different, or that several different jobs seemingly have little in common. However, a carefully conducted job analysis can reveal similarities (and differences) among jobs based on actual tasks performed and skills needed rather than on mere surface impressions. Arvey and Begalla analyzed the job of homemaker with the PAQ, comparing it to 20 other jobs. Using a statistic called D^2 (a measure of similarity between jobs), they were able to show that the job of homemaker is most similar to that of patrol officer. Table 3–2 shows the results comparing the homemaker job to the 20 others (the smaller the D^2 value, the more similar the jobs). This is an example of how job analysis provides accurate insights that casual inspection will not provide.

If there is a final common point of confusion about job analysis, it pertains to what job analysis is sometimes misperceived to be. Job analysis is *not* a way to determine how well employees are performing their jobs (that procedure is called performance appraisal and is the topic of Chapter 7). Nor is job analysis a way to determine the value or worth of a job (that procedure is called job evaluation and will be discussed in the next section). Perhaps the source of the confusion surrounds the fact that criteria, which job analyses identify, are involved in both performance appraisal and job evaluation. Job analysis results are used in perfor-

Table 3–2   *Jobs most similar to a homemaker's job, based on similarity (D^2) scores*

Job	D^2
1. Patrolman	6.69
2. Home economist	7.95
3. Airport maintenance chief	9.96
4. Kitchen helper	9.99
5. Fire fighter	10.21
6. Trouble man	10.23
7. Instrument-maker helper	10.67
8. Electrician, foreman	10.91
9. Maintenance foreman, gas plant	11.12
10. Hydroelectric-machinery mechanic	11.17
11. Transmission mechanic	11.55
12. Lineman, repair	12.25
13. Electric-meter repairman	12.36
14. Instructor, vocational training	12.43
15. Gas serviceman	12.75
16. Inspector, motors and generators	12.84
17. Lifeguard	12.93
18. Fire captain	13.05
19. Repairman, switch gear	13.22
20. Home economist, consumer service	13.47

SOURCE: From "Analyzing the Homemaker Job Using the PAQ" by R. D. Arvey and M. E. Begalla, 1975, *Journal of Applied Psychology, 60*, p. 516.

mance appraisal and job evaluation, but job analysis, performance appraisal, and job evaluation are not equivalent personnel functions.

Another application of job analysis can be seen in the *Dictionary of Occupational Titles* (DOT) (U.S. Department of Labor, 1991). The DOT describes many jobs, each defined in terms of worker traits needed to perform the job. Eleven worker traits are given, including intelligence, verbal ability, numerical ability, finger dexterity, and motor coordination. Job analysts compiled the trait requirement ratings by estimating how much of each of the 11 traits was needed on the job. Made on a 5-point scale, the ratings showed the amount of each trait possessed by various segments of the working population, ranging from 1 (the top 10% of the population) to 5 (the lowest 10%). The DOT also describes jobs in terms of occupational groups, based on similarity of job content. A study by Cain and Green (1983) revealed that these trait ratings were very stable, indicating that they are a sensitive, useful method of understanding jobs.

Job Evaluation

Different jobs have different degrees of importance or value to organizations. Some jobs are critically important, such as company president, and command the highest salary in the organization. Other jobs are less important to the organization's success and thus pay lower salaries. Job evaluation is a procedure that is useful for determining the relative value of jobs in the organization, which in turn helps determine the level of compensation paid. It is beyond the scope of this book to present a complete discourse on compensation. An excellent analysis of compensation from an I/O psychology perspective has been written by Gerhart and Milkovich (1992). I am simply going to review one component of the compensation process: job evaluation. Organizations that wish to attract and retain competent employees have to pay competitive wages. If wages are set too low, competent people will obtain better-paying jobs elsewhere. Similarly, if wages are set too high, the organization will pay more than is necessary to staff itself. How, then, does an organization determine what is a fair and appropriate wage? Basically, two different operations are required. One is to determine *external equity.* Equity means fairness, so external equity relates to what is a fair wage in comparison to what other employers are paying. A wage survey (that is, a survey that reveals what other companies pay employees for performing their jobs) would be used to determine the "going rate" for jobs in the business community. The second operation is to determine *internal equity,* or the fairness of compensation rates within the organization. Job evaluation is used to determine the relative position (from highest paid to lowest paid) of the jobs in the organization; thus, it is used to assess internal equity.

Methods of Job Evaluation

There are several methods of job evaluation. Their common basis is their heavy reliance, implicitly or explicitly, on criteria to assess the relative worth of jobs. Their differences rest primarily on the degree of specificity involved in the comparison process; that is, jobs may be compared either in some global fashion (as in their overall value to the company's success) or along certain specific dimensions (as in how much effort they require, and the working conditions under which they are performed).

In practice, most organizations use evaluation methods that examine several dimensions or factors of work. These dimensions are called *compensable* factors and refer to those factors for which employers pay compensation; that is, various levels of compensation are paid for jobs depending on "how much" of these compensable factors are present in each. Please note a fine distinction here that people often confuse. With a few notable exceptions, organizations do not pay individuals; organizations pay jobs, which individuals fill. The jobs determine the level of compensation, not the people in them.

There is no one fixed set of compensable factors. In theory, organizations can pay jobs for whatever reasons they want. In practice, however, effort, skill, responsibility, problem solving, and working conditions are typical compensable factors. Here is one way in which job evaluation works. Let us say the organization has selected the following four compensable factors: effort, skill, responsibility, and working conditions. Although most or all of the jobs in the organization would be evaluated, we will limit our discussion to two jobs: office secretary and security officer. Results of a job analysis might reveal the major criteria for a secretary's performance are typing, filing, and supervising a clerk. For the security officer, the criteria of job performance might be physically patrolling the office building, remaining vigilant, and maintaining security records. The criteria for both jobs would be evaluated or scored in terms of the degree to which the compensable factors are present. For example, the secretary's job might be evaluated as requiring considerable skill, little effort, modest responsibility, and performance under temperate working conditions. The security officer's job might be evaluated as requiring little skill, modest effort, considerable responsibility, and performance under potentially hazardous working conditions.

Thus, the level of compensation paid for jobs is a function of their status on the compensable factors. Jobs containing high levels of the compensable factors (for example, high effort, great skill) would receive higher rates of pay than jobs that contain low levels of these factors. All the jobs in the company would be evaluated in this fashion and then arranged in a hierarchy from high to low.

Other methods of job evaluation do not require the use of compensable factors, but all methods require that jobs be evaluated along one or more criteria. A (dollar) value is then ultimately attached to the relative position of every job in the hierarchy. Job evaluation attempts to ensure some correspondence between the compensation paid for the job and the value of the job to the organization.

Obviously a key to any job evaluation system is whether the "right factors" are being considered. The evaluations should be made on the basis of factors that truly reflect the jobs' worth, importance, or value. Also, unlike job analysis, which is basically a value-free operation (that is, an *analysis*), job evaluation is heavily laden with values (that is, an *evaluation*). Values are evidenced in terms of the selection of job factors to be evaluated and whether certain factors are considered more important than others. Therefore, job evaluation is an extension of job analysis applied to determining the relative worth of jobs in an organization for the purpose of providing equitable pay.

Research on Job Evaluation

I/O psychological research on job evaluation is not as extensive as that on job analysis. However, a few studies will be described. Gomez-Mejia, Page, and Tornow (1982) compared the relative accuracy and practical utility of seven different job evaluation approaches. Their results indicated that while several job evaluation methods provided useful information, a critical factor was the job analysis data on which the job evaluation system was based. If the job analysis data are of poor quality, their resulting use in job evaluation will also make that process suffer. Hahn and Dipboye (1988) reported most accurate and reliable job evaluation ratings were found to be provided by people who received training in how to evaluate, as well as extensive information about the jobs to be evaluated. Collins and Muchinsky (1993) reported that job evaluation ratings provided consistent assessments of job worth *within* a job family (for example, secretary versus clerk) but produced considerable disagreements about job worth *across* job families (for example, secretary versus electrician). Since large companies often organize their jobs into multiple job families, this finding suggests it is unlikely that a single job evaluation instrument will provide consistent and accurate assessments of worth across all jobs in a company.

I/O psychologists typically regard agreement among people in describing work-related issues as being evidence of the "correctness" of their opinions. However, research on job evaluation reveals the potential fallibility of this perspective. Schwab and Wichern (1983) have suggested that *systematic bias* may be operating in the determination of compensation. For example, let us assume that most secretaries are women and that society as a whole does not highly value the work that women typically perform. Therefore, the wages paid to female secretaries are lower than they "should" be. Additionally, this same bias that operates against female wages also operates to uniformly suppress the judged value of a secretarial job vis-à-vis the compensable factors; that is, secretarial jobs are judged to be relatively low in required effort, skill, and responsibility. Therefore, what looks like a "fair" relationship between the value of the job and the wages paid for it is actually the product of linking biased job evaluation results with biased wages. In other words, as Schwab and Wichern indicate, agreement may masquerade as truth or fairness when it is actually indicating systematic bias. Rynes and Milkovich (1986) concluded that market wages, which often serve as criteria in job evaluation, can be biased by many factors. For example, geographical differences and company pay practices influence market wages, as does the supply and demand of labor, thus dispelling the myth that market wages reflect the true worth of a job.

The issue of systematic bias in job evaluation also relates to the doctrine of *comparable worth*. It is called a "doctrine" because it represents a philosophy of how jobs should be paid. Comparable worth refers to giving people equal pay for performing comparable work (Mahoney, 1983). This is in contrast to giving equal pay for equal work, which is the doctrine underlying the Equal Pay Act, a federal law regarding compensation. The Equal Pay Act states that men and women who perform equal work are to receive equal pay. Proponents of comparable worth believe that rarely are two jobs ever truly equal. They believe it is more reasonable to speak of jobs as having *comparable* or *equivalent* worth. Jobs that are of comparable worth should be paid the same.

To determine the worth of all jobs, you would need to have a common measuring device, such as job evaluation. However, comparable-worth proponents believe that many current job evaluation methods are inherently biased against the work typically performed by females. These people point to labor statistics indicating that females on the average earn about $.60 for every $1 earned by males. This, they assert, is de facto evidence that women are the victims of discrimination caused by job evaluation methods that unfairly undervalue the work they perform. Indeed, Arvey (1986) suggested that the factors selected for consideration in job evaluation may be biased against females. For example, how much physical strength exerted in a job is often used as one factor in job evaluation. Since most males are physically stronger than most females, the rated value of female-dominated jobs may suffer on this factor. Alternatively, many females work in jobs in which eyestrain is a problem, yet amount of eyestrain is typically not a factor included in job evaluation (see Field Note 3). The proponents propose the need for a bias-free system to evaluate jobs that, when applied, would serve to reduce the male/female pay differential by increasing the wages paid to women.

Opponents of comparable worth believe there is no systematic bias operating against "female" jobs. They believe that females are as free to choose whatever jobs they want as are males; they simply settle for lower paying jobs that allow them more latitude for other obligations, such as family duties. In short, the opponents believe the job evaluation system is not at fault; rather, society has socialized men and women to pursue different types of jobs. They further believe there is no way to ever measure jobs in a way that is totally free of any values—that is, to have a totally bias-free assessment.

Most discussions of comparable worth are presented by people who feel strongly about the topic, one way or the other (England, 1992). There are currently no correct answers to this heated debate. At its core is the issue of values applied to job evaluation.

Standards for Criteria

What should criteria be like? This listing by Blum and Naylor (1968) is most representative:

- Reliable
- Realistic

FIELD NOTE 3

At the core of the comparable worth debate is the question of how the worth of a job is determined. A traditional way of determining job worth is through job evaluation. It is common to rate jobs on certain factors (such as effort and working conditions), with each rating being worth a certain number of points. The points are then summed, with the total point value of the job being the measure of its relative worth. Comparable worth advocates believe that the very factors on which jobs are evaluated often serve to slant the final results in favor of jobs traditionally held by men.

For example, on the effort factor, jobs that involve heavy lifting are worth more than jobs that involve light lifting. On the working conditions factor, jobs that are performed under adverse physical conditions (such as outdoor work) are worth more than jobs performed under temperate conditions (as an air-conditioned or heated office). Who is more likely to fill a job requiring heavy lifting—men or women? Typically men. Who is more likely to work outdoors? Typically men. Therefore, men's jobs are more

likely to be worth more points, thus receiving higher wages, than jobs traditionally filled by women. But what if we changed the very factors on which jobs are rated? Two possible factors would be mental stress and handling sensitive/confidential information. Jobs that subject people to high mental stress and require handling of confidential information would be worth more than jobs that don't. Secretaries often work under mentally stressful conditions (that is, a hectic work pace and continual deadlines) and deal with confidential information. Most secretarial jobs are held by women. Therefore, depending on the job factors you wish to consider (effort and working conditions versus mental stress and confidential information), you could arrive at two quite different conclusions regarding the worth of a secretary's job. Job factors are nothing more than criteria, the criteria by which the worth of a job is to be determined. As stated earlier in this chapter, differences of opinion about criteria are at the heart of many disputes. Such is certainly the case regarding comparable worth.

- Representative
- Related to other criteria
- Acceptable to the job analyst
- Acceptable to management
- Consistent from one situation to another
- Predictable
- Inexpensive
- Understandable
- Measurable
- Relevant
- Uncontaminated and bias-free
- Sensitive

This list might be reduced to three general factors; criteria must be appropriate, stable, and practical. The criteria should be relevant and representative of the job. They must endure over time or across situations. Finally, they should not be too expensive or hard to measure. Other authors think other issues are important; for example, the time at which criterion measures are taken (after one month on the job, six months, and so on); the type of criterion measure taken (performance, errors, accidents); and the level of performance chosen to represent success or failure on the job (college students must perform at a "C" level before they can graduate). Weitz (1961) says the choice of criteria is usually determined by either history or precedent; unfortunately, sometimes criteria are chosen because they are merely expedient or available.

Objective Criteria

Objective criteria are taken from organizational records (payroll or personnel) and supposedly do not involve any type of subjective evaluation. Although objective criteria may be devoid of subjective judgment, some degree of assessment must be applied to them to give them meaning. Just knowing that an employee produced 18 units a day is not informative; this output must be compared with what other workers produce. If the average is 10 units a day, 18 units would clearly represent "good" performance. If the average is 25 units a day, 18 units is not good.

Production.   Using units of production as criteria is most common in manufacturing jobs. If there is only one type of job in a whole organization, setting production criteria is easy. But in most companies, there are many types of production jobs, so productivity must be compared fairly. That is, if average productivity in one job is 6 units a day and in another job it's 300 units a day, productivity must be equated to adjust for these differences. Statistical procedures are usually used for this. Other factors can diminish the value of production as a criterion of performance. In an assembly-line job, the speed of the line determines how many units get produced per day. Increasing the speed of the line increases production. Furthermore, everyone working on the line will have the same level of production. In a case like this, units of production are determined by factors outside the individual worker. So errors that are under the worker's control may be measured as the criterion of job performance. However, this is no cure-all for the criterion problem either. Errors are not fair criteria if they are more likely in some jobs than others. Due to automation and work simplification, some jobs are almost "goof-proof." In such jobs error-free work has nothing to do with the human factor.

Sales. Sales are a commonly used performance criterion for wholesale and retail sales work, but a number of variations must be considered. Using the sheer number of sales as a criterion is appropriate only if everyone is selling the same product(s) in comparable territories. A person who sells toothbrushes should sell more units than a person who sells houses. Also, someone selling tractors in Iowa should sell more than a person whose sales territory is Rhode Island. Not only is Iowa bigger than Rhode Island but more farming is done proportionately in Iowa than in Rhode Island. Total sales volume is equally fallible as a criterion. A real estate salesperson can sell a $100,000 house in one afternoon, but how long would it take to sell $100,000 worth of toothbrushes?

The solution to these types of problems is to use norm groups for judging success. A real estate salesperson should be compared to other real estate sales-people in the same sales territory. The same holds for other sales work. If comparisons have to be drawn across sales territories or across product lines, statistical adjustments are needed. Ideally, any differences in sales performance would then be due to the ability of the salesperson, which is the basis for using sales as a criterion of job performance.

Tenure or Turnover. Length of service is a very popular criterion in I/O psychological research. Turnover not only has a theoretical appeal (for example, Hom & Griffeth, 1995) but is also a practical concern. Employers want to hire people who will stay with the company. For obvious, practical reasons, employers don't want to hire chronic job-hoppers. The costs of recruiting, selecting, and training new hires can be extremely high. Turnover is perhaps the most frequently used nonperformance criterion in the psychological literature. Turnover is a valuable and useful criterion because it measures employment stability.

Campion (1991) suggested that many factors should be considered in measuring turnover. One is voluntariness (whether the employee was fired, quit to obtain another job with better promotional opportunities, or quit because of dissatisfaction with one's supervisor). Another factor is functionality (whether the employee was performing the job effectively or ineffectively). Williams and Livingstone (1994) meta-analyzed studies that examined the relationship between turnover and performance and concluded that poor performers were more likely than good performers to voluntarily quit their jobs.

Absenteeism. Absence from work, like turnover, is an index of employee stability. Although some degree of employee turnover is good for organizations, employee absenteeism always has bad consequences.

Rhodes and Steers (1990) and Martocchio and Harrison (1993) have reviewed many studies on why people are absent from work. Absence appears to be the product of many factors, including family conflicts, feelings of job dissatisfaction, alcohol and drug abuse, and personality. However, as Johns (1994) noted, employees are prone to give self-serving justifications for their absence. For example, being absent from work to care for a sick child is more socially acceptable than acknowledging deviant behavior such as drug usage. Accordingly, relying on self-reports of why employees are absent can be highly inaccurate.

Absenteeism is a pervasive problem in industry; it costs employers billions of dollars a year in decreased efficiency and increased benefit payments (for example, sick leave) and payroll costs. Absenteeism has social, individual, and organizational causes, and it affects individuals, companies, and even entire industrial societies.

Accidents.   Accidents are sometimes used as a criterion of job performance, though they have a number of limitations. First, accidents are used as a measure mainly for blue-collar jobs. (Although white-collar workers can be injured at work, the frequency of such accidents is small.) Thus, accidents are a measure of job performance for only a limited sample of employees. Second, accidents are difficult to predict, and there is little stability or consistency across individuals in their occurrence (Senders & Moray, 1991). Third, accidents can be measured in many ways: number of accidents per hours worked, miles driven, trips taken, and so on. Different conclusions can be drawn, depending on how accident statistics are calculated. Employers do not want to hire people who, for whatever reason, will incur job-related accidents. But in the total picture of job performance, accidents are not used as a criterion as often as production, turnover, or absence.

Theft.   Employee theft is a major problem facing organizations, with annual losses estimated at $10 billion (Sackett & Harris, 1985). Hollinger and Clark (1983) administered an anonymous questionnaire regarding theft to employees at three types of organizations. The percentage of employees who admitted to stealing from their employer was 42% in retail stores, 32% in hospitals, and 26% in manufacturing firms. Thus, employee theft is a pervasive and serious problem. From an I/O psychologist's perspective, the goal is to hire people who are unlikely to steal from the company, just as it would be desirable to hire people who have a low probability of having accidents. The problem with theft as a criterion is that we know very little about the individual identity of employees who do steal. Hollinger and Clark based their survey results on anonymous responses. Furthermore, those responses came from people who were willing to admit they stole from the company. Those employees who were stealing but chose not to respond to the survey or who did not admit they stole were not included in the theft results. Greenberg (1990) reported that some employees resorted to theft as a means of offsetting perceived unfairness in their pay. However, the identity of those employees was not known.

Another drawback of using theft as a criterion is that only a small percentage of employees are ever caught stealing. The occurrence of theft often has to be deduced on the basis of calculated shortages from company inventories of supplies and products. In addition, many companies will not divulge any information about theft to outside individuals. That is, while companies will often share

What are the criteria for judging wine? Wine tasters at a California winery.
SOURCE: Courtesy of Chateau Julien Winery

information on such criteria as absenteeism and turnover, theft records are too sensitive to reveal. Despite these limitations, I/O psychologists regard theft as an index of employment suitability, and we will probably witness much more research on theft in the years ahead.

Subjective Criteria

Subjective criteria refer to judgments made of an employee's performance. The judgment is usually a rating or ranking. For example, a supervisor might rate the employees in a department on the basis of overall effectiveness. This rating would then be the standard of job performance. Supervisor ratings are by far the most frequently used judgmental criteria. Lent, Aurbach, and Levin (1971) reported that of the 1,505 criteria used in over 400 studies, 897 (60%) were supervisory ratings. But ratings may also be supplied by peers, subordinates, and workers themselves. The ratings may be on a general factor, such as overall effectiveness, or specific factors, such as quantity of work, quality of work, creativity, practical judgment, and so forth. Some studies have even compared judgments made by two or more sets of raters (for example, supervisors and peers) who evaluate several dimensions of behavior (Lawler, 1967). Such studies normally show that certain raters are more consistent in rating certain aspects of job performance. Supervisors may agree in rating quality of work; peers agree in rating interpersonal relations. Chapter 7 will discuss this issue in greater detail.

Because judgmental criteria are used so often, a great deal of attention has been given to improving the quality of these judgments. If the people doing the judging don't know how to make such decisions, the quality of their decisions will be very low. Spool (1978) reviewed the research on training people to make more accurate judgments of behavior. He found that people can indeed learn to be accurate evaluators. People who are more involved and interested in evaluating behavior make more careful and accurate judgments. Research (for example, Pursell, Dossett, & Latham, 1980) has revealed that a one-day training program can greatly enhance people's skills in observing and interpreting behavior.

From this discussion, it is clear that no single measure of job performance is totally adequate. While each criterion may have merit, each can also suffer from weakness along other dimensions. For instance, few people would say that an employee's absence has no bearing on overall job performance, but no one would say that absence is a complete measure of job performance. Absence, like production or job level, is but one piece of the broader picture. Don't be discouraged that no one criterion meets all our standards. It is precisely because job performance is multidimensional (and each single dimension is an incomplete index of overall performance) that we are compelled to include many relevant aspects of work in establishing criteria.

Relationship among Job Performance Criteria

While several job performance criteria can be identified for many jobs, each criterion frequently assesses a different aspect of performance. These criteria are usually independent of one another. If they were all highly positively intercorrelated—say, $r = .80$ or $r = .90$—there would be no point in measuring them all. Knowing an employee's status on one criterion would give his or her status on the others. Several studies have tried to identify interrelationships among criteria.

A classic study by Seashore, Indik, and Georgopoulos (1960) revealed multiple job performance criteria and also showed that the criteria were relatively independent of one another. For example, Seashore and associates studied 975 delivery men on whom five job performance criteria were available: productivity (objectively measured by time standards); effectiveness (subjectively rated based on quality of performance); accidents, unexcused absences, and errors (based on the number of packages not delivered). The correlations among these five criteria appear in Table 3–3. The data show that the five criteria were relatively independent of one another. The largest correlations were found among the variables of productivity, effectiveness, and errors (.28, −.26, and −.32). These results demonstrate that there really is no single measure of overall performance on the job; each criterion measures a different facet.

Heneman (1986) conducted a major study examining the relationship be-

Table 3–3   *Correlations among five criterion variables*

	Productivity	Accidents	Absences	Errors
Effectiveness	.28	−.02	−.08	−.32
Productivity		.12	−.01	−.26
Accidents			.03	−.18
Absences				.15

SOURCE: Adapted from "Relationship Among Criteria of Job Performance" by S. E. Seashore, B. P. Indik, and B. S. Georgopoulos, 1960, *Journal of Applied Psychology, 44,* pp. 195–202.

tween supervisor ratings of job performance and objective measures of job performance. He reported an average correlation of only .27 between these two types of assessment. Quite clearly, you can arrive at different conclusions about a person's job performance depending on how you choose to assess it.

There is also a relationship between job level and the number of criteria needed to define job performance. Lower level, relatively simple jobs do not have many dimensions of performance; more complex jobs have many. In fact, the number of job performance criteria can separate simple jobs from complex ones. Manual laborers who unload trucks might be measured by only three criteria: attendance (they have to show up for work), errors (they have to know how to stack the material), and speed. More complex jobs, as in the medical field (for example, Taylor, Price, Richards, & Jacobsen, 1964, 1965), might be defined by as many as 15 independent criteria. The more complex the job, the more criteria are needed to define it and the more skill or talent a person has to have to be successful.

Dynamic Criteria

Dynamic criteria refer to changing levels of job performance that occur over time. Job performance is not stable or consistent over time, and this dynamic quality adds to the complexity of making personnel decisions. Figure 3–6 shows the level of three job performance criteria—productivity, absence, and accidents—over an eight-year period. This represents one person's eight-year performance record on a job. You will notice the pattern of behavior for the three criteria differs over time. The individual's level of accidents is stable over time. In this case, accidents would not be a dynamic criterion because of its stability. However, a very different pattern emerges for the other two criteria. The individual's level of productivity increases over the years, more gradually in the early years and then more dramatically in the later years. Absence, on the other hand, follows the opposite pattern. The employee's absence was greatest in the first year of employment and progressively declined over time. Absence and productivity represent dynamic criteria, while accidents represent a static criterion.

When a job applicant is considered for employment, the organization attempts to predict how well that person will perform on the job. A hire/no hire decision is then made on the basis of this prediction. If job performance criteria were static (as with the case of accidents in Figure 3–6), the accuracy of the prediction would be aided by the stability of the behavior. However, if job performance

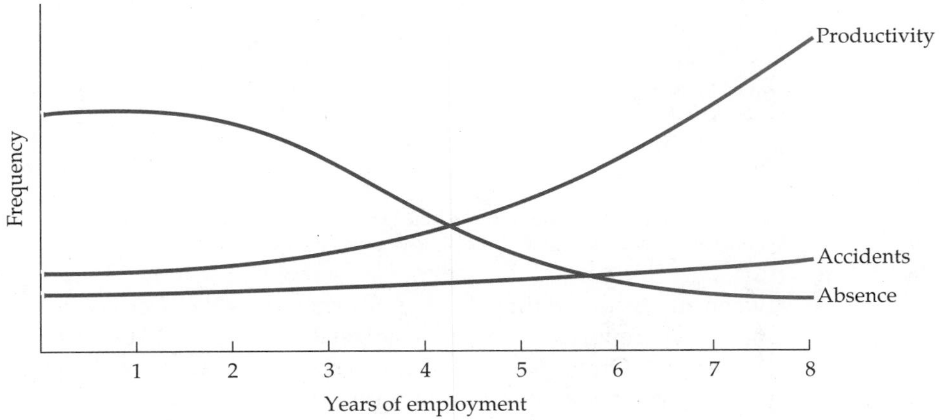

Figure 3-6   *Performance variation in three criteria over an eight-year period*

criteria are dynamic, a critical new element is added to the decision, that of *time*. It may be that initially productivity would not be very impressive, but over time the employee's performance would rise to and then surpass a satisfactory level. The concept of dynamic criteria is equivalent to "hitting a moving target," as the level of the behavior being predicted is continuously changing. Furthermore, the pattern of change may be different *across* individuals. That is, for some people productivity may start off low and then get progressively higher, while for others the pattern may be the reverse.

To what degree are dynamic criteria an issue in I/O psychology? The profession is divided. Some researchers (for example, Barrett, Caldwell, & Alexander, 1985; Barrett, Alexander, & Doverspike, 1992) contend that job performance criteria aren't very dynamic at all, and the problem is not severe. Others (Deadrick & Madigan, 1990; Hofmann, Jacobs, & Baratta, 1993) provide research findings indicating that various criteria of job performance do change over time, as does their predictability. Hulin, Henry, and Noon (1990) believe that time is an underresearched topic in understanding the relationship between criteria. They assert that over time some criteria become more predictable while others decline in predictability. Investigating dynamic criteria requires examining complex research questions that do not lend themselves to simple answers. In general, if criteria operate in a dynamic fashion over time, we need to be sensitive to the difference between prediction of behavior in the short term versus the long term.

Concluding Comments

Austin and Villanova (1992) traced the history of criterion measurement in I/O psychology over the past 75 years. The conceptual problems associated with accurate criterion representation and measurement today are not all that different from those faced at the birth of I/O psychology.

The issue of criteria in I/O psychology is complex and important. Many years ago Nagle (1953) stated that the quality of research is only as good as the criteria. I agree. The quality of our judgments is only as good as the evaluative standards we use to make them. If our goal were to improve the quality of the educational process as shown by the number of students elected to Phi Beta Kappa (a scholastic honorary), we could lower admission standards to this honorary. However, we would only be deluding ourselves. An understanding of criteria and their related problems is basic to I/O psychology.

CASE STUDY   *Who Gets the Scholarship?*

The Rippowam High School principal convened a panel of three teachers to make a most important decision. A local company was willing to award a $10,000 college scholarship to "the most outstanding senior" in the class, with the recipient to be determined by the high school. Walter Plant, Sandra Meltzer, and Jerry Driscoll were given the assignment to select the scholarship recipient. They agreed to meet at 2:30 to discuss their assignment.

Driscoll opened the meeting: "I wish we had more to go on than what they gave us. A student can be outstanding in many ways."

"Well, I assume grades are the most important factor," said Meltzer. "Why don't we start out with the ranking of all students based on their grade point averages? I'd be hard pressed to award $10,000 to any student other than the class valedictorian."

"I don't think it's that easy," said Plant. "I am far more impressed with a student who gets a B+ in honors physics than someone who gets an A in basket weaving. While a student's grade point average is certainly a good measure of academic accomplishments, it's tainted by the difficulty of the courses taken."

"That's not the only problem with the grade point average," Driscoll warned. "I've got some students in my homeroom who will graduate with the minimum number of hours, and I've got some others who branched out and took more than the minimum. I think we should give some consideration to the total number of hours taken in the curriculum."

A deep frown appeared on Plant's face. "I don't see why we should penalize the student who did only what was required by the school. We specify what is needed for graduation, and the students have to comply. I never discourage a student from sticking to the minimum, and I don't think we should devalue their performance for having done so."

"Maybe we're getting too hung up with grades and hours," said Meltzer. "Suzanne Millord won first prize in the regional science fair competition. Shouldn't something like that count, too? I'm more impressed with that than with an 'A' in any class."

"You know," Plant commented, "we are forgetting about some other things, too. How about civic activities, such as participation in student government or interest clubs? We encourage student involvement in these activities to make for a more well-rounded education. I don't feel we should ignore them when it comes time to make an award."

"I feel those activities have their own rewards," said Driscoll. "We want to give this scholarship to the best student, not the most socially active one."

"While we're at it," mused Plant, "how about athletic participation? We also stress physical education as well as social and intellectual development. Maybe we should also include interscholastic athletics. We've got some outstanding athletes in this school, and who's to say that 'most outstanding' can't be defined in terms of athletics?"

"I hardly think this was designed to be an athletic scholarship," Meltzer grumbled. "If you want to make it more complicated, why not throw in financial need; $10,000 is a lot of money, and some families could use it more than others."

Driscoll stared out the window. He knew it would be a long afternoon.

Questions

1. What do you think the conceptual criteria should be in making a scholarship determination?
2. What are some sources of criterion deficiency and contamination in the actual criteria being discussed?
3. Would the criteria for selecting the "most outstanding student" be more biased or less biased by inclusion of financial need? Why?
4. Do you think it's more difficult to identify what the appropriate criteria are, or to determine how to weight the criteria once they have been identified? Why?
5. If you had been invited to this meeting, what suggestions would you make to help the teachers reach a decision?

Predictors: Psychological Assessments

Major Chapter Objectives

- Identify major types of reliability and what they measure.

- Understand major representations of validity and what they measure.

- Be able to categorize major types of psychological tests by administration and content.

- Understand the role of psychological testing in making assessments of people, including ethical issues and predictive accuracy.

- Know the importance of nontest predictors such as interviews, assessment centers, work samples, biographical information, peer assessment, and letters of recommendation.

A *predictor* is any variable used to forecast a criterion. In weather prediction barometric pressure can be used to forecast rainfall. In medical prediction body temperature can be used to predict (or diagnose) illness. In I/O psychology we seek predictors of job performance criteria as indexed by productivity, absenteeism, turnover, and so forth. There is no limit to the variables we can use for this purpose. Although we do not use tea leaves and astrological signs as fortune-tellers do, researchers have explored a multitude of devices as potential predictors of job performance criteria. In this chapter I will review the variables traditionally used, examine their success, and discuss some professional problems inherent in their application.

In this discussion of predictor variables, remember that although their identification is valuable, they are always secondary in importance to criteria. If you think of criteria as being the objective or end point of a conceptual journey, predictors are the roads travelled to reach the criteria. Predictors are merely means to an end. Many years ago Nagle (1953) described the relationship between these two sets of variables:

> Predictors themselves can never be anything but subsidiary to the criterion, for it is from the criterion that the predictors derive their significance. If the criterion changes, the predictors' validity is necessarily affected. If the predictors change, the criterion does not change for that reason. Likewise, it can be seen that if no criteria are used, one would never know whether or not the predictors were selecting those individuals likely to succeed. Research can be no better than the criteria used. One must, therefore, approach the prediction process in a logical fashion, developing criteria first, analyzing them, and then constructing or selecting variables to predict the criteria. When one or more variables show a satisfactory relationship to criteria, such variables may then be used as selection instruments. (p. 273)

Assessing the Quality of Predictors

All predictor variables, like other measuring devices, can be assessed in terms of their quality or goodness. Important features of a good measuring device include consistency and accuracy; that is, predictors should repeatedly yield precise measurements. In psychology we judge the goodness of our measuring devices by two psychometric criteria: reliability and validity. If a predictor is not both reliable and valid, it is useless.

Reliability

Reliability is the consistency or stability of a measure. A measure should yield the same estimate on repeated use when the measured trait has not changed. Even though that estimate can be inaccurate, a reliable measure will always be consistent. Four types of reliability are used in I/O psychology to assess the consistency or stability of the measuring device.

Test-Retest Reliability. Perhaps the simplest way to assess a measuring device's reliability is to measure something at two points in time and compare the scores. We can give an IQ test to the same group of people at two different times and then correlate the two sets of scores. This correlation is called a *coefficient of stability* because it reflects the stability of the test over time. If the test is reliable, those who scored high the first time would also score high the second time, and vice versa. If the test is unreliable, the scores will "bounce around" in such a way that there will be no similarity in individuals' scores between the two trials.

When we say a test (or any measure) is reliable, how high should the reliability coefficient be? The answer is "the higher the better." A test cannot be too reliable. As a rule, reliability coefficients around +.70 are professionally acceptable, though some frequently used tests have test-retest reliabilities only in the +.50 range. "Acceptable" reliability is also a function of the test's use. A test used for individual prediction (to diagnose brain impairment) should be much more reliable than a test used for group prediction (to measure the attitudes of a work group).

Equivalent-Form Reliability. A second type of reliability is parallel or equivalent-form reliability. Here a psychologist would develop two forms of a test to measure the same attribute and give both forms to a group of people. He or she would then correlate the two scores for each person. The resulting correlation, called a *coefficient of equivalence,* reflects the extent to which the two forms are equivalent measures of the same concept. Of the three major types of reliability, this type is the least popular because it is usually challenging to come up with one good test, let alone two. Many tests do not have a "parallel form." However, in the areas of intelligence and achievement testing (to be discussed shortly), equivalent forms of the same test are sometimes found. If the resulting coefficient of equivalence is high, the tests are equivalent and reliable measures of the same concept. If it is low, they are not.

Internal-Consistency Reliability. The third major type of reliability is the internal consistency of the test—the extent to which it has homogeneous content. Two types of internal-consistency reliability are typically computed. One is called *split-half reliability.* Here a test is given to a group of people, but in scoring the test (though not administering it), the items are divided in half, into odd- and even-numbered items. Each person thus gets two sets of scores (one for each half), which are correlated. If the test is internally consistent, there should be a high degree of similarity in the responses (that is, right or wrong) to the odd- and even-numbered items. All other things being equal, the longer a test is, the greater its reliability.

A second technique for assessing internal-consistency reliability is to compute one of two coefficients; Cronbach's alpha or Kuder-Richardson 20 (KR20). Both procedures are similar, although not statistically identical. Conceptually, each test item is treated as a minitest. Thus, a 100-item test consists of 100 minitests. The response to each item is correlated with the response to every other item. Thus, a matrix of interitem correlations is formed whose average is related to the homogeneity of the test. If the test is homogeneous (the item content is similar), it will have a high internal-consistency reliability. If the test is heterogeneous (the items cover a wide variety of concepts), it is not internally consistent and the resulting coefficient will be low. Internal-consistency reliability is frequently used to assess a test's homogeneity of content in I/O psychology.

Inter-Rater Reliability.   When assessments are made on the basis of raters' judgments, it is possible for the raters to disagree in their evaluations. Two different raters may observe the same behavior yet evaluate it differently. The degree of correspondence between judgments or scores assigned by different raters is most commonly referred to as inter-rater reliability, although it has also been called *conspect reliability*. In some situations raters must exercise some judgments in arriving at a score, for example, multiple raters analyzing a job or multiple interviewers evaluating job candidates. The score or rating depends not only on the job or candidate but also on the judgment of the persons doing the rating. The rater characteristics may produce distortions or errors in their judgments. Estimation of inter-rater reliability is usually expressed as a correlation and reflects the degree of agreement among the ratings. Evidence of high inter-rater agreement establishes a basis to conclude the behavior was reliably observed, and in turn we conclude such observations are accurate.

Validity

Reliability refers to consistency and stability of measurement; *validity* refers to accuracy and precision. A valid measure is one that yields "correct" estimates of what is being assessed. However, another factor distinguishes validity from reliability. Reliability is inherent in a measuring device, but validity depends on the use of a test. Validity refers to the test's appropriateness for predicting or drawing inferences about criteria. A given test may be highly valid for predicting employee productivity but totally invalid for predicting employee absenteeism. In other words, it would be appropriate to draw inferences about employee productivity from the test but inappropriate to draw inferences about absenteeism. There are several different representations of validity, and they all involve determining the appropriateness of a measure (test) for drawing inferences.

Criterion-Related Validity.   As its name suggests, criterion-related validity refers to how much a predictor relates to a criterion. It is a frequently used and important type of validity in I/O psychology. The two major kinds of criterion-related validity are concurrent and predictive.

In measuring *concurrent criterion-related validity*, we are concerned with how well a predictor can predict a criterion at the same time, or concurrently. Examples abound. We may wish to predict a student's grade point average on the basis of a test score. So we collect data on the grade point averages of many students, and then we also administer a predictor test. If the predictor test is a valid measure of grades, there will be a substantial correlation between test scores and school grades. We can use the same method in an industrial setting. We can predict a worker's level of productivity (the criterion) on the basis of a test (the predictor).

We would collect productivity data on a current group of workers, administer a test, and then correlate their scores with their productivity records. If the test is of value, we can draw an inference about a worker's productivity on the basis of the test score. In measuring concurrent validity, there is no time interval between collecting the predictor and criterion data. The two variables are assessed concurrently, which is how the method gets it name.

Because the criterion for concurrent validity is always available at the time of using the predictor, why bother to collect predictor data at all? Predictors usually provide a simpler, quicker, or less expensive substitute for criterion data. For example, say the criterion is a salesperson's yearly dollar volume. A predictor that could predict a certain level of sales volume would be much more efficient than having all job applicants serve as salespeople for a year.

In measuring *predictive criterion-related validity*, predictor information is collected and used to forecast criterion performance. A college might use a student's high school class rank to predict the criterion of overall college grade point average four years later. A company could use a test to predict whether job applicants will pass a six-month training program.

Concurrent validity is used to diagnose existing status on some criterion, and predictive validity is used to forecast future status. The primary distinction is the time interval between collecting the predictor and criterion data. The conceptual significance between predictive and concurrent validity in the context of personnel selection will be discussed in the next chapter. The logic of criterion-related validity is straightforward. You determine if there is a relationship between predictor scores and criterion scores based on a sample of employees on whom you have both sets of scores. If there is a relationship, you use scores on those predictor variables to select applicants on whom there are no criterion scores. Therefore, you predict the applicants' future (and thus unknown) criterion performance from their known test scores based on the relationship established through criterion-related validity.

When predictor scores are correlated with criterion data, the resulting correlation is called a *validity coefficient*. While an acceptable reliability coefficient is in the .70 to .80 range, a desirable validity coefficient is in the .30 to .40 range. Validity coefficients less than .30 are not uncommon, but those over .50 are rare. Just as a predictor cannot be too reliable, it also cannot be too valid. The greater the correlation between the predictor and the criterion, the more we know about the criterion on the basis of the predictor. By squaring the size of the correlation coefficient (r), we can calculate how much variance in the criterion we can account for by using the predictor. For example, if a predictor correlates .40 with a criterion, we can explain 16% (r^2) of the variance in the criterion by knowing the predictor. A correlation of 1.0 indicates perfect prediction (and complete knowledge).

Some criteria are difficult to predict no matter what predictors are used; other criteria are fairly predictable. Similarly, some predictors are consistently valid and are thus used quite often. Other predictors do not seem to be of much predictive value no matter what the criteria are, and thus they fall out of use. Usually, however, particular predictors are valid for predicting only certain criteria. Shortly, I will review the predictors typically used in I/O psychology and examine how valid they are for predicting criteria.

Content Validity. Content validity involves the degree to which a predictor covers a *representative sample* of the behavior being assessed. It is limited mainly to psychological tests, but it could also be extended to interviews or other predictors. A test is said to be "content valid" when the content of the test questions covers a representative sample of the content of the job. For example, if the major task dimensions of a secretary's job include knowledge of office procedures, typing, and filing, then a content valid test for this job would include test questions covering office procedures, typing, and filing. There is a strong and obvious link between the process of job analysis (discussed in Chapter 3) and the concept of content validity. First, the domain of job behavior is determined through job analysis. Then test items are constructed that assess the attributes needed to perform the job successfully. The content validity of employment tests is thus a function of the extent to which the content of the job is reflected in the content of the test. Goldstein, Zedeck, and Schneider (1993) assert that content validity is established by the careful linkage between the information derived from job analysis and its associated use in test construction. Content validity purports to reveal that the domain of knowledges, skills, and abilities required to perform well on the job and the employment test are interchangeable.

How is content validity assessed? Unlike criterion-related validity, correlation coefficients are not computed. Content validity is assessed by subject matter experts (SMEs) in the area the test covers. The SMEs render an opinion regarding the degree of content validity manifested in the test. Their judgments could range from "not at all" to "highly valid." Presumably the test would be revised until it showed a high degree of content validity.

A similar type of validity based on people's judgments is called *face validity*. Face validity is concerned with the appearance of the test items: Do they look appropriate for such a test? Estimates of content validity are rendered by subject matter experts, while estimates of face validity are usually rendered by test takers. Because subject matter experts are more knowledgeable than test takers, content validity is more important than face validity. It is possible for a test item to be content valid but not face valid, and vice versa.

Construct Validity. Construct validity is the most theoretical and complex manifestation of validity. A construct is a theoretical concept proposed to explain aspects of behavior. Examples of constructs in I/O psychology are intelligence, motivation, anxiety, and mechanical comprehension. Because constructs are abstractions (ideas), we must have some real, tangible ways to assess them. That is, we need an actual measure of our proposed construct. A paper-and-pencil test of intelligence would be one way to measure the psychological construct of intelligence. Construct validity, in turn, refers to the extent our measure of intelligence (the test) is an accurate representation of the theoretical construct of intelligence. A test that manifests a high degree of construct validity is regarded as faithfully assessing the construct in question.

The construct validity process is the quest to ascertain the linkage between what is measured by the test and the theoretical construct. Let us assume we wish to understand the construct of intelligence, and to do so we develop a paper-and-pencil test we believe assesses that construct. To establish the degree of construct validity of our test, we would want to compare scores on our test with known measures of intelligence, such as verbal, numerical, and problem-solving ability. If our test is a faithful assessment of intelligence, scores on our test should converge with these other known measures of intelligence. More technically, there should be a high correlation between the scores from our new test of intelligence and the existing measures of intelligence. These correlation coefficients are referred to as *convergent validity coefficients*, because they reflect the degree to which these scores *converge* (or come together) in assessing a common concept—intelligence. Likewise, scores on our test should *not* be related to concepts that we know are *not* related to intelligence, such as physical strength, eye color, and gender. That is, scores on our test should *diverge* (or be separate) from concepts that are unrelated to intelligence. More technically, there should be very low correlations between the scores from our new test of intelligence and these concepts. These correlation coefficients are referred to as *divergent validity coefficients*, because they reflect the degree to which these scores diverge from each other in assessing unrelated concepts. Other statistical procedures may also be used to establish the construct validity of a test. After collecting and evaluating much information about the test, we accumulate a body of evidence supporting the notion that the test measures a psychological construct. In turn, we would say the test manifests a high degree of construct validity. Tests manifesting a high degree of construct validity are among the most widely respected and frequently used assessment instruments in I/O psychology.

Binning and Barrett (1989) have described construct validation as the process of demonstrating evidence for five linkages or inferences, as shown in Figure 4–1. Figure 4–1 consists of two empirical measures and two constructs. X is a measure of construct 1, as a test of intelligence purports to measure the psychological

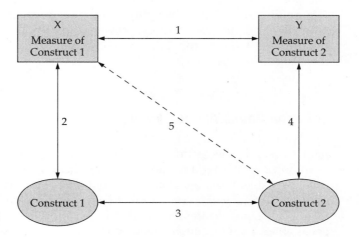

Figure 4–1   *Inferential linkages in construct validation*
SOURCE: From "Validity of Personnel Decisions: A Conceptual Analysis of the Inferential and Evidential Bases" by J. F. Binning and G. V. Barrett, 1989, *Journal of Applied Psychology, 74*, p. 480.

construct of intelligence. Y is a measure of construct 2, as a supervisor assessment of an employee's performance purports to measure the construct of job performance. Linkage 1 is the only one that can be tested directly, as it is the only inference involving two directly measured variables (X and Y). In assessing the construct validity of X and Y, we would be most interested in assessing linkages 2 and 4, respectively. That is, we would want to know that the empirical measures of X and Y are faithful and accurate assessments of the constructs (1 and 2) they purport to measure. For the purpose of constructing theories of job performance, we would be interested in linkage 3, the relationship between the two constructs. Finally, Binning and Barrett note that in personnel selection we are interested in linkage 5, that is, the inference between an employment test score and the domain of performance on the job. Thus, the process of construct validation involves examining the linkages among multiple concepts of interest to us. We always operate at the empirical level (X and Y), yet we wish to draw inferences at the conceptual level (constructs 1 and 2). Construct validation is the continuous process of verifying the accuracy of an inference among concepts for the purpose of furthering our capacity to understand those concepts (Pulakos, Borman, & Hough, 1988). Messick (1995) furthermore believes that issues of construct validation also extend into how test scores are interpreted and the consequences of test use.

There is a tendency to think of test validity as being equivalent to an on/off light switch—either a test is valid or it isn't. The temptation to do so is probably based on other uses of the word *valid* in our language, for example, whether or not a person has a valid driver's license. However, this either/or type of thinking about test validity is not correct. It is more accurate to think of test validity as a dimmer light switch. Tests manifest various degrees of validity, ranging from none at all to a great deal. At some point along the continuum of validity, practical decisions have to be made as to whether a test manifests "enough" validity to warrant its use. To carry the light switch analogy further, a highly valid test sheds much light on the object (construct) we seek to understand. Thus, the test validation process is the ongoing act of determining the amount of "illumination" the test projects on the construct.

Criterion Reliability and Validity

Before we leave this section on reliability and validity, note that these elements are as important to criteria as they are to predictors. The criteria we wish to predict must be stable measures of behavior, not will-o'-the-wisp variables that lack consistency. Similarly, the criteria must be appropriate and relevant. Shoe size is an invalid criterion of intelligence; that is, it would be inappropriate to make inferences about people's intelligence by measuring the size of their feet. However, it may be appropriate to make inferences about a person's height by measuring his or her shoe size. Although the concepts of reliability and validity were deferred until this chapter on predictors, they are equally relevant to criteria.

Psychological Tests and Inventories

Psychological tests and inventories have been the most frequently used predictors in I/O psychology. The difference between the two is that in a test the answers are either right or wrong; in an inventory there are no right or wrong answers. Usually, though, the terms *tests* and *psychological testing* represent the family of tests and inventories.

History of Psychological Testing

Testing has a long multinational history in the field of psychology. Sir Francis Galton, an English biologist, was interested in human heredity. In the course of his research, he realized the need for measuring the characteristics of biologically related and unrelated persons. He began to keep records of people on such factors as keenness of vision and hearing, muscular strength, and reaction time. By 1880, he had accumulated the first large-scale body of information on individual differences. He was probably the first scientist to devise systematic ways of measuring people. In 1890 the American psychologist Cattell introduced the term *mental test.* He devised an early test of intelligence based on sensory discrimination and reaction time. Ebbinghaus, a German psychologist, developed math and sentence-completion tests and gave them to schoolchildren. In 1897 he reported that the sentence-completion test was related to children's scholastic achievement.

The biggest advances in the early years of testing were made by the French psychologist Binet. In 1904 the French government appointed Binet to study procedures for the education of children with mental retardation. To assess mental retardation, Binet (in collaboration with Simon) developed a test of intelligence. It consisted of 30 problems covering such areas as judgment, comprehension, and reasoning, which Binet regarded as essential components of intelligence. Later revisions of this test had a greater sampling of items from different areas. Binet's research on intelligence testing was continued by the American psychologist Terman, who in 1916 developed the concept of intelligence quotient (IQ). These early pioneers paved the way for a wide variety of tests that would be developed in the years to come, many of which were used by industrial psychologists to predict job performance. Although most of the early work in testing was directed at assessing intellect, testing horizons expanded to include aptitude, ability, interest, and personality.

Types of Tests

Tests can be classified either by their administrative aspects or by their content. I will use both methods.

Speed versus Power Tests.   Speed tests have a large number of easy questions; the questions are so easy that the test taker will always get them right. The test is timed (for example, 5-minute limit) and has more items than can possibly be answered in the allotted time period. The total score on such a test is the number of items answered and reflects the test taker's speed of work.

Power tests have questions that are fairly difficult; that is, the test taker cannot get them right just by trying. Usually, there is no time limit. The total score on such a test is the number of items answered correctly. Most tests given in college are power tests. If time limits are imposed, they are done mostly for the convenience of the test administrator.

Individual versus Group Tests.   Individual tests are given to only one person at a time. Such tests are not common because of the amount of time needed to administer them to all applicants. For example, if a test takes one hour and ten people are to take it, ten hours of administration time will be required. The benefits of giving such a test must be judged against the costs. Certain types of IQ tests are individually administered, as are certain tests for evaluating high-level executives. In these tests the administrator has to play an active part (for example, asking questions, demonstrating an object) as opposed to just monitoring them.

Group tests are administered to several people simultaneously and are the most common type of test. They do not involve the active participation of an administrator. The Army Alpha and Beta tests were early group intelligence tests used in World War I. Most tests used in educational and industrial organizations are group tests, because they are efficient in terms of time and cost.

Paper-and-Pencil versus Performance Tests.   Paper-and-pencil tests are the most common type of test used in industrial and educational organizations. They do not involve the physical manipulation of objects or pieces of equipment. The questions asked may require answers in either multiple choice or essay form. The individual's physical ability to handle a pencil should not influence his or her score on the test. The pencil is just the means by which the response is recorded on a sheet of paper.

In a performance test the individual has to manipulate an object or a piece of equipment. The score is a measure of the person's ability to perform the manipulation. A typing test and a test of finger dexterity are examples of performance tests. Sometimes paper-and-pencil and performance tests are used jointly. To get a driver's license, for example, most people have to pass both a written test and a behind-the-wheel performance test.

Ethical Standards in Testing

To prevent misuse of psychological tests, the American Psychological Association has developed guidelines for their use. The ethics of psychological testing are a major responsibility of psychologists, as seen in the APA code of professional ethics (Standards for Educational and Psychological Testing, 1985). Maintaining ethical standards in testing is one of the more important ethical issues confronting the entire profession of psychology (American Psychological Association, 1992).

Depending on the purpose of the testing, test users must have certain qualifications. Sometimes the user must be a licensed professional psychologist, particularly in clinical psychology. Lesser qualifications are sufficient to administer employment tests in industry. To prevent misuse and to maintain test security, restrictions are also placed on who can buy the tests. However, Moreland, Eyde, Robertson, Primoff, and Most (1995) concluded that educational efforts will ultimately be more effective in promoting good testing practices than efforts to limit the use of tests. Test publishers are discouraged from giving away free samples or printing detailed examples of test questions as sales promotions, which could invalidate future test results.

Other ethical issues involve the invasion of privacy and confidentiality. *Invasion of privacy* occurs when a psychological test reveals more information about a person than he or she would want. Tests should be used for precise purposes. They should not be used to learn information irrelevant to performing the job. For example, if a mechanical comprehension test is used to hire mechanics, the company should not also use a personality inventory just to learn about potential employees' personal lives. Using a personality inventory that has no relationship to job performance could be an invasion of the applicant's privacy.

Confidentiality refers to who should have access to test results. When a person takes an employment test, he or she should be told the purpose of the test, how the results will be used, and which people in the company will need to see the results. Problems arise if a third party (another prospective employer, for example) wants to know the test results. The scores should be confidential, unless the test taker gives a written release.

Another problem in this area is the retention of records. Advances in computer technology have made it possible to store large quantities of information about people. Who should have access to this information, and what guarantees are there that it will not be misused? The results of an IQ test taken in sixth grade may become part of a student's permanent academic record. Should a potential employer get the results of this elementary school test? Furthermore, the test probably couldn't predict job performance, so why would anyone want the results? These types of questions are central to problems of confidentiality.

Sources of Information about Testing

Because testing is a rapidly changing area, it is important to keep up with current developments in the field. Old tests are revised, new tests are introduced, and some tests are discontinued.

Fortunately, several key references are available. Perhaps the most important source of test information is the series of *Mental Measurement Yearbooks* (MMY). The MMY was first published in 1938 and has been revised in roughly a five-year cycle. Each yearbook includes tests published during a specified period, thus supplementing the tests reported in previous yearbooks. The *Twelfth Mental Measurements Yearbook* (Conoley & Impara, 1995), for example, deals mainly with tests that appeared between 1989 and 1993. Each test is critically reviewed by an expert in the field and documented with a complete list of references. Information about price, publisher, and versions of the test is also given. The MMY series is the most comprehensive review of psychological tests available in the field.

Less detailed books, such as *Tests in Print* (Murphy, Conoley, & Impara, 1994), resemble bibliographies and help locate tests in the MMY. Other resource books review tests relevant for more restricted applications, as in business and industry (Hogan & Hogan, 1990; Sweetland & Keyser, 1991). Some psychological journals review specific tests, and various professional test developers publish test manuals. The test manual should give the information needed to administer, score, and evaluate a particular test, as well as data on the test's reliability and validity. Although these manuals are useful, they are usually not as complete and critical as reviews in the MMY.

The test user has an obligation to use the test in a professional and competent manner. Tests should be chosen with extreme care and concern for the consequences of using the tests. Important decisions are based on test scores, and the choice of test is equally important. A test should be thoroughly analyzed before it is considered for use.

Test Content

Tests can be classified according to their content. The following sections discuss the major types of tests used in industry along with information on how valid the various types of tests have been in personnel selection as documented from their use in the psychological literature.

Intelligence Tests

Tests of intelligence or cognitive ability have long been used for personnel selection. These tests tend to quite short, often taking less than 30 minutes to administer. Table 4–1 shows some sample test questions from a typical intelligence test.

There has been a long-standing controversy within psychology regarding the construct of intelligence. For more than 100 years psychologists have debated whether there is a single, unitary basis to intelligence or whether intelligence is composed of specific individual cognitive abilities, such as reasoning and perceptual speed. Proponents of the unitary basis to intelligence argue that general intelligence (noted by the symbol g) consistently predicts performance across a wide range of jobs (Ree, Earles, & Teachout, 1994). Similarly, g has been found to predict

Table 4–1   *Sample test questions for a typical intelligence test*

1. What number is missing in this series?
   3–8–14–21–29–(?)
2. SHOVEL is to DITCHDIGGER as SCALPEL is to:
   (a) knife (b) sharp (c) butcher (d) surgeon (e) cut

"Let's put it this way—if you can find a village without an idiot, you've got yourself a job."

SOURCE: Reprinted from *The Industrial-Organizational Psychologist.*

success in job training (Ree & Earles, 1991). In short, general intelligence is regarded to be a ubiquitous predictor of a wide variety of performance criteria, prompting Brand (1987) to observe, "*g* is to psychology what carbon is to chemistry" (p. 257).

Other researchers have argued for the assessment of multiple abilities, including reasoning, spatial ability, perceptual speed, and perceptual/psychomotor ability. Ackerman (1992), for example, reported superior predictive capacity of multiple abilities over general intelligence in complex information processing tasks, such as in the job of air traffic controller. Ackerman and Kanfer (1993) developed a selection test for air traffic controllers based in large part on the assessment of spatial ability. These authors recommended assessing both general and specific abilities in evaluating candidates for hire.

Assessments of general ability appear to be sufficient for predicting success in most jobs, in part because of the ease of administration and the degree of predictive accuracy. However, assessments of specific abilities are also advisable for selected jobs. Landy and Shankster (1994) advise researchers to expand the domain of cognitive abilities assessed for selection, including new methods of making those assessments (see Field Note 1).

Mechanical Aptitude Tests

Mechanical aptitude tests require a person to recognize which mechanical principle is suggested by a test item. One of the more popular tests of mechanical reasoning is the Bennett Test of Mechanical Comprehension (Bennett, 1980). The test is a series of pictures reflecting various issues about mechanical facts and principles. Other tests of mechanical comprehension have also been developed. Sample questions from the Bennett Test are shown in Figure 4–2.

Muchinsky (1993) reported the Bennett Test was most effective in predicting job performance of manufacturing employees who produce electro-mechanical components. A concurrent criterion-related validity coefficient of .38 was reported in the study. Schmitt, Gooding, Noe, and Kirsch (1984) reported an average validity coefficient of .27 for mechanical aptitude tests across many studies. The highest validity coefficients are typically found for vehicle operators as well as trade and craft employees.

Sensory/Motor Ability Tests

Sensory ability tests assess visual acuity, color vision, and hearing sensitivity. These abilities are related to success in certain types of jobs. Perhaps the best

---

FIELD NOTE 1

During the Vietnam War, an elite military unit called Special Forces was called on for assignments that were very important to the military and usually very dangerous. The military was extremely selective in admitting personnel to the Special Forces, typically selecting only 1 out of every 100 candidates. Although several types of tests were used in the selection battery, one in particular was unique. I have never heard of anything like it before or since.

The candidate was given a plain piece of paper with numbered blanks to record answers and a pencil. The test was recorded on a cassette tape, and the test began when the administrator started the tape. The voice on the tape said, "Question number one. A flagpole is 40 feet tall and casts a shadow 40 feet in length on the ground. What is the distance from the top of the flagpole to the top of the flagpole's shadow on the ground?" Eight seconds of silence followed. Then the voice said, "Question number two. What number comes next in this sequence: 4–7–13–25–?" Eight seconds of silence followed. This procedure was repeated for the 100 questions that made up the test.

The questions consisted of basic reasoning

and intelligence items, but what made the test so difficult was its manner of presentation. The questions were spoken once, the candidate had eight seconds to figure out the answer, and never got to go back and check the answers or rethink hard questions. There was one chance to get it correct when it was said, and that was it. Your own chances of getting these two questions correct are greater than the military candidate's because you are reading this and can reread it as often as you like. How would you do if you heard the questions only once and had but eight seconds to figure out each answer?

How was this test constructed, and what does it measure? In combat, members of the Special Forces had to think quickly, correctly, and under pressure. Given these conditions, the test constructors "worked backward" to develop a test that measured these characteristics. The actual content of the questions is almost incidental to the intent of the test. If you think you would be working under stress to take a test such as this, that is exactly what the test developers had in mind. This test was designed to identify who could function effectively under stress and who could not.

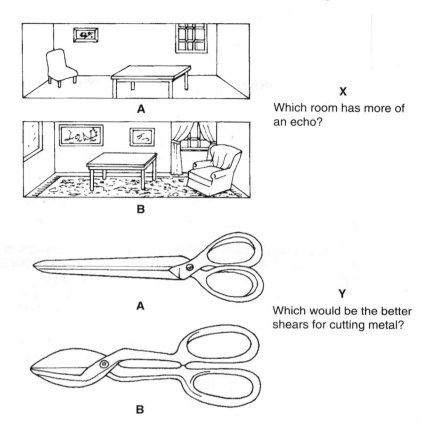

X

Which room has more of an echo?

Y

Which would be the better shears for cutting metal?

Figure 4–2 *Sample test questions from the Bennett Test of Mechanical Comprehension*

known test of visual acuity is the Snellen Eye Chart, a display with rows of letters that get increasingly smaller. The test taker stands 20 feet away from the chart and reads each row until the letters are indistinguishable. A ratio is then computed to express acuity:

$$\text{Acuity} = \frac{\text{Distance at which a person can read a certain line of print (usually 20 feet)}}{\text{Distance at which the average person can read the same line of print}}$$

For example, if the smallest line of print a person can read at 20 feet is a line most people can read from 40 feet, the person's score would be 20/40. Each eye is tested separately, and normal vision is 20/20. The most common way to measure hearing sensitivity is with an instrument called an audiometer, which produces tones of different frequencies and loudness. The tone is gradually raised in intensity. When the test taker signals that the note has been heard, the examiner records

Table 4–2   *Sample test question from a typical perceptual accuracy test*

Which pairs of items are identical?
   17345290—17342590
   2033220638—2033220638
   WPBRAEGGER—WPBREAGGER
   CLAFDAPKA26—CLAPDAFKA26

the level of intensity on an audiogram, which shows the intensity of sound needed to hear tones of different frequency. An audiogram is prepared for each ear. Hearing loss is detected by comparing one person's audiogram with the results from a tested population.

Researchers have also devised paper-and-pencil tests of perceptual accuracy. In these tests two stimuli are presented, and the test-taker must judge whether they are the same or different. The stimuli may be numbers or names. Table 4–2 shows the types of items included in a perceptual accuracy test.

Tests of motor ability assess fine or gross motor coordination. Frequently used motor ability tests include the Purdue Pegboard and the Crawford Small Parts Dexterity Test. In the first part of the Purdue Pegboard, pins are placed into small holes in a pegboard, using the right hand first, then the left hand, and then both hands together. In the second part, the pins are again placed in the holes but with the addition of collars and washers. The first part of the test measures manual dexterity; the second part measures finger dexterity. In the Crawford Small Parts Dexterity Test, pins are first placed in holes in the board, and then metal collars are placed over the pins. In the second part of the test, a screwdriver is used to insert small screws after they have been placed by hand into threaded holes.

Sensory/motor ability tests manifest a typical level of validity between .20 and .25. They are most predictive of job success in clerical occupations.

Personality and Interest Inventories

Unlike the previously cited tests, which have objective answers, personality inventories do not have right or wrong answers. Test takers answer questions about how much they agree with certain statements ("People who work hard get ahead"). In personality inventories similar types of questions normally make up a scale, which reflects a person's introversion, dominance, confidence, and so on. These scale scores are then used to predict job success. The basic rationale is that successful employees have certain interests or personality patterns, and these patterns become the basis for selecting new employees.

The use of personality inventories for predicting job success has undergone a complete cycle. Originally, psychologists thought personality variables were related to job performance. At least on logical grounds, this perspective makes a lot of sense because some people seemingly have the "wrong personality" for a job. Psychologists would use large omnibus personality inventories developed by clinical psychologists to forecast job success. The classic personality inventory of this type is the Minnesota Multiphasic Personality Inventory (MMPI) developed in 1943. The MMPI consists of 550 statements that must be answered "true," "false," or "cannot say." The inventory is scored in terms of ten clinical scales (for example, depression or schizophrenia). The inventory has since been revised (MMPI-2) to reflect advances in personality theory and measurement.

Personality inventories such as the original MMPI were used for many years for personnel selection; in fact, they were overused or misused. They were used indiscriminately to assess a candidate's personality, even when there was no established relationship between test scores and job performance. Soon personality inventories came under attack for invading the test taker's privacy. Some scales of a personality inventory may be useful for personnel selection decisions, but information unrelated to employment success may be revealed in the other scales. Guion and Gottier (1965) concluded that the evidence on personality inventories did not support their use for selecting personnel. Furthermore, influential psychologists such as Mischel (1968) questioned the value of personality assessments in understanding and predicting behavior. The upshot of these criticisms was a marked curtailment in the use of personality inventories for personnel selection.

However, psychologists continued to believe that personality variables were influential in job performance. Previously, they had predicted job performance with conventional personality inventories that were never really intended for industrial use with "normal" adults. Personality inventories like the original MMPI were developed to make clinical diagnoses and to differentiate normal from abnormal personalities. Consequently, their scales weren't refined enough to make accurate predictions about job candidates. Accordingly, I/O psychologists have recently begun developing new personality inventories designed exclusively for use with working populations. The results have been far more impressive than the previous research on clinical personality inventories. For example, Gough (1984) has successfully developed a personality scale to measure managerial potential, as defined by such factors as being organized, capable, mature, and self-confident. Hogan, Hogan, and Busch (1984) created a personality scale designed to measure the disposition to be helpful in dealing with other people, as indexed by such factors as being thoughtful, considerate, and cooperative.

A comprehensive five-factor model of personality structure has been proposed as being useful for predicting job performance. The five factors are extraversion, emotional stability, agreeableness, conscientiousness, and openness to experience. Extensive empirical support for this model's validity has been provided by McCrae and Costa (1987) and Hogan (1991). Personality inventories have also been developed based on this model, including the NEO-PI (McCrae, 1989) and the Hogan Personality Inventory (Hogan & Hogan, 1992). Barrick and Mount (1991) concluded from a meta-analysis that extraversion was a valid predictor of performance in occupations such as managers and salespeople that involve social interactions. Conscientiousness showed consistent relations with job performance criteria for all occupations. Similar empirical support for personality measures as predictors of job performance have been reported by Tett, Jackson, and Rothstein (1991) and Schmit and Ryan (1993).

Integrity Tests

The reemergence of personality assessment for personnel selection is also represented in the recent development and growing use of honesty or integrity tests. Honesty tests are designed to identify job applicants who will not steal from their employer or otherwise engage in counterproductive behavior on the job. These tests are paper-and-pencil tests and generally are designed as one of two types (Sackett & Harris, 1984; Sackett, Burris, & Callahan, 1989). In the first type, an *overt integrity test*, the job applicant clearly understands the intent of the test is to assess integrity. There are typically two sections to such a test. One section deals with attitudes toward theft and other forms of dishonesty (namely, beliefs about the frequency and extent of employee theft, punitiveness toward theft, perceived ease of theft, and endorsement of common rationalizations about theft), and another section deals with admissions of theft and other illegal activities (such as dollar amounts stolen in the past year, drug use, gambling). There is some evidence (Cunningham, Wong, & Barbee, 1994) that the responses to such tests are distorted by applicants seeking to create a favorable impression. The second type of test, called a *personality-based measure*, makes no reference to theft. These tests contain conventional personality assessment items that have been found to be predictive of theft. Because this type of test does not contain obvious references to theft, it is less likely to offend job applicants. These tests are primarily assessments of the conscientiousness personality factor.

The research findings on the validity of integrity tests is positive. Bernardin and Cooke (1993) found that scores on an honesty test successfully predicted theft among convenience store employees. Collins and Schmidt (1993) conducted a study of incarcerated offenders convicted of white-collar crimes such as embezzlement and fraud. Compared to a control sample of employees in upper-level positions of authority, offenders had greater tendencies toward irresponsibility, lack of dependability, and disregard of rules and social norms. In a meta-analytic review, Ones, Viswesvaran, and Schmidt (1993) concluded that integrity tests effectively predict the broad criterion of organizationally disruptive behaviors such as theft, disciplinary problems, and absenteeism.

Numerous problems are inherent in validating tests designed to predict employee theft. First, the issue is very sensitive, and many organizations don't care to make it public. Organizations may readily exchange information on employee absenteeism, but employee theft statistics are often confidential. Second, the criterion isn't really theft as much as being caught stealing, because many thefts go undetected. Third, the percentage of employees caught stealing in an organization is usually very small—2% to 3% would be the norm. Consequently, there are statistical difficulties in trying to predict what is essentially a rare event. Furthermore, Camara and Schneider (1994) noted that test publishers classify integrity tests as *proprietary*, meaning that access to these tests is not provided to researchers interested in assessing their validity. Some people argue that the value of integrity tests for personnel selection is greater than the typical validity coefficient would suggest. They argue that applicants who pass an integrity test are sensitized to the organization's concern for honesty and that other theft-reducing measures (such as internal surveillance systems) may well be used to monitor employees. Such procedures would reduce the occurrence of employee theft but would not be evidenced in the predictive accuracy of the honesty test.

Testing Physical Abilities

Psychological assessment has long been directed toward cognitive abilities and personality characteristics. However, research (for example, Fleishman & Quaintance, 1984) has also examined the assessment of physical abilities, and in particular how these physical abilities relate to performance in some jobs. Hogan (1991a) presented a set of physical abilities relevant to work performance. Among them are:

- *Static strength*. The ability to use muscle force to lift, push, pull, or carry objects.
- *Explosive strength*. The ability to use short bursts of muscle force to propel oneself or an object.
- *Gross body coordination*. The ability to coordinate the movement of the arms, legs, and torso together in activities where the whole body is in motion.
- *Stamina*. The ability of the lungs and circulatory (blood) systems of the body to perform efficiently over time.

An analysis (Hogan, 1991b) revealed that the total set of physical abilities could be reduced to three major constructs: strength, endurance, and movement quality. These three constructs account for most of the variation in individual capacity to perform strenuous activities. Arvey, Landon, Nutting, and Maxwell (1992) established the construct validity of a set of physical ability tests for use in the selection of entry-level police officers. The findings suggested that two factors—strength and endurance—underlie performance on the physical ability tests and performance on the job of police officer. The results further showed that females scored considerably lower than males on the physical ability tests; that is, the tests exhibited an adverse impact against females. However, the findings did not suggest how much importance physical abilities should be accorded in the selection decision compared to cognitive abilities.

In general the research on physical abilities reveals that they are related to successful job performance in physically demanding jobs, as fire fighters, police officers, and factory workers. Future research needs to consider the effects of aging on the decline of physical abilities and the legal implications of differences in physical abilities across groups.

Multiple-Aptitude Test Batteries

A final category of tests is based on their structural composition rather than their item content. *Test batteries* consist of many of the types of tests already discussed: intelligence, mechanical aptitude, personality, and so on. These tests are usually quite long, often taking several hours to complete. Each part of the test measures such factors as intellectual ability and mechanical reasoning. The tests are useful because they yield a great deal of information that can later be used for hiring, placement, training, and so forth. The major disadvantages of the tests are the cost and time involved. The two most widely known multiple-aptitude batteries are the Armed Services Vocational Aptitude Battery (ASVAB) and the Differential Aptitude Test (DAT).

Computerized Adaptive Testing

One of the major advances in psychological testing is called Computerized Adaptive Testing (CAT), or "tailored testing" (Weiss & Vale, 1987). Here is how it works: CAT is an automated test administration system using a computer. The test items appear on the video display screen of the computer terminal, and the examinee answers using the keyboard. Each test question presented is prompted by the response to the previous question. The first question given to the examinee is of medium difficulty. If the answer given is correct, the next question selected from the item bank of questions has been precalibrated to be slightly more difficult. If the answer given to that question is wrong, the next question selected by the computer will be somewhat easier. And so on.

The purpose of the CAT system is to get as close a match as possible between the question-difficulty level and the examinee's demonstrated ability level. In fact, by careful calibration of question difficulty, ability level can be inferred on the basis of the difficulty level of the questions answered correctly. CAT systems are based on complex mathematical models. Proponents believe that tests can be shorter (because of higher precision of measurement) and less expensive and that they have greater security than traditional paper-and-pencil tests. The military is the largest user of CAT systems, testing thousands of examinees monthly.

Although CAT systems represent the "high-tech" approach to psychological assessment, I doubt if they will soon make all paper-and-pencil tests obsolete. In fact, Bartram (1993) suggests that advances in computer technology have outpaced advances in psychological test theory. First, CAT systems were designed to assess abilities and aptitudes. They are not typically used for personality or interest measurement. Second, they obviously require elaborate computer programs, which not all organizations possess. Third, they are most cost efficient for very large employers like the military. And fourth, the mathematical foundations of such systems (called "Item Response Theory") is still a matter of professional debate. CAT systems will never completely replace traditional testing, but they do represent the cutting edge of psychological assessment. Computers have made possible great advances in science, as evidenced in I/O psychology by this major breakthrough in testing. Furthermore, with the creation of national information networks, the traditional practice of using psychological tests late in the selection process may change as it becomes possible to have access to test results at the time a job application is made.

Testing in Retrospect

As Haney (1981) observed, society has tended to imbue psychological tests with some arcane mystical powers that, as the evidence reviewed in this chapter indicate, are totally unwarranted. There is nothing mysterious about psychological tests; they are merely tools to help make better decisions than could be made without them. The psychological testing profession has a large share of critics. Criticism relates more to the inappropriate use of good tests than to using poor quality tests. For example, since the MMPI was never originally intended to predict managerial success, we really shouldn't be too surprised or unhappy when we find it does not. Testing has been oversold as a solution to problems. Many people have decried the "tyranny of testing"—the fact that critical decisions (say, entrance into a college or professional school) that affect an entire lifetime are based on a single test. Testing has its place in our repertoire of diagnostic instruments, but tests should help us meet our needs—not be the master of our decisions. This is sound advice that psychologists have long advocated. However, it is advice that both the developers and users of psychological tests have occasionally ignored or forgotten.

What we have learned about psychological tests from an I/O perspective is that some tests are useful in forecasting job success and others are not. As an entire class of predictors, psychological tests have been modestly predictive of job performance. Yet some authors (for example, Hunter & Hunter, 1984) believe that, all things considered, psychological tests have outperformed all other types of predictors across the full spectrum of jobs. Single-validity coefficients in excess of .50 are as unusual today as they were in the early years of testing. While test validity coefficients are not as high as we would like, it is unfair to condemn tests as useless. Also, keep in mind that validity coefficients are a function of both the predictor and the criterion. A poorly defined and constructed criterion will produce low validity coefficients no matter what the predictor is like. But because of the limited predictive power of tests, psychologists have had to look elsewhere for forecasters of job performance. In the balance of this chapter other predictors psychologists have investigated will be examined.

Interviews

In terms of sheer frequency, interviews are the most popular method of selecting employees. The popularity of the employment interview may also be due to increased legal problems with paper-and-pencil tests. Although most court cases regarding discrimination have involved paper-and-pencil tests, interviews along with other predictors are still regarded as a test by the government and, as such, are subject to the same judicial review. Unlike tests, interviews are highly subjective, so chances for unfair discrimination seem to be greater. Because interviews are used so often in employment decisions, many research studies have been conducted. Some of the major issues inherent in the employment interview are discussed in the following sections.

Format of the Selection Interview

There are several types of interviews, ranging from highly structured to highly unstructured. In a highly structured interview, the interviewer asks predetermined questions of all applicants in the same way and records each response question by question. In an unstructured interview, the interviewer proceeds on the basis of the applicant's response to previous questions. He or she probes and explores the applicant's qualifications in a "play-by-ear" fashion. In theory no two applicants would be asked the same questions. In practice most interviews are halfway between structured and unstructured. That is, the applicants are asked the same general questions, but their responses may cause the interviewer to question them more intensely.

Interviews can also be described in terms of the number of participants or trials. In most cases one applicant and one interviewer have one interview. The interviewer evaluates the applicant and makes a decision. An alternative is for several interviewers to interview the applicant separately. This type of interview is usually conducted for higher-level jobs. The interviewers pool their opinions and reach a decision. A final format is for a panel of perhaps as many as six or seven interviewers to interview an applicant. Again, the interviewers pool their opinions and make a decision. This procedure is typical in government jobs where applicants are often interviewed by a Civil Service evaluation board.

Unlike a paper-and-pencil test, an interview is a dynamic selection device. Interviewers affect the behavior of applicants, and vice versa. The applicant tries to impress the interviewer and thereby effect a favorable decision. The interviewer as well can knowingly or unknowingly alter the applicant's responses by such statements as "You're right," "I agree," or "I disagree." Nonverbal responses (yawning, smiling, frowning, eye contact) can also alter the applicant's behavior. Furthermore, the outcome of the interview can be affected by the interviewer's behavior. Thus, an interviewer's own behavior during the interview may be a determining factor in whether the applicant is hired! Experienced interviewers learn a standardized interview style to minimize the impact of their own behavior on the outcome of the interview.

Schmitt (1976) has developed a graphic model of the determinants of interview decisions, which is shown in Figure 4–3. The interaction of the applicant and the interviewer determines the interview outcome. I will explore some of these factors in greater detail shortly. For the moment, note that many variables that affect the outcomes of interviews do not influence tests. For example, the interviewer's sex may influence who gets offered a job, but the sex of the test scorer would not influence the applicant's score.

Evaluation of the Interview

A classic description of interviews is they are "conversations with a purpose" (Bingham & Moore, 1941). The "goodness" of these conversations as predictors of job performance can be judged by the same criteria used to judge any predictor: reliability and validity.

Reliability.   The reliability of an interview refers to the similarity of judgments made by the same interviewer over time (intra-interviewer reliability) or the simi-

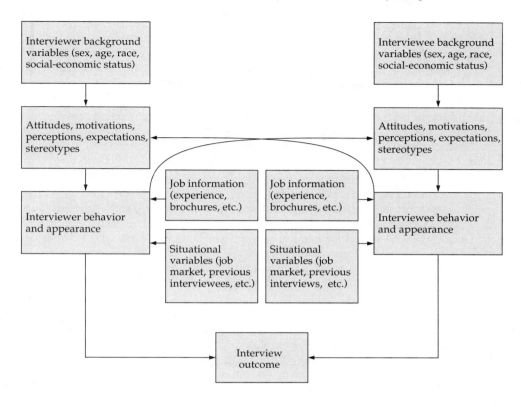

Figure 4–3   *Determinants of interview outcome*

SOURCE: From "Social and Situational Determinants of Interview Decisions: Implications for the Employment Interview" by
N. Schmitt, 1976, *Personnel Psychology, 29*, p. 93.

larity of judgments made by different interviewers about the same job applicant
(inter-interviewer reliability). The two types of reliability address different issues.

Most of the research on intra-interviewer reliability indicates that interviewers are consistent in their evaluations. Whatever they like or dislike about applicants appears stable, so they make consistent evaluations. Carlson (1968) has
shown that interviewer self-consistency increases when (1) the interviewer has a
relative standard (that is, a hypothetical ideal person) that can be used for comparisons, and (2) the applicants' qualifications are diverse (that is, some are good,
some are bad).

While intra-interviewer reliability is typically high, this is not always true for
inter-interviewer reliability. Inter-interviewer reliability assesses the extent to
which different interviewers reach the same decision in evaluating applicants. A
lot of research can be summarized by saying sometimes they agree and sometimes they do not. Some studies report inter-interviewer reliabilities in the .80s;
other studies report inter-interviewer reliabilities as low as .15. A crucial determinant of agreement among interviewers is what specifically they are being asked

to evaluate. If the applicants are being judged in terms of how appropriate their work history is for a given job, most interviewers would probably agree (inter-interviewer reliability would be high). If the applicants are judged on their personality and how it relates to the job, interviewers might disagree (inter-interviewer reliability might be low). This occurs because interviewers have different ideas of what the personality constructs mean and how they are translated into job performance. For example, if interviewers were asked if an applicant was "aggressive" enough to succeed in the job, each might have a different view on what aggressiveness is and how much of it is needed on the job.

Validity.   Care must be exercised in evaluating the validity of the interview process as a whole versus the validity of the interviewer. The validity of interviewers refers to the capacity of individuals to be accurate, sensitive judges of human talent. Research (for example, Zedeck, Tziner, & Middlestadt, 1983) indicates that some interviewers are very good at what they do and that others are poor. The validity of the interview process refers to the extent that all of the information about an applicant that is brought to the attention of the interviewer is predictive of job performance. This would include not only the content of the interview itself but also test scores, letters of reference, and records of past work.

The validity of an interviewer is often tangled up in the validity of these other sources. It's hard to tell how much of the hiring decision was due solely to the interviewer's judgment and how much was due to the other information. Carlson (1972) reported that in reviewing 13 studies where the interviewer was the only source of information, 9 studies had validity coefficients in the .15 to .25 range. However, recent research is reaching a more positive verdict on the validity of the interview. McDaniel, Whetzel, Schmidt, and Maurer (1994) conducted a meta-analysis of interview studies and estimated the validity of the interview to be .37. In particular, their study revealed that highly structured interviews (that is, where all the applicants are asked the same questions) produce higher validity coefficients (.44) than unstructured interviews (.33). Also, situational interviews are especially useful.

In a *situational interview* the applicant is asked how he or she would respond in a particular hypothetical situation. For example, the applicants would be asked what they would do to advise subordinates seeking to apply for a position they were not qualified for. Robertson, Gratton, and Rout (1990) reported a validity coefficient of .43 for predicting managerial potential. Similarly positive conclusions regarding the value of the situational interview for personnel selection were reported by Maurer and Fay (1988) and Harris (1989). Latham and Finnegan (1993) reported that use of the situational interview as a selection method was a source of pride among those who passed and were hired. The current employees having gone through it themselves believed the people being hired were well-qualified for the job.

The interview remains one of the most (if not the most) commonly used personnel selection methods. Arvey and Campion (1982) have postulated several reasons for its persistent use. First, the interview really is more valid than our research studies indicate. However, due to methodological problems and limitations in our research, we can't demonstrate how valid it actually is (Dreher, Ash,

& Hancock, 1988). Second, people generally are prone to place confidence in highly fallible interview judgments; that is, we are not good judges of people, but we think we are, a phenomenon called the "illusion of validity." Finally, although the interview may not be highly valid for selection, it serves other personnel functions unrelated to employee selection, such as selling candidates on the value of the job and of the organization as an attractive employer. Whatever the reasons for the interview's popularity, few companies are willing to do something as important as extending a job offer without first seeing a person "in the flesh."

Factors Influencing Interview Outcomes

Through extensive research involving hundreds of studies, psychologists now know that many factors can influence the outcome of an interview. Schmitt (1976) reviewed the literature on interviews and found a dozen factors (apart from the applicant's qualifications) that affect an interviewer's decision. (The criterion in this research is whether applicants are offered jobs, not whether they turn out to be successful employees.) Here are some major findings from Schmitt's study.

Negative-Positive Nature of the Information. Is it something positive that applicants have said that results in being hired, or is it something negative that they have said that causes their rejection? Research shows that negative information is more important than positive information. Many interviewers look for a reason (information) not to hire an applicant, and when they find it, the applicant is rejected. Suppose a high school graduate said she was on the honor roll for two years. This positive piece of information could be outweighed if she also said that she was expelled from school for two weeks for disciplinary reasons.

Temporal Placement of Information. Does it make a difference when certain information is presented to the interviewer? If interviewers are most influenced by information given early in the interview, this is called a *primacy effect*. If they are most influenced by information given late in the interview, this is called a *recency effect*. It appears that primacy effects tend to occur for general impressions, but recency effects predominate in memory for specific details. Dougherty, Turban, and Callender (1994) reported that interviewers conduct themselves differently in an interview as a function of their initial impression of the candidate. Positive first impressions of the candidate by the interviewer were typically followed by "selling" the company and giving job information. Conversely, negative first impressions were often followed by the interviewer collecting more information about the candidate.

Contrast Effects. Is one applicant's evaluation influenced by preceding applicants? Will an applicant of average credentials appear worse if he or she was preceded by someone with superior credentials? Research indicates that *contrast effects* do occur. Applicants with average credentials appear better to the interviewer if they follow someone with poor credentials, and they appear worse if they follow someone with superior credentials. A more controversial question is how much contrast effects influence interviewers. Some researchers think they exert substantial influence; others think their effects are minimal. It has been suggested that the interviewer's experience controls the impact of contrast effects; that is, more experienced interviewers are less influenced by contrast effects.

Interviewer Stereotypes. Do interviewers have an "ideal" candidate in mind when they interview applicants? The answer seems to be yes. But not all interviewers have the same ideal candidate in mind, even if they are interviewing for the same job. The "ideal candidate" probably contributes to high intra-interviewer reliability, since interviewers are very consistent in evaluating applicants in comparison to their ideal applicant. Whether their conception of the ideal applicant is valid (would result in the best job performance) is another question.

Assessment Center Evaluations

Assessment centers evaluate job candidates, most typically for managerial-level jobs, using several methods and raters. Assessment centers use a group-oriented, standardized series of activities to provide a basis for judgments or predictions of human behaviors believed or known to be relevant to work performed in an organizational setting. In some organizations special rooms have been designed for assessment, while other organizations may use a conference center located away from the normal workplace. Because these centers are expensive, they have mainly been used by large organizations; however, private organizations now conduct assessment center appraisals for smaller companies.

AT&T developed the earliest systematic approach to assessment center evaluation in 1956. It is described in detail by Bray, Campbell, and Grant (1974) and summarized by Bray (1982). Since AT&T's pioneering efforts, hundreds of other organizations have developed centers for the appraisal of upper-level employees.

These characteristics are typical of the assessment center approach:

1. Those employees selected to attend the center (the assessees) are usually management-level personnel the company wants to evaluate for possible promotion, transfer, or training. Occasionally, organizations will send management applicants to the center and then use appraisal information for selection.
2. Assessees are evaluated in groups of 10 to 20. They may be divided into smaller groups for various exercises, but the basic strategy is to appraise individuals against the performance of others in the group.
3. Several raters (the assessors) do the evaluation. They work in teams and collectively or individually recommend personnel action (for example, selection, promotion). Assessors may be psychologists, but usually they are company employees unfamiliar with the assessees. They are often trained in how to appraise performance. The training may last from several hours to a few days.
4. A wide variety of performance appraisal methods are used. Many involve group interactions, for example, leaderless group discussions in which leaders "emerge" via their degree of participation in the exercise. Other methods in-

clude in-basket tests, projective personality inventories, personal history information forms, and interviews. The program typically takes from one to several days.

Given the variety of tests, the assessee provides substantial information about his or her performance. Raters evaluate the assessees on a number of performance dimensions judged relevant for the job in question. These dimensions involve leadership, decision making, practical judgment, and interpersonal relations skills—typical performance dimensions for managerial jobs. Based on these evaluations, the assessors prepare a summary report for each assessee, and then feed back portions of the report to the assessee. Raters then forward their recommendations for personnel action to the organization for review and consideration.

The validity of assessment center evaluations is determined by comparing the judgments of performance made in the center with some criterion of performance back on the job, usually rated job performance, promotions, or salary (Huck, 1973). Validity studies on assessment center evaluations are generally very positive. Byham (1970) reported that correlations of center evaluations of managers with subsequent job performance ratings by superiors ranged from .47 to .64. In their analysis of center evaluations for male and female employees, Moses and Boehm (1975) concluded that assessment centers predicted the future performance for females as accurately as they did for males. Ritchie and Moses (1983) found that assessment center ratings were predictive of the career programs of women seven years later. Huck and Bray (1976) reported a similar finding regarding the fairness of assessment centers in predicting the future job performance of white and black employees. It seems that assessment center evaluations do not have the racial or sex bias of some job performance predictors.

Assessment centers offer promise for identifying persons with potential for success in management. Assessment centers seem to be successful in their major goal of selecting high-talent people. Nevertheless, not all of the research results are totally positive. Drakely, Herriot, and Jones (1988) found that biographical data predicted the success of British navy officers in training as well as the overall assessment rating of a lengthy assessment center procedure. Pynes and Bernardin (1989) reported that paper-and-pencil tests of cognitive ability exhibited greater validity than assessment center ratings for the selection of police officers. Another critical factor seems to be the criterion against which assessment center ratings are validated. For example, Borman (1982) and Tziner and Dolan (1982) found that assessment center ratings were predictive of success in military training and far superior in validity to interviews or psychological tests. We also have known for a long time that assessment center ratings predict the criterion of promotability. Thus, assessment ratings have the capacity to identify individuals who will "get ahead" in the organization. However, Turnage and Muchinsky (1984) found that assessment center ratings were not predictive of actual on-the-job performance measures, as indexed by 21 criteria of supervisory performance. Thus, assessment ratings more strongly predict advancement than performance.

Assessment center evaluations are particularly susceptible to criterion contamination from several sources. One source is basing overall judgments of performance on many evaluation methods (tests, interviews, life history forms, and so on). The validity of the evaluations may stem from the validity of these separate appraisal methods; that is, a valid interview or test might be just as capable of forecasting later job success as the resulting evaluation. But because the incremental value of these methods is "buried" in the overall assessor judgments, it is debatable how much assessors' ratings contribute to predicting future performance beyond these separate methods. There is also evidence (Kleinmann, 1993) that assessees can fashion their behavior to impress assessors when the assessees know what dimensions of their performance are being evaluated.

Klimoski and Strickland (1977) proposed a second source of contamination that is far more subtle. They contend that assessment center evaluations are predictive because both assessors and company supervisors hold common stereotypes of the effective employee. Assessors give higher evaluations to those who "look" like good management talent, and supervisors give higher evaluations to those who "look" like good "company" people. If the two sets of stereotypes were held in common, then (biased) assessment center evaluations would correlate with (biased) job performance evaluations. The danger is that organizations would hire and promote those who fit the image of the successful employee. The long-term effect would be an organization staffed with people who were mirror images of one another. Opportunity for creative people who "don't fit the mold" but might be effective if given the chance would be greatly limited.

After reviewing the literature on assessment centers, Klimoski and Brickner (1987) concluded that assessment evaluations are indeed valid but that I/O psychologists still do not really know why. The authors proposed five possible explanations.

- *Actual criterion contamination.* Companies use the assessment evaluations to make decisions regarding promotions, pay raises, and rated job performance, so it is hardly surprising that assessment evaluations would predict such criteria.
- *Subtle criterion contamination.* As explained by Klimoski and Strickland (1977), both assessors and company supervisors hold common stereotypes of the successful employee, so biased assessment evaluations are related to biased performance evaluations.
- *Self-fulfilling prophecy.* Companies designate their "up-and-coming" employees to attend assessment centers, and after assessment these same people are indeed the ones who get ahead in the company.
- *Performance consistency.* People who succeed in work-related activities do so in many arenas—in assessment centers, in training, on the job, and so on. They are consistently good performers, so success in assessment relates to success on the job.
- *Managerial intelligence.* The skills and abilities needed to be successful in assessment centers and on the job have much in common. Such talents as verbal skills, analytic reasoning, and well-developed plans of action are acquired and cultivated by more intellectually capable people. The authors refer to this construct as "managerial intelligence."

Research on assessment centers has been evolutionary in nature. Early research addressed whether assessment evaluations were predictive of job success and found they were. More recent research addresses the limits of this method of assessment and the reasons that assessment evaluations are predictive. As our knowledge about assessment centers continues to grow, we are beginning to address some complex and intriguing questions of both theoretical and practical significance.

Work Samples and Situational Exercises

Work Samples

Work samples are an exciting approach to personnel selection. Their rationale is simple. Rather than trying to identify predictors of job success that are usually quite different in nature from the criterion they are supposed to predict, a "miniature criterion" is created and used as the predictor. In other words, the goal is to take the content of a person's job, shrink it down to a manageable time period, and let applicants demonstrate their ability in performing this replica of the job. This rationale was presented by Wernimont and Campbell (1968) and has served as the blueprint for later empirical studies.

An excellent example of a work sample was reported by Campion (1972), who wanted to develop a predictor of job success for mechanics. Using job analysis techniques, he learned that the mechanic's job was defined by success in the use of tools, accuracy of work, and overall mechanical ability. He then designed tasks that would show an applicant's performance in these three areas. Through the cooperation of job incumbents, he designed a work sample that involved such typical tasks as installing pulleys and belts, taking apart and repairing a gearbox, and so on. The proper steps necessary to perform these tasks were identified and given numerical values according to their appropriateness (for example, 10 points for aligning a motor with a dial indicator, 1 point for aligning it by feeling the motor, 0 points for just looking at the motor). Using a concurrent criterion-related validity design, each mechanic in the shop took the work sample. Their scores were correlated with the criterion of supervisor ratings of their job performance. The validity of the work sample was excellent: It correlated .66 with use of tools, .42 with accuracy of work, and .46 with overall mechanical ability. Campion showed that there was a substantial relationship between how well mechanics did on the work sample and how well they did on the job. In general, work samples are among the most highly valid means of personnel selection.

But work samples do have limitations. First, they are effective primarily in blue-collar jobs that involve either the mechanical trades (for example, mechanics, carpenters, electricians) or the manipulation of objects. They are not very effective when the job involves working with people as opposed to things. Second, work samples assess what a person can do; they don't assess potential. They seem best suited to hiring experienced workers rather than trainees. Finally, work samples are time-consuming and costly to administer. Because they are individual tests, they require a lot of supervision and monitoring. Few work samples are designed to be completed in less than one hour. If there are 100 applicants to fill five jobs, it may not be worthwhile to give a work sample to all applicants. Perhaps the applicant pool could be reduced with some other selection instrument (for example, a review of previous work history). Yet despite their limitations, work samples are quite useful in personnel selection.

Robertson and Kandola (1982) report another advantage of work samples: applicants respond to them very favorably. Work samples engender a positive reaction from applicants because of their high face validity. Applicants perceive a direct link between how well they perform on a work sample and how well they would perform on the job (that is, the concept of criterion-related validity). Indeed, Cascio and Phillips (1979) reported that one major U.S. city has instituted work-sample selection tests for many city jobs, in part because of the high appeal of the method to applicants.

Situational Exercises

Situational exercises are roughly the white-collar counterpart of work samples; that is, they are used mainly to select people for managerial and professional jobs. Unlike work samples, which are designed to be replicas of the job, situational exercises mirror only part of the job.

Situational exercises involve a whole family of tests that in one way or another assess problem-solving ability. Two good examples are the In-Basket Test and the Leaderless Group Discussion. The In-Basket Test involves having applicants sort through an in-basket of things to do. The contents are carefully designed letters, memos, brief reports, and the like that require the applicant's immediate attention and response. The applicant goes through the contents and takes the appropriate action to solve the problems presented, such as making a phone call, writing a letter, or calling a meeting. A number of observers score the applicant in terms of such factors as productivity (how much work got done) and problem-solving effectiveness (versatility in resolving problems). The In-Basket Test is predictive of job performance of managers and executives, a traditionally difficult group of employees to select. But a major problem with the test is that it takes up to three hours and, like a work sample, is an individual test. If there are many applicants, the time needed to administer the test is prohibitive. Schippman, Prien, and Katz (1990) report the typical validity coefficient for the In-Basket Test is approximately .25.

The Leaderless Group Discussion (LGD) involves having a group of applicants (normally two to eight) engage in a job-related discussion in which no spokesperson or group leader has been named. Raters observe and assess each applicant on such factors as individual prominence, group goal facilitation, and sociability. Scores on these factors are then used as a hiring basis. The reliability of the LGD increases with the number of people in the group. The typical validity coefficient is in the .15 to .35 range.

Although neither the In-Basket Test nor the LGD has the validity of a typical work sample, remember that the criterion of success for a manager is usually more difficult to define. If a mechanic installs a motor upside down, people know about it immediately. If a manager picks the wrong people to do a job, it can be some time before the source of the problem is ascertained. Thus, the lower validities usually found in the selection of managerial personnel are as attributable to problems with the criterion and its proper articulation as anything else.

Biographical Information

The theory of biographical information as a method of personnel selection is based on our development as individuals. Our lives represent a series of experiences, events, and choices, which defined our development. Past and current events shape our behavioral patterns, attitudes, and values. Because there is consistency in our lives regarding behaviors, attitudes, and values, an assessment of these factors from our past experiences will be predictive of such experiences in the future. Biographical information assesses constructs that shape our behavior, such as sociability and ambition. To the extent that these constructs are predictive of future job performance, we can assess previous life experiences that are manifestations of these constructs.

Biographical information is frequently recorded on an application blank. The application blank, in turn, can be used as a selection device on the basis of the information presented. The questions asked on the application blank are predictive of job performance criteria. Mael (1991) recommends that all biographical questions pertain to historical events in the person's life, as opposed to questions about behavioral intentions or presumed behavior in a hypothetical situation. The following questions are typically found on a biographical information questionnaire:

- "How old were you when you got your first job?"
- "Did you ever get fired from a job?"
- "What was your grade point average in high school?"

Some biographical information questionnaires contain as few as 20 questions. Others many include as many as several hundred questions. To determine which questions should be asked, the following research procedure is typically followed. A performance criterion of interest is chosen, usually productivity, turnover, or absenteeism. A sample of current employees who are administered the questionnaire are divided into two groups, as high and low productivity or high and low absenteeism. The next step is to determine if the high- and low-criterion groups differ in terms of the characteristics of the members. If the responses to some biographical questions occur far more often in one group, that question is predictive of job performance. For instance, suppose 80% of the high-productivity group graduated from high school and only 30% of the low-productivity group did. The item "Did you graduate from high school?" would be predictive of productivity and could be used to hire employees.

There are many examples of useful applications of biographical information. Cascio (1976) reported validity coefficients of .77 and .79 for predicting the turnover of white and black workers, respectively. While the magnitude of these validity coefficients is extremely impressive, what is also desirable is that the biographical questionnaire method was fair to members of both racial groups.

Childs and Klimoski (1986) demonstrated that selected early life experiences not only predicted later success in a job but also were predictive of feelings of personal and career accomplishments throughout a lifetime. Other researchers have reported the success of biographical questionnaires in predicting salary earnings, absenteeism, and productivity. Brown and Campion (1994) reported that job recruiters found biographical information to be a useful way to assess whether applicants possessed the attributes needed to perform the job.

While this method of personnel selection has generated considerable interest on the part of researchers (for example, Gunter, Furnham, & Drakeley, 1993; Stokes, Mumford, & Owens, 1994), there are a number of concerns about fairness, legal issues, and honesty of responses. One aspect of the fairness problem concerns equal accessibility of the behavior or experience being questioned by all respondents. For example, assume the response to a question about participation in high school football is found predictive of subsequent performance on a job. The strategy would then be to include this question on an application blank to evaluate job candidates. The problem is that only males are allowed to play high school football, thereby prohibiting females from having potential access to this type of experience. Female job applicants would be disadvantaged in being evaluated by this question. The problem is not that females *didn't* have this experience, but they *couldn't* have it (that is, females didn't have equal access). Asking different questions of male and female applicants is not a solution to this problem, as laws governing fair employment practice emphasize consistency of treatment to all job applicants.

Another concern is that the questions asked should not be invasive. Invasiveness addresses whether the respondent will consider the item content to be an invasion of his or her privacy. As Nickels (1994) notes, items inquiring about religious affiliations, marital status, or dating habits are potentially invasive. Questions perceived to invade privacy invite litigation against the hiring organization by job applicants (see Field Note 2).

A final issue is the question of "fakability"—to what extent do individuals distort their responses to create a more socially desirable impression? Research (Becker & Colquitt, 1992; Kluger, Reilly, & Russell, 1991) reveals that faking does occur in responding to certain types of questions. The questions most likely to be faked in a socially desirable direction were difficult to verify for accuracy and had the appearance of being highly job relevant.

Despite these limitations, biographical information offers a logically defensible strategy to personnel selection. Mumford and Stokes (1992) portray biographical information as revealing consistent patterns of behavior that are interwoven throughout our lives. By assessing that which we have done, we can gain great insight into that which we will do.

Peer Assessment

One alternative to having supervisors evaluate employees is to have employees evaluate one another. This is the basis of peer assessment (Kane & Lawler, 1978).

Though the peer-assessment technique has some peculiar limitations, the method has yielded encouraging results.

Peer assessments are best used when job applicants have known one another for some time. The method is not employed for initial entry into an organization but for selection to advanced positions. It has been used in the military to predict success as an officer and in industry to predict success after training. Applicants answer such questions as "Which of you do you think will make the best officer?" and "Who do you think will score the highest on the final exam in this course?" Responses are tabulated and then correlated with a criterion of performance. Hollander (1965) reported that peer ratings made in the third week of officer training correlated .40 with ratings of success as an officer three years later. Mayfield (1972) found that peer assessments made by life insurance salespeople in a training program correlated .29 with tenure and .30 with production. These ratings, made 18 days after the start of the training program, were predictive of those two criteria one year later.

By far the biggest limitation of peer assessments is that they cannot be used before hiring. Despite this practical limitation, it is apparent that after a brief exposure to one another, candidates have a fairly accurate sense of one another's ability. It is likely that industry will continue to use peer assessments on a limited basis because of their validity and ease of administration.

FIELD NOTE 2

Biographical items sometimes lack content validity to the job in question even though they manifest empirical criterion-related validity. The potential irrelevance of biographical questions is always a concern in personnel selection. Here is a case in point.

A city had developed a biographical inventory that was to be used along with some psychological tests to evaluate police officers for promotion to police detectives. All the questions included on the biographical inventory were predictive of job performance as a detective, as determined by a criterion-related validity study. One of the questions on the inventory was, "Did you have sexual intercourse for the first time before the age of 16?" Some police officers who took this promotional exam and who failed it sued the city for asking such a question in an employment test. The officers said the question had absolutely no relevance to the conduct of a detective's job, and furthermore it was an invasion of their privacy. They had been denied a detective's job because of a totally inappropriate question, and therefore they wanted the entire test results thrown out.

The case was heard at the district court. The judge ruled in favor of the officers, saying that the question was totally lacking in content validity and was an invasion of their privacy. Therefore the officers should be reconsidered for promotion to detective. The city appealed the verdict to the state supreme court. The judge there reversed the lower court ruling and allowed the test results to stand, meaning the officers would not get promoted. The state supreme court judge based his decision on the grounds that the answer to that question did correlate with job performance as a detective. From a practical and legal standpoint, it would be advisable to avoid asking such invasive questions in the first place, even though in this case a lengthy legal battle ultimately resulted in a decision favorable to the city.

Letters of Recommendation

One of the most commonly used and least valid of all predictors is the letter of recommendation. Letters of recommendation and reference checks are as widespread in personnel selection as the interview and the application blank. Unfortunately, they usually lack comparable validity. Letters of recommendation are usually written in behalf of an applicant by a current employer, professional associate, or personal friend. The respondent rates the applicant on such dimensions as leadership ability and written and oral communication skills. The responses are then used as a basis for hiring.

One review of letters of recommendation (Muchinsky, 1979) reported an average validity of .13. Some people even make recommendations that have an inverse relationship with the criterion; that is, if the applicant is recommended for hire, the company would do best to reject him or her! One of the biggest problems with letters of recommendation is their restricted range. As you might expect, almost all letters of recommendation are positive. Most often, the applicants themselves choose who will write the letters, so it isn't surprising that they pick people who will make them look good. Because of this restriction (that is, that almost all applicants are described positively), the lack of predictive ability of the letter of recommendation is not unexpected.

While a few studies using specially constructed evaluation forms have reported moderate validity coefficients, the typical validity coefficient is close to zero. Because of their limited validity, letters of recommendation should not be taken too seriously in making personnel selection decisions. The only major exception to this statement would be the following condition: when applicants are described in positive terms, you will not know if they will be successful on the job. However, on those rare occasions when the applicant is described in negative terms (even if only mildly), such an assessment is usually indicative of future problems on the job. Those types of letters should be taken seriously. On par though, the percentage of letters of recommendation that contain nonsupportive information about an applicant is very small (see Field Note 3).

New and Controversial Methods

The final category is reserved for new and controversial methods of assessing job applicants. Four such methods will be presented.

Drug Testing

Drug testing is the popular term for the detection of substance abuse, which refers to the use of illegal drugs and the improper and illegal use of prescription and over-the-counter medications, alcohol, and other chemical compounds. Substance abuse is a major global problem with far-reaching societal, moral, and economic consequences. The role that I/O psychology plays in this vast and complex picture is the detection of substance abuse in the workplace. Employees who engage in substance abuse jeopardize not only their own welfare but also potentially the welfare of fellow employees and other individuals. I/O psychologists are involved in screening out substance abusers among both job applicants and current employees.

Unlike other forms of assessment used by I/O psychologists that involve estimates of cognitive or motor abilities, drug testing embraces chemical assessments. The method of assessment is based on a urine sample. The rationale is that the presence of drugs will be revealed in a person's urine. Therefore, a sample of urine is treated with chemicals that will reveal the presence of drugs if they have been ingested by the person. There are two basic types of assessments. A screening test assures the potential presence of a wide variety of chemicals. A confirmation test on the same sample identifies the presence of chemicals suggested by the initial screening test. I/O psychologists would not be directly involved with these tests, because they are performed in chemical laboratories by individuals with special technical training. The profession of I/O psychology does become involved in drug testing because it assesses suitability for employment, with concomitant concern about the reliability, validity, legality, and cost of these tests.

Although the issues are very complex, I will briefly describe some concerns. The reliability of the chemical tests is much higher than the reliability of traditional paper-and-pencil psychological assessments. However, the reliability is not

FIELD NOTE 3

I was the director of a graduate program to which about 100 students seek admission annually. One of the requirements for admission is for the applicant to submit letters of recommendation in his or her behalf. Over the years I have received several memorable letters of recommendation, but on one occasion I received a letter (actually, two) that clearly illustrates why such letters have little predictive value. This letter came from the president of a foreign university where the student was enrolled. It made the student sound incredibly strong academically: the class valedictorian, the only recipient of the native king's fellowship program, the only student who received a special citation from the university, and so forth. Needless to say, I was most impressed by this letter.

About two weeks later I got another application for admission from a second student from that same university. Accompanying this application was another letter supposedly written by the university president. This letter was identical in content to the first. The only difference was the name of the student typed at the top of the letter. Thus, both students had been the class valedictorian, both were the only recipient of the fellowship, and so on.

I then called a different academic department and discovered it, too, had received the identical letter on yet a third student from that university who was applying for graduate work in that department. What we had was literally a form letter in which every student in the university was being described, word for word, as the best. The university apparently provided this "service" to its students seeking admission to graduate schools in the United States. Needless to say, such attempts at deception do nothing to portray fairly a candidate's strengths and weaknesses—and most certainly do not enhance the validity of the letter of recommendation as a personnel selection method.

perfect, which means that different conclusions can be drawn about substance abuse as a function of the laboratory conducting the testing. Questions of validity are much more problematic. The accurate detection of drug usage varies as a function of the type of drug involved, because some drugs remain in our systems for days and others remain for weeks. Thus, the timing of the urine sample is critical. It is also possible that diet can falsely contribute to the results of a drug test. For example, eating poppy-seed cake may trigger a confirmatory response to heroin usage because heroin is derived from poppy seeds. The legality of drug testing is also highly controversial. Critics of drug testing contend it violates the U.S. Constitution with regard to unreasonable search and seizure, self-incrimination, and the right to privacy. It is also a matter of debate as to which jobs should be subject to drug testing. Some people argue for routine drug testing; others say drug testing should be limited to jobs that have a potential impact on the lives of others (for example, transportation). Yet another issue involves the criteria for intoxication and performance impairment. What dosage of a drug constitutes a level that would impair job performance? Finally, there is the matter of cost. Screening tests cost about $10 per specimen, but confirmatory tests can cost up to $100 per specimen. These costs will eventually have to get passed on to consumers as part of the price they pay for having their goods and services rendered by a drug-free work force. A major investigation by the National Research Council (Normand, Lempert, & O'Brien, 1994) on drug testing also underscores the particular danger of unfairness to job applicants who are falsely classified as being drug users. Drug testing is thus confronted with trying to delicately balance economic goals of work force productivity with individual rights to fair treatment in the workplace.

Some recent research on drug testing has revealed applicant reactions to such testing and its effectiveness. Murphy, Thornton, and Prue (1991) found that drug testing was judged most acceptable for jobs in which there was the potential for danger to others. Uniform drug testing for all jobs was not viewed favorably. Stone and Kotch (1989) reported that the negative reaction to drug testing by companies can be reduced by giving employees advance notice of scheduled drug tests and responding to detected drug use with treatment programs rather than the discharge of employees. Normand, Salyards, and Mahoney (1990) conducted a study on the effects of drug testing and reported sobering results. A total of 5,465 job applicants were tested for use of illicit drugs. After 1.3 years of employment, employees who had tested positive for illicit drugs had an absenteeism rate 59.3% higher than employees who tested negative. The involuntary turnover rate (namely, employees who were fired) was 47% higher among drug users than nonusers. The estimated cost savings of screening out drug users in terms of reducing absenteeism and turnover costs for one cohort of new employees was $52,750,000. This figure does not reflect the compounded savings derived by cohorts of new employees added each year the drug-testing program is in existence.

As can be seen, drug testing is an exceedingly complex and controversial issue. While the analysis of urine is beyond the purview of I/O psychology, making decisions about an applicant's suitability for employment is not. I/O psychology is finding itself drawn into a complicated web of issues that affects all of society. Our profession may be asked to provide solutions to problems we couldn't even have imagined 20 years ago.

Polygraphy or Lie Detection

A polygraph is an instrument that measures aspects of the autonomic system: physiological reactions of the body such as heart rate and perspiration. In theory these autonomic responses will "give you away" when you are telling a lie. The polygraph is attached to the body with electronic sensors for detecting the physiological reactions. Polygraphs are used more to evaluate people charged with criminal activity in a post hoc fashion (for example, after a robbery within a company has occurred) than to select people into a job, although it is used in the latter capacity as well.

Is a polygraph foolproof? No. People can appear to be innocent of any wrongdoing according to the polygraph but in fact be guilty of misconduct. Research conducted by the Federal Bureau of Investigation (Podlesny & Truslow, 1993) based on a crime simulation reported the polygraph correctly identified 84.7% of the guilty group and 94.7% of the innocent group. Bashore and Rapp (1993) suggested that alternative methods that measure brain electrical activity can be used to complement the polygraph and would be particularly effective in inferring the possession of information in persons attempting to conceal it (that is, the guilty group). In 1988 President Reagan signed into law a bill banning the widespread use of polygraphs for preemployment screening among private sector employers. However, as Honts (1991) reported, polygraph use by the federal government continues to grow. It is used extensively in the hiring process of government agencies involved in national security, as well as in the area of law enforcement.

Graphology

Graphology or handwriting analysis is very popular in Europe as a selection method. Here is how it works. A person trained in handwriting analysis (called a graphologist) examines a sample of a candidate's handwriting. Based on such factors as the specific formation of letters, the slant and size of the writing, and how hard the person presses the pen or pencil on the paper, the graphologist makes an assessment of the candidate's personality. This personality assessment is then correlated with criteria of job success.

Rafaeli and Klimoski (1983) had 20 graphologists analyze handwriting and correlated their assessments with three types of criteria: supervisory ratings, self-ratings, and sales production. While the authors found some evidence of interrater agreement (meaning the graphologists tended to base their assessments on the same facets of handwriting), the handwriting assessments did not correlate with any criteria. Ben-Shakhar, Bar-Hillel, Bilu, Ben-Abba, and Flug (1986) reported that graphologists did not perform significantly better than chance in predicting the job performance of bank employees. Graphology has been found to be predictive of affective states such as stress (Keinan & Eliat-Greenberg, 1993), but its capacity to predict job performance has not been empirically established.

Genetic Screening

Research in the area of genetics indicates that individuals with various genetic makeups are highly susceptible to toxic effects in the work environment. These types of people are much more likely than the average person to develop occupational diseases. Genetic screening in the workplace involves identification of such hypersusceptible individuals for the purposes of minimizing their exposure to these toxic conditions. According to Olian (1984), the value of genetic screening for controlling the frequency of occupational diseases depends on the existence of valid tests capable of detecting genetic predispositions that increase the individual's susceptibility to disease once toxic exposure occurs. "Such individuals could be screened out of chemically dangerous jobs and placed only in positions where environmental toxins do not present special hazards" (p. 424). For example, if a factory uses a certain chemical (such as naphthalene) as part of its manufacturing process, and a job applicant was identified as having a genetic structure that when exposed to this chemical greatly increased the likelihood of disease, the applicant would most likely not be hired for the job. The applicant would have to seek employment elsewhere or would have to be assigned to a job where the degree of exposure was greatly reduced.

Because there is very little research on this subject, I/O psychologists are just beginning to understand how complex the problem is. One aspect is the long latency period of diseases caused by the interaction between genetic material and toxic substances found in the environment. Latency periods of 20 years are common for some diseases such as cancer. Additionally, current federal law prohibits personnel decisions from producing adverse impacts on protected group members. Yet these genetic conditions have been found to fall heavily along gender and racial lines. For example, blacks are over 150 times more likely than whites to develop a form of anemia if they possess a certain genetic condition. Certain chemicals are likely to cause fetal damage, yet only females can be pregnant. Thus, these genetic screens would have a very strong adverse impact, resulting (in these two examples) in a much higher percentage of blacks (than whites) and females (than males) being rejected for employment in such jobs. It is not yet clear from a legal standpoint how much validational evidence would have to be provided to substantiate such decisions.

Most certainly, I/O psychologists are not chemists or geneticists, nor do we pretend to have such expertise. Yet we are being called on to render opinions about suitability for employment, which is our area of expertise, and which is now taking us into new arenas of knowledge. While I/O psychologists will continue to rely heavily on paper-and-pencil means of psychological assessment, we are on the threshold of some frontiers of assessment for which we have no legacy.

Overview and Evaluation of Predictors

Personnel selection methods can be evaluated by many standards. I have identified four major standards that I feel are useful in organizing all the information we have gathered about predictors.

Table 4–3   *Assessment of 12 personnel selection methods along 4 evaluative standards*

Selection Method	Evaluative Standards			
	Validity	Fairness	Applicability	Cost
Intelligence tests	Moderate	Moderate	High	Low
Mechanical aptitude tests	Moderate	High	Moderate	Low
Sensory/motor ability tests	Moderate	High	Low	Low
Personality tests	Moderate	High	Moderate	Moderate
Physical ability tests	High	Moderate	Low	Low
Interviews	Moderate	Moderate	High	Moderate
Assessment centers	High	High	Moderate	High
Work samples	High	High	Low	High
Situational exercises	Moderate	(Unknown)	Low	Moderate
Biographical information	High	Moderate	High	Low
Peer assessments	Moderate	Moderate	Low	Low
Letters of recommendation	Low	(Unknown)	High	Low

The first is *validity*, which refers to the capacity of the predictor to forecast criterion performance accurately. Many authorities would argue that validity is the predominant evaluative standard in judging selection methods; however, the relevance of the other three standards is also substantial.

The second standard is *fairness*, which refers to the capacity of the predictor to render unbiased predictions of job success across applicants in various subgroups of sex, race, age, and so on. I will discuss the issue of fairness in greater detail in Chapter 5.

Applicability, the third standard, refers to whether the selection method can be applied across the full range of job and applicant types. Some predictors have wide applicability in that they appear well suited for a diverse range of people and jobs. Other methods have peculiar limitations that affect their applicability.

The final standard refers to the *cost* of implementing the method. The various personnel selection methods differ markedly in their cost, which has a direct bearing on their overall value.

Table 4–3 presents a summary of the 12 personnel selection methods appraised on each of the 4 evaluative standards. I have partitioned each standard into three levels, labeled low, moderate, and high. This classification scheme is admittedly oversimplified, and in some cases the evaluation of a selection method did not readily lend itself to a uniform rating. Nevertheless, this method should be useful in providing a broadbrush view of all the personnel selection methods.

Average validities in the .00–.20, .21–.40, and over .40 ranges were labeled low, moderate, and high, respectively. Selection methods having many, some, and few problems of fairness were labeled low, moderate, and high, respectively. The applicability standard, the most difficult one to appraise on a single dimension, was classified according to the ease of using the method in terms of feasibility and generalizability across jobs. Finally, direct cost estimates were made for each selection method. Methods estimated as costing less than $20 per applicant were labeled low; $20 to $50, moderate; and over $50, high. The ideal personnel selection method would be high in validity, fairness, and applicability and low in cost. No method has an ideal profile. The 12 methods produce a series of trade-offs among validity, fairness, applicability, and cost. This shouldn't be surprising, for if there were one uniformly ideal personnel selection method, there probably would be little need to consider ten others.

In terms of validity, our best methods are assessment centers, work samples, biographical information, and physical ability tests. However, each of these methods is limited by some problems with fairness, applicability, or cost. Ironically, the worst selection method in terms of validity, letters of recommendation, is one of the most frequently used. However, this method is characterized by high applicability and low cost, which no doubt accounts for its popularity.

Fairness refers to the likelihood the method will yield an assessment unbiased by membership in any group, such as by gender or race. Although the issue of fairness has generated a great deal of controversy, no method is classified as having low fairness. Insufficient information is available on two of the methods (situational exercises and letters of recommendation) to render an evaluation of their fairness, but it seems unlikely they would be judged as grossly unfair. Although several methods have exhibited some fairness problems (thus warranting caution in their use), the problems are not so severe as to reject the method as a means of selecting personnel.

The applicability dimension was the most difficult to assess, and evaluation of this dimension is most subject to qualification. For example, work samples are characterized by low applicability, for they are highly limited to certain types of jobs (that is, jobs involving the mechanical manipulation of objects). However, this limitation appears to be more than offset by the method's high validity and fairness. Simply put, the problem with this method is its feasibility for only a selected range of jobs. Such a limitation seems far more palatable than the problems of low applicability experienced with peer assessments, for example. Peer assessments are limited by their exclusive use as a selection device for entry into secondary or advanced positions, positions that not all organizations have. Alternatively, other methods have high applicability (such as the interview) and qualify as an almost universal means of selection.

The cost dimension is perhaps the most arbitrary. Indirect or hidden costs may be associated with selection methods—costs that were not included in their evaluation but perhaps could have been. The break points in the classification scheme are also subjective. For example, I consider a $40 per applicant cost to be moderate; others might say it is low or high. These issues notwithstanding, you can see a full range of cost estimates in Table 4–3. Some methods do not cost much (for example, letters of recommendation), but they do not appear to be worth much either.

Summary

In this chapter I have examined several major types of predictors used in personnel selection: psychological tests, physical ability tests, interviews, assessment centers, work samples and situational exercises, biographical information, peer assessments, and letters of recommendation. These predictors have been validated against a number of different criteria for a variety of occupational groups. Some predictors have been used more extensively than others. Furthermore, certain predictors have historically shown more validity than others.

In Chapter 3, I listed the attributes of good criteria. A similar list can be derived for predictors.

- Reliable
- Valid
- Bias-free
- Consistent from one sample to another
- Inexpensive
- Not time-consuming

The ideal predictor would be an accurate forecaster of the criterion, equally applicable across different groups of people, and not too lengthy or costly to administer. But predictors rarely meet all these standards in practice.

CASE STUDY   *How Do We Hire Police Officers?*

Bay Ridge, a city with a population of about 125,000, experienced remarkable growth over a short period for two major reasons. First, several large industries had been attracted to the area; with more jobs, there were more people. Second, due to a rezoning plan, several small townships were incorporated into Bay Ridge, which caused a sudden burgeoning in the city's official population.

As a consequence of this growth, the city needed to expand its police force. For many years, Bay Ridge had only a relatively small force and used only a brief interview to select the officers. Recently, however, there had been several complaints against the city's selection interview. Due to the complaints and the need to hire many more officers, the city council decided to abandon the old method of hiring. The city commissioned a job analysis for police officers and determined that three major factors contributed to success on the job. The next step was to develop selection measures to assess each of the three factors. The city council called a meeting with the city personnel director to get a progress report on the selection measures being proposed. Four city council members and Ron Davenport, the city personnel director, attended.

> *Davenport:* I'm pleased to report to you that we have made substantial progress in our study. The job analysis revealed that the following factors determine success on the police force: physical agility, sensitivity to community relations, and practical judgment. We are fairly pleased with the tests developed to assess two of the factors, although one of them is causing us some problems.
>
> *Councilmember DeRosa:* Would you kindly elaborate on what these factors mean?
>
> *Davenport:* Certainly. Physical agility is important in being able to apprehend and possibly disarm a suspect. It is also important in being able to carry a wounded officer out of the line of hostile fire. Sensitivity to community relations involves knowledge of racial and ethnic problems in the city, plus an ability to work with the communiʲ in preventing crime. Practical judgment reflects knowing when it is advisabᵀ pursue a criminal suspect and what methods of action to use in uncertain sitᵀ

Councilmember Flory: How do you propose to measure physical agility?

Davenport: It looks as if we'll go with some physical standard—being able to carry a 150-pound dummy 25 yards, or something similar. We might also use some height and weight requirements. We could have some problems with sex differences in that females are not as strong as males, but I think we can work it out.

Councilmember Reddinger: Are all of these tests going to be performance tests?

Davenport: No, that's the only one so far. For the community relations factor, we're going to use a group interview. We'll ask the candidates how they would go about dealing with some hypothetical but realistic problem, such as handling a domestic argument. The interviewers will grade their answers and give them a total score.

Councilmember Hamilton: What will be a passing score in this interview?

Davenport: We haven't determined that yet. We're still trying to determine if this is the best way to measure the factor.

Councilmember Flory: How do you plan to measure practical judgment?

Davenport: That's the problem case. We really haven't figured out a good test of that yet.

Councilmember DeRosa: How about a test of general intelligence?

Davenport: It appears that practical judgment is related to intelligence, but it's not the same thing. A person can be very intelligent in terms of verbal and numerical ability but not possess a great deal of practical judgment.

Councilmember Reddinger: Hasn't some psychologist developed a test of practical judgment?

Davenport: Not that we know of. You also have to remember that the type of judgment a police officer has to demonstrate is not the same thing as the type of judgment, say, a banker has to show. I guess I'm saying there appear to be different kinds of practical judgment.

Councilmember Hamilton: Could you use some personality inventory to measure it?

Davenport: I don't think so. I doubt that practical judgment is a personality trait. At least I'm not aware of any direct measures of it.

Councilmember Flory: How about using the interview again? A police officer has to demonstrate practical judgment in handling community relations. Can't you just expand the interview a bit?

Davenport: That's a possibility we're considering. Another possibility is to put candidates in a test situation where they have to demonstrate their practical judgment. It could be a pretty expensive method, all things considered, but it may be the best way to go.

Councilmember DeRosa: I have a feeling, Mr. Davenport, that your success in measuring practical judgment will determine just how many good officers we get on the force.

Questions

1. The city would have to validate whatever predictors it developed to select police officers. What method or methods of validation do you think it would use?

2. Do you think that biographical information might be useful in predicting success as a police officer? If so, what types of items might be useful?

3. Describe a work sample or situational exercise that might measure practical judgment.

4. What would be a problem in using peer assessments to select police officers?

5. The personnel department has asked you to assist in developing or selecting predictors of police officer performance. What advice would you give?

Personnel Decisions

CHAPTER 5

Major Chapter Objectives

- Understand the relationship between personnel decisions and employment law.

- Understand the statistical concepts of regression analysis and multiple regression analysis.

- Understand the concept and significance of validity generalization.

- Be able to describe the process of personnel recruitment.

- Identify strategies for selecting employees and understand the process of assessing job applicants.

- Identify the issues pertaining to the determination of the passing score.

- Understand the personnel selection strategies of multiple regression, multiple cutoff, and multiple hurdle.

- Know how the concept and significance of test utility is related to organizational efficiency.

- Be able to describe the personnel functions of placement and classification.

Personnel decisions are decisions that affect people's work lives. In this chapter we will examine the process of making personnel decisions and the factors associated with determining their quality. We will begin the chapter with a discussion of the relationship between personnel decisions and employment law.

Personnel Decisions and Employment Law

For the first 60 years or so of I/O psychology, there was virtually no connection between psychologists and the legal community. Psychological tests were developed, administered, and interpreted by psychologists, and as a profession psychologists governed themselves. However, during the late 1950s and early 1960s, the nation was swept up in the civil rights movement. At that time civil rights concerned primarily the conditions under which blacks lived and worked in this country. Blacks were denied access to colleges, restaurants, and jobs—in short, their civil rights were denied. Presidents Kennedy and Johnson were interested in changing this aspect of American society. In 1964 the Civil Rights Act, a major piece of federal legislation aimed at reducing discrimination in all walks of life, was passed. The section of the law pertaining to discrimination in employment is Title VII, and it is the section most relevant to I/O psychology. In essence, the message was as follows: Blacks were grossly underemployed throughout the country in both private and public sector jobs, particularly in jobs above the lower levels of organizations, and since I/O psychologists had developed the personnel selection methods that seemingly had produced this great underemployment of blacks, the profession held some responsibility for this apparent employment discrimination. To reduce discrimination in employment (one of the mandates of the Civil Rights Act), the federal government began to intervene in the process of employment hiring; in essence, it would monitor the entire procedure to ensure fairness in selection. Thus the interface between I/O psychology and the law began in the 1960s.

The Civil Rights Act was expanded to cover other people as well. In fact, five characteristics were identified for protection: race, sex, religion, color, and national origin. These categories of people are referred to as the *protected groups*. In 1967 the government passed a separate law covering age discrimination called the Age Discrimination in Employment Act. It extends to people aged 40 and over the same type of legal protection granted to the five protected groups under the Civil Rights Act. The Civil Rights Act was also expanded to include all personnel functions—training, promotion, retention, and performance appraisal—in addition to selection. Further, the act was expanded to pertain to any method used for making personnel decisions.

What exactly did the law say? It established a concept called *adverse impact*, which refers to the results of any selection method that causes a disproportionate percentage of people of a given category to be hired compared to another group. Adverse impact is determined by the "4/5ths rule." The rule states that adverse impact occurs if the selection ratio (that is, the number of people hired divided by

FRANK AND ERNEST   SOURCE: Reprinted by permission of Newspaper Enterprise Association, Inc.

the number of people who apply) for any subgroup of people (such as blacks) is less than four-fifths of the selection ratio for the largest group. Suppose 100 whites apply for a job and 20 are selected. The selection ratio is 20/100, or .20. By multiplying .20 by 4/5, we get .16. This means that if fewer than 16% of the black applicants are hired, the selection test has adverse impact. So if 50 blacks applied for the job, at least 8 (50 × .16) would have to be hired to avoid adverse impact.

If adverse impact is found to exist, the employer is obligated to validate the selection procedure to prove that the resulting personnel decisions were indeed based on a correct (that is, valid) method. If adverse impact does not result from the selection method, the employer is not obligated to validate it. Obviously, it is a sound business decision to validate any selection method at any time. A company would always want to know if their method is identifying the best candidates for hire. However, the law requires validation of a method only if it results in adverse impact.

As part of the Civil Rights Act, a federal agency was created called the Equal Employment Opportunity Commission (EEOC). Its mandate was to reduce employment discrimination by ensuring compliance with the law. In 1978 a uniform set of employment guidelines were published for all employers to follow.

Several landmark court cases were based on these employment guidelines. In *Griggs v. Duke Power Company,* the court ruled that individuals who bring suit against a company do not have to prove that the company's employment test was unfair; rather, the company has to prove its test is fair. Thus, the burden of proving the quality of the test rests with the employer. This finding has subsequently been referred to as "Griggs' Burden." In *Albemarle v. Moody,* the court ruled on just how much judicial power the employment guidelines really have. Although they were called guidelines, the court ruled that they be granted the "deference of law," meaning they were in effect the law on employment testing. However, many I/O psychologists believe that a set of testing principles developed by the Society for Industrial and Organizational Psychology (1987) are more technically precise. In *Bakke v. University of California,* the court ruled that whites can be victims of discrimination as well as blacks. Bakke (a white male) sued the University of California on the grounds that his race had been a factor in his being denied admission to their medical school. The court ruled in Bakke's favor and required the University of California to admit Bakke to the medical college. This case was heralded as a classic case of "reverse discrimination," which technically is incorrect. First, it connotes that only blacks can be discriminated against, which obviously is not true. Second, reversal of the process of discrimination results in nondiscrimination. There have been literally thousands of cases adjudicated in the district, appellate, and state and federal supreme courts based on litigation spawned by employment law. These three cases represent a very small sampling.

Here is one way the federal government could become involved procedurally in employment litigation. If a company's selection procedure systematically results in the rejection of a disproportionate number of members of a certain group (most typically race or sex), a rejected applicant can file a complaint against the company with the government. The government then investigates the complaint and tries to reach an agreement with the company regarding use of the test. If the two parties cannot agree, the company can be sued for using unfair selection procedures. The company then has to prove in court that its tests are not unfair and its selection system is valid. Companies that lose such cases have been obligated to pay multimillion-dollar sums. The money is often used to pay the victims of their unfair tests. The financial awards in such cases can be class-action settlements (the person who is suing represents a class of similar people) or back-pay settlements (the company has to pay a portion of what victims would have earned had they been hired). Awards in single lawsuits have reached $20 to $30 million. Needless to say, not everyone who fails an employment test has his or her day in court. A lawsuit must be predicated on "just cause," not simply on the complaints of one disgruntled applicant who failed a test. Also, large employers who affect the lives of many people are more likely to be sued than small employers.

In 1990 the Americans with Disabilities Act (ADA) was signed into law. The ADA is the most important piece of legislation ever enacted for persons with disabilities (O'Keeffe, 1994). A disability is defined by ADA as "a physical or mental impairment that substantially limits one or more (of the) major life activities; a record of such impairment; or being regarded as having such an impairment." Major life activities include seeing, hearing, walking, learning, breathing, and working. An employment test that screens out an individual with a disability must be job-related and consistent with business necessity. The law states that employers must provide persons with disabilities *reasonable accommodation* in being evaluated for employment and in the conduct of their jobs. Employers are required to modify or accommodate business practices in a reasonable fashion to meet their needs. The ADA also extends protection to individuals who are alcoholics and former illegal drug users (Jones, 1994), as well as to individuals with psychiatric disabilities (Carling, 1994). The fundamental premise of the law is that individuals with disabilities can effectively contribute to the work force, and they cannot be discriminated against in employment decisions because of their disabilities. If a reasonable accommodation on the employer's part is needed to meld these individuals into the work force, it is so prescribed by the ADA law. As Klimoski and Palmer (1994) have noted, organizations are expected to act with good will in responding to the ADA and to be committed to making it work effectively. At this time there appear to be legitimate differences of opinion regarding the legal interpretation of the law. These interpretations will become clearer as the courts address cases brought before them regarding the employment rights of people with disabilities. As with all employment laws, the ultimate goal of ADA is to produce a more just and productive society.

Employment laws reflect our societal values as to what we regard as "fairness" in the work world. As our conceptions of fairness have evolved over time, so have the employment laws. The original Civil Rights Act of 1964 provided for equal access to employment by all protected groups. Access to employment is often gained by passing tests used to make employment decisions. Psychological research has revealed that different groups of people do not score equally on standard employment tests. This increases the likelihood that members of these groups will not be hired in equivalent proportions, thereby possibly producing adverse impact. To offset the result of group differences in test scores, some employers responded by using different passing scores for certain groups as a way of avoiding charges of adverse impact. President George Bush signed into law the Civil Rights Act of 1991, which prohibited test score adjustments as a means of attaining employment fairness. Specifically, the Civil Rights Act of 1991 states it shall be an unlawful practice for an employer "in connection with the selection or referral of applicants or candidates for employment or promotion to adjust the scores of, use different cutoffs for, or otherwise alter the results of employment related tests on the basis of race, color, religion, sex, or national origin."

Varca and Pattison (1993) presented a cogent discussion of how the Civil Rights Act of 1991 and more recent court cases such as *Wards Cove Packing Company v. Atonio* have modified both the employee's and the employer's responsibilities in employment discrimination litigation pertaining to issues such as burden of proof. Wigdor and Sackett (1993) describe the development of employment laws as reflecting attempts in reaching ultimate societal goals of work force productivity and providing opportunities for all social groups to achieve their employment potential. Our society is divided on the relative importance that should be attached to attaining these two goals (for example, Gottfredson, 1994; Sackett & Wilk, 1994). In the ensuing years we will witness how the courts adjudicate the complicated interplay between societal goals that surround employment testing. The profusion of laws and court cases testifies to the continuing debate within our country over issues of *social justice* in employment. Social justice in employment will be discussed in several contexts throughout this book.

A Model of Personnel Decisions

Figure 5–1 depicts a model outlining the sequence of factors associated with making personnel decisions. Several of these factors have been discussed in previous chapters. Job and organizational analyses (see Chapter 3) initiate the sequence and establish the context in which personnel decisions will be made. The results of these analyses help provide information useful in determining the criteria of job performance as well as providing insights into those predictor constructs (see Chapter 4) useful in forecasting job performance. The linkage between the

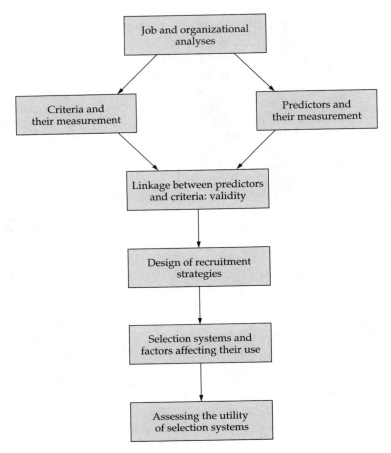

Figure 5–1   *Model of personnel decisions in organizations*

predictors and criteria is the essence of validity—the determination of how well our predictors forecast job performance. We are now in position to continue the sequence used by I/O psychologists, examining issues pertaining to recruitment and designing selection systems and assessing the utility of those systems. However, before I commence a discussion of these issues, let's examine a method of statistical analysis often used by I/O psychologists in assessing the linkage between predictors and criteria, *regression analysis.*

Regression Analysis

The statistical technique used to predict criterion performance on the basis of a predictor score is called regression analysis. While a correlation coefficient is useful for showing the degree of relationship between two variables, it is not useful for predicting one variable from the other. Regression analysis, however, does permit prediction of a person's status on one variable (the criterion) based on his or her status on another variable (the predictor). If we assume that the relationship between the two variables is linear (as it usually is), it can be described mathematically with a regression equation:

$$\hat{Y} = a + bX \qquad \text{[Formula 5–1]}$$

where $\hat{Y}$ = the predicted criterion score,
   a = a mathematical constant reflecting where the regression line intercepts the ordinate (or Y axis),
   b = a mathematical constant reflecting the slope of the regression line, and
   X = the predictor scores for a given individual.

The values of a and b are derived through mathematical procedures that minimize the distance between the regression line (that is, a line useful for making predictions) and the pairs of predictor-criterion data points. To develop a regression equation, you need predictor and criterion data on a sample of people. Let us say we have a sample of 100 employees. Supervisor ratings of job performance are the criterion, while the predictor test we wish to investigate is an intelligence test. We administer the intelligence test to the workers, collect the criterion data, and then see if we can predict the criterion scores on the basis of the intelligence test. On the basis of the predictor-criterion data, we derive the following regression equation:

$$\hat{Y} = 1 + .5X \qquad \text{[Formula 5–2]}$$

The relationship between the two variables is shown in Figure 5–2. Note that the regression line crosses the Y axis at a value of 1 (that is, $a = 1$). Also, for every 2-unit increase in X, there is a corresponding 1-unit increase in Y. Thus, the slope of the regression line, defined as the change in Y divided by the change in X, equals 1/2 or .5 (that is, $b = .5$).

For any value of X, we can now predict a corresponding Y score. For example, if someone scores 12 on the intelligence test, the predicted criterion rating would be:

$$\hat{Y} = 1 + .5(12)$$
$$\hat{Y} = 7 \qquad \text{[Formula 5–3]}$$

If a supervisor rating of 5 represented adequate job performance (and we did not want anyone with a lower rating), the regression equation can be worked backward to get the minimum passing score:

$$5 = 1 + .5X$$
$$X = 8$$

So, if we use the intelligence test to hire, we would not accept any applicants who scored less than 8, because these scores would result in a predicted level of job performance lower than we wanted. There is also another way to find the passing score. In Figure 5–2, locate the value of 5 on the Y axis (the criterion). Move horizontally to the regression line, and then drop down to the corresponding point of the X axis (the predictor). The score is 8.

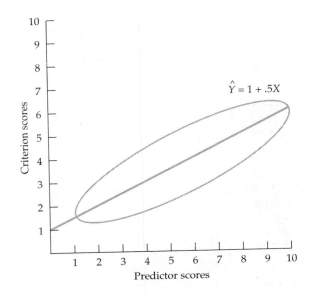

Criterion scores (y-axis, 1–10)
Predictor scores (x-axis, 1–10)

$\hat{Y} = 1 + .5X$

Figure 5–2   *Predictor-criterion scatterplot and regression line of best fit*

In addition to thinking about b as the slope of the regression line, you can think about b in a way that shows the relationship between correlation and regression. Regression is based on correlation. That should make sense because if you can predict one variable from another, those two variables should be related. An alternative conceptualization for b is the correlation between X and Y, times the ratio of the standard deviation of Y, divided by the standard deviation of X; that is,

$$b = r_{xy}\left(\frac{S_y}{S_x}\right)$$

[Formula 5–4]

If the correlation between the intelligence test and the supervisor rating was .60, the standard deviation of the supervisor rating (S_y) was 2.5, and the standard deviation of the intelligence test (S_x) was 3.0, we would have

$$b = .60\left(\frac{2.5}{3.0}\right)$$
$$= .5$$

[Formula 5–5]

In thinking about b this way, you can see that if there were no correlation between the two variables, you could not predict one from the other. If $r_{xy} = .00$, then $b = 0$. If $b = 0$, the regression line would have no slope (it would be parallel to the X axis), and every value of X would yield the same predicted value of Y, thus making prediction of Y pointless. Also, if the standard deviation of the criterion and predictor were equal, then the slope of the regression line would equal the correlation coefficient, or $b = r$. Three different regression lines that demonstrate

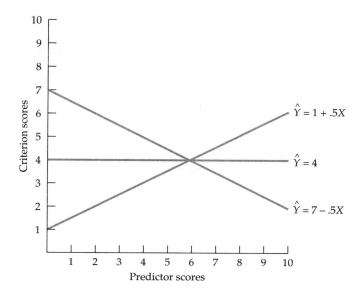

Figure 5–3 *Three regression equations with their mathematical statements*

this relationship are shown in Figure 5–3. Note that the intercept and slope in the graph correspond to their expression in the equation.

Multiple Predictors

Many better personnel decisions are made on the basis of more than one piece of information. How well two or more predictors combined improve the predictability of the criterion depends on their individual relationships to the criterion and their relationship to each other. Suppose two predictors both correlate with the criterion but do not correlate with each other. This relationship is expressed in Figure 5–4.

The shaded area on the left shows how much the first predictor overlaps the criterion. The overlap area is the validity of the first predictor, symbolized by the notation r_{1c}, where the subscript 1 stands for the first predictor and the subscript c stands for the criterion. The shaded area on the right shows the extent to which the second predictor overlaps the criterion; its validity can be expressed as r_{2c}. As can be seen, more of the criterion can be explained by using two predictors. Also note that the two predictors are unrelated to each other, meaning that they predict different aspects of the criterion. The combined relationship between two or more predictors and the criterion is referred to as a *multiple correlation* (R). The only conceptual difference between r and R is that the range of R is from 0 to 1.0, while r ranges from –1.0 to 1.0. When R is squared, the resulting R^2 value represents the

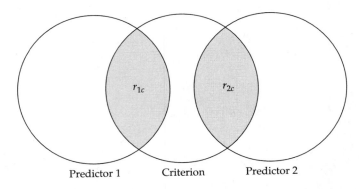

Predictor 1   Criterion   Predictor 2

Figure 5–4 *Venn diagram of two uncorrelated predictors*

total amount of variance in the criterion that can be explained by two or more predictors. When predictors 1 and 2 are not correlated with each other, the squared multiple correlation (R^2) is equal to the sum of the squared individual validity coefficients, or

$$R^2_{c.12} = r^2_{1c} + r^2_{2c}$$ [Formula 5–6]

For example, if $r_{1c} = .60$ and $r_{2c} = .50$, then

$$R^2_{c.12} = (.60)^2 + (.50)^2$$
$$= .36 + .25$$
$$= .61$$ [Formula 5–7]

The notation $R^2_{c.12}$ is "the squared multiple correlation between the criterion and two predictors." In this condition (when the two predictors are unrelated to each other), 61% of the variance in the criterion can be explained by two predictors.

In most cases, however, it is rare that two predictors relating to the same criterion are unrelated to each other. Usually, all three variables share some variance with one another; that is, the intercorrelation between the two predictors (r_{12}) is not zero. Such a relationship is presented graphically in Figure 5–5.

In Figure 5–5 each predictor correlates substantially with the criterion (r_{1c} and r_{2c}), but the two predictors also overlap each other (r_{12}). The addition of the second predictor adds more criterion variance than can be accounted for by one predictor alone. Yet all of the criterion variance accounted for by the second predictor is not new variance; part of it was explained by the first predictor. When there is a correlation between the two predictors (r_{12}), the equation for calculating the squared multiple correlation must be expanded to

$$R^2_{c.12} = \frac{r_{1c} + r_{2c} - 2r_{12}r_{1c}r_{2c}}{1 - r^2_{12}}$$ [Formula 5–8]

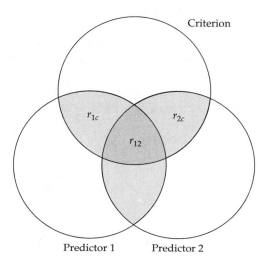

Figure 5–5 *Venn diagram of two correlated predictors*

For example, if the two predictors intercorrelated .30, given the validity coefficients from the previous example and $r_{12} = .30$, we will have:

$$R^2_{c.12} = \frac{(.60)^2 + (.50)^2 - 2(.30)(.60)(.50)}{1 - (.30)^2}$$

$$= .47$$

[Formula 5–9]

As can be seen, the explanatory power of two intercorrelated predictor variables is diminished compared to the explanatory power when they are uncorrelated (.47 versus .61). This example provides a rule about multiple predictors: It is generally advisable to seek predictors that are related to the criterion but are uncorrelated with each other.[1] However, in practice, it is very difficult to find multiple variables that are statistically related to another variable (the criterion) but at the same time statistically unrelated to each other. Usually variables that are predictive of a criterion are also predictive of each other. Also note that the abbreviated version of the equation used to compute the squared multiple correlation with independent predictors is just a special case of the expanded equation, caused by r_{12} being equal to zero.

[1] In point of fact, the statistical relationship between the predictor intercorrelation (r_{12}) and the total predictability of a criterion (R^2) is very complex. Dudycha, Dudycha, and Schmitt (1974) have shown that negative intercorrelations and extreme positive intercorrelations (.95 and greater) enhance the predictability of the criterion beyond what would have been attained with independent ($r_{12} = .00$) predictors. Of course, in reality, the likelihood of finding variables with such statistical properties is extremely small.

Multiple Regression Analysis

The relationship between correlation and regression is the foundation for the relationship between multiple correlation and multiple regression. Just as regression permits prediction on the basis of one predictor, multiple regression permits prediction on the basis of multiple predictors. The logic for using multiple regression is the same as the logic for using multiple correlation: It usually enhances prediction of the criterion.

As noted before, the formula for a regression equation with one predictor is

$$\hat{Y} = a + bX \hspace{4cm} \text{[Formula 5–10]}$$

When we expand this to the case of two predictors, we have

$$\hat{Y} = a + b_1X_1 + b_2X_2 \hspace{3cm} \text{[Formula 5–11]}$$

where X_1 and X_2 are the two predictors and b_1 and b_2 are the regression weights associated with the two predictors. As before, the b values are based in part on the correlation between the predictors and the criterion. In multiple regression the b values are also influenced by the correlation among the predictors. However, the procedure for making predictions in multiple regression is similar to that used in one-predictor (or simple) regression. Suppose we have criterion data on a sample of industrial workers who take two tests we think may be useful for hiring future workers. We analyze the data to derive the values of a, b_1, and b_2 and arrive at the following regression equation:

$$\hat{Y} = 2 + .4X_1 + .7X_2 \hspace{3cm} \text{[Formula 5–12]}$$

If a person scores 30 on test 1 and 40 on test 2, his or her predicted criterion performance would be

$$\hat{Y} = 2 + .4(30) + .7(40)$$
$$\hat{Y} = 42 \hspace{5cm} \text{[Formula 5–13]}$$

The degree of predictability afforded by the two predictors is measured by the multiple correlation between the predictors and the criterion. If the multiple correlation is large enough to be of some value for prediction purposes, we might use the two tests to hire future workers. The company would undoubtedly set a minimum predicted-criterion score at a certain value, say, 40. In this example, the person's predicted job performance score (42) was above the minimum score set by the company (40), so the person would be hired.

Multiple regression is not limited to just two predictors; predictors can be added to the regression equation until they no longer enhance prediction of the criterion. The k-predictor regression equation is simply an extension of the two-predictor regression equation, and all terms are interpreted as before. Such an equation would look like

$$\hat{Y} = a + b_1X_1 + b_2X_2 + b_3X_3 + \cdots + b_kX_k \hspace{2cm} \text{[Formula 5–14]}$$

There comes a point at which adding more predictors will not enhance the prediction of the criterion. Regression equations with four or five predictors usually do as good a job as those with more. The reason is that the shared variance among the predictors becomes very large after four to five predictors, so adding more will not add unique variance in the criterion. If we could find another predictor that was (1) uncorrelated with the other predictors and (2) correlated with the criterion, it would be a useful addition to the equation. Multiple regression is a very popular prediction strategy in I/O psychology and is used extensively.

Concurrent versus Predictive Validity

Issues pertaining to the assessment of validity are not limited to statistical methods, such as regression and multiple regression analysis. There are also issues pertaining to the design of the validation study, and how they affect the inferences we draw from the study. In I/O psychology a particularly compelling issue pertains to the difference between concurrent and predictive criterion-related validity, a topic introduced in Chapter 4.

Criterion or job performance data can be collected in either a concurrent- or a predictive-validity design. The difference between these two validation designs has been the topic of much discussion in personnel selection research. The major distinction is the time interval between collection of the predictor and the criterion data. Although this distinction is technically correct, there are many significant implications within the context of personnel selection and test validation. The concurrent validity of a test is frequently established for practical reasons, but some authors (for example, Guion, 1965) believe that concurrent validity should not be thought of as a substitute for, or even an approximation of, predictive validity. Guion feels the two methods are not even equivalent. Here are some of the reasons.

When a concurrent validity study is undertaken, the present workers take a predictor test for the sake of testing the test. Their scores are correlated with their job performance to obtain an estimate of the test's (concurrent) validity. There are several problems with this method. First, employees who are secure in their jobs are less motivated to do well on the test than ambitious applicants who need work. Applicants' scores can be higher than employees' scores. One research study found that a predictor cutoff for a test that resulted in rejecting 15% of the actual applicants would also have resulted in rejecting 40% of the present employees had they been applying for their own jobs. Second, what an employee learns on the job may influence how he or she responds to a test item. The experience may increase the employee's test score, or it may decrease it if the employee reads too much into the question and thus gets the item wrong. Finally, the range in ability among present employees is restricted. Present employees are the "survivors" of some previous applicant pool. They are more homogeneous (and better) than the original pool of applicants from which they were drawn. This restriction in range causes a reduction in the variability of test scores, which serves to underestimate the test's validity.

Some researchers have tried to establish a new predictor's validity by giving the test to a group of selected applicants who were hired on the basis of some other predictor. No selection decisions are made on the basis of the new predictor score; they are just recorded for later use in a predictive-validity study. This procedure does not completely solve the problem. If scores on the new predictor (being tested) and scores on the other predictor (on which selection decisions were made) are substantially correlated, a significant restriction in range will remain. Only if the two predictors are uncorrelated will there be no restriction in range.

For many years, I/O psychologists have accepted the doctrine of the superiority of predictive validity over concurrent validity (for the reasons cited by Guion, 1965). However, this doctrine has been challenged. Barrett, Phillips, and Alexander (1981) believe the conceptual distinction between predictive and concurrent validity has been exaggerated. The ultimate test of the relative superiority of the two methods involves examining the quality of new employees hired with each method. If better quality workers are hired with tests validated predictively, this method can be considered superior. However, if both methods result in the same quality of new hires, neither method can be declared "better."[2]

Although Barrett and associates do not present any data on the comparability of the two methods, they correctly comment that rarely have any data been presented showing the superiority of predictive validity. Predictive validity seems to be preferable on logical or conceptual grounds, but the authors point out that it has little empirical support and that predictive-validity designs have problems. It remains to be seen whether I/O psychologists will revise their opinions of the long-held doctrine of the deficiency of the concurrent method. Because many validation studies rely on the concurrent method, it would be encouraging to know that the findings from such a design are not "poor substitutes" for or an "approximation" of results from the predictive-validity designs. Concurrent-validity designs have long been used for expedience. Predictive-validity designs have many practical problems for the employer, such as the hiring of all job applicants. If concurrent-validity designs provide an accurate estimate of predictive validity, then they will provide an extremely valuable basis upon which to justify personnel decisions.

Validity Generalization

The concept of validity generalization refers to a predictor's validity spreading or generalizing to other jobs or contexts beyond the one in which it was validated. For example, let us say that a test is found valid for hiring secretaries in a com-

---

[2]Other factors such as cost, however, may also enter into the decision. If two methods result in hiring equally competent workers, the preferred method will be the one that costs less.

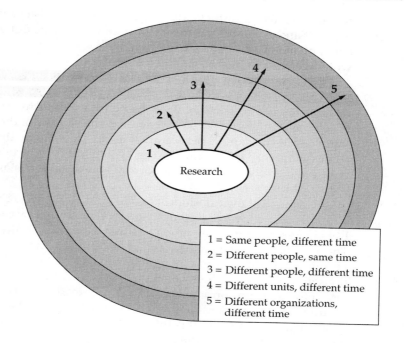

Figure 5–6 *The domains across which validity can generalize*
SOURCE: From *Personnel Selection in Organizations* by N. Schmitt and F. J. Landy, 1993, San Francisco, CA: Jossey-Bass. All rights reserved. Reprinted by permission.

pany. If that same test were found useful in hiring secretaries in another company, we would say its validity had generalized. That same test could also be useful in selecting people for a different job, such as clerks. Here is another case of the test's validity generalizing. In Figure 5–6 Schmitt and Landy (1993) graphically depict the domains across which validity can generalize. The concept of validity generalization has long been a goal of I/O psychologists because it would certainly make our jobs easier. However, when we examined whether a test's validity would generalize across either companies or jobs, we often found that it did not. That is, the test's validity was specific to the situation in which it was originally validated. The implication, of course, was that we had to validate every test in every situation in which it was used. We could not assume that its validity would generalize.

Schmidt and Hunter (1978, 1980) support validity generalization as a means of selecting personnel. They argue that the problem of situational specificity of test validity is based on psychologists' erroneous belief in the "law of small numbers," a belief that whatever results hold for large samples will also hold for small samples. They think this belief is incorrect—that small samples results are highly unstable, resulting in highly variable test validities. Schmidt and Hunter believe that in most cases psychologists use small samples (40 to 50) to validate tests. Indeed, Monahan and Muchinsky (1983) found that in fewer than 10% of the personnel selection validation studies conducted over a 30-year period did the researchers use a sufficiently large sample size, according to the standards Schmidt and Hunter recommend. So situation-specific test validities are obtained. Schmidt and Hunter argue that if tests were validated in large samples, the results would generalize (not be situation specific).

Validity generalization means that there is a single "true" relationship between a test and job performance, such as for a secretary. Let us say that the relationship is a correlation of .40, based on validity studies involving thousands of subjects. In theory, we could generalize the validity of these findings from huge sample sizes to more typical employment situations with small samples. Companies with very large sample sizes would validate certain tests; the rest of the business world would simply "borrow" these validities as a basis for using the tests for hiring.

In support of their position, Schmidt and Hunter (1978) present data based on a sample size of over 10,000 individuals. The sample was drawn from the army. Data were reported on ten predictors that were used to forecast success in 35 jobs. The results indicated highly similar validity coefficients across different jobs, meaning that differences among jobs did not moderate predictor-criterion relationships. The researchers concluded that the effects of situational moderators disappear with appropriately large sample sizes. One psychological construct that is supposedly common for success in all jobs (and which accounts for validity generalizing or spreading) is intelligence, and in particular, the dimension of intelligence relating to information processing.

Few I/O psychologists reject the concept of validity generalization in total. Rather, it is a question of just how far they believe validity can be generalized. At one end of the continuum is the doctrine of situational specificity of validity; that is, there is no validity generalization at all. At the other extreme is validity generalization in its complete form; that is, the validity of a single test can generalize across all jobs. Thus, a cognitive ability test valid for hiring secretaries would also be valid for hiring everyone from plumbers to executives and all jobs in between.

The research of Schmidt and Hunter and their associates compellingly demonstrates that validity is not situation specific. However, going to the other extreme and believing that validity can generalize across all jobs also raises professional skepticism. In other words, *within-occupation* validity generalization (for example, a test valid for predicting success across clerical jobs) seems highly tenable, but *across-occupation* validity generalization is much less so. Tenopyr (1981) rejects the notion of validity generalization in the extreme form, saying that it implies one can use any test to predict success in any job. She believes that I/O psychologists will never resort to having only one test in their assessment repertoire, because 80 years ago precisely that practice led them to develop different tests; that is, no one test was found that could predict success across all jobs. As Burke (1984) states, "Especially in the area of test validity, let us not overcompensate for past excesses (e.g., maintaining that every test must have a local validation study performed) by committing similar excesses in the opposite direction" (p. 113). We still do not have a firm understanding of the limits of validity generalization; it is a matter of professional debate even among I/O psychologists (Schmidt, Pearlman, Hunter, & Hirsh, 1985).

Recruitment

The personnel function of recruitment refers to the process of attracting people to apply for a job. Recruiters can select only from those people who apply. If few people apply for a job, the odds of finding a strong candidate are less than if you have many applicants to choose from.

There is more to recruiting than you might think. Hawk (1967) described the "recruiting yield pyramid" procedure for hiring candidates. A diagram of that pyramid is shown in Figure 5–7. Let us say that the goal is to hire 5 managers. The company has learned from past experience that for every 2 managers who are offered jobs, only 1 will accept. Therefore, the company will need to make 10 offers. Furthermore, the company has learned that to find 10 managers who are good enough to receive an offer, 40 candidates must be interviewed; that is, only 1 manager out of 4 is usually judged acceptable. However, to get 40 managers to travel to the company for an interview, the company has to invite 60 people; that is, typically only 2 out of 3 candidates are interested enough in the job to agree to be interviewed. Finally, to find 60 potentially interested managers, the company needs to get four times as many contacts or leads. Some people will not want to change jobs, others will not want to move, and still others will simply be unsuitable for further consideration. Therefore, the company has to make initial contact with about 240 managerial candidates. Note the mushrooming effect in trying to recruit applicants. Stated in reverse order, 240 people are contacted to find 60 who are interested, to find 40 who agree to be interviewed, to find 10 who are acceptable, to get the 5 people who will accept the offer.

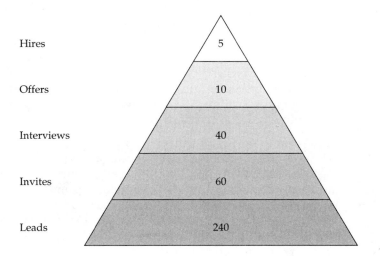

Figure 5–7 *Recruiting yield pyramid*

SOURCE: From *The Recruitment Function* by R. H. Hawk, 1967, New York: AMACOM, a division of American Management Association. All rights reserved. Reprinted by permission.

Obviously these yield ratios (that is, 240:5) will differ, depending on the organization and the job in question. Highly attractive employers will have fewer people decline their offers, and less-demanding jobs will be filled with less selectivity. Also, economic conditions play a big role in whether the company must pursue the applicant or vice versa. Nevertheless, a poor job of recruiting will greatly limit the calibre of people available for hire. Also, from the time a company realizes it needs new employees until the employees show up for work is typically measured in weeks or months rather than days.

Rynes (1993) notes that most of the emphasis on personnel decisions from an I/O perspective centers on how employers can make better decisions when assessing applicants. However, as Rynes observed, the process can be viewed from the opposite perspective, that is, the extent to which applicants consider the company to be a desirable employer. Specifically, what impressions of the company are generated by the company through the use of their recruitment and assessment practices? Schuler (1993) refers to the quality of a selection process that makes it acceptable to job applicants as *social validity*. Applicant reactions to assessment procedures are often vividly personal and highly emotional and clearly influence the applicant's decision to further consider the company as a prospective employer. Rynes (1993) offers the following examples of applicant reactions to the recruiting and assessment tactics of companies:

- A married graduate student with a 3.9+ grade point average reported that the first three questions in a company's psychological assessment procedure involved inquiries about her personal relationship with her husband and children. Although the company asked her what she thought of the procedure before she left, she lied because she was afraid that telling the truth would eliminate her from future consideration. Because of dual-career constraints, she continued to pursue an offer, but noted that if she got one, her first on-the-job priority would be to try to get the assessor fired.
- A student told how he had originally planned to refuse to submit to psychological testing, but was persuaded by his girlfriend that it would be a more effective form of protest to pursue the offer and then pointedly turn it down.
- The first interview question asked of a female student was, "We're a pretty macho organization . . . Does that bother you?" Unfortunately it did, and she simply wrote the company out of her future interviewing plans. (p. 242)

These examples illustrate that job applicants are not merely passive "receptors" of selection procedures. Rather, applicants react to what they are asked to do or say to get a job. Sometimes a negative experience results in withdrawal from the application process. Smither, Reilly, Millsap, and Pearlman (1993) found that applicant reactions to selection methods were positively related to their willingness to recommend the employer to others. Companies and applicants should realize that the recruitment and selection process is *mutual*—both parties are engaged in assessing the degree of fit with each other.

Another area of recruitment addresses what is called the realistic job preview (RJP). The realistic job preview is the opposite of slick promotional advertising that overemphasizes the job's good points and ignores its bad points. Rather, RJPs attempt to portray jobs realistically. The RJP may be in the form of a booklet, a videotape, or an on-site visit. The rationale is that one reason people quit their jobs is due to disillusionment. They were initially led to believe the jobs were going to be highly attractive, but over time reality set in, and the jobs were not so great after all. However, if people can see for themselves from the beginning what the jobs are really like, they will not have such false expectations. In fact, Dugoni and Ilgen (1981) proposed three reasons that RJPs might be effective. First, they lower initial expectations, which in turn increases ultimate job satisfaction. Second, they enhance employees' ability to cope with unpleasant job circumstances. Third, applicants perceive greater openness and honesty with a company that candidly reveals to them what their jobs will really be like. Vandenberg and Scarpello (1990) have postulated that RJPs help attain the match between the individuals' preferences for job rewards and the perception of available job rewards that result in job satisfaction and employment stability.

Are realistic job previews effective in reducing turnover? The results indicate their effect is modest at best. In studying the effect of two types of RJPs (a written description and a videotape) on the turnover of attendants in a facility for the retarded, Zaharia and Baumeister (1981) found that the RJPs had no effect. Reilly, Brown, Blood, and Malatesta (1981) reported that a realistic film and a job visit had no effect on job acceptance rates, employee commitment, or eventual turnover. Dean and Wanous (1984) found that bank tellers who were given an RJP tended to quit their jobs sooner than control-group tellers. However, in the course of a year, there was no difference in the overall turnover of the two groups. Reilly and associates estimated that if RJPs had any effect in reducing turnover, it would be no more than 6%. Breaugh (1983a) felt the value of RJPs was questionable and speculated that some of the inconsistency in the research findings was due to differences in the times at which RJPs were administered. Some companies administer RJPs after a job offer has been extended but before the applicant has accepted it. Other companies give RJPs after a job offer has been accepted. Wanous (1989) concluded that RJPs were more effective when presented through the audiovisual medium rather than in written fashion, when they contained moderate rather than high negativity, and when presented early rather than late in the recruiting process.

In summary, recruitment deals with the process of making applicants available for selection. The ease or difficulty of recruiting depends on such factors as economic conditions, the job in question, the reputation of the organization, and the urgency of filling the job opening. Organizations that have the luxury of a leisurely, deliberate recruiting process will most likely be more successful than those that are rushed into filling a position. Thorough recruiting does not guarantee that the best candidates will be selected; however, haphazard or casual recruiting frequently results in few good candidates to choose from (see Field Note 1).

Affirmative Action

The recruitment function is influenced by a social policy called *affirmative action.* Affirmative action programs are designed to promote active recruiting of all qualified members of the work force and to correct previous wrongs in the composition of the work force. Employers are expected to recruit minority group members as they do others. Recruiters may (1) visit colleges with mainly black or female students, or (2) advertise job openings in magazines or newspapers read by minority groups or on radio or TV programs favored by minorities. Affirmative action programs require employers to recruit minority applicants who might not otherwise seek employment with the companies. Also, companies must prepare affirmative action goals and timetables for employing a certain percentage of minority employees. This is required because many employers have a disproportionately small percentage of minorities in their work forces compared to the population at large. Since affirmative action is not law, a company cannot be sued for not having an affirmative action program. But economic pressures can be brought to bear against the company for lack of participation. If a company receives a portion of its business from government contracts, the government can withhold funds until the company develops an affirmative action program.

Research related to affirmative action issues has revealed some interesting psychological correlates to this recruitment philosophy. Heilman and Herlihy

FIELD NOTE 1

One of the more unusual personnel selection consulting projects I've worked on involved hiring a dentist. A dentist in my town had just experienced an unpleasant breakup with his partner. They disagreed on many major issues surrounding dentistry, including the relative importance of preventive dental maintenance versus treatment, pain management for patients, and so on. Their parting was not amicable. The dentist who remained solicited my help in getting a new partner. He described at great length the characteristics he was looking for in a new partner. Some were more along the lines of possessing certain dentistry skills, while others dealt with attitudinal or philosophical orientations toward dentistry.

I didn't envision any major problems in picking a new partner because the desired characteristics seemed reasonable, and I knew dental schools turned out many graduates each year (thus I would have a large applicant pool). Then came a curve ball I neither anticipated nor understood initially. The dentist then said to me, "And, of course, my new partner must be left-handed." The dumb look on my face must have told the dentist I didn't quite catch the significance of left-handedness. The dentist then explained to me something I never realized

despite all the years I have gone to dentists. Dental partners often share instruments in their practice, and there are both left-handed and right-handed dental instruments. The dentist was left-handed himself, therefore his new partner would also have to be left-handed. I then asked the dentist what proportion of dentists were left-handed. He said he didn't know for sure, but knew it was a small percentage. Suddenly, my task had become much more difficult.

It was one thing to find a new dentist who met the specifications for the job and who would like to set up a practice in a small Iowa town. It was another thing to have the size of the potential applicant pool greatly reduced by such a limiting factor as left-handedness. There is a technical term for left-handedness in this case: "bona fide occupational qualification" (BFOQ). For a qualification to be a BFOQ, it must be "reasonably necessary to the operation of that particular business or enterprise." Thus, an employer could use left-handedness as a BFOQ in dentistry, but left-handedness would not be a BFOQ in accounting, for example. I am happy to tell you I found a dentist who met all the qualifications. The two dentists have been partners for over 15 years now, and their practice continues to grow.

(1984) investigated the reactions of individuals to women who got their jobs on the basis of merit or because of preferential treatment based on gender. Neither men nor women were attracted to jobs when it was believed that women in those jobs had acquired them because of their sex. Heilman, Simon, and Repper (1987) examined the effects of sex-based selection. In a lab study they led women to believe they were selected for a group leader position because of either their sex or their ability. When selected on the basis of sex, women devalued their leadership performance, took less credit for successful outcomes, and reported less interest in persisting as leaders. The findings suggest that when individuals have doubts about their competence to perform a job effectively, sex-based preferential selection is likely to have adverse consequences on how they view themselves and their performance. Heilman, Block, and Lucas (1992) reported that individuals viewed as having been hired on an affirmative action basis were not believed to have had their qualifications given much weight in the hiring process. The stigma of incompetence was found to be fairly robust, and the authors questioned whether the stigma would dissipate in the face of disconfirming information about the individuals' presumed incompetence. Kleiman and Faley (1988) concluded that although granting preferential treatment as part of an affirmative action program may help remedy discrimination inequities at the workplace, it may also affect other important societal and organizational outcomes.

Selection

Selection is the process of choosing for employment a subset of applicants available for hire. Selection implies that some applicants will get hired, others will not. If all the applicants are going to be hired, and it is just a case of which jobs they will fill, then there is no selection. What you have in this context is more appropriately called placement or classification, topics that will be discussed later in the chapter. Selection is predicated on the premise that some applicants are better suited for a job than others, and its purpose is to identify these "better" applicants. If all the applicants are equally suited or can be thought of as interchangeable, then it makes no difference who gets selected. In the vast majority of cases, however, all applicants are not equally suited, so it does matter who gets selected.

Personnel selection is the process of identifying from the pool of recruited applicants those to whom a job will be offered. As long as there are fewer job openings than applicants, some applicants will be hired and some won't. Selection is the process of separating the selected from the rejected applicants. We want the selected employees to be successful on the job and to contribute to the welfare of the organization. Three major factors determine the quality of the newly selected employees and the degree to which they will have an impact on the organization: (1) the validity of the predictor, (2) the selection ratio, and (3) the base rate.

Predictor Validity.   Figure 5–8 shows a predictor-criterion correlation of .80. Along the predictor axis is a line, the *predictor cutoff*, that separates passing from

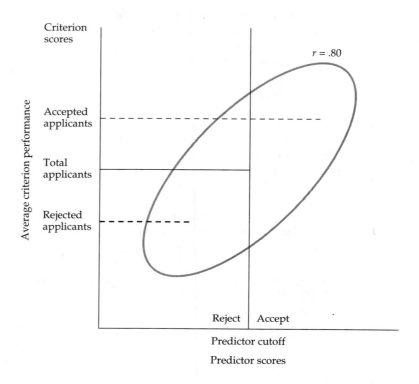

Figure 5–8   *Effect of a predictor with high validity (r = .80) on test utility*

failing applicants. People above the cutoff were accepted for hire; those below it were rejected. Also, observe the three horizontal lines. The solid line, representing the criterion performance of the entire group, cuts the entire distribution of scores in half. The dotted line, representing the criterion performance of the rejected group, is below the performance of the total group. Finally, the dashed line, which is the criterion performance of the accepted group, is above the performance of the total group. The people who would be expected to perform the best on the job fall above the predictor cutoff. In a simple and straightforward sense, that is what a valid predictor does in personnel selection: It identifies the more capable people from the total pool.

A different picture emerges for a predictor that has no correlation with the criterion, as shown in Figure 5–9. Again, the predictor cutoff separates those accepted from those rejected. This time, however, the three horizontal lines are all superimposed; that is, the criterion performance of the accepted group is no better than that of the rejected group, and both are the same as the performance of the total group. The value of the predictor is measured by the difference between the average performance of the accepted group and the average performance of the total group. As can be seen, these two values are the same, so their difference equals zero. In other words, predictors that have no validity also have no value.

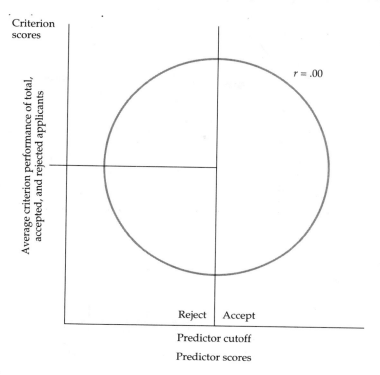

Figure 5-9 *Effect of a predictor test with no validity (r = .00) on test utility*

On the basis of this example, we see a direct relationship between a predictor's value and its validity: The greater the validity of the predictor, the greater its value as measured by the increase in average criterion performance for the accepted group over that for the total group.

Selection Ratio. A second factor that determines the value of a predictor is the *selection ratio* (SR). The selection ratio is defined as the number of job openings (*n*) divided by the number of job applicants (*N*), or:

$$SR = \frac{n}{N}$$

[Formula 5–15]

When the SR is equal to 1 (there are as many openings as there are applicants) or greater (there are more openings than applicants), the use of any selection device has little meaning. The company can use any applicant who walks through the door. But most often, there are more applicants than openings (the SR is somewhere between 0 and 1), and thus the SR is meaningful for personnel selection.

The effect of the SR on a predictor's value can be seen in Figures 5–10 and 5–11. Let us assume we have a validity coefficient of .80 and the selection ratio is

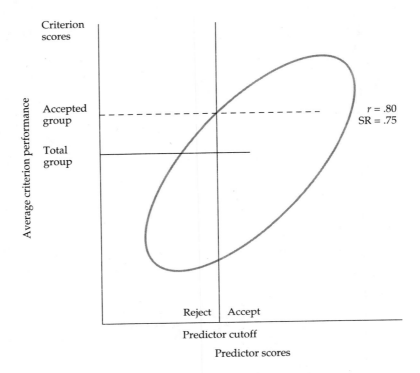

Figure 5–10   *Effect of large selection ratio (SR = .75) on test utility*

.75, meaning we will hire three out of every four applicants. Figure 5–10 shows the predictor-criterion relationship, the predictor cutoff that results in accepting the top 75% of all applicants, and the respective average criterion performance of the total group and the accepted group. By hiring the top 75%, the average criterion performance of that group is greater than that of the total group (which is weighted down by the bottom 25% of the applicants). Again, value is measured by this difference between average criterion scores. Further, by lopping off the bottom 25% (the one applicant out of four who is not hired), the average criterion performance of the accepted group will be greater than for the total group.

In Figure 5–11 we have the same validity coefficient ($r = .80$), but this time the SR is .25; that is, out of every four applicants, we will hire only one. The figure shows the location of the predictor cutoff that results when hiring only the top 25% of all applicants and the respective average criterion performance of the total and accepted groups. The average criterion performance of the accepted group is not only above that of the total group as before, but the difference is also much greater. In other words, when only the top 25% are hired, their average criterion performance will be greater than the performance of the top 75% of the appli-

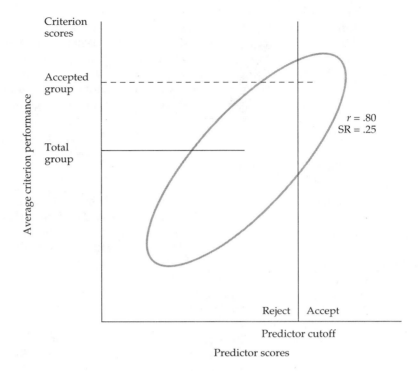

Figure 5-11   *Effect of small selection ratio (SR = .25) on test utility*

cants, and both of these values will be greater than the average performance of the total group.

The relationship between SR and the predictor's value should be clear: The smaller the SR, the greater the predictor's value. This should also make sense intuitively. The fussier we are in admitting people (that is, the smaller the selection ratio), the more likely it is that the people admitted (or hired) will be of the quality we desire.

Base Rate.   The third factor that influences the utility of a predictor is the percentage of present employees who are successful (also called the *base rate*). Management usually decides what constitutes successful job performance. It has in mind a standard or critical value that separates successful from unsuccessful workers. This critical value is the *criterion cutoff*. For example, in most undergraduate colleges, the criterion cutoff separating successful from unsuccessful students is a "C" average (2.0/4.0).

In absolute terms, the largest gains in average criterion performance will occur with a base rate of .50; that is, a new predictor will produce the greatest increase in the number of people who will attain satisfactory performance if the base rate is .50. As the base rate becomes more extreme (high or low), the absolute utility of the predictor decreases. In other words, it is difficult for a predictor to change the actual number of workers who are performing successfully if the current group of employees is performing extremely well or poorly.

In summary, the relationship between the percentage of present employees who are performing successfully and predictor value is as follows: The closer the base rate is to .50, the greater will be the gain in the actual number of new employees who will perform successfully.

Selection Decisions

As long as the predictor used for selection has less than perfect validity ($r = 1.00$), we will always make some errors in personnel selection. The object is, of course, to make as few mistakes as possible. With the aid of the scatterplot, we can examine where the mistakes occur in making selection decisions.

Part (a) of Figure 5–12 shows a predictor-criterion relationship of about .80, where the criterion scores have been separated by a criterion cutoff. The criterion cutoff is the point that separates successful (above) from unsuccessful (below) employees. Again, management decides what constitutes successful and unsuccessful performance.

Part (b) shows the same predictor-criterion relationship, except this time the predictor scores have been separated by a predictor cutoff. The predictor cutoff is the point that separates accepted (right) from rejected (left) applicants. The score that constitutes passing the predictor test is determined by the selection ratio, cost factors, or occasionally by law.[3]

Part (c) shows the predictor-criterion relationship intersected by both cutoffs. Each of the resulting four sections of the scatterplot is identified by a letter representing a different group of people:

Section A: Applicants who are above the predictor cutoff and above the criterion cutoff are called *true positives.* These are the people we think will succeed on the job because they passed the predictor test, and who in fact turn out to be successful employees (vis-à-vis a predictive criterion-related validity paradigm). This group represents a correct decision: We correctly decided to hire them.

Section B: The people in this group are those we thought would not succeed on the job because they failed the predictor test and who, if hired anyway, would have performed unsatisfactorily. This group represents a correct decision: We correctly predicted they would not succeed on the job. These people are *true negatives.*

Section C: People who failed the predictor test (and are thus predicted not to succeed on the job) but who would have succeeded had they been given the chance are called *false negatives.* We have made a mistake in our deci-

---

[3] In some public sector organizations (for example, state governments), the passing score for a test is determined by law. Usually a passing score is set at 70% correct.

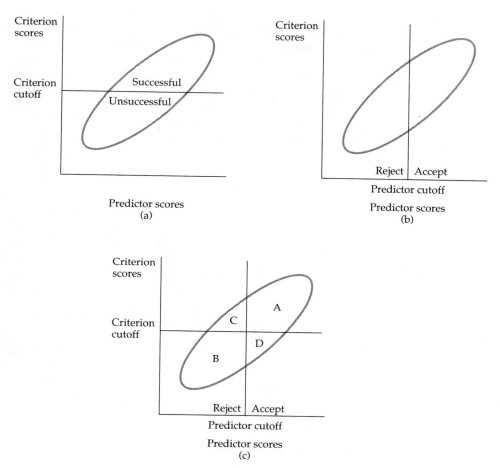

Figure 5–12 *Effect of establishing (a) criterion cutoff, (b) predictor cutoff, and (c) both cutoffs on a predictor-criterion scatterplot*

sion-making process with these people. They would really turn out to be good employees, but we mistakenly decided they would not succeed. These are "the good ones we let get away."

Section D: The people who passed the predictor test (and are thus predicted to succeed on the job) but perform unsatisfactorily after being hired are called *false positives*. We have also erred with these people. They are really ineffective employees who should not have been hired, but we mistakenly thought they would succeed. They are "the bad ones we let in."

Positive/negative refers to the result of passing/failing the predictor test; true/false refers to the quality (good/bad) of our decision to hire the person. In personnel selection we want to minimize the false positives and false negatives.

If there is no difference between making false positive and false negative decisions (that is, letting a bad worker in is no worse than letting a good one get away), it will do no good to "juggle" the cutoff scores. By lowering the predictor cutoff in part (c) of Figure 5–12 (moving the line to the left), we will decrease the size of section C, the false negatives. But by reducing the number of false negatives, we increase the space in section D, the false positives. The converse holds for raising the predictor cutoff (moving the line to the right). Furthermore, classification errors (false positives and false negatives) are also influenced by extreme base rates. For example, when the behavior being predicted occurs very rarely (as employees who will commit violent acts in the workplace), the differential likelihood of one type of error over the other will be great (Martin & Terris, 1991). However, cutoff scores cannot be established solely for the purpose of minimizing false positives or false negatives. Cascio, Alexander, and Barrett (1988) indicate there must be some rational relationship between the cutoff score and the purpose of the test. Issues pertaining to the cutoff score will be discussed next.

For many years, employers were not indifferent about making false positive versus false negative mistakes. Most employers preferred to let a good employee get away (in the belief that someone else who is good could be hired) rather than hire a bad worker. The cost of training, reduced efficiency, turnover, and so on made the false positive highly undesirable. Although most employers still want to avoid false positives, false negatives are also important. The applicant who fails the predictor test and sues the employer on the grounds of using unfair tests can be very expensive. If people do fail an employment test, most employers want to be as sure as possible that they were not rejected because of unfair and discriminatory practices. Denying employment to a qualified applicant is tragic; denying employment to a qualified minority applicant can be both tragic and expensive. Both types of selection errors can be reduced by increasing the validity of the predictor test. The greater the validity of the predictor, the smaller the chance that people will be mistakenly classified.

Determination of the Cutoff Score

Have you ever wondered how certain cutoff or passing scores came to be? That is, why 70% correct is associated with passing a test (as a driver's test), or that in educational institutions the cutoffs of 90%, 80%, and 70% are usually associated with the grades of A, B, and C, respectively? It has been reported that in ancient China several thousand years ago an emperor decreed that 70% correct was needed to successfully pass a test. That 70% correct figure, or relatively close approximations, has been used throughout history in a wide range of assessment contexts as representing a standard to guide pass/fail decisions. While I/O psychologists are primarily limited to assessment decisions in employment contexts, we too have had to wrestle with issues pertaining to the determination of where to set the cutoff score.

Cascio, Alexander, and Barrett (1988) addressed the legal, psychometric, and professional issues associated with setting cutoff scores. As the authors reported, there is a wide variation regarding the appropriate standards to use in evaluating the suitability of established cutoff scores. In general, a cutoff score should be set so as to be reasonable and consistent with the expectations of acceptable job proficiency within the workplace. Also, the cutoff should be set at a point that permits selection of employees who are capable of learning a job and performing it in a safe and efficient manner. Thus, there are undesirable selection consequences associated with setting the cutoff score "too low" (an increase in false positive selection decisions) or "too high" (an increase in false negative selection decisions).

When criterion-related evidence exists of a test's validity, it is possible to demonstrate a direct correspondence between performance on the test and performance on the criterion, which aids in selecting a reasonable cutoff score. Take, for example, the following case in predicting academic success in college. The criterion of academic success is college grade point average, and the criterion cutoff is a C average, or 2.0 on a 4.0 scale. That is, students who attain a grade point average of 2.0 or greater graduate, while those with a grade point average of less than 2.0 do not graduate from college. Furthermore, assume the selection (admission) test for entrance into the college is a 100-point test of cognitive ability. Using a criterion-related validation paradigm, an empirical linkage is established between scores on the test and college grade point average. The statistical analysis of the sets of scores reveals the relationship shown in Figure 5–13. Because a minimal grade point average of 2.0 is needed to graduate and a relationship exists between test scores and college grade point average, we can determine (through regression analysis) the exact test score associated with a predicted grade point average of 2.0. In this example, a test score of 50 is predictive of a grade point average of 2.0. Therefore, a score of 50 becomes the cutoff score on the intellectual ability test.

The task of determining a cutoff score is much more difficult when only content-related evidence of the validity of a given test is available. In such cases it is important to consider the level of ability associated with a certain test score that is judged suitable or relevant to job performance. However, there is an obvious amount of subjectivity associated with such decisions. In general, there is no such thing as a single, uniform, correct cutoff score. Nor is there a single best method of setting cutoff scores for all situations. Cascio et al. (1988) made several suggestions regarding setting cutoff scores. Among them are:

- The process of setting a cutoff score should begin with a job analysis that identifies relative levels of proficiency on critical knowledge, skills, and abilities (KSAs).
- When possible, data on the actual relation of test scores to criterion measures of job performance should be considered carefully.
- Cutoff scores should be set high enough to ensure that minimum standards of job performance are met.

In summarizing the process of determining a passing score, Ebel (1972) noted the following: "Anyone who expects to discover the 'real' passing score . . . is doomed to disappointment, for a 'real' passing score does not exist to be discovered. All any examining authority . . . can hope for, and all any of their examinees can ask, is that the basis for defining the passing score be defined clearly, and that the definition be as rational as possible" (p. 496).

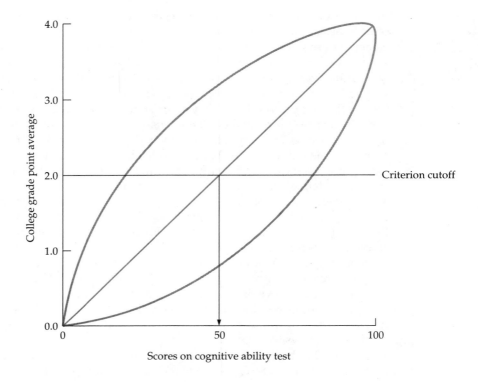

Figure 5–13 *Determining the cutoff score through a test's criterion-related validity*

In addition to measurement issues associated with determining a cutoff score, there are also legal issues to consider. Many of these legal issues pertain to adverse impact. It will be recalled that adverse impact is determined by the "80% rule." That is, adverse impact is said to exist if the selection ratio associated with a particular passing score on a test for one subgroup of job applicants is less than four-fifths (or 80%) of the selection ratio for the largest subgroup of job applicants. Suppose, for example, the passing score of a selection test results in a selection ratio of 70% for male applicants, but only 40% for female applicants. Because 40% is less than four-fifths of 70% (4/5 x 70% = 56%), this passing score has an adverse impact on female applicants. Some organizations mistakenly believed that they could avoid the issue of adverse impact by setting a cutoff score so low that virtually all applicants pass the test (that is, the selection ratio would be extremely high). The courts have recognized this procedure to be futile. If an organization is unable to weed out those individuals who are minimally qualified, there is no justification for using the test in the first place. In the opinion of the courts, setting a very low cutoff score tends to destroy the credibility of the entire testing process.

An alternative to setting low cutoff scores is a procedure called *banding* (Murphy, Osten, & Myors, 1995). The traditional approach to personnel selection is to rank applicants on the basis of their test scores and select the applicants with the highest scores. An alternative approach involves test score banding in which some differences in test scores are ignored, and individuals whose scores fall within the same band are selected on some basis other than the test score (gender or race, for example), thereby eliminating or greatly reducing adverse impact. The width of the band is a function of the reliability of the test. Highly reliable tests produce relatively narrow bands, while less reliable tests produce wider test score bands. Thus a one-point difference in test scores (for example, a score of 90 versus 89) is not judged to be of sufficient magnitude to reflect a meaningful difference in the applicants' respective abilities. This logic can be extended to a two-point difference in test scores, a three-point difference, and so on. Eventually, a certain magnitude of differences in test scores *is* determined to reflect a meaningful difference in ability. This is the point where the band would end; other bands may be formed from the distribution of test scores.

Banding is a controversial method of interpreting test scores. Proponents of the method (for example, Siskin, 1995; Zedeck, Outtz, Cascio, & Goldstein, 1995) argue that banding achieves the objectives of hiring able candidates while avoiding adverse impact. Critics of the method (for example, Schmidt, 1991; Schmidt & Hunter, 1995) contend that banding leads to the conclusion that random selection (that is, ignoring test scores altogether) is logically defensible, which is anathema to the classical principles of measurement. There is also concern (Gottfredson, 1994; Sackett & Wilk, 1994) that banding may lead to an overemphasis of certain types of selection errors relative to others. The ultimate resolution of the question on whether banding is advisable is likely to depend on the organization's values regarding social and economic issues. The controversy also underscores the point raised by Ebel (1972) that there is no one professionally agreed-upon method to determine passing scores on tests.

Personnel Selection Strategies

The question facing a psychologist in making a personnel selection decision is, should this person be hired? Three selection strategies can be used to help with the decision: multiple regression, multiple cutoff, and multiple hurdle. These strategies aid the decision process, for as Guion (1991) notes, personnel selection is always based to some degree on judgments, and they are never as automatic or reflexive as the statistical procedures may suggest (see Field Note 2). These strategies differ in complexity and in their assumptions about predictor-criterion relationships. Each strategy has its own strengths and weaknesses, and each presents a rationale for selecting the "best" person for the job.

Multiple Regression

The multiple regression selection strategy is based on the statistical procedure of multiple regression analysis. Recall that the method involves the use of two or more predictors weighted and added together to enhance the prediction of a crite-

FIELD NOTE 2

This chapter is devoted to explaining how personnel decisions are made. Many factors have been identified and explained, but one has been left out. I've never seen it discussed in any book or article on personnel selection, but (unfortunately) it is sometimes a critical, if not deciding, factor. It is called politics. Consider this experience I had.

I was hired for a very important consulting project: to pick the chief of police for a large city. The job has tremendous visibility, high influence, and great responsibility. I didn't want to "blow it" as the consultant. The city recruited applicants for the opening, and a total of 50 applicants met the minimal qualifications for consideration set by the city. I was handed the 50 applications and told to identify the best candidates in the applicant pool.

My first step was to evaluate each candidate in terms of education and experience using a weighted application-blank procedure. That got the applicant pool down to 25. These 25 quarter-finalists then had to submit written answers to three essay test questions about how they would handle some difficult police problems. These answers were evaluated, and the 15 best applicants proceeded to the semi-finalist stage. Here the candidates took a series of personality inventories and intelligence tests. Based upon those results, 10 finalists were selected and in turn were subjected to a lengthy oral interview. On the basis of all the assessment results, I rank ordered the 10 finalists and submitted the list to the city council, which had the judicial authority to approve the new chief of police. The candidate ranked first was from a different state; the candidate ranked second was currently the assistant chief of police, the second in command. The candidate ranked first was clearly the best person for the job, being far and away better than anyone else. I thought the city council (composed of seven people) had an easy job: to approve the top candidate as the new chief of police. It is here that politics came in, and it got rather dirty.

The assistant chief of police was a close friend of three city council members. They played cards together, as did their wives. From the very beginning, the three city council members had known the assistant chief of police would come out favorably in the selection process. In fact, nearly everyone had thought he would be the next chief of police. When I presented the city council with my list of the 10 candidates, things got very awkward: "Their man" was not first on the list. The press followed the selection process carefully, because it was a hot news item. The media announced the rank order of the 10 finalists. The public's general reaction was to have the city council approve the candidate who had been ranked first. But the head of the city council was not about to sell out his old friend.

The head of the city council (one of the three friends on the council) then made this startling announcement. Because every rookie cop on the force dreams about one day rising to be the chief, to award the chief's job to an "outsider" (that is, a candidate not native to the city) would destroy the morale of the police force and take away every rookie's dream forever. Therefore, he was going to advise the city council to select as the next chief of police not the person ranked first (the outsider) but the person ranked second (the assistant chief, and his friend). This was the first time anyone had made any reference at all to the insider/outsider distinction. It was a new hurdle imposed at the eleventh hour as a means of bumping the top-ranked candidate from the list. Some members of the community howled in protest at this announcement, as did the media, declaring it was a "fix" to install the council's personal choice. All the three city council members had to do was convince a fourth member to vote for the second-ranked person, and he would be in. In a highly electrified meeting of the city council in a council chamber jampacked with reporters and camera crews, the city council members publicly cast their votes. By a vote of 4–3, the number-one-ranked candidate (the outsider) was approved and became the new chief of police.

FIELD NOTE 2 *(continued)*

I would like to believe the four "yes" votes came from people who recognized the quality of the top candidate, but I know better. Politics being what it is, strange things can happen. They voted the way they did not simply because they supported the stronger candidate but because they wanted to get even with the three council members against whom they had held a grudge from a previous political episode. In short, the right decision was made, but for the wrong reason.

I wish to emphasize that there was absolutely nothing in my graduate training to prepare me for this experience. Similarly, there is no section of this book titled "How to Cope with Political Intrigue." But politics is a driving force in all organizations at all levels. Given this fact, sometimes I wonder how I/O psychologists accomplish as much as they do.

rion. Using a two-predictor model and assuming $a = 0$, the multiple regression equation would be

$$\hat{Y} = b_1X_1 + b_2X_2$$

[Formula 5–16]

This approach assumes that (1) there is a linear relationship between the predictors and the criterion (that is, higher scores on the predictors will lead to higher scores on the criterion), and (2) having a lot of the attribute measured by one predictor compensates for having only a little of the attribute measured by the second predictor. Although the former assumption (linearity) is usually met, the latter assumption (compensating predictors) is a more serious limitation.

Given a two-predictor regression equation where $a = 0$, $b_1 = 4$, and $b_2 = 2$, the following equation would be used to select job applicants:

$$\hat{Y} = 4X_1 + 2X_2$$

[Formula 5–17]

Let us say that a predicted criterion score ($\hat{Y}$) of 100 is considered necessary for hiring. Scores on the two predictors that would result in a passing score for four hypothetical applicants are presented in Table 5–1. Applicant A has none of the attribute measured by X_2, but because of the high score on X_1, he or she meets the minimum passing score of 100. Applicant B is just the reverse, having none of the attribute measured by X_1 but a lot of that measured by X_2. Applicants C and D have differing amounts of X_1 and X_2, which compensate for each other in reaching a score of 100.

As can be seen, many combinations of predictor scores result in a passing score on the criterion. Is this notion of "compensating predictors" acceptable for predicting job success? Sometimes it is, and sometimes it is not. For instance, in the case of admission into medical school, a low score on one attribute (verbal ability) may not be compensated for by a high score on a second attribute (numerical ability). But for other jobs, it may be acceptable to trade off low levels of one attribute with high levels of another. Keep in mind that it is rare for a person to

Table 5–1 *How four job applicants with different predictor scores can have the same predicted criterion score using multiple regression analysis*

Applicant	Score on X_1	Score on X_2	Predicted Criterion Score
A	25	0	100
B	0	50	100
C	20	10	100
D	15	20	100

Note: Based on the equation $\hat{Y} = 4X_1 + 2X_2$.

have absolutely no amount of any attribute, so the degree of compensation is usually not as extreme in practice as it could be in theory. Despite this limitation, the multiple regression strategy is a powerful and popular technique in personnel selection.

Multiple Cutoff

The multiple cutoff selection strategy is an alternative to the multiple regression selection strategy. The multiple cutoff method is limited by neither a linear relationship between predictors and criterion nor the problem of compensating predictors. This straightforward and uncomplicated method assumes that a minimal amount of ability on all predictors is needed for job success. Minimal passing score cutoffs are set for each predictor. If an applicant is below the cutoff on any predictor, he or she is rejected. All applicants who have scores at or above the cutoffs are hired. Having a high score on one predictor cannot compensate for having a low score on another.

The advantages of the multiple cutoff technique are that there are no limiting assumptions, and the method is easy to use. No formulas are involved in determining who passes and who fails. The major disadvantage involves determining the cutting scores. Cutting scores are generally set by trial and error, with different ones set for each predictor. However, it is quite difficult to establish the correctness of a cutting score with concurrent-validation procedures when no one in the company hired with the method would have any scores below this score. (If they did, they would not have been hired.) Thus, if it were felt that the cutoffs were set too high, it would be difficult to assess what effect lowering them would have on job performance. This restriction-in-range problem is not limited to the multiple cutoff method, however; it affects all concurrent-validity studies (see Field Note 3).

The multiple regression and multiple cutoff methods can be used in combination. This can take the form of not hiring some people unless their predicted-criterion score was above a certain level (from the multiple regression strategy) and they were above some cutoff on each predictor (from the multiple cutoff strategy). These techniques work best when the selection ratio is low and there are many job applicants. Large numbers of applicants are needed because many will be rejected for one of two reasons: They fell below the cutoff on one or more predictors, or even though they were above each individual cutoff, their predicted-criterion performance was not high enough. This combined approach is often used in selecting students for graduate school. Usually, applicants must have minimally acceptable quantitative and verbal ability as well as an acceptable predicted grade point average in graduate school (a frequently used criterion of success in academia).

Multiple Hurdle

In the multiple hurdle strategy, applicants must get satisfactory scores on a number of predictor variables (or hurdles) that are administered over time. The successful applicant passes each hurdle and is thus ultimately hired. The multiple hurdle approach is not used very often, but when it is used, it is found most frequently in management training programs and in the military. First, people who meet certain basic requirements (perhaps nothing more than interest in the job) are chosen to make up a pool of applicants. The first hurdle is designed to eliminate the least-qualified applicants. In an industrial training program, the first hurdle may be a knowledge test covering the first few weeks of specialized instruction. In the military the first hurdle for prospective paratroopers may be some test of physical fitness. At various points, additional hurdles (that is, evaluations) are presented. To survive in the program, applicants must pass each hurdle; those who do not are dropped. Eventually, a certain number pass all the hurdles, and these people become industrial managers, paratroopers, and so on.

FIELD NOTE 3

The multiple cutoff method of personnel selection is used when the applicants need a minimal amount of ability on two or more factors and thus high scores on one factor cannot make up for low scores on another. I used the multiple cutoff method in a recently completed validation study for a client. The job under investigation was that of retail salesperson. Salespeople must possess some special talents to be successful, and there is no way around not having them.

The results of my study revealed that salespeople had four characteristics that contributed to their success: a very high energy level, a high need for organization, a responsible, take-charge attitude, and high self-esteem. The high energy level means always being on the go, traveling to customers, making calls, and, ultimately, making sales. The organization factor relates to the importance of having a plan, a strategy for selling. It is not just an uncontrolled burst of energy but energy channeled in a carefully mapped-out sequence of customer calls and sales tactics. The high level of responsibility refers to the independence of salespeople. If they do not make the sale, no other employee will. They are responsible for the sales volume in their territory. When sales are good, they do not share the credit; and when sales are bad, they cannot point the finger at anyone else. The self-esteem factor means that salespeople must feel good about themselves. They have to be positive, resilient, "up-beat," and undeterred. They will encounter a lot of rejection in their work; customers will often not buy their products. They cannot internalize these rejections.

The multiple cutoff method provided a way to identify applicants who would be successful. Applicants who did not meet all four standards would not be hired. It is difficult to find people who can meet all four standards—but then, being a successful salesperson is not something just anyone can do.

The advantage is that unqualified people do not have to endure an entire evaluation program before they are rejected. It is best for the organization and the applicant to discover as soon as possible if he or she will not make it on the job. Because many evaluations are made, the company can be more confident in the quality of its final decision. The odds of a false positive's surviving multiple evaluations are much lower than those of surviving one test. The method is used primarily for jobs whose significance to the company warrants an extensive selection program. Lower level jobs are rarely so critical to the company.

The disadvantages are the time and cost involved. Again, the job's value to the company should be a major factor in deciding whether to use this type of program. A problem (although not necessarily a disadvantage) is that the final survivors are extremely similar to one another, so there is a major restriction in range in all their predictor scores. If their predictor scores were correlated with some criterion of job success taken later, the correlation would be very low. One interpretation is that the predictors lack validity. A more likely explanation is that because the survivors are so homogeneous, the similarity of their predictor scores rules out a high correlation with any criterion.

Test Utility and Organizational Efficiency

It is important to remember always that a human resources office is only one part of an organization. Each part must contribute to the organization's overall success. If the company is a profit-making firm (as many are) or just wants to improve operating efficiency (as all organizations should), a basic question involves how much improved personnel-selection techniques contribute to its overall profitability or efficiency. If more productive workers are hired as a result of a new selection technique, how much value or utility will they have to the company? Several studies have shown just how much utility a valid testing program can provide.

Schmidt, Hunter, McKenzie, and Muldrow (1979) estimated the dollar value to the company of using a valid employee-selection program. They analyzed the job of a computer programmer. They asked supervisors to estimate the "worth" (in dollars) of a good, average, and poor-quality computer programmer. Supervisors considered such factors as work speed, number of errors, and so on. The authors used the responses along with the following information they had collected: (1) a certain test useful in hiring computer programmers had a validity of .76, (2) it cost $10 to administer the test to each applicant, (3) more than 4,000 computer programmers were employed by the company (which was, in this case, the federal government), (4) more than 600 new programmers were hired each year, and (5) once on the job, the average programmer lasted about ten years.

Using all this information, the authors compared the expected utility of the test to other tests that had been used in the past and that had validities ranging from .00 to .50. They also examined the effect of various selection ratios ranging from .05 to .80. The dollar value to the government of using the more valid test was astonishing. When the previously used test was assumed to have a validity of

.50 and the selection ratio was .80, the incremental gains in efficiency (that is, the result of hiring better quality people) was $5.6 million in one year. This was the smallest dollar gain, because the previous testing conditions were quite favorable ($r = .50$). Given the poorest testing condition (a previous test with no validity) and a selection ratio of .05, the dollar gain was $97.2 million in one year.

Keep in mind that these dollar values pertain to using just one test to hire people in one job in one organization for just one year. If you extend these principles to testing in general across many jobs and many companies (and also across time), the dollar value extends into the billions. Other studies have shown that the utility of valid tests enhances efficiency by reducing turnover, training time, and accidents. The key element in improved utility is test validity. The impact of test validity on subsequent job performance is dramatic; there is no substitute for using "good" selection techniques.

However, the concept of assessing the dollar value of using valid selection tests has also prompted some admonitions. Boudreau (1991) believes expected utility gains have been *over*estimated because they fail to incorporate certain financial and economic considerations that serve to lower utility estimates. One such consideration would be the increased taxes organizations would have to pay on the increased revenue. Russell, Colella, and Bobko (1993) questioned some of the hiring assumptions underlying utility estimation, such as how consistent the value of job performance is over time. It is possible that the value of high job performance is greatest early in the employment relationship and begins to decline over time. Cascio (1993) challenged the assumption that all applicants who are offered jobs accept and are hired. In practice, lower scoring applicants must be accepted in place of higher scoring applicants who decline offers of employment. When unemployment is low, companies may be forced to lower their minimum hiring requirements to fill vacancies. Lower hiring requirements mean higher selection ratios. Furthermore, Smith, Farr, and Schuler (1993) discussed the difference between considering utility for a particular organization versus society as a whole. In a single organization the worst candidates can be selected out. In the economy as a whole, this is only marginally possible. Even in times of high unemployment (10%), 90% of the economically active population are at work. Selection merely shifts the static pool of talent in favor of organizations that have high selection standards, without any net gain to the economy as a whole. The underlying significance of all these findings is that while utility is a valuable concept for guiding personnel decisions, there are a number of factors that make utility estimates inexact, or at the least contingent upon complicating issues.

A related issue pertains to the degree to which managers find concepts developed by I/O psychologists, such as utility assessment, to be useful in making personnel decisions. Johns (1993) reports that I/O psychologists emphasize the technical merit of their ideas, but technical merit bears little relationship to the actual adoption of innovations designed to enhance administrative efficiency. Johns believes that the products of I/O science are out of alignment with the way organizations make decisions about the class of problems for which I/O innovations are thought to be solutions. Such innovations often fail to address the political or social climate in which adoption decisions are made. Latham and Whyte (1994) found that a sample of experienced managers were unimpressed with utility analysis, even though the analysis indicated that the net benefits from a new procedure were substantial. Managers are suspicious of the credibility of utility analysis methods, which often produce very large estimates of financial gain.

It seems clear to me that the ability of I/O psychologists to translate what they do into a universally understood metric—dollars and cents—enhances our capacity to improve the workplace. Cascio (1991) has demonstrated the economic gains to be accrued from other types of organizational innovations, such as smoking cessation and employee assistance programs. However, I/O psychologists need to direct additional efforts toward understanding the process by which concepts are implemented for actual use. We have emphasized the technical soundness of our science-based findings, while in practice other factors are also influential in the adoption process.

Placement and Classification

The vast majority of research in personnel psychology is on selection, the process by which applicants are hired. Another personnel function (albeit less popular) involves deciding which jobs people should be assigned to after they have been hired. This personnel function is called either placement or classification, depending on the basis for the assignment. In many cases selection and placement are not separate procedures. Usually, people apply for certain fixed jobs. If they are hired, they fill the jobs they were applying for. However, in some organizations (and at certain times in our nation's history), decisions about selection and placement have to be made separately.

Placement and classification decisions are usually limited to large organizations that have two or more jobs an applicant could fill. It must be decided which job would best match the person's talents and abilities. A classic example is the military. Thousands of applicants used to be selected each year, either voluntarily or through the draft. Once in, the next question was where to assign them. Placement and classification procedures are designed to get the best match between people and jobs.

Placement differs from classification on the basis of the number of predictors used to make the job assignment. Placement involves allocating people to two or more groups (or jobs) on the basis of a single predictor score. Many junior high school students are placed in math classes on the basis of a math aptitude test. The aptitude test is usually given during seventh grade. Students with high math aptitude are placed in an algebra class in eighth grade; students with average aptitude do not take algebra until ninth grade; students with low math aptitude do not take algebra until tenth grade, if at all. Applicants for secretarial positions may be placed into job grades (for example, secretary I, secretary II) on the basis of a typing test. The point is that placement decisions are made on the basis of one predictor factor (math aptitude, typing speed, and so on).

Classification involves allocating people to jobs on the basis of two or more valid predictor factors. For this reason, classification is more complex. However, it results in a better assignment of people to jobs than does placement. Classification uses smaller selection ratios than placement, which accounts for its greater utility. The reason that classification is not always used instead of placement is that it is often difficult to find more than one valid predictor to use in assigning people to jobs. The military has been the basis of most classification research. Military recruits take a battery of different tests covering areas such as intelligence, ability, and aptitude. On the basis of these scores, recruits are assigned to jobs in the infantry, medical corps, military intelligence, and so on. Other organizations that have to assign large numbers of people to large numbers of jobs also use this procedure. Given this constraint, relatively few companies need to use classification procedures. Nevertheless, Brogden (1951) has shown that the proper classification is just as important for organizational efficiency as the use of proper selection techniques.

Two sets of issues are particularly important in the areas of placement and classification. The first issue involves the nature of the jobs that need to be filled. Placement and classification decisions are easier when the jobs are very different. It is easier to decide whether a person should be assigned as a manager or a clerk than to decide between a secretary or a clerk. The manager and clerk jobs require very different types of skills, whereas the secretarial and clerk jobs have many similar job requirements. These decisions become more complex if the jobs require successive operations (such as on an assembly line) or coordination among work units. In these cases, we are also concerned about how well all of the people in the work unit fit together to form a cohesive team (Cronbach & Gleser, 1965).

The second issue involves the question of values. What is best in terms of satisfaction and productivity for the individual may not be the best for the company, and vice versa. There can be conflicts between individuals and organizations as to which values underlie manpower allocation decisions. Basically three strategies are possible; each reflects different values.

The *vocational guidance strategy* aims toward maximizing the values of the individual in terms of his or her wants or preferences. College students select their own majors based on the careers they wish to pursue. In other words, no college ever states that a student "must" major in a certain area; the decision is strictly an individual one.

The *pure selection strategy* maximizes organizational values. In this case only the best qualified people are placed in a job. Although the placed people are indeed very good, the method is somewhat impractical. Large numbers of people might not be placed into any job because they are not the "best" of the applicants. The method is inherently wasteful, because many applicants remain unemployed. Both the vocational guidance and pure selection strategies have weaknesses. While the vocational guidance method may work well in educational institutions, it does not work well in industry. If all the applicants wanted to be the company president, large numbers of jobs would go unfilled.

The *successive selection strategy* is a compromise between the first two extremes. In this method all jobs are filled by at least minimally qualified people, and given the available jobs, people are placed in jobs that will make the best use of their talents. Successive selection is a good compromise because the jobs get filled (the organization's needs are met) and individuals get assigned to jobs for which they are suited (the individual's needs are met).

At one time, placement and classification were as important as (if not more so than) selection. During World War II, industry needed large numbers of people to produce war material. The question was not whether people would get a job but what kind of job they would fill. A similar situation occurred in the military as thousands of recruits were being inducted every month. It was of paramount importance to get the right people into the right jobs. Today, the greatest amount of interest in classification continues in the military (Rumsey, Walker, & Harris, 1994). Researchers interested in classification have addressed many of the same issues confronted in selection. For example, Bobko (1994) reports that the most vexing issues facing classification decisions revolve around values—attaining ethnic and gender balance versus performance maximization. The relative importance of general mental ability (*g*) versus consideration of other factors is also a matter of debate in making classification decisions. Zeidner and Johnson (1994) believe other factors besides *g* must be considered in efficiently assigning individuals to jobs. In addition to cognitive ability, Alley (1994) recommends the assessment of personality, interests, and knowledge. The rationale behind placement and classification remains the same: Certain people will perform better in certain jobs than others. To this end, placement and classification are aimed at assigning people to jobs in which their predicted job performance will be the greatest.

CASE STUDY   *Just Give Me a Chance*

Hugh Casey slumped at his desk, totally dejected. He had just read the letter from Fulbright University informing him that his application for admission into their school of medicine had been rejected. It had been his dream since high school to become a doctor, and in particular to be a heart surgeon. Hugh had been an excellent student in high school and was admitted to the highly selective Seymour College despite achieving only a modest score on the college admission test. His interest in medicine was sparked when his father had triple-bypass heart surgery. The surgeon who performed the operation, Dr. Charles Dressen, was a friend of the family. Dr. Dressen had graduated from Fulbright University's medical school, which was nationally renowned for their high standards. Fulbright was the premier medical school in the region. Hugh wanted to emulate Dr. Dressen, to become a heart surgeon who saved lives, just as Dr. Dressen had saved his father's life. Fulbright was not only his first choice for medical school, it was his only choice. Casey felt it almost was his destiny to graduate with a medical degree from Fulbright and follow in Dr. Dressen's footsteps.

At Seymour College Hugh made the Dean's List the previous four semesters. His overall grade point average was 3.60. After a rough freshman year, which many first-year students experience, he settled down and performed very well in the premed curriculum. At the start of his senior year he took the medical college admission test but did not score extremely well. It was the same story with the admission test used by Seymour. He just didn't test well in standardized 3-hour examinations.

However, Hugh felt he had more than proved himself by his performance at Seymour. He believed that doing well over a four-year period should count more in his application to medical school than his performance in a 3-hour test.

Furthermore, three professors at Seymour wrote what they said were very positive letters of recommendation on his behalf. Additionally, even Dr. Dressen, a graduate of Fulbright's medical school, wrote a letter to his *alma mater* in support of Hugh. Finally, Hugh traveled to Fulbright for an interview with the medical school's admission committee. While he was admittedly nervous, Hugh felt the interview had gone very well. He was particularly delighted to tell the committee about his coming to know Dr. Dressen, and how Dr. Dressen had become his inspirational role model. Hugh got goose-bumps when he walked through the halls of the medical school during his visit to Fulbright. He just knew Fulbright was the place for him.

Hugh stared at the rejection letter feeling devastated and angry. How could Fulbright do this to him? How did the admission's committee reach their decision? Hugh earned excellent grades in high school and undergraduate school, and he just knew he would be equally good in medical school. Hugh reasoned that their rejection implied they thought he wouldn't make it through medical school. What would he have to do to prove himself, to prove to the admission's committee he would be a successful medical school student and then a successful heart surgeon? Hugh decided he would ask Fulbright to admit him on a conditional basis, not even knowing if the medical school had such a policy. He would agree to be evaluated after one year in medical school. If he were performing poorly, he would leave Fulbright and accept that the admission committee's initial decision on his application was correct. But if he performed well in that year, then he would want to be fully admitted to the medical school and no longer be under their scrutiny. Hugh wanted to prove to himself, to Fulbright, and to the world that he would become as great a heart surgeon as Dr. Dressen. All he wanted was a chance.

Questions

1. What selection strategy (for example, multiple regression, multiple cutoff) do you think Fulbright uses to evaluate applicants to their medical school? What factors do you think they evaluate in assessing applicants?
2. Do you believe Fulbright thinks Hugh won't be successful in medical school, which is why they rejected his application? Or do you believe Fulbright probably concluded Hugh would be successful in medical school, but there were simply other candidates who had better credentials?
3. If organizations are faced with evaluating many qualified applicants, having more qualified applicants than there are openings, should a personal experience of the type Hugh had with Dr. Dressen be a factor in determining admission? Why or why not?
4. If you were on the admission's committee at Fulbright, how would you make decisions about applicants in a way that is fair and reasonable to both the medical school and the applicants?
5. What do you think about Hugh's plea to be given a chance to prove himself? Is his plea unreasonable? Given the imperfect validity of our selection methods, should organizations give applicants a chance to prove themselves in a trial period on the job (or in school)? Why or why not?

Training and Development

Major Chapter Objectives

- *Understand the relationship between learning and task performance.*

- *Define the strategic value of training and development for organizations.*

- *Be able to assess training needs through organizational, task, and person analysis.*

- *Describe the major methods of training and their associated strengths and weaknesses.*

- *Understand the importance of cultural diversity training, sexual harassment training, 360-degree feedback, and mentoring in management development.*

- *Be able to evaluate training programs, including relevant criteria and research designs.*

- *Understand how legal scrutiny influences personnel training.*

Organizations select employees on the basis of their predicted likelihood of succeeding on the job. While some employees are expected to perform their jobs well immediately upon hire, the vast majority of employees will be granted time to grow into their new jobs. This growth process is expedited by formal organizational training processes designed for that purpose. Goldstein (1991) refers to training processes as "the systematic acquisition of attitudes, concepts, knowledge, roles, or skills that result in improved performance at work" (p. 508). Entry-level employees are hired on the basis of their ability to be successfully trained. For them, the key qualification is their predicted capability to learn how to perform the job. At other job levels, the knowledge and skill demands of work are continually escalating. Accordingly, employees in these jobs must enhance their capabilities to perform their jobs satisfactorily. Training provides opportunities for people to enter the job market with needed talents and perform in new functions.

I share the opinion of others that the relative importance of training to enhance job performance is increasing. A major reason for this emphasis is an increasing reliance on computers in the conduct of work, and the associated repercussions on the human requirements of work. Computer-assisted manufacturing and computer-assisted design represent two major technological innovations in production. Manufacturing employees are now often expected to have some fluency in computer-based operations. Such talents can be acquired only through additional preparation for work. There is a growing emphasis in all areas of work to operate more efficiently (that is, work procedures must require less time or produce less waste) and to enhance the overall quality of our goods and services. Such advances are the basis for enhancing organizational performance in increasingly competitive markets. Training is a process that enhances the degree of fit between job demands and human attributes.

Training and development are both processes for enhancing employee skills, but historically they have somewhat different focuses. The term *development* was generally reserved for skill enhancing processes for managerial-level personnel, while *training* was generally applied to skill enhancement processes in jobs lower in the organizational hierarchy. That is, managers (and above) are "developed," while nonmanagers are "trained." Today this distinction is not as meaningful as it once was. The need for skill enhancement for employees at *all* organizational levels is acute, and all employees should be engaged in the process of expanding their capabilities. Universities and colleges are no longer regarded exclusively as being centers of learning. Learning occurs in all organizations on a continuous basis. It might be advisable to think of your college years as "learning through education," while your working years are "learning through training and development." Some of the classic distinctions between training and development are still relevant, and both processes will be described. But recognizing the need for skill enhancement and knowing how to go about it are more important than the labels affixed to processes.

Learning and Task Performance

Learning can be conceptualized as the process of encoding, retaining, and using information. This perspective of learning prompted Howell and Cooke (1989) to refer to individuals as "human information processors." The specific procedures by which we process information for both short-term and long-term use have been the subject of extensive research in cognitive psychology (Weiss, 1990). I will examine some useful findings from this body of research that can facilitate our understanding of how learning affects the training and development process.

Anderson (1985) has suggested that skill acquisition be segmented into three phases: declarative knowledge, knowledge compilation, and procedural knowledge. *Declarative knowledge* is knowledge about facts and things. The declarative knowledge of skill acquisition involves memorizing and reasoning processes that allow the individual to attain a basic understanding of a task. During this phase, the individual may observe demonstrations of the task and learn task sequencing rules. At this stage of skill acquisition, individuals must devote nearly all of their attention to understanding and performing the task. Performance in the declarative knowledge stage is slow and error prone. Once the person has acquired an adequate understanding of the task, he or she can proceed to the second phase of skill acquisition.

During the second stage of skill acquisition, *knowledge compilation*, individuals integrate the sequences of cognitive and motor processes required to perform the task. Various methods for simplifying or streamlining the task are tried and evaluated. Performance then becomes faster and more accurate than in the declarative knowledge phase. The attentional demands on the individual are reduced as the task objectives and procedures are moved from short-term to long-term memory.

Procedural knowledge refers to knowledge about how to perform various cognitive activities. This final phase of skill acquisition is reached when the individual has essentially automatized the skill, and the task can be efficiently performed with little attention (Kanfer & Ackerman, 1989). After considerable practice, the task can be performed with minimal impairment while attention is devoted to other tasks.

Ackerman (1987) proposed that three major classes of abilities are critically important for performance in the three phases of skill acquisition. *General intellectual ability* is posited to be the most important factor in acquiring declarative knowledge. When the individual first confronts a novel task, the attentional demands placed on the individual are high. As the individual begins to understand the demands of the task and develops a performance strategy, the attentional demands decrease and the importance of intellectual ability for task performance is lessened.

As the individual moves along the skill acquisition curve from declarative to procedural phases, the importance of *perceptual speed abilities* escalates. The individual develops a basic understanding of how to perform the task but seeks a more efficient method for accomplishing the task with minimal attentional effort. Perceptual speed abilities seem most critical for processing information faster or more efficiently at this phase.

Finally, as individuals move to the final phase of skill acquisition, their performance is limited by their level of *psychomotor ability*. Individual differences in final, skilled performance are not necessarily determined by the same abilities that affect the initial level of task performance or the speed of skill acquisition (Kanfer & Ackerman, 1989). Psychomotor abilities (such as coordination) will determine the final level of task performance in the procedural knowledge phase.

Based on these research findings from cognitive psychology, it should be evident that complex relationships exist between individual abilities and phases of task performance. These findings offer an explanation of why some individuals may be quick to acquire minimal competency in a task but subsequently do not develop a high degree of task proficiency. Alternatively, other individuals may initially learn a task slowly but gradually develop a high level of task proficiency. Research by Morrison and Brantner (1992) revealed that learning the requirements of jobs in the military occurred in stages, with plateaus in learning followed by periods of growth. It appears that the relationship between learning and task performance is more complex than many researchers have believed. These findings bear not only on why certain individuals learn at different rates of speed but also on how training and development processes have to be targeted to enhance selected individual abilities.

The Strategic Value of Training and Development

Organizations do not train and develop their employees for the sheer sake of doing so. Rather, it is because employees represent a competitive advantage that enhances organizational performance when managed wisely. The competitive strategy an organization uses is the means by which it competes for business in the marketplace. There is a linkage between the type of competitive strategy an organization uses and its training and development practices (Jackson & Schuler, 1990).

A *speed strategy* offers the customer a competitive value in terms of reduced time for products or services. A training practice that serves this strategic function would emphasize teamwork among employees and methods of streamlined production designed to reduce the time it takes to meet a customer's needs. An *innovation strategy* is used to develop products or services that differ from other competitors'. Its primary business objective is to offer something new and different. The focus of training in this context would be developing new products, services, or technologies. A *quality-enhancement strategy* is designed to provide value on the basis of offering a product or service of higher quality than that offered by competitors. To reach that objective, employees would be trained to provide a consistently high level of service quality devoid of defects. Finally, the objective of a *cost-reduction strategy* is to gain a competitive advantage by being a low-cost provider of services. Under this business strategy, relatively little emphasis would be placed on enhancing employee skills through training. Employees with higher skill levels warrant higher levels of compensation, which serves to increase costs. Since this is the opposite of the desired outcome, organizations pursuing cost-reduction strategies tend to invest few resources in enhancing the skills of their employees.

In reality most organizations adopt a mix of competitive business strategies. Accordingly, training and development activities will be directed to meeting multiple objectives. The fast-food industry is a good example of this mix. However, you should clearly note that an overarching pattern exists between what organizations are trying to accomplish (that is, their strategy for competing) and their philosophy toward training and development. Certain business strategies (innovation) are far more dependent on the quality of their employees than others (cost-reduction). Therefore, the greatest advances and emphases in training technologies are found in those organizations that most highly value their human resources to sustain a competitive advantage.

Pretraining Environment

Tannenbaum and Yukl (1992) reviewed evidence suggesting that events prior to training (that is, the pretraining environment) can influence training effectiveness. Management actions and decisions provide cues that signal employee motivation for training. Employees start to learn about the way training is viewed in the organization early in the socialization process and continue to gather information with each training activity they attend. Some actions signal to trainees whether training is important (for example, supervisory and peer support). Other actions reveal to employees the amount of control, participation, or input they have in the training process (for example, participation in needs assessment).

Cohen (1990) found that trainees with more supportive supervisors entered training with stronger beliefs that training would be useful. Supportive supervisors would discuss an upcoming training course with the employees, establish training goals, provide them release time to prepare, and generally encourage the employees. Baldwin and Magjuka (1991) found that trainees who entered training expecting some form of follow-up activity or assessment afterward reported stronger intentions to transfer what they learned back on the job. The fact that their supervisors would require them to prepare a posttraining report meant they were held accountable for their own learning and apparently conveyed the message that the training was important. The converse is also true. Mathieu, Tannenbaum, and Salas (1990) found that trainees who reported many limitations in their jobs (for example, lack of time, equipment, and resources) entered training with a lower motivation to learn. These trainees had little incentive to learn new skills in an environment where the skills could not be applied.

Another factor defining the pretraining environment pertains to trainee input and choice in training. Baldwin, Magjuka, and Loher (1991) found that allowing trainees to specify what training they wanted increased their motivation to learn, provided they were given the training of their choice. However, trainees who were allowed to choose a course but were then assigned to a different course were

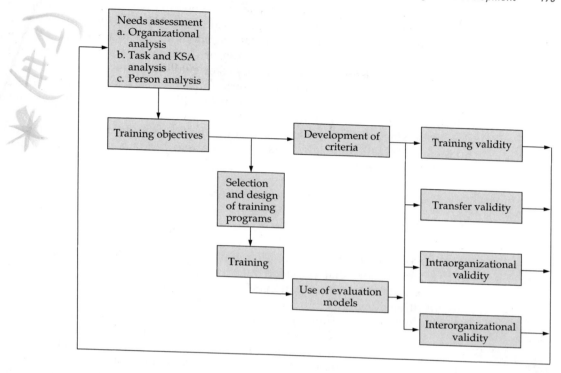

Figure 6–1   *The classic training system*

SOURCE: Adapted from *Training and Organizations: Needs Assessment, Development, and Evaluation* (p. 21) by I. L. Goldstein, 1993, Pacific Grove, CA: Brooks/Cole.

less motivated and learned less than the trainees who did not participate at all in the choice of training. Similarly, Quinones (1995) concluded that one way employee motivation in training can be enhanced is by giving individuals the chance to choose their own training programs and ensuring that these preferences are honored.

As Tannenbaum and Yukl (1992) have articulated, several factors representative of the organizational environment in which training occurs bear directly on its effectiveness. Training does not occur in a vacuum; it is but a means to an end. Factors that strengthen the linkage between training and relevant outcomes can be as critical as the training itself.

Assessing Training Needs

The entire personnel training process is predicated on a rational design (see Figure 6–1) as proposed by Goldstein (1993). The design of personnel training begins with an analysis of training needs and culminates in the assessment of training results. Important steps in between involve developing objectives, choosing methods, and designing an evaluation. Training directors must keep up with the current literature on training methods because previous successes or failures can help shape the selection or design of a training program. It is equally important to determine a means of evaluating the program before it is implemented; that is, evaluative criteria must be selected to serve as the program's scorecard. The bulk of this chapter will discuss the major steps in the design of personnel training.

Assessing training needs consists of a classic three-step process that encompasses organizational analysis, task analysis, and person analysis. Let's consider each of these steps individually.

Organizational Analysis

In the evolution of thinking on training and development, organizational analysis focused on factors that provided information about where and when training could be used in the organization. More contemporary thinking has transformed organizational analysis into an examination of systemwide components that determine whether the training program can produce behavior that will transfer into the organization. Goldstein (1991) observed that persons who participate in training are faced with a problem: They are required to learn something in one environment, the training situation, and to use it in another, on the job. This problem requires an examination of the systemwide components of the organization that may affect a trainee arriving with newly learned skills. Training programs can fail because of organizational constraints that they were not intended to address. For example, trainees will find it difficult to overcome a situation in which they learn a set of behaviors that are inconsistent with the way a manager prefers to have the job performed.

Michalak (1981) believes trainers overemphasize the portion of training that deals with acquisition of skill and place too little emphasis on what happens afterward. Baumgartel and Jeanpierre (1972) found that training is more effective when management provides a supportive climate that encourages trainees to explore new ideas and use their training knowledge. Rouillier and Goldstein (1990) proposed the concept of *organizational transfer climate* to explain why training can differ in its effectiveness. The authors determined that trainees demonstrated more transfer of skills from training to the job in organizational units where they were influenced to use what they had learned and were rewarded for doing so. It was concluded that transfer climate was a potentially powerful tool organizations should consider to facilitate training transfer.

In summary, organizational analysis examines systemwide factors that facilitate or retard the transfer of skills from training to the job. Whatever factors were present in training to facilitate development of new skills should also be present on the job to facilitate maintenance of those skills.

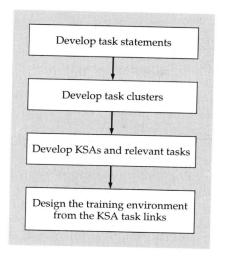

Figure 6–2 *Task and KSA development steps as input for the design of training systems*
SOURCE: Adapted from "Training in Work Organizations" by I. L. Goldstein, 1991, in *Handbook of Industrial and Organizational Psychology*, 2nd ed., Vol. 2, M. D. Dunnette & L. M. Hough (Ed.), Palo Alto, CA: Consulting Psychologists Press.

Task Analysis

A task analysis is used to determine the training objectives that will be related to the performance of particular activities or job operations. The task analysis results in a statement of the activities or work operations performed on the job and the conditions under which the job is performed.

Task analysis involves four major steps as input for developing training programs, as shown in Figure 6–2. Each step will be described.

Develop Task Statements.   The first step in task analysis is to completely specify the tasks performed on the job. (See Chapter 3 for additional discussion on task analysis.) The goal is to write a sentence that conveys *what* the worker does, *how* the worker does it, to *whom* or *what*, and *why* the worker does it. The following two examples of task statements are provided by Goldstein (1991).

> From the job of a secretary: "Sorts correspondence, forms, and reports to facilitate filing them alphabetically." (p. 529)

> From the job of a supervisor: "Inform next shift supervisor of departmental status through written reports so that the number of employees needed at each workstation can be determined." (p. 529)

It would not be unusual to have as many as 100 task statements written to describe the tasks performed in a job. The more varied the job, the greater will be the number of task statements.

Develop Task Clusters.   In this step task statements are grouped into homogeneous clusters to make them more usable and manageable. Subject matter experts (SMEs) are responsible for sorting the task statements into meaningful categories that reflect important dimensions of work. For example, for the job of a secretary one cluster might pertain to tasks involving maintenance of records.

Prepare Knowledge, Skill, and Ability Analysis.   A useful way for specifying the human capabilities needed to perform tasks is by examining the knowledge, skills, and abilities (KSAs) needed. Knowledge (K) refers to the body of information necessary to make adequate job performance possible. Skill (S) refers to the capability to perform job operations with ease and precision, and typically refers to psychomotor abilities. Ability (A) refers to cognitive capabilities necessary to perform a job function. Most often, abilities require the application of knowledge. The purpose of this analysis is to establish the KSAs needed to perform particular tasks. Most often persons who directly supervise the job being analyzed serve as SMEs to provide this information because they often think about what a job incumbent needs to know or what skills and abilities the incumbent needs to perform the tasks. Among the questions asked of SMEs to elicit KSA information would be the following:

- Describe the characteristics of good and poor employees on [tasks in cluster].
- Think of someone you know who is better than anyone else at [tasks in cluster]. What is the reason he or she does it so well?
- What does a person need to know to perform [tasks in cluster]?

The researcher would then develop a linkage between the tasks performed on a job and the knowledge, skills, and abilities needed to perform them.

Develop Training Programs from the KSA Task Links.   The linkage between the KSAs and tasks provides the foundation for directing training to enhance those KSAs critical to job performance. While the relevance of the training for KSA enhancement is established through the linkage, it has been my experience that it is difficult to disentangle what might be a K, S, or A. This seems particularly true with knowledge and abilities. You can generally train people to acquire new knowledge, but it is more difficult to train them in the ability to use that knowledge wisely.

Person Analysis

Person analysis seeks to answer two questions: Who within the organization needs training, and what kind of training do they need? Most of the assessment questions for person analysis are based on the use of performance appraisal systems, because it is necessary to appraise employees to determine their training needs. Performance appraisal is the subject of Chapter 7, and I will soon discuss issues inherent in its use. For the moment, realize that performance appraisal is typically conducted for two reasons. One is to diagnose the employees' strengths and weaknesses as an aid in their development. The other reason is to evaluate the employee for the purpose of making administrative decisions such as pay raises and promotions. Person analysis is predicated on the diagnostic purpose of performance appraisal and is used as a basis for providing learning experiences helpful to the employee. To the extent that person analysis is directed solely to developmental issues and not administrative ones, there is usually little employee resistance to a person analysis, and some evidence suggests that self-evaluations of ability may be of value in identifying individual training needs (Mabe & West, 1982). Finally, it is possible to direct a person analysis of training needs not only to the present but also to the future in terms of what KSAs need to be learned to reach the next level of the organization. In this case, SMEs, usually upper-level managers, would articulate the KSAs needed to perform future job requirements.

In summary, Ostroff and Ford (1989) concluded that the classic tripartite approach of needs analysis (organization, task, and person) is entrenched in the literature as the foundation upon which all subsequent training issues are based. While these three perspectives are still regarded as a useful framework for determining training needs, the specific content of each continues to evolve over time. The most recent advances in training have demonstrated the critical importance of cues and consequences that promote the transfer of skills from training to the job. We are now more aware of the need to examine factors that enable training to be successfully applied to the job. These factors are just as critical (if not more so) as the specific nature of the training.

Methods and Techniques of Training

After determining an organization's training needs and translating them into objectives, the next step is to design a training program to meet these objectives. This isn't an easy task, as each training method has strengths, weaknesses, and costs. Ideally, we seek the "best" method—the one that meets our objectives in the most cost-efficient manner. Many training methods are available, and they can be classified in a number of ways. Where the training takes place is one important aspect of training, and I have chosen it as the best way to organize this discussion of training methods.

On-Site Training Methods

As the name suggests, on-site methods are conducted on the job site. On-site methods usually involve training in the total job, whereas off-site instruction often involves only part of the job.

FRANK AND ERNEST   SOURCE: Reprinted by permission of Newspaper Enterprise Association, Inc.

On-the-Job Training.   On-the-job training is perhaps the oldest and most common form of instruction. Usually no special equipment or space is needed since new employees are trained at the actual job location. The instructors are usually more established workers, and the employees learn by imitation. They watch an established worker perform a task and try to imitate the behavior. One classic principle of training, *transfer of training,* is maximized by this method. Since the training content and location are the same as the job content, there are usually few problems with transfer.

But on-the-job training has several limitations. It is often brief and poorly structured—often little more than "Watch me, and I'll show you how to do it." Also, many established workers find teaching a new recruit to be a nuisance, and the new employee may be pressured to master the task too quickly. On-the-job training is popular partly because it is so easy to administer. But since many new recruits make mistakes while training, the consequences of error must be evaluated.

Vestibule Training.   Vestibule training is a type of instruction sometimes found in production work. A vestibule consists of training equipment that is set up a short distance from the actual production line. Trainees can practice in the vestibule without getting in the way or slowing down the production line. These special training areas are usually used for skilled and semiskilled jobs, particularly those involving technical equipment. One limitation is that the vestibule is small, so relatively few people can be trained at the same time. The method is good for promoting practice, a learning principle involving the repetition of behavior.

Lefkowitz (1970) describes a study comparing vestibule training with on-the-job training for a sample of sewing machine operators. New employees were divided into four groups. The first three groups received one, two, and three days of vestibule training, respectively. The fourth group spent the first day in vestibule training, the second day in on-the-job training, and the third day back in vestibule training before actually starting work. Results showed that the longer the people were in vestibule training the less likely they were to quit, but their average productivity was slightly lower. The best overall results occurred for the people in the fourth group. Their productivity was at or above the other groups', and they had a relatively low quit rate. Lefkowitz concluded that a combination of the two methods was the most effective way to train sewing machine operators.

Job Rotation. Job rotation is a method of training wherein workers rotate through a variety of jobs. They may be in the same job anywhere from a week to a year before they rotate. Job rotation is used with both blue-collar production workers and white-collar managers, and it has many organizational benefits. It acquaints workers with many jobs in a company and gives them the opportunity to learn by doing. Job rotation creates flexibility; during worker shortages, workers have the skills to step in and fill open slots. The method also provides new and different work on a systematic basis, giving employees a variety of experiences and challenges. Employees also increase their flexibility and marketability because they can perform a wide array of tasks. Campion, Cheraskin, and Stevens (1994) found that job rotation was more common for employees early in their career than later. One explanation for this may be that early-career employees are more interested in rotation because they see it as having higher value to their careers than do older employees. Another explanation is that senior management may view job rotation as a better investment when used with early-career employees (that is, there is a bigger organizational payoff due to a longer payback period).

Like any method, job rotation also has its limitations. If workers are paid on a piece rate or commission basis, they may earn more money on some jobs and less on others; that is, due to individual differences, people are not equally suited for all jobs. Workers are then reluctant to rotate out of their "best" job. Job rotation also challenges one of the basic principles of personnel placement: Assign workers to jobs that best match their talents and interests. Some employees are wary of a training system that puts them in jobs they are not good at or do not like. Workers' willingness to learn new jobs is a key factor in the success of a job rotation system.

Apprentice Training. The apprentice system is one of the oldest types of training programs in existence. It is particularly common in the skilled trades. A new worker is "tutored" by an established worker for a long period (sometimes up to five years). The apprentice serves as an assistant and learns the craft by working with a fully skilled member of the trade called a journeyman. Apprenticeship programs are often used in the plumbing, carpentry, and electrical trades. At the end of the apprenticeship program, the person is "promoted" to journeyman. Training is intense, lengthy, and usually on a one-to-one basis. Usually one apprentice is assigned to one journeyman.

One weakness is that the amount of time an apprenticeship lasts is predetermined by the members of the trade. Individual differences in learning time are generally not allowed, so all apprentices have to work for a fixed time before they are upgraded. It has been argued that the apprentice program should be modified to allow more rapid rates of progression for fast learners (Franklin, 1976).

Off-Site Training Methods

There is more diversity in off-site training methods, and they differ markedly in their content and approach to learning.

Lectures. As all students know, the lecture method is a popular form of instruction in educational institutions. It is also used in industry. With this method, large numbers of people can be taught at the same time. In that sense, it is quite cost efficient. However, the more diversified the audience, the more general the content usually becomes. Hence, its utility for imparting specialized knowledge is more limited. A frequent reaction after a lecture on improving sales techniques is, "That idea sounds okay in principle, but how do I put it into operation in my company?" With a more homogeneous audience, a trainer (or teacher) can direct the lecture to specific topics and techniques; this is often more beneficial than using broad-based material. Thus, lectures can be an effective way to train large numbers of people at once, particularly if they have a specific training need.

On the negative side, lectures are usually one-way communication. There is little chance of dialogue, questions, or discussion of individual problems and special interests. Trainees themselves have to understand and personalize the content of the lecture. The lecture method is weak in such classic training principles as practice, feedback, and transfer. Although popular, lecturing is not the best method to use for skill acquisition.

Audiovisual Material. Audiovisual material covers an array of training techniques, including films, slides, and videotapes. It allows participants to see as well as hear and is usually quite good at capturing their interest. This underscores the importance of motivation and interest as necessary conditions for learning. After the initial expense of creating such a program, the cost of repeated use is minimal. Audiovisual material is particularly useful in training people in a work process or sequence. People can more readily trace the pattern of work flow when it is laid out graphically. Konz and Dickey (1969) demonstrated that a slide presentation was superior to verbal and printed instructions in training employees to complete various assembly operations.

On the negative side, it is difficult to modify these training methods. If the training content changes, a whole new film has to be made. Slide presentations are more easily modified, because the outdated slides can be replaced with more current ones. Also, the production cost of training films can be substantial. A half-hour, color film with a sound track can cost $100,000 to produce. However, if the task or job is very important to the company, the film may be cost effective. With the aid of close-up images, stop action, slow motion, and instant replay, delicate and complex tasks can be broken down into discrete and understandable units.

Videotape is particularly useful in recording employees' job behaviors. Their performance can be taped and then observed and evaluated for effective and ineffective behaviors. This method is excellent for providing feedback or letting people know how they are doing. Many studies (for example, Ilgen, Fisher, & Taylor, 1979) suggest that feedback is an important part of the learning process. Kidd (1961) showed that videotape instruction was useful for training people as overseas diplomatic advisers. They learned more effectively and retained more than people who only read a training manual on the same material. Seeing yourself on videotape can also be a most enlightening (and unnerving) experience. The first time I saw a videotape of one of my lectures, my reaction was, "I look like that?'' I quickly saw my weaknesses as a teacher. With new electronic recording equipment, the use of videotape as a training technique is increasing.

Conferences. The conference method of training stresses two-way communication. It is particularly effective if the ratio of trainees to trainers is not very large. This method is useful when the material needs clarification or elaboration or where a lively discussion would facilitate understanding. Sometimes the lecture method can be followed with a conference discussion, giving the participants a chance to share opinions about the material. The trainer can call on people to see if they understand the material, and participants can ask questions. An effective trainer can get all the participants involved, even the less vocal ones. The success of this method depends heavily on the skills and personality of the discussion leader. A dogmatic, abrasive leader can stifle discussion. A good leader knows when to lead the discussion and when to allow others to lead.

The conference method can draw on the learning principles of motivation and feedback. Stimulated participants readily join in the discussion and then receive feedback on their ideas from others in the group. This method is used to enhance knowledge or attitudinal development. The participants' willingness to acquire new knowledge and explore attitude change (and the trainer's ability to facilitate such learning) influences the success of the method. Perhaps because this method does not usually involve any tangible assets other than people, the attitudes, enthusiasm, and verbal communication skills of the participants affect the outcome more than for any other training method.

Programmed Instruction. Programmed instruction (PI) is a newer method of training, but its origin goes back to the research of learning theorist B. F. Skinner. PI may involve an actual piece of equipment (usually called a teaching machine) or a specially constructed paper booklet. In either case, the method has three main characteristics. First, participants are active in the training process. In fact, they determine their own learning pace. Second, the subject to be learned involves many discrete pieces of material, and the participants get immediate feedback on whether they have learned each piece. Third, the material is divided into an organized sequence.

Developing material for PI takes considerable time. Each segment has to facilitate understanding of the total material covered. Thus, the sequence of material is highly integrated and then verified to ensure that each piece contributes to understanding and that the entire process covers a unified theme. Common features of PI are:

- A single piece of information is presented at each stage or *frame.* All of the frames taken together (however many it takes to present the material) are called a *program.* The first frame deals with the first step in some procedure; in industrial training this is usually a work procedure (like operating a piece of equipment). The frames may involve only one question, or they may involve examining some information given in a figure or diagram. A question is then asked about the diagram. The answer is either true/false or multiple choice.
- The participant gives an answer to the question in the first frame. If the answer

is correct, the participant proceeds to the next frame (by turning a knob on the teaching machine or turning the page in a booklet). If the answer is incorrect, the right answer is given along with an explanation of why it is correct.

- The frames are arranged in the exact sequence that occur in the work process. This step-by-step sequence in learning matches the step-by-step sequence followed in performing the task on the job.
- The participant goes through the program at his or her own pace. Emphasis is placed on correct answers rather than work speed. Some people learn best at a slow pace; others can learn more rapidly.
- The participant proceeds through the entire program. After he or she completes it, the number of correct answers is tabulated (either automatically on the machine or by hand with the booklet). Before training, a criterion of mastery has been set, usually 90% or 95% correct. If the participant reaches that level, training on that program is ended for that participant. If the percentage of correct answers falls below the criterion, the participant repeats the program.

Figure 6–3 shows a sample frame from a PI program designed to train workers on the proper way to lift heavy boxes. PI is used in industry, and also with school-children.

Programmed instruction has many advantages as a training method. Participants get immediate feedback. Because the material is presented in a precise and systematic manner, there are no gaps in the presentation. The participants are active learners; there is a constant exchange of information between the participants and the program. When participants make mistakes, they suffer no embarrassment because they are the only ones who know they erred. Fast learners do not have to wait for slow ones to catch up; slow learners do not always have to try to catch up. Finally, PI is an efficient way to train people on material that is structured and rote. It gives a trainer more time to cover unstructured and ambiguous material with a different method (usually the conference).

On the negative side, developing a PI program is time-consuming. The material has to be broken down into a logical sequence. Each frame has to be checked to be sure it is accurate and contributes to overall learning of the material. Some work procedures are hard to break down into an exact sequence because there may be several correct ways to perform the task. Also, the stability or consistency of a structured task must be considered before developing a PI program. PI has its place in a rapidly changing technological area, but it is not a panacea for all training needs (Brethower, 1976).

Computer-Assisted Instruction

Computer-assisted instruction (CAI) is the most recently developed training method. Once restricted in use to mainframe computers, CAI has expanded with the advent of microcomputers. CAI has been used to teach a wide number of skills ranging from how to speak a foreign language to how to fly a helicopter. One CAI program begins by flashing the words "Good Morning." If the trainee fails to press a key that says "Good Morning" in five seconds, the computer

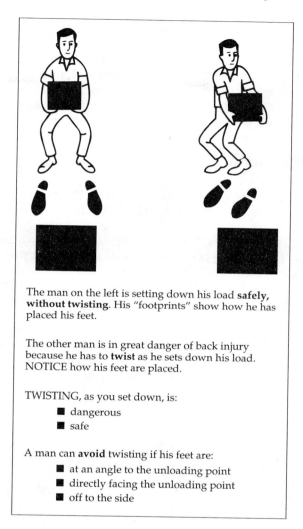

The man on the left is setting down his load **safely, without twisting**. His "footprints" show how he has placed his feet.

The other man is in great danger of back injury because he has to **twist** as he sets down his load. NOTICE how his feet are placed.

TWISTING, as you set down, is:
- dangerous
- safe

A man can **avoid** twisting if his feet are:
- at an angle to the unloading point
- directly facing the unloading point
- off to the side

Figure 6–3 *Sample problem from one of the first programmed instruction safety programs.*
SOURCE: From "A New Approach to Management's Role in Back Safety," 1966, Hicksville, NY: Advanced Learning Systems.

flashes a second message: "What's the matter—kind of grumpy today?" All this has been programmed to make the trainee feel that the computer is not totally impersonal. This, in turn, is designed to enhance motivation.

Hart (1987) describes several advantages to CAI, including individualized instruction, reduced training time, and elimination of travel for training. The advantages to the trainee include being able to work at his or her own pace, to begin and end a lesson when convenient, and to enter a program at his or her current level of achievement. Indeed, Dossett and Hulvershorn (1983) reported the average training time with CAI was less than with the lecture method for training military recruits in electronics. However, training program development lags far behind computer development, and programming for training purposes is still in its early stages. Goldstein (1991) also cautions that successful learning in training systems is not guaranteed by the advent of a new, revolutionary technique alone. It requires careful needs assessment, careful design of training based on those needs, and evaluation efforts to fine-tune the program. While much more work needs to be directed toward fulfilling the potential promise of this method, CAI appears to be a viable technique for enhancing complex skills (see Field Note 1).

Simulation

A simulation is designed to replicate the essential characteristics of the real world necessary to produce learning and transfer. The purpose of the simulation is to produce *psychological fidelity*—that is, to reproduce in the training tasks those KSAs necessary to perform the job. As Goldstein (1991) noted, one important aspect of these simulators is that they permit the environment to be reproduced under the control of the trainer. Environments are created by careful design and planning to provide variation in the essential characteristics of the real situation. Simulation also permits the trainer to expand, compress, or repeat time, depending on the needs of the trainees.

The final behavior to be learned is often too complex to be safely handled by a trainee in a real-life situation. Simulations permit the trainee to be slowly introduced to the essential task characteristics without danger to the trainee, co-workers, or expensive equipment. Simulations also permit the trainee to practice

---

FIELD NOTE 1

Computer-assisted instruction is used by two of my organizational clients. Both companies are in the insurance business and make extensive use of microcomputers. One company continuously works at developing and enhancing its CAI capabilities. It writes new software training programs, conducts analyses of which types of training needs CAI might handle, has developed a CAI library and resource room, and sends some of its employees off to industry-based workshops on the use of CAI. The other company got into CAI as a fad. It purchased some canned CAI programs that it used with some departments. Now those programs are obsolete (because the nature of the insurance business has changed), but the company has not purchased any new programs or taken the time to develop its own. The company has also de-

cided not to purchase any advanced programs to further train those employees who went through the earlier training. Originally treated like a birthday present that captured everybody's interest for a while, CAI fell into disuse once the novelty wore off. For all intents and purposes, CAI is dead as a training method at the second company.

The second company has substantial CAI training material and doesn't know what to do with it. The first company, however, made enough of a commitment in the method to retain its value as a training tool. Like all methods, CAI has to be maintained and adjusted over time. Training methods that are adopted as quick fixes usually wind up stored in the company attic or eventually thrown in the trash bin.

emergency procedures before being exposed to hazardous situations in real life. Flight simulations, for example, manifest a high degree of physical fidelity—the accurate representation of the real world of operational equipment. Flight simulations are so complex that nearly all aspects of flight training can be accomplished on them. Goldberg, Mastaglio, and Johnson (1995) described the development of the Distributed Interactive Simulation (DIS) used by the military to train armor and mechanized infantry units in weapons systems. The DIS combines aviation, combat engineers, air defense, and field artillery simulators to represent the combined arms battlefield.

Many simulations use games. Business games train employees in certain skills. Within the rules of the game, participants try to meet the exercise's stated objectives. Business games can be used to train individuals or groups. Games have been developed to simulate interpersonal relations problems, financial and budgeting issues, and resource allocation decisions. Participants are told the objective (for example, to reach a certain profit level or to maximize financial return with a fixed budget) and then are evaluated on whether they achieve it. Business games are popular for training managers and executives, particularly in financial matters.

A problem with simulations that have a game component is that the participants know it is only a game. Failing at a game is not the same as failing on the job. Participants sometimes behave differently than they would in real life. For example, in a marketing course a business game was created to simulate marketing a product. The class was divided into work teams. The team that showed the greatest profit at the end of the semester received an award. Within the rules of the game (advertising the product, spending on research to improve the product, and so on), the "sales volume" of each work team was posted weekly. As the weeks went by, some work teams gradually fell behind in profit, and members of the losing teams began to take unnatural risks with their companies—risks they probably would not have taken on a real job. They did not care if their actions failed (the company went bankrupt) because it was only a game. And if their wild risks came through, they would receive the award. In this case the game did not include some key components found on the job. Unlike a semester, the life span of a real company does not end on a predetermined date. The consequences of losing one's job (as well as destroying a company) are not the same as simply failing to win a class award. The best simulations are "best" because they provide for a high degree of transfer of training to the actual job. Needless to say, some simulations are easier than others to construct to maximize this transfer.

Role Playing.   Role playing is a training method often aimed at enhancing either human relations skills or sales techniques. As opposed to programmed instruction, which is deliberately geared to the individual, role playing involves many people. Cooke (1987) asserts that role playing is used to demonstrate various skills and concepts in interpersonal relating and communications. The enactment is normally followed by a discussion to determine what happened and why. Participants suggest how the problem could be handled more effectively in the future.

Role playing is less tightly structured than acting, where performers have to say set lines on cue. Participants are assigned roles in the scenario to be enacted. For example, the scenario may be a department store. One person takes the role of an irate customer who is dissatisfied with a recently purchased product. A second person might be assigned the role of the clerk who has to attend to the customer's complaint. Aside from observing some general guidelines about the product, the participants are free to act out their roles however they wish. Their performance is judged by people who do not have an active part in the role playing. In an educational setting the observers may be other students in the class; in a business setting they might be supervisors.

Many variations of role playing are possible. In some exercises participants repeat the enactment several times but switch roles. In other cases participants reverse the role they play in real life—for example, the supervisor plays a union representative. The role forces the participant to adopt the other side's position and then defend it.

Goldstein (1980) describes advances with a technique called behavioral role modeling, which uses role playing as one of its parts. In behavioral role modeling, some points or principles to be stressed in training are identified. The participants watch a model use the principles (often on film) and then rehearse the principles by role playing. The trainer and other group members provide social reinforcement. Latham and Saari (1979) reported a study of behavioral role modeling that was designed to increase interpersonal skills in dealing with employees. Forty first-line supervisors were assigned to either the modeling group or a control group, which received another form of training to meet the same objectives. Results showed that the supervisors trained with behavioral role modeling were more impressed with the training, scored higher on a learning test six months after training, and were judged to be performing better on the job a year later.

The advantages of role playing include the fact that participants are highly active. By "putting their feet in the other person's shoes," participants gain some understanding of what it is like to experience interpersonal conflict in someone else's position. Interpersonal relations skills are among the more difficult ones to enhance with any method. Despite legitimate criticism that some people put more emphasis on acting than problem solving, the method has been quite useful.

Management Development Issues

Management development is the process by which individuals learn to perform effectively in managerial roles. Organizational interest in management development is due in large part to a recognition of its value as a strategy to improve organizational performance. Kotter (1988) argues that the one factor that seems to distinguish excellent companies from others is the amount of time and energy spent in planning, designing, and executing development activities. Baldwin and Padgett (1993) estimate that more than 90% of organizations worldwide engage in some form of development activities for managers. The literature on management development tends to focus on major issues or processes managers address as part of their professional maturation, whereas the literature on personnel training is more concerned with specific methods or techniques of training. However, the larger systems issues of needs assessment, skill enhancement, and transfer are equally applicable to both training and development.

Whetten and Cameron (1991) identified critical management skills and linked them to successful performance on the job. Three *personal skills* were noted: developing self-awareness, managing stress, and solving problems creatively. Four *interpersonal* skills were also identified: communicating supportively, gaining power and influence, motivating others, and managing conflict. The authors point our that these skills overlap and that managers must draw on all of them to perform effectively in a managerial role. Yukl, Wall, and Lepsinger (1990) developed a survey that assesses managerial practices based on these skills. Subordinates and peers describe how much a manager uses these practices and make recommendations on whether the manager's behavioral style should be modified. Managers compare this feedback to their own self-assessment of behavior. Ratings of the importance of these behaviors for the manager's job provide additional information for identifying relevant development activities. Lombardo and McCauley (1988) have proposed that underutilization of selected managerial skills and practices contributes to *derailment*. Derailment occurs when a manager who has been judged to have the ability to go higher fails to live up to his or her full potential and is fired, demoted, or plateaued below expected levels of achievement.

There is also considerable interest in gender differences in management development (Ragins & Sundstrom, 1989). Many organizations have created a managerial hierarchy—composed predominantly of men—which is thought to be a critical structural feature influencing the processes affecting men's and women's managerial advancement. There is evidence that a "glass ceiling" exists for women in their professional advancement through an organization. The existence of this transparent barrier is fostered by organizations that regulate access to developmental experiences as part of a pattern that grooms men for powerful positions. Tharenou, Latimer, and Conroy (1994) reported that development activities had a more positive influence on the managerial advancement of men than women. Men, especially those between the ages of 35 and 54, were more likely than women to attend company-sponsored training courses. Development may lead to advancement for more men than women because men are thought to gain more skills and knowledge from professional development than women do. In turn, men gain skills and knowledge that are more relevant to managerial work, thus becoming better prepared for advancement than women. Organizations need to ensure that women's contributions of education, work experience, and development are perceived as similarly conducive to productivity as men's and, thus, are rewarded with similar advancement.

Four issues of contemporary relevance to the management development process are deserving of discussion. They are cultural diversity, sexual harassment, 360-degree feedback, and the mentoring process.

Cultural Diversity Training

Triandis, Kurowski, and Gelfand (1994) offered an insightful analysis of the consequences of our nation's increasing cultural heterogeneity or diversity. However, dealing with diversity is not a novel issue in this country, as cultural diversity has characterized this nation since its founding. What is novel about modern diversity issues is that managers are encountering it more frequently both within their organizations (their employees) and among their customers. Changes in the composition of the work force are being driven by labor and market trends, legislation, and demographics. Multinational companies increasingly have multinational management, with some top managers from the companies' homelands and some from other countries. The composition of the work force is also changing in the United States at the entry level. White men, who traditionally have constituted the majority of new entrants into the labor force, will be a minority among the new entrants by the year 2000 (Goldstein & Gilliam, 1990). Likewise, the Americans with Disabilities Act may usher in an increase in the percentages of disabled workers.

Historically, there have been two ways to approach cultural differences. One is the color-blind perspective (Ferdman, 1992), which advocates ignoring cultural differences. Its basic rationale is "Do not pay attention to differences." The second approach accepts the presence of cultural differences and proposes to improve relationships by teaching people from each culture to appreciate the perspective of people from other cultures. Research indicates that both perspectives have merit, and an optimal approach may emphasize both what people universally have in common and what makes them different. Triandis and associates (1994) suggest that approximately half of all psychological theories are universally relevant—the other half are the product of Western cultures. The task of cross-cultural psychology is to sort out the two halves.

Triandis (1975) suggested that the ideal problem-solving group is diverse, including members who have been trained to understand the others' point of view. However, diversity has a price: Communication becomes more difficult, and interpersonal attraction is likely to be lower. To increase interpersonal attraction, Triandis recommends individuals be trained to view the behavior of members of other cultures as functional and reasonable within a particular environment. That is, to be able to say, "If I faced that set of circumstances, I would also behave that way." Such a process produces a sense of *similarity* across culturally diverse people, where the psychological processes of adoption are similar but the situations are different. By emphasizing similarities, attraction can be created in two ways: by showing that there are universals and by indicating that the existing cultural differences "make sense."

The goal of diversity training programs is to reduce barriers such as values, stereotypes, and managerial practices that constrain employee contribution to organizational goals and personal development (Noe & Ford, 1992). Diversity training programs differ on the basis of whether attitude or behavior change is emphasized to achieve these goals.

Attitude change programs focus on an awareness of diversity and the personal factors that most strongly influence our behavior toward others. Many programs involve self-assessment of perceived similarities and differences between different groups of employees and attributions for success and failure of minority employees. These programs may also use videotapes and experiential exercises to increase employees' awareness of the negative effects of stereotypes on minority group members. It is assumed that eventually this heightened awareness will result in behavior change.

The *behavioral change approach* emphasizes changing organizational policies and individual behaviors that limit employee productivity. Programs with a behavioral emphasis identify incidents that discourage employees from working to their potential. Perceptions regarding the degree to which the work environment and management practices are congruent with a philosophy of valuing differences among employees are often collected. Specific training programs are then directed at developing employee skills that are needed to create a workplace that supports diversity.

Rynes and Rosen (1995) conducted a major survey of human resource professionals about diversity issues in their organizations. Organizations that had successfully adopted diversity programs had strong support from top management and placed high priority on diversity relative to other competing organizational objectives. Diversity training success was also associated with mandating attendance for all managers, long-term evaluation of training results, managerial rewards for increasing diversity, and a broad inclusionary definition of what is meant by diversity in the organization.

Ronen (1989) discussed a more specialized area of cultural diversity training, that of the individual assigned to an international position. The need for such training has increased for two reasons. One is the increase in the number of individuals so assigned, while the second is the relatively high failure rate of managers in such assignments. Dotlich (1982) reported the difficulties U.S. managers encountered when they lived or traveled abroad on overseas assignments. The following two quotes were representative of the findings:

> Time as a cultural value is something which we don't understand until we are in another culture. It took me six months to accept the fact that my staff meeting wouldn't begin on time and more often would start thirty minutes late and nobody would be bothered but me. (p. 28)

> Communication can be a problem. I had to learn to speak at half the speed I normally talk. (p. 28)

Another problem area is that of family members adjusting to a different physical or cultural environment. From a study of internationally assigned managers from many countries, Arthur and Bennett (1995) determined that family support was the critical factor in accounting for successful international assignments. The results suggest the advisability of including one's spouse and other family members in cross-cultural training and, if feasible, sending them overseas to preview their new environment. Ronen identified four abilities considered critical for successful overseas assignments: tolerance for ambiguity, behavioral flexibility, nonjudgmentalism, and cultural empathy. The selection decision for overseas assignments is usually predicated on the candidate's technical skills in applied functional areas (such as engineering or finance), but the reasons for a failed assignment have little to do with deficient technical skills. Major areas recommended for enhancement through training include information about the host country's geography, political system, history, religion, and generalized customs and habits. It is also recommended that managers learn to understand their own tendencies regarding listening ability, reaction to feedback, and predisposition toward judgmental attitudes. Black and Mendenhall (1990) suggested that cultural novelty, expected degree of interpersonal interaction in the foreign assignment, and the novelty of new jobs and tasks are situational factors likely to influence the appropriateness and effectiveness of cross-cultural training.

Hesketh and Bochner (1994) have proposed that the process of cultural adjustment be viewed as a special case of being socially skilled, reflecting the more basic principle that when individuals interact they are engaged in a mutually organized, skilled performance. *Social competence* is the ability to produce the desired effects on others in social situations. Individuals who are socially inadequate have not mastered the conventions of their society either because they are unaware of the prevailing rules of social behavior or because they are unwilling to abide by them. Therefore, success in international assignments is posited to be a function of the capacity and willingness to learn new social skills. Many specific work-related social skills and attitudes are highly culture-based. For example, Adler, Doktor, and Redding (1986) reported that the Japanese prefer to go from the general to the specific, whereas Westerners like to get the details out of the way before tackling larger issues. Other cultural differences exist with regard to strategies of conflict resolution, bargaining style, and cognitive information processing. Training in social skills can be developed to teach specific culturally relevant behaviors designed to enhance the person's repertoire.

The emphasis on cultural diversity training seems attributable in part to two general factors. One is the increasing awareness of our "differentness" as people, while the second is the reality that we all have to get along with each other to have an amicable and productive society. In a sense it is somewhat of a paradox— seeking ways to find similarities among differences. I believe the importance of addressing this paradox will intensify in the years to come.

Sexual Harassment

The Equal Employment Opportunity Commission (1980) defines sexual harassment as:

> Unwelcome sexual advances, requests for sexual favors, and other verbal or physical conduct of a sexual nature when submission to or rejection of this conduct explicitly or implicitly affects an individual's employment, unreasonably interferes with an individual's work performance, or creates an intimidating, hostile, or offensive work environment.

This definition outlines the two kinds of sexual harassment actionable under federal law: *quid pro quo* sexual harassment and hostile environment harassment.

Quid pro quo harassment occurs when sexual compliance is made mandatory for promotion, favors, or retaining one's job. In the vast majority of cases on this issue, females rather than males have suffered from sexual abuse at work. Such abuse may constitute illegal sex discrimination in the form of unequal treatment on the job. More than 12,500 complaints were filed with the EEOC in 1993, and the cost of investigating and resolving claims of sexual harassment is in the millions of dollars annually. Sexual harassment is not so much about sex as it is about power and the power differentials between managers and employees (Cleveland & Kerst, 1993). Organizations are devoting considerable training resources to deter the likelihood of sexual harassment in the workplace.

Much of the research on sexual harassment has focused on how men and women define it and whether men's definitions differ markedly from women's. Gutek (1985) reported women consistently were more likely than men to label a behavior as sexual harassment. Men and women tend to disagree on whether uninvited sexual teasing, jokes, remarks, or questions represent sexual harassment. Generally, as an act becomes more overt and coercive, women and men are more likely to agree that it is sexual harassment.

Tangri, Burt, and Johnson (1982) described three models used to explain sexual harassment: the natural/biological model, the organizational model, and the sociocultural model. The *natural/biological model* asserts that sexual harassment is simply natural sexual attraction between two people. The *organizational model* argues that sexual harassment is the result of certain opportunities created by the organizational climate, hierarchy, and specific authority relationships. The *sociocultural model* states that sexual harassment reflects the larger society's differential distribution of power and status between the sexes. A test of these models revealed that all three approaches received some empirical support, which led to the conclusion that there is no single explanation for sexual harassment. Gutek, Cohen, and Konrad (1990) proposed a model that includes frequency of interaction between the sexes. They found more sexual harassment in environments where workers had more contact with the opposite sex. Because women are more likely to work with many men than men are to work with many women, women are more likely to be sexually harassed.

Physical attractiveness has also been examined as a factor influencing third-party judgments of sexual harassment. Quinn and Lees (1984) asserted that personnel departments are less likely to take seriously sexual harassment complaints from unattractive female employees than from attractive women. Castellow, Wuensch, and Moore (1990) found that female sexual harassment victims are more likely to win lawsuits against their harassers when the victims are attractive and the harassers are unattractive.

Training in the area of sexual harassment frequently consists of teaching sensitivity to other people's values and preferences. It should not be assumed, for example, that people prefer to be touched (as on the hand or arm) when engaged in conversation. There are also broad cultural differences in the degree to which physical contact between people is regarded as acceptable. There are also differences among people in the degree to which verbal statements, including profanity, are considered offensive or inappropriate. One organizational response to fear of allegations of sexual harassment is to engage in highly defensive behavior, including having a third party present when talking with a member of the opposite sex and interacting with people only in an open, highly visible work area. Other examples include prohibitions on any comments regarding physical appearance (for example, "those are attractive shoes you are wearing") and the reciprocal exchange of gifts among employees on special occasions (for example, flowers or cards on birthdays). Other defensive behaviors are more personalized, such as a male manager refusing to mentor any female protégé. Lobel (1993) has questioned the long-term benefit of these types of prohibitions on male/female relationships in the workplace. In an attempt to limit opportunities for potentially sexual harassing behaviors to occur, Lobel believes that we may also be precluding opportunities for beneficial across-gender relationships to develop. This issue is likely to become a focus of vigorous debate in the years ahead.

360-Degree Feedback

The practice of involving multiple raters, often including self-ratings, in the assessment of individuals is called 360-degree feedback. Typically, feedback about a target manager is solicited from significant others, including the individual's co-workers, subordinates, and superiors. The primary purpose for 360-degree feedback is to enhance managers' awareness of their strengths and weaknesses to guide developmental planning. According to Tornow (1993), 360-degree assessment activities are usually based on two key assumptions: (1) that awareness of any discrepancies between how we see ourselves and how others see us enhances self-awareness, and (2) that enhanced self-awareness is a key to maximum performance as a manager and thus becomes a foundation block for management and leadership development programs.

The name "360-degree feedback" derives from the geometric-shaped rationale for the multiple-rater assessment as shown in Figure 6–4. The target manager is evaluated by other individuals who interact in a social network. The target manager also provides self-assessments. The typical assessment will include evaluations along three dimensions (Van Velsor, Ruderman, & Young, 1991):

- *people:* dealing effectively with people, building good relationships.
- *change:* setting, communicating, and implementing a goal or vision.
- *structure:* structuring and organizing information, time, and work.

The multiple raters would make their assessments of an individual, and then the assessments would be compared. Van Velsor et al. (1991) reported the following findings from their study. These findings are representative of most 360-degree feedback studies:

- Only 10% of the managers saw themselves as others saw them; the rest had substantial discrepancies (that is, more than half of a standard deviation) on one, two, or three of the scales.
- Overrating oneself was the most common profile across scales. This difference was especially noteworthy in the *people* scale, where overrating was almost twice as common as underrating oneself, or showing self-other agreement.

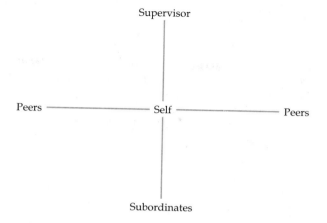

Figure 6–4   *360-degree feedback relationships*

- About 80% of the managers modified their self-assessment in the expected direction on one or more scales after feedback. This change was most pronounced in the area of interpersonal skills.

It is particularly instructive to understand how *disagreement* among raters in 360-degree feedback is interpreted. The classic measurement perspective treats disagreement among raters as error variance; that is, something undesirable that reduces inter-rater reliability. With 360-degree feedback, differences in rater perspective are regarded as potentially valuable and useful and are *not* treated as variation to be reduced. Such differences are treated as an opportunity for professional development and personal learning to understand why individuals are perceived as they are by others.

How important is it that managers see themselves as others see them? Nilsen and Campbell (1993) proposed that job performance is a function of an individual's aptitude, task understanding, decision about how intensely to work, decision about how long to persist in the face of obstacles, and facilitating or inhibiting conditions not under the individual's control. Self-assessments are important because individual's make judgments about themselves relevant to these determinants of performance. Individuals have beliefs about their level of aptitude and whether or not they understand the task they are being asked to perform. If individuals overestimate their aptitude, they will devote less effort to the task than is needed to perform it adequately. Additionally, if individuals believe that they fully understand a task, they will probably devote little or no effort to obtaining additional task-relevant information. If, however, the individuals do not in fact understand what is expected, they may utilize their aptitude and devote their effort, yet still fail to perform the task correctly.

In general, it appears that accurate self-assessors are better able to improve their performance than are inaccurate self-assessors. Self-awareness and self-perception are becoming recognized as critical factors in determining managerial job performance, a job which typically entails working with many other people. However, the issue of exactly what people agree or disagree on is not totally clear. Moses, Hollenbeck, and Sorcher (1993) proposed that it is not simply agreement among people's *observations* that contributes to effective job performance but rather agreement among people's *expectations* of behavior. Thus self-aware managers are knowledgeable of the expectations placed on them by others, including the likelihood that differential expectations will be held by subordinates, peers, and superiors. Dunnette (1993) concluded that 360-degree feedback offers an opportunity to enhance understanding of managerial behavior. Furthermore, the concept provides new methods for identifying areas of individual need for improvement in managerial skills.

Mentoring

A largely successful and frequently used method of facilitating management development is mentoring. *Mentors* are older, more experienced individuals who advise and shepard new people in the formative years of their careers. They are professionally paternalistic and serve in a "godparent" role. Hunt and Michael (1983) discovered four stages of the mentor relationship. First is the initiation phase, where the more powerful and professionally recognized mentor accepts the apprentice as a protégé. The second is the protégé phase, where the apprentice's work is recognized not for its own merit but as the by-product of the mentor's instruction, support, or advice. The third is the breakup stage, where the protégé goes off on his or her own. If the mentor/protégé relationship has not been successful, this will be the final stage. However, if it has been successful, both parties continue on to the lasting-friendship stage. Here the mentor and the protégé have more of a peerlike relationship. The protégé may become a mentor but does not sever ties with the former mentor.

Noe (1988) determined that there are two major dimensions to the mentoring relationship. One is psychosocial, where the mentor serves as a role model who provides counseling, acceptance, and coaching. The other dimension is job-related, where the mentor provides exposure and visibility, sponsorship, and challenging assignments to augment the protégé's career. Most studies report positive results from mentoring. Fagenson (1989) found that mentored individuals had more satisfaction, increased career mobility and opportunity, more recognition, and a higher promotion rate than nonmentored individuals. Similarly, Dreher and Ash (1990) found that individuals who experienced extensive mentoring relationships had higher incomes and were more satisfied with their pay and benefits than individuals who experienced less extensive mentoring relationships. Chao, Walz, and Gardner (1992) demonstrated that informal mentoring programs (for example, a senior-level and junior-level manager found to share similar goals and values) produced more career-related support for the protégé than formal mentoring programs (for example, a pool of potential protégés submit resumés for review by a "match-maker committee"). Personality conflicts and lack of mentor commitment are more likely to occur with assigned mentors than with informal mentors unless the assigned mentors are carefully selected and trained.

Research has also been directed to across-race and across-gender mentoring issues. Thomas (1990) reported white protégés had almost no developmental relationships with persons of another race. Blacks were more likely than whites to form relationships outside the formal lines of authority and their own departments. Same-race relationships were found to provide significantly more psychosocial support than across-race relationships.

Thomas (1993) concluded that the preferred strategy of each party for dealing with racial difference (either denying and suppressing it or discussing it openly) and whether both parties preferred the same strategy influenced the kind of relationship that developed. In some relationships the senior person merely became a sponsor for the protégé, providing career support through advocacy for promotions, feedback, and coaching. In other cases the senior person became a true mentor, offering psychosocial support and friendship along with instrumental career support. Ragins and McFarlin (1990) found that across-gender protégés were less likely than same-gender protégés to report engaging in after-work social activities with their mentors. Compared to other gender combinations, female protégées with female mentors were more likely to agree with the idea that their mentors served a role-modeling function. Ragins and Cotton (1991) reported that women were more likely than men to report restricted access to mentors, in part because initiating a relationship with a mentor might be misinterpreted as a sexual advance.

Given the sensitivity of gender issues and the power differential between senior- and junior-level managers, females may be more likely than males to pursue peer relationships to facilitate their career development. Kram and Isabella (1985) described how peer relationships are important. They identified three types of peers. One is the *information peer,* a person with whom you can exchange information about work in the organization. You share a low level of disclosure and trust, and there is little mutual emotional support. The second type is the *collegial peer,* with whom you have a moderate level of trust and engage in some self-disclosure. Collegial peers provide increased emotional support and feedback and engage in more intimate discussions. The third type is the *special peer,* with whom there are no pretenses or formal roles. You reveal ambivalence and personal dilemmas as you would to few other people in your life. You need not limit peer relationships to members of the same sex, but special peers will most likely be of your sex. Furthermore, the value of peer relationships to career development is not limited to females. However, because of the constraints females have in mentoring relationships, the importance of the peer relationship in career development is accentuated for women.

Posttraining Environment

Tannenbaum and Yukl (1992) noted that the effectiveness of a training program can be influenced by events that occur after a trainee returns to the job. Some employees leave training with new skills and with strong intentions to apply those skills to their jobs, but limitations in the posttraining environment interfere with the actual transfer of training.

Transfer of training can be defined as the extent to which trainees effectively apply the knowledge, skills, and attitudes gained in a training context back to the job. Baldwin and Ford (1988) have noted the distinction between *generalization,* or the extent to which trained skills and behaviors are exhibited in the transfer setting, and *maintenance,* or the length of time that trained skills and behaviors continue to be used on the job. They believe that supervisory support is a major environmental factor that can affect the transfer process. In the posttraining environment, supervisor support could include reinforcement, modeling of trained behaviors, and goal-setting activities. Another factor that could influence transfer is the extent to which the posttraining environment provides opportunities for trainees to apply what they have learned. Ford, Quinones, Sego, and Speer (1991) studied technical trainees after they completed training and found significant differences in opportunities to apply the training and wide variations in the length of time before trainees first performed the tasks for which they had been trained. Tracey, Tannenbaum, and Kavanagh (1995) concluded that posttraining knowledge and behavior were more likely to be transferred to the job in organizations that had strong social support systems. Specifically, transfer of training was enhanced in organizations that regarded themselves as having a culture that recognized the importance of continuous learning.

Some studies have examined whether transfer is facilitated by relapse-prevention training, an approach derived from research on physical addictions (Marx, 1982). Relapse-prevention training is designed to prepare trainees for the posttraining environment and to anticipate and cope with "high risk" situations. Marx and Karren (1988) found that trainees who received relapse-prevention training after a regular training seminar demonstrated more of the trained behaviors than trainees without relapse-prevention training.

It appears that limitations in the posttraining environment may inhibit the application of skills acquired during training (see Field Note 2). Furthermore, supervisory actions taken after one training course may become pretraining cues for subsequent training courses. Tannenbaum and Yukl (1992) recommend that the transfer environment be examined carefully to identify situational facilitators and inhibitors and that trainees should be prepared to deal with the inhibitors or the posttraining environment should be modified to encourage transfer.

Evaluation of Training Programs

As is the case with any assessment or evaluation, some measure of performance must be obtained. Measures of performance refer to criteria, and the criteria used to evaluate training are just as important as those used in personnel selection. Relevance, reliability, and freedom from bias are all important considerations. One distinction between criteria used in personnel selection and criteria used to evaluate training is that training criteria are more varied and are used to evaluate multiple aspects of a training program.

Criteria

Kirkpatrick (1976) identified four levels of criteria used to evaluate training programs: reaction, learning, behavior, and results.

Reaction criteria are the participants' reactions to the program. These criteria measure impressions and feelings about the training; for example, did they believe it was useful or added to their knowledge? Reaction criteria are treated as a measure of the face validity of the training program. Most trainers believe that initial receptivity provides a good atmosphere for learning in the instructional program, but as Goldstein (1991) cautioned, it does not necessarily cause high levels of learning. An evaluation form used to assess participants' reactions is shown in Figure 6–5.

Learning criteria evaluate how much has been learned in the training program. A final exam given at the end of a training program is an example of a learning criterion. With some training methods, such as programmed instruction, the learning criterion is built right into the program; the participant must reach a certain level of proficiency (for example, 90% correct) before training is complete. With other methods, such as role playing directed at improving attitudinal skills,

---

FIELD NOTE 2

When I was in graduate school, I helped a professor with a study of the coal mining industry. Many on-the-job accidents occurred in coal mines, and our assignment was to develop a safety training program to reduce them. My personal assignment was to observe and interview the coal miners about their work. While down in the mines, I noticed that the miners engaged in dangerous behaviors, such as not wearing their hard hats, leaving off their masks (which filtered out coal dust), and smoking in the mine (where an open flame could trigger an explosion). In addition to being unsafe, some of these behaviors were blatant violations of safety rules.

After the miners finished their work shifts, I interviewed them about their jobs. I was particularly interested in why they did such seemingly hazardous things. Since our goal was to develop a training program that would reduce accidents, I felt that eliminating these unsafe behaviors would be an obvious place to start. So I asked them why they didn't wear safety equipment at times. I did not expect their answer. They said they believed there was no relationship between what they did in the mine and what happened to them. They felt their lives

were in the hands of luck, fate, or God, and it did not really matter how they conducted themselves. They all seemed to have personal anecdotes about other miners who were extremely safety conscious (that is, always wore all the safety equipment and were exceedingly cautious people in general) yet suffered serious injuries or death in accidents through no fault of their own, such as a cave-in. In short, the miners were highly fatalistic. They believed that if "your number was up," you would get hurt or killed, and there was nothing you could do about it. While a hard hat was a fine thing to wear, it would not do much good if five tons of rock fell on you. Therefore, they were not interested in engaging in safe behavior, because their behavior did not matter one way or the other.

This experience taught me many lessons about training. The major one is, if people are not motivated to learn new behaviors, it is pointless to try. The coal miners simply did not want to learn new behaviors, because in their minds their lives and welfare were determined by factors beyond their control. Trainers are like chefs: They can prepare the finest meals, but they cannot make you eat if you are not hungry.

ACME TRAINING PROGRAM

Trainer _____   Subject _____
Date _____

1. Was the subject pertinent to your needs and interests?

   ☐ No   ☐ To some extent   ☐ Very much so

2. How was the ratio of lecture to discussion?

   ☐ Too much lecture   ☐ OK   ☐ Too much discussion

3. Rate the leader on the following:

	Excellent	Very Good	Good	Fair	Poor
A. How well did he/she state objectives?					
B. How well did he/she keep the session alive and interesting?					
C. How well did he/she use the blackboard, charts, and other aids?					
D. How well did he/she summarize during the session?					
E. How well did he/she maintain a friendly and helpful manner?					
F. How well did he/she illustrate and clarify the points?					
G. How was his/her summary at the close of the session?					

What is your overall rating of the leader?

☐ Excellent   ☐ Very Good   ☐ Good   ☐ Fair   ☐ Poor

4. What would have made the session more effective?

_____

_____

_____
Signature (optional)

Figure 6–5   *Participant evaluation form*

SOURCE: Adapted from "Evaluation of Training" by D. L. Kirkpatrick, 1976, in *Training and Development Handbook*, 2nd ed., R. L. Craig (Ed.), New York: McGraw-Hill. Copyright © 1976. Used by permission.

there may be no formal evaluation of how much was learned; or participants might simply be asked if they changed their attitudes because of the training. Collectively, reaction and learning criteria are called *internal criteria*; that is, they refer to assessments internal to the training program itself.

Behavioral criteria refer to actual changes in performance once the employee is back on the job. These criteria address such questions as, "To what extent are the desired changes in the job behaviors of the trainee realized by the training program?" If the goal of the training program is to increase production, the behavioral criterion assesses output before and after training. Other types of behavioral criteria include absenteeism, scrap rate, accidents, and grievances. All of these are *objective criteria*. They can be measured easily and have relatively clear meaning (see discussion in Chapter 3). But if the goal of the training program is to increase managers' sensitivity toward hiring the handicapped, "increased sensitivity" has to be translated into some objective behavioral criteria. Also, note that scores on learning criteria and on behavioral criteria do not always correspond. Some people who perform well in training do not transfer their new knowledge or skills back to the job. This is particularly true with training programs aimed at changing attitudes or feelings.

Results criteria refer to the economic value of the training program to the company. Cascio (1989) developed a procedure to apply utility analysis to the assessment of training outcomes. One premise is that if the training program has any effect, the average job performance of the trained group should exceed that of the untrained group. Cascio proposes use of a break-even analysis to determine that the economic value of the training program to the organization is greater than zero. Utility analyses are based on a careful assessment of the costs associated with developing training, training materials, training time, and production losses. While such analyses are often difficult to perform, the failure to analyze training programs in dollars makes it more likely that training will be viewed as a cost rather than as a benefit to the organization. Collectively, behavioral and results criteria are called *external criteria*; they are evaluations external to the training program itself.

Consideration of all four of these criteria sometimes produces different conclusions about the effectiveness of training than a judgment reached by considering just one or two criteria. For example, Campion and Campion (1987) compared two methods for improving a person's interview skills. An experimental group received multiple instruction techniques on improving their interview skills, while a control group engaged in self-study of relevant material. The results revealed that the experimental group performed better on reaction and learning criteria, but the two groups were equivalent with regard to behavioral and results criteria. Alliger and Janak (1989) concluded that training criteria are causally related; that is, attitudes toward training influence how much is learned and to what extent behavior is changed.

A survey conducted by Catalanello and Kirkpatrick (1968) revealed how companies evaluate their human relations training programs using four types of criteria. Out of 110 organizations responding to the survey, 78% attempted to measure trainee reactions, and about 50% attempted to assess learning, behavior, or results criteria. The results of the survey are shown in Figure 6–6. A large number of companies tried to assess learning before and after training, but they

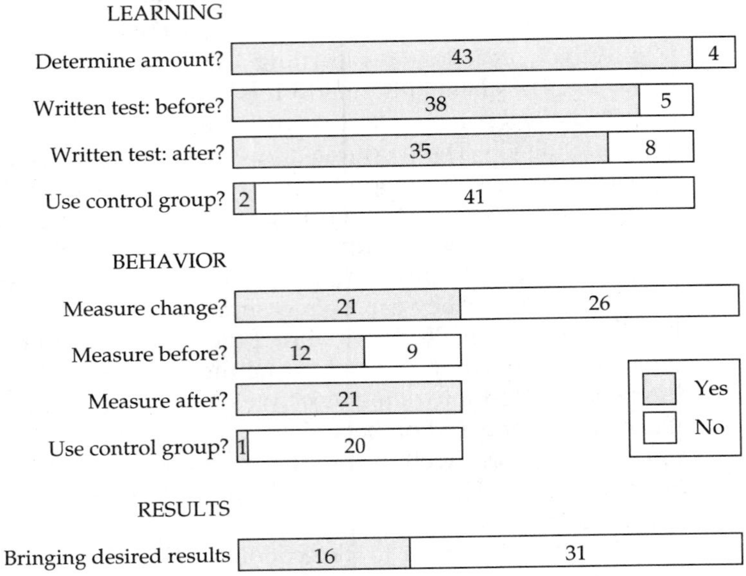

LEARNING

Determine amount?	43	4
Written test: before?	38	5
Written test: after?	35	8
Use control group?	2	41

BEHAVIOR

Measure change?	21	26
Measure before?	12	9
Measure after?	21	
Use control group?	1	20

☐ Yes
☐ No

RESULTS

Bringing desired results	16	31

Figure 6–6 *Evaluation of human relations training programs*

SOURCE: From "Evaluating Training Programs: The State of the Art" by R. E. Catalanello and D. L. Kirkpatrick, 1968 (May), *Training and Development Journal*, 22, pp. 2–9. Copyright © 1968 by Training and Development Journal, American Society for Training and Development. Reprinted by permission. All rights reserved.

were less involved with measuring change in behavior. Results of human relations training are disappointing; 31 of 47 companies reported that they did not achieve the desired results. But note that control groups were rarely used, which indicates that companies seldom used adequate experimental designs. (More will be said about experimental designs shortly.) Saari, Johnson, McLaughlin, and Zimmerle (1988) examined the management training practices of 1,000 U.S. companies. Less than one-third conducted a needs assessment to determine the training needs of their managers. Relatively few companies attempted to evaluate training programs and, among those that did, most evaluations assessed only the participants' reactions to training.

Goldstein (1978) illustrated the importance of assessing training effectiveness from multiple perspectives. He created some hypothetical complaints to show the many viewpoints by which the success of any training program can be judged:

From a trainee: "There is a conspiracy. I just finished my training program. I even completed a pretest and a posttest. My posttest score was significantly better than the scores of my friends in the on-the-job control group. However, I lost my job because I could not perform the work."

From a trainer: "There is a conspiracy. Everyone praised our training program. They said it was the best training program they ever attended. The trainees even had a chance to laugh a little. Now the trainees tell me that management will not let them perform their jobs the way we trained them."

From an administrative officer in the company: "There is a conspiracy. My competition used the training program, and it worked for them. They saved a million. I took it straight from their manuals, and my employees still cannot do the job."

Each of these people asserts that the program did not have the intended effect.
Goldstein (1991) says that the validity of any training program can be assessed along four dimensions:

- *Training validity.* Did the trainees match the criteria established for them in the training program? This dimension is concerned with what Kirkpatrick (1976) referred to as internal criteria and addresses the extent to which the trainees mastered the training.
- *Transfer validity.* Did the trainees match the criteria for success when they were back on the job? This dimension involves external criteria and addresses the extent to which employee performance on the job was enhanced by training.
- *Intraorganizational validity.* Is the training program equally effective with different groups of trainees within the same organization? This dimension is concerned with the internal generalizability of the training, such as the effectiveness of sensitivity training for sales versus production workers in the same organization.
- *Interorganizational validity.* Is the training program equally effective with different trainees in companies other than the one that developed the training program? This dimension involves the external generalizability of the training, such as the degree to which a training program that is successful for a manufacturing company would also be successful for a financial organization.

In a review of studies that examined the effectiveness of managerial training programs, Burke and Day (1986) concluded that managerial training is moderately effective in improving learning and job performance, but we have relatively little knowledge about the intra- and interorganizational validity of such programs. The question of training program success is not simple. I think that transfer validity is the ultimate test of training program effectiveness. But depending on the company's objectives, intra- and interorganizational validity can also be important.

Research Designs

The basic issue in the design of training research is whether differences in criterion behavior are indeed the result of training. A research design assesses whether a training program has achieved its intended objectives. Many research designs can be used to measure training effectiveness, but the more sensitive the design is in assessing differences in performance between groups the more confidence we have that the change in job performance is due to the effects of the training program (Arvey & Cole, 1989).

The simplest research design is shown in Figure 6–7. One group of people is

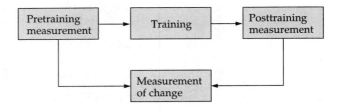

Figure 6–7   One-group pretest/posttest experimental design

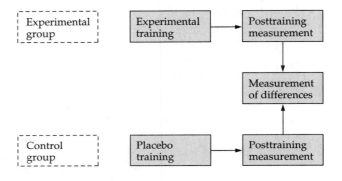

Figure 6–8   Two-group experimental design with no pretest

assessed before and after training. We attribute the difference between pre- and posttraining scores to training. But such a conclusion may be wrong; the change may be due to a Hawthorne effect. Also, employees may change over time simply because they have more job experience, acquire new skills or knowledge, increase their self-confidence, and so on. These types of factors refer to maturation; that is, people may become more productive or make fewer errors just because they develop on the job, which has nothing to do with training. For these reasons, simple pretest/posttest designs are usually inadequate.

A research design that can be used to address a Hawthorne effect is shown in Figure 6–8. This is a two-group design. One group receives the experimental training; the other receives placebo training (that is, some form of training other than that being studied). Since a Hawthorne effect is still possible, placebo training is better than no training at all for that group. In this design both groups experience the novelty of training. This design is preferable to the one-group design, but it, too, has limitations. The two groups are used as a basis for comparison, but we do not know if the groups are comparable to begin with. Perhaps one group of people was more intelligent, more motivated, or more highly skilled from the start; we have no premeasure of performance to indicate the initial comparability of the two groups.

Other, more complex research designs are also available. They differ mainly in the use of multiple control groups, but they are not too practical in personnel training. It is sometimes difficult to divide intact employee work units into different groups. For example, if there is substantial interaction among people in a work group, there will be practical problems if some of the people get experimental training and others get placebo training. Employees talking among themselves about their training can alter motivation and otherwise contaminate the design. In fact, some evidence (Hand & Slocum, 1972) suggests that experimental groups often outperform control groups because people in the control group lose motivation; they are jealous or angry that they were not chosen for the experimental training.

Sussman and Robertson (1986) concluded that no one research design is uniformly the best, and we should try to use the most appropriate design that is feasible to assess the effects of training. Sackett and Mullen (1993) believe that oftentimes in real life trade-offs have to be made between the need for training evaluation information and organizational constraints (for example, it is just not possible to utilize a second group of employees to serve as a control group in training). Rather than abandoning all attempts to evaluate training, it is preferable to communicate to organization decision makers both the strengths and the limitations of whatever training evaluation data are obtained. As Goldstein (1986) noted, "the job of the training analyst is to choose the most rigorous design possible and to be aware of its limitations" (p. 144).

Equal Employment Opportunity and Training

Though far more lawsuits have charged unfair discrimination in the selection process, personnel training is subject to the same legal scrutiny. Employers must show the fairness and validity of their training procedures as well as their selection procedures. One major case before the U.S. Supreme Court, *Kaiser Aluminum & Chemical Co. v. Weber,* involved charges of unfair discrimination in a company's training programs. Weber, a white male, alleged that he was denied the same access to Kaiser's training program as black employees. Without the training, employees were not promoted to higher positions. Kaiser's system of admitting employees to its training program involved taking the same proportion of black employees as white employees. Kaiser felt that it did not have enough black employees at higher levels, so it set up a racial quota system to help resolve the problem. Weber alleged that this system represented unfair discrimination. He contended that admission to the training program was in part determined by race and, as the EEOC guidelines state, race cannot be a factor in making personnel decisions. The Supreme Court ruled in favor of Kaiser Aluminum. It said, in effect, that race can be used as a factor in personnel decisions when it is done to compensate for previous inequities in the composition of the company's work force.

Some organizations select applicants on the basis of their predicted success in a training program as opposed to their actual job performance. An example would be the use of a test to predict success in police academy training. As Russell (1984) notes, the courts have rendered mixed verdicts on the appropriateness of success in training as a criterion for validating selection tests. One interpretation indicates that training success is a sufficient criterion, while another requires that it also be validated with job performance. Goldstein and Gilliam (1990) predict that by the year 2000 much of the litigation surrounding training will involve age discrimination, as individuals between the ages of 45 and 64 increase by 25% over their current percentage.

Bartlett (1978) decomposed the training process into its constituent parts and showed how each part has a potential for discrimination. Possibilities exist with regard to whether training is a job prerequisite, who gets admitted to a training program, comparable treatment of individuals in the training program, who passes and who fails training, placement of employees into jobs as a result of training, and promotion, advancement, and compensation after training. Bartlett warns that a company must be prepared to defend its reasons at each stage of the training process. Personnel training, like personnel selection, must conform to fair employment practices.

CASE STUDY   *Train or Select?*

The senior management staff at Barstow Industries faced a long-standing problem within the company. The company was large, employing approximately 11,000 people nationwide. Barstow hired a large number of people in their professional and scientific classification of employees: salespeople, engineers, accountants, and chemists. The management staff was divided on the type of person to hire. About half the staff favored hiring people directly out of college with the company training them in their jobs. The emphasis would be on training. The basic requirement was that the people had to be bright—bright enough to learn the job quickly. The other half of the staff favored hiring people with extensive job experience. There would be little need for training because the new employees would have already demonstrated their ability to perform the job.

Both sides had good arguments. Those who favored the training approach argued that the company could save money on payroll costs because new, unproven employees could be hired at lower salaries than their experienced counterparts. Furthermore, by making the training company-specific, there was less chance the employees would be hired away by a competitor. It was also argued that the company had good training facilities, including trainers, that were resources the company should not underutilize.

Those who favored the selection of experienced employees proposed powerful counterarguments. They cited statistics showing that a sizable proportion of new college graduates don't last long with their first employer. They argued that they didn't want the company to act as a proving ground by weeding out the unsuccessful employees. Whatever increased salary costs were associated with hiring proven, experienced employees were offset by their increased job performance. It was argued that their competitors would identify the "keepers," and Barstow could raid those companies' talent by offering a higher salary.

It was difficult to argue against the lower payroll costs the company would have by hiring new, unproven people. But it was also difficult to argue with the higher job performance and lower turnover obtained by hiring experienced employees. Every time it came to filling an open position, the same arguments would be presented by both sides. Individual managers in charge of filling positions within their departments had their own views on the issue, but it seemed there was always a person in authority above them who supported the other approach. Everyone seemed to believe there should be a uniform company position on the matter, but there certainly was no consensus on what the company should do. The only group that held a single view was the Human Resources Department. This was highly understandable because one of their major functions was to provide training. Everyone hoped the senior management staff would reach a decision shortly, but everyone also knew that many people would be unhappy with whatever decision was made.

Questions

1. What are some additional benefits and liabilities of hiring young employees and training them to fit a company's needs?
2. What are some additional benefits and liabilities of hiring experienced employees who have received most of their professional training elsewhere?
3. What are the benefits and liabilities of Barstow Industries staffing their organization using each approach?
4. Do you think certain types of jobs (for example, sales) more readily lend themselves to one approach over the other? Why?
5. Give some examples of company-specific training and consider to what degree the training could be generalized to another company.

Performance Appraisal

Major Chapter Objectives

- *Understand why organizations have performance appraisal systems.*

- *Know the sources of performance appraisal data and understand the associated limitations of each.*

- *Understand the purpose of rater training.*

- *Understand the bases of rater motivation.*

- *Know the strengths and weaknesses of self-appraisal and peer appraisal.*

- *Understand the objectives of performance appraisal interviews.*

Employee performance is continually appraised, whether on a formal or an informal basis. Appraisals may be made from haphazard observation, memory, hearsay, or intuition. Alternatively, a formal and rational system may be used. Formal appraisals are more accurate, fair, and useful to all concerned. This chapter deals with formal programs, methods, and techniques for appraising employee performance.

Murphy and Cleveland (1995) believe that performance appraisals can help organizations in several ways. These factors are the primary reasons most organizations have formal performance appraisal systems.

First, performance appraisals can enhance the quality of organizational decisions ranging from determining pay raises to promotions to discharges. The purpose of the human resource function in an organization is to maximize the contributions of employees to the goals of the organization, and assessments of employee job performance can play a major role in accomplishing that function.

Second, performance appraisals can enhance the quality of individual decisions, ranging from career choices to development of future strengths. Accurate performance feedback is an important component of success in training, providing critical input for forming realistic self-assessments in the workplace. Performance feedback is also a key to maintaining high levels of work motivation.

Third, performance appraisals can affect employees' views of and attachment to their organization. An organization that has a successful performance appraisal system may help to build employee commitment and satisfaction. Employees who believe that an organization's decisions are irrational or unfair are unlikely to develop a strong commitment to that organization.

Finally, formal performance appraisals provide a rational, legally defensible basis for personnel decisions. As discussed in Chapter 5, personnel decisions must be based on reason, not capriciousness. There must be a defensible explanation for why some employees are promoted, are discharged, or receive differential pay raises compared to others. As will be discussed shortly, personnel decisions based on performance appraisals are subject to the same legal standards as tests. Both tests and performance evaluations are used as techniques in the administration of the personnel function. While performance appraisals may trigger discordant reactions from some employees, the alternative of making personnel decisions devoid of a rational basis is simply unacceptable.

Using the Results of Performance Appraisals

Results of a performance appraisal program may be applied to many other management functions (see Figure 7–1). As discussed in Chapter 3, criteria are derived from job analysis procedures; the criteria, in turn, are the basis for appraisals. Let's take a closer look at the major uses of performance appraisal information.

Personnel Training. Perhaps the main use of performance appraisal information is to provide employee feedback, the basis for person analysis discussed in the previous chapter. Feedback highlights employees' strengths and weaknesses.

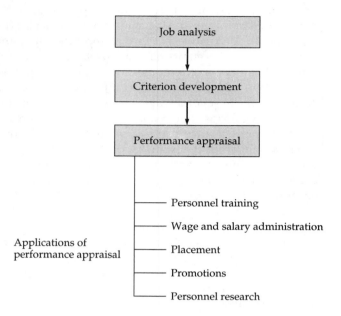

Figure 7–1   Development of performance appraisal information and its applications

Of course, the appraisal should pertain to job-related characteristics only. Deficiencies or weaknesses then become the targets for training. Training should involve only those areas where poor performance can be attributed to the individual and not to aspects of the work environment. The supervisor plays a key role in helping to develop the employee's skills. Although, by definition, performance appraisals are evaluative, in this context they serve more as diagnostic aids. Since some employees will not acknowledge their weaknesses, a supportive supervisor is more effective than one who is threatening or critical. More will be said about this later in the chapter.

Wage and Salary Administration.   Perhaps the second most common use of performance appraisals is to evaluate employees for raises. Pay increases are often made, in part, based on job performance. Appraisal programs can be designed so that there will be a direct relationship between the evaluation and the size of the raise. For example, an employee who is judged to be performing in the top 10% of the work force might get a 12% raise. Conversely, an employee who performs in the bottom 10% might get only a 2% raise.

Unfortunately, the "personnel development" and "salary administration" aspects of appraisal are often uncomfortable partners. Many employees attach far more meaning to raises because they are more immediate and real than they do to revelations about weaknesses on the job. If the two functions are combined in the same appraisal, employees can become defensive. When admitting weaknesses means getting a smaller raise, personnel development may take a backseat in importance.

In a classic article, Meyer, Kay, and French (1965) talked about the need for "split roles" for supervisors in conducting appraisals. One role is a counselor or coach in discussing employee development or performance improvement. The other role is a judge in making salary decisions. Evidence shows that most supervisors cannot play both roles simultaneously. The problem may be addressed by having two appraisals—for example, one in January for employee development, the other in June for salary. Or the supervisor may handle development, while the personnel department handles salary. Although both functions are important, it has customarily been assumed that they should not be conducted at the same time by the same person. However, some research by Prince and Lawler (1986) has challenged the view that salary discussion hinders the developmental function of performance appraisal. These researchers contend that employees prefer less ambiguity in the evaluation-to-reward connection; therefore, it may be advisable to combine the administrative and diagnostic functions of performance appraisal.

Placement.   Performance appraisal information is vital for placement decisions. New employees (such as management trainees) are often exposed to many new tasks or jobs. Over a 12-month period, a trainee might have jobs in marketing, finance, and accounting. After being appraised in each, the trainee might be permanently assigned to that area where he or she performed best. By identifying the employee's strengths, performance appraisal indicates where the person's talents might best be used.

Promotions.   Promotions may be based on how well an employee performs in his or her current job. Appraisals identify the better-performing employees, and an employee who cannot perform well in his or her current job will not be considered for promotion. However, performance is not the sole reason for promotion. Promotions are usually granted on a combination of seniority and merit. If based strictly on seniority, there is nothing to ensure that competent people get promoted. Promotions based strictly on performance are more defensible, but most experts agree that experience in a job is also worth considering.

Discharge.   Termination of employment must be predicated on just cause. A typical basis of just cause is inadequate job performance, as determined through performance appraisal. It is also highly advisable for organizations to document the efforts made to enhance the employee's performance and show that the decision to terminate employment was the organization's last resort. Many lawsuits stemming from performance appraisals allege the fired employee was the victim of a "wrongful discharge." In such cases the organization must demonstrate the fairness, job-relatedness, and accuracy of the performance appraisal process that led to the termination decision.

Personnel Research.   In many criterion-related validity studies, assessments of the criterion are derived from performance appraisals. Recall that the criterion is a measure of job performance, and that is what performance appraisals are supposed to measure. When I/O psychologists want to validate a new predictor test, they correlate scores with criterion measures, which are often exhumed from a company's performance appraisal files. The value of any selection device is only as good as the criterion it tries to predict. So the appraisal must be a relevant measure of job success. Harris, Smith, and Champagne (1995) found that for the purpose of personnel research, specially constructed performance appraisal instruments yielded more useful and less biased information than did evaluations originally collected for administrative purposes (for example, salary administration). Harris and colleagues recommend that more attention be given to the purposes behind performance appraisal, and how these purposes influence the quality and usefulness of the evaluation (see Field Note 1).

FIELD NOTE 1

Performance appraisals are always conducted for a purpose; that is, the appraisal information is put to some use in terms of giving feedback to employees on their own job performance, in determining merit pay raises, or some other application. There should be a high degree of correspondence between the extensiveness of the appraisal process and how extensively the resulting information is used. When there is little correspondence between the two, major problems typically ensue. Here is a case in point.

One organization I am familiar with prided itself on the thoroughness of its performance appraisal process. Performance appraisal information was used to determine merit-pay raises, making the amount of the raise a function of an employee's merit. The company had a highly extensive performance appraisal program, using a frequency count of units of production where applicable and also considering attendance. The program relied heavily on rated performance—from the supervisors, from peers, even self-evaluations. Both behavioral and trait rating scales were used, and employees were rank-ordered on the basis of overall performance. In short, employees were judged along every conceivable performance dimension with a multitude of methods.

All of the information was finally brought together, and the employees were ordered from high to low. The top person typically had three times the level of performance of the bottom person. All this information was now going to be used to determine salary raises. After careful deliberation based on all the information, the company awarded a 5% pay raise to the bottom performer and a 7% pay raise to the top performer, with everyone else falling in between. The lengthy, tedious performance appraisal process turned out to be a farce (at least insofar as the pay raise issue was concerned). The difference between a 5% and 7% pay raise was trivial and certainly not worth all the ballyhoo the company had gone through. If the top performer was truly three times better than the bottom performer (as their highly detailed evaluations indicated), then the top performer's raise should have been about three times greater than that of the bottom performer—that is, about 15%, not 7%. Since the company wanted to use merit-pay raises to motivate the employees to perform well, it should have made superior performance "worth it" to them. Instead, the company communicated the opposite message. The employees figured, "Why bother?" If being the best performer was worth only a few dollars more than being the worst, it simply wasn't worth it to perform well. The merit-pay system based on a thorough performance appraisal system blew up in the company's face, and they soon abandoned the system.

Performance Appraisal and the Law

Federal law on fair employment practices also pertains to performance appraisal. Unfair discrimination can occur not only on the predictor (test) side of the equation but also in the job behavior the test is trying to predict.

Holley and Feild (1975) discussed the relationship between performance appraisal and the law and raised concerns about several possible areas for discrimination. First, the appraisal system must be relevant to the job. As an example, security guards who were appraised on the pleasantness of their personalities could seriously question the relevance of the appraisal. Second, supervisors should not evaluate aspects of an employee's performance that are not observable. This precludes the possibility of biases and misconceptions. Finally, evaluations should not be based on subjective, vague factors like "desire to succeed." This desire can take many forms for different people. The clearer the factors, the more likely the supervisor's attention will be centered on the pertinent aspects of job behavior.

Kleiman and Durham (1981) reviewed 23 court cases involving charges of discrimination in performance appraisal. They sought to determine the standards set by the courts in assessing performance appraisal systems. They discovered that the courts (1) have a strong interest in appraisal systems regardless of their adverse impact; (2) emphasize job analysis procedures for identifying relevant appraisal criteria; and (3) want employers to demonstrate the construct validity of their performance appraisal evaluations. These legal findings support the results from empirical research on sex and race bias in performance appraisal (Schmitt & Lappin, 1980). Schmitt and Lappin demonstrated that raters of different races evaluate members of their own racial group differently from members of other racial groups. Black raters gave higher ratings to blacks than to whites; the opposite effect was observed for white raters. With such an empirical demonstration of race-linked bias, it should be apparent that performance appraisal, like personnel selection and training, is another possible avenue for unfair discrimination in employment.

Feild and Holley (1982) examined the effects of 13 appraisal system characteristics on the verdicts rendered in 66 employment discrimination cases. They found five factors that determined whether the judgments were for the plaintiff or the defendant: (a) the use of job analysis to develop the appraisal system, (b) trait versus behavioral orientation of the appraisal instrument, (c) whether evaluators were given specific written instructions, (d) whether the appraisal results were reviewed with employees, and (e) whether the defendant was an industrial or nonindustrial (for example, governmental) organization (nonindustrial defendants were more likely to win). In a review of major court cases with performance appraisal issues, Barrett and Kernan (1987) identified six dimensions to a professionally sound performance appraisal system:

- Job analyses should be conducted to identify characteristics necessary for successful job performance.

- These characteristics should be incorporated into the evaluation instrument.
- Supervisors should be trained in how to use the evaluation instrument.
- Formal appeal mechanisms should be created to reconsider any evaluation.
- The performance evaluations should be clearly documented.
- The organization should provide corrective guidance for poor performers.

In summary, organizations must justify personnel decisions based on employee performance appraisal. EEOC guidelines state that performance appraisal must not be discriminatory (Latham & Wexley, 1981). The number of court cases involving alleged discrimination in performance appraisal is not as great as those involving personnel selection. But the number is growing, and that trend is likely to continue.

Sources of Performance Appraisal Information

Job performance can be characterized by many criteria. Three different types of measures are possible: objective production data, personnel data, and judgmental data. Each of these job performance measures will be described, along with information about their validity.

Objective Production Data

Using objective production data as an index of how well an employee is performing on the job is limited in its frequency and value. For a person holding the job of a machine operator, job performance may be measured by counting the number of objects produced per day, per week, and so forth. Similarly, salespeople are appraised in terms of assessing (counting) their sales volume over a given period. It is even possible to evaluate the performance of firefighters by counting the number of fires they extinguish.

Although each of these objective production measures has some degree of intuitive appeal, none is a complete measure of job performance. Two problems in particular affect each of these measures. First, we would like to assume that differences in performance across people reflect true differences in terms of how well these people perform their jobs. Unfortunately, variability in performance can be due to factors beyond the individual's control. One machine operator may produce more because he or she works with a better machine. A salesperson might have a large sales volume because his or her territory is better. Firefighters who put out few fires might be responsible for an area with relatively few buildings. This problem of variation in performance stemming from external factors should sound familiar; it represents a form of criterion contamination (a topic discussed in Chapter 3).

The second problem with objective performance measures is that they rarely tell the whole story. A machine operator who produced more objects per day but who also produced more defective objects would not be described as the "best."

Quality may be as important as quantity, but this cannot be recorded in a simple count of objects produced. A salesperson spends a lot of time recruiting new customers, an aspect that must be weighed against simply making calls on established customers. Creating new customers can be as important as maintaining business with old ones. Sales volume might be less at first, but in the long run the new customers will increase total sales volume. Extinguishing fires is but one aspect of a firefighter's job; preventing fires is another one. The "best" firefighters conceivably may not have put out many fires but might have contributed heavily toward preventing fires in the first place.

There is growing use of electronic performance monitoring (EPM) to assess the performance of workers engaged in computer-based tasks. An EPM system records the objective aspects of performance on computer-based tasks, such as volume and speed of entries (Lund, 1992). Westin (1992) has revealed that such systems are regarded as unfair and inaccurate assessments of work performance because they ignore the discretionary or judgmental component of work inherent in all jobs. In short, all of these actual criteria suffer from criterion deficiency. They are deficient measures of the conceptual criteria they seek to measure.

Relevance of Objective Production Data.   For the jobs mentioned, objective production data have some relevance. It would be absurd to say that sales volume has no bearing on a salesperson's performance. The salesperson's job is indeed to sell. The issue is one of degree of relevance. It is a mistake to give too much importance to objective production data in performance appraisal (see Field Note 2). This is sometimes a great temptation because these data are usually very accessible, but the meaning of those clear-cut numbers is not always so evident. Finally, for many jobs, objective performance measures do not exist, or if they do, they have little relevance to actual performance. The issue of criterion relevance is a question of judgment. For some jobs, objective performance data are partially relevant measures of success; in many others, such relevance is lacking.

Personnel Data

The second type of appraisal information is personnel data, the data retained by a company's personnel office. The three most common indexes of performance are absenteeism, turnover, and accidents. The critical issue with these variables is criterion relevance. To what extent do they reflect differences in job performance? Absenteeism is probably the most sensitive measure of performance. In almost all jobs, employees who are often absent are judged as performing worse than others, all other factors being equal. Indeed, an employee can be fired for excessive absence.

Most organizations have policies for dealing with absenteeism, which attests to its importance as a variable in judging overall performance. However, the measurement and interpretation of absenteeism are not clear-cut (Muchinsky, 1977b). Absences can be "excused" or "unexcused" depending on many factors pertaining to both the individual (for example, seniority) and the job (for example, job level). An employee who has ten days of excused absence may still be appraised as performing better than an employee with five days of unexcused absence.

Whether the absence was allowed must be determined before performance judgments are made. Measuring absenteeism is a thorny problem, but it is seen as a highly relevant criterion variable in most organizations.

Turnover is also used to measure performance. It too involves measurement problems. Some turnover is voluntary (the employee quits); some is involuntary (the employee is fired). An employee who quit would probably be appraised "better" than an employee who was fired. Some organizations will let an employee resign to improve his or her chances of getting another job. This clouds the value of turnover as a measure of performance. The meaning attached to a chronic job-hopper has also changed over the years. Twenty years ago, job-hoppers were viewed with some suspicion at the management level; they seemed unstable and unable to hold a job for long. Today, however, job-hoppers are regarded more positively. Exposure to different jobs is taken to mean that they have more breadth of experience. This is an example of how the same behavior (turnover) acquires different interpretations over time.

Accidents can be used as a measure of job performance but only for a limited number of jobs. Frequency and severity of accidents are both used as variables, as are accidents resulting in injury or property damage. Accidents are a more relevant criterion variable for blue-collar than for white-collar jobs. People who drive delivery trucks may be evaluated in part on the number of accidents they have, but this variable can be contaminated by many sources. Road conditions, miles driven, time of day, and condition of the truck can all contribute to accidents. While relevance is limited to certain jobs, accidents can contribute greatly to appraisal. Companies often give substantial pay raises to drivers with no accidents and fire those with a large number.

Relevance of Personnel Data.   There is no doubt that factors such as absence, turnover, and accidents are meaningful measures of job performance. Employees

FIELD NOTE 2

We usually think of high performance in terms of a positive score, a gain, or some improvement over the status quo. Conversely, when individuals perform "worse" than they did last year, it is tempting to conclude that they didn't perform as well. However, such is not always the case. Performance must be judged in terms of what is under the control of the individuals being evaluated versus those influences on performance that are beyond their control. There can be broad, pervasive factors, sometimes of an economic nature, that suppress the performance of everyone being judged. One example is in sales. If there is a general downturn in the economy and products or services are not being purchased with the same frequency as they were in the previous year, sales could be down, for example, by an average of 15%. This 15% (actually −15%) figure would represent "average" performance. Perhaps the best salesperson in the year had only a 3% drop in sales over the previous year. "Good" performance in this situation represents a smaller loss compared to some average or norm group. This example illustrates why there is always some judgmental or contextual component to appraising performance. Relying solely on objective numbers can be misleading.

may be discharged for incurring excessive absences or accidents and may be rewarded for perfect attendance or a perfect safety record. However, as was the case with production data, personnel data rarely reveal a comprehensive picture of the employee's performance. There are often other highly relevant aspects of job performance that are not revealed by personnel data. It is for this reason that judgmental data are most often relied upon to offer a more complete assessment of job performance.

Judgmental Data

Judgmental data are usually used for performance appraisal. Lent, Aurbach, and Levin (1971) reported that in 1,500 criterion measures used in I/O research, almost 900 (60%) were supervisory ratings of subordinates' performance. Judgmental data are popular in performance appraisal because finding relevant objective measures is difficult. Subjective assessments can also apply to almost all jobs. Those who do the assessments are usually supervisors, but some use has also been made of self-assessment and peer assessment.

Relevance of Judgmental Data. The relevance of judgmental data in performance appraisal, as is true of the relevance of any type of performance appraisal data, refers to the extent to which the observed data are accurate measures of the "true" variable being measured. The "true" variable can refer to a global construct, such as overall job performance, or a dimension of job performance, such as interpersonal relations ability. One method of assessing the relevance of judgmental data is to correlate them with performance appraisals from another method, such as objective production or personnel data. In studies that have conducted this type of analysis, the resulting correlations have been only moderate in magnitude. While these results may be interpreted to mean that judgmental data have only moderate relevance, the key question is whether the objective production data or the personnel data can be assumed to represent "true" ability. Those types of data might be just as incomplete or remotely relevant as judgmental data. Since we never obtain measures of the conceptual criterion (that is, "true" ability), we are forced to deal with imperfect measures that, not surprisingly, yield imperfect results. Weekley and Gier (1989) have shown the existence of rater disagreement and halo error even among such expert raters as Olympic judges who are intensely trained to make accurate evaluations.

Borman (1978) had another approach to assessing the relevance of judgmental data. He made videotapes of two employment situations: a manager talking with a problem employee, and a recruiter interviewing a job candidate. Sixteen videotapes were made, eight of each situation. Each tape showed a different degree of performance—for example, from a highly competent recruiter to a totally inept one. Similar degrees of performance were shown of the manager/subordinate meeting. Professional actors were used in the tapes. The same actor played the recruiter in all eight tapes, but a different actor played the new employee in each tape. Thus, the performance level (the "true" ability of the manager or recruiter) was "programmed" into the scripts.

Raters were asked to rate the performance of the manager and the recruiter with a series of rating scales. The evaluations were correlated with the performance levels depicted. Correlations between ratings and levels of performance across several job dimensions (organizing the interview, establishing rapport, and so on) ranged from .42 to .97. The median was .69. Although this study used a simulation as opposed to actual job performance, it did show that various types of rating procedures were susceptible to differences in validity. The study also revealed that certain dimensions of performance were more accurately evaluated ("answering recruitee's questions," $r = .97$) than others ("reacting to stress," $r = .42$). Borman was led to conclude that raters are limited in their ability to appraise performance; they could not accurately evaluate the levels of "true" performance that were acted out in the scripts. He suggested a practical upper limit to validity that is less than the theoretical limit ($r = 1.0$).

Performance Appraisal Methods

Researchers from several disciplines (for example, those interested in management, communication, and education) have addressed performance appraisal. The contributions of I/O psychologists are particularly manifested in designing performance appraisal methods. A wide variety of appraisals have been developed, all intended to provide accurate assessments of how people are performing. The major systems used in performance appraisal are graphic rating scales, employee-comparison methods, and behavioral checklists and scales. Although these performance appraisal methods require relatively few administrative costs, there can be expenses associated with training individuals to use these methods, as well as the possibility of a few unanticipated costs (see Field Note 3).

Graphic Rating Scales

Graphic rating scales are the most commonly used system in performance appraisal. Individuals are rated on a number of traits or factors. The rater judges "how much" of each factor the individual has. Usually performance is judged on a 5- or 7-point scale, and the number of factors range between 5 and 20. The more common dimensions rated are quantity of work, quality of work, practical judgment, job knowledge, cooperation, and motivation. Examples of typical graphic rating scales are shown in Figure 7–2.

In making appraisals with rating scales, the rater may unknowingly commit errors in judgment. These can be placed into three major categories: halo errors, leniency errors, and central-tendency errors. All three stem from rater bias and misperception.

Halo Errors.   Halo errors are evaluations based on the rater's general feelings about an employee. For example, the rater may generally have a favorable attitude toward an employee that will permeate all evaluations of this person. Typically, the rater has strong feelings about at least one important aspect of the employee's performance. This is then generalized to other performance factors, and the employee is judged (across many factors) as uniformly good or bad. The rater who is impressed by an employee's idea might allow feelings about this one incident to carry over to evaluation of leadership, cooperation, motivation, and so on. This occurs even though the "good idea" is not related to these other factors.

Raters who commit halo errors do not distinguish among the many dimensions of employee performance. However, a compounding problem is that there are two types of halo. One type is truly a rating error and refers to the failure to differentiate an employee's performance across different dimensions. The second type refers to giving uniformly consistent ratings to an employee when these ratings are in fact justified; that is, the employee truly performs well across many dimensions. Bartlett (1983) refers to these as *invalid* and *valid halo*, respectively. Murphy and Reynolds (1988) concluded that for the most part true (valid) halo does not greatly affect the observance of halo error (invalid) in ratings.

In general, halo errors are considered to be the most serious and pervasive of all rating errors (Cooper, 1981). Recent research on halo error has revealed that it is a more complex phenomenon than initially believed. Murphy and Anhalt (1992) concluded that halo error is not a stable characteristic of the rater or ratee but rather is the result of an interaction of the rater, the ratee, and the evaluative situation. Balzer and Sulsky (1992) contend that halo may not be a rating "error"

FIELD NOTE 3

Many times there are unexpected costs associated with performance appraisal. Here is the story of one of the more unusual expenses I have ever encountered in a research study.

One of the uses of performance appraisal information is as a criterion of job performance. In turn, criteria of job performance may be used to validate selection tests. A colleague needed to collect both performance appraisal (criterion) data and test score (predictor) data to develop a selection test battery for a company. He traveled to the company and had all the supervisors convene in the company cafeteria. He explained the nature of the performance ratings he wanted them to make. Then he explained that all their subordinates would be taking a 30-minute test, and the scores would be correlated with the supervisors' performance appraisal ratings, as is done in a concurrent criterion-related validity study. My colleague then asked the supervisors if they wanted to take the same test their subordinates would be taking just to get a feel for what it was like. They agreed. He then passed

out the test and informed them they would have 30 minutes to complete it. He wanted the testing procedure to be very exact, giving everyone precisely 30 minutes. His watch did not have a second hand. He was about to ask if he could borrow someone else's watch when he spied the company's microwave oven on the wall in the cafeteria. He went over to the microwave, set the timer for 30 minutes, told the supervisors to begin the test, and started the microwave.

About 20 minutes into the test, a terrible odor began to fill the cafeteria. Somebody noticed it was coming from the microwave. My colleague had failed to place anything in the microwave when he started it, so for 20 minutes the microwave cooked itself, ultimately suffering terminal meltdown. The microwave cost $800 to replace and is one of the more unusual test-validation expense items I have ever heard of. Incidentally, the test turned out to be highly predictive of the performance appraisal ratings, so the exercise was not a complete waste.

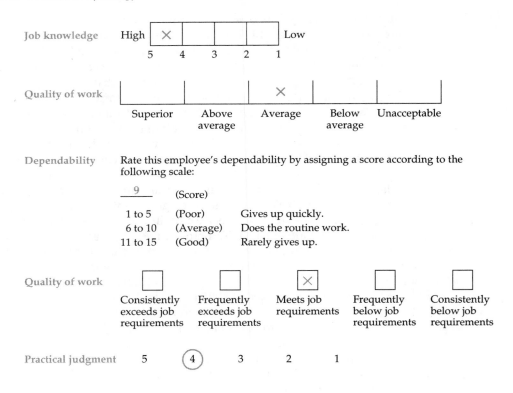

Figure 7–2   *Examples of graphic rating scales for various performance dimensions*

as much as it is an indicator of how we cognitively process information in arriving at judgments of other people. That is, the presence of halo does not necessarily indicate an inaccuracy in the ratings. In a related view, Lance, LaPointe, and Fisicaro (1994) note there is disagreement as to whether halo error is a product of the rater or of the cognitive process of making judgments of similar objects. Murphy, Jako, and Anhalt (1993) recommend that great attention be paid to examining the rating contexts that produce halo effects.

Leniency Errors.   Some teachers are "hard graders," and others are "easy graders." So too can raters can be characterized by the leniency of their appraisals. Harsh raters give evaluations that are lower than the "true" level of ability (if it can be ascertained); this is called *severity* or *negative leniency*. The easy rater gives evaluations that are higher than the "true" level; this is called *positive leniency*. These errors usually occur because the rater has applied personal standards derived from his or her own personality or previous experience.

Central-Tendency Errors.   Central-tendency errors refer to the rater's unwillingness to assign extreme—high or low—ratings. Everyone is "average," and only the middle (central) part of the scale is used. This may happen when raters are asked to evaluate unfamiliar aspects of performance. Rather than not respond, they play it safe and say the person is average in this "unknown" ability.

Despite the fact that we have long been aware of halo, leniency, and central-tendency errors, there is no clear consensus on how these errors manifest themselves in ratings. Saal, Downey, and Lahey (1980) observed that researchers define these errors in somewhat different ways. For example, leniency errors are sometimes equated with skew in the distribution of ratings; that is, positive skew is evidence of negative leniency and negative skew of positive leniency. Other researchers say that an average rating above the midpoint on a particular scale indicates positive leniency. The exact meaning of central tendency is also unclear. Central-tendency errors occur if the average rating is around the midpoint of the scale, but there is not much variance in the ratings. The amount of variance that separates central-tendency errors from "good" ratings has not been defined. Saal and associates feel that more precise definitions of these errors must be developed before they can be overcome. To help combat these errors, other appraisal methods have been developed.

Employee-Comparison Methods

Rating scales provide for evaluating employees against some defined standard. With employee-comparison methods, individuals are compared with one another. Variance is thereby forced into the appraisals, and the concentration of ratings at one part of the scale caused by rating error is avoided. However, all methods of employee comparison involve the question of whether variation represents true differences in performance or whether it creates a false impression of large differences when they are in fact small. There are three major employee-comparison methods: rank order, paired comparison, and forced distribution.

Rank-Order Method. With the rank-order method, the rater ranks employees from high to low on a given performance dimension. The person ranked first is regarded as the "best," and the person ranked last as the "worst." However, because rank-order data have only ordinal-scale properties, we do not know how good the "best" is or how bad the "worst" is. We do not know the level of performance. For example, the Nobel Prize winners in a given year can be ranked in terms of their overall contributions to science, but we would be hard-pressed to conclude that the Nobel laureate ranked last made the worst contribution to science. Rank-order data are all relative to some standard, in this case excellence in scientific research. Another problem is that it becomes quite tedious and perhaps somewhat meaningless to rank-order large numbers of people. What usually happens is that the rater can sort out the people at the top and the bottom of the pile. However, for the rest with undifferentiated performance, the rankings may be somewhat arbitrary.

Paired-Comparison Method. With the paired-comparison method, each employee is compared to every other employee in the group being evaluated. The rater's task is to select which of the two is better on the dimension being rated.

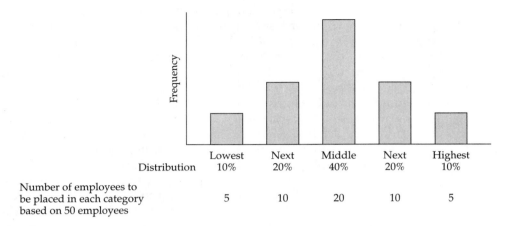

Distribution	Lowest 10%	Next 20%	Middle 40%	Next 20%	Highest 10%
Number of employees to be placed in each category based on 50 employees	5	10	20	10	5

Figure 7–3   *The forced-distribution method of performance appraisal*

The method is typically used to evaluate employees on a single dimension: overall ability to perform the job. The number of evaluation pairs is computed by the formula $n(n-1)/2$, where n is the number of people to be evaluated. For example, if there are 10 people in a group, the number of paired comparisons is $10(9)/2 = 45$. At the conclusion of the evaluation, the number of times each person was selected as the better of the two is tallied. The people are then ranked by the number of tallies they receive.

A major limitation is that the number of comparisons made mushrooms dramatically with large numbers of employees. If 50 people are to be appraised, the number of comparisons is 1,225; this will obviously take too much time. The paired-comparison method is best for relatively small samples.

Forced-Distribution Method.   The forced-distribution method is most useful when the other employee-comparison methods are most limited—that is, when the sample size is large. Forced distribution is typically used when the rater must evaluate employees on a single dimension, but it can also be used when multiple dimensions are required. The procedure is based on the normal distribution and assumes that employee performance is normally distributed. The distribution is divided into five to seven categories. Using predetermined percentages (based on the normal distribution), the rater evaluates an employee by placing him or her into one of the categories. All employees are evaluated in this manner. The method "forces" the rater to distribute the employees in all categories (which is how the method gets its name). Thus, it is impossible for all employees to be rated excellent, average, or poor. An example of the procedure for a sample of 50 employees is shown in Figure 7–3.

Some raters react negatively to the method, saying that the procedure creates artificial distinctions among employees. This is partly because the raters feel that performance is not normally distributed but rather negatively skewed; that is, most of their employees are performing very well (see Field Note 4). The dissatisfaction can be partially allayed by noting that the lowest 10% are not necessarily performing poorly, just not as well as the others. The problem (as with all comparison methods) is that performance is not compared to a defined standard. The meaning of the differences among employees must be supplied from some other source.

Behavioral Checklists and Scales

Most recent advances in performance appraisal have involved behavioral check-lists and scales. The key term is *behavior*. Behaviors are less vague than other factors. The greater the agreement on the meaning of the performance appraised, the greater the chance that the appraisal will be accurate. All of the methods in this group have their origin directly or indirectly in the critical-incidents method.

Critical Incidents.   Critical incidents are behaviors that result in good or poor job performance. Flanagan (1954) developed the critical-incidents method. Supervisors record behaviors of employees that greatly influence their job performance. They either keep a running tally of these critical incidents as they occur on the job or recall them at a later time. Critical incidents are usually grouped by aspects of

---

FIELD NOTE 4

Although it is rarely discussed in performance appraisal, one problem regarding employee evaluation deals with the shape of the distribution of employee job performance. As discussed in Chapter 2, some statistical distributions depart from normality, with a skewed distribution being the most common. Some performance appraisal methods are premised on employee performance being normally distributed; the forced-distribution method is a case in point. In fact, most psychologists probably believe that variables are normally distributed unless they have reason to believe otherwise. However, there are some strong arguments that lead us to conclude that job performance is not normally distributed but negatively skewed. That is, far more employees perform their jobs successfully than unsuccessfully. Why? Think about it. I/O psychology addresses itself to the attraction, selection, and development of successful employees. We try to recruit applicants from sources and in ways that will result in good candidates. We carefully select employees who we predict will succeed on the job. Once on the job, employees are given training to improve their job performance further. Individuals who don't perform well are often dismissed. All these forces combine to shift the overall distribution of job performance to the high end of the scale. There are always some employees who don't perform their jobs as well as the company would like, but they typically are in the minority. Consequently, the distribution of job performance in most companies is far more negatively skewed than normal (Muchinsky, 1994). One of the problems with performance appraisal methods predicated on a normal distribution is that one assumption of the method (normality) just doesn't fit reality in some cases. I/O psychologists should give more thought to the underlying distribution of job performance and how it affects evaluation of job performance. Although many variables in psychology are normally distributed, I don't believe job performance is necessarily one of them.

"Barkley, I perceive my role in this institution not as a judge but merely as an observer and recorder. I have observed you to be a prize boob and have so recorded it."
SOURCE: Reprinted by permission of Tribune Media Services.

performance: job knowledge, decision-making ability, leadership, and so on. The end product is a list of behaviors (good and bad) that constitute effective and ineffective job performance.

The original method did not lend itself to quantification (that is, a score reflecting performance). It was used to guide employees in the specifics of their job performance. Each employee's performance can be described in terms of the occurrence of these critical behaviors. The supervisor can then counsel the employee to avoid the bad and continue the good behaviors. For example, a negative critical incident for a machine operator might be "leaves machine running while unattended." A positive one might be "always wears safety goggles on the job." Discussing performance in such clear terms is more understandable than vague statements such as "poor attitude" or "careless work habits."

Weighted Checklist.   A weighted checklist is simply an attempt to quantify performance using the critical-incidents technique. The procedure for developing a weighted checklist begins with a list of critical incidents. Once the list has been developed, a panel of "experts" (usually supervisors) rates each critical incident in terms of just how "good" the good ones are and just how "bad" the bad ones

Table 7-1 *Checklist of weighted critical incidents for a secretarial job*

Critical Incident	Scale Value
Knows the difference between correcting the grammar in the boss's letter and correcting the writing style.	+6.5
Knows various postal rates and mails material in a cost-efficient manner.	+4.2
Knows what typing is to be done on plain paper versus company letterhead.	+3.1
Keeps a running count on the use of office supplies.	+2.5
Opens all mail whether or not it is marked "confidential."	−1.9
Confuses priorities on typing that needs immediate attention and projects that have no established deadlines.	−3.8
Files away correspondence so that it can rarely be found for later reference.	−5.2
Leaves many mistakes in typing from failing to proofread the typed copy.	−7.1

are. Thus, a scale value is derived for each incident reflecting its relative degree of importance to the job. The scale values are usually derived by averaging the ratings made by the supervisor. Table 7–1 shows some examples of items from a weighted checklist for a secretarial job.

Supervisors then evaluate employee performance by checking off observed behaviors. The values for all checked behaviors are added to yield the employee's score. The ideal employee would exhibit all the positive and none of the negative behaviors. The method gives information that can be used in many ways, including counseling employees on how to improve performance. Employees can be ranked on total scores, thus providing information on the range of performance. The scores can be averaged for a measure of "typical" performance, which can serve as a standard for judging individual employees.

Behaviorally Anchored Rating Scales. Behaviorally anchored rating scales (BARS) are a combination of the behavioral-incident and rating-scale methods. Performance is rated on a scale, but the scale points are anchored with behavioral incidents. The development of BARS is time consuming, but the benefits make it worthwhile. BARS are developed in a five-step process:

1. A list of critical incidents is generated in the manner discussed previously.

2. A group of people (usually supervisors—either the same people who generated the critical incidents initially or another group) clusters the incidents into a smaller set of performance dimensions (usually five to ten) that they typically represent. The result is a given number of performance dimensions, each containing several illustrative critical incidents.

3. Another group of knowledgeable people is instructed to perform the following task. The critical incidents are "scrambled" so they are no longer listed under the dimensions described in Step 2. The critical incidents might be written on separate note cards and presented to the people in random order. The raters' task is to reassign or retranslate all the critical incidents back to the original performance dimensions. This step is a variation of the Smith and Kendall (1963) procedure wherein the goal is to have critical incidents that clearly represent the

performance dimensions under consideration. A critical incident generally is said to be successfully retranslated if some percentage (usually 50% to 80%) of the raters reassign it back to the dimension from which it came. Incidents that are not retranslated successfully (that is, where there is ample confusion as to which dimension they represent) are discarded.

4. The people who retranslated the items are asked to rate each "surviving" critical incident on a scale (typically 7 or 9 points) in terms of just how effectively or ineffectively it represents performance on the appropriate dimension. This rating phase is similar to the process used to derive the scale weights in the weighted checklist. The ratings given to each incident are then averaged, and the standard deviation for each item is computed. Low standard deviations indicate high rater agreement on the value of the incident. Large standard deviations indicate low rater agreement. A standard deviation criterion is then set for deciding which incidents will be retained for inclusion in the final form of the BARS. Incidents that have a standard deviation in excess of 1.50 typically are discarded because the raters could not agree on their respective values.

5. The final form of the instrument consists of critical incidents that survived both the retranslation and the standard deviation criteria. The incidents serve as behavioral anchors for the performance dimension scales. The final BARS instrument consists of a series of scales listed vertically (one for each dimension) and anchored by the retained incidents. Each incident is located along the scale according to its established rating. An example of a BARS for patrol officer performance is shown in Figure 7–4. As can be seen, behaviors are listed with respect to what the employee is expected to do at various performance levels. For this reason, BARS are sometimes referred to as "behavioral expectation scales."

One of the major advantages of the method does not involve performance appraisal. It is based on the high degree of involvement of persons developing the scale. The participants must carefully examine specific behaviors that lead to effective performance. In so doing, they may reject false stereotypes about ineffective performances. The method has face validity for both the rater and ratee and also appears to be useful for training raters. However, one disadvantage is that BARS are job specific; that is, you need to develop a different behaviorally anchored rating scale for every job.

Behavioral-Observation Scales.   Another development in appraisal is the behavioral-observation scale (BOS). Like BARS, it is based on critical incidents. With BOS the rater must rate the employee on the frequency of critical incidents. The rater observes the employee over a certain period, such as a month. Here is an example of a 5-point critical-incident scale used in appraising salespeople (Latham & Wexley, 1977):

Knows the Price of Competitive Products

Never	Seldom	Sometimes	Generally	Always
1	2	3	4	5

Job knowledge: Awareness of procedures, laws, and court rulings and changes in them

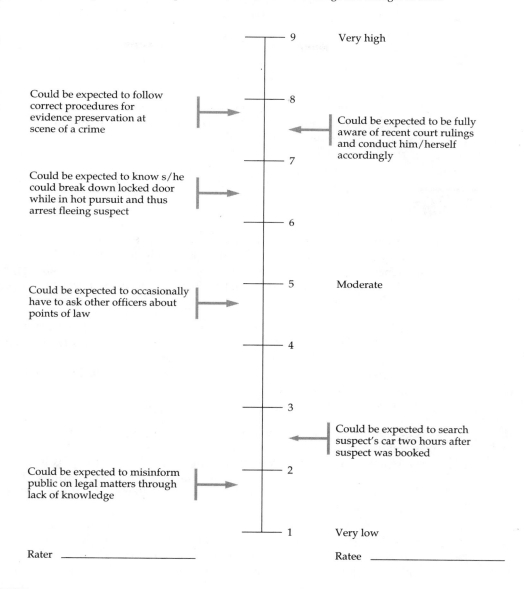

Figure 7–4 *Example of a behaviorally anchored rating scale for appraising patrol officers*
SOURCE: From *Psychology of Work Behavior*, rev. ed. (p. 128), by F. J. Landy and D. A. Trumbo, 1980, Pacific Grove, CA: Brooks/Cole.

Raters evaluate the employees on several such critical incidents, recording how often they observed the behavior. The total score is the sum of all the critical incidents. The final step is to correlate the response for each incident (a rating of 1, 2, 3, 4, or 5) with the total performance score. This is called *item analysis*. It is meant to detect the critical incidents that most influence overall performance. Those incidents that have the highest correlations with the total score are the most discriminating factors in performance. They would be retained to develop criteria for job success.

Latham, Fay, and Saari (1979) suggested advantages to performance appraisals with BOS. Like BARS, BOS are developed by those using the method for evaluation, who understand they are committed to using the scales. Second, BOS information can be used to teach new employees the behaviors most critical to the job. Finally, BOS are content valid; the aspects of performance appraised are derived directly from the job. This satisfies the EEO requirement that appraisal methods be job relevant.

Rater Training

Can you train raters to make better performance appraisals? The answer appears to be yes. Most rater-training studies seek to train appraisers to make fewer halo, leniency, and central-tendency errors. For example, Latham, Wexley, and Pursell (1975) randomly assigned 60 managers who appraised performance to one of the following three groups:

- *Workshop group.* This group was shown videotapes on evaluating individuals. Members then discussed appraisal procedures and problems in making appraisals, with the intent of reducing rating errors.
- *Discussion group.* This group received training similar in content, but the main method was discussion.
- *Control group.* This group received no training.

Six months later, the three groups were "tested." They were shown videotapes of several hypothetical job candidates along with job requirements. The managers were asked to evaluate the candidates' suitability for the jobs in question. Major differences in rating errors were made by each of the groups. The workshop group had no rating errors. The control group performed the worst, making three types of errors.

Zedeck and Cascio (1982) considered the purpose for which performance appraisal ratings were made—merit raise, retention, or development—and found that training works better for some purposes than for others. Training typically enhances the accuracy of performance appraisals, as well as their acceptability to those who are being appraised.

However, not all research on rater training is positive. Bernardin and Pence (1980) reported that raters who were trained to reduce halo errors actually made less accurate ratings after training. This seems to be due to the fact that, as Bartlett (1983) noted, there are two types of halo; reduction of invalid halo will increase accuracy, but reduction of valid halo will decrease it. Hedge and Kavanagh (1988) concluded that certain types of rater training reduced classical rating errors such as halo and leniency but did not increase rating accuracy. This underscores the uncertain relation between rating errors and accuracy due to our inability to know what "truth" is (Sulsky & Balzer, 1988).

One type of rater training appears to be particularly promising. *Frame-of-reference training* (Sulsky & Day, 1992) involves providing raters with common reference standards (or frames) by which to evaluate performance. Raters are shown vignettes of good, poor, and average performance and are given feedback on the accuracy of their ratings of the vignettes. The intent of the training is to "calibrate" raters so that they agree on what constitutes varying levels of performance effectiveness for each performance dimension. Research by Woehr (1994) and Day and Sulsky (1995) supported the conclusion that frame-of-reference training increased the accuracy of individual ratees on separate performance dimensions. In a meta-analytic review of rater training for performance appraisal, Woehr and Huffcutt (1994) examined the effectiveness of rater training methods on the major dependent variables of reduced halo error, reduced leniency error, and increased rating accuracy. They concluded that rater training had a positive effect on each dependent variable. However, the training strategies were differentially effective in addressing the aspect of performance ratings they were designed to meet.

Rater Motivation

It is not unusual for the majority of employees in a company to receive very high performance evaluations. These inflated ratings are often interpreted as evidence of massive rater errors (for example, leniency or halo) or a breakdown in the performance appraisal system. The typical organizational response for rating inflation is to make some technical adjustment in the rating scale format or to institute a new training program for raters. However, there is another explanation for rating inflation that is unrelated to rater errors.

Murphy and Cleveland (1995) posit that the tendency to give uniformly high ratings is an instance of adaptive behavior that is, from the rater's point of view, an eminently logical course of action. Thus, deficiencies in ratings are more likely to be a result of the rater's *willingness* to provide accurate ratings than of their *capacity* to rate accurately. If the situation is examined from the rater's perspective, there are many sound reasons to provide inflated ratings.

First, there are typically no rewards from the organization for doing accurate appraisals and few if any sanctions for inaccurate appraisals. Official company policies often emphasize the value of good performance appraisals, but organizations typically take no specific steps to reward this supposedly valued activity. Second, the most common reason cited for rating inflation is that high ratings are needed to guarantee promotions, salary increases, and other valued rewards. Conversely, low ratings will result in these rewards being withheld from subordinates. Raters are thus motivated to obtain valued rewards for their subordinates. Third, raters are motivated to give inflated ratings because the ratings received by subordinates are a reflection of the *rater's* job performance (Latham, 1986). One of the duties of managers is to develop their subordinates. If managers consistently rate their subordinates as less than good performers, it can appear as if the managers are not doing their jobs. Thus high ratings make the rater look good, and low ratings make the rater look bad. Fourth, raters tend to inflate their ratings because they wish to avoid the negative reactions that accompany low ratings (Klimoski & Inks, 1990). Negative evaluations typically result in defensive reactions from subordinates, which can create a very stressful situation for the rater. The simplest way to avoid unpleasant or defensive reactions in appraisal interviews is to give uniformly positive feedback (that is, give inflated ratings).

There is no simple solution to offset the motivation to inflate ratings. The problem will not be solved by just increasing the capability of raters. In addition, the environment must be modified in such a way that raters are motivated to provide accurate ratings. Murphy and Cleveland (1995) believe accurate rating is most likely in an environment where the following conditions exist:

- Good and poor performance are clearly defined.
- The principle of distinguishing among workers in terms of their levels of performance is widely accepted.
- There is a high degree of trust in the system.
- Low ratings do not automatically result in the loss of valued rewards.
- Valued rewards are clearly linked to accuracy in performance appraisal.

Murphy and Cleveland know of organizations in which *none* of these conditions is met, but they don't know of any in which *all* of them are met. It is clear that we need more research on the organizational context in which performance appraisals are conducted.

Mero and Motowidlo (1995) also reported findings that underscored the importance of the context in which ratings are made. They found that raters who were held accountable for their performance ratings made more accurate ratings than raters who were not held accountable. The ultimate solution to the problem of rating inflation will come through changing the context in which ratings are made—not through changing the rater or the rating scale.

Contextual Performance

Borman and Motowidlo (1993) contend that individuals contribute to organizational effectiveness in ways that go beyond the activities that comprise their jobs. They can either help or hinder efforts to accomplish organizational goals by doing many things that are not directly related to their main functions. However, these contributions are important because they shape the organizational or psychological context that serves as a catalyst for work. Consideration of these contributions is a valid component of overall job performance, yet they transcend the assessment of performance in specific tasks. Examples of contextual performance include:

- Persisting with enthusiasm and extra effort as necessary to complete one's own task activities successfully.
- Volunteering to carry out task activities that are not formally part of one's own job.

- Helping and cooperating with others.
- Endorsing, supporting, and defending organizational objectives.

Borman and Motowidlo believe that an accurate assessment of job performance must include contextual factors as well as task performance. Motowidlo and Van Scotter (1994) found that both task performance and contextual performance contributed independently to overall performance in a sample of U.S. Air Force mechanics. Experience was more highly related with task performance than with contextual performance, while personality variables were more highly related with contextual performance than with task performance. Borman, White, and Dorsey (1995) concluded that supervisors weight contextual performance approximately as highly as task performance when making overall performance ratings. In general it appears that knowledgeable raters are sensitized to the general contributions employees make in enhancing organizational welfare. Consideration of these contributions are as important in determining an overall evaluation as is performance in the more narrow and specific behavior associated with task performance.

Self- and Peer Appraisals

Most research on judgmental performance appraisal deals with evaluations made by a superior (supervisor, manager). However, there is also information on the value of performance appraisals made by colleagues or peers. Self-evaluations have also been discussed. Our knowledge is somewhat limited, but these methods do offer added understanding of performance appraisal.

Self-Assessments

With self-assessment, as the term suggests, each employee appraises his or her own performance. The procedure most commonly used is some type of graphic rating scale. Meyer (1980) reported a study in which 92 engineers rated their performance against their views of the performance of other engineers in the company. On average, each engineer thought he or she was performing better than 75% of the rest of the engineers in the study. Statistically, it is quite a trick to have 100% of the work force in the top 25% of job performers. This underscores the biggest problem with self-assessment: *positive leniency.* Most people have higher opinions of their own performance than others do.

Anderson, Warner, and Spencer (1984) demonstrated in a clever study just how prevalent and pervasive inflation bias is in self-assessments of ability. They asked applicants to rate their own abilities in real clerical tasks as well as in bogus tasks that sounded real but were nonsense. Some of the bogus tasks were "operating a matriculation machine," "typing from audio-fortran reports," and "circumscribing general meeting registers." The clerical applicants rated themselves high on the real tasks (where their ability was not verified) and also in the tasks that did not even exist! Steel and Ovalle (1984) found that there was less positive leniency in self-assessments when there was a high degree of feedback from supervisors. In other words, employees who get little feedback from their supervisors think more highly of their own abilities than employees who receive a lot of feedback. Mount (1984) found that managers evaluate themselves more leniently compared both to how they evaluate their supervisors and to how their supervisors evaluate them.

Thornton (1980) reports that despite leniency problems, there are fewer halo errors with self-appraisals. People apparently recognize their strengths and weaknesses and appraise themselves accordingly. Thornton also reported little agreement in most studies comparing self-assessments and supervisor assessments. Superiors do not evaluate employees in the same way that employees evaluate themselves. This does not mean that one appraisal is "right" and the other "wrong." It just means that the two groups do not agree in evaluating the same performance. Thornton suggests that this may be healthy because it provides a basis for discussing differences and may foster an exchange of ideas. Campbell and Lee (1988) concluded that self-assessments were of greater value when used for developmental rather than administrative purposes.

Peer Assessments

In peer assessment members of a group appraise the performance of their fellows. According to Kane and Lawler (1978), three techniques are commonly used. One is peer nomination, in which each person nominates a specified number of group members as being highest on the particular dimension of performance. Peer ratings have each group member rate the others on a set of performance dimensions using one of several kinds of rating scales. The third technique is peer ranking, where each member ranks all others from best to worst on one or more performance dimensions.

The reliability of this method is determined by assessing the degree of interrater agreement. Most studies report high reliabilities (coefficients in the .80s and .90s), indicating that peers agree about the job performance of group members. Validity of peer assessments is determined by correlating the peer assessments with criterion measures usually made later—such as who successfully completed a training program, who got promoted first, the size of raises, and so on. What is uncanny is that group members who have known one another a relatively short time (two to three weeks) can be quite accurate in their long-term predictions about one another. Validity coefficients are fairly impressive, commonly in the .40 to .50 range. The peer nomination technique appears to best identify people with extreme levels of attributes as compared to other members of the group. Peer ratings are the most applicable but have only marginal empirical support. It has been suggested that their use be limited to giving feedback to employees on how others perceive them. Relatively few data are available on the value of peer rankings, although they may be the best method for assessing overall job performance.

There is some evidence that peer assessments are biased by friendship (that is, employees evaluate their friends most favorably), but friendships may be formed on the basis of performance. Also, many work group members do not like to evaluate one another, so part of the method's success hinges on impressing participants with its value. Indeed, Cederblom and Lounsbury (1980) showed that lack of user acceptance may be a serious obstacle in using this otherwise promising method. They found that a sample of college professors felt peer assessments were heavily biased by friendship. They thought peers would rate and be rated by their friends more favorably than would be justified. Problems with knowing the people to be rated and fostering a "mutual admiration society" caused the professors to question the value of peer assessment. They also felt that the method should be used for feedback, not for raises and promotions. Despite reluctance to use peer assessments for administrative decisions, research continues to support their predictive accuracy. Shore, Shore, and Thornton (1992) found peer assessments to be superior to self-assessments of job advancement.

Peer assessment, like self-assessment, is part of an overall performance appraisal system. The information generated cannot be isolated from information gained using other methods. Holzbach (1978) showed that superior, peer, and self-assessments all contribute information about performance. But information from each source involved halo errors. Borman (1974) showed that peers, superiors, and subordinates (if any) hold unique pieces of the puzzle that portray a person's job performance. Thus, rather than having raters at just one level of the organization, it is better to have each level contribute the portion that it is able to perform most effectively. Each performance dimension should be defined precisely enough to obtain the information unique to the relevant source. Overlap with dimensions better assessed by other sources should be avoided. The appraisal system should include compatible and mutually supporting segments. Each segment should be assigned the role to which it is best suited (Kane & Lawler, 1978). Performance appraisal should not be seen as simply selecting the best method. What is "best" varies with the use made of the information, the complexity of the performance appraised, and the people capable of making such judgments.

Feedback of Appraisal Information to Employees

In the final step of appraisal, the employee and his or her superior review and discuss the evaluation, usually referred to by the misnomer "performance appraisal interview." Performance was appraised before the interview; the interview is a means of giving the employee the results. Both superior and subordinate are usually very uneasy about the interview. Employees often get defensive about negative performance aspects. Superiors are often nervous about having to confront employees face to face with negative evaluations. However, for an appraisal system to be effective, interview objectives must be met with the same rigor as the other system objectives.

The interview typically has two main objectives. The first is reviewing major job responsibilities and how well the employee has met them. The second objective is future planning, or identifying goals the employee will try to meet before the next review. Both employee and superior should provide input in setting goals.

There has been much research on factors that contribute to success in meeting the two objectives of the interview. Feedback on job performance has two properties: information and motivation. That is, feedback can tell the employee how to perform better as well as increase his or her desire to perform well. Ilgen, Fisher, and Taylor (1979) showed that how the employee perceives the superior can greatly influence his or her response to feedback. They feel credibility and power are the most important aspects here. Credibility is the extent to which the superior is seen as someone who can legitimately evaluate performance. It is enhanced when the superior is seen as having expertise about the employee's job and being in a position to evaluate performance. Power is the extent to which the superior can control valued rewards. Ilgen and associates believe that credibility and power influence (1) how well the employee understands feedback, (2) the extent to which the feedback is seen as correct, and (3) the willingness of the employee to alter behavior as suggested by the feedback.

Other factors can also influence employee reactions to the performance appraisal interview. Kay, Meyer, and French (1965) studied the relationship between criticism and employee defensiveness. They found that the more critical the superior, the more defensive the employee became. However, praise per se did not make employees more at ease. Most criticism was buried in a "praise sandwich" (that is, praise/criticism/praise). The superior would praise the employee ostensibly to make him or her feel more at ease, then criticize some aspect of the employee's performance, then praise the employee again so that he or she left with a "good feeling." But employees became conditioned to the fact that when they were praised, it was a signal that some criticism was just around the corner.

Another area of research interest is nonverbal communication. Nonverbal communication refers to the messages we communicate without words. They are powerful and often unintended indicators of how we feel. It has been suggested that while we all can use words to deceive, our nonverbal communications reveal the truth about ourselves. Birdwhistell (1970) presented three major categories of nonverbal communication: kinesics (body movements such as eye contact, head nodding, posture, and gestures), paralanguages (such as saying "mm-hmm" or "un-huh"), and proxemics (the physical distance between people). We are just beginning to understand what role nonverbal behaviors play in organizational life.

DeMeuse (1987) concluded that the frequency of smiling and head nodding is related to overall performance evaluation. Smiling, approving, accepting people seem to receive higher evaluations than their more reserved counterparts. Research on proxemics indicates that distances of 4 to 5 feet seem most comfortable for many North Americans; greater distance is perceived as aloofness. Gifford, Ng, and Wilkinson (1985) reported that employment interviewers rated job applicants as having greater motivation and social skills when the applicants smiled more, used hand gestures, dressed stylishly, and were talkative. Vetter (1969) has shown that people attribute meaning to these nonverbal cues, although the meaning may not accurately reveal the affective state of the cue sender. For example, if an employee slouches in the chair during the interview, the superior can interpret the behavior to mean that the employee is indifferent or bored. The superior who does not smile during the meeting may be perceived by the employee as having a rejecting feeling about him or her. Both parties could be wrong in their attributions of meaning. The slouching employee may be very nervous, not bored. The unsmiling superior may only be trying to avoid the image that the interview is a lighthearted affair that should not be taken seriously. Sometimes nonverbal cues are seen as complementing the verbal message. ("I got praised up and down, and he never quit smiling the whole time.") At other times, they may be a mixed signal. ("I can't quite figure it out—he said I was doing great, but he didn't smile at me once.")

Cederblom (1982) found that three factors seem consistently useful in producing effective performance appraisal interviews: the supervisor's knowledge of the subordinate's job and performance in it, the supervisor's support of the subordinate, and a welcoming of the subordinate's participation. However, just conducting a performance appraisal interview will not resolve all problems in evaluating subordinate performance. Ilgen, Peterson, Martin, and Boeschen (1981) found that even after the performance appraisal interview, subordinates and supervisors sometimes disagreed on the level of subordinate performance, with subordinates feeling that their performance was at a higher level.

In a review of performance evaluations, Greenberg (1986) identified seven characteristics that contributed to employees' accepting their evaluations and feeling they were fair:

- Solicitation of employee input prior to the evaluation and using it.
- Two-way communication during the appraisal interview.
- The opportunity to challenge/rebut the evaluation.
- The rater's degree of familiarity with the ratee's work.
- The consistent application of performance standards.
- Basing ratings on actual performance achieved.
- Basing recommendations for salary/promotions on the ratings.

I fully concur with Greenberg's findings. My experience with effective performance appraisal systems underscores the importance of all these characteristics and clearly reveals that there is much more to performance evaluation than making a check mark on an appraisal instrument. Russell and Goode (1988) concluded that managers' reactions to performance appraisal systems were affected by their overall satisfaction with them (that is, their attitude toward the systems' ability to document the performance of their subordinates) and the appraisal's improvement value. Likewise, Dickinson (1993) found that the most important determinant of employee attitudes about performance appraisal is the supervisor. When the supervisor is perceived as trustworthy and supportive, attitudes about performance appraisal are favorable.

Concluding Comments

The topic of performance appraisal has attracted strong research interest among I/O psychologists over the past 30 years. However, the primary focus of the research has changed across time. Latham, Skarlicki, Irvine, and Siegel (1993) noted that earlier research on performance appraisal tended to address the psychometric properties of the various types of rating instruments. Such studies included the effects of rating scales on reducing rater errors and enhancing accuracy. More recent research has addressed the broader organizational context in which performance appraisals are conducted including user reactions, perceptions of fairness, and the process of how evaluations can be used to develop employees. Ilgen, Barnes-Farrell, and McKellin (1993) believe that the major problems facing performance appraisals do not lie in rating scale construction or the cognitive processes raters use to make evaluations. Rather, more attention should be given to the values and expectations generated by the social context in which raters find themselves. Factors such as the extent to which raters desire to be liked by ratees and beliefs about freedom to be open and honest in making evaluations are under-researched. It appears that future research on performance appraisal will continue down the path of examining how evaluations are shaped by the organizational context in which they are made.

CASE STUDY   *What Do You Do with Poor Performers?*

Anita Douglass was the regional sales manager for a national chain of fitness centers. Her job was to direct a sales force that sold fitness center franchises to operators. The salesperson's job was to recruit responsible, ambitious people who would invest their own time and money into operating a center. Each operator would pay a franchise fee to the company. The company, in turn, would lease the building, supply all the equipment, and would help with the financing, if needed. Sales throughout the nation were very strong, as there was a heavy demand for fitness training. Douglass's sales territory was second-best in the nation. All her salespeople were doing very well, except two. Marty Crane and Julie Forester consistently failed to meet their sales goals. Both were running out of excuses, and Douglass was running out of patience. Douglass was angered and embarrassed over their poor performance. She figured that the only reason her boss hadn't inquired about Crane and Forester was because she could "bury" their performance within the overall performance of her sales territory. If these two salespeople had been at the top of the pile instead of the bottom, her sales territory would be number one in the nation.

Despite their common substandard performance, Douglass viewed them somewhat differently. After Crane's first bad performance evaluation, she undertook additional training. While the extra training didn't seem to help, at least she tried. Crane seemed to be working hard but getting nowhere—described in her last performance review as "an ineffectual diffusion of energy," otherwise known as "spinning your wheels." Crane had a pleasing demeanor, which may have been part of her problem. Douglass thought that perhaps Crane was more concerned with having people approve of her than making a sale. Maybe Crane would perform better for the company in a job outside of sales, she thought.

Forester, on the other hand, seemed rather indifferent about failing to meet her sales goals and attributed her poor performance to everyone except herself. If Forester ever worked up a sweat, it went unnoticed by Douglass. Forester conveyed the impression that the company was lucky to have her, although the reasons for this privilege were indiscernible. None of the other salespeople wanted anything to do with Forester. They wouldn't trade sales territories with her, and they didn't want Forester covering for them when they went on vacation.

Douglass thumbed through the personnel files of Crane and Forester. It was becoming increasingly more difficult to justify not firing them. If only one of them got the axe, Douglass decided it would be Forester. Then Douglass caught herself in midthought. The performance of both these salespeople was equally bad. How could she justify keeping one and firing the other? Douglass surmised that the only difference between Crane and Forester was that she liked one more than the other. Douglass had the reputation of being tough but fair. She couldn't understand why this was becoming a difficult decision for her, and why she was considering being more charitable to Crane than to Forester.

Questions

1. What is it about Crane that makes Douglass view her differently from Forester?
2. Are these issues relevant in judging job performance? Should they matter?
3. If you were Douglass, what would you do with Crane and Forester?
4. Do you think Douglass's boss would be critical of Douglass for tolerating poor performance, or admire her for being patient with members of her staff?
5. What other information would you like to have before deciding whether Crane and Forester should be retained or fired?

ORGANIZATIONAL PSYCHOLOGY

SECTION

3

Organizations and Work Teams

Major Chapter Objectives

- *Be able to explain the three major theories of organization.*

- *Be able to explain Mintzberg's theory of organizational structure.*

- *Be able to explain downsizing and its effect on organizations.*

- *Understand the components of social systems: roles, norms, and culture.*

- *Understand the concept of work teams and their principles.*

Many academic disciplines have contributed to the study of organizations, including I/O psychology, sociology, economics, and political science, but their contributions tend to differ in terms of the specific constructs investigated. The most common I/O perspective is to examine individual behavior and attitudes within an organizational context. A related topic of interest to I/O psychologists is how work groups function within organizations. Work groups may be examined in terms of how they are formed and how effectively they perform. Larger scale analyses of organizations (most often conducted outside of I/O psychology) include the relationships between organizations, as well as the relationship of organizations to larger social structures such as society.

Davis and Powell (1992) note that the study of organizations is relatively recent, having begun in the 1950s. During that time, psychologists began to appreciate how much influence organizations exerted on the behavior of employees. And in 1970 the profession of "industrial" psychology officially became "industrial/organizational" psychology, thus defining the scope of I/O psychology as we know it today. Formal recognition of the "O" in I/O psychology compelled us to gain a better understanding of the social bases of behavior. This chapter is devoted to explaining how two social concepts—organizations and work teams—influence and shape the behavior of their members. In this chapter I will examine various organizing concepts ranging from the formal structure of an organization to the social dynamics of work groups.

Three Theories of Organization

It is probably easier to state why organizations exist rather than to define what they are. In their simplest form, organizations exist as vehicles for accomplishing goals and objectives; that is, organizations are collectivities of parts that accomplish goals more effectively when organized in a larger structure. This organizing process has been examined in a variety of ways, producing various schools of thought or theories about organizations. There are three major schools of thought about organizations, with many variations and emphases (Scott, 1992): classical, neoclassical, and systems theories of organization. These schools of thought take markedly different views of the same phenomenon.

Classical Theory

Classical theory, which emerged in the first few decades of the 20th century, focuses mainly on structural relationships in organizations. Classical theory begins with a statement of the basic ingredients of any organization and then addresses how the organization should best be structured to accomplish its objectives. Classical theory posits four basic components to any organization:

> *A system of differentiated activities.* All organizations are composed of the activities and functions performed in them and the relationships among these

activities and functions. A formal organization emerges when these activities are linked together.

People. While organizations are composed of activities and functions, people perform tasks and exercise authority.

Cooperation toward a goal. Cooperation must exist among the people performing their various activities to achieve a unity of purpose in pursuit of common goals.

Authority. Authority is established through superior-subordinate relationships, and such authority is needed to ensure cooperation among people pursuing their goals.

Given that four ingredients are the basis of any organization, classical theory addressed itself to various structural properties by which the organization should best reach its goals. Four major structural principles are the hallmarks in the history of organizational theory.

Functional principle. The functional principle is the concept behind division of labor; that is, organizations should be divided into units that perform similar functions. Thus, work is broken down to provide clear areas of specialization, which in turn improves the organization's overall performance. Similar work activities often represent themselves as departments, which enhances coordination of activities and permits more effective supervision and a more rational flow of work. It is the functional principle that accounts for the fact that work functions are often grouped into such units as production, sales, engineering, finance, and so on; these labels describe the primary nature of the work performed within each unit. The functional principle refers to the horizontal growth of the organization, that is, the formation of new functional units along the horizontal dimension.

Scalar principle. The scalar principle deals with the organization's vertical growth and refers to the growth of the chain of command that results from levels added to the organization. Each level has its own degree of authority and responsibility for meeting organizational goals, with higher levels having greater degrees. Each subordinate should be accountable to only one superior, a tenet referred to as the *unity of command*. Classical theorists thought that the best way to overcome organizational fragmentation caused by division of labor was through a well-designed chain of command. Coordination among factions would be achieved by people occupying positions of command in a hierarchy. Figure 8–1 provides a graphic representation of both the functional and the scalar principles.

Line/staff principle. One way to differentiate organizational work functions is by whether they are line or staff. Line functions have the primary responsibility for meeting the major goals of the organization, like the production department in a manufacturing organization. Staff functions support the line's activities but are regarded as subsidiary in overall importance to line functions. Typical staff functions would be personnel and quality control. That is, while it is important to have good employees and to inspect products for their quality, the organization was not created to provide people with jobs

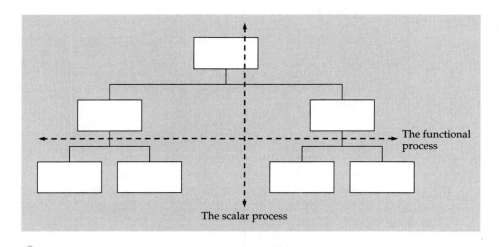

The functional process

The scalar process

Figure 8–1 *Pyramid of organization*

SOURCE: From *Organization Theory: A Structural and Behavioral Analysis* (p. 32) by W. G. Scott, T. R. Mitchell, and P. H. Birnbaum, 1981, Homewood, IL: Richard D. Irwin.

or products to inspect. It was created to manufacture products (a line function), and personnel and quality control are but two staff functions designed to support this larger goal.

Span-of-control principle. The span-of-control principle refers to the number of subordinates a manager is responsible for supervising. A "small" span of control would be 2 subordinates; a "large" span of control might be 15. Large spans of control produce flat-shaped organizations (that is, few levels between the top and bottom of the organization); small spans of control produce tall-shaped organizations (that is, many levels). A diagram showing how the span of control affects the shape of the organization is shown in Figure 8–2.

Classical theory is credited with providing the structural anatomy of organizations. It was the first major attempt to articulate the form and substance of organizations in a comprehensive fashion. There is little that is "psychological" about this view of organizations. Indeed, none of the classical organizational theorists were psychologists. The influence of psychology became apparent in neoclassical theory, the next school of thought. Nevertheless, while current organizational researchers regard classical theory as antiquated, its four principles are deeply ingrained in the real-life structure of organizations. Problems of line/staff relationships, number of organizational levels, division of labor, coordination, and spans of control are still of major concern. Further thinking about organizations occurred because organizations were more complex than the four classical principles would suggest. This desire to add richness and realism to organizational theory gave rise to neoclassical theory.

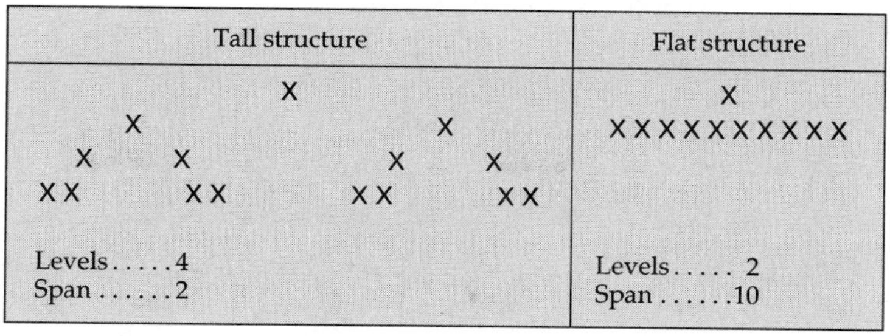

Tall structure		Flat structure
X		X
X	X	X X X X X X X X X X
X X	X X	
X X X X	X X X X	
Levels.....4		Levels..... 2
Span......2		Span 10

___

Figure 8–2 *Span of control and organizational structure*
SOURCE: From *Organization Theory: A Structural and Behavioral Analysis* (p. 34) by W. G. Scott, T. R. Mitchell, and P. H. Birnbaum, 1981, Homewood, IL: Richard D. Irwin.

Neoclassical Theory

Neoclassical theory had its birth in the 1950s, but its origins rest with findings from the Hawthorne studies. Neoclassical theory was identified with scholars who recognized the deficiencies in the classical school of thought. In fact, the name *neoclassical* connotes a modernization or updating of the original (classical) theory, while still acknowledging its contributions.

It is a misnomer to call neoclassical theory a "theory" because there really is no formal theory. Rather, it is a recognition of psychological/behavioral issues that question the rigidness with which the classical principles were originally stated. The neoclassicists examined the four major principles of classical theory and found evidence that challenged their apparent unassailability. This evidence was based primarily on psychological research and an examination of "real-life" organizational problems.

The neoclassicists noted that while division of labor causes functional interdependence among work activities, it also depersonalizes these activities so that the individual finds little meaning in them. People develop a sense of alienation from highly repetitive work, which ultimately results in dissatisfaction with their work. In turn, this dissatisfaction can result in decreased efficiency caused by lowered productivity and increased absence. In short, the neoclassicists argued for a less rigid division of labor and for more "humanistic" work in which people could derive a sense of value and meaning from their jobs.

The scalar principle was questioned on the grounds that other systems operate on people in organizations besides those imposed by formal superior-subordinate relationships. Individuals are influenced by interpersonal activities that extend well beyond those prescribed by the formal organizational structure. In short, while the scalar principle prescribes formal lines of authority, in reality many sources operating in an organization influence the individual.

The line/staff principle was perhaps the easiest for the neoclassicist to challenge. The black and white theoretical distinction between line and staff functions is not always so clear in practice. Take, for example, the sales function. A manufacturing company's purpose is indeed to produce, but if it does not sell what it produces, the company cannot survive. What, then, is the sales function—a major line function or an ancillary staff function? The neoclassicists illustrated that many staff functions are critical to the success of the organization, so the value of the distinction between line and staff is not as great as originally proposed.

Finally, deciding what contributes to a satisfactory span of control seems far more complex than picking a number. The neoclassicists noted that it depends on such issues as the supervisor's managerial ability (poor managers cannot supervise many subordinates) and the intensity of the needed supervision (one could effectively manage many more subordinates who do not require much direction than those who do require intensive direction). Psychological factors such as leadership style and capacity would greatly influence the determination of effective spans of control.

The primary contribution of neoclassical theory was to reveal that the principles proposed by classical theory were not as universally applicable and simple as originally formulated. The neoclassicists drew heavily on behavioral research that revealed the importance of individual differences, but they did not overtly reject classical theory. Rather than attempting to change the theory, they tried to make it fit the realities of human behavior in organizations. However, the neoclassicists were limited by commencing their conceptualization about organizations from the classical perspective. By the mid-1960s, it became apparent that an entirely new approach to thinking about organizations was necessary. Organizations were more complex than even the neoclassicists portrayed them; this led to the formation of a radically different school of thought called systems organization theory.

Systems Theory

Modern organization theory adopts a complex, dynamic view of organizations called the "systems approach." Systems theory had its origins in the biological sciences and was modified to meet the needs of organizational theory (Kast & Rosenzweig, 1972). Systems theory views an organization as existing in an interdependent relationship with its environment: "It is impossible to understand individual behavior or the activities of small groups apart from the social system in which they interact. A complex organization is a social system; the various discrete segments and functions in it do not behave as isolated elements. All parts affect all other parts. Every action has repercussions throughout the organization, because all of its elements are linked" (Scott, Mitchell, & Birnbaum, 1981, p. 44). In fact, the idea that all parts of the system are interdependent is the key to understanding the systems approach. All of the parts and their interrelatedness make up the "system," which is how the theory gets its name.

Systems theory asserts that an organizational system is composed of five parts:

The system

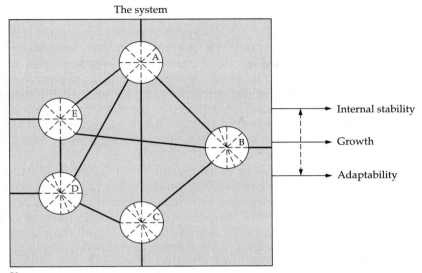

Internal stability

Growth

Adaptability

Key:
  1. Circles represent parts of the system.
  2. Broken lines represent intrapart interactions, i.e., individuals with other individuals.
  3. Solid lines represent interpart interaction.
  4. Both the solid and broken lines are the processes that tie the parts of the system together.

Figure 8–3   *The framework of systems analysis*

SOURCE: From *Organization Theory: A Structural and Behavioral Analysis* (p. 48) by W. G. Scott, T. R. Mitchell, and P. H. Birnbaum, 1981, Homewood, IL: Richard D. Irwin.

- *Individuals.* Individuals bring their own personalities, abilities, and attitudes with them to the organization, which influences what they hope to attain by participating in the system.
- *Formal organization.* The formal organization is the interrelated pattern of jobs that provide the structure of the system.
- *Small groups.* Individuals do not work in isolation but form memberships in small groups as a way to facilitate their own adaptability within the system.
- *Status and role.* Status and role differences exist among jobs within an organization and define the behavior of individuals within the system.
- *Physical setting.* The physical setting includes the external physical environment and the degree of technology that characterizes the organization.

Figure 8–3 illustrates the five parts of the system and their interrelatedness. Complex interactions exist among all parts of the system. Individuals interact to form small groups, members of the groups are differentiated by status and roles, the physical environment affects the behavior of individuals and groups, and all exist within the framework provided by the formal organization.

With all of these parts making up the system, it is necessary to have a means to provide coordination and linkage among them. Such functions are accomplished through communication and decision making; they permit the various parts of the system to "talk" to each other. Organizational communication occurs through a series of networks that often bear little resemblance to formal lines of authority. Similarly, decisions often get made in ways that deviate from formal lines of authority. That is, the reality of how organizations actually conduct themselves is usually quite different from the principles established by classical organizational theory. Also, the Achilles' heel of most large organizations is a failure to communicate. This makes considerable sense given the systems perspective of organizations wherein communication is the means by which the system can be responsive to its environment.

Finally, systems theory instructs us that the parts and interactions of a system do not exist for themselves. Rather, they exist to meet the system's larger goals, which are to attain stability, growth, and adaptability. A living organism has to be stable in the sense that its parts are harmoniously integrated. Growth reflects a sense of vitality and vigor. Adaptability is critical if the organism is to respond to environmental changes, because adaptability enables the organism to survive in times of rapid change. Thus, a healthy, successful organization is not only "effective" in meeting its business objectives but also stable, growing, and adaptable. These are the characteristics of all living organisms, be they organizations, animals, plants, or societies.

Systems theory offers a radical departure from the classical and neoclassical schools of thought. Systems theory views organizations as living organisms. The purpose of an organization is to reach stability, to grow, and to adapt, as all living organisms must do to survive. Note the abstractness of systems theory. There are no direct references to anything quite as simple as a span of control, for example. This abstractness is deliberate, for only at some degree of generality can we attempt to equate such diverse entities as organizations, plants, and animals. Modern organizational theorists believe that an understanding of something as complex as an organization requires the type of conceptualizations offered by systems theory. A systems perspective of organizations permits us to understand phenomena of organizational life that earlier theories did not address.

Despite the distinctiveness of the three schools of thought on organizations, each school offered critical concepts that are of great relevance today. These schools of thought are more than historical milemarkers in the evolution of organizational theory. In particular, the concept of small groups from systems theory has been greatly amplified to provide a primary focal point of interest, that of the work team. The concept of work teams and their significance will be discussed later in this chapter.

Organizational Structure

Mintzberg (1993) has offered a comprehensive and lucid explanation of how organizations evolve in reaching a certain form and shape. These characteristics are the "structure" or formal component of an organization. Various types of structure are possible, and organizations continuously seek a structure that is an optimal match to its environment. That is, the structure of an organization is an adaptive mechanism that permits the organization to function in its surroundings. Organizations with maladaptive structures will ultimately cease to exist. Since individuals assume roles within organizations, individuals (most notably employees) feel the brunt of change caused by the continuing evolution of an organization's structure. It is in this regard that I/O psychology is involved in matters of organizational structure.

Coordinating Mechanisms

Mintzberg (1993) defines the structure of an organization as "the sum total of the ways in which its labor is divided into distinct tasks and then its coordination is achieved among these tasks" (p. 2). While many structures are possible for an organization, the number of effective structures for a particular organization are relatively few. Five coordinating mechanisms have been proposed to explain the fundamental ways organizations coordinate their work. These are considered to be the most basic elements of structure—the glue that holds organizations together.

1. *Mutual adjustment.* Mutual adjustment achieves coordination of work by the process of informal communication among employees. As the term implies, it is the process by which employees coordinate their efforts to produce an outcome. Two people paddling a canoe would be an example of the mutual adjustment between individuals needed to propel the canoe through water.

2. *Direct supervision.* Direct supervision achieves coordination by having one person take responsibility for the work of others, issuing instructions to them and monitoring their actions. As an organization outgrows its simplest state, it turns to this second mechanism of coordination. In effect one brain coordinates several hands, as the coxswain (stroke caller) of a six-person rowing crew.

3. *Standardization of work processes.* Work processes are standardized when the contents of the work are specified. The production assembly line of a manufacturing company would be one such example. A worker inserts a bolt into a holed piece of metal. There is only one action to perform, and there is no room for individual discretion as to how the work is performed. The work is designed in such a way that the same process is followed no matter who is performing the job.

4. *Standardization of work output.* Outputs are standardized when the results of the work, for example, the dimensions of the product or the performance, are specified. The fast food industry would be an example. A hamburger ordered from a particular fast food vendor should look and taste the same whether it was purchased day or night, in July or December, in Cleveland or San Diego. The work is designed in such a way that the same output is achieved irrespective of differences in time or location.

5. *Standardization of skills and knowledge.* Skills and knowledge are standardized when the kind of training required to perform the work is specified. In this case coordination is achieved before the work is undertaken. Organizations insti-

tute training programs for employees to standardize the skills needed to perform work, thereby controlling and coordinating the work. By example, there is rarely communication between an anesthesiologist and a surgeon in an operating room while removing an appendix. They hardly need to communicate, because by virtue of their medical training they know what to expect of each other.

According to Mintzberg, these five coordinating mechanisms manifest themselves in a rough order. As organizational work becomes more complicated, the means of coordination shifts from mutual adjustment to direct supervision. This is followed by standardization of work processes, then outputs, and finally skills. A person working alone has no need for any coordinating mechanisms. The addition of a second person requires that the two individuals adjust to each other. As the group gets larger, however, it becomes less able to coordinate informally. A need for leadership arises. Control of the work group passes to a single individual, as direct supervision becomes the favored coordinating mechanism. As the work becomes more involved, a transition occurs toward standardization. When the tasks are simple and routine, the organization relies on the standardization of the work processes themselves. However, increasingly complex work may preclude this, compelling the organization to turn to standardization of the outputs. In very complex work, the outputs often cannot be standardized either. Therefore, the organization must settle for standardizing the skills of the worker.

Organizations cannot rely on a single coordinating mechanism. Most use all five. A certain amount of direct supervision and mutual adjustment is always required. Contemporary organizations simply cannot exist without leadership and informal communication. In the most automated (that is, fully standardized) factory, machines break down, employees fail to show up for work, and schedules must be changed at the last minute. Supervisors must intervene, and workers must be free to deal with unexpected problems.

Classic organization theory emphasized both direct supervision and standardization as coordinating mechanisms. The concepts of span of control, line/staff, and unity of command characterize the components of an organization's *formal structure*. Frederick Taylor (1911) sought to achieve coordination through standardization, specifying the work operations (as body movements and when to take work breaks) of pig-iron handlers and coal-shovelers. According to scholars in the beginning of the 20th century, organizational structure defined a set of official, standardized work relationships built around a tight system of formal authority.

However, neoclassic organizational theory revealed the significance of the most primary means of attaining coordination, that of mutual adjustment. That is, other activities take place among workers that are not in line with the official organizational structure. Thus, the presence of unofficial relationships within work groups (an *informal structure*) established that mutual adjustment serves as an important coordinating mechanism in all organizations. In fact, as you will see in Chapter 13, the mechanism of standardization, a long-standing hallmark of formal organizational structure, was actually detrimental to the psychological and physical health of the worker. It was not until the creation of systems theory that a balance between the classic and neoclassic perspectives was attained and all five coordinating mechanisms were regarded as viable.

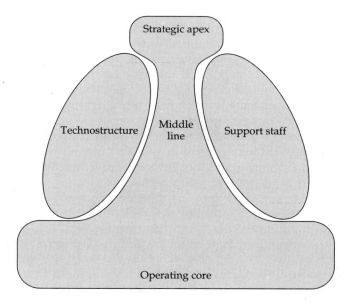

Figure 8–4   *The five basic parts of an organization*
SOURCE: From *Structure in Fives: Designing Effective Organizations* (p. 11) by H. Mintzberg, 1993, Englewood Cliffs, NJ: Prentice Hall.

Five Basic Parts of an Organization[1]

Consistent with systems theory, organizations are structured to define the interrelationships among the parts of the systems. Mintzberg (1993) proposes that all organizations consist of five basic parts, as shown in Figure 8–4.

1. *Operating core.* The operating core of the organization encompasses those members, the operators, who perform the basic work related directly to the production of products and services. The operators secure the inputs needed for production (buy the raw material), turn inputs into outputs (assemble individual parts into complete units), and distribute the outputs (sell the product). The operating core is the heart of every organization, the part that produces the essential outputs that keep it alive.

2. *Strategic apex.* The strategic apex is charged with ensuring that the organization serves its mission in an effective way. Here are found those people charged with *overall* responsibility for the organization—the president and any other top-level managers whose concerns are broad. The strategic apex plays the most important role in providing direction to the organization, serving as the organization's brain.

[1]Mintzberg (1993) notes that the number "five" often appears in the study of organizational structure (indeed, it is the basis of his book's title, *Structure in Fives*). While the number five is not magical, it does represent the number of concepts used to explain various aspects of organizational structure. The interested reader is encouraged to explore the profound insights Mintzberg offers in his book about organizational structure.

3. *Middle line*. The strategic apex is joined to the operating core by the chain of middle-line managers with formal authority. This chain runs from the senior managers to the first-line supervisors, who have direct authority over the operators, and embodies the coordinating mechanism of direct supervision. In theory, one person at the top of the strategic apex can supervise all operators. In practice, direct supervision requires close personal contact between manager and operator, with the result that there is some limit to the number of operators any one manager can supervise. An organizational *hierarchy* is built, as a first-line supervisor is put in charge of a number of operators to form a basic organizational unit. In turn, another manager is put in charge of a number of these units to form a higher level unit, and so on. Eventually all the remaining units come under a single person at the strategic apex to form the whole organization.

4. *Technostructure*. In the technostructure are found the analysts who serve the organization by affecting the work of others. These analysts are removed from the operating work flow. They may design the work, plan it, or train the people who do it, but they do not do it themselves. The technostructure is effective only when it can use its analytical techniques to make the work of others more effective. In general, the more standardization the organization uses to facilitate coordination, the more it relies on its technostructure. Standardization of skills plays a major role in coordinating the analysts own work, because analysts are typically highly trained specialists.

5. *Support staff*. The support staff exists to provide services to aid the basic mission of the organization. These typically would include the mailroom, switchboard, security, and janitorial services. Many times the support staff is lumped together with the technostructure and labeled the "staff" (vis-à-vis the line/staff distinction). However, support units are decidedly different from the technostructure. The support staff is not directed toward giving advice. Rather, its function is to perform. The support staff does not use a single coordinating mechanism. Rather, each unit relies on whatever mechanism is most appropriate for itself, such as standardization of skills in the legal department and standardization of work processes in the cafeteria.

In many organizations decision-making power is highly centralized; that is, it flows from the strategic apex, down through the middle line of the hierarchy, to the operating core. Centralization is the tightest means of coordinating decision making in the organization. Decisions are made by one person and then implemented through direct supervision. However, strong pressures can exist to decentralize, to push decision-making power lower down the organizational hierarchy. Mintzberg (1993) cites three reasons for this. One is that not all of an organization's decisions can be understood at the strategic apex. Sometimes the necessary information just cannot be brought to the apex. People at the bottom of the hierarchy with the necessary knowledge end up having to defer to managers at the top who are out of touch with the immediate situation. Second, decentralization allows the organization to respond quickly to local conditions. The transmission of information to the apex and back takes time, which may be critical. Third, decentralization is a stimulus for motivation. The organization can attract and retain intelligent people only if it gives them considerable power to make decisions.

Giving power to middle-line managers trains them in decision making, which is an increasingly important skill as an individual moves up the organizational hierarchy. However, as Mintzberg cautions, centralization and decentralization should not be treated as absolutes but rather as two ends of a continuum. In reality most organizations manifest some of the properties of both, with one being more prominent.

Reorganizing and Downsizing

The structure of an organization is its means of adapting to its environment. Accordingly, when the environment changes (for example, because of greater competition or regulatory control), it is common for the organization's structure to change in response. The structure of an organization has a great impact on individuals (most notably its employees), and an organization may choose to expand because of greater opportunities to sell its products or services. This would necessitate hiring more employees at the operating core and middle-level management, and typically more staff employees to serve their needs. It is also possible that as employees move up the organizational hierarchy, reporting relationships may change among the employees. These types of changes in the organizational structure are referred to as *reorganizing,* implying that the organization is reconfiguring itself to better adapt to its environment.

However, another form of reorganization also greatly affects the lives of employees and involves the loss of jobs. An organization may believe it has too many employees to be effectively responsive to its environment. The most common cause for the decision to cut jobs is the conclusion that the organization can "do more with less" (that is, have greater efficiency with fewer employees). For most organizations the single largest expense is wages and salaries paid to employees. By eliminating jobs, an organization can reduce costs. The work that would have been accomplished by the departed employees will now have to be performed by the remaining employees, or through technical changes in work processes (for example, automation). The terms given to this process of job loss include *downsizing, reduction-in-force,* and *right-sizing.* The term *right-sizing* implies there is a size for the organization that is "right" or correct for its environment. It is not uncommon for large organizations to reduce their size by several thousand employees at one time.

Where do the jobs that are eliminated come from within an organization? All five parts of the organization are targeted, with the greatest losses typically coming from the middle line, technostructure, and support staff. Job loss can also occur in the operating core as jobs become automated or are reassigned to other countries that pay lower wages. The strategic apex may also be reduced, but generally the fewest job losses occur at this level. As noted previously, the support staff consists of such jobs as security personnel and cafeteria workers. Rather than organizations hiring their own employees to work in these jobs, organizations contract (in effect, "rent") the services of these people through other organizations, such as a company that offers security guards or food preparers to other organizations. Contracting the services of these individuals is less costly to the

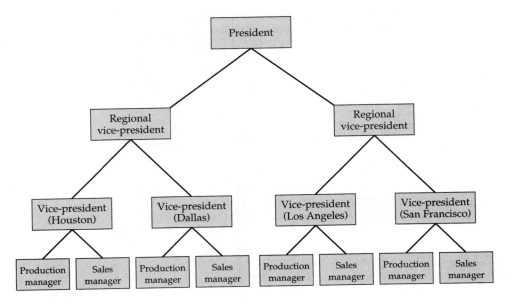

Figure 8–5   *Top part of organizational chart for manufacturing company before downsizing*

organization than hiring their own employees to perform these services. Similar reductions occur in the technostructure. With fewer employees to advise (the primary function of the technostructure), there is less need for "advisers." You may recall from Chapter 1 that in recent years the number of I/O psychologists working in organizations has decreased, while the number working for consulting firms has increased. In essence, organizations have reduced the number of jobs typically filled by I/O psychologists, and in turn contracted their services through consulting firms.

However, most of the job loss has occurred in the middle line. The middle line serves as a means of direct supervision for lower-level employees. How can an organization survive without the middle line? The answer lies in the coordinating mechanisms. Direct supervision is one of the five coordinating mechanisms. By eliminating much of the middle line, the coordinating mechanism shifts from direct supervision to standardization. The coordination formerly achieved through personal contact with a supervisor is now achieved through greater standardization of the work process, the output, or employee skills.

Another manifestation of reorganization through downsizing is larger spans of control. With larger spans of control, fewer managers are needed, the organizational hierarchy becomes smaller, and the shape of the organization becomes flatter. It is also common for decision making to become more decentralized following downsizing. Figure 8–5 shows the top part of an organizational chart for a manufacturing company. The company is structured to be organized by both function (production and sales) and location (California and Texas). There are small spans of control. Each person below the president has two subordinates.

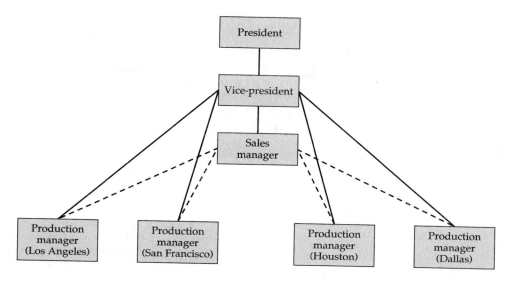

Figure 8–6   *Top part of organizational chart for manufacturing company after downsizing*

With such a configuration, a total of 15 people are needed to staff this part of the organization. Figure 8–6 shows the same company following reorganization, in this case, downsizing. A total of 8 jobs have been eliminated by this reorganization. The sales function has been consolidated into one job. The plant manager at each of the four locations now reports directly to the vice-president. Each plant manager now also provides information directly to the sales manager (as indicated by the dotted lines), but administratively the plant managers report to the vice-president. The vice-president now has a span of control of five. The jobs lost in this reorganization include one vice-president, three sales managers, and the entire layer of (middle) managers.

What consequences might we expect from this reorganization? There would be less administrative control because of the loss of managerial jobs. There would be greater pressure on the organization's parts to coordinate with each other because of the loss of direct supervision. There would probably be more stress placed on the surviving employees to work harder and find new ways to do the work of the other employees whose jobs were eliminated. The organization would have fewer salary expenditures because eight jobs were eliminated. Eight people would be out of work.

How would you feel if you lost your job because you were fired? Probably not very good, but in all likelihood you would have received some signals along the way that you were not performing satisfactorily. In turn, you probably would have had some control over whether to change your job behavior. How would you feel if you lost your job because it was eliminated? You could have been an exemplary employee, but you lost your job through no fault of your own. *You* were not released, rather the *job* you were filling was eliminated to make the

DILBERT   SOURCE: Dilbert ® reprinted by permission of United Feature Syndicate, Inc.

organization more efficient. In the next chapter I will examine the psychological reactions to downsizing, both from the perspective of the survivors and of those whose jobs were eliminated.

Organizational structure exerts a great influence on the lives of individuals. When organizations are expanding in size to better adapt to their environments, new jobs are created eventually culminating in the recruitment, selection, training, and appraisal of new employees. When organizations are contracting in size, the overall social order of employment is altered. As a rule, organizations that are downsizing reduce the number of middle managers needed to run the business. These displaced middle managers will not necessarily find new jobs as middle managers in other companies; rather, the *job* of middle manager is being reduced in frequency. Holders of middle management jobs may be forced to enter new jobs, not new positions in the same job family. This may necessitate professional retraining, learning new skills to fill jobs that continue to exist. Thus, issues of organizational structure affect not only I/O psychology but also the sociology of employment and the economics of across-occupation mobility.

While organizations are defined in large part by their structures, division of labor is not the only concept needed to understand the functioning of organizations. Organizations also have social systems that influence the conduct of their employees. This is the topic of the next section.

Components of Social Systems

A social system is a structuring of events or happenings; it has no formal structure apart from its functioning. Physical or biological systems (cars or human beings) have structures that can be identified even when they are not functioning (electrical or skeleton structures); that is, they have both an anatomy and a physiology. There is no anatomy to a social system. When a social system stops functioning, no identifiable structure remains. It is hard for us to think of social systems as having no tangible anatomy, because it is easier to understand concepts with concrete and simple components (Katz & Kahn, 1978). Social systems do indeed have components, but they are not concrete and are sometimes referred to as the *informal components* of an organization. Three components of social systems are

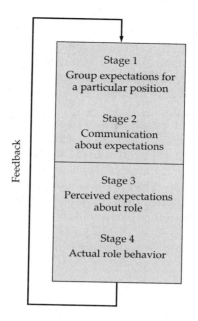

Figure 8–7   The role episode
SOURCE: From *Organization Theory: A Structural and Behavioral Analysis* (p. 103) by W. Scott, T. R. Mitchell, and P. H. Birnbaum, 1981, Homewood, IL: Richard D. Irwin.

particularly important and will be discussed in detail here. Keep in mind that these are abstract components embodied only in their functioning.

Roles

When an employee enters an organization, there is much for that person to learn. This includes expected performance levels, recognition of superiors, dress codes, and time demands. Roles ease the learning process. Roles are usually defined as the expectations of others about appropriate behavior in a specific position (Scott et al., 1981). Each of us plays several roles simultaneously (parent, employee, club member, and so on), but I will focus on job-related roles here.

Scott and associates (1981) listed five important aspects of roles. First, they are impersonal; the position itself determines the expectations, not the individual. Second, roles are related to task behavior. An organizational role is the expected behaviors for a particular job. Third, roles can be difficult to pin down. The problem is defining who determines what is expected. Since other people define our roles, opinions differ over what our role should be. How we see our role, how others see our role, and what we actually do may differ. Fourth, roles are learned quickly and can produce major behavior changes. Fifth, roles and jobs are not the same—a person in one job might play several roles.

We learn our role through a *role episode*, shown in Figure 8–7. Group members have expectations about job performance, which they communicate either formally or by having the role occupant observe others in similar roles. In stage 3, the role occupant internalizes the behavior he or she believes is appropriate. If the behavior (stage 4) differs widely from the group's expectations (stage 1), the occupant gets feedback from the group regarding the discrepancy. This feedback is intended to alter behavior toward meeting group expectations. The role episode is ongoing. Expectations may change over time, as might the employee's behavior.

Another aspect of role behavior is role differentiation. This is the extent to which different roles are performed by employees in the same subgroup. One person's job might be to maintain good group relations, such as a work-unit coordinator. His or her role might require providing emotional or interpersonal support to others. Another's role might be setting schedules, agendas, and meeting deadlines; such a person is usually an administrator. When all roles in a work group fit together like the parts of a puzzle, a smoothly running, effective group results. However, all the parts may not fit together. In the next chapter, I will examine the ways some organizational pressures produce role problems.

Norms

Norms are shared group expectations about appropriate behavior. While roles define what is appropriate for a particular job, norms define acceptable group behavior. Roles differentiate positions; norms establish behavior expected of everyone in the group, such as when employees take coffee breaks, how much they produce, when they stop for the day, and what they wear. Norms are unwritten rules that govern behavior. A no-smoking sign is not a norm but a formal written rule of behavior. If employees smoke despite the sign, there is a norm that sanctions such behavior in spite of the formal rule.

Norms have several important properties. First, there is "oughtness" or "shouldness"—that is, prescriptions for behavior. Second, norms are usually more obvious for behavior judged to be important for the group. A norm might exist for when employees stop work before lunch. But there probably would not be a norm about what employees eat. Third, norms are enforced by the group. Much expected behavior is monitored and enforced through formal rules and procedures. With norms, group members regulate behavior. Sometimes formal rules and group norms clash. The no-smoking rule and the group norm sanctioning smoking is an example. Unless the organization imposes sanctions on smokers (that is, rule breakers), the group norm would probably prevail. Finally, the degree that norms are shared and the degree that deviation is acceptable vary. Not all smokers might smoke in proscribed areas, and those who do not might be as accepted by the group as those who do.

There is a three-step process for developing and communicating norms. The norm must first be defined and communicated. This can be done either explicitly ("Here is the way we do things around here") or implicitly (the desired behavior is observed). Second, the group must be able to monitor behavior and judge whether the norm is being followed. Third, the group must be able to reward conformity and punish nonconformity. Conformity enhances predictability of be-havior within the group, which in turn promotes feelings of group cohesion.

Compliance with norms is enforced by positive reinforcement or punishment. Positive reinforcement can be praise or inclusion in group activities. Punishment can be a dirty look, a snide remark, or actual physical abuse. (Workers who ex-ceeded the group norm for productivity in the Hawthorne studies were hit on the arm, which was called "binging.") Another form of punishment is exclusion from group activities. The group will often try to convince the nonconforming em-ployee (referred to as a *deviant*) to change his or her behavior. The group will try to alter the deviant's opinion through increased communication, verbal or nonver-bal. The clearer and more important the norm, the more cohesive the group and the greater the pressure will become. Eventually, the deviant will either change or be rejected. If rejected, the deviant will become an isolate, and the pressure to conform will stop. Because the group may need the isolate to perform work tasks, they will usually reach a truce; the isolate will be tolerated in work but excluded from group activities and relations. The isolate can quit the job and try to find a better match between his or her values and a group or continue in an uncomfort-able work situations.

Finally, norms are not always contrary to formal organization rules or inde-pendent of them. Sometimes norms greatly aid organization goals. For example, there may be a norm against leaving for home before a certain amount of work has been done. Although quitting time is 5:00 P.M., the group may expect employ-ees to stay until 5:15 or 5:30 and finish a certain task. In this case the deviant is one who conforms to the formal rule (that is, leaving at 5:00 P.M.) instead of the group norm. When group norms and organization goals are complementary, high de-grees of effectiveness can result.

Organizational Culture

The concept of culture was originally proposed by anthropologists to describe societies, but it is also useful for describing organizations. Culture consists of the language, values, attitudes, beliefs, and customs of an organization. It represents a complex pattern of variables that, when taken collectively, give each organization its unique "flavor" (see Field Note 1). Several definitions of organizational culture have been proposed, but the most straightforward was offered by Deal and Ken-nedy (1982): "The way we do things around here."

Furnham and Gunter (1993) propose several features of organizational cul-ture. First, an organization's culture can be traced to its founders. These people usually possess dynamic personalities, strong values, and a clear vision of what the organization should look like. They play a big role in initial hiring of employ-ees, and their ideas and values are readily transmitted to new employees. Second, culture develops out of an organization's experience with the external environ-ment. Every organization must establish its own identity in its industry and in the marketplace where it operates. As it struggles to do so, some values and practices will be more effective than others. Third, culture also develops from the need to maintain effective working relationships among its employees. Depending on the nature of the organization's business and the characteristics of the types of people it must hire, different expectations and values develop.

Communication processes are deeply ingrained within organizational culture, for it is through communication that culture is transmitted. It is through interactions with long-time organizational members that new recruits are enculturated. This is how new members learn the language and appropriate behavior of the group, hear its stories and legends, and observe the organization's rites and rituals. Beyer and Trice (1987) believe that the culture of an organization can best be understood by analyzing its tangible and visible rites of passage including hiring and basic training, degradation (dismissal), renewal (organization development activities), conflict reduction (collective bargaining), and integration (office Christmas party). New members must determine what is appropriate dress, how to arrange their office, and how much latitude they have in being on time for

FIELD NOTE 1

To illustrate the importance of culture in defining "the way we do things around here," let's look at two companies whose cultures are extraordinarily different from each other.

One company is in the telephone communications business. It is only about 15 years old and was created as a result of the breakup of AT&T. All the officers are bright, young (only two over age 40), extremely ambitious entrepreneurs. Their (unofficial) company motto is "Ready, Fire, Aim." They make major business decisions on the basis of hunches, insight, and savvy. For example, I attended one board meeting where they decided they wanted to publish their own version of the Yellow Pages, a business telephone directory. One person was given the assignment of finding a building, another one would purchase the needed equipment, a third (the personnel director) was told to hire and train 180 new employees to staff the department. They decided to have this department operating in six weeks! A standing joke in the company is that if you don't like the way things are going today, don't worry because by next week things will be different. They refer to themselves as "cowboys," people who ride roughshod over the business terrain.

The other company is in the insurance business and has been in business for more than 100 years. All the officers are much older—no officer is under age 55. They all worked their way up the corporate ladder. Being made an "officer" is the product of having worked at least 25 years within the company. They don't have a corporate motto, but if they did it would be "Slow but Sure." Everything they do in the company is checked and rechecked. Memos are examined and edited by people one, two, and sometimes three administrative levels above the memo writer. They start to plan their annual office Christmas party in February. There is a manual, an office procedure guide, a handbook, and a written policy for every conceivable business situation or decision.

To say that these two companies have grossly different cultures is an understatement. Each organization has its own values and behaviors, and each attracts a different type of employee. If you like rapid change and the resulting dynamic tension such change produces, you would be extremely frustrated working in the insurance company. If you like stability and predictability, you would be most anxious working in the communications business.

Travel agents promote their business by saying you should travel to far-away countries to experience different cultures. As a consultant, I have experienced many different (organizational) cultures, and I haven't had to travel too far to do it.

appointments and in meeting deadlines (Barnett, 1988). Culture may also be communicated through other channels, such as in-house memos, official policies, statements of corporate philosophy, and any other means of value expression (see Field Note 2).

Because organizational culture is the product of historical behavior patterns, it cannot be instantly created or changed. If it is deemed advisable to change an organization's culture, the most frequently used strategy is to change the people in the organization. This is accomplished either through the dismissal of influential individuals in the organization (caretakers of the old culture) or by changing people's positions in the organization (particularly at upper organizational levels). I/O psychologists believe that an organization's culture is strongly related to its success. However, it is both a cause and a consequence of this success.

Summary of Social System Components

Organizations have physical structures, but these alone do not define them. The social fabric—norms, roles, and culture—is a significant influence on the conduct of organization members. These components are not tangible entities, but they are as much attributes of an organization as is its size. Organizations differ in norms, roles, and culture. Norms influence behavior, increasing consistency and predictability. Roles prescribe the boundaries of acceptable behavior and enhance con-

---

FIELD NOTE 2

Organizational culture embraces the values and character of the organization. Sometimes the culture of an organization is communicated in a subtle way, at other times the communication is loud and unambiguous. One company, founded about 90 years ago, was started through the efforts of one man. He created the company when he was about 30 and served as the company's president until his death at age 80. The company manufactures world-class building supplies. Today their products are sold nationally and the company employs about 3,000 people. The company was founded on the value of making the finest product in the market, for which they charge a high price. Their marketing orientation is strictly top-of-the-line—if you want the best, you think of them. The culture of the organization today still follows the philosophy of the founder. The founder and his philosophy are so revered that the company turned his small office into something of a shrine. Cordoned off with a thick velvet rope, the office is preserved as it was when the founder was leading the company. The office telephone, lamp, desk, chair, briefcase, and fountain pen are all period pieces. The decor of the office is not ostentatious or sumptuous, but rather understated elegance, like their products. There is a 1952 calendar hanging on the wall. While the office is no longer in active use, it serves an extremely valuable purpose for the company. It is a constant reminder, a physical embodiment, of the person whose values continue to guide the company today, long after his death. The orientation for all new employees includes a visit to this office as a way of communicating the heritage of the company. It doesn't take long for anyone (including an outsider like me) to grasp what this company is all about. Sometimes you have to dig to unearth the culture of an organization. Not this one.

formity. These constructs help produce uniformity and consistency in individual behavior. This is necessary in part to ensure that all organizational members are pursuing common goals. Individuals give up some freedom in joining an organization, and these constructs represent ways through which freedom is limited. Organizations differ in culture just as individuals differ in personality. Similarly, just as certain personality types are better suited for some jobs, certain cultures foster certain behaviors. Together, these three constructs define an organization's social system; they are intangible but potent determinants of behavior.

Work Teams

Historically, I/O psychology has tended to make individuals the object of their attention. That is, we were concerned with finding the right person for the job, training the individual, and subsequently monitoring his or her performance on the job. While the existence of informal work groups was acknowledged in the Hawthorne studies, for the most part interest in groups was limited to social psychology. However, there is a growing trend in organizations to use work groups, not just individuals, as the organizing principle through which work is accomplished. Guzzo and Shea (1992) point to the growing use by organizations of project teams, focus groups, autonomous work groups, and multifunctional work teams. Ultimately, this perspective could lead to groups (rather than individuals) being hired, trained, appraised, rewarded, promoted, and fired. Although formal group-oriented organizations are not yet the prevailing reality of organizational life, there are many indications that we are moving in that direction (see Field Note 3).

Guzzo (1995) notes that there is no real distinction between the terms *groups* and *teams*. Psychology has tended to use the term *groups*, as witnessed by the study of group dynamics and group processes. Teams, on the other hand, tend to describe groups with a narrower focus or purpose. I will use both terms interchangeably.

Groups are bounded social units that work within a larger social system—the organization. A group within an organization has an identifiable membership (that is, members and nonmembers alike clearly know who is a member and who is not) and an identifiable task or set of tasks to perform. Tasks may include monitoring, producing, serving, generating ideas, or other activities. The group's work requires that team members interact by exchanging information, sharing resources, and coordinating with and reacting to one another in the course of accomplishing the group task. Furthermore, there is always some degree of interdependence among the teams in an organization; that is, the product of one team's efforts will influence the conduct of another team.

Types of Teams

Larson and La Fasto (1989) propose three basic types of teams, each having a somewhat different objective.

Problem-resolution teams require each member of the team to expect that interactions among members will be truthful and embody a high degree of integrity. Each member must believe that the team will be consistent and mature in its approach to dealing with problems. The members must have a high degree of trust in a process of problem resolution that focuses on issues rather than on predetermined positions or conclusions. Diagnostic teams at the Centers for Disease Control are an exemplar of this type of team.

Creative teams are responsible for exploring possibilities and alternatives, with the broad objective of developing a new product or service. A necessary feature of the team's structure is autonomy. For a creative team to function, it is necessary to have autonomy from systems and procedures, as well as to create an atmosphere in which ideas do not become prematurely quashed. Creative teams need to be insulated within the organizational structure to remain focused on the result to be achieved rather than on organizational processes. The development of the IBM PC was the result of a creative team that endured many failures before arriving at a successful product. The design team needed protection from typical organizational pressures that reflected impatience with failure. The "incubation period" for the PC was many years, and it could not have been accelerated by performance expectations imposed by others.

Tactical teams are responsible for executing a well-defined plan. To do so there

---

FIELD NOTE 3

The growing use of work teams by organizations may be aided by a transformation in the way we are enculturated in our society. Teamwork emphasizes deliberate cooperation, sharing mutual resources for collective gains, and sublimating individual interests. These are not characteristics typically associated with Western cultures. It is fair to ask, to what degree are these values and behaviors nurtured by social institutions prior to our entering the work world?

In the United States, education stresses *individual*, not collective, accomplishment. In college, students are graded on the basis of their own academic performance. Some individuals do better than others. I am not aware of any professor who treats an entire class as one "team," yokes the assessment of each individual student to the overall performance of the class, and accordingly gives the same grade to all students in the class. It is individual students who graduate from college—one individual's name appears on the degree, not all the members of some team.

Several individuals who are now functioning as team members in organizations have described the difficulties inherent in the individual-to-team-member transition. New values and behaviors have to be learned, including mutual trust, interdependence, and cultivating a collective mentality. One new team member described how she had to overcome her reluctance to aid a fellow team member who was obviously struggling with an assignment. She said that had she extended the same assistance to a college classmate during a test, such behavior would have constituted "cheating." A behavior that two years earlier in one context would have warranted punishment is now encouraged and rewarded in another.

The successful implementation of work teams in organizations could be greatly ameliorated by increasing the exposure of individuals to contexts and situations where collective thinking and behavior is valued, particularly early in life. But with the exception of team sports such as soccer and football, Western cultures have been slow to recognize the value of teamwork.

Table 8–1   *Characteristics of three types of teams*

Broad Objective	Dominant Feature	Process Emphasis	Example
Problem resolution	Trust	Focus on issues	Centers for Disease Control
Creative	Autonomy	Explore possibilities and alternatives	IBM PC team
Tactical	Clarity	Directive Highly focused tasks Role clarity Well-defined operational standards Accuracy	Cardiac surgery team

SOURCE: From *Teamwork* (p. 43) by C. E. Larson and F. M. La Fasto, 1989, Newbury Park, CA: Sage.

must be high task clarity and unambiguous role definition. The success of tactical teams depends on a high degree of responsiveness from team members, a clear understanding of who does what, and a clear set of performance standards. An example of a tactical team would be a police SWAT team or a cardiac surgical team. Each operational procedure must be well defined, and each task must be highly focused and very specific. Furthermore, the standards of excellence must be clear to everyone, and ways of measuring success or failure must be understood by the entire team. Table 8–1 shows the basic characteristics of the three major types of teams.

Nature of Decision Making in Teams

Decision making is a major activity contributing to team effectiveness. Morgan and Bowers (1995) identified four components of team decision making that serve as a useful model. These components are situation assessment, metacognition, shared mental models, and resource management. According to this model, team decision making begins with *situation assessment*, which refers to the detection and interpretation of cues to recognize the existence of a problem. *Metacognition* involves developing the definition of the problem and creating a strategy to solve it. This process leads to the development of *shared mental models*, or the ability of team members to develop a common understanding of the problem as well as a strategy for solving it. Finally, team decision making requires *resource management*, which is the efficient utilization of the team's skills and abilities in the execution of the task.

Guzzo (1995) asserts that decision making in teams is distinct from individual decision making. In teams, information is often distributed unequally among members and must be integrated. Choosing among alternatives is made more complicated by having to integrate the differing perspectives and opinions of team members. The integration process usually must also include dealing with uncertainty, dealing with the effects of status differences among members, and by the failure of one member to appreciate the significance of the information he or she holds. Ambiguity, compressed amounts of time, heavy workloads, and other factors may become sources of stress that affect the group's ability to perform its task. Furthermore, Hollenbeck, Ilgen, Tuttle, and Sego (1995) identified social distraction among members as a reason for lowered performance in a team decision-making task. When confronted with a task that was perceived to be boring, the presence of others provided a sense of distraction that ultimately led to a performance breakdown at a critical juncture.

Principles of Teamwork

McIntyre and Salas (1995) conducted extensive research on U.S. Navy tactical teams and identified several principles of teamwork. Five of these principles are also relevant for other organizations employing teams.

Principle 1. Teamwork implies that members provide feedback to and accept it from one another. Effective teamwork implies that team members feel free to provide feedback. That is, the climate within the group must be such that neither status nor power stands as an obstacle to team members' providing feedback to one another. Effective teams engage in tasks with an awareness of their strengths and weaknesses. When team leaders show the ability to accept constructive criticism, they establish a norm that this type of criticism is appropriate.

Principle 2. Teamwork implies the willingness, preparedness, and proclivity to back fellow members up during operations. Better teams are distinguishable from poorer teams in that their members show a willingness to jump in and help when they are needed, and they accept help without fear of being perceived as weak. Team members must show competence not only in their own particular area but also in the areas of other team members with whom they directly interact.

Principle 3. Teamwork involves group members' collectively viewing themselves as a group whose success depends on their interaction. Team members must have high awareness of themselves as a team. Each member sees the team's success as taking precedence over individual performance. Members of effective teams view themselves as connected team members, not as isolated individuals working with other isolated individuals. Effective teams consist of individuals who recognize that their effectiveness is the team's effectiveness, which depends on the sum total of all team members' performance.

Principle 4. Teamwork means fostering within-team interdependence. Fostering team interdependence means that the team adopts the value that it is not only appropriate but essential for each team member (regardless of status within the team) to depend on every other team member to carry out the team's mission. Contrary to what may take place in the rest of the organization, interdependence is seen as a virtue—an essential characteristic of team performance—not as a weakness.

Principle 5. Team leadership makes a difference with respect to the performance of the team. Team leaders serve as models for their fellow team members. If the leaders openly engage in teamwork—that is, provide and accept feedback, and provide and accept supportive behaviors—other team members are likely to do the same. Team leaders are vital and have tremendous influence on teams. When team leaders are poor, so are the teams.

McIntyre and Salas (1995) believe that these principles provide for a theory of teamwork. In their attempts to implement or improve team-based performance, organizations need to think specifically about how organization members can effectively serve in the capacity of team members. It requires the incorporation of a theory of teamwork into the organization's operating philosophy. Teamwork will take place within the organization only to the extent that the organization fosters it and builds upon it.

Personnel Selection for Teams

Much of what I/O psychologists have learned about the selection of individuals for organizations is not wholly transferable to the selection of teams. Traditional job analytic methods identify the KSAs needed for individual job performance, yet these methods tend to be insensitive to the social context in which work occurs. Groups or teams, by definition, are social entities that interact within a larger social context. Klimoski and Jones (1995) believe that choosing team members on the basis of individual-task KSAs alone is not enough to ensure optimal team effectiveness. For example, Guzzo and Shea (1992) indicated that considerable interest has been evidenced in using the Myers-Briggs Type Indicator (which assesses cognitive style) in selecting team members. Successful teams also depend on those characteristics of individual members that facilitate team functioning. Consideration should also be given to such group process factors as learning ability, tolerance for stress, and risk-taking propensity.

Successful selection of team members requires identifying the best mix of personnel for effective team performance. Thus, selection requirements for particular individuals may involve complementing the abilities other individuals will bring to the task. Creating the right mix can also mean considering those factors that account for interpersonal compatibility. Establishing team requirements would involve identifying and assessing the congruence among members with regard to personality and values. Prieto (1993) asserts that five social skills are particularly critical for individuals to enhance the performance of the group. They must know how to:

- gain group acceptance,
- increase group solidarity,
- be aware of the group consciousness,
- share the group identification, and
- manage others' impressions of him or her.

Our knowledge of methods of personnel selection for team membership is not as advanced as it is for individual selection. Prieto recommends the use of group exercises to assess the behavior of the group of applicants as a whole and of each applicant influenced by that group. Klimoski and Jones (1995) believe that the assessment center method as well as personality inventories (of the type discussed in Chapter 4) may be particularly useful. Furthermore, these authors also address the issue of *deselection*—eliminating individuals from team membership who, although otherwise qualified, bring hidden agendas into the group's deliberations. To date there is little in the way of research findings to guide us on the social and political aspects of groups while still preserving the idea of selection based on competence.

Concluding Comments

The conversion from an individual to a team perspective of work embraces more than just a reconsideration of our personnel selection procedures. In fact, we will have to reexamine our knowledge about all facets of human resource management from identification of team training needs to team training methods to techniques of appraising team performance. Furthermore, while some of our concepts might generalize directly from individuals to groups (for example, Campion, Medsker, & Higgs, 1993), it is conceivable that some procedures might be incompatible. One purpose of performance appraisal is to identify performance differences across individuals and to differentially reward them accordingly. If we strive for teamwork and a sense of unity across group members, we should then *not* differentially reward the "best" individual team members. We will have to develop appraisal and reward processes that treat all members of a group as a single entity, not as individuals. Organizations get what they reward. If they choose to appraise and reward individual job performance, they should then not decry a lack of teamwork and cooperation among their employees (Kerr, 1995). I/O psychology must gird itself for a journey of understanding into how work is best performed by teams. New psychological concepts or adaptations of existing concepts that currently have unknown validity when generalized to groups must be explored.

CASE STUDY   *Should We Use Work Teams?*

Terry Porter was the founder and president of a small financial services company. The company was created about 10 years ago and grew in size to 16 employees. The purpose of the company was to provide financial services such as billing, payment disbursement, collection, and record keeping to other organizations. Terry discovered there was a need to provide these services, as larger companies were finding less expensive ways to perform these needed business functions. The organizations could substantially downsize their accounting departments by contracting the work to companies that specialized in this business. As other organizations increasingly contracted financial services to specialized firms, companies such as Terry's continued to prosper.

Business was growing at such a rate that Terry decided the time had come to consider changing the way the company was structured. Over the past few years several new employees had been hired as the workload grew. However, the additional employees seemed to create some problems of work flow coordination. Also, the potential for attaining greater business volume was evident, and what was needed was an organized method to obtain and service the new accounts. Terry contemplated reorganizing the staff into two work teams of seven employees each. Only Terry and the receptionist would not be team members. The primary responsibility of one team member would be to recruit new business. Other team members would be involved in performing the mainstream functions of the business, which would be better coordinated by the assignment of specific roles. Terry further considered having each team target itself to the two different market segments that comprised the business: manufacturing organizations and health-related services. In this way the company would be organized around the two major bases of business, and each team would have clearly defined objectives. The two teams would be called "Team Alpha" and "Team Beta," respectively. Their motto would be "There is no 'I' in our team."

Terry had never been involved with work teams before and had several concerns about how they operate. For example, Terry wasn't sure how to decide which employees would be assigned to each team. All the employees seemed to get along very well, but would the spirit of goodwill continue if they were divided? Would an unhealthy sense of competitiveness emerge between the two teams? Terry also didn't know how the employees would feel about such a reorganization. They all would have more specific duties and responsibilities compared to before. Terry also wondered about the use of special incentives for team performance. Should there be special incentives for recruiting the most new business? If so, the deck would be stacked in favor of Team Beta because of the greater growth of companies in health-related services. Perhaps, Terry concluded, this would just make Team Alpha try harder.

The potential gains from using work teams seemed great, but Terry conceded that the conversion to work teams was perhaps more daunting than she originally believed.

Questions

1. What conditions or factors are present that are driving the consideration of work teams?
2. What benefits do you think might flow to the company by creating work teams?
3. Could these same benefits be derived by *not* reorganizing into work teams? If so, how might this happen?
4. By organizing into work teams, what are some other potential problems for Terry's company?
5. Have you ever been a member of a team? What was your assessment of the benefits and liabilities of the team?

Organizational Behavior

Major Chapter Objectives

- *Be able to explain the concept of organizational justice.*

- *Understand the concept of organizational citizenship behavior and its relationship to other concepts.*

- *Understand the concept of the psychological contract in employment and its changing nature.*

- *Understand organizational mergers and acquisitions and their effects on I/O psychological concepts.*

- *Explore the basis for violence in the workplace.*

In the previous chapter I examined several conceptual approaches to organizations, including the structure, configuration, and social mechanisms that permit their functioning. In this chapter I will examine various psychological concepts that have emerged within organizations. I will focus on concepts that not only have theoretical value but also have been found to influence a wide array of practical matters relating to work behavior. The term *organizational behavior* is somewhat of a misnomer, as technically organizations do not behave. Rather, the term refers to the behavior of individuals and groups within an organizational context.

Deciding which concepts should be addressed in a chapter on organizational behavior is difficult. The field is very broad (Mowday & Sutton, 1993; Wilpert, 1995) and covers a diverse array of subjects. The primary criteria for my selection of concepts included the following. First, a concept should help explain and integrate material presented not only in this chapter but also in other chapters of this book. Second, there had to be a sufficient body of content that a balanced and informative presentation was possible. And finally, the selected concepts had to represent the most recent thinking by researchers and practitioners on salient organizational issues. Thus, the purpose of this chapter is to explain concepts that have been found to be useful in understanding behavior in organizations.

Organizational Justice

Organizational justice is concerned with the fair treatment of people in organizations. It can be thought of as a more limited application of social justice, a concept that has been debated by philosophers for hundreds of years. Within an organizational context there are always competing goals and objectives. A case in point would be personnel selection. Job applicants are in the role of seeking to obtain employment with an organization. The organization, in turn, is in the role of offering employment to some applicants and denying the opportunity to others. This decision is made through an assessment of the applicants. Both the outcome of the selection decision (that is, who was offered employment and who wasn't) and the process (that is, whether the assessment was rendered via a psychological test, interview, or some other means) can be questioned in terms of fairness: Was a just and fair outcome reached through the use of just and fair methods? Justice has been claimed to be "the first virtue of social institutions" (Rawls, 1971, p. 3). In this section I will examine the conceptual basis of organizational justice and discuss its application to understanding behavior in organizations.

Distributive Justice

Justice has been conceptualized from two major perspectives. The first is called *distributive justice*, which refers to the fairness of the outcomes, results, or ends achieved. Distributive justice, like all forms of justice, is heavily predicated on values. These values refer to the rules or standards by which judgments of fairness are rendered. Three rules have been identified as the basis to distribute justice; they are equity, equality, and need.

Equity. The *equity distribution rule* suggests that people should receive rewards that are consistent with the contributions they make or bring to a situation. Consider a university that wants to award a financial scholarship to two students. Using the equity distribution rule, the two students judged most qualified on the basis of their abilities would be offered the scholarships. These two individuals would be judged to be able to contribute the most to the university in terms of ability (as determined by high school grades, standardized test scores, and so forth), so they are rewarded with the scholarship offers. Using the equity distribution rule, it is "fair" that the two most qualified students were offered the scholarships.

Equality. The *equality distribution rule* suggests that all individuals should have an equal chance of receiving the outcome or reward, regardless of differentiating characteristics such as ability. In the truest sense, the equality rule would require random selection of the scholarship recipients rather than selection based on ability. Since universities don't award scholarships randomly, a modified equality rule must be used. Since in this example there are two scholarships, the students would be divided into two categories, for example, by gender. The university would then offer a scholarship to the most qualified male and the most qualified female. The "most qualified" consideration is derived from the equity rule, while the one male/one female consideration is derived from the equality rule. Applying the equality rule, it is "fair" that one person from each gender was offered a scholarship.

Need. The *need distribution rule* states that rewards should be distributed on the basis of individual need. The special consideration the needy individual receives would be perceived as the basis of fairness. In the scholarship example, the university would assess the financial need of all the students and offer scholarships to the two neediest students (irrespective of ability or gender). Applying the need distribution rule, it is "fair" that the two financially neediest students were offered the scholarships.

As you might imagine, there can be legitimate differences of opinion among people regarding what is the "fairest" rule to use in awarding scholarships. One possible resolution might be to segment the scholarships, that is, to offer one based on ability and the other based on need. If the most academically qualified student is a female, the other scholarship could be awarded to the financially neediest male student. With such a distribution, the scholarships would have been awarded on the basis of equity, equality, and need. However, some people might say that it is *unfair* to weight equity and need the same and that both scholarships should be awarded solely on the basis of need (or equity). Another person might say it is unfair to consider gender in such decisions and that the most qualified student and the neediest student should be offered the scholarships independent of gender.

These types of disagreements among people regarding what is fair (and unfair) about distributions are not at all uncommon. Since distribution rules are based on values, no rule is inherently right or wrong. Organizations typically address differences of opinion regarding distribution rules by seeking to gain consensus on which rule is the "fairest" to follow or by distributing different rewards by different rules. As you will see, it is often difficult to reach consensus on fairness, and there can be far-reaching implications for organizations regarding differing views on what constitutes fairness in their practices (see Field Note 1).

FIELD NOTE 1

What does it mean to be "fair?" Most certainly there are ways to consider fairness, and I was party to one situation that evoked multiple perspectives.

A wealthy individual died and bequeathed $3 million to a university to support students who attended the school. The university invested the $3 million such that it earned 6% interest, or $180,000, per year. Every year the university could grant $180,000 to students to support their education without having to expend the original $3 million gift. The university convened a committee to determine the fairest way of dispersing the $180,000 per year. I was a member of that committee. Three distinct schools of thought emerged as to what constituted the "fairest" disbursement of the money.

Proponents of the first school of thought recommended that the financial award be granted to the most academically talented applicants, as indexed by high school grades and standardized test scores. This university had highly reputable programs in engineering and agriculture, majors that typically attract more males than females. Because these programs attracted many of the most highly qualified applicants to the university, and because the vast majority of these applicants were male, the financial award recipients would be very heavily represented by males.

Proponents of the second perspective said that the university ought to embrace all groups in society—across genders, racial groups, age groups, the physically disabled, and so forth. Therefore, the financial support should be intentionally allocated to individual students representative of the various groups. In this way the university would show its support for recruiting a diverse student body.

In the third perspective proponents said that the money should be allocated based on financial need. It was proposed that the best use of the money would be to provide a vehicle for students who could not otherwise afford it to obtain a college education. Therefore, the recipients of the financial support should be the financially neediest students.

I was struck not only by how different the recipients would be depending upon which strategy was followed but also by the inherent plausibility of each strategy. Each position had some intuitive appeal—each one made some sense to me. The three groups argued over such matters as the difference between a scholarship versus financial aid and what the intentions of the deceased benefactor were in disbursing his money. The final decision by the committee reflected a compromise—a (fair) resolution of conflicting standards of fairness. A portion of the funds were set aside to be allocated on the basis of need. Other funds would be allocated on the basis of academic ability, with members of the various groups being represented in the funding. It was not a decision the committee enthusiastically endorsed, but one it could live with.

If you had been on that committee, what position would you have taken in allocating the funds? Why do you think your position is the "fairest" one?

Procedural Justice

The second major type of justice is *procedural justice,* which is the fairness of the means used to achieve the results. As the name suggests, it is directed to the perceived fairness of the policies and procedures used to make decisions. In essence, the distinction between distributive and procedural justice is the difference between content and process that is basic to many of the philosophical approaches to the study of justice.

Folger and Greenberg (1985) describe two approaches to conceptualizing procedural justice. One emphasizes the role of the individual's "voice" in the process. Procedures are perceived to be more fair when the affected individuals have an opportunity to either influence the decision process or offer input. The other approach emphasizes the structural components of the process, whereby procedural justice is a function of the extent to which a number of procedural rules are satisfied or violated. These procedural rules suggest that decisions should be made consistently, without personal biases, with as much accurate information as possible, and with an outcome that could be modified. Also included in procedural justice is the treatment the individual receives during the process, reflecting issues of personal respect and the propriety of questions asked.

In applying the concept of procedural justice to a personnel selection system, for example, a number of components might contribute to a "fair" selection process (Gilliland, 1993). Ideally the selection test should be job-related (or more precisely from the applicant's view, face valid), should allow the candidate to demonstrate his or her proficiency, and should be consistently scored across applicants. Furthermore, candidates should receive timely feedback on their applications for employment, should be told the truth, and should be treated respectfully in the assessment process. Note that these procedural justice issues pertain to the selection process, not the outcome of whether the applicant was accepted or rejected (which would be a matter of distributive justice). Figure 9–1

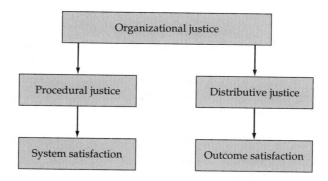

Figure 9–1 *Two major types of organizational justice and reactions to them*
SOURCE: Adapted from "Employee Theft as a Reaction to Underpayment Inequity: The Hidden Costs of Pay Cuts" by J. Greenberg, 1990, *Journal of Applied Psychology, 75.*

	Focal determinant	Category of justice	
		Procedural	**Distributive**
	Structural	Systemic justice	Configural justice
	Social	Informational justice	Interpersonal justice

Figure 9–2   *Taxonomy of justice classes*
SOURCE: Adapted from "The Social Side of Fairness: Interpersonal and Informational Classes of Organizational Justice" by
J. Greenberg, 1993, in *Justice in the Workplace: Approaching Fairness in Human Resource Management* (p. 83) edited by R. Cropanzano,
Hillsdale, NJ: Erlbaum.

graphically depicts the two major types of organizational justice and individual
reactions to them.

A Taxonomy of Justice Classes

Greenberg (1993) developed a taxonomy of justice classes based on two factors.
One is the type of justice, distributive or procedural. The second is the immediate
focus of just action, structural or social. In the case of structural determinants,
justice is sought by focusing on the context within which interaction occurs. In
contrast, the social determinants of justice focus on the treatment of individuals.
The act of following a prevailing rule of justice (for example, distributing rewards
equitably) is structurally fair, while the act of treating others in an open and honest fashion is socially fair. The taxonomy of justice classes is shown in Figure 9–2,
and the categories are explained in greater detail here.

   Systemic justice. Systemic justice is the variety of procedural justice that is
accomplished via structural means. These structural means include making
sure decisions are made such that they: (a) are consistent over people and
time, (b) are based on accurate information, (c) represent the concerns of all
parties, and (d) are compatible with prevailing moral and ethical standards.
These are the means of structuring the context to promote systemic justice.

   Configural justice. Configural justice refers to the variety of distributive
justice that is accomplished via structural means. It addresses the pattern of
resource allocations perceived as fair under various circumstances. The allocation rules of equity, equality, and need would be one illustration. These are
all ways of structuring the context of reward allocations so certain distributive patterns will result.

   Informational justice. Informational justice refers to the social determinants
of procedural justice. Informational justice may be sought by providing
knowledge about procedures that demonstrate regard for people's concerns.
This can be accomplished by providing people with adequate accounts and
explanations of the procedures used to determine desired outcomes. For ex-

planations to be perceived as fair, they must also be recognized as genuine in intent (without any ulterior motives) and be based on sound reasoning. Because it is typically the open sharing of information that promotes this class of procedural justice, the term *informational* is used to identify it.

Interpersonal justice. Interpersonal justice refers to the social aspects of distributive justice. Interpersonal justice may be sought by showing concern for individuals regarding the outcomes they received. Ostensible displays of politeness and respect for citizens' rights have enhanced their perceptions of fair treatment by authorities, such as the police and the courts. Similarly, apologies are a tactic for enhancing interpersonal justice, because they involve expressions of remorse and serve to distance individuals from the negative effects of their actions. This social determinant of justice that deals with *outcomes* is different from justice dealing with *procedures*.

I will conclude this section with how our knowledge of selected organizational issues has been aided by viewing them from Greenberg's taxonomy of justice.

The first organizational issue is that of performance appraisal. Greenberg (1986) proposed that beliefs about what makes a performance evaluation perceived as being fair were based in part on the procedures by which the evaluations are determined. Greenberg asked participants in management training seminars to think of an incident in which they received either a particularly fair or unfair performance evaluation on the job. These identified incidents were subsequently rated by other managers regarding their importance in producing fair performance appraisals. Five procedural factors reflective of systemic justice were identified: (1) soliciting input from the ratee prior to the evaluation and using it, (2) two-way communication during the interview, (3) ability to challenge/rebut the evaluation, (4) the rater's familiarity with the ratee's work, and (5) the consistent application of standards. In keeping with Greenberg's class of systemic justice, these five factors were used to structure the context of performance appraisal to produce a fair evaluation system.

A second study by Greenberg (1994) demonstrates informational and interpersonal justice in promoting acceptance of a work site smoking ban. Announcements of a work site smoking ban were made to employees of a large company. The announcements differed in the amount of information given about the need for the ban and the degree of interpersonal sensitivity shown over the personal impact of the ban. Some employees received a great deal of information about the reason for the smoking ban, while others received only the most cursory information. Furthermore, some employees received a personally sensitive message: "We realize that this new policy will be very hard on those of you who smoke. Smoking is an addiction, and it's very tough to stop. We are quite aware of this, and we do not want you to suffer." Other employees received a message showing less personal concern: "I realize that it's tough to stop smoking, but it's in the best interest of our business to implement the smoking ban. And, of course, business must come first." Immediately after the announcement, surveys were completed to assess employees' acceptance of the ban. Although heavy smokers were found least accepting of the ban, they showed the greatest incremental gain in acceptance after exposure to thorough information presented in a highly sensitive manner. By contrast, nonsmokers' acceptance of the ban was uniformly unaffected by the way it was presented to them. Regardless of how much they smoked, all participants recognized the procedural fairness associated with giving thorough information in a socially sensitive manner.

Perhaps the best illustration of Greenberg's fourth class of justice, configural justice, is found in the national debate on societal values in employment. Configural justice refers to how resources are allocated to achieve a fair outcome. The debate on societal values can be viewed as whether the resource of jobs (or employment) is best allocated on the basis of equity or equality. Proponents of the equity rule of allocation argue that jobs should be filled strictly on the basis of ability, irrespective of such demographic groups as race, age, and gender. If selection of the most qualified applicants results in a distribution of jobs filled predominantly by members of one group, the equity rule would evince such an outcome as fair. Alternatively, the equality rule of allocation argues that society is comprised of members of different groups based on race, age, and gender. Therefore, to be fair, the distribution of people holding jobs should be approximately equal to the distribution of people in society. Application of such a rule might require hiring someone who is a member of a certain race, age, or gender group with less ability than someone with greater ability from some other group. It is argued that all groups deserve a fair share of society's benefits, and jobs are among those benefits.

As others have observed (for example, Gottfredson, 1994; Sackett & Wilk, 1994), discussions of technical issues in personnel selection (such as where to set the passing score on a test) are really superfluous to the larger issue of what objectives are guiding the offering of employment. If the objective is to pursue the equity rule of allocation of jobs, certain selection decisions will be made. However, if the equality rule of allocation of jobs is followed, other selection decisions may be made. The societal debate about jobs and who fills them must squarely face issues of configural justice, with the realization that there is often more than one way to judge what is fair.

Organizational Citizenship Behavior

The classic approach to thinking about a job is in terms of the tasks performed that comprise the job. In fact, one purpose of job analysis (described in Chapter 3) is to establish or identify these tasks. In turn, performance appraisal (discussed in Chapter 7) is concerned with assessing how well employees perform the tasks that comprise their jobs. However, organizational researchers have discovered that some employees contribute to the welfare or effectiveness of their organization by going beyond the duties prescribed in their jobs. That is, they give extra discretionary contributions that are neither required nor expected. The most frequently used term for this phenomenon is *organizational citizenship behavior*. It is also referred to as *prosocial organizational behavior* and *extra-role behavior*. Organ

(1994) refers to a person who engages in organizational citizenship behavior as a "good soldier."

Five dimensions are frequently proposed to define what constitutes citizenship behavior (Organ, 1988; Van Dyne, Graham, & Dienesch, 1994). The first is *altruism*, which reflects willfully helping specific people with an organizationally relevant task or problem. The second is *conscientiousness*, which refers to being punctual, having attendance above the group norm, and judiciously following company rules, regulations, and procedures. *Courtesy* is the third dimension, reflecting being mindful and respectful of other people's rights. *Sportsmanship* refers to avoiding complaints, petty grievances, gossiping, and falsely magnifying problems. The final dimension is *civic virtue*, which is responsible participation in the political life of the organization. Civic virtue reflects not only keeping abreast of current organizational issues but also more mundane issues such as attending meetings, attending to in-house communications, and speaking up on issues. It has been suggested that civic virtue is the most admiral manifestation of organizational citizenship behavior because it often entails some sacrifice of individual productive efficiency.

Employees who exhibit prosocial behavior are highly valued by their managers. Indeed they should be, as they contribute above and beyond the normal requirements and expectations of the job. An empirical study of performance evaluation revealed the degree to which citizenship behavior influences judgments of job performance. MacKenzie, Podsakoff, and Fetter (1991) examined three objective measures of weekly productivity relating to sales volume for a sample of insurance agents. Also obtained for these agents was an evaluation of the dimensions of organizational citizenship behavior, as well as a managerial assessment of their overall job performance. The results indicated that the managers' subjective evaluations of the agents' job performance were determined as much by the agents' altruism and civic virtue as by objective productivity levels.

It is reasonable to question the origins of organizational citizenship behavior. That is, are manifestations of such prosocial behavior a product of our individual dispositions (which are fairly immutable), or can organizations conduct themselves in ways that bring out such behavior in employees? Research supports both the dispositional and situational antecedents of organizational citizenship behavior. Support for dispositional antecedents comes from the Big 5 model of personality (discussed in Chapter 4). Two of the Big 5 dimensions appear relevant to organizational citizenship behavior. One, agreeableness, pertains to the ease or difficulty a person has in getting along with people, or how good-natured a person is with respect to interpersonal relationships. The second, conscientiousness, pertains to reliability, dependability, punctuality, and discipline. Evidence indicates that some people, given selected aspects of their personality, are more likely to engage in organizational citizenship behaviors than are others. As McNeely and Meglino (1994) noted, organizations can promote prosocial behavior by selecting applicants with high scores on agreeableness and conscientiousness.

The second explanation for organizational citizenship behavior, situational antecedents, has at its basis the concept of organizational justice. That is, if employees believe they are being treated fairly, they will be more likely to hold positive attitudes about their work. Organ (1988) hypothesized that fairness per-

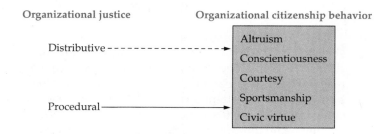

Figure 9–3   *Relationship between organizational justice and organizational citizenship behavior*

SOURCE: Adapted from "Relationship Between Organizational Justice and Organizational Citizenship Behavior: Do Fairness Perceptions Influence Employee Citizenship?" by R. H. Moorman, 1991, *Journal of Applied Psychology, 76,* p. 849.

ceptions may influence prosocial behavior by prompting employees to define their relationship with the organization as a social exchange. In exchange for being treated fairly, employees would engage in discretionary gestures of organizational citizenship behavior. However, to the extent that unfairness is perceived in the relationship, the tendency would be to recast the relationship in terms of a more rigidly defined exchange. Thus, in a trusting relationship with the organization, the employee contributes more to the exchange than is formally required. However, to the degree that the organization is perceived as lacking fairness, the employee retreats to contributing to the exchange only that to which he or she is obligated.

In a test of this proposition, Moorman (1991) examined the relationship between forms of organizational justice (distributive and procedural) and organizational citizenship behavior. A graphic portrayal of the relationship between organizational justice and prosocial behavior is presented in Figure 9–3. It was proposed that employees will engage in citizenship behavior because they perceive the organization to be fair (both distributively and procedurally). Moorman discovered that organizational citizenship behavior was related to perceptions of procedural justice, but not to distributive justice. Furthermore, the courtesy dimension of citizenship behavior was most strongly related to procedural justice. Employees who believed that their supervisors personally treated them fairly appeared to be more likely to exhibit citizenship behaviors.

The major implication of the study is that supervisors can directly influence employees' citizenship behavior. The perception of justice was based on whether supervisors used procedures designed to promote fairness. Moorman concluded that if supervisors want to increase citizenship behavior among their employees, they should work to increase the fairness of their interactions with employees. Subsequent research has strengthened the conclusion of a reciprocal exchange between the employee and the organization. Organizations perceived as being equitable and that recognize desirable behavior in their employees reap the benefits of having employees engage in higher levels of citizenship behavior.

Research on citizenship behavior captures the richness of examining workplace behavior from an organizational or social perspective. Organ and Ryan

(1995) have proposed that organizational citizenship behavior unifies several organizational constructs. At the organizational level it may be the equivalent of what g (general mental ability) is at the individual level. It is clear from the MacKenzie et al. (1991) study that evaluations of job performance cannot be divorced from the social context in which they occur. Citizenship behavior is related to perceptions of organizational justice and can be viewed as one dimension of the social exchange between the employee and the organization. A related aspect of this social exchange is the psychological contract, the topic of the next section.

Psychological Contract

Rousseau (1995) describes the psychological contract as the exchange relationship between the individual employee and the organization. It is not a formal written contract between the two parties but an implied relationship based on mutual contributions. The psychological contract is the employee's perception of the reciprocal obligations existing with the organization. Employees have beliefs regarding the organization's obligations to them as well as their obligations to the organization. Employees may believe that the organization has agreed to provide job security and promotional opportunities in exchange for hard work and loyalty. The psychological contract is oriented toward the future. Without the promise of future exchange, neither party has incentive to contribute anything to the other, and the relationship may not endure. The contract is comprised of a belief that some form of promise has been made and that the terms and conditions of the contract have been accepted by both parties.

Beliefs or perceptions regarding implied promises and acceptance are the basis of the psychological contract. Each party believes that both parties have made promises and that both parties have accepted the same contract terms (Rousseau, 1989). However, this does not necessarily mean that both parties share a common understanding of all contract terms. Each party only *believes* that they share the same interpretation of the contract. The psychological contract is not made once but rather is revised throughout the employee's tenure in the organization. The longer the relationship endures and the two parties interact, the broader the array of contributions that might be included in the contract. Rousseau and Parks (1993) found that employment itself was perceived as a promise (that is, the implied contract of continued future employment) and that an employee's performance is perceived as a contribution (a way of paying for the promise). Robinson, Kraatz, and Rousseau (1994) examined how psychological contracts change over time. They found that during the first two years of employment, employees came to perceive that they owed less to their employer while the employers in turn owed them more.

Rousseau has suggested that psychological contracts lie along a continuum, ranging from the transactional to the relational. Transactional contracts are characterized by short time frames and specific obligations. Financial resources are the primary vehicle of exchange. Relational contracts are characterized by long-term

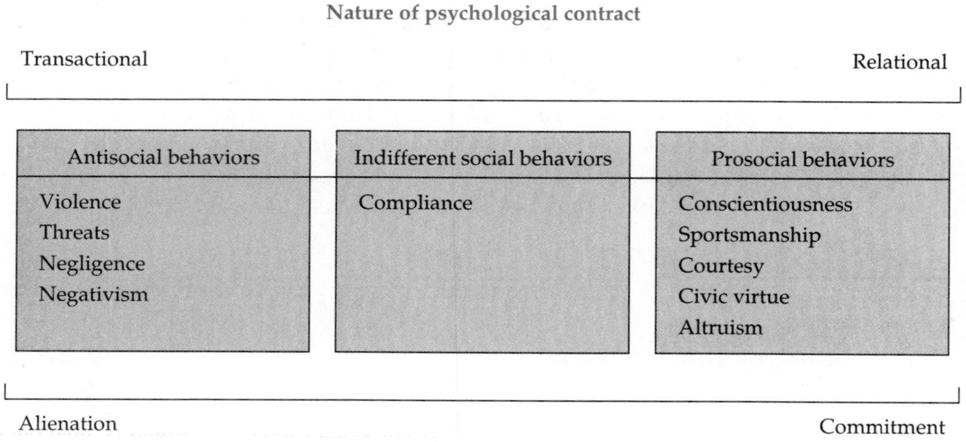

Nature of psychological contract

Transactional   Relational

Antisocial behaviors	Indifferent social behaviors	Prosocial behaviors
Violence Threats Negligence Negativism	Compliance	Conscientiousness Sportsmanship Courtesy Civic virtue Altruism

Alienation   Commitment

Figure 9–4   *Relationship between psychological contract and range of social behaviors*
SOURCE: Adapted from " 'Till Death Do Us Part . . . ': Changing Work Relationships in the 1990s" by J. M. Parks and D. L. Kidder, 1994, in *Trends in Organizational Behavior* (p. 120) edited by C. L. Cooper and D. M. Rousseau, New York: Wiley.

relationships with diffuse obligations. Transactional contracts are predicated on a prescription of total self-interest, while relational contracts implicitly acknowledge the value of the relationship itself, in which one party may put the immediate interests of the other party ahead of his or her own. At the relational end of the continuum, obligations are ambiguous and constantly evolving. These contracts are long term in nature and exchange not only financial resources but also socioemotional resources such as loyalty and affiliation. Figure 9–4 shows the continuum of psychological contracts and the range of social behavior within an organization.

There is also an element of power in all contracts. Power can be distributed either equally (symmetrically) between the two parties or unequally (asymmetrically). Asymmetrical power is most common in employment relationships. Power asymmetries affect the perceived voluntariness of the exchange relationship, dividing the two parties into categories of contract makers (relatively powerful) and contract takers (relatively powerless). As contract takers, employees cannot easily exit the employment relationship. This may result in a perceived loss of control in the relationship, which is likely to intensify feelings of mistreatment and injustice when violations are perceived. Because the employer is the more powerful party, terms of the contract can be dictated to the less powerful employee, who must either accept them or exit the relationship.

Violation of the Psychological Contract

Violation of the psychological contract occurs when one party in a relationship perceives another as failing to fulfill promised obligations. Table 9–1 lists typical

Table 9–1   *Violations of the psychological contract*

Violation Type	Definition	Examples
Training/development	Absence of training, or training experience not as promised	"Sales training was promised as an integral part of marketing training. It never materialized."
Compensation	Discrepancies between promised and realized pay, benefits, bonuses	"Specific compensation benefits were promised and were either not given to me, or I had to fight for them."
Promotion	Promotion or advancement schedule not as promised	"I perceived a promise that I had a good chance of promotion to manager in one year. While I received excellent performance ratings, I was not promoted in my first year."
Job security	Promises regarding degree of job security one could expect were not met	"The company promised that no one would be fired out of the training program—that all of us were 'safe' until placement (in return for this security we accepted lower pay). The company subsequently fired four people from the training program."
Feedback	Feedback and reviews inadequate compared to what was promised	" . . . (I did) not receive performance review as promised."
People	Employer perceived as having misrepresented the type of people at the firm in terms of things such as their expertise, work style, or reputation	"It was promised as dynamic and as having a challenging environment . . . rubbing elbows with some of the brightest people in the business . . . a big lie. The true picture started to come out . . . after the initial hype . . . of working at one of the best 100 companies in the U.S. had worn off."

SOURCE: Adapted from "Violating the Psychological Contract: Not the Exception But the Norm" by S. L. Robinson and D. M. Rousseau, 1994, *Journal of Organizational Behavior, 15,* p. 256.

organizational violations of the psychological contract and quotes from employees reflective of them. The failure of one party to comply with its obligations to another can be expected to erode both the relationship and the affected party's belief in the reciprocal obligations of the two parties. Violations by an employer may affect not only what an employee feels he or she is owed by the employer but also what an employee feels obligated to offer in return. Violation of a psychological contract undermines the very factors (for example, trust) that led to emergence of a relationship. If the employer reneges on an implied promise, the employer's integrity is questioned. A violation signals that the employer's original motives to build and maintain a mutually beneficial relationship have changed or were false to begin with. The psychological contract binds the employee and the employer— a form of guarantee that if each does his or her part the relationship will be mutually beneficial. Violations weaken this bond.

"I've got it, too, Omar . . . a strange feeling like
we've just been going in circles."

THE FAR SIDE   SOURCE: The Far Side cartoon by
Gary Larson is reprinted by permission of Chronicle
Features, San Francisco, CA. All rights reserved.

Shore and Tetrick (1994) posited that three factors determine the employee's reaction to violations in the psychological contract. The first is the type of psychological contract in effect. Violation of a primarily transactional contract, particularly of short duration, may be less intense and more amenable to revision than violation of long-standing relational contracts. Rousseau (1989) believes that violation of a relational contract produces deep feelings equivalent to moral outrage. The second factor is the perceived magnitude of the violation. A minor violation would probably induce the employee to seek restoration of the contract; in effect, to resolve the perceived misunderstanding. However, a gross violation would prompt the employee to focus on the emotional hurt of the violation, not its resolution. The third factor is the extent to which the employer is perceived to be directly responsible or accountable for the violation. If the organization is perceived as having involuntarily broken the psychological contract, the magnitude of the violation will be less than if the organization is perceived as doing so voluntarily or deliberately. For example, if some employees lose their jobs because the organization was damaged by a natural disaster (for example, a fire), the sense of violation will be less than if the employer were to discharge the employees for another reason.

What is the typical employee response to violations of the psychological contract? Robinson et al. (1994) found that psychological contracts became less relational and more transactional following violations. Employees turned away from the socioemotional aspects of work and focused on the monetary benefits of the relationship. This has the effect of increasing the psychological distance between the employee and the employer, making the contract more transactional. A sequential pattern of five employee responses to violations has been identified. The first is *voice*; the employee will voice his or her concern over the violation and will seek to reinstate the contract. If unsuccessful, voice is followed by *silence*. Silence connotes compliance with the organization, but with a loss of commitment. Silence is followed by *retreat*, as indicated by passivity, negligence, and shirking of responsibility. *Destruction* may then occur, whereby the employee retaliates against the employer through theft, threats, sabotage, and in extreme cases, homicidal violence against individuals perceived as contributing to the violation. The topic of workplace violence will be discussed in greater detail later in this chapter. Finally, in the *exit* stage, the employee quits the organization or provokes the organization to invoke his or her dismissal.

Research has shown that justice perceptions exert a role in responses to violations of the psychological contract. In particular, procedural justice is of primary importance to employees whose relational contracts were violated. The use of fair and equitable procedures by organizations can lessen the impact of the contract violation on the employee. For example, pay is one of the most fundamental metrics of exchange between employer and employee, and a reduction in pay is regarded as a major violation of a psychological contract. Greenberg (1990) described a situation where because of the loss of lucrative business relationships, a manufacturing company was forced to reduce its payroll by temporarily (for 10 weeks) by cutting wages by 15%. At one plant of the company, the problem was explained in great detail. Employees were shown respect, and their questions were answered with sensitivity. At a second plant of the same company, the pay cut was simply announced to the employees, with no attempt to share expressions of remorse or apology. Greenberg reported that the employees of the second plant responded to their feelings of frustration and resentment by committing many more acts of theft against the employer compared to employees at the first plant. The loss of income was no less at the first plant, but those employees perceived a greater sense of justice and fair play than did their counterparts at the second plant.

Parks and Kidder (1994) noted three major underresearched issues regarding the psychological contract. One is the *employer* side of the contract, and the employer's perceptions of violations by the employees. For the most part research has examined the contract from the employee's perspective. Second is what happens when the psychological contract is *kept*. It is unclear whether a contract becomes more relational as goodwill is enhanced by kept promises. Finally, we don't know very much about whether, once violated, a psychological contract can be *healed*. More research on all three of these issues is necessary to better understand contract violations.

Individual Responses to Organizational Downsizing

One fundamental violation of a psychological contract is the organization's decision to reduce employment through layoffs or downsizing. Such decisions are based on huge power differentials between employer and employee and involve the complete loss of control by the employee. As noted in the previous chapter, downsizing affects thousands of employees annually and is changing the nature of the psychological contract as we know it.

Organizational downsizing has targeted middle-level managers and professional staffs as well as blue-collar employees. These developments are harbingers of fundamental change in the evolution and nature of organizational behavior. In this section I will examine downsizing from the perspective of the individual employee, in terms of both those who have lost their jobs as well as the survivors (Kozlowski, Chao, Smith, & Hedlund, 1993).

There is an inherent paradox associated with downsizing. Downsizing is a deliberate organizational decision to reduce the work force. It is intended to improve organizational performance, yet it has a profound negative impact on the lives of individual employees. At the core of this paradox lies a challenge to a long-standing principle of work and employment—namely, that work can be structured in ways that are beneficial to both the individual and the organization. Downsizing produces the cold and brutal realization that the goals of the individual and the goals of the organization need not necessarily align.

Terminated Personnel.   The individuals most directly affected by downsizing are those who lose their jobs. Downsized employees face the immediate prospect of a loss of income. The lead time employees have upon hearing that their jobs have been eliminated and the date of their termination is often only a matter of weeks, and there is little time to search for a new job. Buss and Redburn (1987) reported that eight years after a plant closing, 27% of the affected work force was still unemployed. Furthermore, those that do find some employment may only be able to obtain less attractive and lower-paying jobs. Individuals with skills that do not readily transfer outside the organization and those with less education have suffered great financial losses.

Employment has a number of psychological benefits that are lost when an individual becomes unemployed. Individuals who lose their job suffer physical symptoms caused by the strain of unemployment. Indicators of the stressful experience of unemployment include the incidence of headaches, stomach problems, and high blood pressure. Unemployed individuals have been found to exhibit patterns of learned helplessness, lower feelings of self-worth, and increased depression. Older, white-collar employees experience particularly acute feelings of betrayal by their organization, demoralization, and cynicism. I will discuss issues of stress and well-being in greater detail in the next chapter.

Surviving Personnel.   While downsizing has more direct implications for the individuals who lose their jobs, employees who remain with the organization will also be affected by downsizing strategies intended to make the organization run more efficiently. Survivors often respond with reduced trust and commitment because the organization broke its psychological contract with them (see Field Note 2). The reactions of these survivors to the downsizing process, as well as their reactions to the organization's treatment of terminated employees, can adversely affect future organizational effectiveness.

While the surviving employees are still employed by the organization, their conditions of employment may be different from before. To remain with the organization, some individuals may be demoted into lower-level jobs, which is often accompanied by a salary reduction as well. Other downsizing strategies targeted to reduce costs include job sharing, part-time schedules, and reduced hours. Although affected employees may experience a reduction in income, this is less painful than the total loss of employment.

Brockner and Greenberg (1990) developed a conceptual model of survivor reactions to downsizing based on organizational justice. Survivors may question whether the downsizing was a necessary response to an economic downturn, whether terminated employees were adequately forewarned, whether the rules used to choose those to be laid-off were fair, and whether or not the organization provided "caretaking activities" (for example, counseling, severance pay) to help individuals adjust to the job loss. Brockner, Davy, and Carter (1985) found that survivors felt guilt when a fellow worker was laid-off, resulting in increased pro-

---

FIELD NOTE 2

To understand the impact of downsizing on the surviving members of an organization, consider the following analogy. The employees of an organization are one of its resources (which is why they are often referred to as "human resources"). The organization uses these employees to accomplish its objectives. Individuals have resources as well. One resource we all have in common is time. Every person has 24 hours in each day to accomplish his or her objectives. Organizational downsizing that results in the loss of 20% of the work force would not be unusual. How would you deal with a 20% loss in your time resources? That is, instead of a 24-hour day, your day has been "downsized" by 20% (or 5 hours) to become a 19-hour day. You still have to do everything you did before, but now you have five fewer hours in which to do it. How would you live your life differently? If you normally sleep 8 hours, would you now sleep only 3 hours? If you need 8 hours of sleep and have to continue working an 8-hour day, that leaves 3 hours for everything else, including eating, transportation time, and recreation. Do you think you would feel stressed under these conditions? Do you think you might not be as fully committed to your activities under these conditions? While we all probably waste some time each day, it is questionable whether we waste 20% of it. Therefore eliminating 20% of our day would not necessarily make us that much more efficient. It might compel us to use our time more wisely, but it would also exact a cost on us. That is, we would probably have to "give" on some other aspects of life. Such is the predicament faced by the surviving members of organizational downsizing. They face increased pressure to perform the work that was once performed by a larger work force.

ductivity. However, survivors also feel less commitment to the organization, and often seek elsewhere for employment with greater security.

In addition to the impact on survivors individually, downsizing affects the functioning of groups as well. Krantz (1985) described the tendency for groups to engage in defensive behavior to relieve the stress of downsizing. The defensiveness manifests itself in a greater reluctance to be flexible and accommodating in performing group tasks. There is also evidence that work teams become more cohesive and resistent to change in response to environmental threats. Increased resistance to change can greatly impede the functioning of teams specifically created to be responsive to changing conditions.

Rather than staffing permanent employees, Smither (1995) reports that many organizations are making greater use of contingency (temporary) workers. Contingent workers provide services for a specific time period to perform particular tasks. The need for their services varies as a function of the organization's work flow. Contingent workers may work through temporary employment agencies that allocate their services to organizational clients in need of them. They are the modern day industrial equivalent of migrant farm workers, people who obtain temporary employment by following the harvesting of crops across the nation. Contingent workers receive lower salaries than if they were permanent employees performing the same work, and they rarely receive fringe benefits such as medical insurance or pensions. Contingent workers are disproportionately young, female, and from minority groups. They exemplify the transactional psychological contract as they have a short-term outlook on their involvement with an organization. The future holds little promise for them.

While contingent workers may increase organizational flexibility and decrease labor costs, there is a price to pay. The price includes a withdrawal of prosocial behaviors, or worse, engaging in antisocial behaviors. Furthermore, a common reaction of surviving employees after downsizing is to feel overworked. Schor (1992) reports that surviving employees often must take up the work of terminated individuals. Additionally, they feel compelled to accept being overworked in the expectation that it will result in their own continued employment. These workers may in turn reassess their own psychological contracts and may perceive their own contracts as transactional, whether or not it was intended as such by the employer.

Downsizing has forced both organizations and individuals to reassess the nature of the employment relationship. One consequence has been an apparent increase in transactional psychological contracts, with an accompanying decrease in the number of individuals who feel a sense of loyalty and commitment to their employers. It has been argued that downsizing is a necessary response to organizational structures that have become bloated and economically inefficient. Organizations that resist downsizing as a means of addressing their imperiled conditions risk orchestrating their total demise (and the loss of even more jobs). However, downsizing has become bitter medicine for individuals in the treatment of organizational maladies. Its presence and frequency of use has prompted a major reassessment by I/O psychologists on long-held tenets regarding the nature of the employment relationship.

The Psychology of Mergers and Acquisitions

One strategy organizations can use in response to environmental pressures is to become smaller, that is, to downsize. Another strategy organizations can use in response to environmental pressures is to become larger. But rather than just becoming a larger version of what the organization already is, organizations can choose to "marry" another organization as a way of increasing their size. The logic behind an organizational marriage is similar to that of the marriage of individuals—that is, the overall quality of life for both parties will be enhanced by the marriage. Organizational marriages encompass the concepts of mergers and acquisitions. The technical distinction between mergers and acquisitions is slim. A *merger* is the marriage or joining of two organizations of equal status and power. Their union is mutually decided. Both organizations think they will be more prosperous by their formal association with the other. An *acquisition* is the procurement of property (in this case, an organization) by another organization. The purchasing organization is in the dominant or more powerful role. Unlike a marriage of individuals, acquisition can be a marriage between two organizations where only one party agrees to the new relationship. The dominant organization thus acquires an unwilling partner to enhance its financial status in what is called a "hostile takeover." Other acquisitions are characterized by more friendly relations between the two organizations, but nevertheless the more powerful organization still acquires the less powerful organization. The acquiring organization is referred to as the "parent," while the organization being acquired is the "target." For the purposes of this discussion, mergers and acquisitions will be portrayed as the combining of two companies, regardless of the difference in power between the two. There is relatively little research on this topic. What we do know applies mainly to the characteristics of the two organizations as they affect the quality of their marriage and the individual responses of employees to their organization being united with another.

Some characteristics of parent firms have been found to affect the way they implement the integration of the two companies (Hogan & Overmyer-Day, 1994). Two prominent issues are the parent's culture and the parent's arrogance toward the target. Some parent cultures are more likely to impose themselves on the target companies than others. Parent organizations with strong consensus on beliefs and values, as well as strong socialization of members into these beliefs and values, are particularly likely to attempt to impose these on targets. The unity of a parent's culture, as well as its tolerance for diversity, is related to how the parent treats the target. Some parent companies have been found to exhibit characteristics of arrogance and presumption—they "know what's best" for the target. Jemison and Sitkin (1986) proposed three types of organizational arrogance: interpersonal ("We're better than you"), cultural ("Our values, practices, and beliefs are superior"), and managerial ("Our administrative systems are better"). Arrogance influences parent managers to act condescendingly toward targets, increasing their tendencies to impose solutions and negatively affecting morale, turnover, and performance. Arrogance also increases target resistance to being

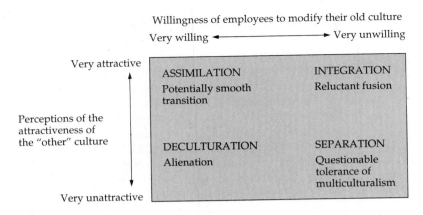

Figure 9–5   *Modes of interaction between two organizational cultures in mergers and acquisitions*

integrated into the parent company. Buono and Bowditch (1989) suggested that the more important the target to the parent, the more likely the parent is to exert control of the target and thus increase the likelihood of conflict.

The elements of a target's culture pertaining to the identification of its heroes, leadership style, feelings of "family" among workers, and degree of mentoring among managers are likely sources of problems when integration is attempted. It has been suggested that management's attitude toward risk and the degree of responsibility for decision making are major areas where cultural clashes are most evident. Each organization being unaware of the other's culture appears to be responsible for the majority of problems faced when integrating two organizations. During negotiations between the two organizations, issues of "strategic fit" (that is, shared or complementary business strategies, financial goals) typically dominate discussion. However, issues of "organizational fit" (that is, the compatibility of the cultures and the match between work forces) are often neglected.

Cartwright and Cooper (1994) have proposed two factors that account for the degree of success in merging two organizational cultures. One is the willingness of organizational members to modify their existing culture, while the second is the attractiveness of "the other" (parent or target) culture. These two factors result in four possible modes of interaction between organizational cultures, which are shown in Figure 9–5. The four modes, respectively, reflect a harmonious blending of cultures (assimilation), a reluctant fusion of cultures (integration), the loss of cultural identify (deculturation), and the emergence of a multicultural organization (separation).

On an individual level, turnover is the most common behavioral outcome of mergers. Those individuals most likely to face involuntary removal are target employees situated near the top of the organizational hierarchy. Individuals in staff positions (for example, legal, human resources, accounting, and so forth) are most likely to face job loss because these functions are easily absorbed by the parent's operations (see Field Note 3). However, removal of key personnel from these functional specialties may create integration problems for the parent if the terminations are conducted too hastily or in an insensitive manner. Individuals in these high-level positions often possess knowledge of the target organization's culture or operations that could prove useful to the parent when implementing integration plans. If these positions are terminated too quickly by the new parent, it may communicate an undesirable message of corporate ruthlessness and callousness. The perceived lack of organizational justice can damage the image of the parent and increase resistance to integration.

Research has shown, however, that the majority of target employees who leave do so voluntarily. Baytos (1986) estimated that 50 to 75% of key managers from acquired organizations voluntarily leave the new organization within a few years of the merger. Many managers who quit their jobs cited a loss of managerial autonomy as a major reason behind their decision to leave. The voluntary turn-

---

FIELD NOTE 3

Job loss has plagued workers for decades, although the circumstances change over time. In the late 1920s and early 1930s, the nation experienced what is referred to as the Great Depression. Millions of workers lost their jobs in what was an extremely difficult time in our nation's history. Many farmers went out of business because of enduring droughts during these years. A farmer who lost his farm advised his son to leave the family farming business. The father said that there were just too many things that could go wrong in farming—droughts, floods, freezes—over which there was no control. The farmer advised his son to pursue a career in an industry where he could join a large company and enjoy employment stability. The father was embittered over the loss of his farm business, and he did not want to see his son suffer the same fate. His son became an employee at a huge steel mill, one of thousands of employees who worked at the mill. For many years the steel industry prospered, as did the son, who got married and had a son of his own. In the late 1960s, U.S. steel companies began to experience intense competition from Japanese steel companies. The Japanese produced steel at a lower cost, which prompted U.S. steel companies to cut back in size because of the loss in business.

The man lost his job (along with many other employees) and became embittered about industries that were victimized by foreign competition. He in turn advised his own son to enter an industry that would be relatively unaffected by conditions of nature and not prone to job loss because of foreign competition. He advised his son to go into the tobacco or alcohol distilling business, because he believed that no matter what the economic climate, people still like to smoke and drink. The son took his advice, and became an accountant for a distillery. The company produced high-quality alcoholic beverages and was highly successful. The company was so successful it became attractive to other, larger companies. The distillery was eventually acquired by a much larger company, which employed many accountants of their own, and the son's job was eliminated.

Three generations of this family incurred job losses, but all for very different reasons. None of the individuals were fired because of poor job performance; rather, the jobs they once held disappeared. Corporate mergers and acquisitions represent an updated version of the uncontrollable forces that can affect individual employees in the 1990s just as droughts affected family farmers in the 1930s.

over of highly productive workers is considered by some as indicative of failure in the integration process. In cases where an acquisition is utilized in part to gain the skills and talents possessed by another company, the attrition of top performers undermines the achievement of that goal.

The psychological response of employees to the announcement that their company has been acquired has been compared with the sense of loss experienced following bereavement (Mirvis, 1985). As in models of individual bereavement, it is posited that employees pass through stages of grief beginning with disbelief and denial, followed by anger, emotional bargaining, depression, and finally acceptance. The loss of individuals' identification with their organization may produce stress associated with the loss as well as a nostalgic impulse in employees to hold on to what they have. Collective employee grief is likely to increase cohesiveness and resistance to change and make new cultures even more difficult to introduce.

It has been estimated that during the 1980s at least 25% of the U.S. work force was affected by merger and acquisition activity (Fulmer, 1986). As with downsizing, I/O psychologists have little experience in dealing with how individuals respond to this type of organizational activity. In the past 10 to 15 years we have had to address new aspects of organizational behavior about which we had little knowledge. The depth and magnitude of these issues on the psychology of work have had a profound impact on the profession of I/O psychology.

Violence in the Workplace

I conclude this chapter with one of the darkest manifestations of organizational behavior—violence in the workplace. The growing epidemic of violent crime has not spared the workplace. As reported by Mantell (1994), the National Safe Workplace Institute determined that there were more than 111,000 violent workplace incidents in 1992. Of these, 750 individuals were murdered by their coworkers. The number of employees who killed their managers has doubled in the last decade. Reporting appropriate statistics on crime has the subtle effect of making them appear somewhat dry and impersonal. Consider these descriptions of specific acts of violence in the workplace (Mantell, 1994, pp. 2–4):

- A Tampa, Florida man returned to his former workplace and shot three of his supervisors as they sat eating their lunches. He wounded two others before killing himself.
- A Sunnyvale, California worker of a defense contractor shot and killed seven people in the office after a female coworker turned down his romantic advances.
- A woman in a Corona, California hospital opened fire with a .38-calibre handgun, wounding a nurse and spraying the infant nursery with bullets.
- A terminated Woodlawn, Maryland car mechanic came back to the garage and fired into a crowd of workers, killing two and wounding one.

It may be tempting to dismiss these accounts as somewhat sensationalized reporting of isolated events. However, the frequency and severity of workplace violence is escalating, both nationally and internationally. Most of the literature on workplace violence is not based on empirical research of a psychological nature (Thomas, 1992). In fact, I/O psychologists are just beginning to study this problem.

A starting point for understanding the psychology of workplace violence is with the topic of aggression. Cox and Leather (1994) state, "Human aggression is typically the product of interpersonal interactions wherein two or more persons become involved in a sequence of escalating moves and countermoves, each of which successively modifies the probability of subsequent aggression" (p. 222). Thus, aggressive acts are frequently the retaliatory response to a previous act or acts by the aggressor. A violent act is therefore conceptualized as sequenced within an integrated series of social acts. The retaliatory response can be understood in part by the concepts of organizational justice and the psychological contract. Perpetrators of workplace violence often see themselves as victims of some injustice in the workplace. They may be particularly inclined to perceive the organization as having violated the principles of procedural justice. In fact, Johnson and Indvik (1994) posit that violation of the psychological contract is one of the leading causes of workplace violence. A term frequently associated with perpetrators of workplace violence is "disgruntled." Mantell (1994) reports that acts of physical violence are invariably preceded by symptoms of anger or betrayal, such as verbal threats or sullenness. Perpetrators seemingly want more from the organization in terms of personal identity and purpose than the organization can provide, and in turn they personalize their sense of rejection when their needs are unmet. They tend to see themselves as having had their relationship (contract) with the organization violated, but they accept little or no responsibility for their own behavior. It also appears to be the case that perpetrators of violent workplace crimes often have maladaptive personalities and have experienced interpersonal conflict in other aspects of their lives.

Looking for systematic patterns among perpetrators of workplace violence has led to the identification of consistent characteristics among these individuals. A problem with this profile approach is that while it may indeed describe perpetrators, the identified characteristics may describe many other individuals as well. That is, many employees may "fit" the profile but in fact do *not* engage in workplace violence. For example, most employees whose jobs were downsized feel a sense of rejection and injustice, yet they do not commit violent acts. Hindsight or "postdiction" may give the impression that perpetrators were obvious candidates to commit such crimes and should have been identified and deterred from their actions, but predictive accuracy is never so easily attained. Despite the prevalence of workplace violence, its occurrence is still relatively rare in the total constellation of employed individuals. Therefore, correct prediction of such events is far more problematic than "looking backwards" after their occurrence might suggest.

Aggression is the product of both individual and situational factors. Among the situational factors identified are population density, noise, heat, and alcohol usage. Both laboratory and field research (for example, Geen, 1990) indicate that aggression becomes increasingly likely under conditions of perceived crowding, uncontrollable noise, and high ambient temperatures. However, it is the research on the relationship between alcohol usage and aggression that is most declarative.

Pernanen (1991) posits that alcohol produces a complete modification of an individual's ability to understand a social situation. Alcohol leads to both a narrowing of perception of the situation at hand and a dampening of intellectual and verbal ability. Alcohol encourages an overinflated evaluation of a person's sense of control, power, and mastery over the world. The inebriated individual may be led into aggression by both a biased interpretation of the situation and an increased confidence in being able to cope by largely physical means (Cox & Leather, 1994). Many perpetrators of workplace violence were found to have consumed alcohol prior to commission of their act.

Some researchers believe that violence in the workplace is part of the larger category of psychosocial hazards organizations must be responsive to. Cox and Leather (1994) proposed three strategies organizations should adopt in dealing with the complex hazards of workplace violence:

- *Preventive strategies* (such as employee training) remove the hazard or reduce its impact on employees or their likelihood of exposure.
- *Reactive strategies* (such as formal organizational emergency plans) improve the organization's ability to recognize and deal with problems as they arise.
- *Rehabilitative strategies* (such as counseling) help employees cope with and recover from existing problems.

Violence in the workplace is a complex phenomenon. Like drug usage in the workplace, it spills over into other disciplines traditionally removed from I/O psychology. It remains to be seen how big a role we will play in addressing this topic. If primary emphasis is placed on the act (criminal violence) rather than its location, the role of I/O psychology will probably not be large. However, if examined primarily in terms of its location (the workplace), I/O psychology will be called upon to help understand and control this serious problem.

Concluding Comments

Organizational behavior encompasses a broad range of topics. Some scholars find it useful to conceptualize studies of organizational behavior along a continuum, ranging from what is referred to as "micro to macro." The micro approach emphasizes the individual and his or her relationship with the organization. The psychological approach to the study of organizational behavior reflects this perspective. For example, the psychological contract is defined in terms of an individual's expectations for the employment relationship. The macro approach examines organizational behavior from a broader perspective and is reflective of a sociological orientation to organizations. Mowday and Sutton (1993) believe that the sociological perspective can offer new insights into concepts that have long been viewed from the individual perspective. For example, Pfeffer (1991) suggests that the attitudes employees develop about the job can be construed to be a consequence of social contagion processes and that the emphasis should be on investigating who employees come into contact with in the organization.

It has also been suggested that researchers learn to distinguish between strong and weak organizational contexts in influencing behavior. That is, some aspects of behavior exhibited in organizations may be extensions or generalizations of the same type of behavior individuals exhibit outside of a work context. We may be highly consistent in certain behaviors and demonstrate them irrespective of a work or home context. Other manifestations of behavior may be limited primarily to the organization. The importance of this distinction is evident when considering violence in the workplace. Perhaps employees who commit criminal acts of violence in the workplace also commit aberrant behavior outside of the workplace. If such is the case, a comprehensive personnel selection system might be used to identify such people and limit their access to the organization. However, if otherwise well-adjusted people become driven to commit workplace violence because of perceived injustice and extreme stress, a different course of action would be warranted.

In the next chapter I will examine not only stress but also the process by which individuals attempt to balance the conflicts between work and home life. This work/home conflict in itself has been found to be a major source of stress for individuals.

CASE STUDY   *Where Should the Ax Fall?*

Ted Simmons stared pensively at two personnel files. Simmons was the vice-president of finance for Savannah Mills, a long-time business leader in the textile industry. Savannah Mills had just endured another difficult year, and sales and profits were again lower than projected. Simmons had just returned from a staff meeting where he was told that the company would be downsizing its staff to reduce expenses. Simmons had to eliminate one of his two financial manager positions, and other job losses were to follow down the line in his department. In fact, all the major departments at Savannah Mills would incur job losses, some more than others.

Simmons had the pleasure of working with two exemplary managers, and eliminating one of these jobs from the company would be extremely difficult and unpleasant. Warren Davis had been with the company for almost 25 years. He had devoted his entire career to Savannah Mills, starting to work there after high school. His dedication and commitment to the company were almost legendary. He earned a bachelor's degree in general business, attending college on a part-time basis while holding a full-time job at Savannah Mills. Whatever the company asked Davis to do, he did with vigor and good cheer. He willingly accepted assignments where the company needed him and always expressed sincere gratitude for the chance to be with Savannah Mills. His father had been an employee of the company for more than 40 years when he retired, and the Davis children grew up playing on company-sponsored recreational teams. Warren Davis was also very active in the community, representing Savannah Mills on various civic projects. Davis was once referred to as a "walking billboard" for the company, so deep was his loyalty to the company that meant so much to him and his family.

The other manager was Barry Steele. Steele had a very different history with the company. Steele was 29 and had been with Savannah Mills for five years. He earned an MBA from a highly prestigious university in New England. Upon graduation Steele had many job offers but chose Savannah Mills because of their expressed intent to more strongly professionalize the financial operations at the company. This would give Steele the opportunity to put his talents to work. Steele delivered on all the expectations of him, and in fact exceeded these expectations. He revolutionized the company's system of managing their financial assets through the use of automated control principles he learned in graduate school. It was through Steele's shrewd assessments that Savannah Mills avoided even bigger financial losses, and he positioned the company to return to profitability. Steele was known as "the wonder kid" because of his accomplishments, but he never acted arrogant or pompous. He was not active in company or civic affairs, but quietly went about his business. If there were ever a young employee who seemed destined for a highly successful future with Savannah Mills, it was Steele.

Simmons faced a dreadful choice. He didn't have to fire one of his managers; poor job performance was not the issue. Rather, he had to choose to eliminate the job of a person whose contributions to the company were very positive. Simmons argued with the company president on the merits of keeping both managers. His arguments were to no avail. The issue was one of reducing expenses, and all departments were to suffer the loss of good employees. Simmons felt this was one of the toughest calls he had ever had to make. No matter which way it went, the decision would speak loudly about what type of employee Savannah Mills valued the most.

Questions

1. Recall the concept of the psychological contract. What aspects of the contract are at issue in this case?
2. If Davis's job is eliminated, what message will that send to the other employees at Savannah Mills?
3. If Steele's job is eliminated, what message will that send to the other employees at Savannah Mills?
4. Recall the concept of organizational citizenship behavior. To what degree does this concept influence your thoughts about a just decision in this case?
5. If you were Simmons, whose job would you eliminate, and why?

CHAPTER

10

Stress and Well-Being at Work

Major Chapter Objectives

- *Be able to explain environmental influences on mental health.*

- *Be able to explain the concept of mental health.*

- *Identify the dispositional factors in mental health.*

- *Understand the concept of work stress.*

- *Understand the basis of work/family conflict.*

- *Be able to discuss issues pertaining to dual-career families.*

- *Understand the psychological effects of unemployment.*

Sigmund Freud was once asked what he thought a "normal" person should be able to do well. He is reported to have said *"Lieben und Arbeiten"* ("to love and to work") (Erikson, 1963, p. 265). Freud believed that is through one's family that love-related needs are gratified, and that work had a more powerful effect than any other aspect of human life to bind a person to reality. Therefore, Freud's call for a normal person to love and to work can be interpreted as an emphasis on work and family for healthy psychological functioning (Quick, Murphy, Hurrell, & Orman, 1992).

A person's work and occupational stature play a critical role in an individual's sense of identity, self-esteem, and psychological well-being. Work is the central and defining characteristic of life for most individuals. Work may have intrinsic value, instrumental value, or both. The intrinsic value of work is the value an individual finds in performing the work, in and of itself. Instrumentally, the value of work is found in providing the necessities of life and serving as a channel for the individual's talents, abilities, and knowledge.

It has been suggested that the split in a person's work and home identities dates back to the Industrial Revolution era. It was then that it became necessary for a person to leave the home and "go to work." However, work and home commitments need not necessarily be at odds with each other. Kanter (1977) proposed that knowledge of the tension and illness-producing features of one system, either work or family, can be used to understand a person's adjustment to the other system. It seems clear that most workers do not leave the pressures of the job behind after leaving work.

The purpose of this chapter is to examine the sense of well-being at work and to explain how work stress can threaten this well-being. Central to the discussion is the balance between "love and work" needed for well-being and how work-related issues can lead to imbalance in this relationship.

Environmental Influences on Mental Health

Warr (1987) has proposed that a sense of well-being from work must first be understood in terms of the general environmental determinants of mental health. Warr identified nine environmental determinants of mental health, which can be viewed as the basis for developing psychological well-being.

1. *Opportunity for control.* The first determinant of mental health is the opportunity provided by an environment for a person to control activities and events. Mental health is enhanced by situations that promote personal control. The opportunity for control has two main elements: the opportunity to decide and act in one's chosen way, and the potential to predict the consequences of action. Absence of the second element produces a specific form of uncontrollability—a person has freedom of decision and action but cannot predict the outcome. Not knowing the consequences of behavior, the individual cannot control what will happen.

2. *Opportunity for skill use.* A second feature is the degree to which the environment inhibits or encourages utilization and development of skills. Restrictions

on skill use may be of two kinds. First are those that prevent people from using skills they already possess, permitting instead only behaviors that are only routine. Second are restrictions on the acquisition of new skills, requiring people to remain at low levels of skilled performance despite their potential for extending into more complex activity.

3. *Externally generated goals.* The third feature assumed to underlie mental health is the presence of goals or challenges generated by the environment. An environment that makes no demands on a person offers no challenge and encourages no activity or achievement. Conversely, an environment that gives rise to the establishment and pursuit of goals is assumed to lead to activities that may have a positive impact on mental health, both intrinsically and through their consequences.

4. *Variety.* Some environments generate repetitive and invariant goals and associated activities. Required activity of a repetitive kind is unlikely to contribute to mental health to the same degree as more diverse requirements, which introduce novelty and break up uniformity of activity and location. Therefore, the fourth determinant of mental health is environmental variety.

5. *Environmental clarity.* The fifth feature is the degree to which a person's environment is clear. Clarity includes two components. One is the availability of feedback about the consequences of one's actions. Second is the clarity of role requirements and normative expectations about behavior, and the degree to which standards are explicit and accepted within one's environment.

6. *Availability of money.* Severely restricted access to money can give rise to many processes likely to impair mental health. The presence of money does not ensure mental health, but the absence of money often produces extensive psychological problems. Poverty reduces the opportunity for personal control in one's life, which is a previously identified determinant of mental health.

7. *Physical security.* A seventh feature is a physically secure living environment. The environment needs to protect a person against physical harm and to provide an adequate level of security with respect to eating, sleeping, and residing. The environment also needs to be reasonably permanent, providing security into the future.

8. *Opportunity for interpersonal contact.* Environments differ in the opportunity they provide for contact with other people. Such contact meets needs for friendship and reduces feelings of loneliness. Interpersonal contact also provides social support that is both emotional and instrumental (contributing to the resolution of problems through practical help and advice). Also, many goals can be achieved only through the interdependent efforts of several people. Membership in groups makes possible the establishment and attainment of goals that could not be realized by an individual alone.

9. *Valued social position.* The ninth aspect considered to be important is a position within a social structure that carries some esteem from others. Esteem is generated primarily through the value attached to activities inherent in a role and the contribution they make. Role membership also provides public evidence that one has certain abilities and meets certain social obligations. There is often widespread agreement about the level of esteem that derives from a particular position.

Warr (1987) recognized some overlap among these nine dimensions but felt a recognition of each was necessary to understand how environments affect mental health. If you were interested in changing environments to enhance mental health, these nine features would be useful targets to produce beneficial change.

The Concept of Mental Health

No single definition of mental health exists. It is easier to understand the meaning of mental health by referencing its determinants. Societal standards contribute to the meaning of mental health (many derived from contemporary Western society), and standards proposed by the medical profession regarding mental illness also shape this concept. I will not explore the varied contributions of these sources in conceptualizing mental health; rather, I will examine the overall perspective of mental health proposed by Warr (1987) and focus on its five major components.

1. *Affective well-being*. Affective well-being is referenced by two separate dimensions, pleasure and arousal. A particular level of pleasure may be accompanied by high or low levels of arousal, and a particular level of arousal may be either pleasurable or unpleasurable. Figure 10–1 portrays this two-dimensional view of affective well-being. A feeling of affective well-being derives from both dimensions. For example, depressed feelings are characterized by low status on each dimension (being located in the bottom left-hand section of Figure 10–1), and anxiety may be described in terms of a low status on pleasure and high status on arousal (in the top left-hand section). The highest levels of affective well-being are associated with the top right-hand section, reflecting high pleasure and high arousal. Terms such as *happy* and *full of energy* are indicative of the individual's status on these two dimensions. In general, a person's affective well-being over a given period can be described in terms of the proportion of time spent in each of the four sections of Figure 10–1.

2. *Competence*. Good mental health is partly viewed in terms of acceptable degrees of success or competence in different spheres of activity, such as interpersonal relations, problem solving, paid employment, and so on. The competent person has adequate psychological resources to deal with life's pressures. It has been suggested that good mental health becomes apparent only when a person faces adversity. Successfully responding to pressures requires having appropriate cognitive and psychomotor skills, as well as beliefs and opinions consistent with reality.

3. *Autonomy*. Autonomy refers to a person's ability to resist environmental influences and to determine his or her own opinions and actions. The tendency to strive for independence and self-regulation is a fundamental characteristic of a mentally healthy person. Autonomy is the tendency for an individual to feel and act on the assumption that he or she is influential rather than helpless in the face of life's difficulties. The contribution of autonomy to mental health is given greater importance in Western than in Eastern societies.

4. *Aspiration*. The mentally healthy person is viewed as someone who engages with the environment. He or she establishes goals and makes active efforts to attain them. A raised aspiration level is reflected in high motivation, alertness to new opportunities, and a commitment to meet personal challenges. Conversely, low levels of aspiration are exhibited in reduced activity and an acceptance of the

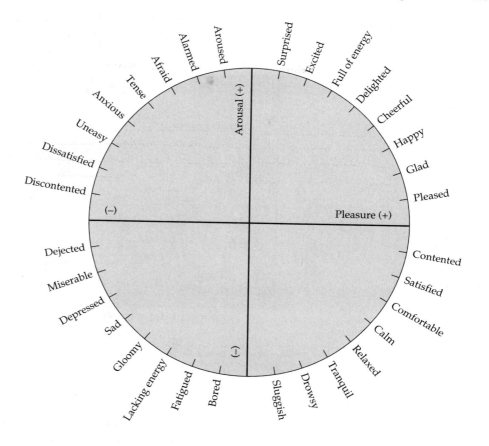

Figure 10–1 *Two-dimensional model of affective well-being*
SOURCE: From *Work, Unemployment, and Mental Health* (p. 27) by P. B. Warr, 1987, Oxford: Clarendon.

present state no matter how unsatisfactory it appears. In striving to achieve personal goals, an individual may face stressful situations and, indeed, may create them when pursuing difficult challenges. The importance of raised aspiration level to good mental health is particularly clear in circumstances adverse to the individual, where the desire for change is likely to be viewed as central to a healthy response.

5. *Integrated functioning.* The final component of mental health is the most difficult to define and is most unlike the other four components. Integrated functioning refers to the person as a whole. People who are psychologically healthy exhibit balance, harmony, and inner relatedness. In relation to Freud's statement about love and work, it has been suggested that the healthy person is someone who can balance the importance of these two areas. Integrated functioning may also be considered across time, typically in terms of a balance between accepted strain during difficult phases of goal attainment and relaxation during the intervening periods.

"Wendell ... I'm not content."

Warr's (1987) portrayal of mental health represents a comprehensive assessment of the major dimensions of psychological well-being. Competence, autonomy, and aspiration reflect aspects of a person's behavior in relation to the environment and often determine the level of a person's affective well-being. For example, an inability to cope with current difficulties (a form of low competence) may give rise to distress (an aspect of low affective well-being). Affective well-being has its roots in medical criteria, including the person reporting a sense of feeling well and also not being impaired psychologically or physically. Integrated functioning, however, deals with the multiple relationships among the four components and covers broader issues. Throughout the balance of this chapter I will examine how work-related factors facilitate or inhibit psychological well-being as defined from this five-factor perspective.

Dispositional Factors in Mental Health

While there is a vast amount of research attesting to environmental influences on our mental health and work affect, recent research also indicates that there is a genetic component to how we feel about work-related issues. That is, our mental health and responses to work may not be solely due to environmental influences. Rather, we each bring our own dispositions to the workplace, which in turn influences our affective response. A major question deals with just how strongly these dispositional factors affect our feelings about work. This is the I/O psychology version of the environment/heredity or nature/nurture controversy that has intrigued psychologists for decades.

Arvey, Bouchard, Segal, and Abraham (1989) studied 34 pairs of identical twins who had been reared apart from an early age to test the hypothesis that there is a significant genetic component to work affect. The results indicated that approximately 30% of the variance in work affect was due to genetic factors. The authors also reported a tendency for the twins to hold similar jobs. In a subsequent study Keller, Bouchard, Arvey, Segal, and Dawis (1992) examined 43 reared-apart twin pairs to test the hypothesis that genetic factors were associated with work values. Work values assessed the importance of such factors as achievement, status, safety, and autonomy to the individual. The results revealed that on average 40% of the variance in work values was related to genetic factors, whereas 60% of the variance was associated with environmental factors. The findings indicate a genetic predisposition to prefer certain work outcomes over others. The findings from these two studies suggest that a person's genetic makeup is associated with job satisfaction and the outcomes a person wants on the job.

Work affect is not immutable, that is that we are born to feel a certain way about work. To the contrary, work affect is malleable by environmental factors, and these factors produce a larger effect than genetic influences. However, these findings provide insights into why individuals respond differently to motivation and incentive programs. Bouchard, Arvey, Keller, and Segal (1992) summarized their research by stating, "A message that flows from the findings of genetic influence on human behavior is that human individual differences are genuine and complex in origin . . . and that differences cannot be explained away with a simple wave of the hand or the assertion that they are due to x, y, or z environmental variables" (p. 92). For the most part I/O psychology has not addressed itself to the genetic component of work behavior. However, the results of these studies indicate that there may be limits to the extent to which we can modify individual behavior and attitudes by altering the workplace.

Work Stress

Psychological disorders in the workplace have been identified as being among the ten leading work-related diseases and injuries in the United States (National Institute for Occupational Safety and Health, 1988). Ilgen (1990) stated, "The health of the work force is one of the most significant issues of our time" (p. 273). Recognition of the psychosocial risk of work has prompted a long stream of medical, psychological, and behavioral stress research. Pelletier (1977) reported that stress and psychosocial factors play a far more central role in chronic disorders than they do in acute and infectious diseases. As a consequence, both employees and organizations have become increasingly aware of the negative effects of work-related stress. A nationwide survey by the Northwestern National Life Insurance Company (1991) showed that nearly 46% of American workers felt that their jobs were very or somewhat stressful, whereas nearly 27% reported that their jobs were the single greatest source of stress in their lives. Nearly 72% of those surveyed experienced frequent stress-related physical and mental conditions.

A very large amount of research has been conducted across many disciplines on work stress. Research has examined the causes, symptoms, and consequences of work stress as well as interventions designed to reduce its effect on individuals. Furthermore, there is no agreed-upon definition of stress or how to conceptualize it. For example, it is not the case that all work demands on individuals are undesirable. If it were, the preferred state of the individual would be inactivity, which we know to be untrue. People seek activity, including the kinds of activities that use abilities they value. However, some activities or situations produce undesirable effects such as emotional tension, sleep disorders, and a decrease in job performance. Selye (1982) sought to distinguish "good stress" from "bad stress" by referring to them as "eustress" and "distress," respectively. I will limit my focus here to distress and to understanding its negative effect on individuals.

Because of the many issues related to stress, researchers have proposed conceptual models of stress designed to integrate a diverse array of research findings. Many such models have been developed, and one by Kahn and Byosiere (1992) will guide this discussion. This model is presented in Figure 10–2. Stress in organizations is conceptualized in terms of seven major categories, with numerous linkages among the categories. This reflects one of the primary research findings about stress—there are complex associations between the antecedents of stress, individual differences in how people respond to stress, and the consequences of stress. A causal sequence is hypothesized to exist among these categories. I will examine each of the seven categories presented in the model along with findings pertaining to the prevention of stress.

Organizational Antecedents to Stress.   Research on the organizational antecedents to stress is generally directed toward understanding how broad-based and abstract factors induce stress. Brenner and Mooney (1983), for example, have examined the relationship between economic conditions (economic growth, instability, and unemployment levels) and social indicators of health (diseases and death) in nine countries: Australia, Canada, England, Denmark, Finland, France, Germany, Sweden, and the United States. The variables are examined in what are referred to as *lagged relationships;* that is, changes in economic conditions produce changes in health several years later. Unemployment and business failures predicted death from heart disease in eight of the nine countries, with a one-year to four-year lag while controlling for such variables as alcohol consumption.

Cobb and Kasl (1977) conducted a longitudinal study on U.S. plant closings for the purpose of understanding the relationship between impending job loss and health. Workers in plants that did not close were compared with those in plants that were marked for closing. Five waves of data were collected over a two-year period, spanning the sequencing of events from rumor to actual job loss and (in most cases) reemployment. Psychological measures of health were collected along with self-reported information. The results showed that the threat of unem-

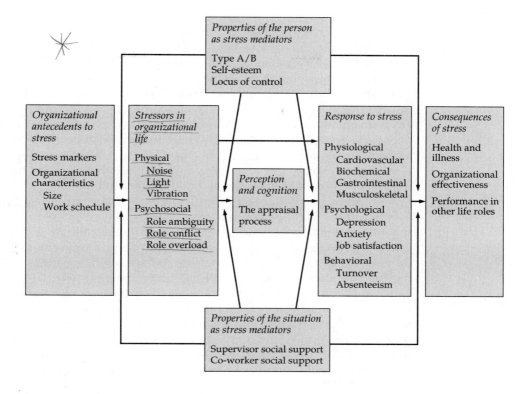

Figure 10-2 Theoretical framework for the study of stress in organizations

SOURCE: Adapted from "Stress in Organizations" by R. L. Kahn and P. B. Byosiere, 1992, in *Handbook of Industrial/Organizational Psychology* (p. 592) edited by M. D. Dunnette and L. M. Hough, Palo Alto, CA: Consulting Psychologists Press.

ployment triggered some physiological changes long before actual job loss occurred and that most physical indicators returned to normal after new job stability was attained. For most people, involuntary loss of a job was an event that generated stress, both directly and indirectly.

Stressors in Organizational Life. The term *stressors* designates stimuli generated on the job and having negative consequences, physical or psychological, for significant proportions of people exposed to them. Kahn and Byosiere (1992) reduced stressors to two major types. The first, *task content*, includes such dimensions as simplicity-complexity and monotony-variety. The second, *role properties*, refers to the social aspects of the job and includes supervisory relations and role conflict.

Research findings have demonstrated a relationship between ill-health (most notably heart disease) and jobs characterized by highly repetitive, monotonous work that require sustained vigilance (see Field Note 1). Shift work and physical stressors (cold, heat, and noise) also produce stress at work. These factors will be discussed in greater detail in Chapter 15 on working conditions. Nevertheless, ill-health has also been associated with working in air-conditioned offices, a phenomenon referred to as the "sick building syndrome." Hedge, Erickson, and Rubin (1992) reported that the sick building syndrome produces the following symptoms: sensory irritation; skin irritation; neurotoxic effects such as headaches, nausea, and drowsiness; and hyperactivity reactions such as runny eyes, runny nose, and asthma-like symptoms. Research has demonstrated that the sick building syndrome is not caused solely by indoor pollutants but may be related to the electromagnetic fields from video display terminals, which attract irritating fibers and particles to the screens. The syndrome may also be related to respiratory ailments associated with recirculated air. There is also a growing body of research (for example, Soine, 1995; Stenberg & Wall, 1995) that suggests that women are more susceptible than men to sick building syndrome.

However, it is with regard to role properties that most organizational stressors have been identified. *Role conflict* consists of perceptual differences regarding the content of the role or the relative importance of its elements. Such differences occur between the individual and other people in a work group who do not hold the same role expectations. Such conflict generates negative affect, tension, and often physical symptoms on the part of the focal person. Conflict between the demands of different roles filled by the same individual can also occur. Such conflicts have been reported most often in occupations such as military service, police work, and teaching, where the compartmentalization of time between work and family cannot be easily or dependably arranged. *Role overload* is a variant of role conflict in which conflict is experienced as a necessity to compromise either quantity, time schedule, or quality. For example, consider a

FIELD NOTE 1

Jobs requiring sustained vigilance have been found to produce marked stress. Research on firefighters indicates that a major source of stress is not responding to fire calls but waiting for a call to come in. The tension and anxiety associated with waiting to use their skills is often far more stress-inducing than responding to hazardous situations. A metropolitan fire department may get several calls per day, usually representing nonthreatening or mildly threatening situations, but occasionally those involving large fires or hazardous materials. It is the continuous stream of relatively "minor" incidents that breaks the tedium associated with vigilance and reduces the level of job stress.

However, fire departments located at major airports (both commercial and military) face a somewhat different situation from their urban counterparts. Firefighters who work at airports may go several weeks before having to respond to any incident, and when the incident occurs it is invariably more threatening than rescuing a cat from a tree. Some military planes contain armaments that could explode in the event of a fire or crash landing. The potential loss of life in a commercial airline accident can be very high. When not responding to such potentially perilous situations, airport firefighters endure the stress of waiting for something dramatic to happen. The Greek writer Homer presaged airport firefighters as those who live "between Scylla and Charybdis"—two equally perilous alternatives, neither of which can be passed without encountering and probably falling victim to the other.

supervisor who says to an employee, "I want this report finished by tomorrow, and I want it done well." There will be conflict between the time deadline and the request for high quality work. Findings from many studies reveal that over-loaded individuals describe their work demands as excessive and their reactions as negative.

Perceptions and Cognitions: The Appraisal Process.   The appraisal process seeks to explain that different people react differently to stressors that are objectively the same. Furthermore, the stressors encountered within organizations are often em-bedded in complex situations. Successful coping requires the ability to analyze both positive and negative features and to decide on a course of action. Researchers have examined the stages through which individuals perceive and evaluate situations in assessing stress. Lazarus and Folkman (1984) have proposed primary and second-ary appraisal processes based on temporal sequence. Primary appraisal consists of the initial determination that a stimulus (person, event, situation) is positive (be-nign), negative (stressful), or neither (irrelevant) in its implications for well-being. Secondary appraisal is a judgment about what might and can be done to minimize gain. The appraisal process may be cyclical as the individual takes into account a previous coping strategy or some new information.

The importance of the appraisal process as a predictor of stress outcomes is well illustrated by a study of patients who had undergone surgery for breast cancer (Vinokur, Threatt, Vinokur-Caplan, & Satariano, 1990). Neither the objec-tive stage of the disease nor the extent of surgery predicted the person's appraisal of threat, but that appraisal was a major predictor of subsequent anxiety and depression. Other studies have indicated that appraisal plays a similarly impor-tant role in predicting the outcome of job-generated stress.

Responses to Stress.   Researchers have identified three major categories of possible responses to stress: physiological, psychological, and behavioral. The physiological responses include cardiovascular symptoms such as blood pressure and cholesterol level; biochemical measures such as catecholamines and uric acid; and gastrointestinal symptoms such as peptic ulcers. Higher heart rates have been reported under conditions of role conflict, ambiguity regarding future develop-ments on the job, and overall reported stress at work. Catecholamines change very rapidly and respond to a variety of stimuli. Unpredictability at work, level of control over pace and method, and distracting noise have all been associated with increased levels of catecholamines. Air traffic controllers, for example, have been found to show significant associations between daily levels of cortisol secretion and work variables such as load and pace. Research on gastrointestinal symptoms has shown less consistent results compared to the other two types of physiologi-cal response.

Psychological responses to stress at work most typically involve assessments of affective variables, with job dissatisfaction being most common. Stress has also been found to influence more intense and aroused affective states such as anger, frustration, hostility, and irritation. More passive but perhaps no less negative responses include boredom, burnout, fatigue, and depressed mood. The psychological effects of work-related stress have also been found to produce lowered self-confidence and self-esteem.

Behavioral responses to stress at work have not been studied as frequently as have psychological responses. However, five broad categories of behavioral responses have been examined: the work role (job performance, accidents, drug use at work), oppressive behavior at work (theft, purposeful damage), flight from the job (absenteeism, turnover), degradation of other life roles (spouse and child abuse), and self-damaging behaviors (alcohol and drug abuse). Some of the findings, such as drug usage at work, have not been studied extensively and may be underreported for reasons of social acceptability or the avoidance of punishment. Dompierre and Lavoie (1994) also reflected on the methodological and ethical difficulties of conducting research on work stress and family violence. Nevertheless, the research results indicate that work-generated stressors have behavioral effects that are manifested both on the job and away from it, and they impose substantial costs on organizations.

Consequences of Stress.   The consequences of stress typically involve performance of the individual on the job and in other life roles. Other ramifications involve the health of the individual, as affected by prolonged exposure to physical stressors and through responses to recurrent psychological stressors. Researchers in Sweden (Alfredsson & Theorell, 1983), for example, have developed standardized measures of job characteristics for 118 occupational groups on a nationwide basis. Men in jobs characterized by high demand and low control (low autonomy) were at twice the risk for heart attacks in comparison with men in the same age range (40–54) employed in all other occupations. The next step is to discover ways of reducing such sources of stress.

It is also highly plausible that nonwork stresses can affect attitudes and behavior at work. Research findings suggest that such relationships are particularly evident for single-parent families and for families in which both parents are employed. Research is also being conducted that shows the combined effects of work and nonwork stressors on health. Frankenhaeuser (1988), for example, showed that the characteristic elevation of catecholamines as the stresses of the work day accumulate are sharply reduced at the end of the work day for men, but for married employed women the elevation persists until the household responsibilities are also fulfilled.

Properties of the Person as Stress Mediators.   The recognition of individual differences in resistance to stress has long been identified. Two personality characteristics have been clearly identified as mediating the effects of stress. The first is *Type A behavior*—a personality type that intensifies the effects of various job stressors. Type A people walk, eat, and talk rapidly. They are aggressive, competitive, and constantly feel under time pressure (see Field Note 2). Type B people are less concerned about time; play for fun, not to win; and can relax without guilt. Type A people have a higher standing pulse rate than Type B people and are twice as likely to develop heart disease. Wright (1988) concluded that Type A people have a high, possibly insatiable need for achievement. They experience early (no later than adolescence) success, which seems to breed a greater-than-usual sense of hope that striving efforts will eventually pay off. Type A individuals cannot control themselves when exposed to work-related stimuli. In assessing the proclivity of Type A individuals to feel stress from work he said, "What is needed are ways of training ourselves and others to maintain diligence with pacing—that is, to run the race of life like a marathon and not a series of 100-yard dashes" (p. 13).

The second personality characteristic that mediates stress is *locus of control.* Locus of control differentiates between people who believe that they themselves are primarily responsible for what happens to them and those who believe that major events in their lives are mainly determined by other people or forces beyond themselves. People whose locus of control is primarily internal will respond to stress differently from those whose locus of control is external. Those who are internally oriented are more likely to take action against the source of the stress itself or to mitigate its effects in other ways. Those who are externally oriented are more likely to see effective actions as being beyond their powers and thus endure rather than act.

Properties of the Situation as Stress Mediators.   In addition to characteristics of individuals, certain properties of situations can mediate or buffer the effects of a stressor. The buffering effect can reduce the tendency of organizational properties to generate specific stressors, alter the perceptions and cognitions evoked by such stressors, mediate the responses that follow the appraisal process, or reduce the health-damaging consequences of such responses. The primary variable hypothesized to provide this buffering effect is social support. Social support reduces the relationship between various job stressors and indicators of mental and physical health (anxiety, depression, and irritation). Social support did not reduce the relationship between job stressors and boredom or job dissatisfaction. Sutton and Kahn (1987) have proposed three other situational variables as potential buffers

FIELD NOTE 2

Research has shown that Type A individuals often thrive in highly competitive jobs. Their unrelenting striving for achievement often results in high levels of job performance. However, the downside of the Type A personality is that achievement striving runs to excess. They cannot control themselves and incur a wide variety of work-related ailments such as stress, ulcers, and heart attacks. There are paper-and-pencil tests that identify Type A personality types. Imagine you are an I/O psychologist who is developing a test battery to hire new employees. Would you include the test that identifies Type A personality applicants and hire them because their personality is predictive of job success? Would you include the test and *not* hire Type A individuals because of their proclivity for incurring work-related ailments? Or would you not use the personality test in the selection battery but use it as a diagnostic test to help identify individuals after they have been hired who might benefit from therapeutic counseling? Identification of the Type A personality has the potential to be an ethical dilemma. We want to hire individuals who will be successful on the job, and the Type A personality is predictive of performance in some jobs. However, we also have an ethical obligation not to deliberately place individuals into situations hazardous to their health. What is your view on this issue?

against stress: (a) the extent to which the onset of a stressor is predictable; (b) the extent to which it is understandable; and (c) the extent to which aspects of the stressor are controllable by the person who must experience it. Of these three proposed relationships, the strongest support has emerged for the predictability of a stressor. If the occurrence of a stressful event can be predicted, its absence can also be predicted. Thus, the individual knows when it is safe to relax and not maintain a constant state of vigilance or anxiety.

Prevention and Intervention.   This final category is not part of the model of organizational stress proposed by Kahn and Byosiere (1992), but it does represent a major source of professional activity in stress management. For the most part, stress management has been more concerned with reducing the effects of stress rather than reducing the presence of stressors at work. As a consequence, the major effort has been directed at increasing individual resistance to stressors generated at work.

Stress management initiatives directed at *preventing* stress may include on-site physical fitness, exercise, meditation, and time management programs. Ross and Altmaier (1994) also report a growing use of techniques designed to lower arousal to stressors, such as deep breathing, progressive muscle relaxation, biofeedback, and yoga. Stress *intervention* initiatives most typically involve counseling, social support groups, and employee assistance programs. Of course, many organizations utilize both prevention and intervention programs. Kahn and Byosiere concluded from a review of stress management studies that most programs are directed toward reducing the cognitive appraisal of stressors and their subsequent effects rather than with reducing or eliminating the stressors themselves. Employee assistance programs, for example, attempt to repair damage already done, usually by alcohol or drug abuse.

In general both the quality and quantity of research on the effectiveness of stress management programs is not as high as the research on other aspects of stress. Nevertheless, there are indications that stress management programs are successful. Those programs in stress management that have been rigorously evaluated show significant reductions in subjective work stress and psychophysiological indicators. Their effects on job satisfaction and performance are less clear.

Work/Family Conflict

Over the past two decades the American family has undergone significant structural and functional changes (Thomas & Ganster, 1995). These changes have not been accompanied by equally dramatic shifts in organizational policies. Many companies continue to be guided by traditional workplace policies fashioned when the father worked outside the home while the mother stayed home to care for the house and the children. Such arrangements are distinctly different from today's diverse workplace, which is increasingly populated with women, single parents, and dual-career couples. The potential for conflict and stress increases as most workers struggle with the demands of paid employment and home responsibilities.

Interest in family-related issues by I/O psychologists is a relatively new concern, manifesting itself primarily in the past 15 years. For many years we tended to limit our focus to work-related issues (tasks, jobs, occupations, organizations), and left the subject of domestic matters (family) to other areas of professional study. However, I/O psychologists began to see legitimate linkages or connections between the two spheres of work and family and have expanded into these areas of inquiry. Zedeck (1992) described the following three topics as targets of research and practical matters.

The effect of work on family. This area examines what impact work factors have on family matters. To express this relationship in terms of research design, *work* is regarded as the independent variable, and family is the dependent variable. This perspective is most typical of I/O psychological research. A common finding is that aspects of work (such as job stress and work schedules) have negative effects on families.

The effect of family on work. This perspective is the opposite of the former and generally focuses on how structural or developmental aspects of the family have an impact on work behavior. For example, some researchers have viewed family life as a "shock absorber" in that, if home life is positive, it blocks disappointment at work. Others view family responsibility as a major determinant of work absenteeism and tardiness.

The family/work interaction. This third perspective views work and family as interacting and concludes that no simple or direct causal link exists between work and family matters. One view of the family/work interaction concerns the compatibility or incompatibility of family/work relations and its impact on other processes such as the transition between roles (Jones & Butler, 1980).

Regardless of which of these three perspectives is emphasized, researchers have offered conceptual models to explain the relationship between work and family. Three basic types of models have been proposed, and they represent different perspectives on how we fill both work and family roles.

Spillover model. The spillover model asserts that there is similarity between what occurs in the work environment and what occurs in the family environment. It also proposes that a person's work experiences influence what he or she does away from work. It is assumed that attitudes at work become ingrained and carried over into home life, affecting a basic orientation toward the self and family members. In general, spillover is a notion of positive relationships between work and family variables such that an individual's satisfaction with work enhances family life.

Compensation model. The compensation model is most often contrasted with the spillover model. It proposes an *inverse* relationship between work and family. It further assumes that individuals make differential investments of themselves in the two settings so that what is provided by one makes up for what is missing in the other. Thus, deprivations experienced in work are made up or compensated for in nonwork activities.

Segmentation model. The segmentation model proposes that the work and non-work spheres are distinct; an individual can be successful in one without any influence on the other. The two spheres exist side by side and for all practical purposes are separated from each other. This separation, either in type, space, or function, allows a person to effectively compartmentalize his or her life. The dominant view is that the family is the realm of intimacy and empathy, whereas the work world is impersonal and instrumental.

Barling (1990) observed a historical trend when each of these three models was proposed. Barling concluded: (1) the suggestion that work and family affect each other had emerged by the 1930s; (2) the pervasive assumption during the 1950s was that work and family are independent; (3) by the 1970s the assumption was that work and family roles were intertwined; and (4) today, considerable empirical evidence attests to the overlap between work and family for most individuals.

However, none of the models clearly specify the psychological processes by which work and family affect each other. Repetti (1987) addressed this shortcoming by proposing four processes through which work and family may be linked. One process is the direct transfer of mood from one sphere to another. If negative affect develops as a result of stressors in one sphere, it is subsequently transported to the other sphere. The second process is described through role conflict, which is based on the premise that people have limited supplies of physical, mental, and emotional resources and that work and family systems must strike a balance in their quest for such resources. The third process is a socialization process whereby skills and values learned in one sphere, in which they are adaptive and functional, are applied in another setting. The fourth process is somewhat in opposition to the socialization process. Here the skills and values that assist functioning in one sphere do not generalize to the other. Repetti's processes underlying work/family linkages are primarily directed to the mechanisms of adaptation to stress and conflict.

Empirical tests of the three models generally reveal some degree of support for each. Zedeck (1992) suggests that the models need additional refinement and clarity to effectively assess their veracity. Among the unspecified questions underlying the models are the following:

1. Can more than one explanatory model be appropriate for the same individual? That is, can there be spillover for some aspects of the employing organization or family but compensation for others?
2. If more than one model is applicable to an individual, can the models function simultaneously, or must they be sequential? That is, before there is compensation for some factors, do other factors need to have been spilled over?
3. Do the models hold at different times or stages for individuals? Both work and family activities develop over time and pass through stages, such as initiation

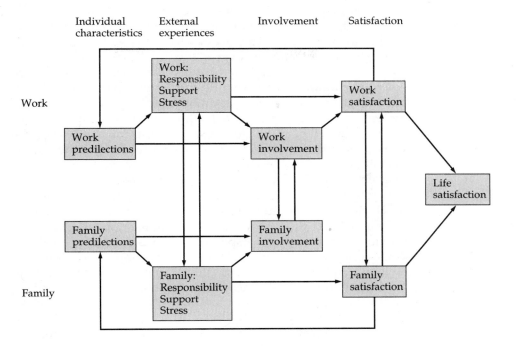

Individual   External   Involvement   Satisfaction
characteristics   experiences

Figure 10–3   *Proposed model of work-family relationships*
SOURCE: Adapted from "Work and Family Crossroads Spanning the Career" by A. Howard, 1992, in *Work, Families, and Organizations* (pp. 70–137) edited by S. Zedeck, San Francisco: Jossey-Bass.

and maturity. What happens to the relationship between work and family if the stages of each are (or are not) synchronized?

Zedeck (1992) believes that reactions to work and nonwork are not totally stable but vary over time and conditions. Instead of focusing on which model is "correct" in describing the work/family relationship, research needs to address the social and psychological factors associated with the different ways individuals experience this relationship.

Several researchers (for example, Frone, Russell, & Cooper, 1992a) have proposed more specific models that address the relationship between work and family. One such model was developed by Howard (1992) and is presented in Figure 10–3. Howard proposes that work and family are mirror images reflected along life's path. The two spheres culminate in the hopeful expression of life satisfaction. The causal flow of Figure 10–3 is from left to right, beginning with individual characteristics and ultimately resulting in life satisfaction. In between are concepts pertaining to work and family experiences, involvement, and satisfaction. Howard conducted two major assessments of the model. One was of the model's *symmetry*, which meant that both work and family influences were comparable in affecting overall life satisfaction. The second assessment was the *consistency* of the relationship between work and family over the lifetime of the individual. The model was tested with a large sample of managers whose lives were followed over a 30-year period. Howard used a broad array of measures to assess stress, involvement, and satisfaction. The results revealed complex patterns between work and family over time. Work and family involvement were inversely related; greater absorption in work is accompanied by less involvement in the family. But work and family were found to move in the same direction at the crossroads of satisfaction and stress. Satisfaction with work generalizes or spills over into contentment with the family. However, the overall results between work and family were *not* found to be symmetrical, in that work involvement and satisfaction affected the family but the reverse was not true. Work had more influence on the family than vice versa. A similar conclusion was reached by Frone, Russell, and Cooper (1992b). The family may be as potent as work only when there is high stress. The opportunities work provides encourages development of new abilities. Involvement in the family domain can lead to satisfaction and a sense of peace. However, involvement in the work realm can escalate to even more work involvement and to neglect of the family domain. Left unchecked, the more work/less family spiral can lead to diminishing life returns or the phenomenon of career success and personal failure.

The managers were divided into four groups, based on having high or low work involvement and high or low family involvement. Those managers who had advanced the farthest in the organizational hierarchy were characterized by high work involvement and low family involvement. Those managers who placed their families in the forefront paid a price in terms of advancement in management. The groups also differed in terms of reports about opportunities missed in their career. The professionally successful high work–low family involvement group most often reported missed career opportunities, as if their desires for career challenge and success had become to some extent insatiable. The low work–low family group was found to be the least adjusted, as they lacked the seriousness of purpose that would build commitments to either a career or family. In general the results revealed that overall happiness in life can be attained through various combinations of work and family interests, and there is no one best approach to balancing work and family commitments.

Friedman and Galinsky (1992) noted some of the major changes in the labor force and how organizational efforts have had to change to recruit and retain a productive work force. By the year 2000 about two-thirds of the new entrants into the work force will be women, and about three-fourths of them will become pregnant at some point during their working years. More than half of these women will return to work before their child's first birthday. An estimated 20% of workers—mostly women—will be responsible for their aging parents. While women still perform most family tasks, 60% of men have wives who work.

The pressures of work and family are accelerating, and families, which already have born the greater burden of conflicts experienced between home and work, can do little more to sustain the balance. Changes in the social pattern of worker participation have necessitated that companies make accommodations to their workers. These accommodations are directed toward reducing the conflict between home and family, which, if unattended to, would ultimately lead to lower efficiency in the workplace. Such inefficiency would be caused by greater tardiness, absenteeism, turnover, and stress-related decrements in job performance.

Four major organizational responses to reducing home/family conflict have been developed. The first is on-site or near-site child-care centers. Companies may develop such centers exclusively for their own employees or in a consortium with other employees for use by several participating companies. There are approximately 1,400 on-site or near-site child-care centers by employers in the United States. While their number is growing, many companies are too small to have the resources to provide such a center.

A second type of assistance to employees is family leave. In 1993, President Clinton signed into law The Family and Medical Leave Act, whereby employees can withdraw from the work force to attend to family needs without risking loss of their jobs. The law gives workers up to 12 weeks of unpaid leave each year for birth, adoption, or foster care of a child; care for a spouse, parent, or child with a serious health condition; or the employee's own serious health condition. The law is designed to be of particular use to parents of newborn children. Research has shown that the single most important predictor of job retention following childbirth is the availability of job-guaranteed maternity leave. One company with an excellent leave policy found that only 5% of new mothers did not return to their jobs. Grover and Crooker (1995) reported in a national survey of workers that in organizations offering family-responsive human resource policies such as child-care assistance, employees showed significantly greater organizational commitment and expressed lower intentions to quit their jobs. The findings also were evidenced for employees *without* children, which the authors interpreted as supporting the theory that offering assistance to employees in need symbolizes concern for employees and positively influences attachment to the organization.

While only a few hundred companies have responded to the elder-care needs of their employees, the number is likely to grow dramatically in the future. Caring for elderly relatives may be more complex than child care because it involves the coordination of a variety of social services, such as transportation, medical, legal, housekeeping, and personal services. Most of the companies responding to employees' elder-care needs provide information and counseling about the array of available services. Some companies coordinate such services.

Finally, some use is being made of telecommuting: the arrangement to perform work at home. Such jobs often involve computer operations, but they need not be computer-based. The employees may perform work-at-home operations on an occasional basis to handle emergencies or planned-for family obligations. Companies carefully screen work-at-home candidates for initiative and ability to take responsibility, train participants, and often require regular time in the office to maintain communication. Parents who work at home acknowledge that this option does not preclude the need for child-care assistance. However, it does offer greater flexibility in balancing work and home obligations.

Dual-Career Families

Balancing the demands of work and family can be an arduous experience for most individuals. Issues of adjustment can be further compounded when both partners have careers. Oakley (1974) estimated that mothers with young children work an average of 77 hours per week in the home. Adding a career to that workload can create extraordinary pressures on both parties to have fulfilling work and home lives.

Silberstein (1992) concluded that in most dual-career families there is an emphasis on a work-oriented lifestyle prior to the birth of children. However, once there are children, the dual-career family system undergoes a profound shift. The pragmatic demands of home life increase dramatically and cannot be postponed, rescheduled, or ignored. Both men and women report that the arrival of children creates the greatest conflict between work and family. For the majority of both men and women, having children translates into fewer hours at work. However, the extent to which this occurs and the meanings of this shift differ for men and women. Karambayya and Reilly (1992), for example, reported that more women than men accommodated their careers to fit their families. The felt need to make an accommodation influenced the women's choice of a career (for example, assuring a flexible schedule) or of a work site. However, many women have reported that their work environments are not willing or able to bend to the demands of family. Additionally, some women have described hostile reactions from work colleagues to pregnancies.

Men, on the other hand, tend to differentiate their feelings of conflict over family and career from their wives' feelings. This difference between husbands and wives stems from expectations in men that work is primarily for men, and family is primarily for women. Silberstein (1992) offers the following statement from a man in his mid-30s:

> I have the suspicion that it's more difficult for a woman. If you're a traditional, career-oriented man, you're supposed to spend a lot of time in the office, and bring work home, and commute long distances. And the man has less time for the family, which is not a good thing, but that's how it is traditionally. Whereas for a woman, there's always the other side of the mirror, which is the woman who is at home, spending hours and hours with her children, and is always there when they need her. And that imposes some degree of guilt on a woman who is successful in her career. (p. 100)

Silberstein (1992) reports that differences in the degree that wives and husbands accommodated their careers for children has become a central marital tension. Differential investment in career and family is the recurrent issue around which arguments occur, and it demands constant renegotiation. In the dual-career marriage, both spouses arrive at their own definition of what is required for work success and what level of involvement in the family feels right. Each partner, therefore, argues from personal experience about the appropriate balance of work and family, whereas in the one-career marriage, the spheres of wife and husband are less comparable.

Dual-career couples often cite a lack of temporal control over their lives. There appears to be insufficient time to fulfill the obligations of both work and family. The creation of time schedules to coordinate activities can be facilitative, but adherence to the schedules can be a source of tension in itself. Other time-related issues pertain to the lack of personal time for individual activity (such as recreation or leisure) and coordinated social activities. Time constraints are also associated with reformulating role activities in the marriage such as the division of domestic labor. The lack of time also contributes to a couple's decision to seek external support services such as child care and assistance with household chores.

In examining the benefits and costs of dual-career marriages, Silberstein (1992) reported that most marriages were aided by the self-fulfillment each spouse derived from pursuit of a career. Each spouse experiences an independent source of self-esteem, and they benefit as a couple from the combined stimulation of each partner's work life (see Field Note 3). Both partners are also likely to feel that each is contributing in a similar fashion to the welfare of the marriage. However, the costs of dual-careers are considerable, with most sacrifices being associated with losses of time and energy. In particular, dual-career couples are prone to save the least amount of time and energy for their own personal relationship, attending first to the demands of work, children, and the managerial aspects of domestic life. This sentiment was expressed by a woman in her early 40s:

> I hesitate to use the analogy, but right now I feel we are more business partners than husband and wife. It's like we operate this small corporation together, but the intimate aspect is somewhat lacking. (Silberstein, 1992, p. 147)

The Psychological Effects of Unemployment

The possibility of job loss is a major concern for the contemporary worker. Thousands of employees lose their jobs annually through layoffs and organizational

FIELD NOTE 3

The profusion of dual-career couples has spawned a new dimension in personnel recruitment. Dual-career couples are often reluctant to move unless there are meaningful jobs for both members. Organizations seeking to attract one member are at a strategic advantage if they can help secure a job for the other member. Some organizations, particularly in urban areas, have formed networks or alliances to help recruit dual-career couples. One member of the couple will work for one organization in the network, while the second member will work for another organization in the network. Organizations comprising the network represent various industries as a way to increase the likelihood of job placement. It is rare that both members of the dual-career couple will get their "first-choice" of a job in this fashion, but it does help to ensure that they both will find something satisfactory. Participating organizations benefit as well by increasing the likelihood of sustained employment by the member. A major reason for turnover among dual-career couples is that one member can't find a good job. By forming such a recruitment alliance, organizations enhance their own positions. The recruitment of dual-career couples through organizational alliances represents an unusual example of not only inter-organizational but also interindustry cooperation.

downsizing (see Chapter 9). Perilous economic conditions have resulted in large-scale job loss both domestically and globally. What have we learned about the meaning of work to individuals as a result of involuntary unemployment? I will conclude this chapter with a discussion of the psychological effects of unemployment.

Jahoda (1981) asserts that being employed has both intended and unintended consequences for the individual. Earning a living is the most obvious intended consequence of employment, but the primary psychological meaning of work derives from the unintended or latent consequences:

- imposing a time structure on the waking day,
- regularly sharing experiences and contacts with people outside the nuclear family,
- linking individuals to goals and purposes,
- defining aspects of personal status and identity, and
- enforcing activity.

Jahoda claims that these unintended consequences of employment are functions that "meet human needs of an enduring kind." Accordingly, when a person is unemployed and is deprived of these functions, his or her enduring human needs are unsatisfied. Furthermore, as Winefield (1995) has noted, the issue is more complex than unemployment versus employment. Individuals who are employed (or become re-employed) in highly tenuous and insecure jobs do not have the same sense of psychological well-being as those individuals who enjoy stable employment. It is thus argued that stable employment is the major institution in society that reliably and effectively provides these supports to psychological well-being.

Fryer and Payne (1986) offered a somewhat different explanation as to why unemployment is psychologically devastating. Their explanation was based on a loss of discretionary control and is heavily tied to the loss of income associated with unemployment. Financial problems are one of the outstanding worries for most unemployed people, and lack of money is one of the underlying causes of problems in maintaining relationships. While the loss of adequate income is certain for most unemployed people, there is also uncertainty as to how long the low income will persist. The poor resources of the unemployed means that they have much less discretion or freedom to pursue various decision options, such as food or clothes to purchase. The act of choosing is severely restricted by unemployment. Attempting to solve problems with limited resources frequently means that the quality of the solution is poorer, which can engender a sense of failure and lowered self-esteem. Thus, the loss of financial resources serves to limit choices, thereby enhancing feelings of limited control over a person's life. Lowered psychological health follows from this condition.

Both the explanations offered by Jahoda (1981) and by Fryer and Payne (1986) are represented in Warr's (1987) nine environmental factors needed for mental health. A loss of employment has been found to trigger changes in eight of the nine environmental determinants of psychological well-being.

The opportunity for control is clearly lessened by unemployment. Lack of success in job-seeking, the inability to influence employers, and increased dependence on social welfare programs all contribute to a reduction in people's ability to control what happens to them. The opportunity for skill use is also likely to be reduced during unemployment. Occupational skills are generally not used during unemployment, although there may be opportunities to use certain skills in domestic activities. People becoming unemployed from jobs that demand a high level of skill are likely to suffer a greater reduction in this feature than people whose previous employment required only limited skill. Unemployment produces a reduction in externally generated goals, because fewer demands are placed on the individual. Since external demands are often linked to particular points (such as family mealtimes or the start of a work day), a general reduction in demands is often accompanied by a loss of temporal differentiation. Time markers that break up the day or week and indicate an individual's position in it are no longer as frequent or urgent.

A loss in variety is partly due to having to leave the house less often and partly to the loss of contrast between job and nonjob activities. Those domestic demands that do impinge on the person are likely to be similar and unchanging from day to day, with standard routines and an absence of novelty. Environmental clarity is also likely to be reduced during unemployment. Information relating to the future permits planning within predictable time schedules and reduces the anxiety typically generated by uncertainty. Planning for the future is difficult when uncertainty exists about a person's occupational or financial position in the months to come. Payment for work is at the heart of the employment contract, and the standard of living of almost all adults below retirement age is principally determined by income received from a job. Unemployment removes that income, and in almost all cases this has a serious and wide-ranging impact on the availability of money.

Physical security is usually associated with the availability of money. A general need for some personal and private territory contributes to a stable self-concept and enhanced well-being. Reduced income can give rise to loss of adequate housing or the threat that this will happen. The only determinant of mental health that appears to be unaffected by unemployment is the opportunity for interpersonal contact. Younger and middle-aged unemployed individuals typically report no change in the amount of interpersonal contact before and after job loss. Some research findings (for example, Warr & Payne, 1983) indicate that social contacts even *increase* in frequency for these groups during unemployment. They report spending more time with neighbors and family members. However, older individuals (particularly women) report a reduction in social contacts after becoming unemployed, typically spending their days alone at home. On becoming unemployed a person loses a socially approved role and the positive self-evaluations that go with it. The new position is widely felt to be one of lower prestige, deviant, second-rate, or not providing full membership to society. Even when social welfare benefits remove the worst financial hardships, shame may be attached to receipt of funds from public sources and a seeming failure to provide for one's family.

As based upon these assessments provided by Warr (1987), there is a strong linkage between unemployment and mental health. Work provides a sense of meaning and purpose to life, and the removal of that purpose lowers the quality of life. In the next sections I will examine how unemployment affects four sub-groups of the population: middle-aged men, women, teenagers, and the long-term unemployed.

Middle-Aged Men.   Research (for example, Jackson & Warr, 1984; Warr & Jackson, 1985) has consistently revealed the negative impact of unemployment on the affective well-being of middle-aged men, especially those with families in need of financial support. The financial demands of middle-aged men are likely to be particularly great, as many of them have growing children in need of support. Middle-aged men's social position is also strongly affected by unemployment, since they lose their valued role as provider for the family in addition to their positions as contributors to a work group. Their uncertainty about the future is compounded by the fact that their unemployment produces ambiguity that extends into the lives of all family members. Plans can less easily be made, and the future is less clearly predictable.

Women.   Historically, more men than women have been the subjects of unemployment research. Nevertheless, research indicates that the impact of unemployment on affective well-being is as negative for women as it is for men. The findings for women are somewhat complicated by marital status and position as a primary wage-earner. Women who are unmarried or are primary wage-earners respond to unemployment in a fashion similar to that of men. However, women who are married and are not primary wage-earners may experience somewhat different responses to unemployment, as they do to employment. The primary differences involve the factors of esteem and externally generated goals. Esteem from one's social position does not always increase after a married woman gets a job. This depends both on the nature of her employed role and on the attitude taken by important people in her life. Married women whose domestic environments make few demands on them are likely to find that their mental health is enhanced by employment. In contrast, married women whose home environments are already very demanding are likely to suffer from the addition of job-related goals.

Leana and Feldman (1991) reported that women were not less traumatized by job loss than men, and there were no substantial differences between men and women in psychological and behavioral stress symptoms. There were differences, however, in how each group coped with the job loss. Men relied more on problem-focused activities such as job search, while women relied more on seeking social support.

Teenagers.   The position of unemployed teenagers compared to middle-aged people is less problematic. Teenagers have relatively good opportunities for interpersonal contact, as they often maintain a network of friends and established patterns of leisure activities. Their financial requirements are generally less than for older groups. Although unemployed teenagers experience the lack of valued social position, which is common during unemployment at all ages, they may see themselves as members of a large group of unemployed youth who have been victimized by bad economic conditions. Because of widespread unemployment of teenagers, personal responsibility and social stigma are liable to be less strongly felt. Winefield, Tiggemann, and Winefield (1992), for example, reported that teenagers who gave externally based justifications for their unemployment displayed higher self-esteem and less hopelessness than those who gave internal justifications (that is, those who felt responsible for their unemployed status).

Despite these conditions, unemployment has a significant negative impact on teenagers' affective well-being. However, it is those components of mental health that explicitly involve behavior in social roles—autonomy, competence, and aspiration—that appear to be of greatest concern. Gaining a job is of special significance for adolescents, marking the end of childhood dependence and representing entry into the adult world. Independence is enhanced through the income provided by employment. Autonomy is thus retarded by joblessness after leaving school. The development of competence may also be inhibited, as new skills acquired from a job are denied to teenagers who fail to obtain paid work. There is also the fear that aspirations will be stunted, as teenagers without paid work may become adjusted to a relatively inactive life. The loss of aspiration in teenagers has generally not been supported by research, but the harmful impact of teenage unemployment on autonomy and competence appears to be substantial.

The Long-Term Unemployed. Warr (1987) reported that 40% of unemployed people in Britain had been continuously out of paid work for more than one year, and 25% had been continuously unemployed for more than two years. Research has indicated that the impact of job loss on affective well-being is typically rapid. Further deterioration is likely in the period after job loss, until a plateau of poor mental health is reached between three and six months. This pattern is particularly marked for middle-aged men. The time frame for impaired mental health for unemployed teenagers appears to be longer. Winefield and Tiggemann (1990) reported that Australian teenagers did not exhibit substantially lower self-esteem or affective well-being after two years of unemployment compared to when they were students in school. However, after the third year of unemployment, the mental health of the teenagers deteriorated markedly. Related findings were reported by Schaufeli and Van Yperen (1992) in a sample of Dutch teenagers. In general it appears that overall levels of mental health among the long-term unemployed are particularly low and that their environments in terms of the nine features proposed by Warr (1987) remain chronically impoverished.

A closing note on the national origins of unemployment research is in order. It will be recalled from Chapter 2 that research topics in I/O psychology often emerge out of experience with practical problems. The vast majority of high-quality research on the psychological effects of unemployment has been conducted by international researchers, most notably in Britain (Warr) and Australia (Winefield). One reason for this is that unemployment rates are often higher in other countries compared to the United States. Warr (1987) also notes that there are cultural differences in the availability of public money for the unemployed. For example, welfare benefits continue indefinitely in Britain and Australia, while in the United States substantial reductions occur after six or nine months. As such, there may be different degrees of mental health impairment caused by unemployment across nations.

Concluding Comments

Work stress is not only a frequent problem for employees, it appears to be growing in acceptance as part of the price individuals pay for employment. The fact that stress management programs are directed not at making work less stressful but at increasing our capacity to deal with stress suggests that few people believe stress can be eliminated or drastically reduced from work. As discussed in Chapter 9, one of the consequences of organizational downsizing is that fewer employees have to do the work that was once performed by a greater number of employees. The prevailing sentiment is that organizations are expected to do more (work) with less (resources). Technological advances (particularly relating to computer-based operations) have also accelerated the speed at which work is performed. These changes have the potential to diminish overall mental health by reducing autonomy or control. In the evolution of work design, employees are becoming increasingly more controlled by situational factors as opposed to exerting control over their work environments. As the research on mental health and stress revealed, the reductions in self-regulation (feeling "out of control") impairs psychological well-being (Murphy, Hurrell, & Quick, 1992). Rather than denying the reality of work stress or assuming no responsibility for it, organizations are becoming increasingly committed to addressing it. The annual health care costs in this country alone exceed $500 billion, with business paying about one-half the cost. The annual cost of stress-related illnesses to the American economy is estimated to be $150 billion (Joure, Leon, Simpson, Holley, & Frye, 1989). It is simply cheaper to promote healthful behavior than to pay the costs associated with not promoting it.

CASE STUDY   *Two Siblings, Two Lifestyles*

Joe Vesco rarely got to see his older sister, Rita. Although they lived only 70 miles apart, their visits seemed primarily limited to family holidays. Rita was 31, married, and had two boys, ages 6 and 3. She was a supervisor for a telemarketing company, overseeing the work of 15 sales agents. Rita put in long hours, typically 50 to 60 hours per week. She frequently worked until 8:00 P.M., because many sales calls were made in the early evening. She had a departmental sales quota to reach and also had to monitor the individual sales quotas of each of her agents. Work was very stressful. She also experienced considerable guilt and anxiety over how her work life was affecting her family. Her husband picked the children up from day care and fed them dinner. The younger child was often asleep before Rita arrived home. She and her husband had discussed at length whether Rita should look for another job with more conventional hours. It always seemed to come down to money. They needed both incomes to maintain their family, and Rita's job was particularly well-paying. She was paid partly on commission, and because she frequently exceeded her department's sales quota, Rita received about 20% additional income over her base salary. No other job would pay as well.

Joe had a very different life. He was single, 24, and worked as a surveyor for the county. He had his own apartment, had just recently purchased his first new car, and loved his sense of independence. The job didn't pay very well, but the hours were stable. He left work every day at 4:30. Joe didn't worry about being fired or losing his job. The county employed only a few surveyors, and no one could remember anyone in his department ever having been fired or laid off. It was a highly secure job, but not very challenging. Joe didn't think he would make a career out of the job, but for the present it suited him very well.

Joe and Rita got together at their parents' anniversary party. Joe hadn't seen Rita for quite some time and was surprised at how stressed-out she looked. He remembered his sister as always being a stabilizing influence on him while growing up. She always seemed to be in control of her life. That apparent control, whether real or just imagined by Joe, was no longer evident. Rita complained about not being able to leave her work problems at work and worrying about her children while at work. She acknowledged taking medication to help her get to sleep, which had never been a problem before. Rita also talked about going back to smoking, after having given up cigarettes for almost seven years.

Joe reflected on his own life in comparison to his sister's. He didn't make nearly the money she did, but his biggest concern in life seemed to be which sporting event he would watch on TV when he came home from work—and car payments. Joe remembered his own mother always being home when he got back from school. He wondered how his nephews would respond to their mother's absence after school. Joe concluded that Rita was wondering the same thing.

Questions

1. What are the primary sources of work/family conflict in Rita's life?
2. To what degree does gender play a role in Rita's work/family conflict? Why?
3. What are the rewards and drawbacks for both Rita and Joe in the jobs they hold?
4. To what do you attribute the difference in lifestyle between Joe and Rita: age? gender? marital status? children? income?
5. Do you think Rita made a conscious choice to pursue her lifestyle, or do you think she was subtly drawn into it over time? What does your answer suggest about the nature of work/family conflict?

Work Motivation

Major Chapter Objectives

- *Be able to explain five critical concepts central to work motivation.*

- *Be able to explain the conceptual basis and degree of empirical support for the following motivational theories: need hierarchy, equity, expectancy, reinforcement, and goal setting.*

- *Be able to provide an overview and synthesis of work motivation theories.*

Interest in the study of motivation has waxed and waned since the early part of this century (Kanfer, 1990). During the 1930s and 1940s, the study of motivation was preeminent in American psychology. In the 1950s and 1960s, interest in motivation in the workplace was kindled. Some authors contend that "work motivation" cannot be understood apart from motivation in the broader context. However, for purposes of this discussion, I will limit the focus of motivation to contexts endemic to the workplace. Over the past 35 years there has been a profusion of work motivation theories. These theories offer markedly different explanations for the same aspect of human behavior. Work motivation theories have been proposed from environmental, social, dispositional, and cognitive perspectives. In the past five to ten years, however, attempts have been made to identify consistency in the psychological constructs that underlie the theories. As you will see, certain psychological constructs coalesce more readily across theories than do others.

Motivation is not directly observable. It must be inferred from an analysis of behavior and the products of those behaviors. Motivational processes can be inferred only from analysis of a continual stream of behavior that is determined by both environment and heredity and is observed through their effects on personality, beliefs, knowledge, abilities, and skills. There is no universally agreed-upon definition of motivation. Generally speaking, *motivation* may be defined as individual variability in behavior *not due solely* to individual differences in ability or to overwhelming environmental demands that compel action (for example, escaping a burning building).

The study of work motivation has generally been directed to three dependent variables. The first is *direction of behavior,* which addresses the choice of activities we make in expending effort. That is, why we might choose to work diligently at some tasks and not at others. The second is *intensity of action,* which addresses how much effort we will expend on a task. The third is *persistence of behavior* over prolonged time periods, addressing behavior that is not the product of a one-time choice between courses of action (direction) nor produced by devoting constant, high levels of effort to a single task (intensity). A comprehensive understanding of work motivation requires an integration of these three orientations.

Five Critical Concepts

It is relatively easy to misunderstand or confuse concepts critical to work motivation. The distinctions among these concepts are not always easily seen and can become blurred. To help you differentiate them throughout the chapter, let's take a closer look at these five critical concepts.

> *Behavior.* Behavior is the substance through which we infer motivation. The behavior in question may be typing speed, firing a rifle at a target, or any other of a very broad constellation of human activities.
> *Performance.* Performance entails some evaluation of behavior. The basic unit of observation is behavior, but coupled with the behavior is an assessment

of the behavior as judged against some standard. For example, if the behavior is typing 40 words per minute, a judgment can be made as to whether this *level of performance* is adequate/inadequate to hold a job. The behavior is appraised within some organizational context, and implies that 40 words per minute might represent adequate performance in some jobs and inadequate performance in others. Most organizational theories tend to be concerned with performance, not just behavior. Performance, however, is determined by factors that transcend behavior.

Ability. Ability is one of three determinants of behavior. It is generally regarded as fairly stable within individuals and may be represented by a broad construct such as intelligence or a more specific construct such as physical coordination.

Situational constraints. Situational constraints are the second determinant of behavior and refer to environmental factors or opportunities that facilitate or retard behavior (and ultimately performance). Examples would include tools, equipment, procedures, and the like, which, if present, facilitate behavior and, if absent, diminish it. If no situational constraints are present, behavior has the potential to be maximized. Individual behavior manifests itself within some environmental or situational context that influences the conduct of behavior but is beyond the control of the individual.

Motivation. Motivation is the third determinant of behavior. You can think of ability as reflecting what you *can* do, motivation reflects what you *will* do (given your ability), while the situation controls what you are *allowed* to do.

Each of the three components is critical to the manifestation of behavior. Maximal behavior is observed when a person has high ability, exhibits high motivation, and is in an environment supportive of such behavior. The judgment of "poor performance" could be attributed to four factors. First, the organization in which the behavior occurs may have high standards, which in another organization may result in a more positive evaluation of the behavior. Second, the individual may lack the needed ability to exhibit the desired behavior. (I was never very good at catching fly balls in baseball.) Third, the individual may lack the motivation to exhibit the desired behavior. (Countless hours of practice didn't seem to enhance my ball-catching behavior.) Fourth, the individual may lack the needed equipment or opportunity to exhibit the behavior. (An expensive new baseball glove didn't help either.)

Work Motivation Theories

I will present five different theories of work motivation. They differ markedly in terms of the psychological constructs hypothesized to account for motivation (see Field Note 1). Each theory will be presented in terms of three sections: a *statement* of the theory, *empirical tests*, and an *evaluation*. At the conclusion of this presentation, I will examine points of convergence among the theories and discuss the fundamental perspectives that have been taken in addressing work motivation.

FRANK AND ERNEST   SOURCE: Reprinted by permission of Newspaper Enterprise Association, Inc.

Need Hierarchy Theory

Statement of the Theory.   One of the major theories of motivation was developed by Abraham Maslow (1987). It is called the need hierarchy theory. Most of Maslow's writing was not concerned with work motivation. Only later in his career did Maslow become interested in applications of his theory. Most of its uses were derived from other researchers' examinations of its relevance for industrial organizations. According to Maslow, the source of motivation is certain needs. Needs are biological or instinctive; they characterize humans in general and have a genetic base. They often influence behavior unconsciously. What causes people to behave as they do is the process of satisfying these needs. Once a need is satisfied, it no longer dominates behavior and another need rises to take its place. Need fulfillment is never ending. Life is a quest to satisfy needs.

Much of Maslow's theory identifies needs, but the second component explains how the needs relate to one another. Maslow proposes five types of needs: physiological, safety, social, self-esteem, and self-actualization. Physiological needs are the most basic; their fulfillment is necessary for survival. They include the need for air, water, and food. Safety needs include freedom from threat, danger, or deprivation. They involve self-preservation. Today, most of our safety needs are met, but people experiencing disasters like hurricanes or riots have had their safety needs threatened. Social needs include the desire for association, belonging, and companionship. These involve an individual's ability to exist in harmony with others. Self-esteem needs include self-confidence, recognition, appreciation, and the respect of one's peers. Satisfaction of these needs results in a sense of adequacy; their thwarting produces feelings of inferiority and helplessness. The last type of need is self-actualization—the best known and least understood in Maslow's scheme. Self-actualization is realization of one's full potential—in Maslow's (1970) words, "to become more and more what one is, to become everything that one is capable of becoming."

The second part of the theory concerns how these needs are related. According to Maslow (1987), needs exist in a hierarchy. At the base are the physiological needs, which must be met first and continuously. The remaining needs are placed in order, culminating with the highest need, self-actualization. Physiological and safety needs are referred to as basic needs; social, self-esteem, and self-actualization needs are higher order needs. The need hierarchy theory is illustrated in Figure 11–1.

Maslow proposed several points regarding the need hierarchy:

- Behavior is dominated and determined by the needs that are unfulfilled.
- An individual will systematically satisfy his or her needs by starting with the most basic and working up the hierarchy.
- Basic needs take precedence over all those higher in the hierarchy.

The first proposition is fundamental: Once a need is fulfilled, it will no longer motivate behavior. A hungry person will seek food. Once the hunger is satisfied, it will no longer dominate behavior. The second proposition involves fulfillment progression. That is, a person will progress through the needs in order, moving on to the next one only after the preceding one has been fulfilled. We all spend our lives trying to fulfill these needs because, according to Maslow, only a small percentage of people have fulfilled the self-actualization need. Maslow also says that this need can never be fully satisfied. The third proposition stresses that the needs basic to survival always have a higher priority.

Maslow's theory has several implications for work behavior. When pay and security are poor, employees will focus on those aspects of work necessary to fulfilling their basic needs. As conditions improve, the behavior of supervisors and their relationship with the individual take on increased importance. Finally, with a much

---

FIELD NOTE 1

There are two perspectives on motivation. One approach is to regard motivation as a characteristic trait or a personality dimension. Thus, people vary in terms of how much of this characteristic they have, ranging from little, if any (these people are called "lazy"), to a lot (these people are called "ambitious"). Many job announcements seem to endorse this perspective as they clamor for "eager, hard-driving, high-energy, go-getter" candidates who will bring to the jobs the levels of motivation needed for success. This trait is often deemed highly critical for managerial jobs.

The alternative approach is based on the idea that forces in the environment will motivate people. These forces can range from inspiring talks and speeches (the athletic coaching profession is a classic example) to the characteristics of certain tasks that motivate people to do a good job (these will be reviewed in Chapter 13). The assumption underlying this approach is that just about anyone can be transformed into a charged-up performer when exposed to the proper stimulation. Thus, people can attend "motivation clinics" designed to unleash the driving potential that supposedly resides within everyone. This "unlocking mechanism" has been the object of intensive search for decades.

Imagine yourself as a company president. Would you want to hire people who were already motivated to succeed before joining your company? Lee Iacocca, a popular and respected corporate executive, refers to these people as those in whom "a fire burns in their belly." Alternatively, would you turn your attention to the workplace itself and seek to staff the organization with inspiring managers who will "turn on" the work force? Perhaps you would try to design work to motivate the people who perform it? The answers to these questions have intrigued I/O psychologists since the inception of the profession and have profound economic and social consequences.

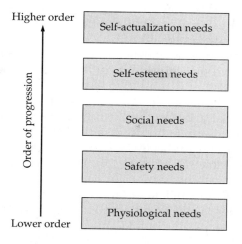

Figure 11–1 *Maslow's need hierarchy*
SOURCE: From *Motivation and Personality* (3rd ed.) by A. H. Maslow, 1987, New York: Harper & Row.

improved environment, the supervisor's role diminishes and the nature of the work reemerges. However, work is now important in self-actualization and not in fulfilling basic needs.

The theory also predicts that as people move up in the management hierarchy, they will be motivated by increasingly higher level needs; thus, managers at various levels should be treated differently. Additionally, employees can be expected to always want more. The organization can never give enough in terms of individual growth and development. It is the nature of the self-actualization need that once activated and satisfied, it stimulates an even greater desire for satisfaction. Thus, it is a continuing source of motivation.

Empirical Tests of the Theory.   The ultimate test of any theory is empirical support, but a problem with Maslow's theory involves measuring the variables. Because he did not provide operational definitions of his variables, other researchers must measure them and test the theory.

Lawler and Suttle (1972) sampled a group of lower level managers at two points in time separated by six months. The median stability (test/retest reliability) of the need measures over this six-month period was found to be only .38. This is evidence that either the managers' needs changed over the six months or the measurement was somewhat unreliable. Lawler and Suttle also found that needs exist in a two-level hierarchy (as opposed to the five Maslow proposed). The basic biological needs are on the bottom, and all other needs are on the top.

Betz (1984) found mixed support for the theory. On the negative side, she found that need importance was not related to need deficiency. Yet, as the theory predicts, Betz found a positive correlation between need fulfillment and life satisfaction. Finally, Wahba and Bridwell (1976) reviewed all earlier research on Maslow's theory. They concluded that the theory had received little clear or consistent support. Some of Maslow's propositions were totally rejected; others received mixed or questionable support. Most support was for the importance of the basic needs; the least evidence was for the higher level needs. The number of needs appeared questionable, as did the idea of fulfillment progression.

Evaluation of the Theory.   It is tempting to dismiss most of Maslow's theory, given the lack of support, but a few points suggest a more positive verdict. First, it is not a theory in the usual sense. Maslow did not propose testable hypotheses. As Wahba and Bridwell (1976) said, "Maslow's need hierarchy theory is almost a nontestable theory" (p. 234). It was based on logical and clinical insights into human nature rather than on research findings. Furthermore, Maslow did not discuss any guidelines for empirical tests of his theory. Many questions remain, and the way the theory is tested is open to interpretation. For example, what is the time span for the unfolding of the hierarchy? Is there a relationship between age and the need we are trying to satisfy? How does the shift from one need to another take place? Do people also seek to fulfill needs by going down the hierarchy? These questions are very important; they affect how we would use the theory in the work environment.

The theory's vagueness also leaves some nagging issues unanswered. According to Maslow, we systematically progress from one need to the next, yet we all need to eat, drink, and breathe every day. We never really have our physiological needs satisfied. We try to fulfill our self-esteem needs even if our social needs are not fully satisfied. Rather than going through the hierarchy in stages, perhaps we attempt to satisfy all needs concurrently. Maslow did not deal with this speculation.

Maslow's theory, a highly abstract statement about humankind, is far more philosophical than empirical. But his notion of self-actualization is well ingrained in the way we think about our mission in life. His writing has generated a great deal of thought about the nature of humankind in general. While Maslow's theory is deficient in explaining day-to-day behavior at work, his contributions to the field of psychology as a whole should not be ignored.

Equity Theory

Statement of the Theory.   Adams (1965) proposed a theory of work motivation drawn from the principle of social comparison; how hard a person is willing to work is a function of comparisons to the effort of others. The theory has perceptual and social bases, since motivation is a function of how a person sees himself or herself in comparison to other people. Adams has suggested that motivation has a social rather than a biological origin.

Equity theory has four major parts:

1. Because it is a perceptually based theory, the individual perceives himself or herself in comparison to others. The person who does the perceiving is called "Person."
2. It is postulated that Person compares himself or herself to another individual. This other person is called "Other."

3. All of the assets Person brings to the job constitute the third component; collectively, these assets are referred to as "Inputs." Inputs can include Person's education, intelligence, experience, skill, seniority, effort level, health, and so on. They are anything of perceived value or importance that Person brings to the job.

4. All benefits Person derives from the job are the fourth component, collectively referred to as "Outcomes." Outcomes can include pay, benefits, working conditions, status symbols, seniority benefits, and so forth. They are those factors Person perceives as being derived from employment.

The theory states that Person forms a ratio of his or her inputs to outcomes and compares it to perceptions of Other's inputs:outcomes ratio. Adams assumes that people can quantify both their inputs and outcomes into common scale units. For example, Person will consider all the inputs she brings to the job; let us say they total 50. Person will assess her outcomes in the same manner; again let us assume they total 50 units. Person's ratio is therefore 50:50. Person then compares her ratio to what she perceives Other is putting into his job and deriving in outcomes from it. Let us assume Person assesses Other's inputs and outcomes to be 50 units each. We now have two ratios as assessed by Person:

Person, 50:50 and *Other,* 50:50

The equality of the ratios as perceived by Person represents equity (literally, "fair"). If Person perceives Other as deriving 200 units of outcomes from his job (due to more pay, higher status) but also contributing 200 units of inputs (due to greater education, more experience), this would also represent equity to her. Other is getting more out of the job than Person but is also putting more into it; that is, 50:50 equals 200:200.

What happens if Person's ratio is different from Other's—that is, 50:50 versus 50:75? Both Person and Other are perceived as contributing the same amount of inputs (50 units), but Other is deriving more outcomes (75 units). According to Adams, this situation would represent inequity, or "unfairness," in the sense that Person perceives Other to be getting more out of the job, although both are contributing the same number of inputs.

According to Adams, feelings of inequity cause tension, which Person will become motivated to reduce. The greater the inequity between Person and Other, the greater the tension and the greater the motivation to reduce it. Thus, for Adams, the source of motivation is feelings of tension caused by perceived inequity. Feelings of inequity are necessary for motivation to occur, for if Person perceives herself as being in an equitable relationship with Other, she will not be motivated.

Adams proposed two types of inequity. Underpayment refers to Person's perception of herself as deriving fewer outcomes from a job than Other, when both are contributing comparable inputs. An example of underpayment inequity would be

Person, 50:50 and *Other,* 50:75

Overpayment refers to Person's perception of herself as deriving more outcomes from a job than Other, when both are contributing comparable inputs. An example of overpayment inequity would be

Person, 50:75 and *Other,* 50:50

Adams felt that people could alter their motivation levels in an attempt to bring feelings of inequity back into line. The drive to reduce the tension caused by inequity would manifest itself in more or less effort being put into the job, which is a form of input. Adams said that how inequity was reduced would be a function of the method of payment: hourly (wages determined per unit of time, such as $5 per hour) and piece rate (wages determined per unit of production, such as 25 cents per object).

Most research done on equity theory was conducted in laboratory or field experiment paradigms. To test the theory, feelings of overpayment and underpayment had to be induced in the subjects. This was accomplished using the following types of manipulations. The experimenter, posing as a manager or supervisor of some fictitious company, would place an ad in a local newspaper announcing part-time job openings. At the employment interview, subjects (who did not know this was a psychology experiment) would be told the job paid a certain hourly rate (such as $5 per hour) or piece rate (such as 25 cents per object produced). They would then start work at this rate. After a few days the experimenter would say, "We just received a large contract from the government, and we can now pay you more money. Starting tomorrow, you will make $8 per hour (or 40 cents per object)." This manipulation was meant to induce feelings of overpayment. Subjects would be paid more for doing the same job. To induce feelings of underpayment, the experimenter would say, "We have just experienced a major cutback in financial support due to the loss of a contract. Starting tomorrow, we can pay you only $2 per hour (or 15 cents per object)." These experimental instructions would be given to some subjects but not to others. Some people would work at the "new" rate, and others would continue to work under the original rate. The first few days of employment were designed to set base rate expectations about the job. After this period, the amount of compensation for the same work would either go up (in the overpayment condition) or down (in the underpayment condition). The question to be answered was, What would these people do as a result of feelings of inequity? Given two types of inequity (underpayment and overpayment) and two compensation systems (hourly and piece rate), four sets of hypotheses were proposed for how Person would reduce feelings of inequity:

Overpayment—hourly. Subjects would try to reduce the inequity caused by overpayment by working harder or expending more effort. By increasing their inputs (effort level), they would reduce feelings of inequity. The increased effort was predicted to manifest itself in increased quantity or quality of production.

Overpayment—piece rate. To reduce feelings of inequity, subjects would work harder as a means of increasing their inputs. However, if their increased effort resulted in greater quantity of output, the feelings of inequity would be magnified. Thus, subjects in this condition would produce fewer but higher quality objects than before.

Underpayment—hourly. Subjects would decrease their effort to accommodate the decrease in outcome. Decrements in product quantity and quality
would result.

Underpayment—piece rate. To compensate for the loss in pay, subjects would
produce more but appreciably lower quality objects.

Empirical Tests of the Theory.   A fairly large number of studies have tested
some or all of the predictions made by equity theory. Researchers used both payment systems in studying the effects of inequity on performance of interviewers.
Certain groups of subjects were made to feel overpaid or underpaid; others were
made to feel they were paid equitably. For the most part, the data supported the
theory. Overpaid subjects conducted significantly more interviews when paid by
the hour. The quality of the interviews (measured by completeness and detail)
was higher for those overpaid when a piece-rate system was used.

Most studies found that equity predictions held up best in the underpayment
conditions. Also, the results of studies using hourly payment were stronger than
those with piece-rate payment. These findings have important implications,
which I will discuss shortly.

The original theory proposed that people expend more or less effort to reduce
inequity. These are called behavioral ways of reducing inequity. As mentioned,
one way to reduce inequity would be to adjust the level of effort expended—
changing inputs, as the theory postulates. A second way would be for Person to
alter outcomes, such as by asking for a raise if Person felt underpaid. A third
technique would be to get Other to change his or her inputs or outcomes by using
peer pressure to get Other to work faster or slower. Finally, if all else failed, Person
could always quit a job if it was perceived as too inequitable.

Research has shown, however, that there are also cognitive ways to reduce
inequity. That is, a person does not have to "do" anything; rather, he or she reduces inequity through mental processes. One way is for Person to distort views
of his or her inputs or outcomes. For example, Person could think, "I'm not really
working that hard. After all, I spend a fair part of my day just talking to my
friends." Outcomes could also be distorted in a similar way. A second technique is
for Person to distort Other's inputs or outcomes: for example, "She really has to
put up with a lot from her supervisor that I don't have to take." It has also been
observed that, given the difficulty of making comparisons across jobs, the distortion of inputs (such as time and effort) is more common than the distortion of
outcomes (such as salary increases and promotions). Finally, if a particular Other
made Person feel inequitable, Person could always find a new Other for comparison. Equity theory does not state who that Other has to be. The methods of reducing inequity (both behavioral and cognitive) are listed in Table 11–1.

Most experiments on equity theory have supported the predictions. Problems
occur not because the theory is "wrong" but because hypotheses and predictions
are not very precise. There are several ways of reducing inequity, and the theory
does not specify which way will be chosen. A second problem involves time.
Many experiments studied behavior for short periods, from 10 minutes to
30 days. As with any motivation theory, we are interested in the long-term effects
on behavior. Some of the implications of this will be addressed in the next section.

Table 11–1   *Modes of reducing inequity*

Behavioral modes of inequity reduction:
1. Change inputs
2. Change outcomes.
3. Get Other to change inputs or outcomes.
4. Quit job for more equitable one.

Cognitive modes of inequity reduction:
1. Distort own inputs or outcomes.
2. Distort Other's inputs or outcomes.
3. Change comparison Other.

Evaluation of the Theory. Numerous authors have expressed concern over both the theory's substance and implications. To date, the research on equity theory has addressed the outcome of financial compensation. Yet financial compensation is but one of many outcomes derived from a job. Most studies have found fairly strong support for the underpayment predictions but less support for the overpayment ones. One consequence of inequity caused by underpayment is an increase in job dissatisfaction. We know that this is associated with increased absenteeism and turnover. We will have accomplished very little in the work force if, in the name of increased motivation, people feel underpaid and then are absent from work or quit.

In theory, feelings of overpayment will cause a person to work harder to produce more or higher quality products. However, research has shown that such feelings do not last very long. People seem to have a very high threshold for overpayment (that is, it takes a large increment for people to feel overpaid) but a low threshold for underpayment (that is, it takes a small decrement for people to feel underpaid). Given that feelings of overpayment are short-lived, an organization that doubled the wages of its employees every two months to make them feel consistently overpaid would soon be bankrupt. Huseman, Hatfield, and Miles (1987) suggest that individuals differ in their sensitivity to feeling over- or underrewarded. They believe that "benevolents" are employees who more likely feel a sense of being overrewarded than do "entitleds."

Finally, the whole issue of organizations deliberately manipulating their employees to induce feelings of inequity raises serious moral and ethical questions. Few employees would like working for an organization that willingly made them experience inequity (see Field Note 2).

Recent research has shown that the principles of equity theory extend to nonmonetary outcomes. Greenberg (1988) examined employees who were randomly reassigned on a temporary basis to the offices of either higher, lower, or equal status co-workers while their own offices were being remodeled. Relative to those workers reassigned to equal status offices, those reassigned to higher status offices raised their performance (a response to overpayment inequity) and those reassigned to lower status offices lowered their performance (a response to underpayment inequity). Greenberg (1990) measured employee theft rates in manufacturing plants during a period in which pay was temporarily reduced by 15%. Compared with pre- or postreduction pay periods (or with control groups whose pay was unchanged), groups whose pay was reduced had significantly higher theft rates. When the bases for the pay cuts were thoroughly and sensitively explained to employees, feelings of inequity were lessened and the theft rate was reduced as well. In this study the data supported equity theory predictions regarding likely responses to underpayment.

Despite the problems, people expend effort in relation to the effort of others in the work force. Social comparison is valid, because what we do is in part a product of what others around us do. The theoretical origins of equity are both justified and accurate in that there is a social component to motivation. Equity theory should be lauded for its attempt to consider this phenomenon as a basis for work motivation. Consistent with the concept of organizational justice, equity theory postulates that how hard a person is willing to work is in part determined by perceptions of what is fair or just. There should be equity or fairness in the relationship between what you put into a job and what you get out of it in comparison to other people.

FIELD NOTE 2

Most formal studies of equity theory have occurred in field experiment or laboratory conditions. However, some researchers have used the tenets of equity theory to explain naturally occurring phenomena. Lord and Hohenfeld (1979) applied equity theory to explain the on-the-field performance of some major league baseball players.

A major league player signs a contract for a certain duration (say, three years) at a specified salary. At the end of the contract term, both the player and the team must negotiate a new contract. Sometimes the player and the team cannot agree on a new contract, because the player feels he is worth more money than the team offers. In short, the player feels underpaid in comparison to what other players are receiving. In this case the player may engage in a process known as "playing out his option"; that is, he will continue to play for the same team for one more year without a contract. This year is called the "option year." At the end of the option year, the player is free to sign with any other baseball team in the major leagues. However, during the option year, the player receives a lower salary than he did when he was under contract. Therefore, his feelings of underpayment are intensi-

fied for two reasons. First, he feels he is worth more than he was being paid under the old contract. Second, he is paid even less than before during the option year.

According to equity theory, perceptions of underpayment should produce lower performance. Lord and Hohenfeld studied a sample of 23 baseball players who were unable to reach an agreement with their teams for a new contract and thus played out their option year. The authors selected four criteria of job performance: batting average, home runs, runs batted in, and runs scored. They compared the players' performance on these criteria before the option year with their performance during it. Equity theory would postulate that because the players felt underpaid, their performance on these four factors would be lower during the option year. The results supported the hypothesis for the first three performance indexes but not for runs scored. The findings were consistent across the players, over time, and over the performance indexes. They indicated that, at least in this sample, feelings of underpayment did produce lower job performance, as equity theory would have predicted.

Expectancy Theory

Statement of the Theory.   Expectancy theory originated in the 1930s, but at that time it was not related to work motivation. Vroom (1964) brought expectancy theory into the arena of motivation research. In the past 30 years, expectancy theory has been the most popular and prominent motivation theory in I/O psychology. Since Vroom's formulation, several other researchers have proposed modifications. I will not examine all the variations but will focus on some key elements.

Expectancy theory is a cognitive theory. Each person is assumed to be a rational decision maker who will expend effort on activities that lead to desired rewards. Individuals are thought to know what they want from work and to understand that their performance will determine whether they get the rewards they desire. A relationship between effort expended and performance on the job is also assumed.

The theory has five major parts: job outcomes, valence, instrumentality, expectancy, and force.

Job Outcomes. Job outcomes are things an organization can provide for its employees, such as pay, promotions, and vacation time. Theoretically, there is no limit to the number of outcomes. They are usually thought of as rewards or positive experiences, but they need not be. Getting fired or being transferred to a new location could be outcomes. Outcomes can also refer to intangibles, such as feelings of recognition or accomplishment.

Valence. Valences are the employee's feelings about the outcomes and are usually defined in terms of attractiveness or anticipated satisfaction. The employee generates valences; that is, he or she would rate the anticipated satisfaction from (that is, ascribe a valence to) each outcome considered. Rating is usually done on a −10 to +10 scale. The individual can indicate whether an outcome has positive or negative valence. If the employee anticipates that all outcomes will lead to satisfaction, varying degrees of positive valence will be given. If the employee anticipates that all outcomes will lead to dissatisfaction, varying degrees of negative valence will be assigned. Last, if the employee feels indifferent about the outcomes, a valence of zero will be given. The employee will generate as many valences as there are outcomes.

Instrumentality. Instrumentality is defined as the perceived degree of relationship between performance and outcome attainment. This perception exists in the employee's mind. Instrumentality is synonymous with the word *conditional* and literally means the degree to which the attainment of a certain outcome is conditional on the individual's performance on the job. For example, if a person thought that pay increases were totally conditional on performance, the instrumentality associated with that outcome (a pay raise) would be very high. If a person thought that being transferred was totally unrelated to job performance, the instrumentality associated with that outcome (a transfer) would be very low. Like valences, instrumentalities are generated by the individual. He or she evaluates the degree of relationship between performance and outcome attainment on the job. Instrumentalities are usually thought of as probabilities (which therefore range between 0 and 1.0). An instrumentality of 0 means that attainment of that

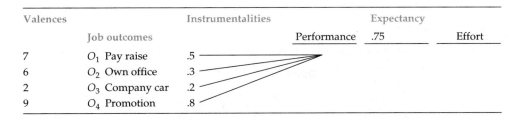

Figure 11–2   *An example of Vroom's expectancy theory*

outcome is totally unrelated to job performance; an instrumentality of 1 means that attainment of that outcome is totally conditional on job performance. Just as there are as many valences as there are outcomes, there are as many instrumentalities as there are outcomes.

Expectancy. Expectancy is the perceived relationship between effort and performance. In some jobs there may not seem to be any relationship between how hard you try and how well you do. In others there may be a very clear relationship: The harder you try, the better you do. Expectancy, like instrumentality, is scaled as a probability. An expectancy of 0 means that there is no probability that an increase in effort will result in an increase in performance. An expectancy of 1 means that an increase in effort will be followed by a corresponding increase in performance. As with the valence and instrumentality components, the individual generates the expectancy for his or her job. After thinking about the relationship between effort and job performance, the individual makes an assessment (ascribes an expectancy). Unlike the previous components, usually only one expectancy value is generated by the person to reflect the effort-performance relationship.

Force. Force, the last component, is the amount of effort or pressure within the person to be motivated. The larger the force, the greater the hypothesized motivation. Mathematically, force is the product of valence, instrumentality, and expectancy, as expressed by the following formula:

$$\text{Force} = E \left(\sum_{i=1}^{n} V_i I_i \right) \qquad \text{[Formula 11–1]}$$

This formula can better be explained with the aid of the information in Figure 11–2.

The components that constitute expectancy theory—job outcomes (O), rated valences, instrumentalities, and expectancy—are presented for a hypothetical employee. To compute this individual's force, multiply the valence for an outcome by its corresponding instrumentality and then sum these numbers. Therefore,

$$(7 \times .5) + (6 \times .3) + (2 \times .2) + (9 \times .8) = \sum_{i=1}^{4} V_i I_i = 12.9 \qquad \text{[Formula 11–2]}$$

Then multiply 12.9 by the listed expectancy of .75, which yields a force score of

$$E\left(\sum_{i=1}^{4} V_i I_i \right) = .75(12.9) = 9.7$$

[Formula 11–3]

This product, 9.7, represents the amount of force within the person to be motivated. It is the end product of the information on valence, instrumentality, and expectancy.

Now that we have this force score, what do we do with it? Think of it as a predictor of how motivated a person is. As with any predictor, the next step is to correlate it with some criterion. Because the force score predicts effort, the criterion must also measure effort. The most common measure of effort is a subjective assessment, usually a rating: the individual renders a self-assessment of his or her effort, the individual's supervisor makes the judgment, or peer assessments are used. For example, the number of hours spent studying each week has been used to predict the motivation of students. In one type of validation paradigm of expectancy theory, force scores and criterion measures of effort are calculated for a group of people. If the theory is valid, the greater the person's force score, the greater the effort should be. The theory's validity is typically assessed by correlating the force scores with the criterion of effort. High correlations between the two variables substantiate the theory; low correlations disconfirm it. I will examine the validation process more closely in the next section.

Expectancy theory provides a rich rational basis for understanding motivation in a given job. Each component is a framework for analyzing the motivation process. First, consider the outcomes and their rated valences. If a person feels indifferent about the outcomes (a low valence), there is no reason to work hard to attain them. According to expectancy theory, therefore, the first ingredient for motivation is desired outcomes. Second, the person must believe that there is some relationship between job performance and attainment of outcomes (instrumentalities must be high). If a person wants the outcomes but does not see performance as a means of getting them, there is no link between what is done and what is wanted. Reward practices and the supervisor are crucial in establishing high instrumentalities. If a supervisor says, "Your performance has been very good lately; therefore, I will reward you with a raise [or promotion]," the individual will see that the attainment of a pay raise or a promotion is conditional on (instrumental to) good performance. Conversely, if a supervisor says, "We don't give pay raises or promotions on the basis of performance; we grant them only on the basis of seniority," the individual will not be motivated to perform well to attain these outcomes. Perhaps the only motivation will be to work hard enough not to be fired, so these outcomes would eventually be attained through increased service with the organization. When outcomes are made contingent on performance and the individual understands this relationship, expectancy theory predicts that job performance will be enhanced.

Finally, the notion of expectancy is crucial. People must see a relationship (an expectancy) between how hard they try and how well they perform. If expectancy is low, it will make no difference to them whether they work hard because effort and performance seem unrelated. When I first started college, I was a chemistry major. I desired certain outcomes (for example, good grades, a sense of accomplishment). I also realized that attaining these outcomes was conditional on my performance in classes. I had high valences for both the outcomes and the perceived high instrumentalities. However, after three agonizing semesters, my expectancy was near zero. It did not seem to matter how hard I tried; I just could not alter my (low) performance in chemistry classes. My overall motivation fell dramatically along with my performance, and I eventually chose a new major. In retrospect, I realize I lacked the abilities to perform well as a chemist. All the motivation I could muster would not lead to good performance.

The idea of expectancy also explains why some jobs seem to create high or low motivation. On assembly lines, group performance level is determined by the speed of the line. No matter how hard a person works, he or she cannot produce any more until the next object moves down the line. The employee soon learns that he or she need only keep pace with the line. Thus, there is no relationship between individual effort and performance. Alternatively, sales jobs are characterized by high expectancy. Salespeople who are paid on commission realize that the harder they try (the more sales calls they make), the better their performance (sales volume). Expectancy theory would predict that motivation is greatest in jobs with high expectancies.

In summary, expectancy theory is very good at diagnosing the components of motivation. It provides a rational basis on which to assess people's effort expenditure.

Empirical Tests of the Theory. Research has focused on the specific predictions the theory tries to make. One approach assumes that the theory tries to distinguish the "most-motivated" from the "least-motivated" people in a group. With one force score derived for each person, supposedly the person with the highest score is the most motivated, and the person with the lowest score is the least motivated. This type of approach is called an *across-subjects design,* because predictions are made across people.

The second approach tests the theory differently. Here the theory assumes that each person is confronted with many tasks and then predicts on which tasks the person will work the hardest and on which he or she will expend the least effort. The theory is expanded to derive a force score for each task under consideration, and a criterion of effort is obtained for each. For each person, a correlation is computed between predictions of effort made by the theory and actual amounts of effort expended on the tasks. This type of approach is called a *within-subjects design;* predictions are made for each individual separately.

Validation studies generally find better predictions for the within-subjects design than the across-subjects design. Average validity coefficients for the across-subjects design are usually in the .30s to .40s, while average validity coefficients for within-subjects designs are usually in the .50s to .60s. The theory seems better at predicting various levels of effort an individual will expend on different tasks than at predicting gradations of motivation across different people (Kennedy, Fossum, & White, 1983). These validity coefficients are quite impressive; they are generally higher than those reported for other motivation theories.

In a major study on incentive motivation techniques, Pritchard, De Leo, and Von Bergen (1976) reported that a properly designed, successful program for motivating employees will have many of the attributes proposed by expectancy theory. Among the conditions they recommend for a program to be successful are the following:

1. Incentives (outcomes) must be carefully sought out and identified as highly attractive.
2. The rules (behaviors) for attaining the incentives must be clear to both those administering the system and to those actually in it.
3. People in the system must perceive that variations in controllable aspects of their behavior will result in variations in their level of performance and, ultimately, their rewards.

In somewhat different words, these three conditions for an effective incentive motivation program reflect the concepts of valence, instrumentality, and expectancy, respectively. The importance of having desired incentives is another way of stating that the outcomes should have high valence. The clarity of the behaviors needed to attain the incentives reflects the strength or magnitude of the instrumentalities. The ability to control levels of performance through differential effort expenditure is indicative of the concept of expectancy. In short, expectancy theory contains the key elements of a successful incentive system as derived through empirical research. Although not all research on expectancy theory is totally supportive, the results have tended to confirm its predictions.

Evaluation of the Theory.   Expectancy theory is a highly rational and conscious explanation of human motivation. People are assumed to behave in a way that will maximize expected gains (attainment of outcomes) by exhibiting certain job behaviors and expending certain levels of effort. To the extent that behavior is not directed toward maximizing gains in a rational, systematic way, the theory will not be upheld. Whenever unconscious motives deflect behavior from what a knowledge of conscious processes would predict, expectancy theory will not be predictive. Researchers suggest that people differ in the extent to which their behavior is motivated by rational processes. This was quite apparent in one of my own studies (Muchinsky, 1977a). I examined the extent to which expectancy theory predicted the amount of effort college students put into each of their courses. Using a within-subjects design, the average validity of the theory for all students was .52; however, for individual students it ranged from −.08 to .92. Thus, the theory very accurately predicted the effort expenditure of some students but was unable to predict it for others. This supports the idea that some people have a very rational basis for their behavior, and thus the theory works well for them; others appear to be motivated more by unconscious factors, and for them the theory does not work well (Stahl & Harrell, 1981).

Empirical support for expectancy theory is strong. There is some evidence (Kernan & Lord, 1990) that the underlying links between valence, instrumentality, and expectancy may vary as a function of the complexity of the goals the individual is pursuing. That is, qualitatively different cognitive processes may be operating in trying to attain single versus multiple goals. Despite these problems, the prevailing consensus is that expectancy theory is one of the dominant motivation theories in I/O psychology today.

Reinforcement Theory

Statement of the Theory. (Reinforcement theory is one of the older approaches to motivation,) what is novel is its application to industrial workers. Also referred to as *operant conditioning* and *behaviorism,* reinforcement theory has its origins in B. F. Skinner's work on conditioning animals. It was not until the 1970s, however, that I/O psychologists began to see some potential applications of reinforcement theory to the motivational problems of employees.

The theory has three key variables: stimulus, response, and reward. A *stimulus* is any variable or condition that elicits a behavioral response. In an industrial setting, a *response* would be some measure of job performance, like productivity, absenteeism, or accidents. A *reward* is something of value given to the employee on the basis of the elicited behavioral response; it is meant to reinforce the occurrence of the desired response. Most attention has been paid to the response-reward connection. Based on research with animals, four types of response-reward connections or contingencies have been found to influence the frequency of the response:

Fixed interval. The subject is rewarded at a fixed time interval, such as every hour. Those paid on an hourly basis can be thought of as being rewarded on a fixed-interval basis.

Fixed ratio. The subject is rewarded as a function of a fixed number of responses. For example, a real estate salesperson who gets a commission after each sale is rewarded on a fixed-ratio schedule. In this case the reward schedule is said to be continuous.

Variable interval. The subject is rewarded at some time interval, which varies.

Variable ratio. Reward is based on behavior, but the ratio of reward to response is variable. For example, the above salesperson might sometimes be paid after each sale and at other times after two or three sales. The person would be paid on the basis of the response (that is, making a sale), but the schedule of payment would not be constant.

Advocates of reinforcement theory believe that the magnitude of the subject's motivation to respond can be shaped by manipulating these reinforcement schedules.

A number of authors have discussed the potential benefits and liabilities of using reinforcement theory as a basis for motivating employees. The theory entails placing the control of employee motivation in the organization's hands, since organizations can "regulate" the energy output of employees by manipulating reinforcement schedules. Most people would like to feel as if they are in control of their own lives rather than being manipulated into certain behavior patterns by the organization. The issue of responsibility for controlling behavior is very sensitive, because it entails ethical considerations for employee welfare. If employees work to exhaustion through mismanagement of their efforts, they are responsible for their actions. However, if they are manipulated into expending excessive effort, they have been victimized by a force beyond their control, and the organization should be held responsible for their condition. Issues of ethical responsibility for behavior are not central to the theory, but they are important when it is ap-

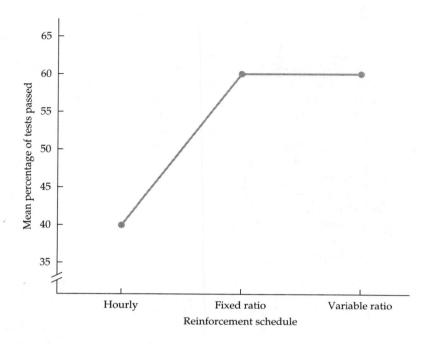

Figure 11–3   *Percentage of tests passed under different reinforcement schedules*

SOURCE: From "The Effect of Varying Schedules of Reinforcement on Human Task Performance" by R. D. Pritchard, D. W. Leonard, C. W. Von Bergen, and R. J. Kirk, 1976, *Organizational Behavior and Human Performance, 16,* p. 218.

plied in daily life. Whenever anything is "done" to someone by an outside agent, the question of whose values (the individual's or the agent's) are being optimized arises.

Empirical Tests of the Theory.   Empirical tests of reinforcement theory have involved determining which schedule of reinforcement has the greatest effect on increasing the occurrence of the desired behavioral response. In a series of studies involving tree planters, Yukl and Latham (1975) and Yukl, Latham, and Pursell (1976) compared the effectiveness of various schedules of reinforcement. Some planters were paid on a fixed-interval schedule (hourly pay); others were paid based on the number of trees they planted. Employees paid on a ratio schedule were significantly more productive (planted more trees). Pritchard, Leonard, Von Bergen, and Kirk (1976) examined the effect of different payment schedules on employees' ability to pass self-paced learning tests of electrical knowledge. Some employees were paid a flat hourly wage, while others were paid according to the number of tests they passed. Two types of ratio-payment schedules were used: fixed (the employee was paid after passing every third test), and variable (the employee was paid after passing a variable number of tests). The results of the study are shown in Figure 11–3. Employees paid contingently (that is, based on their performance) passed 60% of the tests; those paid by the hour passed about

40%. Results also showed no difference in test performance between fixed- and variable-ratio reinforcement schedules.

Research on reinforcement theory is not limited to measures of productivity. Pedalino and Gamboa (1974) described how the theory could be used to decrease absenteeism. The authors devised a plan whereby every employee who came to work on time was dealt one card from a poker deck. Each day, the attending employees were dealt a new card. At the end of the week, the employee with the best poker hand won $20. In this case the desired response (attendance) was reinforced through monetary reward. Attendance under this plan was greater than before the program was introduced.

Evaluation of the Theory. Research clearly indicates that the principles of reinforcement theory do "work." However, the theory suffers from some limitations in industrial settings. As Mawhinney (1975) noted, current applications of reinforcement theory tend to ignore individual differences in what is valued as a reward. In the Pedalino and Gamboa study, for example, it was assumed that all the employees were interested in playing poker and would respond positively to a gambling or lottery situation. Vast individual differences in preferences would have precluded the success of any such program. In addition, reinforcement has primarily been limited to studies of quantity of production. We don't know very much about how quality of performance is affected, the long-term effects of various reinforcement schedules, or people's attitudes toward such incentive methods.

The use of reinforcement theory in industry has its share of supporters and detractors. Advocates cite its wide applicability for solving problems. Its uses include absence and turnover reduction, productivity enhancement, and improvement of supervisory training. Emery Air Freight is one of the biggest reinforcement theory success stories. Emery reported $3 million in cost savings after adopting a system of positive reinforcement. Other companies have also reported successful applications. What seems to be of concern are possible ethical matters associated with the reinforcement of behavior. How ethical is it for an organization to use a payment system that increases productivity but may cause adverse side effects? Sweden has condemned piece-rate payment schedules because they cause tension and ultimately damage workers' mental and physical well-being. There is also evidence that workers in short-cycle, monotonous jobs prefer hourly rates to piece rates. They complain that piece-rate systems "control" them (or at least their behavior), which is the precise intent of the system. Despite these legitimate ethical concerns, reinforcement theory has a history of producing desired changes in work behavior. Unlike other motivational theories, its focus is not on the individual but on environmental factors that shape or modify behavior. While implementation problems exist, they address only the theory's applicability rather than its validity (see Field Note 3).

Goal-Setting Theory

Statement of the Theory. Goal setting is a motivation theory based on the assumption that people behave rationally. The crux of the theory rests on the relationship among goals, intentions, and task performance. Its basic premise is that conscious ideas regulate a person's actions. Goals are what the individual is consciously trying to attain, particularly as related to future objectives.

According to Locke and Latham (1990), goals have two major functions: They are a basis for motivation, and they direct behavior. A goal provides guidelines for deciding how much effort to put into work. Goals are intended behaviors; in turn, they influence task performance. However, two conditions must be met before goals can positively influence performance. First, the individual must be aware of the goal and know what must be accomplished. Second, the individual must accept the goal as something he or she is willing to work for. Goals can be rejected because they are seen as too difficult or too easy or because the person does not know what behaviors are needed to attain them. Acceptance of the goal implies that the individual intends to engage in the behavior needed for goal attainment.

Locke and Latham's theory of goal setting states that more difficult goals lead to higher levels of job performance. The authors believe that commitment to a goal is proportional to its difficulty. Thus, more difficult goals engender more

FIELD NOTE 3

Reinforcement theory is premised on rewarding desired behavior. The stronger the link between the behavior and the reward, the greater the probability of attaining that behavior. However, in an organizational context it is sometimes difficult to tie rewards to a particular behavior, because many behaviors are typically elicited concurrently. It is thus possible to obscure the connection between the reward and the desired behavior, which decreases the probability of the behavior occurring. In an extreme case everything gets turned around: The behaviors organizations have tried to encourage are punished, and those that they have tried to discourage are actually rewarded. Kerr (1995) described how this can happen.

Orphanages are organizations created as residences for children before they are placed in private homes. The orphanage, therefore, is theoretically interested in placing as many children as possible in good homes. Orphanages receive state funds to assist them in their operations. Since the primary goal is to place children in good homes, the means by which the orphanage is run should be directed toward this objective. However, such is not the case—the reward system created by the orphanage's management of-ten drives the process in reverse for the following reasons:

- The number of children enrolled in the orphanage often is the most important determinant of the size of its allocated budget.
- The number of children under the director's care will affect the size of the support staff, which also is a determinant of the budget.
- The total organizational size will largely determine the director's prestige at annual conventions, in the community, and so on.

Therefore, to the extent that staff size, total budget, and personal prestige are valued by the orphanage's executive personnel, it becomes rational for them to make it difficult for children to be adopted. The reward system reinforces the exact opposite of the behavior for which the orphanage was created—that is, the placement of children.

Vast amounts of research indicate that schedules of reinforcement can indeed motivate behavior to occur in certain patterns. However, the direction of that behavior is not always consistent with organizational goals.

commitment to their attainment. Goals can also vary in specificity. Some goals are general (for example, to be a good biology student), and others are more specific (to get a "A" on the next biology test). The more specific the goal, the more concentrated the individual's effort in its pursuit and the more directed the behavior. It is also important for the person to receive feedback about task performance; this guides whether he or she should work harder or continue at the same pace.

According to goal-setting theory, the following factors and conditions would induce high motivation and task performance. Goals are behavioral intentions that channel our energies in certain directions. The more difficult and more specific the goal, the greater will be our motivation to attain it. Feedback on our performance in pursuit of the goal tells us whether our efforts are "on target." The source of motivation, according to goal setting, is the desire and intention to attain the goal; this must be coupled with the individual's acceptance of the goal. Rather than dealing with motivation as a product of innate needs, feelings of inequity, or schedules of reinforcement, goal setting assumes that people set acceptable target objectives and then channel their efforts in pursuit of them. In particular, the emphasis in goal-setting theory is on the direction of behavior.

Empirical Tests of the Theory.   For the most part, empirical tests of the theory are quite supportive. As an example, Latham and Baldes (1975) studied truck drivers hauling logs to lumber mills. Performance was studied under two conditions. First, drivers were told only to "do their best" in loading the trucks. After a time, they were told to set a specific, difficult goal of loading their trucks up to 94% of the legal weight limit. (The closer to the legal limit, the fewer trips were needed.) Each truck driver got feedback by means of a loading scale indicating tonnage. Figure 11–4 shows the drivers' performance over a 48-week period. At the onset of goal setting, performance improved greatly; however, the cause is not clear-cut. One explanation is that performance improved due to the effects of goal setting. Another could be a sense of competition among the drivers as to who could load the truck closest to the legal limit. (The decline in performance between the fourth and fifth blocks was due to the truck drivers' "testing" of management to gauge its reaction.) In any case, the study clearly showed that performance under goal setting was superior to the "do-your-best" condition.

Wright (1990), however, has concluded that assigned goals produce greater increases in performance than self-set goals. Also, Hollenbeck, Williams, and Klein (1989) reported that commitment to difficult goals was higher when goals were stated publicly rather than privately. While variation does exist in terms of task behaviors and acceptance of goal setting, research indicates that goal setting produces better performance than the absence of goals or very general goals. As Latham and Marshall (1982) have stated, the key issue appears to be not how a goal is set but whether the goal is set.

Evaluation of the Theory.   You should be struck by the elegance and simplicity of goal-setting theory. There are no references to innate needs, perceived instrumentalities, or comparison others. As Latham and Locke (1991) observed, goal-setting theories lie within the domain of purposefully directed action. The theory focuses on the question of why some people perform better on work tasks than do

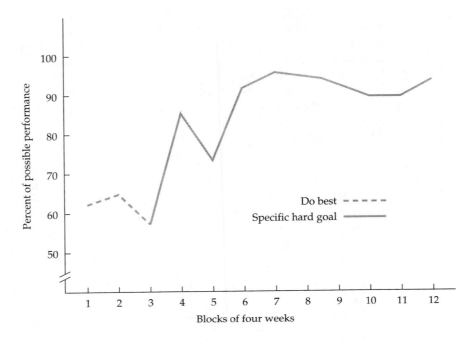

Figure 11–4 *The effect of specific, hard goals on productivity*
SOURCE: From "The Practical Significance of Locke's Theory of Goal Setting" by G. P. Latham and J. J. Baldes, 1975, *Journal of Applied Psychology, 60,* p. 123.

others. If they are equal in ability and environmental conditions, then the cause must be motivational. The theory states that the simplest and most direct motivational explanation of why some people perform better than others is because they have different performance goals. Difficulty and specificity of the goal influence performance, as do the amount and nature of feedback. There are some differences in performance between goals that are assigned and those that are self-selected. Different types of people also prefer different types of goals. But it is clear that goal setting elicits better performance.

Goal setting seems to be generalizable as a theory of motivation. It is not limited in applicability to highly rational people, although it does assume that people follow through with their intentions. The theory has a cognitive basis: Employees must think about the goals they want to pursue; they must decide whether the goals are acceptable; they must understand what behaviors they have to exhibit to attain the goal; and they must know how to evaluate feedback on their progress. Research has shown that feedback is critical for optimal performance but that people differ in their ability to use the information provided. There is also evidence that goal setting is effective for groups. Thus, a work group can set a goal to decrease scrap rate, for example, or to increase productive output. Group goals can be more difficult to attain, however, because in many cases the success of the overall group depends on more than just the success of individual members. A basketball team may set a goal of winning a certain number of games in a season, but its success will be determined by more than just the number of points scored by each player. Member coordination and integration must also be considered. One player might help the team by passing, another by rebounding, and the others by shooting.

Certain situational factors must also be present. A production worker, for instance, cannot increase the speed of an assembly line. In some cases effort or desire alone may not be enough for goal attainment. Reasonable opportunity must be provided. Perceptions of this opportunity may be a deciding factor in whether a person accepts a goal.

Locke, Shaw, Saari, and Latham (1981) reviewed 12 years of goal-setting research studies and came to the following conclusion: 90% of the studies show that specific and challenging goals lead to higher performance than do easy goals, "do-your-best" goals, or no goals. Goal setting was found to improve task performance when (1) subjects have sufficient ability, (2) feedback is provided on progress in relation to goals, (3) rewards are given for goal attainment, (4) management is supportive, and (5) individuals accept assigned goals. Tubbs (1986) concluded that the concepts of goal difficulty, goal specificity, and participation in the goal-setting process were all supported by empirical research studies. However, the principles of goal setting were empirically supported more often in laboratory than in field studies. Tubbs also discovered that individuals are more willing to accept and work for an extremely difficult goal when they know that they will not have to do so for any extended period. In summary, the overall verdict on the value of goal setting as a theory of motivation is overwhelmingly positive. Quite clearly, setting goals does enhance performance. Attention has also been turned to why goals enhance performance (Mento, Steel, & Karren, 1987), and how people become committed to reaching a goal (Hollenbeck & Klein, 1987).

Pritchard, Jones, Roth, Stuebing, and Ekeberg (1988) noted that most research on improving productivity through goal setting has involved studying relatively simple jobs with the individual as the unit of analysis. Because most jobs are more complex and given the interdependencies in work, they feel that group-level intervention studies are needed. The authors studied work group productivity for nine months. They introduced a group-level intervention designed to enhance group productivity consisting of three parts: feedback, group goal setting, and incentives (time off from work). Group-level feedback was found to increase productivity by 50% over the baseline, and goal setting plus feedback increased productivity by 75% over the baseline. The combined effect of feedback, goal setting, and incentives increased productivity by 76% over the baseline. The study showed that the principles of goal setting, proven useful with individual performance, also hold for group performance.

Overview and Synthesis of Work Motivation Theories

On the basis of the five theories of work motivation presented, it is reasonable to ask if there are unifying themes that run through them. Kanfer (1992) has pro-

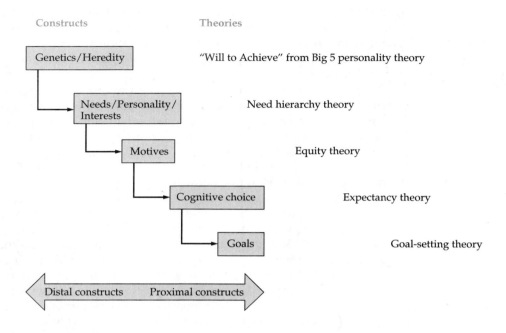

Constructs   Theories

Genetics/Heredity   "Will to Achieve" from Big 5 personality theory

Needs/Personality/   Need hierarchy theory
Interests

Motives   Equity theory

Cognitive choice   Expectancy theory

Goals   Goal-setting theory

Distal constructs   Proximal constructs

Figure 11–5   *A framework of motivation constructs and theories*
SOURCE: Adapted from "Work Motivation: New Directions in Theory and Research" by R. Kanfer, 1992, *International Review of Industrial and Organizational Psychology*, p 4.

posed that the theories can be examined along a continuum of their conceptual proximity to action. The end points of the continuum are distal (distant) and proximal (near) constructs. Distal construct theories such as personality theory exert indirect effects on behavior. Proximal construct theories begin with the individual's goals rather than with the factors that have shaped the individual's objectives. Figure 11–5 reveals the motivational constructs and associated theories arrayed along the distal/proximal continuum proposed by Kanfer.

At the extreme distal end is the construct of genetics/heredity. I did not formally examine a genetics-based theory of motivation, but you are familiar with it from another area. A contemporary interpretation of personality is represented in the Big 5 theory. One personality factor of considerable interest to I/O psychologists is Conscientiousness, as it is the basis for integrity tests. Another name for Conscientiousness is Will to Achieve (Digman & Takemoto-Chock, 1981). This name implies that individuals who are attentive to detail, rule-abiding, and honest also exhibit high ambition. Accordingly, this view of motivation is that the capacity to be motivated is genetically determined, is an enduring component of personality, and can be assessed with a paper-and-pencil personality inventory.

Maslow's theory is predicated on a universal set of basic human needs, arranged in a hierarchy. Interindividual differences in motivation are attributed to differences in the particular needs people are trying to satisfy. Equity theory asserts that there is a social component to motivation; that is, how hard we are willing to work is in part a function of how we perceive other people in our environment. Based on a social comparison of what other people are giving and getting, we make an assessment of how much effort we are willing to exert. Implicit in the concept of equity theory is a sense of fairness (that is, equity) or justice, which embeds this theoretical perspective of motivation within the same conceptual framework as that offered by the research on organizational justice.

As we continue down the continuum toward proximal constructs, there is increasing reliance on the assumption that people make conscious, deliberate, controllable choices about how much effort they choose to expend. It is the antithesis of a genetic/dispositional orientation toward motivation. Proximal theories are heavily predicated on a cognitive explanation for motivation. Expectancy theory postulates that individuals are consciously aware of the results or outcomes they wish to attain, perceive relationships between their behavior and attaining those outcomes, and also perceive a relationship between their effort and their behavior. The theory elevates motivation to a conscious choice made by the individual. Goal-setting theory also exemplifies this orientation and offers motivation as an opportunity to engage in self-control or self-regulation. The capacity to control one's own life was noted in the previous chapter as one of the determinants of mental health. Goal-setting theory postulates one way that we can assume some control over our lives is to decide how hard we are willing to work. Locke (1991) offers the following description of how prevalent individual choice or volition is in our lives:

> For example, people can choose . . . what their needs are and how to satisfy them; what values they should pursue and the validity of the values other people have told them to pursue; whether and how to apply their values to a specific situation; what goals to set, how to develop plans to reach them, and whether to commit to the goals and plans; what their performance capacity is for a specific task and how to raise it; what their performance means and who is responsible for it; the adequacy of their rewards and the relation of these rewards to their values; the causes of their affective reactions to their performance and rewards; and how to modify these reactions (e.g., by changing their performance or changing their value standards). (pp. 297–298)

As can be witnessed from the arrangement of motivational theories in Kanfer's framework, there is an array of explanations for motivation based on consideration of the individual ranging from genetic predisposition to individual conscious choice. Noticeably absent from Kanfer's framework is where reinforcement theory fits in. Reinforcement theory is predicated on environmental factors that shape behavior through patterns of reward. According to reinforcement theory, the role of the individual, either through genetic make-up or cognitive processes, is not regarded as essential or necessary to understand motivation. Much current thinking in psychology asserts that the cognitive perspective is more insightful in understanding motivation and that the operant (reinforcement) perspective is too insensitive to individual differences, particularly with regard to volition.

Other theoretical advances are also being made in the study of work motivation, mostly representing modifications or derivatives of the theories I reviewed. For example, from the dispositional perspective, Kuhl and Beckmann (1994) have proposed a construct called *action control.* Individual differences in action control

Table 11–2   Summary and evaluation of work motivation theories

Theory	Source of Motivation	Empirical Support	Industrial Applicability
Need theory	Unconscious, innate needs	Weak: Little support for proposed relationships among needs.	Very limited: Theory lacks sufficient specificity to guide behavior.
Equity theory	Drive to reduce feelings of tension caused by perceived inequity	Mixed: Good support for underpayment inequity, weak support for overpayment inequity.	Limited: Social comparisons are made, but feelings of inequity can be reduced through means other than increased motivation.
Expectancy theory	Relationship among desired outcomes, performance-reward, and effort-performance variables	Moderate-strong: More strongly supported in within-subject than across-subject experiments.	Strong: Theory provides a rational basis for why people expend effort, although not all behavior is as consciously determined as postulated.
Reinforcement theory	Schedule of reinforcement used to reward people for their performance	Moderate: Ratio reinforcement schedules evoke superior performance compared to interval schedules, but little difference exists among various ratio schedules.	Moderate: Contingent payment for performance is possible in some jobs, although ethical problems can be present in an organization's attempt to shape employee behavior.
Goal-setting theory	Intention to direct behavior in pursuit of acceptable goals	Moderate-strong: Performance under goal-setting conditions usually superior to conditions under which no goals are set.	Strong: Ability to set goals is not restricted to certain types of people or jobs.

refer to dispositional tendencies in the context of an individual's cognitions associated with anticipated or on-going activity. Persons who are high in action control are posited to direct attention toward task resolution rather than to internal emotional states unrelated to task accomplishment. From the cognitive choice perspective, Lord and Kernan (1989) have posited a theory of self-regulation based on the notion of a negative (discrepancy-reducing) feedback loop. Comparisons between a person's standard or goal and perceived performance results in cognitive and behavioral output toward the reduction of discrepancies between the goal and the perceived state of affairs. This orientation toward motivation is referred to as *cybernetic control theory*. Finally, it should be added that some researchers (for example, Klein, 1991) attempt to integrate the propositions of the existing motivational theories (as expectancy and goal-setting theories) as opposed to formulating new theories. A general summary of the major theories of work motivation discussed in the chapter is presented in Table 11–2.

Katzell and Thompson (1990) analyzed the vast body of research and theory on motivation and identified seven practices that can raise the level of motivation of people in work organizations:

- Ensure that workers' motives and values are appropriate for the jobs on which they are placed.

- Make jobs attractive and consistent with workers' motives and values.
- Define work goals that are clear, challenging, attractive, and attainable.
- Provide workers with the personnel and material resources that facilitate their effectiveness.
- Create supportive social environments.
- Reinforce performance.
- Harmonize all these elements into a consistent sociotechnical system.

No one theory of work motivation presented in this chapter lends itself to all seven of these practices. However, each theory can be directed to some of them, leaving us with the conclusion that each theory of work motivation offers something of value in understanding this most complex construct. It is the inherent mystery of why people are motivated to behave as they do that has intrigued psychologists for decades.

CASE STUDY   *What to Do with Harry?*

Joe Collins, production manager of York Tool and Die Company, tapped Harry Simpson on the shoulder.

> *Collins:* Harry, I'd like to talk to you in my office.
> *Simpson:* Right now?
> *Collins:* Right now.

Simpson took off his safety goggles and put them on the rack. He was a line foreman, and it was unusual to be called away from his line. He figured it had to be something big; otherwise, Collins would have waited until break.

> *Simpson:* Hey, Willie, cover for me, will you? I've got to talk to Joe.

Simpson walked into Collins' office and sat down. The look on Collins's face told him it wasn't going to be good news.

> *Collins:* Harry, I've known you for eight years. You've always kept your nose to the grindstone. You've been conscientious and diligent. I've had fewer problems with you than with most of the other foremen. But lately things have been different. You've come to work late five times in the past month. You've been late turning in your weekly production sheets. The scrap rate of your line has been going up too. I was also told that Willie had to spend a lot of time breaking in the two new guys. That's your job. What's going on, Harry?
> *Simpson:* I didn't realize these things were happening.
> *Collins:* You didn't know you were late? You've been coming to work at 7:30 for eight years. When you punch in at 7:45, you're late, and you know it.
> *Simpson:* I don't know, Joe, I just haven't felt with it lately. Doris says I've been moping around the house a lot lately too.
> *Collins:* I'm not here to chew you out, Harry. You're a valuable man. I want to find a way to get you back in gear. Anything been bugging you lately?
> *Simpson:* Well, I've finally figured out I'm not going to make it to supervisor. At least not in the near future. That's what I've been working for all along. Maybe I've hit my peak. When Coleman made it to supervisor, I figured I'd be the next one up. But

it never happened. I'm not sore—Coleman is a good man and he deserved it. I just feel kind of deflated.

Collins: You're well respected by management, Harry, and your line thinks you're great too. You've set a tough example to live up to. I want you to keep it up—we need people like you.

Simpson: I know I have an important job. But I figure I can't get ahead anymore, at least not on how well I do my job. I guess it boils down to luck or something.

Collins: What if I give you a new line to run? Would that give you a new challenge?

Simpson: No, I wouldn't want that, Joe. I like my line, and I don't want to leave them.

Collins: All right, Harry, but here's the deal. I want you to cut back on the lateness, pronto. Get your production reports in on time, and watch the scrap. With the price of copper going up, we've got to play it tight. Oh, and give Willie a break. He's got enough to do. Does this sound okay to you?

Simpson: Yeah. You're only telling me to do what I'm supposed to be doing.

Collins: Keep at it, Harry. In two more years, you'll get a ten-year pin.

Simpson: It won't pay the rent, but I'd like to have it.

Simpson walked back to the line. Willie looked up and saw him coming.

Willie: What'd Joe want?
Simpson: Oh, nothing much.

Willie knew Simpson was hiding something, and Simpson figured Willie knew what it was.

Questions

1. Which theory of motivation do you feel best explains Simpson's recent behavior?
2. What would equity theory have predicted about Simpson's behavior following Coleman's promotion?
3. In terms of expectancy theory, how would you describe Simpson's valence for a promotion and its instrumentality?
4. What psychological needs did Collins appeal to in talking to Simpson?
5. How might you use reinforcement theory to shape Simpson's behavior in the areas needing attention?

Leadership

Major Chapter Objectives

- Be able to explain the major topics of interest among leadership researchers.

- Be able to explain the major theoretical approaches to the study of leadership, including: leadership traits, behavioral theory, power and influence, situational theory, transactional and charismatic leadership, implicit leadership, and substitutes for leadership.

- Be able to explain the points of convergence among leadership approaches.

- Understand cross-cultural leadership issues.

- Understand diversity issues in leadership.

When you think of leadership, many ideas come to mind. Your thoughts might relate to power, authority, and influence. Maybe you think of actual people—Washington, Lincoln, Kennedy, King—or what effective leaders do. The concept of leadership evokes a multitude of thoughts, all of which in some way address causes, symptoms, or effects of leadership.

In this chapter I will examine how I/O psychologists have tried to grapple with the multifaceted concept of leadership, particularly as it relates to behavior in the world of work. Research on leadership has been diverse, because investigators have approached the concept from different perspectives. Some research has examined what strong leaders are like as people by looking at demographic variables, personality traits, types of skills, and so on. Without followers, there can be no leaders; accordingly, some research has examined leader-follower relations. Presumably "strong" leaders accomplish things that "weak" leaders do not; thus, another area of research is on the effects of leadership. An interesting question addresses contextual effects in leadership—for example, is leadership of a prison more demanding than that of a business organization? Thus, the situation in which leadership occurs has attracted much attention. Other areas of interest within the domain of leadership research have also been investigated. While such diversity of interest expands our basis of understanding, it also creates ambiguity as to exactly what leadership is all about.

Interest in leadership concerns the I/O practitioner as well as the scientist. In fact, leadership is one of the richer areas of interplay between the two—it has had a healthy influx of ideas from both camps. Identifying and developing leaders is a major concern of industry today. Companies often train their higher level personnel in skill areas (interpersonal relations, decision making, planning) that directly affect their performance as leaders. In Greensboro, North Carolina, there is an organization called the Center for Creative Leadership whose purpose is to enhance, through training, the leadership abilities of key business personnel. Not surprisingly, the military is also greatly concerned with leadership. It sponsors a wide variety of research projects that have the potential for increasing our understanding of this subject. In summary, the balance between the theory and practice of leadership is fairly even as a result of this dual infusion of interest.

Major Topics of Interest in Leadership Research

Because of the many facets of leadership, researchers have focused on selected areas. These studies can be grouped into six major categories: positional power, the leader, the led, the influence process, the situation, and leader emergence versus leader effectiveness. Let's look at each of these areas in more detail.

Positional Power

Some investigators view leadership as an exercise of positional power: The higher the position in the organizational hierarchy, the more power the position has. In the leadership context we are most concerned with legitimate power, the formal power given to a position. The positional power of a company president exceeds that of a manager; in turn, the manager has more power than a secretary. Viewing leadership in terms of positional power separates the person from the role. Little attention is given to the individual's attributes; most is aimed at the use of positional power. Organizational theorists speak of such terms as the power of the presidency and administrative clout, issues not really related to the people in such positions. Sometimes history judges leaders on their inability to use all the power their positions give them. Other leaders try to exceed the power granted their positions. In some countries leaders emerge by seizing power through military or political coups. Within this perspective, leadership is inherent in an organizational position based on the concept of power.

In the total spectrum of leadership research, a relatively small number of studies have been done on positional power. Many I/O researchers find it hard to separate leadership itself from the characteristics of people in leadership positions. But research on positional power has shown that some leadership issues transcend individual differences.

The Leader

Characteristics of individual leaders has been one of the most researched areas of leadership. Most leadership theories are based on understanding the differences among personal traits and behaviors. This is almost the opposite of emphasis on positional power, which minimizes individual differences. Many early studies leaned toward demographic and personality variables. Others studied what behaviors individual leaders exhibited that influenced the judgment of whether they were strong or weak leaders. Statements like "Strong leaders radiate confidence" or "Weak leaders are indecisive" reflect the school of thought that stresses the importance of the leader in examining the leadership process. Research has been done on the selection of people into leadership positions; other research has been devoted to training people to enhance their leadership skills. The significance here is the focus on leader characteristics or behavior and their influence on others. This is a classic I/O psychology perspective, and it is the most popular in leadership research literature.

The Led

Another area of interest is that of the characteristics of the followers, or the led. This is quite a shift in emphasis from the preceding area, in that leadership is construed more in terms of who is led than who does the leading. Casual observation suggests that some people are easier for leaders to work with than are others. Military leaders have long known that some groups of recruits are more responsive, cohesive, or productive. Teachers have noted variations among student classes. Industrial training directors have found this among various trainee groups. A leader's performance is not the same across different groups of followers. We might label this class of studies "followership" research.

As an example, consider the case of a high school science teacher. The material may remain fairly constant over time, but the teacher's behavior may vary depending on the students. One year the teacher may have a class of bright, motivated students who quickly grasp the material. The teacher may respond by offering the class more advanced topics, laboratory experiments, or field trips. Another year the teacher could have students who have difficulty learning the material. The teacher may have to instruct at a slower pace, use more examples, and hold help sessions. Other variables include class size, disciplinary problems, and student backgrounds. Thus, attributes of the led (the students) as indexed by their intelligence, motivation, number, interpersonal harmony, and background would be examined as factors affecting the behavior of the leader (the teacher).

We do not know as much about followers as we do about leaders. Studying followers usually involves studying groups as opposed to individuals, and groups are far more variable and difficult to study. Viewing the leadership process from the perspective of those who are led is fairly new in I/O psychology, but we are learning that followers can influence leaders just as we have long known the converse to be true.

The Influence Process

Rather than focusing on either the leaders or the led, some researchers have found it instructive to examine the relationship or link between the two parties, particularly as they influence each other. Here researchers give their attention to the dynamics of this relationship, although they may also consider characteristics of both leaders and followers. In a general sense, what leaders "do" to a group is influence its members in pursuit of some goal. Research on the influence process examines how this is enacted.

The concept of influence entails how one person's actions affect another's. There are several methods of influence, including (1) coercion, (2) manipulation, (3) authority, and (4) persuasion. *Coercion* involves modifying behavior by force. *Manipulation* is a controlled distortion of reality, as seen by those affected. People are allowed to see only those things that will evoke the kind of reaction desired. In the case of *authority*, agents appeal to a mutual decision, giving them the right to influence. *Persuasion* means displaying judgment in such a way that those exposed to it accept its value. Researchers study how these methods are used in leader-follower relations. As an example, Greene and Schriesheim (1980) studied two types of leader behavior: instrumental and supportive. In instrumental leadership a leader clarifies the group's goals. A supportive leader is friendly and considerate of others' needs. Greene and Schriesheim classified various work groups by size. The results showed that relatively small groups were most influenced by a supportive leader and that instrumental leadership worked better in larger groups (perhaps because it brings order and structure to the group).

Like the above study, research on the influence process tends to be fairly complex. It usually involves analysis of several variables. Perhaps more than any other leadership area, this research has shown the intricacies and many facets of leader-group relations.

The Situation

Leadership research has also been directed at the situation or context in which leader-group relations occur. These factors can greatly affect the types of behaviors a leader has to exhibit to be effective. Imagine the leader of a Boy Scout troop, the supervisor of a production crew, and the warden of a prison. Each faces a different situation. Research on situational factors has tried to identify how various contexts differ and what effect they have on leader behavior.

The context in which leadership occurs will influence the type of leader behavior called for. As an example, Green and Nebeker (1977) studied two types of leadership situations: one favorable and one unfavorable. In the favorable situation, leaders emphasized interpersonal relations and were supportive of the group members. In the unfavorable situation, the leaders became more task-oriented and more concerned with goal accomplishment than with interpersonal relations. Green and Nebeker were able to show that different situations evoke different styles of leadership behavior.

SOURCE: Reprinted by permission of Tribune Media Services.

Leader Emergence versus Leader Effectiveness

The final category is effectiveness versus emergence of leaders. Some leadership researchers are interested in the dynamics of what causes leaders to emerge within a group. This emergence process can be either formal (that is, a person is designated to be the leader) or informal (that is, a person evolves as the leader of a group without having been so designated). Researchers would examine characteristics such as the leader's age, sex, and physical appearance, or they would consider verbal and nonverbal behaviors associated with the subsequent emergence. Also of interest might be the characteristics of the group from which the leader emerged. For example, Goktepe and Schneier (1989) reported no difference in the proportion of men and women who emerged as leaders. However, group members with masculine gender-role characteristics emerged as leaders significantly more often than did those with feminine gender-role characteristics. In short, leader emergence is concerned with the process that results in someone's being regarded as the leader of a group.

Research on leader effectiveness is concerned with the performance of the leader. In this line of research, the characteristics of the leader (or the group) associated with evaluation of leader quality and establishing the criteria for effective leaders are of interest. In the former case, effective leaders might be identified as possessing certain characteristics, such as verbal fluency, sensitivity, decisiveness, and so on. In the latter case, effective leadership might be regarded as success in task completion (that is, an effective leader gets the job done) or acceptance by the group (that is, an effective leader has group support). Issues associated with both leader emergence and leader acceptance have long been of interest to I/O psychologists.

Overview

Leadership researchers do not limit their studies or theories to just one of these six areas. A researcher interested in influence processes might consider in which situations influence attempts will be successful. Interest in leader traits may also include consideration of follower traits. My purpose in describing these areas is to highlight major categories of leadership research and acknowledge their different units of analysis while realizing that the areas are not mutually exclusive. Table 12-1 summarizes the six major research areas and lists the topics and questions each area tends to address.

Theoretical Approaches to Leadership

Several theoretical approaches have been developed to explain leadership. These orientations are presented in terms of their dominant focus and contribution to

Table 12–1   *Topics and associated issues in leadership research*

Topic	Unit of Analysis	Variables of Interest	Research Questions
Position power	Organization roles and positions	Influence tactics; use of power	Under what conditions will organizations resort to strong influence attempts?
The leader	Individual leaders	Personality characteristics; leader behaviors	What traits or behaviors differentiate effective versus ineffective leaders?
The led	Work groups and subordinates	Group size; experience of subordinates	What types of subordinates desire close supervision?
Influence process	Superior-subordinate interface	Receptivity to influence; nature of influence attempts	Under what conditions are leaders most susceptible to subordinate influence attempts?
The situation	Environment or context in which leadership occurs	Situational effects on leader behavior; factors defining favorable situations	How do various situations modify behavior?
Leader emergence versus effectiveness	Individuals or groups	Group dynamics and individual characteristics	How do individuals become recognized as leaders?

the study of leadership. Yukl and Van Fleet (1992) offer an expanded version of these approaches (and related issues) in their excellent review of leadership research.

The Trait Approach

The trait approach emphasizes the personal attributes of leaders. Early leadership theories attributed success to possession of abstract abilities such as energy, intuition, and foresight. Some differences were found between leaders and nonleaders on selected traits, but for the most part the relationship between traits and leadership success did not reveal a particular set of universally relevant traits to be successful.

Advances in trait research led to a change of focus from abstract personality traits to specific attributes that can be related directly to behaviors required for effective leadership in a particular situation. This more directed approach revealed that some traits increase the likelihood of success as a leader, even though none of the traits guarantee success (Kirkpatrick & Locke, 1991). The relative importance of different traits for leader effectiveness appears to depend in part on the leadership situation.

Individual traits that appear to be related to leadership success include high energy level, stress tolerance, integrity, emotional maturity, and self-confidence. *High energy level* and *stress tolerance* help people cope with the hectic pace and demands of most leadership positions, frequent role conflicts, and the pressure to make important decisions without adequate information. Leaders with high emotional maturity and integrity are more likely to maintain cooperative relationships with subordinates, peers, and superiors. *Emotional maturity* means that a leader is less self-centered, has more self-control, has more stable emotions, and is less defensive. *Integrity* refers to a person's behavior being consistent with expressed values and that the person is honest and trustworthy. *Self-confidence* makes a leader more persistent in pursuit of difficult objectives, despite initial problems and setbacks.

Motivation is another aspect of personality related to leader effectiveness. The classic research of McClelland and his colleagues (for example, McClelland & Boyatzis, 1982) identified three leader motives: need for power, need for achievement, and need for affiliation. Someone with a high *need for power* enjoys influencing people and events and is more likely to seek positions of authority. Someone with a high *need for achievement* enjoys attaining a challenging goal or accomplishing a difficult task, prefers moderate risks, and is more ambitious in terms of career success. Someone with a high *need for affiliation* enjoys social activities and seeks close, supportive relationships with other people. Similar results were found in another study on managerial motivation conducted by Berman and Miner (1985).

A related line of research addresses leader skills, as opposed to the possession of personality traits, in the belief that it requires skill to implement the traits in leadership roles. Three basic categories of skills have been proposed: technical, conceptual, and interpersonal. *Technical skills* include knowledge of work operations, procedures and equipment, and knowledge of markets, clients, and competitors. *Conceptual skills* include the ability to analyze complex events and perceive trends, recognize changes, and identify problems. *Interpersonal skills* include understanding of interpersonal and group processes, the ability to maintain cooperative relationships with people, and persuasive ability. In general, the research supports the conclusion that technical, conceptual, and interpersonal skills are necessary in most leadership positions. However, the relative importance of specific skills varies greatly depending on the situation.

In general, the trait approach was dominant in the early days of leadership research, then fell out of favor for a long time, and only recently has regained some credibility through the advances in personality assessment. Traits offer the potential to explain why people seek leadership positions and why they act the way they do when they occupy these positions. It is now evident that some traits and skills increase the likelihood of leadership success, even though they do not assure success. Despite this progress, the utility of the trait approach for understanding leadership is limited by the elusive nature of traits. Traits interact with situational demands and constraints to influence a leader's behavior, and this behavior interacts with other situational variables to influence group process variables, which in turn affect group performance. It is therefore difficult to understand how leader traits can affect subordinate motivation or group performance unless we examine how traits are expressed in the actual behavior of leaders. Emphasis on leadership behavior ushers in the next era of research on leadership.

Table 12–2 Sample items from the Leader Behavior Description Questionnaire

Structure	Consideration
1. He schedules work to be done.	1. He is friendly and approachable.
2. He emphasizes the meeting of deadlines.	2. He makes group members feel at ease when talking to them.
3. He lets group members know what is expected of them.	3. He does little things to make it pleasant to be a member of the group.

The Behavioral Approach

The behavioral approach emphasizes what leaders actually do on the job and the relationship of this behavior to leader effectiveness. Major lines of behavior research include the classification of leadership behaviors into taxonomies and identification of behaviors related to criteria of leadership effectiveness.

A major question in behavior research is how to classify leadership behavior in a way that facilitates research and theory on leadership effectiveness. Early research conducted during the 1950s at Ohio State University sought to identify relevant aspects of leadership behavior and measure these behaviors with a questionnaire completed by subordinates of leaders. The results revealed that subordinates perceived the behavior of their leader primarily in terms of two independent categories, one dealing with task-oriented behaviors (initiating structure) and the other dealing with people-oriented behaviors (consideration). The questionnaire that resulted from this research, called the Leader Behavior Description Questionnaire (LBDQ), is a hallmark in the history of leadership research. Sample questions from the LBDQ are presented in Table 12–2. The two-factor taxonomy of task-oriented and people-oriented behavior provided a good starting point for conceptualization of leadership behaviors, but the two dimensions eventually proved too abstract to provide a basis for understanding how leaders handle the specific role requirements confronting them. More recent advances in the assessment of leadership from the behavioral perspective are evidenced in the Leadership Practices Inventory developed by Kouzes and Posner (1995). Further progress in behavior research required a shift in focus to more specific aspects of behavior. Yukl, Wall, and Lepsinger (1990) proposed an integrating taxonomy with 11 generic categories of behavior applicable to any leader. Yukl and associates asserted that the relative importance of each category varies across situations and that categories of behavior can be enacted in different ways in different situations. The taxonomy is presented in Figure 12–1, and the major purposes of the leader behaviors is presented in Table 12–3.

An increasing amount of research has examined how specific types of leadership behavior are related to leader effectiveness. This research suggests that managerial effectiveness is predicted better by specific behaviors relevant to the leadership situation (for example, clarifying, monitoring, and problem solving) than by broad measures such as initiating structure and consideration. Clarifying is the primary component of initiating structure, and a number of studies have

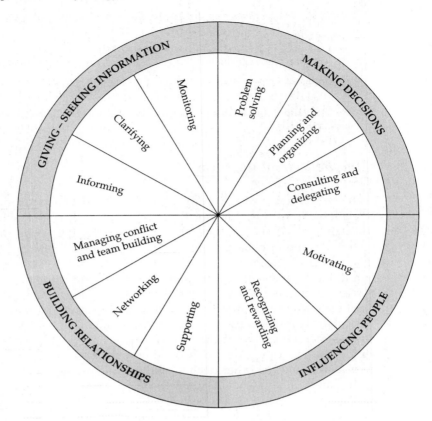

Figure 12–1   *Integrating taxonomy of leader behaviors*
SOURCE: From *Leadership in Organizations* (2nd ed.) (p. 129) by G. Yukl, 1989, Englewood Cliffs, NJ: Prentice-Hall.

been conducted on the use of clarifying behavior by leaders (for example, explaining responsibilities, assigning work, giving instructions, and setting priorities, deadlines, and standards). Setting specific challenging but realistic goals is an important component of providing clarification, and in the motivation literature there is ample evidence from field experiments that goal setting results in better performance than no goals or "do your best" instructions.

Several studies found relationships between planning and leadership effectiveness, although effective planning was usually informal and flexible rather than formal and rigid. Behaviors such as coaching, mentoring, and team building have also been found important for developing subordinate confidence and strengthening their identification with the organization's mission.

As was found in trait research, the behavior research also suffers from a tendency to look for simple answers to complex questions. Most research on leadership effectiveness has focused on behaviors individually rather than on examining how effective leaders use patterns of specific behaviors. It is likely that

Table 12–3   *Major purposes of leadership behaviors in the integrating taxonomy*

Managerial Behavior	Internal Context	External Context
Networking	Good relations with subordinates	Good relations with peers, superiors, outsiders
Supporting	Good relations with subordinates, stress tolerance by subordinates	Good relations with peers, superiors, outsiders
Managing conflict and team building	Good relations with subordinates, group cohesiveness, cooperation among subordinates	Good relations with peers, superiors, outsiders
Motivating	Subordinate effort	Cooperation and support from peers, superiors, and others
Recognizing and rewarding	Subordinate effort and role clarity, good relations with subordinates	Cooperation and support from peers, superiors, and others
Planning and organizing	Unit efficiency and coordination	Adaptation to environment, external coordination
Problem solving	Stability of operations, unit efficiency and coordination	Adaptation to environment, external coordination
Consulting and delegating	Decision quality, subordinate effort	Decision quality and implementation
Monitoring	Detection of problems, evaluation of performance	Detection of problems and opportunities
Informing	Decision quality, unit efficiency and coordination	External coordination, enhance unit reputation
Clarifying	Role clarity, unit efficiency and coordination	External coordination

SOURCE: From *Leadership in Organizations* (2nd ed.) (p. 131) by G. Yukl, 1989, Englewood Cliffs, NJ: Prentice-Hall.

specific behaviors interact in complex ways and that leadership effectiveness cannot be understood unless these interactions are studied. For example, monitoring is useful for discovering problems, but unless something is done to solve problems when they are discovered, it will not contribute to the effectiveness of the leader. Delegating is unlikely to be effective unless the leader clarifies the subordinate's new responsibilities, ensures that the subordinate accepts them, monitors progress in an appropriate way, and provides necessary resources.

Because of the growing realization of the importance of influencing others to attain goals, the next major direction in leadership research was to gain a better understanding of leader power and influence.

The Power and Influence Approach

The power possessed by a leader is important not only for influencing subordinates but also for influencing peers, superiors, and people outside the organization, such as clients and suppliers. Major questions in research on power include identification of different types of power, an understanding of how different amounts and types of leader power are related to leadership effectiveness, and an understanding of how influence behavior is related to effective leadership.

Power and Leader Effectiveness.   Efforts to understand power usually involve distinctions among various forms of power. A classic power taxonomy, proposed by French and Raven (1960), differentiated five types of power: reward, coercive, legitimate, expert, and referent.

Reward power. This is the capacity of an organization (or a member in a specified role) to offer positive incentives for desirable behavior. Incentives include promotions, raises, vacations, good work assignments, and so on. Power to reward an employee is defined by formal sanctions inherent in a superior's role.

Coercive power. The organization can punish an employee for undesirable behavior. Dismissal, docking pay, reprimands, and unpleasant work assignments are examples. This capacity to punish is also defined by formal sanctions inherent in the organization.

Legitimate power. Sometimes referred to as authority, this means that the employee believes the organization's power over him or her is legitimate. Norms and expectations help define the degree of legitimate power. If a boss asked an individual to work overtime, this would likely be seen as legitimate, given the boss's authority. However, if a co-worker made the same request, it might be turned down. The co-worker has no legitimate authority to make the request, although the individual might agree out of friendship.

Expert power. The employee believes that some other individual has expertise in a given area and that he or she should defer to the expert's judgment. Consultants are called on for help in handling problems because they are seen as experts in certain areas. The source of expert power is the perceived experience, knowledge, or ability of a person. It is not formally sanctioned in the organization. There are also differences in the perceived boundaries of expertise. One employee may be seen as the expert on using tools and equipment; others will turn to him or her for help with technical problems. However, that expertise may not be seen as extending to other areas, such as interpersonal relations.

Referent power. This is the most abstract type of power. One employee might admire another, want to be like that person, and want to be liked by him or her. The other worker is a referent, someone the employee refers to. The source of referent power is the referent's personal qualities. Cultural factors may contribute to these qualities. Younger people will often defer to an older person partly on the basis that age per se is a personal quality that engenders deference. Norms can also generate referent power. An employee may wish to identify with a particular group and will bow to the group's expectations.

Table 12–4 presents the five sources of power and their likely outcomes in dealing with subordinates. Yukl (1994) notes that the success of an influence at-

Table 12–4 *Sources of leader power over subordinates and likely outcomes*

| Source of Leader Influence | Type of Outcome | | |
	Commitment	Compliance	Resistance
Referent power	Likely,* if request is believed to be important to leader.	Possible, if request is perceived to be unimportant to leader.	Possible, if request is for something that will bring harm to leader.
Expert power	Likely,* if request is persuasive and subordinates share leader's task goals.	Possible, if request is persuasive but subordinates are apathetic about task goals.	Possible, if leader is arrogant and insulting, or subordinates oppose task goals.
Legitimate power	Possible, if request is polite and very appropriate.	Likely,* if request or order is seen as legitimate.	Possible, if arrogant demands are made or request does not appear proper.
Reward power	Possible, if used in a subtle, very personal way.	Likely,* if used in a mechanical, impersonal way.	Possible, if used in a manipulative, arrogant way.
Coercive power	Very unlikely.	Possible, if used in a helpful, nonpunitive way.	Likely,* if used in a hostile or manipulative way.

*Indicates most common outcome.

SOURCE: From *Leadership in Organizations* (2nd ed.) (p. 44) by G. Yukl, 1989, Englewood Cliffs, NJ: Prentice-Hall.

tempt is a matter of degree. It produces three qualitatively distinct outcomes. *Commitment* describes an outcome in which an individual (the target) internally agrees with a request from another individual (the agent) and makes a great effort to carry out the request effectively. *Compliance* describes an outcome in which the target is willing to do what the agent asks but is apathetic rather than enthusiastic about it and will make only a minimal effort. *Resistance* describes an outcome in which the target person is opposed to the request rather than merely indifferent about it and actively tries to avoid carrying it out.

Research on legitimate power indicates that it is a major source of daily influence on routine matters for managers in formal organizations (Yukl & Falbe, 1991). Research on positive reward behavior, which is based on reward power, finds that it has beneficial effects on subordinate satisfaction. Punishment, which is based on coercive power, can be used to influence the behavior of individuals who jeopardize the mission of the organization or threaten the leader's legitimate authority. Referent and expert power are used to make nonroutine requests and motivate commitment to tasks that require high effort, initiative, and persistence.

Some researchers have proposed that the manner in which power is exercised largely determines whether it results in enthusiastic commitment, passive compliance, or stubborn resistance. Effective leaders use combinations of power in a subtle fashion that minimizes status differentials and avoids threats to the self-esteem of subordinates. In contrast, leaders who exercise power in an arrogant and manipulative manner are likely to engender resistance.

Organizations differ in the extent to which they use the various bases of power. Authoritarian managers rely on reward and coercive power. Managers with a participative style rely on expert and referent power. The military relies heavily on the legitimate power inherent in military rank. Stahelski, Frost, and Patch (1989) reported that university administrators used referent and expert power to influence subordinates more than legitimate, reward, or coercive power.

Ragins and Sundstrom (1989) examined gender differences in the use of power within organizations. They concluded that power seems to grow incrementally through the accumulation of multiple resources over the span of a career. For women, the path to power contains many impediments and barriers that can be characterized as an obstacle course. The path to power for men contains fewer obstacles that derive from their gender and may actually contain sources of support unavailable to their female counterparts.

Leader-Member Exchange Theory.   Graen and his associates (for example, Dansereau, Graen, & Haga, 1975) proposed a theory of leadership based on mutual influence called leader-member exchange (LMX) theory. The theory postulates that leaders differentiate their subordinates in terms of (1) their competence and skill, (2) the extent to which they can be trusted (especially when not being watched by the leader), and (3) their motivation to assume greater responsibility within the unit. Subordinates with these attributes become members of what Graen calls the in-group. *In-group members* go beyond their formal job duties and take responsibility for completing tasks that are most critical to the success of the work group. In return, they receive more attention, support, and sensitivity from their leaders. Subordinates who do not have these attributes are called the *out-group;* they do the more routine, mundane tasks and have a more formal relationship with the leader. Leaders influence out-group members by using formal authority, but this is not necessary with in-group members. Thus, leaders and subordinates use different types and degrees of influence depending on whether the subordinate is in the in- or out-group.

In a review of the theory, Dienesch and Liden (1986) concluded that there are three psychological bases for the "exchange" between the superior and subordinate. *Personal contribution* refers to the perception of the amount, direction, and quality of work-oriented activity each member puts forth toward the mutual goals of the dyad. *Loyalty* is the expression of public support for the goals and personal character of the other members. *Affect* is the degree of liking members of the dyad have for each other. These three dimensions are referred to as the "currencies of exchange" within the dyad.

In a modification of LMX theory, the development of relationships in a leader-subordinate dyad was described in terms of a *life-cycle model* with three possible stages (Graen & Scandura, 1987). The relationship begins with an initial testing phase in which the leader and the subordinate evaluate each other's motives, attitudes, and potential resources to be exchanged; changes in the role of the subordinate are negotiated through a series of mutually reinforcing behavior cycles. If the relationship proceeds to the second stage, the exchange arrangement is refined, and mutual trust, loyalty, and respect develop. Some exchange relationships advance to a third (mature) stage, wherein exchange based on self-interest is transformed into mutual commitment to the mission and objectives of the work unit.

Table 12–5   *Definition of influence tactics*

Tactic	Definition
Rational persuasion	The agent uses logical arguments and factual evidence to persuade the target that a proposal or request is viable and likely to result in the attainment of task objectives.
Inspirational appeals	The agent makes a request or proposal that arouses target enthusiasm by appealing to target values, ideals, and aspirations or by increasing target self-confidence.
Consultation	The agent seeks target participation in planning a strategy, activity, or change for which target support and assistance are desired, or is willing to modify a proposal to deal with target concerns and suggestions.
Ingratiation	The agent uses praise, flattery, friendly behavior, or helpful behavior to get the target in a good mood or to think favorably of him or her before asking for something.
Personal appeals	The agent appeals to target feelings of loyalty and friendship toward him or her when asking for something.
Exchange	The agent offers an exchange of favors, indicates willingness to reciprocate at a later time, or promises a share of the benefits if the target helps accomplish a task.
Coalition tactics	The agent seeks the aid of others to persuade the target to do something, or uses the support of others as a reason for the target to agree also.
Legitimating tactics	The agent seeks to establish the legitimacy of a request by claiming the authority to make it or by verifying that it is consistent with organizational policies, roles, practices, or traditions.
Pressure	The agent uses demands, threats, frequent checking, or persistent reminders to influence the target to do what he or she wants.

SOURCE: From *Leadership in Organizations* (3rd ed.) by G. Yukl, 1994, Englewood Cliffs, NJ: Prentice-Hall.

LMX theory has never been clear about the desirability of having sharply differentiated in-groups and out-groups. A sharply differentiated in-group is likely to create feelings of resentment and undermine team identification among subordinates who are excluded from the in-group (Yukl, 1989b). It is likely that effective leaders establish a special exchange relationship with all subordinates, not just with a few favorites. A leader can use some aspects of a special exchange, such as greater delegation of responsibility and sharing of administrative functions with a few subordinates while also developing a relationship of mutual trust, supportiveness, respect, and loyalty with other subordinates. It is not necessary to treat all subordinates exactly the same, but each should perceive that he or she is an important and respected member of the team rather than a "second-class citizen."

Influence Tactics.   A bridge between the power and behavior approaches is research on influence tactics. The choice of tactics for a particular influence attempt depends somewhat on the status of the target person and the objective of the influence attempt. The most common tactics are defined in Table 12–5.

Pressure is used more in downward influence attempts than in lateral or upward influence attempts, consistent with the greater amount of position power leaders have over subordinates than over peers or superiors. Some tactics, such as ingratiation, rational persuasion, and personal appeals, tend to be used more in initial influence attempts, whereas tactics such as pressure, exchange, and coalitions tend to be used more often in follow-up influence attempts after the agent has met initial resistance by the target (Yukl & Tracey, 1992).

Some tactics are more effective than others in gaining commitment, although the outcome of any influence attempt will likely depend in part on the specific situation, the relationship between agent and target, the agent's power over the target, and the perceived legitimacy and relevance of the agent's request. Yukl and Tracey (1992) reported that the most effective tactics for obtaining target commitment were rational persuasion, consultation, and inspirational appeals; the least effective tactics were pressure, coalition tactics, and legitimating tactics.

Influence is a fundamental concept in leadership, and the power influence approach appears to provide unique insights about leadership emergence and effectiveness. Conceptualization of power still remains somewhat unclear, however, as power may be construed as potential influence or enacted influence. That is, power may be viewed as influence over the attitudes and behaviors of people or as influence over events. We need to learn more about the way power changes over time as a result of the leader's use and misuse of it.

The Situational Approach

The situational approach emphasizes the importance of contextual factors such as the leader's authority and discretion, the nature of the work performed by the leader's unit, the attitudes of subordinates, and the nature of the external environment. Situational research and theory falls into two major subcategories. One line of research, path-goal theory, treats leader behavior as a dependent variable; researchers seek to discover how the situation influences behavior and how much variation occurs in leader behaviors across different types of positions. The other line of research, cognitive resources theory, seeks to discover how situational variables moderate the relationship between leader attitudes (for example, traits, behaviors) and measures of leader effectiveness.

Path-Goal Theory.   According to path-goal theory (House, 1971), leaders motivate higher performance in subordinates by acting in ways that influence them to believe valued outcomes can be attained by making a serious effort. Aspects of the situation such as the nature of the task, the work environment, and subordinate attributes determine the optimal amount of each type of leader behavior for improving subordinate satisfaction and performance.

Using this theory, a leader must be able to manifest four different styles of behavior, which have been derived from previous research on work behavior:

Directive behavior. The leader provides specific guidelines to subordinates on how they perform their tasks. The leader should set standards of performance and provide explicit expectations of performance.

Supportive behavior. The leader must demonstrate concern for subordinates' well-being and must be supportive of them as individuals.

Participative behavior. The leader must solicit ideas and suggestions from subordinates and invite their participation in decisions that directly affect them (see Field Note 1).

Achievement-oriented behavior. A leader must set challenging goals, emphasize improvements in work performance, and encourage high levels of goal attainment.

Effective leaders need all four of these styles, because each one produces different results. But when should a leader use which style? It depends on a number of situational factors. Two types of situational factors have been identified. Some relate to subordinate characteristics, others to environmental factors. Leader behavior is motivating to the extent that it helps subordinates cope with environmental uncertainties or frustrations. What effect do these leader behaviors have? The leader can influence subordinates' perceptions of their jobs by (1) removing obstacles from the paths to the desired goals, (2) rewarding them for attaining their goals, and (3) helping them clarify paths to valued goals. Thus, the leader

FIELD NOTE 1

One leader style proposed by path-goal theory is participative leadership, which allows subordinates to participate in the decision-making process. I/O psychologists have experienced considerable difficulty in figuring out the conditions under which this style is effective. Many factors seem to contribute to its success. We can start with the leader. Some individuals like to retain the decision-making authority inherent in their leadership roles. One basis for their feelings is that as leaders they have more expertise than their subordinates, so why dilute the quality of the decision by delegating it to others? Some leaders solve this problem by giving subordinates the authority to make trivial decisions, or what is sometimes called "throwing them a bone."

Another problem is the subordinates. Most of us like to have our feelings solicited in matters that pertain to us, but there are wide individual differences. Some subordinates like to get involved in fine-grained details of decisions, and others do not. Some subordinates resent having to make all sorts of decisions. If they are going to be burdened with the responsibility for making administrative decisions, then they want the salary and title that traditionally come with it. When invited by the boss to participate in certain decisions, they are inclined to feel "That's your job, not mine." Willingness to participate is also moderated by the nature of the problem. Some problems are fair game for employee involvement, and others are not.

Finally, there are cross-cultural differences in the acceptance of participative leadership. A leading U.S. company once opened a production plant in Latin America. Using the latest leadership ideas from the United States, company officials invited the native employees to participate in a wide range of work-related decisions. Within a short period, turnover was running exceedingly high. When the company investigated the cause of the turnover, it was shocked to learn that its own management practices were primarily responsible. The employees interpreted management's participative style as evidence of its ignorance about running the plant. The employees were saying, in effect, "We're the workers, not management. If you don't know how to run your own plant, how do you expect us to know?" Effective use of the participative leadership style is more complex than you might think.

helps subordinates do the things that must be done to obtain the desired rewards.

However, path-goal theory has a number of conceptual limitations. The theory focuses on subordinate motivation as the explanatory process for the effects of leadership, and it ignores other explanatory processes, such as a leader's influence on the organization of work, resource levels, and skill levels. It has been suggested that greater empirical support would be found for the theory if some key propositions were stated in more narrowly defined behaviors such as clarifying work roles as opposed to the broader concept of initiating structure.

Cognitive Resources Theory. Fiedler and Garcia (1987) proposed the cognitive resources theory of leadership. Cognitive resources refer to the leader's intelligence, technical competence, or job-relevant knowledge. The theory addresses how and under what conditions leaders should use their cognitive resources to lead their groups. Fiedler and Garcia propose that when leaders employ directive behavior, are not under stress, and enjoy the support of their followers, they will make the most effective use of whatever cognitive resources they possess.

This theory focuses on unraveling the conditions for optimum use of leader abilities. The theory asserts that leaders have two general types of resources to help resolve problems: prior experience and intelligence. When a group is under stress because of the tense relationships between leaders and subordinates, leaders rely on prior experience in leading the group and do not make effective use of their intelligence. Fiedler believes that stress is a variable that can be managed effectively. Thus, through stress management, it is possible to increase the application of intelligence by leaders—that is, to make fuller utilization of cognitive resources. The theory postulates under which conditions leaders should draw more heavily on either prior experience or intelligence to solve leadership problems. Fiedler incorporated both situational and personal variables into this theory. You can think of cognitive resource theory as a specification of the process leaders should use in dealing with various types of situations to effectuate the success of the group.

In a test of the theory, Vecchio (1990) found that under stress a leader's job-relevant experience (rather than intellectual ability) had a stronger influence on group performance. However, when the group is supportive of the leader, there is a stronger association between leader intelligence and group performance. Yukl and Van Fleet (1992) state that the theory is new, with relatively little research having been conducted to assess it. However, some conceptual weaknesses also exist in the theory. For example, the intervening processes used to explain critical relationships are still incomplete, and likely differences among leaders in their reactions to stress are not recognized.

Wagner and Sternberg (1990) proposed a concept that seemingly has considerable relevance to cognitive resources theory. They proposed the concept of "street smarts" or practical intelligence. Practical intelligence differs from traditional academic intelligence in terms of its capacity to predict success in solving problems that don't have a single, correct solution. The two types of intelligence are not unrelated, but academic intelligence is more strongly associated with solving academic problems in a formal classroom setting, whereas practical intelligence is more strongly associated with solving practical problems outside the classroom. The basis for "street smarts" is the acquisition of tactic knowledge: work-related practical know-how that is learned informally on the job. Perhaps future research on cognitive resources theory will reveal that "street smarts" is a major type of cognitive resource that an individual can draw on to lead a group. In general, Sternberg (1995) believes that the role of intelligence in leadership has yet to be fully understood and that intelligence and experience can be complementary, rather than antagonistic, resources.

Transformational and Charismatic Leadership

Transformational leadership refers to the process of influencing major changes in the attitudes and assumptions of organization members and building commitment for major changes in the organization's objectives and strategies. Transformational leadership involves influence by a leader on subordinates, but the effect of the influence is to empower subordinates who also become leaders in the process of transforming the organization. Thus, transformational leadership is usually viewed as a shared process, involving the actions of leaders at different levels and in different subunits of an organization.

Charismatic leadership is defined more narrowly and refers to follower perception that a leader possesses a divinely inspired gift and is somehow unique and larger than life. Followers not only trust and respect the leader but also idolize or worship the leader as a superhuman hero or spiritual figure (Bass, 1985). According to House (1977), the indicators of charismatic leadership include a follower's trust in the correctness of the leader's beliefs, unquestioning acceptance of the leader, affection for the leader, and willing obedience. Thus, with charismatic leadership the focus is on an individual leader rather than on a leadership process that may be shared among multiple leaders.

Transformational Leadership.   Bass (1985) defined transformational leadership in terms of the leader's effect on followers. Leaders transform followers by making them more aware of the importance and value of task outcomes, by activating their higher order needs (in Maslow's sense), and by inducing them to transcend self-interest for the sake of the organization. As a result of this influence, followers feel trust and respect toward the leader, and they are motivated to do more than they originally expected to do.

Bass views transformational leadership as more than just another term for charisma. *Charisma* is defined as a process wherein a leader influences followers by arousing strong emotions and identification with the leader. Bass considers some charisma to be a necessary but not sufficient condition for transformational leadership. Two other components of transformational leadership are intellectual stimulation and individualized consideration. *Intellectual stimulation* is a process wherein leaders increase follower awareness of problems from a new perspective. *Individualized consideration* is a subset of behaviors from the broader category of consideration, and it includes providing support, encouragement, and developmental experiences to followers. Charisma, intellectual stimulation, and individualized consideration interact to influence changes in followers, and the combined effects distinguish between transformational and charismatic leadership. Transformational leaders seek to empower and elevate followers, whereas in charismatic leadership the opposite sometimes occurs. That is, some charismatic leaders keep followers weak and dependent and try to instill personal loyalty rather than commitment to ideals.

Charismatic Leadership.   House (1977) proposed a theory that identifies how charismatic leaders behave, how they differ from other people, and the conditions under which they are most likely to flourish. As noted earlier, the theory specifies indicators of charismatic leadership that involve attitudes and perceptions of followers about the leader. The theory also specifies leader traits that increase the likelihood of being perceived as charismatic, including a strong need for power, high self-confidence, and strong convictions. Behaviors typical of charismatic leaders include (a) impression management to maintain follower confidence in the leader, (b) articulation of an appealing vision that defines the task in terms of ideological goals to build follower commitment, (c) communication of high expectations for followers to clarify expectations, and (d) expression of confidence in followers' abilities to build their self-confidence.

Charismatic leaders give their followers a vision of the future that promises a better and more meaningful life. Conger and Kanungo (1987) believe that charismatic leaders are regarded as "heroes" who exhibit unconventional behaviors and transform people to share the radical changes they advocate. Manz and Sims (1991) add that such leaders should also be viewed as hero makers, and the spotlight should be on the achievements of the followers as well as the leaders. House, Spangler, and Woycke (1991) examined the personality and charisma of U.S. presidents and their effectiveness as leaders. They concluded that personality and charisma did make a difference in the effectiveness of the presidents.

However, Hogan, Raskin, and Fazzini (1990) cautioned that there is a "dark side" to charismatic leaders. Because they have excellent social skills, sometimes to the point of being charming, they are readily liked by their followers, but lurking behind the mask of likability may be a person with pronounced adjustment problems. Only after these people fail in their leadership roles do we ever learn of their maladjustment, which was cleverly concealed by their ability to manipulate people to like them. Musser (1987) described the differences between positive and negative charismatics in terms of whether they seek to instill commitment to ideological goals or to themselves. Conger (1989) described the following problems that are likely to occur with negative charismatics.

- They start grandiose projects to glorify themselves, and the projects are often unrealistic due to the leader's inflated self-assessment and unwillingness to seek and accept advice from others. They tend to ignore or reject evidence that a plan or strategy is encountering serious difficulties, thereby reducing the chance of correcting problems in time to avert a disaster.
- These leaders are willing to spend time in high visibility activities to promote a vision but are unwilling to spend the time necessary to guide and facilitate implementation of a vision. They tend to vacillate between extremes of loose

delegation when things are going well and overcontrolling behavior when trouble occurs with a project.

- They fail to develop competent successors. These leaders try to keep subordinates weak and dependent, and they remove people with the leadership qualities of a potential successor. Thus, a leadership crisis is likely to occur when the leader dies or departs.

The similarities and differences between charismatic and transformational leaders is not totally clear. For example, is it possible to be transformational and highly charismatic at the same time? Bass proposed that charisma is a necessary component of transformational leadership, but the research on transformational leaders suggests that many of them are not perceived by their followers as charismatic. Perhaps the attribution of charisma is weakened when a leader reduces the dependence of followers on the leader by empowering them, building their commitment to new values and organizational objectives, and instituting changes in the organizations.

Implicit Leadership Theory

The previous theories of leadership presume that leadership is something that is really "out there," and the various theories are merely different ways to explain what it is. A radically different view is that leadership exists only in the mind of the beholder, usually the follower. It may be that leadership is nothing more than a label we attach to a set of outcomes. That is, we observe a set of conditions and events and make the attribution that leadership has occurred or exists. Implicit leadership theory regards leadership as a subjectively perceived construct rather than an objective construct. Implicit leadership theory is also referred to as the attribution theory of leadership and social information processing theory.

Lord and his associates have made the greatest contribution to this view of leadership. For example, Lord, Foti, and Phillips (1982) concluded that individuals hold conceptions of prototypic leaders (that is, what they think leaders are like) and then evaluate actual leaders according to their conceptions. People judged as "good" leaders are likely to be those whose actions and demeanors conform to the conception we hold. Thus, "effectiveness" in leadership is not determined objectively but through confirmation of expectations. Phillips and Lord (1981) discovered that individuals develop global impressions of leader effectiveness and then use those global impressions to describe specific dimensions of leader behavior. Thus, individuals make confident judgments of behavior they had no opportunity to observe in much the same way halo error operates in performance appraisal. Meindl and Ehrlich (1987) discussed what they called "the romance of leadership" as it relates to assessments of organizational performance. In their study subjects gave better evaluations to performance outcomes attributed to leadership factors than they gave to the same outcomes when they were attributed to nonleadership factors. The authors concluded that leadership has assumed a heroic, larger-than-life quality in people's minds. Meindl and Ehrlich believe that leadership may serve more of a symbolic role, causing people to feel assured and confident that the fate and fortune of an organization are in good hands. They contend that leadership may not account for as much of an organization's success as we believe, but leadership has a symbolic value in producing subordinate support, which may then paradoxically produce organizational effectiveness.

Implicit leadership theory poses a vexing dilemma for the assessment of leaders through questionnaires such as the LBDQ. We don't know if what these questionnaires measure is the actual behavior of the leader or the cognitive set of the rater. While Lord (1985) and Foti and Lord (1987) have proposed strategies to aid in measurement of leaders, the issues raised by implicit leadership theory challenge the very foundation on which most of our knowledge of leadership is based.

Substitutes for Leadership

Kerr and Jermier (1978) have asked what it is that organization members need to maximize in seeking organizational and personal outcomes. They conclude that employees seek both guidance and good feelings from their work settings. Guidance usually comes from role or task structuring; good feelings may stem from any type of recognition. Although these factors must be present, they do not necessarily have to come from a superior. Other sources may provide guidance and recognition as well. In these cases the need for formal leadership is diminished. The authors reference substitutes for leadership and highlight the point that a leader is merely a vehicle for providing these services. Indeed, some organizations have been experimenting with abandoning foremen and supervisor positions, leaving such traditional leadership positions in the hands of employees organized into special work teams. Such operating procedures are implicit testimony to the practical feasibility of having substitutes for formal leaders.

Although not all leadership positions have been abandoned in these organizations, there is evidence that the concept of leadership does not have to be vested in a formal position. Howell and Dorfman (1981) tested the validity of whether leader substitution can replace or "act in the place of" a specific leader (see Field Note 2). They examined whether having a closely knit cohesive work group and tasks that provide feedback concerning performance took the place of a formal leader. The authors found partial support for the substitution of leadership, giving some credence to the idea that leadership need not always reside in a person.

Pierce, Dunham, and Cummings (1984) provided further support for leader substitutes. They examined four environmental sources from which employees get structure and direction in how to perform their work: the job itself, technology, the work unit, and the leader. The authors found that only when the first three sources of structure were weak did the influence of the leader strongly affect employees. It seems that employees can derive typical leader qualities (that is, structure and direction) from inanimate sources in their environments and that leadership functions need not be associated with someone in authority. It is thus possible to envision a successfully operating leaderless group in which the job itself provides direction in what to do (initiating structure) and the work group members support and tend to one another (consideration). Taylor, Friedman, and Couture (1987) described a three-year experiment involving running an office without first-level supervisors, using 100 telephone operators, one manager, and a revolving committee of seven members. Compared with similar facilities, there were lower rates of absenteeism, fewer grievances, and fewer customer complaints. The experiment resulted in more employee involvement in decision mak-

FIELD NOTE 2

I once had an unintended firsthand exposure to what I/O psychologists refer to as "substitutes for leadership." I was on vacation and had the opportunity to tour a small company that made handcrafted shoes. The production area looked like something out of a fairy tale. The company employed about 20 cobblers. Cobblers make shoes on what is called a last. For example, lace shoes would be made on one last, loafers on another, boots on another, and so on. Each cobbler was hunched over his last, fashioning a pair of shoes from leather stock. The room was saturated with the rich aroma of leather. The youngest cobbler had been working there for 16 years, the oldest for more than 40 years. Their fingers were calloused and stained from continuously working with leather. They worked slowly but methodically, developing shoes from a pattern (customers would trace their feet on a piece of paper, which served as the pattern). There was no automated equipment, only hand tools. Every cobbler was an expert in making a certain style of shoe and generally stayed with making one style. There were some seasonal variations in orders; more boots were made in the winter and more casual shoes were made in the summer. Every cobbler was a craftsman in the truest sense of the word. The year was 1986, but it might as well have been 1886.

Although I visited the company as a tourist, the I/O psychologist in me began to creep out. I asked the person who showed me around, "To whom do these cobblers report?" I was told, "No one. We all used to report to the president and founder of the company, but he died eight years ago." I said, "Who tells these cobblers what to do?" He said, "No one. They know

what to do. That's why they work here." I said, "Who runs staff meetings?" He said, "No one. We don't have meetings. Hilda answers the phone and sends out the bills. I order the leather from our suppliers and keep the books. Everyone else makes shoes." I said, "How do you evaluate the work of these cobblers?" He said the finished pair of shoes provided an assessment of the cobbler's work. If the shoes didn't look right, they would be remade. He couldn't remember the last pair of shoes that were defective. If a customer says the shoes don't fit properly, the cobbler who made them reworks them until they do fit. I concluded my visit by asking two cobblers what they liked most about their jobs. What I had envisioned as an endless series of shoes, they saw differently. They said it felt gratifying to make something useful with their hands. Each pair they made was a measure of their work, and they took great pride in their work. They also said that no two pairs of shoes were ever the same. Since they were custom-made shoes, people differed in the size of their feet and their preference for color.

My experience at the shoe company reaffirmed that in some circumstances formal leadership is not necessary. That is, the functions that leadership provides, such as a sense of direction for one's work and providing support for doing it, can be derived from other sources. The cobblers didn't need direction in how to do their work, and the nature of the work they did provided feedback and support. Thus, as the research suggests, there can indeed be substitutes for leadership. The fact that some work groups can prosper without leaders gives us a clue to the conditions under which leadership is needed.

ing within the company, longer spans of control, more experimentation, and a sense that things can be done differently.

There is also evidence that some individuals are capable of directing themselves, a concept called "self-leadership." Manz (1986) found that some employees could lead themselves if their values and beliefs were congruent with those of the organization. In summary, the research on substitutes for leadership suggests that leadership can be thought of as a series of processes or functions for facilitating organizational and personal effectiveness. These processes or functions need not necessarily emanate from a person in a formal leadership role but may be derived from characteristics of the work being performed by the group members.

The concept of self-leadership is related to many of the issues discussed in Chapter 8 on organizations and work teams. The concept of organizational downsizing has resulted in broader spans of control and flatter organizational structures. As a consequence, there is less direct supervision of employees, as other control mechanisms must become operative to ensure that organizational goals are met. Small spans of control produce closer supervision but also add layers to the organization's structure. Reducing the middle management layer of organizations puts greater pressure on the other parts of the organization to accomplish what middle management once performed—namely, providing direction and control.

How might such direction and control be provided? One answer is through different organizing concepts such as self-managed work teams. The work team provides a sense of direction or structure to the group's efforts and provides feedback and support to the team members. As the literature on substitutes for leadership has revealed, while structure and support are necessary for organizational functioning, they need not emanate from a formal leadership position.

It should also be recognized that today's work force is more highly educated and trained than ever before. With education and training comes knowledge and skills that the employee can bring to the task, lessening the need for a supervisor to tell employees what to do and to monitor their performance. Employees who know what needs to be done and have the resources to do it do not need extensive supervision.

Finally, do not equate supervision with leadership. One dimension of leadership is oversight or supervisory responsibilities. However, leadership entails more than just monitoring and directing others. It embraces a sense of vision, an understanding of how the organizational unit can function and even prosper in its environment. Leadership is more inclusive than supervision. Self-directed work teams ameliorate the need for direct supervision, but they do not obviate the need for organizational leadership.

Points of Convergence among Approaches

Despite the profusion of leadership approaches and related empirical findings, Yukl (1994) notes that there is convergence in the findings from different lines of leadership research. Yukl identified three consistent themes in the findings from leadership research.

Importance of Influencing and Motivating.   Influence is the essence of leadership. Much of the activity of leaders involves attempts to influence the attitudes and behaviors of people, including subordinates, peers, and outsiders. Motivating behavior includes a variety of social influence techniques for developing commitment to organizational objectives and compliance with requests. Much of the influence behavior of charismatic leaders falls into the motivating category, including inspiring commitment to new objectives and strategies, modeling exemplary behavior for followers to imitate, and appealing to values and aspirations.

Situational factors determine the importance of leader efforts to motivate subordinates. Leader influence on subordinate motivation is much less important when the task is intrinsically appealing. Motivation is more important for a very difficult task that frustrates and discourages subordinates. For these types of tasks, the subordinate's performance will suffer unless the leader intervenes to arouse enthusiasm and confidence.

Some of the traits and skills predictive of leader effectiveness are relevant to the use of power. Leaders with a high need for power and high self-confidence make more influence attempts. Self-confidence, persuasive ability, relevant expertise, and political insight facilitate the effectiveness of influence attempts. Interpersonal skills are necessary to articulate an appealing vision and to persuade people of the need for change.

Importance of Maintaining Effective Relations.   Effective leaders establish cooperative relationships characterized by high levels of mutual trust and loyalty. Power research indicated the importance of referent power as a source of influence over the effect and commitment of subordinates. Referent power over subordinates is developed gradually over time as a result of dyadic social exchange processes in which the leader demonstrates trust and provides benefits to a subordinate while avoiding forms of influence that cause resentment. Behavior research found that subordinates are usually more satisfied with a leader who is friendly and helpful, shows trust and respect, and demonstrates concern for their needs and feelings. Situational research showed that the effects of leader behavior depend in part on the needs and values of subordinates. Supportive behavior is likely to have a stronger effect on subordinate satisfaction when the subordinate has a stressful, difficult task and lacks self-confidence.

Several of the traits and skills predictive of leadership effectiveness appear to be important for developing favorable relationships with subordinates, peers, and superiors. Relevant interpersonal skills include tact and diplomacy, listening skills, and social sensitivity. A leader with a positive regard for others is more likely to develop friendly relationships with people. Leaders who are preoccupied with personal ambition tend to do things that jeopardize relationships with people (for example, betraying a trust or reneging on a promise to increase their personal gain).

Importance of Decision Processes.   Much of the activity of leaders involves decision making, but leaders seldom make important decisions at a single point in time except for problem solving in response to immediate crises. In dealing with day-to-day decisions, effective leaders are guided by their long-term objectives and strategies.

People who effectively solve problems or develop successful strategies gain status and power. The reputation for expertise gained from successful decisions made in the past gives a person greater influence over subsequent decisions. Situational theories and research on group decision making outline the conditions under which participation is most likely to improve the quality of a leader's decisions. The potential benefits from group decisions are greater for complex, important decisions than for routine ones. Participation results in better decisions when the participants have relevant information and clear ideas lacked by the leader, when they are willing to cooperate in finding a good solution, and when there is ample time for the participative process to be carried out.

Several of the traits and skills predictive of leadership effectiveness are relevant for decision making. Leaders with extensive technical knowledge and cognitive skills are more likely to make high-quality decisions. These skills are important for analyzing problems, identifying causal patterns and trends, and forecasting likely outcomes of different strategies for attaining objectives. Self-confidence, tolerance for ambiguity, and stress tolerance help leaders cope with the responsibility for making major decisions on the basis of incomplete information.

Cross-Cultural Leadership Issues

Because of the growing number of organizations that conduct business on an international basis, we are now learning about cross-cultural issues in leadership. Much of our knowledge is derived from situations where international managers are assigned to positions in the United States. Graen and Wakabayashi (1994) studied companies that have manufacturing plants located both in the United States and in Japan, such as Toyota. These plants, which use Japanese organization methods and mostly American employees, require cross-cultural leadership to be successful. A *Japanese transplant* is a manufacturing plant owned by a Japanese parent company and located in a foreign country. Leadership presents special problems for Japanese transplants in the United States because of cultural differences between the two countries. Some of the problems found in Japanese transplants in the United States were identified by Graen and Wakabayashi:

1. *Language differences complicate communications and cooperation at managerial levels.* Very few domestic managers are able to interpret communications from the Japanese home office, and few Japanese managers can discuss abstract issues in English. Communication is therefore restricted to concrete issues without the benefit of any rationale or subtlety. The array of unresolved language problems keep managers from confronting underlying cultural issues.

2. *Japanese managers and workers are shocked by what they perceive as American managers' seemingly underdeveloped sense of obligation to their company and co-workers.* Japanese managers often believe that American managers place their personal interests above those of the company and their co-workers. For example, one

company launched a new product during deer hunting season and asked its hourly workers to postpone taking days off until the product launch was completed. The Japanese managers were pleased that absenteeism increased by only 5% for production workers but were aghast that absenteeism among American managers also increased by 5% during this period. The Japanese managers complained that the American managers should feel a stronger obligation to the company and lead the workers by setting a good example. This perceived underdeveloped sense of obligation makes it difficult for Japanese managers to trust or rely on domestic managers to perform critical tasks.

3. *American managers have difficulty with the absence of punishment for insubordination as an ideal.* According to Japanese management principles, workers should not necessarily be punished for resisting a legitimate request by their managers. Instead, their philosophy considers the possibility that it is the manager who may be at fault for making a request that is resisted. Without insubordination as a punishable offense, a manager must develop a sense of obligation and ownership in his or her workers through leadership development activities. Such activities build mutual obligations that render insubordination superfluous.

4. *American managers see a lack of office perks as a loss of status.* The absence of status symbols, such as private offices, reserved parking spaces, and management meeting rooms, reduces the gulf between hourly workers and management. In addition, some companies require all plant management personnel to work on the shop floor at least one day per month and get their hands dirty. Though domestic managers understand at a conceptual level that such equal treatment helps reduce the social distance between hourly workers and managers, they feel the loss of status associated by a lack of perks at an emotional level. Compared to their cohorts in domestic companies, they feel that their situation is inferior and that they are not treated as well.

5. *American managers do not commit their entire career to a single company.* One of the most serious challenges Japanese transplants face pertains to the issue of management mobility in the United States. Japanese transplants very carefully recruit and select domestic managers for home and staff functions. They hope that everyone hired will retire with the company. When domestic managers leave the transplant for another company, Japanese managers feel the loss doubly. First, they must repair their extensive networks by assuming the obligations of their departed peer and prepare for a new person to grow into the numerous company networks. This kind of adjustment is especially difficult for the Japanese leadership system because it is based on stable teams of committed managers. Second, many Japanese managers have difficulty accepting that a domestic manager can proclaim allegiance to a company and then leave within a year or two for another company—especially if it is a direct competitor.

Graen and Wakabayashi believe that American and Japanese managers face different fears when confronted with a culture clash. The Americans fear that adopting the Japanese system could subvert traditional American values of individualism. Alternatively, the Japanese fear that adopting the American management system could undermine traditional Japanese values of teamwork. The authors point out that functional solutions to this dilemma can be reached when both parties are willing to learn each other's culture and work together to create a hybrid culture.

Diversity Issues in Leadership

Hogan, Curphy, and Hogan (1994) questioned the role of leadership within organizations in the 21st century. They made the following observations. Historically, the typical American worker has been a white male with a high school education employed in a manufacturing job. Our knowledge of leadership largely focuses on how to lead that kind of person in those kinds of jobs in those kinds of organizations. Demographic trends suggest, however, that the national economy will shift from manufacturing to service jobs and that the work force will become older, more diverse, and more female (Offerman & Gowing, 1990). The labor market for skilled workers will tighten, and there will be increased competition for talented personnel. As noted in Chapter 8, as organizations shrink, fewer middle managers will be needed, and the responsibilities of first-line managers will expand.

We do not have extensive knowledge on the best way to manage female and minority employees in service organizations. Moreover, we will likely have the same percentages of women and minorities in management as are currently in the work force. Are there significant gender or cultural differences in leadership style, and will these styles be more or less effective for building teams in tomorrow's organizations? Eagly, Makhijani, and Klonsky (1992) provided some answers to these questions. They examined research on the evaluation of men and women who occupy leadership roles. While holding organizational characteristics constant and examining the gender of the leader, the research assessed whether people are biased against female leaders. Although the findings showed only a small overall tendency to evaluate female leaders less favorably than male leaders, this tendency was more pronounced under certain circumstances. Specifically, women in leadership positions were devalued relative to their male counterparts when leadership was carried out in stereotypically masculine styles, especially when this style was autocratic or directive. Also, the devaluation was greater when leaders occupied male-dominated roles and when the evaluators were women. In a meta-analysis of studies examining gender and effectiveness of leaders, Eagly, Karau, and Makhijani (1995) reported that the congruence of leadership roles with leaders' gender enhanced effectiveness. Men were more effective than women in roles that were defined in more masculine terms, and women were more effective than men in roles that were defined in less masculine terms.

Concluding Comments

While a number of approaches have been examined to better understand leadership, in all these approaches we can see that leadership is a vital process in directing work within organizations. There appear to be boundary conditions regarding when formal leadership is most effective, as well as processes leaders use to galvanize the members of their organizations. It is also insightful that current thinking about leadership considers leaders not only as heroes but also as hero makers. Thus leadership need not be a phenomenon vested exclusively in upper level positions; rather, it is a contagious process that can manifest itself throughout all levels of an organization. Perhaps future research will be directed toward understanding the contagion of leadership.

Chemers and Murphy (1995) note that one explanation for gender differences in leadership is cultural. This view holds that because of their roles as family caretakers, women are socialized to be sensitive, nurturing, and caring. When they carry that socialization over into organizational roles, women are likely to be warmer, more considerate, democratic leaders. An alternative explanation proposed that observed differences in leadership style between men and women are more a function of biases in the observation process than the result of true differences. If we are more likely to notice and remember behaviors consistent with our categorical stereotypes, our observation of male and female leaders may be biased in attention, selection, memory, or recall. Although minor differences may exist in leadership styles between men and women, our biases exaggerate the perception of these differences.

CASE STUDY   *Which Direction Should We Follow?*

Wayne LaPoe, president of Americom, studied his notes in preparation for the company's annual business planning and strategy meeting. It was at this meeting that most of the major goals for the next year would be set. As a diversified company in the communications field, there were several different directions the company could take. However, they basically boiled down to two possible avenues. One was to develop a wider range of products in anticipation of changing market needs. The other was to increase the sales and marketing of their existing products. Each direction had its own champion within the company, and the decision on which path the company should take would be decided at the meeting where two executive vice-presidents would state their cases.

Brandon McQuaid, vice-president of Sales and Marketing, was a dominant force within the company. McQuaid stood 6' 4", was perfectly trim, always appeared slightly tanned, and had an engaging smile and a resonant voice. He was impeccably dressed in the latest styles. He inspired tremendous loyalty among his staff. Always warm and gregarious, McQuaid was liked by everyone. It would be difficult not to like McQuaid, thought LaPoe. McQuaid had a knack for making everyone feel good about themselves, and he usually got a great deal of support for his ideas.

Ralph Pursell was vice-president of Research and Development. An engineer by training, Pursell was about as different from McQuaid as night from day. Pursell was 5' 7", at least 30 pounds overweight, and often appeared unkempt. No one ever accused Pursell of making a fashion statement. While his interpersonal skills were minimal, lurking behind his chubby face was the mind of a brilliant product designer. It was under his guidance for product development that Americom captured a huge share of the market in fiber optics. He was the most highly respected employee in the company. While some made snide remarks behind his back about his physical appearance, many employees realized that they owed their jobs to Pursell's genius.

LaPoe anticipated how the planning meeting would go. He had seen it unfold the same way in past years. Pursell would make a pitch for developing some new products using language that only he understood. The other executives in the room would simply take it on faith that Pursell knew what he was talking about. Then McQuaid would have his turn. Radiating confidence and optimism, would not take long for McQuaid to have just about everyone eating out of his hand. He would argue that the company hadn't begun to scratch the surface in marketing Pursell's current trendsetting products. After 15 minutes of this charm there would be a lot of smiling and head nodding in the room. When all was said and done, it was usually McQuaid's position that the management staff voted to adopt. Pursell would go back to his lab and wonder why the rest of the company didn't see things his way.

LaPoe questioned whether his management staff responded more to McQuaid's form than to Pursell's substance. He didn't want to alienate his staff by overturning their approval of McQuaid's position, yet LaPoe wondered how much longer Pursell would continue to live with losing battles to McQuaid. LaPoe felt somewhat trapped himself. He needed the loyalty and commitment inspired by McQuaid, yet it was Pursell's ideas that McQuaid sold. LaPoe concluded that if it were possible to combine Pursell's technical ability with McQuaid's interpersonal skills, Americom would probably have a new president.

Questions

1. Is the management staff blinded by McQuaid's engaging leadership style, or is charm a legitimate component of leadership?
2. Should all leaders have a fairly large amount of interpersonal skills, or is someone like Pursell entitled to a leadership position on the basis of technical expertise?
3. If you were LaPoe, would you recommend Pursell get some training in interpersonal skills and communication to enhance his credibility? Why or why not?
4. Why are so many people at Americom "taken" with McQuaid? What does this suggest about why we accept people as leaders?
5. Is there a difference between having influence and being a leader? In what ways are these concepts related and unrelated?

THE WORK ENVIRONMENT

Job Design and Organization Development: Creating High-Performance Organizations

CHAPTER

13

Major Chapter Objectives

- *Be able to explain the rationale of job design as reflected in job enlargement and job enrichment.*

- *Understand the logic and formulation of the job characteristics model.*

- *Know how to redesign jobs.*

- *Understand the rationale of organization development.*

- *Understand the concepts of the change agent, the client, and the intervention.*

- *Be able to discuss organizational culture change and total quality management (TQM).*

- *Be able to discuss values and ethics in organization development.*

Organizations constantly try to maximize the "fit" between worker and workplace. The better the fit, the more likely it is that the organization will be effective and smooth running. Thus far, our discussion of increasing the fit centered on the worker. Using the peg-and-hole analogy, I discussed finding new pegs that fit existing holes (personnel selection) or reshaping existing pegs for better fit (personnel training). However, the problem of fit can be approached by trying to change the shape of the hole. It is possible to change the workplace instead of, or in addition to, changing the worker. The overall purpose is to create a high-performing organization, manifesting itself in greater productivity, lower cost, increased satisfaction, less turnover, and so on. However, change is never easy, and in fact it is often unwelcomed. The status quo is comfortable, and organizations must overcome resistance to change. The major reason for change in contemporary organizations is to achieve a competitive advantage in their business operations. External pressures impinging on organizations are the driving force to initiate change.

In this chapter I will examine two approaches to changing the workplace. One approach, *job design,* focuses on changing a job. The other approach, *organization development,* has a larger scope and involves more than just a job. The two approaches are not unrelated; some consider job design as part of organization development. However, organization development usually involves reorganizing many components of the workplace; job design has a narrower scope.

To Alter the Worker or the Workplace?

The choice of whether to change the worker or the workplace is not easy. It is also not strictly an either/or choice; efforts to change the work environment may be made at the same time that workers are being changed. Usually, though, there is more emphasis on changing one or the other. There is no magic formula telling the I/O psychologist which side deserves more attention. This is a matter of professional judgment, best guided by the psychologist's experience with the organization.

The history of the organization's problems is usually the best place to begin. If a company has been successfully manufacturing a product or providing a service, it would be better to replace a few workers who do not perform well than to revamp the entire organization. If large parts of the work force have difficulty adjusting to work demands, personnel training may be the best method of raising skill levels to match organization needs. However, when problems seemingly reappear independent of who performs the work, thought must be given to altering the workplace. As a rule, it is more difficult to alter the workplace than the workers. Changing one part of an organization usually will have intended as well as unintended effects on the rest of the organization.

Because organizations are designed to have interchangeable human parts, their life spans exceed the working life spans of their employees. The complexities of personnel selection, placement, and training notwithstanding, the workplace is less alterable than the work force. Successful organizations learn to alter both as conditions demand. In this chapter, I will look at ways of changing the workplace, recognizing that the constant search for good "fit" warrants giving attention to both sides of the relationship.

Job Design

Historical Overview

Job design originated in the early 1900s. Frederick Taylor believed that efficiency could be improved by carefully designing work to increase productivity. Taylor (1911) advocated structuring jobs for simplification and standardization. Simplification meant breaking jobs into small tasks and then having each worker perform a small part of a total operation. A worker does the task repeatedly; the result is extreme specialization. For example, a job might be to connect two pieces of metal with a bolt. This is one part of an entire operation, and it might be repeated 100 times every hour. Other workers perform similar specialized tasks until the entire product is finally produced through the total efforts of all workers. The work process is also standardized; that is, the sequence of activities performed is the same.

Taylor's approach did improve productivity. Workers were able to produce more goods, the skill levels needed for these specialized tasks were lower, and less time was needed to train the workers. In the short run, this approach resulted in economic efficiency. In Taylor's time economic conditions were not good, jobs were relatively scarce, and people were grateful for whatever work they could get. However, this approach also produced problems. Workers rebelled at highly specialized, routine jobs. Monotony produced boredom, which, when coupled with lack of challenge and a sense of depersonalization, led to dissatisfaction. The behavioral consequences of work simplification and standardization are presented in Figure 13–1.

The dissatisfaction resulting from Taylor's approach showed itself in ways that detract from efficiency: lateness, absenteeism, turnover, stress, drug use, and sabotage. Over time, the problems were exacerbated by changing worker populations. At the turn of the century, workers were relatively uneducated and jobs

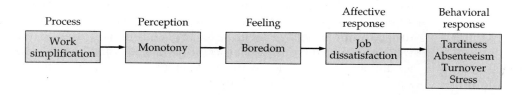

Figure 13–1 *Behavioral consequences of work simplification*

were scarce; thus, workers were not very critical of the jobs. As workers became more educated and more jobs became available, they were no longer content with jobs that provided little other than income. The economic gains of increased efficiency were offset by reactions to the simplified jobs. Indeed, Melamed, Ben-Avi, Luz, and Green (1995) have proposed that monotonous jobs produce a form of stress they believe relates to "underload"—a condition caused by an insufficient amount of stimulation on the job. Wong and Campion (1991), in turn, proposed that jobs should be designed to be in a mid-range of stimulation, being neither too low nor too high in the demands placed on workers. In general, research on job design describes attempts to make jobs "better" by making them inherently motivating and satisfying to perform.

Job Enlargement and Job Enrichment

In the 1940s and 1950s, organizations began to realize that the structure of jobs must be changed from specialization of work to greater satisfaction of employee needs. During this time, two "job change" strategies became popular: job enlargement and job enrichment. In theory the two are different; in practice they have a lot in common. Job enlargement means increasing the number and variety of tasks a worker performs. Job enrichment means increasing a worker's control over the planning and performance of a job and participation in setting organization policy. Job enlargement involves expanding the scope of a worker's job duties. An example might be a production worker's responsibility for assembling several parts of a piece of equipment as opposed to one part. Job enrichment involves giving the worker more autonomy and decision-making power over when and how work operations are performed. At the core of both programs was the belief that motivation would be better if workers had a greater sense of achievement in their work.

Many early studies examined the effects of job enlargement and enrichment on worker behavior and attitudes. These field studies compared on-site performance before and after job change. Several studies reported increases in either attitude or performance as a result of job design changes. However, the research was not of the best quality, because it rarely used control groups. A company would often introduce new technology along with changes in work operations. It was thus impossible to tell whether the changes in performance and attitude were due to changes in technology or to job design changes.

The incomplete research designs and the inability to determine causes for change led people to question the value of job enrichment and enlargement. Both strategies seemed to produce changes in worker response, but the reasons were unclear. Further, changes often lasted for only a limited time. As a result, attention was focused on the changes in specific parts of jobs and how these affected behavior and attitudes. More research was directed toward explaining why job design succeeded or failed. There were fewer large-scale job enlargement and job enrichment programs. Researchers began to identify the structure of jobs and how changing structure would lead to changes in performance.

FRANK AND ERNEST   SOURCE: Reprinted by permission of Newspaper Enterprise Association, Inc.

Task Attributes

As the name suggests, research on task attributes was meant to identify characteristics of the task components of jobs that influence worker behavior. In an early
study, Turner and Lawrence (1965) identified six task attributes that they thought
were related to satisfaction and attendance: variety, autonomy, required interaction, optional interaction, knowledge and skill required, and responsibility.
They conducted interviews and made field observations of these six attributes for
47 different jobs. Each attribute was scaled, yielding a score reflecting "how
much" of it was present in each job. Jobs that scored high on these variables were
positively correlated with high worker satisfaction and attendance. Yet a curious
finding also emerged: This relationship held only for workers from factories in
small towns and not for urban workers. Turner and Lawrence concluded that
worker reactions to task attributes were influenced by cultural factors. This gave
impetus to investigating what "types" of people respond most positively to redesigned jobs. The findings from such studies will be discussed shortly.

Following the Turner and Lawrence study, other researchers investigated how
certain task attributes influence performance. Hackman and Lawler (1971) identified four core dimensions of jobs: variety, autonomy, identity, and feedback. They
concluded that jobs high on these core dimensions, performed by individuals
desiring satisfaction of higher order needs (in the Maslow sense of achievement,
recognition, and so on), yielded the greatest satisfaction, motivation, attendance,
and performance.

It was apparent that motivation was influenced by job structure. Further, it
seemed possible to design jobs to increase motivation. In this sense job design
efforts can be viewed as attempts to increase motivation, as discussed in Chapter
11. Research studies produced evidence that jobs providing variety, autonomy,
identity, and feedback increased motivation among some employees. This manifested itself in greater organizational commitment and job involvement, as well as
in increased attendance and job satisfaction.

It also became apparent that not all people responded in the same way. Why
people differed in responses to jobs with comparable task attributes had to be
explained. Researchers focused on the role of human needs in determining the

"type" of job a person would want. It was thought that people trying to satisfy higher order needs would want more stimulating jobs. They would thus respond more positively to enriched jobs. Jobs providing high levels of certain task attributes seemingly satisfied such needs.

Several scales were developed to identify people who would want an enriched job and would respond positively to (be more motivated by) it. Hackman and Oldham (1975) developed one such scale, the Higher-Order Need Strength Questionnaire B. The relative strength of growth needs is reflected in the choice of jobs characterized by opportunities for decision making, need for a variety of skills and abilities, freedom and independence, and factors such as high pay, fringe benefits, job security, and friendly co-workers. Results of studies testing the effect of these needs suggest that people with strong higher order needs do derive more satisfaction from enriched jobs. However, not all research has been supportive. It appears that an individual's desire (need) to be challenged at work does affect reactions to an enriched job, but this alone does not account for all variance.

Job Characteristics Model

Clearly, there has been no one theoretical explanation of why and how task attributes affect workers. The way jobs influence motivation could partially be explained by several existing theories, including Maslow's need hierarchy and expectancy theory. To integrate and synthesize much of the literature on this topic, Hackman and Oldham (1976) proposed a model to explain how jobs influence attitudes and behavior. Called the job characteristics model, it is probably the most researched explanation of job enrichment.

According to Hackman and Oldham, any job can be described by five core dimensions:

Skill variety. The number of different activities, skills, and talents the job requires.

Task identity. The degree to which a job requires completion of a whole, identifiable piece of work—that is, doing a job from beginning to end, with visible results.

Task significance. The job's impact on the lives or work of other people, whether within or outside the organization.

Autonomy. The degree of freedom, independence, and discretion in scheduling work and determining procedures that the job provides.

Task feedback. The degree to which carrying out the activities required results in direct and clear information about the effectiveness of performance.

The second part of the model deals with the effect of the core job dimensions on the individual. Core job dimensions are said to influence three critical psychological states. The experienced meaningfulness of work is high when the job involves skill variety, task identity, and significance. The experienced responsibility for work outcomes is influenced mainly by the amount of autonomy. Knowledge of results of work activities is a function of feedback. According to the theory, high

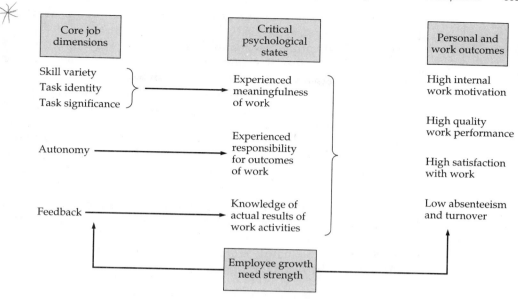

Figure 13-2   The job characteristics model

SOURCE: From "Motivation Through the Design of Work: Test of a Theory" by J. R. Hackman and G. R. Oldham, 1976, *Organizational Behavior and Human Performance, 16*, p. 256.

levels of the critical psychological states will lead to favorable personal and work outcomes. These include high internal motivation, work performance, satisfaction, and low absence and turnover.

The final part of the Hackman and Oldham model is an individual difference variable called growth need strength (GNS), which reflects a desire to fulfill higher order needs. As had others before them, Hackman and Oldham felt that people with high needs for personal growth and development should respond more positively to jobs high on the core dimensions. Only people with high GNS should strongly experience the critical psychological states associated with such jobs. The entire job characteristics model is portrayed in Figure 13–2.

Hackman and Oldham developed an equation for indexing the potential of a job to motivate its holder. The equation is based on the five core dimensions. Hackman and Oldham refer to their index as the motivating potential score (MPS) and define it as

$$\text{MPS} = \frac{\text{Skill Variety} + \text{Task Identity} + \text{Task Significance}}{3} \times \text{Autonomy} \times \text{Feedback}$$

The first three core dimensions are averaged because they all contribute to the experienced meaningfulness of work, the first critical psychological state. The other two dimensions, autonomy and feedback, reflect the remaining critical states and thus are not averaged.

The job's motivating potential will be very high when each component of the formula is high. Because the components are multiplied, low scores on any one will yield a low motivating potential score. A score of zero on any of the major components (for example, a job completely lacking in autonomy) reduces the MPS to zero; the job has no potential for motivating incumbents.

Finally, as shown in Figure 13–2, the entire effect of the job characteristics model is moderated by the strength of growth need. Only employees trying to satisfy higher order needs will respond favorably to a job high in motivating potential.

Empirical Tests of the Model.   A number of studies have tested the relationships and predictions of the model. Empirical support is mixed. Certain parts of the model are substantiated more than others.

Hackman and Oldham (1976) provided validation evidence for their own theory. In general, the results were moderately supportive:

1. The core job dimensions relate to the critical psychological states. Skill variety, task identity, and task significance combined to predict the level of perceived meaningfulness. The authors were thus able to identify those factors contributing to "meaningful work," a frequent desire of employees.
2. The three critical psychological states related to selected personal and work outcomes. In particular, high levels were associated with satisfaction and internal motivation.
3. Individual differences in GNS have a moderating effect. In particular, high GNS employees were more likely to have favorable personal and work outcomes after experiencing the critical psychological states.

However, not all findings were supportive:

1. The core dimensions of autonomy and feedback were not clearly related to the corresponding critical psychological states of experienced responsibility and knowledge of results. Some of the other dimensions predicted these states as well or better.
2. The critical psychological states were only weakly related to absence and performance.

In general, the results showed that jobs high on the core job dimensions were associated with high levels of personal and work outcomes. Individuals with high GNS responded most favorably to these types of jobs. The importance of the intervening critical psychological states was not strongly supported.

Based on a review of more than 200 studies that tested the model, Fried and Ferris (1987) arrived at the following three conclusions. Research suggests the existence of multiple job characteristics, but it is not clear how many there are. Second, the linkage between the job characteristics and the critical psychological states is not as strong as originally hypothesized. Third, the personal and work outcomes specified in the model are indeed related to the job characteristics.

Measurement of Job Design Variables

It is virtually impossible to get pure, objective measures of task characteristics. The variety and autonomy present in a job are usually best ascertained by asking incumbents. In the final analysis, what is important is how workers perceive their jobs, for it is on the basis of these perceptions that they develop feelings about their work. Therefore, many measurement issues involve the extent to which workers see common dimensions in their jobs.

When Hackman and Oldham (1976) proposed the job characteristics model, they also developed a questionnaire called the Job Diagnostic Survey (JDS). This assessed the variables in the model. Hackman and Oldham (1975) felt that the JDS would provide a reliable and valid assessment of core dimensions, critical psychological states, and strength of individual growth needs. Perhaps the most critical issue was the number and nature of core job dimensions, for it is these that supposedly are the basis for enriched and meaningful work. Hackman and Oldham had proposed five core job dimensions; other researchers tried to confirm their existence.

In testing the validity of the JDS, Dunham (1976) could find little difference in the measures of variety and autonomy. This suggests that the two dimensions are not as distinct as Hackman and Oldham proposed. Dunham also felt that all five dimensions could be subsumed in a single dimension reflecting *job complexity* without losing the meaning of enriched work; that is, it could be said that an enriched job is simply more complex than a routine job. The five core factors proposed by Hackman and Oldham did not appear every time. I/O psychologists seem to agree that certain key factors define enriched work, but they do not seem to concur on what or how many factors there are.

There has also been research on other instruments useful in job design (for example, Sims, Szilagyi, & Keller, 1976). But exactly what factors we should measure in designing jobs is also debatable. Sims and associates identified six core job factors, using an instrument they called the Job Characteristics Inventory. As did Hackman and Oldham, they identified variety, autonomy, feedback, and task identity as four core job factors. However, they also identified two factors unique to their study: dealing with others and friendship. Kulik, Oldham, and Langner (1988) modified some of the items in the JDS to produce scales that more closely conformed to the five-factor structure. However, the revised JDS did not improve the prediction of satisfaction, motivation, or productivity. Taber and Taylor (1990) reached this general conclusion: "The JDS has facilitated the development of a large and fruitful body of research into the meaning of work. There will continue to be an important function served by instruments such as the JDS that assess subjective perceptions of job characteristics, but research may have progressed as far as it can go using exclusively subjective measures" (p. 495). The authors recommend additional measures of job characteristics that are assessed more objectively, reliably, and specifically. A related conclusion was reached by Spector and Jex (1991). Indeed, Spector (1992) asserts that perceptual measures of job characteristics are affected by attitudes, moods, cognitive processes, and dispositions.

In summary, attempts to determine the important variables in job design have been only moderately successful. In a general way we know the types of variables

FIELD NOTE 1

The process of job enrichment produces an interesting paradox from the standpoint of monetary compensation. Let us say we have a boring, distasteful job that pays $7 per hour. We decide to enrich the job, making it more inherently pleasurable and satisfying to perform. The changed job now involves greater skill variety and decision-making responsibility. The question now becomes, in which direction should we alter the wage paid to this job after the enrichment? The more common answer would be to increase the wage, perhaps to $8 per hour, because the job now requires more talent and responsibility. However, it can also be argued that the wage should be decreased, perhaps to $6 per hour. Here is why.

There are two major forms of compensation or reward: extrinsic (financial) and intrinsic (nonfinancial) rewards. Because the job initially provided very little intrinsic reward, the employer had to offer a substantial wage. However, after enrichment the job became more intrinsically rewarding. Thus, to keep the overall level of compensation (extrinsic and intrinsic) constant, the extrinsic compensation should be lowered. The extreme case of this logic would be a job that is so intrinsically gratifying that we will perform it for free (that is, no extrinsic compensation at all).

How do you feel about this paradox? Do enriched jobs provide a certain level of their own (intrinsic) reward such that increases in financial compensation are not necessary? Or do we "double dip"—that is, pay higher wages for jobs that are also more satisfying to perform?

critical to enriched work. Precisely what these variables are differs for different types of jobs. So long as measurement problems persist, it will be difficult to develop a single verifiable model as the foundation for job design. Our limited ability to generalize across different jobs necessitates a more situation-specific approach. This will not preclude "reshaping holes," but it will certainly not make our job any easier (see Field Note 1).

How to Redesign Jobs

Given some understanding of what constitutes an enriched job, the next step is to actually change a job to make work more stimulating. The process of job redesign is by no means simple or routine; many factors must be considered. Aldag and Brief (1979) recommend the following procedures for redesigning a job:

1. The need to redesign the job should be assessed. Presumably there is a reason to alter a job, like unsatisfactory turnover, absence, performance, or accident levels. If such a need exists, the redesigned job should meet the following criteria:

    a. It should be simple, demanding a low skill level and short-cycle completion sequences. Such a job is often seen as monotonous.

    b. Altering production methods and procedures should be economically feasible. If redesign entails huge new capital investments (for example, in equipment and facilities), the expected gains in performance might not offset the costs of technology.

    c. Jobholders should accept and be ready for job redesign. This means seeing increased variety, autonomy, and so on, as desirable. The incumbents must also have (or be capable of learning) the aptitudes and skills needed to perform the redesigned work.

2. If a job meets these criteria, a committee or task force should be formed to investigate the prospects further. The task force should include management, labor, and outsiders as needed. Those holding the job in question are ideal candidates. The task force's main responsibility is to intently study the job in question, particularly the tasks to be performed. The best source of information is a structured job analysis, which may already have been done for another reason, such as for personnel selection, performance appraisal, or training. The task force should identify exactly which activities will directly contribute to perceptions of task attributes like autonomy, variety, and feedback. Since the job was chosen because it was seen as monotonous, efforts should be made to understand what it is about it that produces lack of autonomy, task identity, feedback, and so on. The task force should focus on the link between the activities performed and the holders' reactions to the job along core task dimensions.

3. The task force should then plan some possible redesign aimed at improving the job in terms of task attributes; that is, changes in work performance that can increase feelings of autonomy, variety, feedback, and task identity. Perhaps different changes would contribute to each task attribute. The goal of this phase is to come up with new procedures that will allow workers to get their jobs done and also result in stronger perceptions of the task attributes. The changes may involve expanding the scope of job duties, new sequences of work procedures, or developing a new production system.

4. The task force should choose the criteria used to judge whether redesign has succeeded. Many factors can be included: employee attitudes; objective individual indexes like absence, turnover, and performance; and organization indexes like cost efficiency. These factors will be the "score card" for the redesign program. Changes should then be made and employee performance closely monitored. If the efforts were successful, thought might be given to expanding the program to other jobs.

The entire job redesign strategy is presented in Figure 13–3.

    Job redesign takes a fairly long time to plan, execute, and monitor—months or years rather than days or weeks. Rigid standards for evaluating the program are also necessary. An organization must be sure that job redesign is truly "worth it" before undertaking major changes. If the changes are attributable only to a Hawthorne effect, the organization would be wise to tread softly; that is, it should be sure that the changes are not due simply to the novelty of new ways of working. Intelligent decisions can be made only by using good information; this in turn necessitates using appropriate evaluation procedures.

    Finally, it is not uncommon for changes in one area to have repercussions throughout the whole organization. Job redesign should not be done in a vacuum. Shortly, I will examine how job redesign can have "ripple effects."

    Huse and Cummings (1985) describe an example of a job redesign and its outcome. A company manufactured laboratory hot plates, which are used in sci-

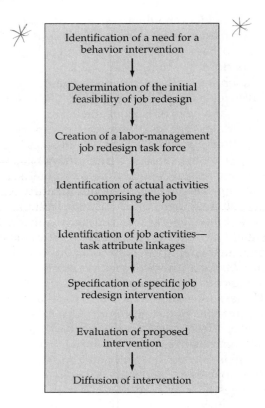

Figure 13–3 *Strategy for redesigning jobs*
SOURCE: From *Task Design and Employee Motivation* by R. J. Aldag and A. P. Brief, 1979, Glenview, IL: Scott, Foresman. Copyright ©
1979, Scott, Foresman and Company. Reprinted by permission.

entific research. The task of assembling the hot plates was highly fractionated;
individual employees would repeatedly add one component to each unit as it
passed before them in a continuous assembly line. This method of production was
highly routinized, according to the concepts of work simplification and standardization. However, the company was dissatisfied with the level of productivity, the
number of defective products, and the degree of absenteeism.

As a means of enhancing efficiency, the company took steps to redesign the
job by forming new and larger modules of work. All of the previously separate
tasks were combined so that each operator could completely assemble, inspect,
and ship a hot plate. The operators would then attach their personal name tags to
the hot plate. The redesigned job resulted in an 84% improvement in productivity,
controllable rejects dropped from 23% to fewer than 1%, and absenteeism
dropped from 8% to less than 1%.

A sophisticated analysis indicated that the changes were due to the intervention. In accordance with the tenets of the job characteristics model, the process of
combining tasks increased the variety of skills used on the job. Allowing the em-

ployees to attach their name tags and personally ship the finished product increased task identity. Self-inspection of the product added greater task significance, autonomy, and feedback from the job itself. While not all job redesign efforts are as successful as this one was, major gains in organizational efficiency can be attained through job redesign.

Effectiveness of Job Redesign Programs

Does job redesign "work"? Does it produce the intended positive outcomes? The number of studies conducted on job enrichment has increased in recent years, and we are now in a position to examine their cumulative findings. The major outcome of redesigned work appears to be an increase in job satisfaction. Loher, Noe, Moeller, and Fitzgerald (1985) reported average correlations between scores on the five core job dimensions of the job characteristics model and reported job satisfaction of around .40. In other words, it seemed that the more jobs are enriched (defined as higher scores on the core job characteristics), the more satisfied the people are who perform them. The research relating job characteristics to changes in job performance has produced mixed findings. Locke, Feren, McCaleb, Shaw, and Denny (1980) estimated that across all jobs there is a 17% improvement in productive output after enrichment. However, Griffin, Welsh, and Moorhead (1981) report less supportive findings. Griffin and associates feel that poorly designed measures of job performance contribute to the ineffectiveness of some job enrichment programs.

What can we conclude about the effectiveness of job redesign? Probably the safest conclusion is that results vary depending on the criterion, and we cannot simply assume that such programs will have a common outcome. Most studies report mixed findings (improvements in some areas but not in others), but total failures have also been cited. Job redesign is complex; it is difficult to generalize findings across diverse situations. Differences can exist not only in redesign techniques but also in employees (age, experience, education, skill level) and workplace (jobs, organizations, union status). In trying to improve the worker/workplace fit by changing the workplace, we should exercise the same caution and concern used in evaluating workers. Just as we know that a given test is not valid for hiring many different kinds of workers, we should also realize that a given job redesign technique will not necessarily work for different jobs. Unfortunately, there are no universal procedures for selecting or modifying pegs or for reshaping holes.

Organizational Implications of Job Redesign

Organizations are complex systems composed of interdependent parts. If you alter one part of an organization, changes (often unanticipated) in other parts will likely ensue. As a simple example, suppose job redesign were successful in increasing the output of a production department. The organization would have to accommodate the growing supply of manufactured goods, which would create a warehousing and space problem. It would likely be pressured to increase the sale of these goods as the stockpile increased. If the sales department were successful, the responsibility of the accounting and bookkeeping departments would be increased. Thus, changes in production would have implications for the rest of the organization; such ripple effects are not at all uncommon. Organizations often do not understand the consequences of making changes in selected areas.

Furthermore, there are multiple theoretical perspectives to job design that have the potential for grossly differing organizational implications. As reported by Campion and Thayer (1985), jobs can be designed to increase psychological stimulation (that is, make them more challenging to perform) or to decrease the likelihood of accidents and errors (that is, make them simpler to perform). (This study is discussed more fully in Field Note 2.) Each approach to job design influences different outcomes, and each approach has costs as well as benefits. Trade-offs are inevitable. Campion (1988) states that a comprehensive theory of job design must be interdisciplinary in nature. Psychological approaches strive to produce jobs that are stimulating and mentally demanding, but they may have the unintended consequences of

FIELD NOTE 2

The study by Campion and Thayer (1985) reveals a contradiction between two fundamental approaches to work design, both of which have a strong psychological heritage. The first approach is called the human-factors paradigm (and is presented in greater detail in Chapter 15). This approach emphasizes the design of work in terms of increasing efficiency. It typically involves designing tasks to avoid complicated movements, intensive decisions, and other factors that often lead to errors. In general, the human-factors paradigm strives to maintain functional simplicity, forthrightness, and directness in the design of task duties. The more complicated the system, the more things that can go wrong; thus, designers strive to keep things simple and straightforward. This philosophy tends to produce tasks that are easy to perform (with the ultimate goal of being "goof-proof") or that are at least as uncomplicated as possible.

The second approach is the job enrichment paradigm; it, too, seeks to enhance efficiency. However, its tack is very different from the human-factors approach. The job enrichment paradigm seeks to provide a sense of challenge and stimulation. It is precisely because many jobs have been designed with simplicity in mind that they are perceived as boring and monoto-

nous. Thus, using a job enrichment rationale, tasks are designed to provide some diversity of human response and, in the process, literally increase the variability in operator behavior—the very thing that the human-factors paradigm seeks to minimize.

As Campion and Thayer discovered, these two approaches make almost polar-opposite recommendations for task design. Is there a middle ground resolution to these conflicting views? Not directly. In the extreme, both approaches are dysfunctional. If every work task were designed to be so simple that it required no human thought or discretion, we would have created a very sterile and unappealing environment. On the other hand, when I get behind the wheel of my car, I am grateful that human-factors psychologists have designed the steering mechanism such that when I want the car to turn left, I simply turn the wheel to the left. I would not want the steering mechanism "enriched" to the point where it would take simultaneous foot, knee, hand, and arm movements to get the car to turn left. In short, each approach has its place in work design, but there are occasions and situations in which it is not clear which paradigm should prevail.

increasing training times and creating staffing difficulties. The mechanistic approach errs in the other direction, because jobs may be designed inadequately in terms of satisfaction and potential growth. Campion and McClelland (1991) experimentally redesigned jobs to examine the consequences. The enlarged jobs were better from a motivational perspective but worse from a mechanistic (engineering) perspective. The redesigned jobs had the benefits of providing more job satisfaction, less boredom, and greater chances of catching errors but also had the costs of higher training requirements, higher basic skills, and higher compensable factors. Clegg and Wall (1990) found that relatively poor mental health was associated with workers performing jobs that had been simplified, but only for those who saw their work as not using their skills. Campion and Berger (1990) reported that jobs characterized by higher scores on the core job dimensions were also associated with higher aptitude levels and higher pay. When an organization wants to make jobs more challenging, they should realize that they will need people with more talent and ability to perform them. Furthermore, increased employee talent will also demand more pay; more talented people are worth more. Schneider, Reichers, and Mitchell (1982) and Campion (1989) confirmed that elevating the core characteristics of jobs also increased the aptitudes of individuals needed to perform the jobs successfully. Schneider and associates feel that some job enrichment programs may fail because they increase the aptitude requirements beyond the levels incumbents possess. However, Campion and McClelland (1993) concluded that the trade-off between higher aptitude and higher wage levels need not be direct. They proposed a distinction between task enlargement and knowledge enlargement. Knowledge enlargement referred to adding requirements to the job for understanding procedures or rules relating to different products sold by the organization. Knowledge enhancement was found to increase employee motivation and satisfaction, but without the direct effect of escalating wage rates as found with task enlargement. Campion and McClelland were optimistic that jobs could be designed to enhance motivation and satisfaction but suggested that the effects of such efforts may take several years to manifest themselves.

Organization Development

In the first part of this chapter, I discussed job design—changing jobs to make them more motivating and meaningful for the worker. Job design is one way to improve organization effectiveness, but it is by no means the only way. Sometimes the problems facing organizations require solutions beyond making a job the unit of change. The topic of organization development, often referred to as simply OD, concerns the ways in which organizations can grow, change, and develop to function more effectively. In this part of the chapter, I will examine OD.

What Is Organization Development?

Definitions of OD tend to be rather long and cumbersome. This is because OD is a multifaceted concept that defies a simple yet accurate definition. One useful definition by Huse and Cummings (1985) defines OD as "a system-wide application of behavioral science knowledge to the planned development and reinforcement of organizational strategies, structures, and processes for improving an organization's effectiveness" (p. 2). Porras and Robertson (1992) indicate that most definitions of OD embody several themes. The *purpose* of OD is improvement in the organization's effectiveness, its ability to adapt, its self-renewing processes, and its development of new and creative organizational solutions. Its *scope* is overall organizational or systemwide change. Its *conceptual* underpinnings derive from behavioral science theory, research, and technology. Its *process* is planned, value-based, consultant-aided, and directed or supported by top management. Finally, its *targets* are the organization's culture, structure, strategy, and processes. As the foregoing suggests, OD is broadly based and ultimately designed to facilitate the organization's well-being.

The Need for OD

To understand why OD was invented requires some understanding of the social times and conditions through which it has evolved. The evolution of OD has been chronicled by Mirvis (1990). In the 1950s theories of management and organization evolved out of a cold, sterile, and solely quantitative perspective to include consideration of social, human factors. OD was born as an attempt to better understand the process of group dynamics. The preferred means of understanding group dynamics was through behavioral science training, also called the T-group ("T" for training). Individuals unknown to each other would come together with no set agenda, no clear leadership, and no established mode of operation. Their function was to learn about themselves and the dynamics of social interaction in an unstructured medium by creating their own rules and roles. The logic behind the T-group was that if people could learn to understand themselves and how groups operated, this knowledge could be applied to work organizations to enhance their effectiveness. However, it eventually became apparent that the capacity to enhance self-learning and affect change in a small group would not necessarily generalize to larger, more complex social systems such as those found in most organizations.

Although OD sought to humanize work at the group level, it was largely unsuccessful in doing so. It took a major series of social and economic changes to reroute the direction of OD. Such changes began to take place in the 1980s, as evidenced by massive organizational restructuring and downsizing. As discussed in Chapter 8, the primary result of economic pressures caused by foreign competition was that millions of jobs were eliminated. Organizations sought to staff themselves with fewer employees as a means of controlling costs. However, there is a psychological cost to treating employees as if they are highly disposable—the employees feel little in the way of loyalty and commitment to the organization. In its place develop feelings of self-interest and cynicism about trust in the workplace. Levinson (1994), in fact, describes the failure of American corporations to adapt to changed economic circumstances as a social catastrophe. In the final analysis no organization can prosper in the long run without a committed work force. It therefore fell to OD to reestablish the relationship between employees and organizations that culminates in sustained growth and development. Today OD is guided by attention to what some individuals regard as the "softer" sides of organizations—values, vision, culture, and integrity. Thus, OD finds itself directed to the process of organizational transformation, transforming organizations into being attendant to both financial criteria of success and the social dynamics required to sustain such success. Not surprisingly, there is a strong connection between OD and the concept of transformational leadership, as discussed in Chapter 12.

The driving mechanism behind OD is the manifestation of organizational *excellence* in its many forms. Organizations seek to attain excellence in the products they make, the services they provide, the customers they satisfy, and the individuals they employ. The concept of excellence is the unifying theme for integrating the facets of running an organization. I will examine the concept of organizational excellence and OD practices used to pursue it later in the chapter.

Three Basic Concepts

Three concepts are invariably evident in all OD literature. Each has been the subject of extensive investigation and is an integral part of any OD effort. Collectively, they are the ingredients of all OD programs.

The Change Agent.   The change agent (sometimes referred to as the interventionist) is the person who initiates the change. This is usually someone outside the organization (for example, a hired consultant), but occasionally it may be a person within it. The agent is usually involved in diagnosing and classifying problems, identifying courses of action, recommending change procedures, and in some cases actually implementing the changes.

Effective change agents should possess the following qualities: diagnostic ability, basic knowledge of behavioral science, empathy, knowledge of the theories and methods of their own disciplines, goal-setting ability, and problem-solving skills. Agents must strive to build trust among organization members; they must be seen as being sincerely concerned with improving the organization's well-being. Without this trust, organization members will resist attempts at change.

Also, the agent must intervene only to the extent required to effect enduring solutions to the problem at hand. If the agent's role is to help the organization diagnose problems and plan strategies for improvement, he or she should not impose predetermined "solutions" with supposed "guaranteed" results. The change agent should never try to exceed the limits of his or her role; these should be mutually agreed on at the start of the program.

The Client.   The client is the recipient of the change effort. This may be an individual, a group, or possibly the entire organization. You might not think it would be a problem, but sometimes it is not exactly clear who the client is. For example, an organization may at first hire a consultant to diagnose why an important manager suffers from excessive role overload. The agreement may also include the consultant's offering strategies for alleviating the problem. In diagnosing the problem, the consultant discovers that the manager has assumed increasing responsibility because his or her subordinates are seen as incompetent. Rather than overseeing a poor job, the manager gradually assumes responsibility for doing it. At this point, there are three parties (besides the consultant) involved: the manager, the subordinates, and the organization employing these people.

To help people, an agent must interact with and influence them. If the agent's authority does not extend to interacting with subordinates, the real problem probably will not be resolved. Perhaps the true issue in the situation described is incompetent subordinates, but it could also be a manager who has distorted views of the quality of subordinates' work. Perhaps the manager is not good at delegating, irrespective of subordinates' merits. In this case, how can the consultant help the client, and who in fact is the client? In practice, there may be more than one client. The manager may be the key client, but there may be various ancillary clients, all part of the total organization. In some cases helping one client may conflict with enhancing the well-being of another. The agent must decide how the organization can best be helped, realizing that this is not always an easy decision.

The Intervention.   Intervention is what the change agent does on behalf of the client. The change agent can engage in a broad range of activities. The major intervention types include:

- Diagnostic activities: fact-finding to ascertain the state of the system, the status of a problem, the "way things are."
- Intergroup activities: to improve the effectiveness of interdependent groups.
- Education and training activities: to improve skills, abilities, and knowledge.
- Coaching and counseling activities: to help people define learning goals, learn how others see their behavior, and learn new behavior to see whether it improves goal attainment.
- Life- and career-planning activities: to enable individuals to focus on life and career objectives and how they might achieve them.

Each of these interventions includes many activities and exercises. They all use conceptual material and actual experience with the phenomenon being studied. Some are directed toward specific targets, problems, or processes. For example, intergroup activities are directed toward work teams; life-planning activities, toward individuals. In general, interventions are structured activities in which selected units (target groups or individuals) engage in a series of tasks directed toward organization improvement.

A Model of Planned Organizational Change

As Porras and Robertson (1992) noted, to change an organization you must understand at least three basic sets of variables. The first are the variables that can be manipulated or changed by the OD intervention. The second are the outcomes

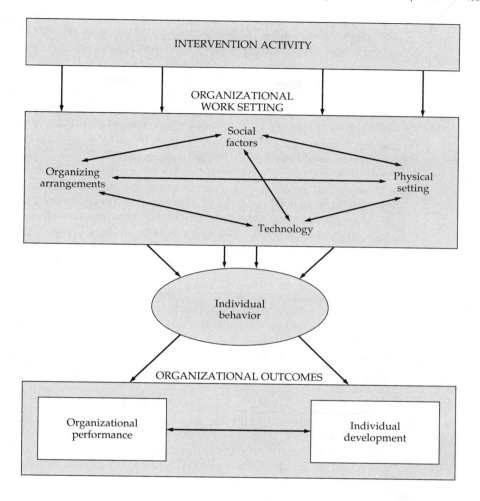

Figure 13–4   *A conceptual model of the dynamics of planned organizational change*
SOURCE: From "Dynamics of Planned Organizational Change: Assessing Empirical Support for a Theoretical Model" by P. J. Robertson, D. R. Roberts, and J. I. Porras, 1993, *Academy of Management Journal, 36,* p. 621.

intended by the change effort. Third are the variables that influence the degree to which the manipulated variables can alter the outcome variables.

Robertson, Roberts, and Porras (1993) have proposed a model to explain how organizations can be changed through OD intervention, and it is shown in Figure 13–4. Let's examine the components of this model in more detail.

Organizational Work Setting.   The work setting consists of four sets of characteristics. The first are *organizing arrangements,* which consist of the structure, strategies, administrative systems, and reward systems of the organization. The second are *social factors,* which include the organization's culture and management style. Third is the *physical setting*, which includes the space configuration of the organization, interior design, and physical ambiance. *Technology* is the fourth component and includes equipment, machinery, and work-flow design. These four broad categories of organizational characteristics make up the internal work setting of the organization. The four categories affect each other such that the design of one influences the functioning of the others. Accordingly, a change in one factor will usually result in changes in the others. The interaction of the four categories affects the behavior of organizational members. If the different characteristics are congruent, they will complement each other. If they are not aligned well, they will likely result in ineffectiveness.

Individual Behavior.   The members of the organization are influenced by the work setting as it relates to their individual behavior. Changes in the work characteristics that produce seemingly incompatible demands (for example, to perform very high quality work very rapidly) will produce stress, which in turn leads to lower job performance, illness, or withdrawal from work. The first major outcome of OD is increased organizational performance.

Organizational Performance.   According to Porras and Robertson (1992), if individual members work hard, take responsibility and initiative, learn their jobs well, and commit themselves to their jobs, then the likelihood that the organization as a whole will perform well is enhanced. A key goal of any change process must be to create work settings that will promote and facilitate adoption of these behaviors.

Individual Development.   The second major outcome of OD is enhanced individual development. The nature of the organization in which a person works encourages some types of behavior and inhibits others, which in turn have an important influence on the person's psychological health and personal development. While much of the focus has been primarily on organizations that have a negative impact on their members, organizations can also be designed to provide positive experiences for their members.

The final relationship indicated in Figure 13–4 is the mutual effect between organizational performance and personal development. These two outcomes affect each other, and over the long run one cannot improve without the other. The interdependence of the two is reflected in an observation by Mirvis (1988): "In OD of the 1960s, it was assumed that by developing people we could create healthier and more effective organizations. Today many advocate that we must develop organizations to create healthier and more effective people" (pp. 17–18).

The process of intervening into organizational systems, creating changes in organizational components that will in turn result in changes in the work behaviors of organizational members, constitutes the primary activity of OD (Porras & Robertson, 1992). However, individual behavioral change is not the singular goal of OD. Change in individual behavior is necessary to affect change in organizational outcomes. To maintain high levels of one outcome without correspondingly high levels of the other is not possible. In a test of the model shown in Figure 13–4,

Robertson et al. (1993) conducted a meta-analysis of planned change interventions. The results supported the overall validity of the model. Interventions were found to generate positive change in the work setting variables, and there was a positive relationship between individual behavior change and organizational outcome change. Mixed support was found for changes in work settings influencing individual behavior changes. Robertson et al. believe that their model provides useful insights into understanding which variables can be manipulated, the types of outcomes that result from OD interventions, and those variables that influence the linkage between organizational change and outcome attainment.

Typology of OD Interventions

Change agents deal with different kinds of clients (individuals, groups, total organizations), fill different roles, and direct their efforts to different problems. Consequently, researchers have tried to integrate the various OD interventions into a typology to promote better understanding of the relationships among them. In OD, typologies have classified interventions on such factors as role of the change agent, type of client, types of problems addressed, kinds of interventions, and so on. A typology of OD interventions is shown in Figure 13–5.

A cube is created from the three dimensions of OD interventions. The first dimension is the recipient of the change effort: the client. Basically, agents try to

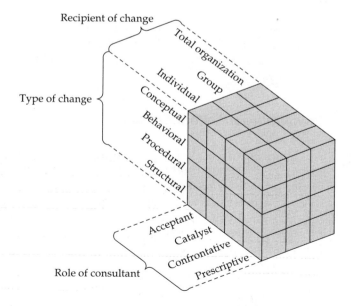

Figure 13–5   *Typology of organization development interventions*

change either selected individuals, groups of workers, or entire organizations. The second dimension is the level or nature of change. This can be conceptual (new information or knowledge), behavioral (new skill), procedural (new policy or practice), or structural (including organization reporting relationships). The third dimension includes four roles of the change agent. In an acceptant role the consultant offers passive support, permitting clients to explore problems and feelings in the presence of an accepting outsider. In a catalyst role the consultant stimulates self-examination by providing feedback on the client's problems; in general, the agent functions as a catalyst for change. In the confrontive role the consultant challenges client attitudes or procedures by asking probing questions, presenting discrepant data, and proposing alternatives that will motivate clients. Finally, in the prescriptive role, the consultant serves as an expert, controls the situation, and prescribes what should be done.

As researchers have commented, a change agent's intervention will not fit neatly into one of the boxes in the cube. In an intervention the key client may be an individual, but that person's relationship to a subgroup may also become an issue. Finally, during the intervention a consultant may support, stimulate, challenge, or direct the client, depending on the problem and the stage of intervention. Nevertheless, a typology is often helpful in ordering the dimensions of a concept. You may find that Figure 13–5 serves such a purpose, recognizing that it is only an approximation and not a mirror of reality.

Major OD Interventions

There are many intervention strategies for a consultant to draw on. It is beyond the scope of this discussion to describe all or even most of them. However, I have chosen two OD interventions that are representative of major types of initiatives in this field.

Organizational Culture Change

As discussed in Chapter 8, the culture of an organization embodies its values, beliefs, and attitudes and is the driving force behind its behavior. When the behavior or conduct of the organization no longer serves to attain its larger objectives, it becomes necessary for the organization to behave differently. A change in organizational behavior usually necessitates a change in the organization's culture. It is often difficult to bring about a change in organizational culture, because it necessitates altering underlying values and beliefs that have long guided the organization (see Field Note 3). Although change is difficult to effect, several authors (for example, Appelbaum & Batt, 1993; Kotter & Heskett, 1992) have identified the critical features of the change process.

1. *A strong leader.* Perhaps the most important feature is the need for a strong

leader to initiate and sustain the cultural change. The leaders must recognize that the environment and organizational members will exert significant energy to maintain the status quo. However, it is critical that the leader does not waver from the plan for change. A vital component of the leader's role is to influence others in examining prevailing assumptions and values. New approaches or perspectives often threaten or worry organizational members. Nevertheless, the leaders must persevere in their endeavor with missionary zeal. It is often the case that the culture change is initiated with one strong leader at the helm, but other influential leaders emerge in the process.

    2. *A clear vision of what needs to be done*. It is also critical that there be a sense of vision or direction as to where the organization is headed. It is not enough to have intense energy provided by a leader to initiate the culture change. What must also be present is a shared belief in what the new culture will be like. The vision may arise from the values of the leader, or it may emerge out of a crisis that must be

---

FIELD NOTE 3

I once heard a presentation by a chief executive officer (CEO) describing what it was like to change a major corporation. The company was a long-time leader in the aerospace industry. It had a lengthy history of profitable years and high organizational prestige. The company then began to lose money because of foreign competition and other external pressures. Two previous CEOs tried and failed to change the culture of the company. Both had been long-time leaders of the company who were successively promoted into the CEO position. Both CEOs failed to change the organizational culture because in part they *were* the culture. Each person had been very influential within the company, and to change the organizational culture entailed "undoing" much of what they had already done.

The company's third attempt at a change in leadership entailed bringing in an outsider to the company, someone who was not steeped in its traditions and values. He encountered massive resistance on many fronts and hired two I/O psychologists to facilitate the change process. He successfully persuaded a few top executives to embrace his vision of the company, and the change process began—albeit slowly. The new CEO stated that the company was profitable not because of its actions but in spite of them. The company had relied on its esteemed industry reputation to get away with actions (such as not vigorously developing new products) that served to hurt it in the long run. When foreign competition increased in intensity, the "long run" became the "short run." There was still substantial resistance to the new vision, as some people claimed the company had endured downturns before. On those occasions the company weathered the storms and eventually returned to economic prosperity. In short, some employees viewed the current crisis as a temporary problem that would work itself out. It didn't. Shortly thereafter a major unit of the company was sold off, affecting the lives of several hundred employees. Many were laid off by their new employer. This action got the attention of the remaining employees of the company, and the change process began in earnest. The company as a whole came to realize that the need for change wasn't just talk. Many changes began to occur in the way work was performed, particularly with regard to new product development and cost reductions. The company also began to change its self-image, going from one of self-assured smugness to being aware of its own vulnerability. The new CEO felt that other changes would be in the offing but believed that the company was more receptive to continued change after having overcome its inertia to change at all.

handled to save the business. The *process* of cultural change is more important than the *product*. Because change is continuously needed by organizations to adapt to their environments, the organization must develop some fluency in learning how to change. While moving from X to Y may be the initial object of attention, eventually the organization will also have to move from Y to Z.

The vision process entails not only charting the destination but also generating commitment from all organizational members to be players in the change process. The enrollment of all employees to actively cultivate change is often accelerated by a clear understanding of what will occur if change does not take place. It is not the case that leaders will "punish" employees who fail to participate but rather that the organization as a whole will suffer (most notably through the loss of jobs or the demise of the organization).

3. *New work procedures are developed.* It is necessary for the organization to develop new work procedures that buttress the new cultural values being espoused. If the organization does not "do" anything different besides verbally expressing its desire to do so, it will basically be "business as usual" within the organization. The organization must be prepared to "walk the talk" in the change process. New work procedures help break allegiance to old values from which the organization seeks to depart. These new work procedures may include the extensive use of teams. Moving to team-based operations necessitates major changes in organizational behavior including communication, cooperation, and decision making, as well as new organizational policies pertaining to selection, training, and compensation.

Another possible change in work procedures may entail job redesign. In this case the employees will have the structure of their jobs altered, usually giving them greater decision-making authority over the conduct of their work operations. Such new procedures for performing work provide a venue for organizational members to reframe their values, attitudes, and beliefs about the organization and what it is trying to accomplish. A failure to change how work is performed even though new values and beliefs have been expressed often results in "back-sliding." Back-sliding is the return to the old ways of thinking and feeling, and ultimately behaving, from which the organization needs to evolve.

4. *The organization is open to learn.* Everyone in the organization, from the leaders on down, must accept the fact that no one has all the answers. The organization must be prepared to go through periods of groping, grasping, and stumbling and to learn from these difficult times. Rather than viewing these occasions as representations of shortcomings in vision, intelligence, or fortitude, the organization must view itself as learning, adapting, and growing. In so doing, mistakes will be made. However, instead of viewing the mistakes as punishable offenses or signs of weakness, they should be regarded as part of a normal and healthy change process. Senge (1990) speaks to the need for "learning organizations," organizations that are not only comfortable with the growth process but also treat their members in a nurturing (as opposed to sanctioning) manner. The organization must accept that good ideas and opportunities for growth can and do originate at all levels of the organization, not just from top management.

Total Quality Management

Total quality management (TQM) is a comprehensive approach to organization development that not only embraces behavioral concepts but also those of business strategy, using statistical information to aid in decision making. The principles of TQM were originally developed for manufacturing organizations, but subsequently they have been adapted to service organizations (including educational institutions) as well. In service organizations TQM is also referred to as "continuous process improvement."

The roots of TQM are varied and are from multiple disciplines. An emphasis on employee involvement in making operating decisions about the organization comes from psychology. That is, as the research on participative decision making and leadership revealed, there are issues in which employees have expertise on matters that can be accessed to improve organizational efficiency. Effective decision making is rarely, if ever, a strictly top-down affair. From the field of statistics the concept of statistical quality control was developed. An American physicist named W. Edwards Deming is credited with formulating the concept. It involves the use of rudimentary statistical analyses to aid in understanding organizational processes. The most critical statistical index is that of variation (discussed in Chapter 2). If an organization wants to provide a high quality service or product, the quality should *not* vary across products. That is, *consistency* is regarded as a precursor of quality. For example, if a fast food restaurant made hamburgers that sometimes tasted good and sometimes tasted bad, there would be too much variation in the quality of the hamburger. The hamburgers should taste the same all the time. In addition to reducing variation, the organization should strive to elevate the mean quality of the product. Thus, the goal would be to produce hamburgers that always tasted the same, and always tasted good. These two simple statistical concepts of reducing variation and raising the mean are the foundation of using statistical quality control to improve organizational performance.

From marketing came the concept that the primary focus of the organization should be to satisfy its customers. Satisfied customers are the key to the retention and growth of business. Marketing research also revealed that there can be differences between what customers really want from a product (a tasty hamburger) and what the organization believes its customers want (a hamburger delivered to the customer in less than 45 seconds). Customer service and satisfaction is the driving force behind TQM. Finally, from the area of business strategy came the concept that all parts of the organization, including its overall mission, operating technology, support services, organizational culture, and employee training and rewards, must be aligned to work together to produce an effective outcome. For example, it would be dysfunctional for the organization to say it strives to produce a high quality product, yet train and reward employees to produce a large quantity of products irrespective of quality. Thus TQM is the confluence of concepts and ideas from many disciplines brought together to aid in the development and direction of organizations.

Lawler, Mohrman, and Ledford (1995) concluded that four factors needed to be present to have an effective system of employee involvement, upon which

TQM is based. The first is *sharing of information* about business performance, plans, and goals. It is impossible for employees to make good suggestions about how products and services can be improved without access to business information. It is also difficult for employees to alter their behavior in response to changing conditions and get feedback about the effectiveness of their performance. In the absence of business information, individuals are usually limited simply to carrying out prescribed tasks and roles in a relatively automatic way. It is imperative that relevant business information be shared at all levels of the organization and not be the sole province of upper management.

Second is the need for *developing knowledge*. It is critical that employees at all levels be involved in a continuous process of skill development. Without the proper skills, it is unwise for individuals to participate in a business and influence its direction. Particularly important skills include group decision making, team building, and leadership. These skills are critical because most employee involvement programs involve meetings, interpersonal interactions, group problem solving, and influencing others.

Third is the need to *reward organizational performance*. Basing rewards on organizational performance is one way to ensure that employees are involved in and care about the performance of their company. Individual incentive plans do not tie the individual into the overall success of the business; moreover, they can interfere with teamwork and problem solving. Team incentives can be supportive of employee involvement activities, such as work teams and problem-solving groups. Profit sharing and employee stock ownership are widely used to link employees more closely to the success of the business and reward them for it.

The need to *redistribute power* is the fourth factor. Moving power downward in organizations often requires structural changes. Job enhancement and self-managed work teams involve a substantial change in the basic structure of the organization and are aimed at moving important decisions into the hands of individuals and teams performing the basic manufacturing or service work of the organization. Job enhancement programs have typically been targeted at routine assembly and clerical jobs, while self-managed work teams are used in a broader array of jobs.

Lawler et al. (1995) note that the effective utilization of employee involvement requires the simultaneous use of these four practices, not just the selective use of one or two of them. Interrelated patterns of mutually reinforcing practices are necessary to encourage and sustain employee behavior. Casual or fleeting use of these practices will be ineffectual and will not produce the sustained and systematic efforts needed to produce enduring organizational change.

Lawler and associates conducted a major study of organizations that have adopted TQM. A very high percentage (83%) of those companies with TQM programs reported that their experience with them has been positive or very positive. The overall findings from their study are reported in Table 13–1. It seems evident that organizational interest in TQM is not a passing fad or the "flavor-of-the-month" panacea for organizational ills. The U.S. government annually grants the Malcolm Baldridge National Quality Award to the company that demonstrates the greatest advances in improving the quality of their products. Competition for

Table 13–1 *Summary of responses to question, "Overall, how positive has your experience been with total quality management?"*

Very Negative	0%
Negative	1%
Neither Negative nor Positive	16%
Positive	66%
Very Positive	17%

SOURCE: From *Creating High Performance Organizations* (p. 75) by E. E. Lawler, S. A. Mohrman, and G. E. Ledford, 1995, San Francisco: Jossey-Bass.

Table 13–2 *Characteristics of high-performing organizations*

They are performing excellently against a known external standard.
They are performing excellently against what is assumed to be their potential level of performance.
They are performing excellently in relation to where they were at some earlier time.
They are judged by informed observers to be doing substantially better qualitatively than other comparable systems.
They are doing whatever they do with significantly fewer resources than it is assumed are needed.
They are perceived as exemplars of the way to do whatever they do, and this becomes a source of ideas and inspiration for others.
They are perceived to fulfill at a high level the ideals for the culture within which they exist—that is, they have mobility.
They are the only organization that has been able to do what they do at all, even though it might seem that what they do is not that difficult or mysterious a thing.

SOURCE: From "The Purposing of High-Performing Systems" by P. Vaill, 1982, *Organizational Dynamics, 2 (2), p. 25.*

the Baldridge Award is intense, and the recipients are highly regarded in the business community.

Reeves and Bednar (1994) note that there is not a universal definition of quality; rather, different definitions of quality are appropriate under different circumstances. They believe that there are organizational trade-offs in accepting one definition of quality over another. Despite multiple definitions of quality, Vaill (1982) identified eight characteristics of high performing organizations that embody the principles of TQM. Vaill based his findings on a study of diverse organizations including universities, a Coast Guard unit, hospitals, marching bands, drug rehabilitation agencies, and stock brokerages. His findings are summarized in Table 13–2. It is these characteristics that all OD programs, directly or indirectly, try to develop in organizations.

Empirical OD Research

Porras and Robertson (1992) reviewed 63 empirical research studies on OD over a 14-year period to assess the impact of interventions. The interventions were grouped into four categories: organizing arrangements, social factors, technology,

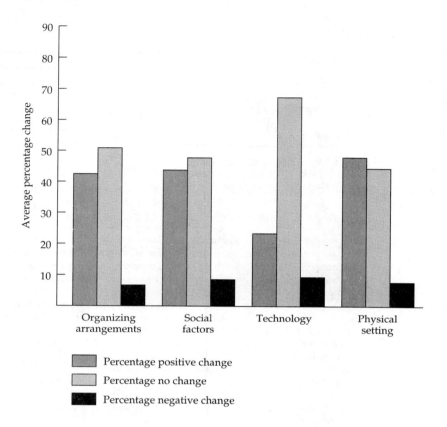

Figure 13–6   *OD-induced change in key organizational work setting variables*

SOURCE: From "Organizational Development: Theory, Research, and Practice" by J. I. Porras and P. J. Robertson, 1992, *Handbook of Industrial and Organizational Psychology, 4*, p. 787.

and physical setting. *Organizing arrangements* included the creation of new committees, task forces, or work teams. *Social factors* most typically included team building and process consultation. *Technology* was most often represented by job redesign. Finally, *physical setting* involved changes in office layout, such as from a closed-office (with partitions) to an open-office layout. The dependent variables included individual and organizational outcomes. The results of the study are presented in Figure 13–6. Several findings are evident. One is that a common outcome of an OD intervention is that no change occurred approximately 25 to 50% of the time. Second, the percentage of studies reporting a negative change (that is, the OD intervention produce negative outcomes) was very small. A subsequent analysis of these overall findings revealed that social factor interventions resulted in the most frequent positive change, while physical setting interventions had the most frequent negative changes. These findings are deserving of two comments. First, given the problems of accurately measuring change, it is conceivable that at least some of the findings that produced no change may have been based on measures that were insensitive to the types of change occurring. Second, it is precisely because specific interventions in technology produced no change in outcomes that organizations have moved toward large-scale, multifaceted, comprehensive change efforts such as TQM.

One conclusion that may be drawn from this study is that singular OD interventions are not likely to produce large-scale changes in individual and organizational outcomes. This is not really surprising given that organizations tend to be resistant to change. Macy and Izumi (1993) argue that to be successful, organizational change efforts must be directed to systemwide design and transformation strategies. To significantly change and transform organizations, there must be change in the power, control systems, and decision making of the organization. Change efforts that start at the work site (office, plant, production line) are generally not as successful as those that start at the corporate level. TQM, and other systemwide initiatives aimed at large-scale organizational change, seemingly hold the greatest promise for success.

Values and Ethics in OD

It is appropriate to end the discussion of OD with a comment on values and ethics. Whenever change is deliberate, someone's values and beliefs are being acted on. The act of change itself is based on a value (that is, change is good or necessary). OD is saturated with values. Sometimes these are implicit, sometimes they are explicit, and sometimes they clash. The operative values include: (1) cooperation is preferable to conflict, (2) openness is preferable to suppression, and (3) the level of trust and support in most groups and organizations is lower than necessary or desirable. Psychologists have long known that behavior manifests values. The behaviors of the change agent and the client in an OD intervention are also guided by values. All parties involved should discuss their values before discussing possible choices. Some conflicts over strategies occur because participants disagree about fundamental values. Many times agreement is assumed when, in fact, it does not exist. A manager I knew preferred creating a feeling of competition among his subordinates to see who would come up with the best idea for a project. It would have been foolish to engage in team building to enhance intragroup cooperation when that value was not endorsed by the manager.

White and Wooten (1986) proposed a conceptual model to explain the domain of professional ethics. Ethics evolve from the intersection of four constructs: values, norms, science, and laws. This model is depicted in Figure 13–7, and the constructs are defined in Table 13–3. The model proposes that values, norms, science, and laws are necessary prerequisites for an ethical system to exist within

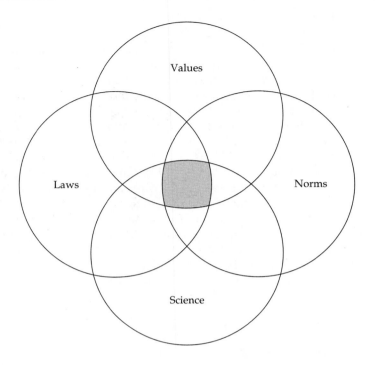

Figure 13–7   *The domain of professional OD ethics*

SOURCE: From *Professional Ethics and Practice in Organizational Development* (p. 73) by L. P. White and K. C. Wooten, 1986, New York: Praeger.

a profession. Each of these constructs has significantly influenced the development of professional ethics.

Since OD is directed to planned organizational change, it is instructive to consider the ethics of change. Lippitt (1982) offered the following observation:

> No person or group of persons, however empowered, can prevent change from occurring. At best, they can only hasten or delay it. More important, they can cope with change at all only if they are aware of its nature and probable effect. In this sense, those responsible for the management of our organizations are faced with extraordinary difficulties in being always correctly informed and situationally knowledgeable. Organizational changes faithfully reflect the needs and interests of some of the people, but not necessarily all of them; therefore, they inevitably produce inequities. Since everything is the result of a change, competent managers cannot afford to overlook any change whatsoever, because every change is a seed from which some part of tomorrow's organization will grow. (p. 385)

Given this inevitability, interventionists must confront the question of the ethicality of change itself, particularly on organizational participants. As presented in the model shown in Figure 13–7, values play an integral role in the formation of any ethical system. While it may be tempting to get caught up with the techniques associated with the latest intervention, the fundamental values that drive accep-

Table 13–3   *Definition of five constructs used in describing professional OD ethics*

Construct	Definition
Values	Beliefs or ideals held by individuals or groups concerning what is good, right, desirable, or important in an idea, object, or action.
Norms	An idea, conceptualization, belief, or a statement enforced by the sanctions of members of a group concerning their behavioral rules, patterns, and conduct, which is referenced in the form of what should be done, what ought to be done, what is expected, and the level of action or expectation under specific circumstances.
Science	A body of knowledge that is characterized by the use of the scientific method, which seeks out goal-oriented information through systematic, unified, and self-correcting processes.
Laws	A system of social rules, norms, or standards of behavior concerning the right and wrong of human conduct that is put in codes enforced by sanctions imposed through recognized authority.
Ethics	Concepts and standards held by individuals or groups concerning the values surrounding the rightness and wrongness of modes of conduct in human behavior and the result of human behavior or actions.

SOURCE: From *Professional Ethics and Practice in Organizational Development* (p. 75) by L. P. White and K. C. Wooten, 1986, New York: Praeger.

tance of the intervention must be articulated. For example, when an organization downsizes and 20% of the work force lose their jobs, the consequences of this action for the laid-off employees (as well as those who weren't) must be evaluated in terms of the values that underlie a sense of fairness and justice. OD cannot be used blindly as a technique of change insensitive to the ethical consequences of its use.

The issue of ethics is also vitally important to the individual OD consultant. Like any professional working with people's lives, the OD consultant must have integrity. Conflicts can arise that directly involve ethical issues. One of the toughest decisions for a change agent is when to end a consultant/client relationship (White & Wooten, 1983). On the one hand, the consultant likes to "be there" to help; on the other hand, there comes a point when the client must break free of the consultant. If the consultant leaves the system too soon, the client may not have the internal resources to solve problems. If the consultant prolongs the relationship (all the while being paid a fee), he or she may create a state of being "needed" by the client to survive. When to end a relationship is a matter of professional judgment. No formula will provide the answer. While ethical matters are rarely a case of black or white, they are the substance of the consultant's professional character.

CASE STUDY   *How Do I Create Teamwork?*

Alex Rowland gazed pensively out of his office, which overlooked the production area of his company. Seven years ago, he had founded Microtechnics, Inc., a high-tech company that produced microchips for use in computers. Rowland, an engineer by training, prided himself on assembling one of the finest engineering design departments in his industry. He handpicked his people from the finest universities in the country, gave them a free hand in product design, and paid them extremely well. While many companies feared losing their engineers to competitors, Rowland had the luxury of knowing many engineers were just waiting for a chance to join his company. In an industry where product quality and capacity were critical, Microtechnics was regarded as an industry leader in product design.

But all was not well. What was once the strongest asset of the company was bordering on becoming a liability. Rowland wondered if he had created a monster. The problem was that the company was lagging far behind in production and in having its products hit the market at opportune times. The apparent cause was the Engineering Department, the very department that had put Microtechnics on the map. The engineers were very prideful and territorial. They would not release a new product for production until they thought it was perfect down to the last detail. The engineers did not want the Production Department grabbing one of their "babies" until they were ready to release it. There was a constant struggle between the Engineering and Production departments regarding the release of products for manufacturing and distribution. Although Rowland knew the value of superior products, he also knew that consumers paid for products, not great ideas, and if Microtechnics didn't put the product in the consumers' hands, soon there would be no Microtechnics. The Production Department repeatedly approached Rowland about missed production deadlines. Sales were way down because other companies were getting their products out the door first. They often lacked the quality of a Microtechnics product, but they still made great inroads into new markets by being there first. Microtechnics was developing a reputation of being the caboose in product delivery, and in a highly competitive industry its tardiness was killing it financially.

The Engineering Department viewed Production as a bunch of bureaucrats, people who failed to understand the importance of superior workmanship. The engineers at Microtechnics had earned numerous patents on their products and in the span of seven short years had garnered three industry awards for product design. They were good, they knew it, everyone knew it. The problem was that Microtechnics wasn't just in the business of thinking up new products. It also had to produce them and get people to buy them.

Rowland stared out over a cup of coffee. He felt that he was running two separate companies: one in engineering, the other in production. They certainly weren't working together. Rowland knew that he couldn't kill the goose that laid his golden eggs. Without his engineers, his company would be nothing. But if he couldn't get his engineers to realize that they were in the manufacturing business, they wouldn't stay in business. Rowland felt trapped. He couldn't live without his engineers, and he wasn't living too well with them. If he couldn't find a way to unite his company, he knew it wouldn't be long before he joined a long list of former company presidents who had great ideas but didn't know how to run a business.

Questions
1. What exactly is the problem facing Microtechnics?
2. What factors are operating to reinforce the way the Engineering Department is operating?
3. What intervention strategies do you feel might benefit Microtechnics, and how would you implement them?
4. Do you believe the situation at Microtechnics requires involvement of a change agent external to the company, or should Rowland create a permanent job within the company to address this situation? Why do you feel as you do?
5. If the intervention strategy is successful, how would the operation of Microtechnics be conducted differently than it is now?

Union/Management Relations

Major Chapter Objectives

- *Be able to explain the nature and formation of a labor union.*

- *Be able to describe the functions of a labor contract.*

- *Understand the strategies of impasse resolution in the collective bargaining process.*

- *Be able to describe responses to impasse.*

- *Be able to describe the nature of grievances and grievance arbitration.*

- *Understand the impact behavioral research results have had on union/management relations.*

Over the years, I/O psychologists have been involved in a broad range of topics relating to work. Strangely enough, one not often addressed is union/management relations. This area cannot be dismissed as "tangential" to work; for many organizations, union-related issues are among the most crucial. Many practitioners have observed that there is a great imbalance in I/O psychologists' interest between union and management problems. The two are not mutually exclusive, but I/O psychology seems to be more aligned with management, as this list of professional activities of I/O psychologists shows: managerial consulting, management development, use of assessment centers to identify those with management ability, and determination of criteria of managerial success. However, I/O psychology has not spurned the advances of unions or been unreceptive to them. Shostak (1964) described the relationship as "mutual indifference." Unions appear to be reluctant to approach I/O psychologists for help in solving their problems. Rosen and Stagner (1980) think this is caused partly by the belief that I/O psychologists are not truly impartial and partly by a reluctance to give outsiders access to union data.

The reasons for the unions' attitudes are not totally clear. One explanation is that the development of industrial psychology is closely tied to the work of Frederick Taylor. Criticisms of "Taylorism" have been raised by union workers; they see it as exploiting workers to increase company profits. There can be an adversarial relationship between unions and management, a "we/them" perspective. Unions may still see I/O psychology as a partner of "them." Also, some factors may appear to place I/O psychologists more in the management camp. I/O psychologists are often placed in management-level positions. Also, management invariably sees the need for, explains problems to, and pays the consultant. In short, I/O psychology has been more involved with management than with unions (to the point that some authors refer to I/O psychology as a "management tool"). This is most apparent in the conspicuous absence of psychological research on unions. A summary of the major reasons that I/O psychologists have not worked well with unions was offered by Huszczo, Wiggins, and Currie (1984) and is presented in Table 14–1.

Table 14–1   *Reasons unions distrust I/O psychologists*

Their association with management.

Their association with F. W. Taylor's scientific management (that is, emphasis on efficiency, time and motion studies).

Unions are ignored in textbooks and journals of I/O psychology.

Their association with moralistic intellectuals who want social reform.

Methods (for example, attitude surveys) used to avoid or beat union-organizing attempts or lower pay demands.

Their association with job enrichment techniques that interfere with job classification and standards systems.

Methods of psychological testing emphasize differentiation among workers (hence, antisolidarity and antiseniority systems).

Many psychologists have not had work experience similar to that of union members, which causes suspicion and creates communication barriers.

SOURCE: "The Relationship Between Psychology and Organized Labor: Past, Present, and Future" by G. E. Huszczo, J. G. Wiggins, and J. S. Currie, 1984, *American Psychologist, 39,* p. 434.

FIELD NOTE 1

I am of the opinion that unions have been given inadequate attention by educators. When the topic of labor unions comes up, students are more likely to have heard of Jimmy Hoffa (a union leader with reputed criminal connections) than Walter Reuther (a major contributor to organized labor). Why? There are probably many reasons, but one seems fundamental. Schools, colleges, and higher education in general are founded on scholarly intellectual values. They produce learned people, many of whom rise to become business leaders. Unions, on the other hand, got their start representing relatively uneducated workers, the rank-and-file employees, rather than business leaders. Rightly or wrongly, unions have had the image of representing the "common man" in labor over the "privileged intellectuals." Some union leaders become suspicious and skeptical of the motives of formally educated people, feeling that they are more likely to share values held by management.

Textbooks that offer more than a passing look at organized labor are rarely found in this country. It seems that the "we/they" dichotomy between labor and management has also filtered down into textbook writing; unions simply are infrequently discussed in books. This book, in fact, is one of the few I/O psychology textbooks to devote a chapter to union/management issues. However, the anti-intellectual attitude that some unions hold is costing them in ways beyond exposure in education. Unions rarely hire outside professionals; they generally promote from within their own ranks. If you were an I/O psychologist who wanted to work full time for a union, I doubt if you would have many employment possibilities. Furthermore, unions are currently experiencing a decline in membership. An unprecedented number of unions are being decertified, and unions are losing their effectiveness compared to previous years in negotiating for desired employment conditions. In short, unions are in need of some fresh ideas. They could benefit from some OD-type interventions. But unless unions are willing to look beyond their own ranks for expertise, I doubt that they (like any organization) will have sufficient internal strength to pull themselves up by the bootstraps. The paradoxical split between I/O psychology (the study of people at work) and labor unions (which represent a large portion of workers) has been detrimental to both parties.

In the past several years, interest in unions has increased. Whether the "thaw" will continue and grow remains to be seen. I suspect current interest stems from the realization that worker/workplace problems need not be dealt with from an either/or perspective. Unions and management can benefit from jointly solving problems that affect them. If our discipline is successful in overcoming its "promanagement" image, we can and will make greater inroads in understanding unions. Current research suggests that such changes are beginning (see Field Note 1).

In this chapter I will examine the nature of unions, the factors influencing union/management relations, recent research on unions, and how unionization affects many topics discussed earlier.

What Is a Union?

Unions are organizations designed to promote and enhance the social and economic welfare of their members. Basically, unions were created to protect workers from exploitation. Unions originally sprang from the abysmal working conditions in this country 100 years ago. Workers got little pay, had almost no job security, had no benefits and, perhaps most important, worked under degrading and unsafe conditions. Unions gave unity and power to employees. This power forced employers to deal with workers as a group, thereby providing a basis for improvement in workers' welfare. Federal laws forced employers to stop certain activities (such as employing children) and engage in others (such as making Social Security contributions). Collectively, labor unions and labor laws brought about many changes in the workplace. Although the problems facing the North American worker today are not as severe as they were 75 years ago, unions continue to give a sense of security and increased welfare to their members.

Why do workers join unions? What can unions accomplish? Unions have consistently contributed to the attainment of certain outcomes. Bok and Dunlop (1970) feel that unions have made the following contributions to worker welfare:

- They have increased wages; in turn, employers have raised the wages of some nonunion workers.
- They have bargained for and gotten benefits such as pensions, insurance, vacations, and rest periods.
- They have provided formal rules and procedures for discipline, promotion, wage differentials, and other important job-related factors. This has led to less arbitrary treatment of employees.

Other contributions unions have made include providing better communication with management, obtaining better working conditions, increasing employee unity, and raising morale. Other authors cite social reasons, like belonging to a group with whom workers can share common experiences and fellowship. Thus, there are both economic and personal reasons for joining unions.

Unions as Organizations

Approximately 20 million U.S. citizens belong to labor unions, representing about 25% of the nonagricultural work force. In Canada, union membership is over 2 million. The largest labor union is the American Federation of Labor-Congress of Industrial Organizations (AFL-CIO). Of all union members, 83% belong to an AFL-CIO affiliate. Other large unions include the United Auto Workers and the United Mine Workers. While unions are strongest among blue-collar employees, some white-collar workers (particularly government employees and teachers) are also being unionized, as witnessed by the growth of the American Federation of State, County, and Municipal Employees. However, union membership has declined both nationally and internationally in recent years. Van der Veen and Klandermans (1995) reported that union membership in the United States is less than half what it was 40 years ago. The decline in unionization is attributed to a reduction in the manufacturing sector (a traditional stronghold of labor unions) and a rise in service industries and knowledge workers, who are not typically represented by unions.

Each union has a headquarters, but its strength is its many locals. A local may represent members in a geographic area (for example, all tollbooth collectors in Philadelphia) or a particular plant (for example, Amalgamated Beef Packers at Armour's Dubuque, Iowa, slaughterhouse). The local elects officials. If it is large enough, it affords some officials full-time jobs. Other officials are full-time company employees who may get time off for union activities. The shop, or union, steward has a union position equivalent to that of a company supervisor. The steward represents the union on the job site; he or she handles grievances and discipline. Usually the steward is elected by members for a one-year term. Mellor (1995) reported that women join U.S. unions at a higher rate than do men (currently 3 to 1), yet women are underrepresented as elected union officers. It appears that the "glass ceiling" phenomenon experienced by women seeking to enter management positions has its counterpart in staffing union leadership positions.

A union represents an organization (for example, a labor organization) within another organization (the company). The local depends on the company for its existence. Large companies often have a multiunion labor force and thus multiple organizations within themselves. In this case the employer must deal with several collectively organized groups—for example, production workers, clerical workers, and truck drivers. Each union negotiates separately, trying to improve the welfare of its members. A large, multiunion employer is a good example of how organizations are composed of interdependent parts. Each union has a certain degree of power, which can influence the behavior of the total organization.

Union members pay membership dues, which are the union's chief resource. The union can also collect money for a strike fund, a pool members can draw from if they are on strike and do not get paid. (I will discuss strikes in more detail shortly.) Unions use their funds to offer members such things as special group automobile insurance rates or union-owned vacation facilities. Unions are highly dependent on their members. Increased membership gives a union more bargaining clout, generates more revenue, and provides a greater range of services for members. Without members, a union cannot exist—indeed, declining membership can threaten its very survival.

Formation of a Union

When employees want to consider joining a union, they follow a standard procedure. First, they invite representatives to solicit union membership. Federal law allows organizers to solicit membership as long as this does not endanger employees' safety or performance. Solicitations usually occur over lunch or at break time. It is illegal for employers to threaten physically, interfere with, or harass organizers. It is also illegal to fire employees for having prounion sentiments.

Both the union and the company typically mount campaigns on behalf of their positions. The union stresses how it can improve the workers' lot. The company mounts a countercampaign stressing how well off the employees already

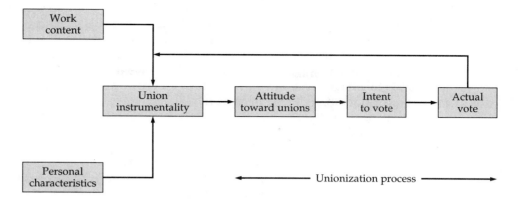

Figure 14–1   *A model of the determinants of the unionization process*
SOURCE: From "A Predictive Study of Voting Behavior in a Representation Election Using Union Instrumentality and Work Perceptions" by T. A. DeCotiis and J. Y. LeLouarn, 1981, *Organizational Behavior and Human Performance, 27,* p. 109.

are, the costs of union membership, and loss of freedom. Then a federal agency, the National Labor Relations Board (NLRB), gets involved. The NLRB sends a hearing officer to oversee the union campaign and monitor further developments.
Employees are asked to sign cards authorizing a union election. If fewer than 30% sign the authorization cards, the process ends. If 30% or more sign, an election is held to determine whether a union will represent the employees. The NLRB officer must determine which employees are eligible to be in the union and thus eligible to vote. Management personnel (supervisors, superintendents, and managers) are excluded. The hearing officer schedules the election, provides secret ballots and ballot boxes, counts the votes, and certifies the election. If more than 50% of the voters approve, the union is voted in. If the union loses the election, it can repeat the entire process at a later date. A union that lost a close election would probably do so.
Brief and Rude (1981) proposed that the decision to accept or reject a union is not unlike other choices facing an individual. Employees will support a union to the extent that they see it as a way of getting outcomes important to them without prohibitive costs. Over 50 years ago Bakke (1945) stated this most eloquently:

> The worker reacts favorably to union membership in proportion to the strength of his belief that this step will reduce his frustrations and anxieties and will further his opportunities relevant to the achievement of his standards of successful living. He reacts unfavorably in proportion to the strength of his belief that this step will increase his frustrations and anxieties and will reduce his opportunities relevant to the achievement of such standards. (p. 38)

DeCotiis and LeLouarn (1981) developed the model of the determinants of unionization shown in Figure 14–1. The work context includes employee reaction to work, organization culture, perceived organization structure, and supervision. Personal characteristics include age, sex, and race, as well as feelings of job satisfaction. The work context and personal characteristics determine union instrumentality—that is, the extent to which a union is seen as improving the employee's welfare. Instrumentality affects the employee's attitude toward unions; in turn, this affects the employee's intent to vote for a union. The actual vote is determined by the sequence shown in the model. DeCotiis and LeLouarn were able to explain over 54% of the variance in perceptions of union instrumentality by consideration of the concepts in their model.

Summers, Betton, and DeCotiis (1986) found that union instrumentality can be lowered when different unions are competing among themselves for the right to represent employees. They discovered that employees are likely to take anti-union information more seriously if its source is another union rather than management. Premack and Hunter (1988) carefully studied the unionization decision by means of elaborate statistical methods. They concluded that some employees hold strong attitudes toward unions, both pro and con, and their attitudes are usually not altered one way or the other during the course of the organizing campaign. However, other employees are uncertain about their attitudes toward unions, and their attitudes can be altered by the behavior of both parties during the organizing campaign. Premack and Hunter note that these employees' votes are critical to the outcome of the election because most union representation elections are decided by a small number of votes.

The Labor Contract

Once a union is recognized, its officials are authorized to negotiate a labor contract. This is a formal agreement between union and management specifying conditions of employment over a set period.

Both sides prepare a preliminary list of what they want included; the union presents its demands and the employer its offers. The union tends to ask for more than it knows it can get; management tends to offer less. While both sides seek a satisfactory agreement, they often resort to bombast, which is a hallmark of such negotiations. Union officials may allege that management is making huge profits and taking advantage of workers. Management may allege that malicious union leaders have duped the good workers and that their policies may force the company into bankruptcy. Over time, both sides come to an agreement; the union often gets less than it wanted and management gives more. When agreement is not reached (an impasse), other steps are taken, as will be discussed.

Contract negotiations take place between two teams of negotiators. The union side typically consists of local union officials, shop stewards, and perhaps a representative of the national union. Management usually fields a team of a few personnel and production managers who follow preset guidelines. The contract contains many articles; there are also many issues to bargain over. The issues can generally be classified into five categories: compensation and working conditions, employee security, union security, management rights, and contract duration. Table 14–2 gives examples of these and the positions typically taken by each side.

Table 14–2 *Typical bargaining issues and associated positions taken by union and management*

Issue	Union's Position	Management's Position
Compensation and working conditions	Higher pay, more fringe benefits, cost-of-living adjustments	Limit company expenditures by not yielding to all union demands
Employee security	Seniority is the basis for promotions, layoffs, and recall decisions	Merit or job performance is the basis for these decisions
Union security	A union shop in which employees must join the union when hired	An open shop in which employees can choose to join the union
Management rights	Union wants more voice in setting policies and making decisions that affect employees	Management feels certain decisions are its inherent right and does not want to share them with the union
Contract duration	Shorter contracts	Longer contracts

Each bargaining team checks with its members during the process to see whether they will compromise on initial positions. Each side may be willing to yield on some points but not others. Eventually, they reach a tentative agreement. Union members then vote on the contract. If they approve it, the contract is ratified and remains in effect for the agreed-on time (typically two to three years). If members reject the contract, further negotiation will be necessary. Martin and Berthiaume (1995) examined factors that union members consider in ratifying a labor contract. The results showed that both the material aspects of the contract (that is, better wages) and whether the union was perceived to represent union members influenced the ratification vote.

Determining whether a contract will be ratified typically depends on industry practices, community practices, and recent trends. If the union represents truck drivers and a critical issue is wages, the union will collect data needed to judge the proposal. What other companies in the industry pay truck drivers, what other companies in the community pay them, and whether prices and wages are rising or falling will be considered. Stagner and Rosen (1965) classically referred to the area of compromise as the bargaining zone; this is presented in Figure 14–2. Both parties must move toward a compromise without exceeding their tolerance limits; this is the point beyond which the contract will be unacceptable. If both parties reach a compromise within their expectations, there will be agreement. If, however, one side exceeds its tolerance limit, the proposed contract will not be acceptable.

Both sides will use whatever external factors are available to influence the contract in their favor. If there is high unemployment and the company could replace workers who go on strike, management has an advantage. If the company does much of its business around Christmas, the union may choose that time to negotiate a contract, knowing that the company can ill afford a strike then. Each side looks for factors that will bolster its position.

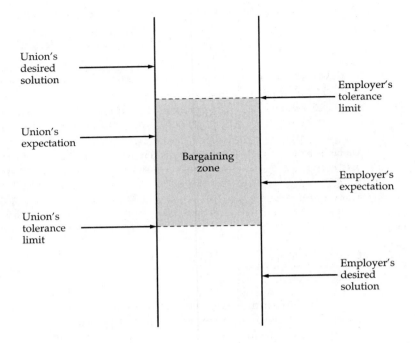

Figure 14-2   *Desires, expectations, and tolerance limits that determine the bargaining zone*
SOURCE: From *Psychology of Union-Management Relations* (p. 96) by R. Stagner and H. Rosen, 1965, Belmont, CA: Wadsworth. Reprinted by permission of the publisher. Brooks/Cole Publishing Company, Pacific Grove, California.

Collective Bargaining and Impasse Resolution

Whether the bargaining process runs smoothly is often due to the parties' approaches. Pruitt (1993) distinguishes between distributive and integrative bargaining postures. *Distributive bargaining* is predominant in the United States. This assumes a win/lose relationship; whatever the employer gives the union, the employer loses and vice versa. Because both sides are trying to minimize losses, movement toward a compromise is often painful and slow. The alternative is *integrative bargaining*. Both sides work to improve the relationship while the present contract is in effect. Contract renewal is not seen as the time and place for confrontation. Instead, both parties seek to identify common problems and propose acceptable solutions that can be adopted when the contract expires. These bargaining postures are not formally chosen; rather, they are implied by behavior in the workplace. While it is not always a strictly either/or decision, distributive bargaining is far more characteristic of union/management relations than is integrative bargaining.

What happens if the two parties cannot reach an agreement? In some cases the labor contract may stipulate what will be done if an impasse is reached. In other cases union and management must jointly determine how to break the impasse. In either case there are three options, all involving third parties: mediation, fact-finding, and arbitration.

Mediation. Mediation is the most used and the least formal third-party option. A neutral third party (a mediator) assists union and management in reaching voluntary agreement. A mediator has no power to impose a settlement; rather, he or she facilitates bringing both parties together.

Where do mediators come from? The Federal Mediation and Conciliation Service (FMCS) provides a staff of qualified mediators. An organization contacts FMCS for the services of such a person. The mediator need not be affiliated with FMCS; any third party acceptable to labor and management may serve. Generally, however, both parties prefer someone with training and experience in labor disputes, so FMCS is often called on.

How a mediator intervenes is not clear-cut. Mediation is voluntary; thus, no mediator can function without the trust, cooperation, and acceptance of both parties. Acceptance is important, because the mediator must obtain any confidential information that the parties have withheld. If the information is used indiscriminately, the parties' bargaining strategy and leverage could be weakened. The mediator tries to reduce the number of disputed issues; ideally, he or she reaches a point where there are no disputes at all. The mediator encourages information sharing to break the deadlock. Without a mediator, it is often difficult for parties to "open up" after assuming adversary roles. The mediator facilitates the flow of information and progress toward compromise. If the mediator is unsuccessful, both parties may engage in the next phase: fact-finding.

Fact-Finding. Fact-finding is more formal than mediation. A qualified mediator may also serve as a fact finder, but his or her role will change. In fact-finding the third party reviews the facts, makes a formal recommendation to resolve the dispute, and makes the recommendation public. It is presumed that if the recommendation is public, pressure will be brought on the parties to accept it or use it for a negotiated settlement. However, fact-finding has not produced the desired pressure. Public interest is apparently aroused only when a strike threatens or actually imposes direct hardship on the public.

Fact-finding may be most useful when one party faces internal differences and needs recommendations from an expert to overcome opposition to a settlement. There appears to be a difference in the effectiveness of fact-finding between private- and public-sector employers. In the public sector, fact-finding has met with limited success. Parties learn that rejecting a fact-finding recommendation is not politically or economically costly, so they are unlikely to value the opinion of the fact finder. In the private sector, fact-finding can be helpful primarily because the final technique of settlement (arbitration) is strongly opposed by unions and management. However, fact-finding is not used very often in the private sector.

Arbitration. Arbitration is the final and most formal settlement technique. Both parties must abide by the decision of the neutral third party. "Final and binding" is usually associated with arbitration. The outcome of arbitration is binding on both parties. Use of arbitration may be stipulated in the labor contract;

it may also be agreed on informally. This is called interest arbitration because it involves the interests of both parties in negotiating a new contract.

Arbitrators must have extensive experience in labor relations. The American Arbitration Association (AAA) maintains the standards and keeps a list of qualified arbitrators. Arbitrators listed by AAA often also serve as mediators listed by FMCS. Effective mediators, fact finders, or arbitrators all need the same skills. What distinguishes the services is the clout of the third party.

There are many forms of interest arbitration. With *voluntary arbitration,* the parties agree to the process. This form is most common in the private sector in settling disputes arising while a contract is still in effect. *Compulsory arbitration* is legally required arbitration, and it is most common in the public sector.

There are other types of arbitration as well. In *conventional arbitration,* the arbitrator creates the settlement he or she deems appropriate. In *final-offer arbitration,* the arbitrator must select the proposal of either union or management; no compromise is possible. For example, suppose the union demands $8 per hour and the company offers $7. In conventional arbitration the arbitrator could decide on any wage but will probably split the difference and decide on $7.50. In final-offer arbitration, the arbitrator must choose either $7 or $8. An additional variation also holds for final-offer arbitration. The arbitrator may make the decision on a *total package;* that is, he or she must choose the complete proposal of either the employer or the union on all issues. Alternatively, the decision may be made on an *issue-by-issue basis.* In this case the arbitrator might choose the employer wage offer but select the union demand on vacation days. Decisions on voluntary versus compulsory arbitration, conventional versus final-offer arbitration, and total-package versus issue-by-issue arbitration are determined by law for public-sector employers and by mutual agreement in the private sector (see Field Note 2).

Interest arbitration is more common in the public sector. Historically, the private sector has been opposed to outside interference in resolving labor problems that are "private" affairs. Thus, private-sector employers will readily seek the advice of a mediator but shun strategies that require certain courses of action. The public sector, however, is quite different. Strikes in the public sector (for example, police) can have devastating effects on the general public. Since they are often prohibited by law, other means of settlement (fact-finding, arbitration) are provided. Some public-sector employees have gone on strike (sometimes legally but usually illegally), but strikes are more often the outcome of impasses in the private sector.

Next I will consider the options available if no settlement is reached through standard procedures.

Responses to Impasse

Consider the situation in which union and management cannot resolve their disputes. They may or may not have used a mediator. Assume that the private sector is involved, because mediation, fact-finding, and arbitration might be required in the public sector. What happens if the two parties cannot agree?

Collective bargaining entails realizing that both sides can take action if they are not pleased with the outcome. These actions are weapons with which to bring about favorable settlements. What the union can do is go on strike. Union members must vote for a strike. If members support a strike and no settlement is reached, they will stop work at a particular time. That point is typically the day after the current contract expires. Taking a strike vote during negotiations brings pressure on management to agree to union demands.

The right to strike is a very powerful tool, because losses from a long strike may be greater than the concessions made in a new contract. Also, unions are skilled in scheduling their strikes (or threatening to do so) when the company is particularly vulnerable (such as around Christmas for the airline industry). If employees do strike, the company is usually closed down completely. There may be limited production if management performs some jobs. It is also possible to hire workers to replace those on strike. These replacements are called "scabs." Given the time it takes to recruit, hire, and train new workers, replacements will not be hired unless a long strike is predicted.

While a strike hurts management, it is unpleasant for the workers as well.

FIELD NOTE 2

Interest arbitration can be a seductively simple means of resolving impasses—so simple, in fact, that some people fear it is overused. Let us say that the union wants a 50-cent-per-hour pay increase and management offers 10 cents per hour. From past experience both sides believe that an arbitrator would likely split the difference between the two, settling on 30 cents per hour. It has been suggested that the more arbitration is used to resolve impasses and the more splitting that occurs, the more likely it is that parties will not bargain seriously between themselves; that is, they will opt for the effortless remedy, arbitration. Thus, the parties will disregard the mediation and fact-finding stages and go directly to arbitration. Arbitration becomes an addictive response to impasse; this phenomenon has been labeled the "narcotic effect" of arbitration.

How do you weaken the narcotic effect of arbitration? One solution is to have arbitrators not split the difference in making decisions. However, arbitrators are free to fashion whatever decisions they think are fair. Splitting the difference is often perceived as the fairest thing to do, and it increases the acceptability of the arbitrator for future cases since neither party will have received preferential treatment. Thus, with each split decision, the narcotic effect becomes stronger. One way to weaken the narcotic effect is to prohibit split decisions, which is what happens in final-offer arbitration. Here, the arbitrator is bound to accept either the 50-cent or 10-cent position and not any figure over, under, or in between. Given this, it has been hypothesized that negotiators will offer more serious, reasonable proposals, knowing that the alternative is to have an arbitrator choose one position over the other. An absurd offer would never get chosen. In total-package, final-offer arbitration, the arbitrator must choose the entire package of either the union or management. This tends to drive both parties into compromise. The alternative version of issue-by-issue, final-offer arbitration produces its own type of split decisions; that is, since there can be no within-issue splits, the arbitrator splits between issues: The union position is accepted on one issue, and management's position on another. Creation of total-package, final-offer arbitration is presumed to have greatly decreased reliance on arbitration for impasse resolution.

THE WIZARD OF ID   SOURCE: The Wizard of ID by Brant Parker and Johnny Hart. By permission of Johnny Hart and Creators Syndicate, Inc.

Since they are not working, they do not get paid. The employees may have contributed to a strike fund, but such funds are usually only a fraction of regular wages. A strike is the price employees pay to get their demands met. It sometimes also limits their demands. By the time a union faces a strike, it is usually confronted with two unpalatable options. One is to accept a contract it does not like; the other is to strike. Employees may seek temporary employment while they are on strike, but such jobs are not always available. On the basis of labor economists' studies of the costs of strikes to both employees and employers, it is safe to say that strikes rarely benefit either party. Sometimes the company suffers the most; in other cases the union does. There are rarely any "winners" in a strike. Stagner and Rosen (1965) have illustrated the consequences for both union and management in accepting each other's alternatives, particularly as they relate to a strike (see Table 14–3).

One study examined some of the dynamics associated with strikes. Stagner and Effal (1982) looked at the attitudes of unionized automobile workers at several times, including when contracts were being negotiated, during an ensuing strike, and seven months after the strike ended. They found that union members on strike (1) had a higher opinion of the union and its leadership than before the strike, (2) evaluated the benefit package more highly after the strike, (3) became more militant toward the employer during the strike, and (4) reported more willingness to engage in union activities. The results of this study support predictions based on theories of conflict and attitude formation.

Management is not totally defenseless in case of a strike. If it anticipates a strike, it might boost production beforehand to stockpile goods. Most public-sector employees, on the other hand, perform services, and services cannot be stockpiled. This is one reason strikes are illegal in some parts of the public sector. Sometimes a strike uncovers information about the quality of the work force. When one company replaced strikers with temporary help, new production records were set. In this case the strike revealed a weakness in the employees.

A strike is not the only option available to the union. *Work slowdowns* have also been used wherein workers operate at lower levels of efficiency. Workers may simply put out less effort and thus produce less, or they may be absent to reduce productivity. Since strikes are illegal in the police force, police officers dissatisfied with their contracts have called in sick en masse with what has become known as

Table 14–3 Union and company alternatives and related consequences

Company	Union
Alternative 1	
Perceived consequences of giving in to union demands:	Perceived consequences of accepting company counteroffer:
1. Lessening of investor return.	1. Loss of membership support.
2. Loss of competitive standing.	2. Loss of status within union movement.
3. Setting bad precedent.	3. Setting bad precedent.
4. Avoiding costly strike.	4. Avoiding costly strike.
5. Avoiding government and public ill will.	5. Avoiding government and public ill will.
Alternative 2	
Perceived consequences of refusing to accede to union demands:	Perceived consequences of sticking to original demands:
1. Due to potential strike, loss of investor return.	1. Prove strength and determination of union to members.
2. Due to potential strike, loss of competitive standing.	2. Due to potential strike, loss of member income.
3. Loss of government and public good will.	3. Due to potential strike, loss of member support.
4. Maintenance of company prerogatives.	4. Loss of government and public good will.
5. Breaking union power.	5. Teach company a "lesson."

SOURCE: From *Psychology of Union-Management Relations* (p. 103) by R. Stagner and H. Rosen, Belmont, CA: Wadsworth. Reprinted by permission of the publisher, Brooks/Cole Publishing Company, Pacific Grove, California.

the "blue flu." Such tactics can exert great pressure on management to yield to union demands.

Sabotage is another response to impasse in negotiations. Stagner and Rosen (1965) describe a situation in which factory production was increased from 2,000 to 3,000 units per day by modifying a drill press. However, wages were not increased, and workers resented it. They found that bumping the sheet metal against the drill would eventually break the drill. The employee handling the drill would have to wait idly for a replacement. By some curious accident, average production continued around 2,000 units per day. However, management got the "message." While sabotage is not a sanctioned union activity, like a strike, it is a way of putting pressure on management to accept demands.

Management also has a major tactic to get the union to acquiesce. It is called a *lockout*, and it is considered to be the employer's equivalent of a strike. The company threatens to close if the union does not accept its offer. Employees cannot work and thus "pay" for rejecting the employer's offer. A threatened lockout may put the pressure of a majority of workers on a minority holding out against a contract issue. Like strikes, lockouts are costly to both the company and the union, and they are not undertaken lightly. They are management's ultimate response to an impasse.

Before I leave this topic, note that strikes, slowdowns, sabotage, and lockouts represent failures in the collective bargaining process. These actions have been taken because a settlement was not reached. Like most responses to frustration, they are rarely beneficial in the long run. Some unions may want to "teach the company a lesson"; some companies want to break a union. But both parties have a symbiotic relationship. A company cannot exist without employees, and without a company, employees have no jobs. Collective bargaining reflects the continual tussle for power, but neither side can afford to be totally victorious. If a union exacts so many concessions that the company goes bankrupt, it will have accomplished nothing. As Estey (1981) put it, "Labor does not seek to kill the goose that lays the golden eggs; it wants it to lay more golden eggs, and wants more eggs for itself" (p. 83).

If management drives employees away by not making enough concessions, it will not have a qualified work force. Industrial peace is far more desirable for all parties than warfare. Conflict can provide opportunities for change and development, but if conflict gets out of hand, it can be devastating. Union/management relations are not all typified by infighting and power plays. Nothing unites opposing factions faster than a common enemy. Because the United States is losing some economic battles to foreign competition, some union/management relations have become far more integrative. For example, unions in the auto industry have given up some concessions gained before the current contract expired. The industry, in turn, used the money saved to become more competitive. By remaining solvent, the industry continued to provide jobs. Both management and labor could pursue some common goals. Collective bargaining is a delicate process. Neither side should lose sight of the total economic and social environment, even though short-term, narrow issues are often at the heart of disputes.

Disputes over Contract Interpretation

Collective bargaining is mainly directed toward resolving disputes over new labor contracts; however, disputes also occur over clauses in a current contract. No matter how clearly a labor contract is written, disagreements invariably arise over its meaning or extent. Developing a clear and precise contract involves writing skills in their highest form. Despite the best intentions of those involved, events occur that are not clearly covered in a labor contract. For example, companies often include a contract clause stating that sleeping on the job is grounds for dismissal. A supervisor notices that an employee's head is resting on his arms and his eyes are closed. The supervisor infers that the employee is asleep and fires him. The employee says he was not sleeping but felt dizzy and chose to rest for a moment rather than risk falling down. Who is right?

If the supervisor dismissed the employee, the employee would probably file a *grievance,* or formal complaint. The firing decision can be appealed through a grievance procedure, which is usually a provision of a labor contract (Ash, 1970). First, the employee and the supervisor try to reach an understanding. If they do not, the shop steward represents the employee in negotiating with the supervisor. This is often done whether or not the steward thinks the employee has a "case"—above all, the steward's job is to represent union members. If it is not resolved, the case may then be taken to the company's director of industrial relations, who will hear testimony from both sides and issue a verdict. This may be a compromise—such as, the employee keeps his or her job but is put on probation. The final step is to call in an arbitrator. He or she examines the labor contract, hears testimony, and renders an opinion. This process is called *rights* or *grievance arbitration;* it involves the rights of the employee. The labor contract usually specifies that union and management share the cost of arbitration, which may be $2,000 per hearing. This is done to prevent all grievances from being routinely pushed to arbitration. Each side must believe it has a strong case before calling in an arbitrator (see Field Note 3).

The arbitrator must be acceptable to both sides; this means that he or she must be seen as neither prounion nor promanagement. The arbitrator may decide in favor of one side or issue a compromise decision. The decision is final and binding. If an arbitrator hears many cases in the same company and repeatedly decides in favor of one side, he or she may become unacceptable to the side that always loses. Articles of the labor contract that are repeated subjects of grievance (due mainly to ambiguous language) become prime candidates for revision in the next contract.

Dalton and Todor (1982) have proposed a model of the grievance process that emphasizes the role of the union steward. This is shown in Figure 14–3. Some incident occurs that is seen as a possible grievance. A management representative

---

FIELD NOTE 3

For many years, rights arbitration has been used as a means of resolving disputes over grievances filed in unionized companies. The arbitrator is called in, hears both sides of the story, and renders a decision. This decision is final and binding to both parties. Why? Because both parties have agreed to this means of dispute settlement in the labor contract and therefore must accept the arbitrator's decision.

Over the past few years, the arbitration model of dispute settlement has been used to resolve an ever-widening range of problems. These problems are not limited to unionized companies, to employment issues, or even to any companies. Actually, all that is needed are two (or more) disputants, an acceptable third party who will serve as an arbitrator, and an agreement by the parties to accept the arbitrator's decision.

Here is an example. Let us say you take your car to a repair shop. It charges you $500 for the work, which you pay, but you discover the car still does not run properly. You want to either get your money back or have the car fixed to your satisfaction, but the repair people say that your car must have a new problem because it worked fine when it left the shop. You now have a dispute on your hands.

What can you do about it? One approach would be to try to work it out with the repair shop, but you probably will not get too far since the repair people already feel strongly about their position. Another approach would be for you to bring a legal suit against the repair shop. This could take a long time, and both parties would have to pay associated legal fees. A third alternative would be to use an arbitrator, someone whose opinion both you and the repair people respect and whose decision you would agree to abide by. Furthermore, you and the repair shop owners would agree to share the cost of the arbitrator's fee.

What if you did not like the arbitrator's decision and later decided to seek relief in court? Could you? Possibly—but it would be brought to the court's attention that you reneged on the arbitrator's decision, which would certainly detract from your perceived honesty and credibility. Arbitrators generally offer disputants greater speed and less cost in reaching a resolution than many other systems of dispute settlement. Is there any guarantee that you will be satisfied with the resolution? No, but if you did not like the solution, you probably would not consider that arbitrator an acceptable choice for any future disputes. This is the way arbitrators are found unsatisfactory in industrial disputes: They have alienated one of the disputing parties.

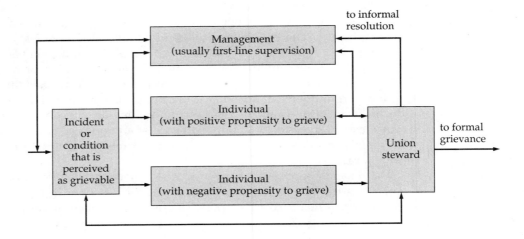

Figure 14–3   *Model of the grievance process*
SOURCE: From "Antecedents of Grievance Filing Behavior: Attitude/Behavioral Consistency and the Union Steward" by D. R. Dalton and W. D. Todor, 1982, *Academy of Management Journal, 25,* p. 166.

may try to reduce grievances by resolving the problem informally with the union steward's consent. If the employee wants to pursue a grievance (has a positive propensity), the steward might discourage this action but would probably support it. If the worker has a negative propensity to file a grievance, the steward may encourage the individual or may file in the name of the union without the worker's consent. Finally, the bottom link in the model shows that a steward can bypass any worker propensities (positive or negative) and file a grievance in the union's name. In such a case, the steward's propensity alone determines the action. Dalton and Todor feel that the union steward holds a key role in the union member-grievance relationship, one that until recently has not been well understood.

A few studies have examined the extent to which the work environment contributes to number and types of grievances. In an early study Ronan (1963) studied grievance activity over a five-year period in two plants that manufactured heavy equipment. He found that the plants did have a significant effect on the number of grievances but the kind of work did not. Employees at both plants submitted grievances for similar reasons and seemed to follow the same pattern in terms of rate. Muchinsky and Maassarani (1980) found that depending on the type of work, certain articles of a contract are more likely to be grieved. Public employees who work as prison guards and attendants in state mental hospitals were more likely to file grievances about their own safety and disciplinary actions than were employees in a transportation department. But transportation department employees filed more grievances about hours of work and wages. Thus, allegations are directly related to type of work. The most "sensitive" aspects of work are likely to differ from one organization to another.

Think of grievances as a somewhat contaminated index of the quality of union/management relations. In general, when the working relationship is good, grievances will be fewer. However, as Gordon and Miller (1984) have noted, in some organizations work problems get resolved informally between the conflicting parties and never develop into formal grievances. While formal grievances are usually indicative of conflict, their absence does not always reflect a problem-free work environment. Also, the more ambiguous the labor contract, the more likely conflicts will ensue. A poorly written or inconsistently interpreted contract invites grievances. There can be much grievance activity in a recently unionized organization; employees will use grievances to "test" management's knowledge of the labor contract (Muchinsky & Maassarani, 1981). Particularly in the public sector, where collective bargaining is relatively new, officials are expected to act as "management" even though they have little or no training in dealing with labor. Such an imbalance contributes to errors in contract administration. Gordon and Bowlby (1989) found that employees were more likely to file grievances when management actions against them were perceived as a threat and when employees attributed the discipline to a manager's personal disposition (animus toward the worker). Employees were less likely to file grievances when they perceived managers as simply following rules that required punishment for the specific worker behavior.

Employee concern over capricious management decisions is one of the major reasons employees opt for union representation. Fryxell and Gordon (1989) reported that the amount of procedural justice afforded by a grievance system was the strongest predictor of employee satisfaction with a union. Gordon and Bowlby (1988) also challenged the dictum that grievances are best resolved at the lowest step of the grievance process. Grievants who won their cases at higher levels of the grievance process showed greater faith in the fairness and perceived justice of the dispute resolution process. Finally, Klaas (1989) reported that at higher levels in the grievance process managers were influenced by the grievant's work history as documented in their performance appraisals, even when that history was not relevant to evaluating the merits of the grievance. In conclusion, while there is much publicity about strike-related issues, members feel that the union's highest priority should be better ways of handling grievances. Unions serve many purposes, but the most pressing need they fill seems to be ensuring fair treatment in employment. Of course, this is a primary reason unions appeal to workers.

Influence of Unions on Nonunionized Companies

Even if they do not have unionized employees, companies are still sensitive to union influence. Companies that are unresponsive to employees' needs invite unionization. A nonunion company that wants to remain so must be receptive to its workers' ideas and complaints. If a company can satisfy employees' needs, a union is unnecessary; that is, the company does voluntarily what a labor union would force it to do. In a given community or industry, there is often a mix of union and nonunion companies. If unionized employees get concessions from management on wages, benefits, hours, and so on, these become reference points for nonunionized employees, and a nonunion company may feel compelled to raise wages to remain competitive. If a labor contract calls for formal grievance procedures, a nonunion company may well follow suit. Workers are aware of employment conditions in other companies, which gives them a frame of reference for judging their own. If a company does not offer comparable conditions, employees may see a union as a means of improving their welfare. This is not to say that nonunion companies must offer identical conditions. There are costs associated with a union (for example, dues); a nonunion company might set wages slightly below those paid in a unionized company so the net effect (higher wages minus dues) is comparable. What economists call the "union/nonunion wage differential" has been the subject of extensive research. Jarrell and Stanley (1990) reported that the union/nonunion wage differential varied with the national unemployment rate and ranged from 8.9% to 12.4%.

Although a prudent nonunion employer will keep abreast of employment conditions in the community and the industry, a company cannot act to keep a union out "at all costs." There is much labor relations legislation. Many laws (like the National Labor Relations Act) were enacted to prohibit unfair practices on both sides. For example, an employer cannot fire a worker just because he or she supports a union. The history of labor relations is full of cases of worker harassment by unions or management to influence attitudes toward unionization. But both sides can suffer for breaking the law.

Behavioral Research on Union/Management Relations

Thus far, I have examined the structure of unions, collective bargaining, and various issues in union/management relations. For the most part, I have not discussed psychological issues; with the exception of grievances, there is little behavioral research on union/management relations. However, over the past few years, interest in this area has increased. We are beginning to see an interdisciplinary approach to topics that historically were treated with parochialism (Brett, 1980). In the next few pages, I will examine research on union/management relations with a strong behavioral thrust.

Employee Support for Collective Bargaining

Numerous studies have dealt with why employees support a union, particularly with regard to personal needs and job satisfaction. Feuille and Blandin (1974) sampled the attitudes toward unionization of more than 400 college professors at a university experiencing many financial and resource cutbacks. The items measured were satisfaction with areas like fairness of the university's personnel decisions, adequacy of financial support, representation of faculty interests in the state legislature, and salary. The professors were also asked to rate their inclination to accept a union. Professors who were dissatisfied with employment conditions were much more likely to support a union. Respondents also were consistent in their attitudes toward a union and perceptions of its impact and effectiveness. Proponents of a union saw it as an effective way of protecting employment interests and as having a positive impact. In general, results indicated that unionization is attractive as employment conditions deteriorate.

Using a similar research design and sample, Bigoness (1978) correlated measures of job satisfaction, job involvement, and locus of control with disposition to accept unionization. Bigoness also found that feelings of dissatisfaction related to acceptance of unionization. In particular, dissatisfaction with work, pay, and promotions each correlated .35 with attitude toward unionization. Additionally, unionization was more appealing to people who were less involved in their jobs and had an external locus of control. Combining all independent variables in a multiple-regression equation, Bigoness accounted for more than 27% of the variance in attitudes toward unionization.

Hamner and Smith (1978) examined union activity in 250 units of a large organization. In half the units there had been some union activity; in the other half no activity was reported. Using an immense sample of more than 80,000, Hamner and Smith found that employee attitudes were predictive of level of unionization activity. The strongest predictor was dissatisfaction with supervision. Schriesheim (1978) found that prounion voting in a certification election was positively correlated with dissatisfaction; also, dissatisfaction with economic facets was more predictive than dissatisfaction with noneconomic factors. Furthermore, research by Youngblood, DeNisi, Molleston, and Mobley (1984) and Zalesny (1985) showed the importance of two other factors in union support. The first factor is attitude toward collective bargaining in general. The more acceptable unions are in general to a person, the more likely he or she will be to vote for unionization. The second factor is attitude toward unions as instrumental in enhancing worker welfare. Employees may not be satisfied with their employment conditions, but they may feel that unions can do little to aid them.

What these studies have in common is that they all show that dissatisfaction with employment conditions is predictive of support for unionization. The more satisfied workers are, the less likely they are to think a union is necessary or that it will improve their welfare. These results are not surprising. They do reveal the facets of dissatisfaction associated with a disposition toward unions. Some authors tout the social benefits of unions (for example, association with similar people), but it is mainly the perceived economic advantages that give unions their appeal. Not all support for unions, however, is based on dissatisfaction with economic conditions. Hammer and Berman (1981) found that the faculty at one college wanted a union mainly because they distrusted administrative decision making and were dissatisfied with work content. Prounion voting was motivated by a faculty desire for more power in dealing with the administration.

Union Influence

What influence do unions have on enhancing employee welfare? Various studies have produced somewhat different conclusions. Gomez-Mejia and Balkin (1984)

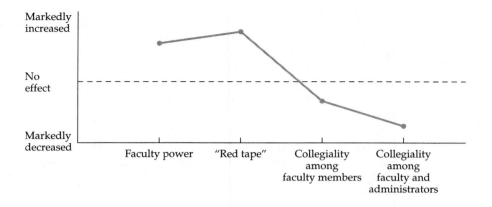

Figure 14–4   *Perceptions of the effects of faculty unionization*

SOURCE: "The Relationship Between Faculty Unionism and Organizational Effectiveness" by K. Cameron, 1982, *Academy of Management Journal, 25*, p. 13.

found that samples of unionized and nonunionized college teachers were equally satisfied with all job facets except pay; unionized faculty were more satisfied with their wages. Carillon and Sutton (1982) found a strong positive relationship between union effectiveness in representing teachers and their reported quality of work life. Allegedly, college administrators fear that faculty unionization will affect organization effectiveness. Cameron (1982) dealt with this in 41 colleges; faculty were unionized in 18 colleges and nonunionized in 23. Cameron proposed nine indexes of effectiveness for a college, involving student academic development, faculty and administrator satisfaction, and ability to acquire resources. Nonunion colleges were significantly more effective on three of the nine indexes; unionized colleges were not significantly more effective on any. Cameron also collected attitude data from faculty members on five factors relating to their work. These results are presented in Figure 14–4. Faculty power and red tape were seen as increasing since unionization; collegiality was seen as decreasing. The study revealed some major differences in effectiveness of union and nonunion colleges; however, the cause was not determined. Unionization may "cause" colleges to be less effective, which would be a strong argument against unions. However, the less effective colleges may turn to unions for improvement, which is obviously an argument supporting unionization. As discussed in Chapter 2, causality is difficult to determine. Raelin (1989) noted that the literature on this topic seems to suggest that less effective colleges turn to unions in an attempt to restore their professional status, although it is questionable whether a union by itself can return an established profession to its original status prior to perceived deprofessionalization.

Fullagar, Gallagher, Gordon, and Clark (1995) tested the proposition that new organizational members are socialized to consider joining a union. Two types of socialization exist. The first is *institutional*, which refers to the collective and formal practices organizations use to provide newcomers with a common set of experiences and information to elicit standardized responses. In contrast, *individual* socialization practices are idiosyncratic and informal. Individual socialization is informal in that learning takes place on the job through interactions with other organizational members. Fullagar and associates found that individual socialization practices had a positive impact on both affective and behavioral involvement in the union. However, institutional socialization practices were shown to be either ineffective or counterproductive. The practical implications are that important interactions occur between union officials and new members in developing new members' affective attachment to the union and later participation in union activities. Informal and individual socialization tactics may be undertaken by active or interested rank-and-file members and not necessarily by union stewards. Institutional socialization efforts (for example, an orientation program to the union) seemingly are more effective in increasing awareness, while individual socialization efforts are more effective in producing involvement (Fullagar, Clark, Gallagher, & Gordon, 1994).

Dispute Settlement

I/O psychologists have examined the process by which disputes are settled in both laboratory and field settings. As in some other areas of I/O research, the generalizability of laboratory findings is somewhat limited. Gordon, Schmitt, and Schneider (1984) feel that the value of laboratory studies is to prepare people for undertaking actual collective bargaining in the future and to help develop questionnaires for later field use in dispute settlement. They noted that the limitations of laboratory and field research on dispute settlement are the classic ones discussed in Chapter 2. There is questionable generalizability from laboratory studies, and field studies fail to identify causal relationships.

There have been several studies on mediation and arbitration as a means of dispute settlement. Bazerman and Neale (1982) asked whether strategies of personnel selection and training can improve negotiating effectiveness. They proposed selecting negotiators on the basis of their ability to take a broad perspective on problems and training them not to be overconfident about effecting a resolution. The authors found that training increased the number of concessions negotiators were willing to make and concluded that it may be a useful tool in dispute settlement. Neale (1984) determined that when the costs of arbitration are high, negotiators are more likely to reach a resolution on their own before resorting to arbitration. However, when cost is not much of an issue, they are more likely to accept arbitration. Researchers have also discovered the behavioral implications of the different types of arbitration. Starke and Notz (1981) reported that subjects anticipating final-offer arbitration were closer to agreement at the conclusion of their bargaining than subjects anticipating conventional arbitration. In fact, Grigsby and Bigoness (1982) concluded that final-offer, conventional, total-package, and issue-by-issue arbitration all produced different bargaining outcomes even though they are all variations of the same resolution process (arbitration). These behavioral studies on dispute settlement have enhanced our understanding in ways that traditional labor economic research has been unable to do. In fact, Brett, Goldberg, and Ury (1990) discuss how I/O psychologists can be used to resolve disputes. They propose that a dispute-system designer organize procedures in a low-to-high cost sequence and work with parties to help them acquire new motivation, negotiation skills, and recourses to new procedures. The individual may even recommend changes in the broader organization that will facilitate the success of a dispute resolution system.

Commitment to the Union

The concept of employee commitment to a union addresses the notion of dual allegiance: Can a person be loyal to both a labor union and the employing company? For several years, researchers have examined the antecedents of both union and company commitment. For example, Fukami and Larson (1984) discovered that it was more difficult to explain workers' commitment to their union than their commitment to their employer.

A big stride in our understanding of union commitment was made through a major study by Gordon, Philpot, Burt, Thompson, and Spiller (1980). These researchers developed a questionnaire for measuring commitment that was completed by more than 1,800 union members. Responses were factor analyzed, and union commitment was found to be composed of four dimensions: loyalty, responsibility to the union, willingness to work for the union, and belief in unionism. The research had at least two major benefits for unions. First, unions could use questionnaires to assess the effect of their actions and estimate solidarity, especially before negotiations. Second, the research revealed the importance of socialization to new union members. The authors felt that union commitment increases when both formal and informal efforts are made to involve a member in union activities soon after joining. Co-worker attitudes and willingness to help are crucial to the socialization process. Improving the socialization of new members improves their commitment, which is one index of union strength. In a follow-up study by Ladd, Gordon, Beauvais, and Morgan (1982), the questionnaire was administered to nonprofessional and professional members of a white-collar union. The results revealed the same factors as those found in the original study despite the sample differences, although other researchers have arrived at somewhat different conclusions (Friedman & Harvey, 1986). Thacker, Fields, and Tetrick (1989) and Thacker, Fields, and Barclay (1990) further established the construct validity of the union commitment scale, and Klandermans (1989) found the scale useful for understanding unionism in Holland.

Mellor (1990) studied membership decline in 20 unions. The unions with the greatest decline in membership showed the strongest commitment to the union by the surviving members. Members in locals with more severe losses expressed a greater willingness to participate in future strikes. Fullagar and Barling (1989) reported that union loyalty was best predicted by union instrumentality, extrinsic job dissatisfaction, and early socialization experiences with unions. They proposed that greater union loyalty caused greater formal participation in union activities. In a study of dual allegiance, Margenau, Martin, and Peterson (1988) found that satisfied workers felt allegiance to both the company and the union, whereas dissatisfied workers showed allegiance only to the union. Tetrick (1995) proposed that union members become committed to their unions for many of the same reasons individuals become committed to their companies. Tetrick believes that commitment to a union can be understood in terms of union citizenship behaviors that are developed in a context of organizational justice. Finally, Gordon and Ladd (1990) provided a cautionary note about professional ethics to researchers studying dual allegiance. They said that researchers should be fully aware of the reasons that either the union or the company would encourage research on allegiance. I/O psychologists should not allow themselves to be "used" by either side to further their own aims by the conduct of such research.

I/O Psychology and Industrial Relations

Hartley (1992) has proposed several areas where I/O psychology can contribute to the field of industrial relations. These include many of the issues already examined: why workers join unions, dispute settlement, and dual commitment. I will now examine three traditional I/O topics from a labor union perspective: personnel selection, training, and employee involvement.

Personnel Selection. In both union and nonunion companies, management determines the knowledge, skills, and abilities needed to fill jobs. The personnel office usually determines fitness for employment in lower level jobs. For higher level jobs, responsibility is spread through various units of the company. However, in a union company the labor contract may stipulate that those hired for jobs represented by the union must join the union. This is a union shop; the employee has no choice about joining.[1] In other unionized companies the employee has the choice of joining a union; these are open shops. However, considerable pressure can be brought on an employee to join. In many cases, it is also to the employee's advantage to join the union for the benefits and protection it affords.

Union influence in personnel selection can affect both applicants and companies. Those who do not endorse unions (or who are uncertain about them) may not apply for jobs in unionized companies. Obviously, the applicant pool for unionized companies will be reduced if such feelings are widespread. The extent of this problem will vary with antiunion sentiment and the availability of other jobs.

Union influence can also work in reverse. One company I know of prides itself on remaining nonunionized. It believes that unionization is encouraged by employees with prior union experience and therefore carefully screens job applicants for union membership. Those who have been union members are not con-

---

[1] However, some states have "right-to-work" laws prohibiting union shops.

sidered (however, they are not told why). The company wants applicants with the talent needed but places a higher priority on avoiding unionism. Whether the company can continue this without adversely affecting the quality of the work force will depend on the job openings and the number of applicants for employment with the company. Thus, from the perspectives of both the applicants and the company, unions can and do ultimately influence who gets hired.

Personnel Training.   One area in which unions have direct and significant influence is personnel training. One of the oldest forms of training is apprenticeship, and unions have a long history of this kind of training, especially in trades and crafts. Apprenticeship is governed by law; at the national level, it is administered by the Department of Labor. The Bureau of Apprenticeship and Training works closely with unions, vocational schools, state agencies, and others. According to the U. S. Department of Labor (1994), there are more than 475 apprenticed occupations employing approximately 280,000 apprentices. Apprentices go through a formal program of training and experience. They are supervised on the job and are given the facilities needed for instruction. There is a progressive wage schedule over the course of apprenticeship, and the individual is well versed in all aspects of the trade. Some authors (for example, Franklin, 1976) think apprenticeship training is unnecessarily long; but there is little doubt that such programs turn out highly skilled artisans.

Most apprenticeship programs are in heavily unionized occupations (construction, manufacturing, transportation); thus, unions work closely with the Bureau of Apprenticeship and Training. Figure 14–5 shows the cooperation among various organizations and agencies in the carpentry trade. Although not all unions are involved in apprenticeship programs, the link between unions and apprenticeship is one of the oldest in the history of American labor.

Employee Involvement.   Employee involvement embraces some of the newer management concepts, such as employee ownership of companies, employee profit-sharing plans, self-managed work teams, and total quality management. It is reasonable to question whether the increased interest in workers' participation in management has resulted in a reduction of "them" versus "us" attitudes on the part of employees. Kelly and Kelly (1991) concluded that employees express positive attitudes toward particular innovations (such as self-managed work groups) but that these attitudes are specific to the innovation and do not generalize to broader "them and us" attitudes and the industrial relations climate. Kelly and Kelly believe that the proper conditions have not been present for fostering broader cooperative attitudes. They note that attitude change is more likely to occur where there is a perception of personal choice and control, but economic conditions and management directives have not provided the conditions for generating employee perception of choice and control. That is, there is a perception among workers that management has been compelled because of economic pressures to try new concepts that reduce the power differential between workers and management. Given this, the amount of sincere trust between workers and management is insufficient to warrant a major enhancement in cooperation between parties in some companies. In a related vein, Fields and Thacker (1992) examined

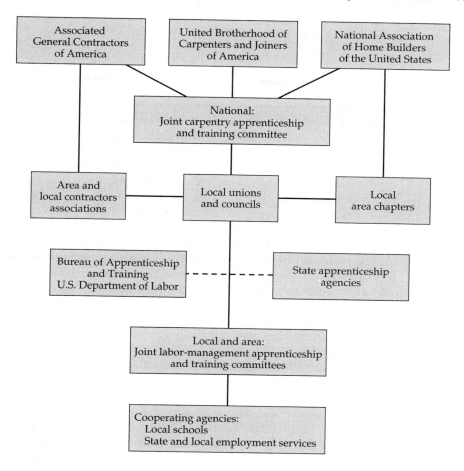

Figure 14–5 *Cooperation among unions, industry, and government in the apprenticeship system of the carpentry trade*

SOURCE: From *Apprenticeship: Past and Present* (p. 25) by U.S. Department of Labor, Washington, DC: Government Printing Office.

changes in union and organizational commitment after the implementation of a joint union/management quality-of-worklife program. The results indicated that company commitment among unionized workers increased only when participants perceived the program as successful, but union commitment increased irrespective of the perception of the program's success. In general, it appears that while unionized employees recognize the benefits of employee involvement programs, participation in them does not mean that the boundaries between union and management are less well-defined.

In this chapter I have examined a topic long neglected by I/O psychologists. Whatever the legitimate or illegitimate reasons, the tide appears to be turning. I hope that interest in research on unions will continue. Because I/O psychologists profess interest in human problems in the work world, we simply cannot ignore the impact of unions in this environment. Indeed, as Gordon and Nurick (1981) stated, knowledge of organization behavior is incomplete without an understanding of union influence.

CASE STUDY   *Should We Let in a Labor Union?*

Carl Dwyer and Ann Stovos were faculty members at Springdale College. The college had been in existence for about 30 years, and Dwyer had been on the staff almost from the beginning. Stovos was a relative newcomer, just completing her third year as a faculty member. For the past two years, there had been talk about unionizing the faculty. Much of the interest was sparked by two events. First, the college had experienced financial cutbacks due to low enrollment. Without tuition revenue, it was facing hardships paying the faculty. As a result, six teaching positions had been eliminated. The faculty understood the college's financial problems, but they felt that cutbacks should be made in other areas, such as eliminating some administrative positions. The faculty was also critical of how the college determined which teaching positions were eliminated. The other event was that for the third year in a row the faculty were given only a 5% raise. Other colleges in the state were giving bigger raises, and some of the Springdale faculty felt that they were getting the short end of the stick.

Various union representatives had been on campus; there was enough support for a representation election to be held in about a month. The faculty really seemed divided. Some openly supported a union, some were openly opposed, but the majority did not voice their sentiments. Dwyer was opposed to the idea of collective bargaining; Stovos supported it. Since they were officemates, the topic came up quite often. On this particular day, they were discussing whether the goals of unions were compatible with the goals of higher education.

> *Dwyer:* I just don't think there is any place in a college for burly picketers carrying placards and threatening to beat up anyone who crosses the picket line. A college is a place for quiet, scholarly thought, an opportunity to teach interested students and to contemplate some of the deeper values. I've been here since we had only 5 buildings and a staff of 20. I don't want to see this place turned into a playground for skull crushers.
>
> *Stovos:* You've been watching too many movies, Carl. No one is going to turn Springdale into a battlefield. I want the same things you do. I didn't come here to be physically intimidated. I wouldn't like that any more than you do. But I also want to be treated fairly by the administration. I'd like some security from arbitrary decisions. There's nothing immoral about that, is there?
>
> *Dwyer:* Do you think a union can prevent layoffs and get us 25% yearly raises?
>
> *Stovos:* No, I don't. But a union can force the drafting of fair and equitable policies if layoffs have to occur. And if everyone else is getting 10% raises, maybe they can help us there too. A union won't work miracles, but it can help prevent injustice.
>
> *Dwyer:* You don't understand, Ann. A college is not a factory. Different ideals run a college. It's not profit but scholarship. We have to foster a climate for inquisitive

minds, learning, and personal growth. If I were interested only in making a buck, I wouldn't have become a college professor.

Stovos: Whether you like it or not, Carl, we are employees like all other working people. What's wrong with trying to ensure fair treatment at work? We have bills to pay and families to support just like everyone else. I don't understand why a college is somehow "different" from all other employers.

Dwyer: That's the problem in a nutshell. A college is not just an employer, and we don't just have jobs. We have careers, and the success of our careers depends on an environment that supports what we are trying to do. Union organizers, picket lines, labor contracts, and mediators have no place in a college.

Stovos: I don't see why a college is somehow "immune" from having to treat its employees fairly like every other employer. What makes a college so special?

Dwyer: Twenty years ago—10 years ago, even—the very thought of a union would have been absurd. The fact that we're now considering one is just proof that the quality of education in this country is going downhill. I can just see it now: "Sorry, class, this is our last meeting. I'm going on strike Monday."

Dwyer got up from his desk, grabbed his coat and hat, and headed off for a meeting.

Stovos: I suppose you'd feel better if you met your class for the last time because you were one of the ones whose position got eliminated.

Dwyer didn't answer, but he slammed the door on the way out.

Questions

1. Do you feel that Dwyer is correct in believing that a union would interfere with the goals of higher education?
2. What benefits does Stovos see from unionization?
3. Do you believe that some organizations, because of their purpose and goals, should not have unionized employees? If so, which ones, and why?
4. Do you think the respective lengths of time that Dwyer and Stovos have spent at the college have any relation to their attitudes? Why or why not?
5. When you think of unions, what thoughts come to mind? Why do you feel as you do?

Ergonomics and Work Conditions

Major Chapter Objectives

- *Be able to describe ergonomic approaches to work design.*

- *Be able to explain psychological approaches to accident reduction.*

- *Be able to identify the physical stressors in the workplace.*

- *Understand how various work schedules influence worker attitudes and behavior.*

- *Understand the impact of alcoholism and drug abuse in the workplace.*

#1)

Ergonomics (or human factors psychology) is the study of the interface between individuals and their work environment. The environment may refer to a work tool or piece of equipment or to the spatial surroundings in which work is conducted. Ergonomics has experienced remarkable growth as a profession in the past ten years due to the recognition that contributions in this area can improve the quality of our lives. Howell (1993) views ergonomics as being responsive to social changes, as witnessed by increased computerization, automation, and information display. Reschetyuk (1992) and Haigh (1993) have described a growing interest in the design of products for individuals of 50 years of age, the fastest growing segment of the population. An evaluation of research conducted in gerontology (aging) indicates deterioration of vision and hearing, hand function, and mental abilities in older populations. Ergonomic research findings can guide designers in the specifications of products that are functional, efficient, safe, and attractive to older and younger users alike. Reschetyuk refers to the study of product design for older populations as "gero-ergonomics." However, ergonomics is not limited strictly to issues of product design. Annett (1994) described the application of ergonomic principles to sports science, and in particular the role of mental imagery for enhancing motor skills. Becker and Steele (1995) noted that organizations are making increased use of teams for conducting business operations, yet most offices are still designed for individual use. These researchers describe a variety of office space layouts found to facilitate teamwork, making the physical design of the workplace congruent with its organizing principles. Finally, Wang (1993) discussed recent trends in ergonomics in China, including its close link to economic and social reform. In short, ergonomics has emerged as a broad-based paradigm for facilitating the performance of individuals and groups within a diverse range of environments.

People work under a broad array of conditions. For example, most people work indoors, but some work outdoors. Some jobs require exposure to intense heat, cold, and noise; others offer temperate conditions. Many people work from 8:00 A.M. to 5:00 P.M., but other hours are also common. Some jobs involve a high risk of injury or illness; others are low risk. How do these different conditions affect attitudes and behavior? What have I/O psychologists learned about responses to variations in working conditions? This chapter is devoted to examining how work conditions affect the employee.

Research in these areas has been conducted in a wide range of professions. Though I/O psychology has made many contributions to the area, so have engineering, physiology, and medicine. Engineers have designed tools, equipment, and work procedures to minimize employee stress and fatigue. Physiologists have studied the effects of heat, cold, noise, and other forms of physical stress on the human body. Physicians studying industrial medicine examine the relationship between certain illnesses and types of work, such as black lung disease among coal miners and cancer among asbestos workers. Thus, research on working conditions and employee behavior is interdisciplinary. Many of the questions addressed extend beyond I/O psychology, but our profession is a primary contributor to the area.

Ergonomic Approaches to Work Design

The ergonomic perspective to achieving person/environment congruence is to hold the individual as a constant and mold the work environment to the person. The theory behind ergonomics is that environments are more malleable than people; thus, the environment is adapted to the limitations and qualities of people. Personnel selection and training approaches take the opposite perspective; that is, people are either selected or "shaped" to fit the environment. In reality, of course, successful person/environment fits require a combination of both approaches.

Grandjean (1986) presents four major objectives of ergonomics:

#1)
- To fit the demands of work to the efficiency of people to reduce stress.
- To design machines, equipment, and installations so that they can be operated with great efficiency, accuracy, and safety.
- To work out proportions and conditions of the workplace to ensure correct body posture.
- To adapt lighting, air-conditioning, noise, and so on to suit people's physical requirements.

The "environment" includes a wide variety of physical situations—the physical conduct of work, equipment design, workplace layout—in short, the arena in which people operate. When I/O psychologists speak of an environment (that is, a machine or work site) as having been "ergonomically designed," we mean it was developed or designed with special regard for its impact on the operator's physical or psychological well-being (see Field Note 1). Imada (1990) recommends that

FIELD NOTE 1

The field of ergonomics is experiencing a rejuvenation. About 30 years ago our nation's interest in the space program triggered a large outpouring of interest in ergonomics. Designing space capsules that could be operated by an astronaut captivated a great deal of attention. In one space flight the astronauts were instructed to flip a switch "up" to conduct some flight operation. Upon doing so the capsule began to shake violently, so the astronauts flipped the switch "down," contrary to what they were supposed to do. The capsule's operation returned to normal, and no one knew what went wrong. Then someone figured it out. In the weightlessness of space, the astronauts happened to be floating upside-down at the time. Thus, the "up" and "down" positions of the switch became reversed from their vantage point. This was a condition no one on gravity-bound Earth had anticipated when the system was being designed.

The military has been a continual user of ergonomic research, but after our nation's interest in the space program began to wane, there was a concomitant reduction of interest in ergonomics. However, that trend appears to be reversing again. With the boom in high-tech equipment, such as computers, copiers, and electronic recreational products, there is renewed interest in designing these products from a human perspective—that is, to be "user friendly," a phrase reflecting an ergonomic orientation. There are a growing number of jobs for psychologists in the field of ergonomics. What the space program did for ergonomics in the 1960s is being recreated by the high-tech companies of the 1990s.

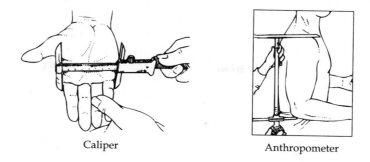

Caliper   Anthropometer

Figure 15–1   *Two instruments used to assess body measurements*
SOURCE: From *Engineering Physiology* by K. H. Kroemer, H. J. Kroemer, and K. E. Kroemer-Elbert, 1986, New York: Elsevier.

ergonomics be promoted to top management as a method of reducing costs and increasing user appeal of products.

Researchers from many disciplines other than psychology contribute to ergonomics. These disciplines have contributed heavily to the development and utilization of three fundamental paradigms that guide the ergonomic analysis and design of work. These paradigms are the anthropometric, biomechanical, and physiological bases of work design. Each will be briefly explained in the following sections, and illustrative examples of work design from each paradigm will be presented.

Anthropometric Approach

Anthropometry is the study of people in terms of their physical dimensions. It includes the measurement of human body characteristics, such as size, breadth, girth, and distance between anatomical points. Anthropometrists take a large number of measurements on individuals (for example, the distance between shoulder and elbow, between the eyes, and so forth) to create a sizable database. The measurements are categorized by demographic variables such as sex, age, and ethnicity because of their relationship to the variables being measured. That is, males are typically physically bigger than females, our bodies change shape as we get older, and different races have differing physical proportions. Figure 15–1 shows the measurement of two body characteristics, one using a caliper and the other using an anthropometer. With descriptive statistics as percentiles, figures are calculated representing major points in the distribution of anthropometric data. Thus, we can describe individuals according to their body characteristics compared to their norm group. For example, a person who is at the 80th percentile in height but the 30th in weight would have a tall, slender build.

The compilation of anthropometric measurements becomes the basis for equipment design, used in either work or leisure. Countless examples abound for the application of anthropometric measures. The size of the keys on a typewriter and the spacing between the keys was determined through anthropometry. Men with stubby fingers sometimes have difficulty typing because most keyboards were designed for people with smaller hand features. Figure 15–2 shows ten hand/object couplings. The size of the object would be designed in accordance with anthropometric data about people's hands. The width of airline and theater seats are similarly determined through examination of the measures of relevant body parts. The leisure industry also draws heavily on anthropometric data to determine the size of football helmets, golf clubs, tennis racquets, and so forth.

The military makes great use of anthropometrics. Because people in the military come in a broad range of sizes, weapons and equipment have to be designed to accommodate a broad range of individual differences. I once heard an ergonomist comment on the problems of designing an adjustable monitor screen and chair that could accommodate operators (either male or female) who were in the 10th percentile in height and the 90th percentile in weight, or vice versa. This system had to be workable (that is, a readable screen and a comfortable chair) for people who were short and heavy, tall and thin, or anything in between.

There are also civilian, commercial applications of anthropometrics. For example, Roebuck (1995) describes the development of a system for the photographic recording of body silhouettes and for applying computer analysis techniques to develop flat clothing patterns from body outlines. The customer enters a booth where a side-view and a front-view photograph are taken. The resulting outline contours are then matched as closely as possible to one of a series of standard silhouettes. A computer analysis of differences then estimates the necessary deviations from the standard flat clothing patterns to fit the individual. The suit or other clothing is then custom-tailored to the individual.

Biomechanical Approach

Biomechanics is defined as the application of mechanical principles (such as levers and forces) to the analysis of body-part structure and movement. Where anthropometrics is utilized in equipment design, biomechanics helps determine the physical movements required in work. Furthermore, as opposed to body measurements, biomechanics is concerned with the effect of movement and force on human muscles, tendons, and nerves. Its focus is on how the conduct of work affects these body parts and, in turn, the best way to design work to minimize stress, pain, or fatigue.

Biomechanics entails the use of complex sensing instruments designed to measure the effects of movements on the body. For example, there are instruments that measure how much force your arms can exert as a function of the angle of your elbow, how much stress is applied to your shoulders as a function of the position of your arms, and so on. Extensive use is also made of motion pictures and video recorders that focus on close-up views of the body at work. Through this information, biomechanics provides a way to design work that is most compatible with the physical limits of the human body.

The biomechanical approach to work design goes well beyond the domain of psychology into such disciplines as physics and human anatomy. As such, biome-

1. Finger Touch: One finger touches an object without holding it.

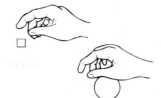

2. Palm Touch: Some part of the inner surface of the hand touches an object without holding it.

3. Finger Palmar Grip (Hook Grip): One finger or several fingers hook(s) onto a ridge, or handle. This type of finger action is used where thumb counterforce is not needed.

4. Thumb-Fingertip Grip (Tip Grip): The thumb tip opposes one fingertip.

5. Thumb-Finger Palmar Grip (Pinch or Plier Grip): Thumb pad opposes the palmar pad of one finger (or the pads of several fingers) near the tips. This grip evolves easily from coupling #4.

6. Thumb-Forefinger Side Grip (Lateral Grip) or Side Pinch: Thumb opposes the (radial) side of the forefinger.

7. Thumb-Two-Finger Grip (Writing Grip): Thumb and two fingers (often forefinger and index finger) oppose each other at or near the tips.

8. Thumb-Fingertips Enclosure (Disk Grip): Thumb pad and the pads of three or four fingers oppose each other near the tips (object grasped does not touch the palm). This grip evolves easily from coupling #7.

9. Finger-Palm Enclosure (Collet Enclosure): Most, or all, of the inner surface of the hand is in contact with object while enclosing it.

10. Power Grasp: The total inner hand surface is grasping the (often cylindrical) handle which runs parallel to the knuckles and generally protrudes on one or both sides from the hand.

Figure 15–2   *Ten couplings between hand and object*

SOURCE: From *Engineering Physiology* by K. H. Kroemer, H. J. Kroemer, and K. E. Kroemer-Elbert, 1986, New York: Elsevier.

chanics is an interdisciplinary approach to designing work; as its very name would suggest, it is a fusion of mechanical principles and living organisms. The research methods of this approach also depart considerably from those of traditional I/O psychology. For example, Viano, Lau, Asbury, and King (1989) studied the effects of simulated automobile accidents on chest and pelvic injuries by subjecting unembalmed cadavers to blunt lateral impacts. In many ways the biomechanical approach to work design is the classic human factors perspective: designing the physical requirements of work to be compatible with the capabilities and limitations of the human body.

Physiological Approach

The physiological approach to work design focuses on the underlying systemic aspects of the body, such as circulation, respiration, and metabolism. From this perspective, work is designed with regard to such parameters as oxygen flow, blood flow, heart rate, and blood pressure. As is characteristic of ergonomics in general, there is extensive reliance on measurement—in this case the measurement of physiological responses of the body. Rather than speaking about issues such as muscle fatigue or back strain, physiologists address the specific neurochemical conditions that produce the symptoms of fatigue and strain. Therefore, "work" is thought of in terms of the flow of nerve impulses, sugar metabolism, and acid secretion.

A good illustration of the physiological perspective is shown in Figure 15–3. Pictured are three ways to carry a satchel and their associated effects on oxygen consumption. Carrying the satchel as a backpack results in the lowest amount of oxygen (and thus energy) consumption. Carrying the satchel slung over the shoulder consumes 82% more energy. Finally, carrying the satchel as a briefcase uses the most energy. We can also use Figure 15–3 to compare the anthropometric, biomechanical, and physiological approaches to work design. Anthropometrics would seek to design the satchel to be approximately equal to the width of a person's back, biomechanics would consider the strain caused by the satchel on the body, and physiologists would address themselves to energy depletion.

Another example of the physiological perspective would be the analysis of the causes of muscle fatigue. Muscle fatigue is caused by the production of lactic acid at a faster rate than oxygen can be delivered through the circulatory system. Energy is provided as a result of burning nutrients from food with oxygen (aerobic) and without (anaerobic). Most oxygen is delivered to the muscle cells from the circulatory system, with blood flow to the muscles matching the muscular demands for oxygen after a few minutes of work. By measuring the amount of oxygen a person uses during work, the amount of aerobic metabolism taking place can be calculated. Thus, work tasks requiring moderate or heavy effort are designed to keep the demands low enough to permit aerobic metabolism to supply the necessary energy. If the demands exceed what aerobic metabolism can

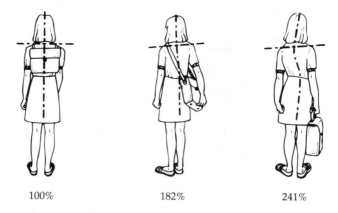

100%   182%   241%

Figure 15–3   *Effect of effort on energy consumption for three ways of carrying a school satchel*
SOURCE: From "Carrying of School Bags by Children" by M. S. Malhotra and J. Sengupta, 1965, *Ergonomics, 8*, p. 56.

provide, the anaerobic metabolic system helps produce energy but also produces lactic acid in the process. Hence, it is common for workers in jobs requiring intense bursts of energy (such as firefighters) to experience fatigue quickly. Work designers therefore try to distribute the intensity and duration of peak energy demands to reduce these fatigue-producing conditions. In jobs where intense energy bursts are unavoidable, attention is given to using equipment to help ease the energy demand or to providing backup personnel to permit adequate recovery. Markowitz (1989) compared a sample of firefighters who fought a large polyvinyl chloride (a dangerous chemical) fire versus an unexposed sample. The results suggested a strong relationship between psychological distress experienced shortly after a toxic exposure event and longer term symptoms. Lim, Ong, and Phoon (1987) examined heart rate and urinary catecholamine levels as stress indicators among firefighters. The results suggested that stress levels were higher on work shifts where there were no fires, indicating that boredom and anxiety contribute to stress.

The physiological perspective approaches work design from the most molecular perspective. As with biomechanics, it embraces scientific methods not usually found in the more traditional areas of I/O psychology. Because all work activities have an inherent physiological basis, this perspective is particularly well adapted to studying all types of jobs. With recent advances in computerization, many people now make use of video display terminals (VDTs) in their jobs. A growing body of literature suggests that extensive use of VDTs leads to visual strain and physical discomfort in the neck and shoulder area (Stellman, Klitzman, Gordon, & Snow, 1987). In addition to visual and skin problems associated with VDT usage, Bramwell and Cooper (1995) reported the possibility that extensive

VDT usage may produce a greater risk of problems in pregnancy. This latter finding is of special concern, because a large portion of VDT users are women of childbearing age. Grandjean (1987) has examined the physiological effects of VDTs on vision as a function of various characteristics of VDTs, such as brightness, contrast, and flicker. He reports definite patterns between photometric characteristics and physiological responses and recommends that VDTs be designed from an ergonomic perspective as well as from a purely mechanical one. Grandjean also has studied the effects of hand placements and positions and believes they also contribute to operator efficiency and satisfaction. He believes the VDT workstation has become the launch vehicle for ergonomics in the office world.

Overview

The anthropometric, biomechanical, and physiological perspectives in work design are simply three ways to modify the environment to accommodate people's characteristics and limitations. While each approach has its own distinctive focus, they are not mutually exclusive. Anthropometric information can be of great help in the design of work from a biomechanical perspective. However, think of these approaches as three tacks researchers have found useful to modify the environment to fit people in the conduct of work. Anthropometrics relies on a descriptive inventory of bodily measurements, biomechanics examines major body parts and movements in terms of mechanical principles, and the physiological perspective deals with the effect of work on the body's fundamental systems.

Human/Computer Interactions in the Workplace

It is estimated that the majority of all U.S. workers will deal daily with a computer by the end of this century. Computers are greatly affecting the lives of blue-collar and white-collar workers alike. Freese (1987) states that technology is driven to its limits to automatize as completely as possible. The rest that cannot (yet) be done by technical means or is so uneconomical to do with machines is being left to humans. He feels that computerization is creating a major ethical concern for the blue-collar sector of the work force. Turnage (1990) argues that technological innovation will not be readily adopted (and thus will not improve productivity) unless due regard is given to the users of technology. She proposes the concept of "high tech/high touch"—whenever technology is introduced, there must be a counterbalancing human response (such as high touch) or the technology will be rejected. Turnage argues that sophisticated technology will not work unless the proper balance is struck between human and machine systems.

Computers are also being used to conduct a form of performance appraisal, a concept called "computer-aided monitoring." Computer-aided monitoring provides continuous assessment of an employee's performance, sometimes on a minute-by-minute basis. Chalykoff and Kochan (1989) found that management views such monitoring as a system to develop the employee and to gauge the quality of work. However, some employees feel they are being spied on, and the monitoring tends to provide negative, not positive, feedback. Larson and Callahan (1990) found that computer-aided monitoring serves as a cue to signal the perceived importance of a task, which in turn affects the amount of effort devoted to it. Also, some employees regard computer-aided monitoring as a major source of job stress.

Parsons and Kearsley (1982) addressed the issue of division of labor between humans and a growing segment of the work force—robots. They recommend studying the relationship between humans and robots with regard to not only performance and output but also human/robot communication, job satisfaction, and organizational impact. Chao and Kozlowski (1986) found that low-skill workers reacted negatively toward implementation of robots, perceiving them largely as threats to their job security. High-skill workers reacted more positively toward robots, perceiving their implementation as providing opportunities to expand their skills. Research on the human/robot interface may become the Hawthorne studies of the future, and Shenkar (1988) considers robotics to be one of the major challenges facing I/O psychology.

Safety and Accidents

Industrial safety and accidents are among the oldest topics in I/O psychology, dating back to the turn of the century. One of the first responsibilities of psychologists was to develop safer working conditions. Engineers also contributed greatly, particularly in equipment design and plant layout. Although we have made big strides in improving work safety, industrial accidents still are a major concern. The National Safety Council has published some alarming statistics (DeReamer, 1980):

1. Approximately 1 million productive person-years are lost annually through work accidents.
2. Accidents cost the nation at least $51.1 billion in lost wages, medical expenses, property damage, and insurance costs.
3. One American worker dies every eight minutes from an industrial accident.
4. Injuries to U.S. workers each year have the same economic impact as if the nation's entire industrial community were to shut down for one full week.
5. In the United States, loss of life from accidents during this century far exceeds that from wars, earthquakes, floods, tornadoes, and other natural catastrophes combined.

Researchers in different disciplines address the problem of industrial accidents from various perspectives, but all are concerned with reducing frequency and severity of accidents. I/O psychologists focus on individual characteristics associated with accidents and investigate various traditional approaches (personnel selection, work design, and training) in accident reduction. Industrial hygienists view occupational diseases as consequences of recurring events or accidents. Safety engineers see accidents as results of a sequence of acts or events with undesirable consequences including personal injury, property damage, or work interruption.

Accidents and injuries are not synonymous. Injury is the consequence of an accident, but many "no-injury" accidents also occur. Though psychologists are concerned with accidents whether or not they result in injury, they generally pay more attention to those accidents involving injuries. In an attempt to make people more aware of the likelihood of accidents, researchers have computed the objective probability of incurring an accident as a function of, for example, miles driven, trips taken, and so on. However, Sheehy and Chapman (1987) found that an increase in the objective probability of an accident seems to generate a proportional denial of its likelihood (that is, perceived probability) among people, thereby mitigating its capacity to sensitize people to its occurrence.

Further, when accidents and injuries do occur, there is often a strong impetus to assign blame for their occurrence and to search out their cause. As Senders and Moray (1991) have noted, it is often very difficult to identify a single cause of accidents, particularly those involving human error. Reason (1994) reports that only recently has society witnessed a growing openness on the part of the medical profession to acknowledge physician error in mishaps to patients. Reason stated, "This new spirit of *glasnost* has led to an increasing number of fruitful research partnerships between doctors (particularly anesthetists) and human factor specialists" (p. *vii*). In short, social, legal, and political forces often operate to retard our ability to understand the causes of human error, which in themselves are inherently difficult to identify.

Safety Legislation

State and federal laws protect the welfare of the worker. The major one is the Occupational Safety and Health Act (OSHA), which became effective in 1971. OSHA was meant to integrate federal and state legislation under a federal program establishing uniform codes, standards, and regulations. The purpose of the act is "to assure, as far as possible, every working woman and man in the nation safe and healthful working conditions, and to preserve our human resources." To accomplish this, there are provisions for safety and health standards, research, information, and education and training in occupational safety and health.

OSHA is comprehensive, covering such things as record keeping, inspection, compliance, and enforcement of safety standards. It lists more than 5,000 safety and health standards, ranging from density of particles in the air to the height at which a fire extinguisher is to be mounted. Some critics suggest that the act is too concerned with trivial standards that burden employers without really protecting

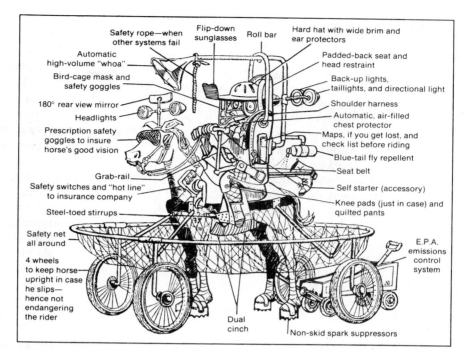

Safety rope—when other systems fail
Flip-down sunglasses
Roll bar
Hard hat with wide brim and ear protectors
Automatic high-volume "whoa"
Padded-back seat and head restraint
Bird-cage mask and safety goggles
Back-up lights, taillights, and directional light
180° rear view mirror
Shoulder harness
Headlights
Automatic, air-filled chest protector
Prescription safety goggles to insure horse's good vision
Maps, if you get lost, and check list before riding
Blue-tail fly repellent
Grab-rail
Seat belt
Safety switches and "hot line" to insurance company
Self starter (accessory)
Steel-toed stirrups
Knee pads (just in case) and quilted pants
Safety net all around
E.P.A. emissions control system
4 wheels to keep horse upright in case he slips—hence not endangering the rider
Dual cinch
Non-skid spark suppressors

COWBOY AFTER OSHA

workers. Others consider OSHA one of the most important and influential pieces of legislation ever enacted. The law provides for safety inspections and fines for noncompliance. Trained officers conduct 100,000 inspections annually. Companies can be fined for maintaining improper safety records and for willfully violating standards. In 1987 financial penalties totaling more than $3 million, the largest sum ever levied against an employer, were proposed against a beef-packing plant for having more than 100 serious safety violations.

Other laws involving safety (for example, workers' compensation) exist, but none of them has the far-reaching impact of OSHA. It has given new status and responsibility to safety and health practitioners. OSHA has increased concern among employers and unions over safety and health problems, as well as compliance with safety regulations. Has OSHA been effective in enhancing industrial safety? Cascio (1995a) noted that OSHA has been the subject of controversy since its inception. Investigations by Congress have found that OSHA has made few lasting reductions in lost workdays or injury rates. However, because of OSHA and other agencies concerned with industrial safety, we know more about dangerous workplace substances such as vinyl chloride, PCBs, and asbestos. As a result, companies have taken at least the initial actions needed to protect workers from them.

Psychological Approaches to Accident Reduction

Throughout this book, I have stressed three approaches to achieving a better fit between worker and workplace. The first is based on individual differences and involves selecting people who have the characteristics thought to be necessary or desirable for specified work demands. This is the personnel selection approach, the analog of finding the right "pegs" to fit the "holes." The second approach is that of training people in the necessary skills, knowledge, or attitudes. This is the personnel training approach, the analog of "reshaping the pegs" to fit the "holes." The third approach is modifying the workplace to provide a better match with abilities and characteristics. This is the engineering psychology or work design approach, the analog of "reshaping the holes" to fit the "pegs." These approaches are all used to reduce industrial accidents and create a safer work environment. Given that 50% to 80% of all accidents are attributable to human error (Spettell & Liebert, 1986), an examination of accidents from a human perspective is most reasonable. I will now examine in some detail I/O research to achieve greater person/environment congruence.

Personnel Selection Approach

The personnel selection approach is the search for individual differences predictive of accidents. This paradigm has proceeded along two paths: group prediction and individual prediction. *Group prediction* (also called actuarial prediction) has been remarkably successful in forecasting accidents. It is the basis on which insurance companies operate, and it works as follows. Based on hundreds of thousands of cases from national samples, insurance companies calculate the probability of incurring automobile driving accidents as a function of many variables, such as age, sex, marital status, and so on. From a purely statistical standpoint, it is calculated that young (under 25), single, male drivers are more likely to incur accidents than are persons with some other combination of characteristics. Therefore, the cost of the insurance sold to members of various cohorts is adjusted to reflect the differential likelihood of having an accident. In the extreme case, an insurance company might refuse to cover people who have extremely high probabilities for accidents. As you can imagine, these demographically constituted categories cover millions of people nationwide and are very coarse groupings. Consequently, insurance companies, being highly competitive, seek additional predictors of accidents to refine their assessments (and thus lower the cost of insurance). For example, if you are a college student with a "B" or better grade point average, you are a member of a group that has fewer accidents than less academically accomplished students. Accordingly, the cost of your insurance can be reduced somewhat. Some companies offer cost reductions for nonsmokers, infrequent drivers (that is, 7,500 miles per year or less), and graduates of driver education classes. They do so because these variables have been found to be predictive of accidents on an actuarial basis.

The second avenue of the personnel selection approach to accidents is *individ-*

ual prediction. Here predictions are made regarding the likelihood of certain individuals' having accidents. I/O psychologists would most likely contribute to this approach. Beirness (1993) examined research findings pertaining to the role of personality factors in driving behavior and accidents in an attempt to relate driving style to lifestyle. Six broad dimensions of personality appeared to be strongly and consistently related to accidents: thrill seeking, impulsiveness, hostility/ anger, emotional instability, depression, and loss of control. High levels of these personality factors predispose individuals to high-risk driving situations and to react to situations in the driving environment that place them at high risk. Personality factors were found to account for 10 to 20% of the variance in accidents and up to 35% of the variance in risky driving.

Recent research on the value of personality tests to predict accidents has yielded some encouraging findings. For example, Hansen (1989) developed personality scales from the MMPI assessing a state of distractibility that was correlated with accidents in a sample of chemical workers. Hilakivi and colleagues (1989) examined the validity of a personality test to select drivers for the Finnish military. The personality factors of impulsivity, adventurousness, naiveté, and excessive trustfulness were correlated with motor vehicle accidents.

In keeping with the personnel selection approach, variables predictive of accidents would be used to hire people for jobs having high accident risk. People would be hired for transportation jobs (chauffeurs, bus drivers, pilots) and jobs having a high risk factor (handling of hazardous chemicals) based on their likelihood of having accidents.

Ergonomic Approach

Designing a safer work environment is one of the oldest and most prominent objectives of ergonomists or engineering psychologists. I will review a few examples of their work.

Many industrial workers use tools in the conduct of their jobs. If the tools are not designed with the limitations of the human body in mind, injuries can result. A common work-related injury is carpal tunnel syndrome, a painful injury to the wrist. It is found more frequently in people whose jobs require extensive finger and hand movements. Figure 15–4 shows three ergonomically designed knives for meat cutting and packing jobs that reduce the amount of stress on the wrists, particularly over extended use.

Voevodsky (1974) described a study that tried to reduce the number of times taxicabs are struck from behind. Cab drivers often stop faster than drivers behind them anticipate. Voevodsky installed yellow warning lights on the trunks of 343 cabs. These lights began to blink when the cab slowed down. The rate of blinking was proportional to the rate of deceleration; faster blinking implied more rapid deceleration. A control group of 160 cabs was not fitted with the lights. After ten months, accident statistics on the two groups of cabs were compared. On three major performance dimensions (number of rear-end collisions, cost of repairs necessitated, and injuries to cab drivers), the experimental cabs outperformed the control cabs. The size of the difference was also very impressive: Accidents were

Figure 15–4   *The handles on these knives are designed to utilize the larger muscle groups of the forearm and upper arm. This design also allows an improved power grip that can help reduce grip force.*
SOURCE: Courtesy of The Saunders Group.

reduced by over 60%. The statistics on the control cabs were unchanged during the study. To see whether the differences were due simply to greater caution on the part of the drivers of the experimental cabs, comparisons were made of front-end collisions. No significant differences were found between experimental and control cabs. The author thus concluded that the cab drivers had not changed their driving, but the motorists behind them had.

These two examples are good illustrations of the ergonomic approach to safety. The researchers modified the equipment used, and the changes resulted in fewer accidents and injuries. Engineering psychology has shown that performance can be improved by designing the workplace to complement human skills, be it in terms of muscle usage or reaction time.

Personnel Training Approach

Personnel training involves more than selecting a method to improve skills. It also involves creating an atmosphere in which training is supported and trained persons are rewarded for improvement. The personnel training approach to safety involves everything I discussed about other types of training and represents a major approach toward accident reduction. As is the case in all training, employees must be motivated. With safety training, employees must have a reason for behaving safely. Training is thus directed toward making safety a desirable outcome.

All training programs are conducted within a climate that places some degree of importance on training. In some organizations training may be highly valued; in others it may be treated with only mild interest. Dedobbeleer and Beland (1991) reported that an effective safety climate was one in which management had a strong commitment to safety and the workers were heavily involved in safety issues. Janssens, Brett, and Smith (1995) examined variation in the relationships among constructs affecting the perceptions of worker safety in the U.S., French, and Argentine plants of the same division of a multinational organization, all affected by the same corporatewide safety policy. Management's concern for safety had the least effect on accidents in France and the greatest effect in Argentina. The authors proposed that cultural differences in managerial style and decision making across the three plants contributed to the variation in how workers perceived the company's safety policy.

Zohar (1980) developed a questionnaire to assess organizational climates regarding safety. Employees at 20 companies rated their perceptions of the safety climate. A team of four experienced safety inspectors evaluated each organization on safety practices and accident-prevention programs. Scores on the questionnaire were then compared with inspectors' judgments. The results revealed that management's commitment to safety is a major factor in the success of safety programs. Organizations with a strong safety climate have job training programs, give executive authority to safety officials, have high-level managers on safety committees, and consider safety in job design. Zohar feels that attempts to improve safety (for example, by new regulations or poster campaigns) without management commitment will probably not succeed. As I stated in Chapter 6, the role of management is critical to any training program, and safety training is no exception.

These studies attest to the importance of an environment conducive to safety training. Employees quickly pick up cues on the importance of safety. Scrap or waste on the floor, unprotected wires, and failure to wear hard hats contradict bulletin board posters saying "Safety First." Organizational attitudes toward safety are conveyed by what people do. The studies show that management behavior and attitudes relate to employee feelings about safety and to accidents.

In terms of actual safety training, Komaki, Barwick, and Scott (1978) showed the efficacy of goal setting, positive reinforcement, and feedback. They studied employees in two departments of a food manufacturing plant: production (makeup) and wrapping. After analyzing the jobs in both departments, they identified safe and unsafe behavior and made slides showing these behaviors. Workers saw two slides per task and discussed each type of behavior. After reviewing their current accident rate, employees in both departments set goals for safe behavior. The goals were plotted on a large graph conspicuously displayed at the work site. The researchers then observed behavior, provided feedback and encouragement, and plotted behavior on the graph.

The results are shown in Figure 15–5. In the wrapping department the baseline of safe behaviors jumped from 70% to 95% after training; in the makeup department the percentage increased from 77% to 99%. After termination of the program, safe behavior reverted to its pretraining levels. Komaki and associates (1978) reported that worker motivation was very high throughout the study, and pressure was put on co-workers not to "ruin" the graph. The results clearly indicate that safe behavior can be enhanced through training aimed at increasing motivation and sensitivity, but safe behavior requires continuous attention. In this case unsafe behavior returned to its base rate immediately following the end of the program (labeled "Reversal" in the figure).

Other studies document the value of safety training. Reber, Wallin, and

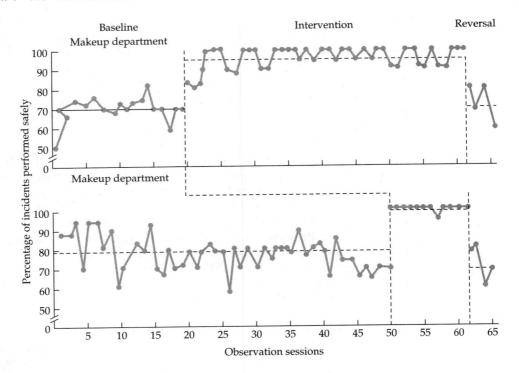

Figure 15–5   *Percentage of employees' safe behavior in two departments of a food manufacturing plant during a 25-week period*

SOURCE: From "A Behavioral Approach to Occupational Safety: Pinpointing and Reinforcing Safe Performance in a Food Manufacturing Plant" by J. Komaki, K. D. Barwick, and L. R. Scott, 1978, *Journal of Applied Psychology, 63,* p. 439.

Chhokar (1984) developed checklists of safe and unsafe behaviors at work. Employees were asked to set hard but attainable goals for improved safety performance. They were shown slides of the safe and unsafe behaviors, identified by means of the checklists, and were instructed to select the safe behaviors in conducting their jobs. Their safety performance was fed back to them, giving them knowledge of their results on the job. The training produced a 54% reduction in lost-time injuries. McAfee and Winn (1989) reviewed 24 studies that examined the use of positive incentives and feedback to improve safety and decrease accidents in industry. All studies found that incentives or feedback were successful in improving safety conditions or reducing accidents.

   An interesting common denominator of all these safety training studies is that they focused on the conduct of positive (safe) behavior rather than railing against violations of safety rules (negative behavior). That is, they all conclude that training should be directed toward enhancing safe behavior rather than eradicating unsafe behavior.

Overview

Organizations need not limit themselves to one approach to reducing accidents. In fact, Peters (1991) suggested that the prudent organization would adopt a comprehensive program using multiple approaches. Each approach has its own merits; when used in combination, they improve the likelihood of reducing accidents. Hollenbeck, Ilgen, and Crampton (1992) recommended the use of a comprehensive system of multiple approaches to reduce the frequency of lower-back disability, a widespread phenomenon that has dramatic impacts on employer costs. Research indicates that there are some useful variables for predicting which people are most likely to incur accidents. To the extent that these differences can be reliably predicted, the personnel selection approach can help us staff organizations with people who exhibit safe behavior. The engineering-psychology approach entails modifying the tools, equipment, and machinery to eliminate unsafe conditions. Machines must be designed to complement human skills and limitations. The training approach is based on the belief that safety skills, like all skills, can be improved through training. This approach stresses the importance of an environment conducive to safety and of acquiring the knowledge and skills needed to reduce accidents. Each method approaches safety from a different perspective, but all three have proved effective in reducing accidents.

Despite all the advances made in recent years in equipment, tools, machinery, and technology in general, safety is not totally a technical issue per se. Actually, it is primarily a people issue. Smith, Cohen, Cohen, and Cleveland (1978) identified seven factors that were found to differentiate low-accident from high-accident companies. These factors are listed in Table 15–1. Note how many relate to people. While the topic of safety certainly transcends individual differences, and the value of technical advances in equipment design should not be underestimated, eventually the ultimate responsibility for maintaining a safe work environment rests with people. Cohen (1977) cogently summarized this point when he said, "Maximally effective safety programs in industry will be dependent on those practices that can successfully deal with 'people' variables" (p. 168). The world's

Table 15–1 *Characteristics of successful safety programs*

Greater management commitment and involvement in safety programs
A more humanistic approach in dealing with employees, stressing frequent positive contact and interaction
Better employee selection procedures
More frequent use of lead workers versus supervisors to train employees
A much greater degree of housekeeping and general plant cleanliness
Better plant environment qualities
Lower turnover and absenteeism among a more stable work force

SOURCE: "Characteristics of Successful Safety Programs" by M. J. Smith, H. H. Cohen, A. Cohen, and R. J. Cleveland, 1978, *Journal of Safety Research, 10*, pp. 5–15.

best seat belts will save no lives if people won't wear them or if they find ways to circumvent their use (see Field Note 2).

Physical Stressors in the Workplace

Stress is highly complex and multifaceted. The causes of stress include work demands, role pressures, and organization characteristics. I discussed how role pressures contribute to stress in Chapter 10. In this chapter I will examine how work demands (noise, heat, and cold) and some organization characteristics (most notably, work hours) contribute to stress. There are wide individual differences associated with perceptions of stress. That is, one person may feel stressed by a hectic schedule; another may enjoy the challenge and variety. Any stimulus (for example, work pace, noise, role pressure) that elicits a stress response is a stressor. Stressors associated with the physical conditions of work elicit fairly consistent stress responses. However, the degree of stress is often moderated by individual differences.

FIELD NOTE 2

I spent some time studying miners of bituminous coal (see Chapter 6). In the course of my work, I discovered that the miners would occasionally feel compelled to take some major risks that could result in accidents and fatal injuries. Here is what would happen.

The machinery used to extract coal from the ground was electrically powered. Down on the mine floor (several hundred feet below the surface), miners operated tremendously powerful machinery that required large amounts of electrical current. The electrical current was supplied by a cable that was attached to the rear of the machinery. In much the same way that an upright vacuum cleaner is moved over a carpet, the mining equipment was moved back and forth on the mine floor to extract the coal from the coal face.

The miners were supposed to mount the electrical cable on hooks elevated above the mine floor. But because there were organizational pressures to extract the coal from the ground as quickly as possible, the miners sometimes took a "shortcut" and left the cables on the mine floor. Mounting the cables on hooks would take time away from their work, so they skipped this step to save time and be more productive. Why was this important? Returning to the vacuum cleaner analogy, when you are pushing and pulling the vacuum across the carpet, sometimes you may inadvertently back it over the attached electrical cord. However, nothing happens because the weight of the vacuum is not great enough to slice through the cord and give you an electrical shock. Mining equipment, on the other hand, is very heavy (several tons) and could easily cut into the power cable. This is precisely what could have happened to the miners. When moving the machinery back and forth, the operator inadvertently could have run over the power cable trailing on the mine floor, which would have sent several thousand volts of electricity into the machinery, electrocuting the operator. The miners told me that as they became more experienced in operating the machinery, they "kind of got the feel" for where the cables were and would not back over them. However, should they have ever "missed" in their judgments, a lethal injury would have awaited them.

Noise

Noise is defined as "unwanted sound." But before presenting the effects of noise on performance, let's review the characteristics of sound. Two physical characteristics are frequency and intensity; their psychological counterparts are pitch and loudness. Sound emanates in waves. If the sound is "pure" (like a tuning fork), a graph of the wave looks like a sine (sinusoidal) wave. Low frequency sounds have fewer wave repetitions per unit of time than do high frequency sounds. In fact, the number of waves per second is the frequency. Frequency is usually measured in cycles per second (cps) or Hertz (Hz). Impure sounds have more complex wave patterns because they are composed of differing frequencies. The psychological analog of frequency is pitch; we recognize this by saying that a tenor has a different pitch than a soprano.

Intensity of sound is usually measured in decibels (dB) and reflects differences in sound energy. The decibel scale is constructed so that a change of 10 dB means a tenfold change in sound power. Differences in frequency are represented by differences in waves per second; differences in intensity are represented by differences in the height of the waves. "Loud" sounds have more intensity than "soft" sounds. Figure 15–6 shows various sounds and associated decibel values.

The Effects of Noise. It is difficult to say definitely what effect noise has on performance since "performance" has been examined in many contexts. Some aspects of performance are more affected by noise than others. Noweir (1984) examined the effects of noise (80–99 dB) on employees in three textile mills. Employees with high noise exposure (above 90 dB) had more disciplinary actions, accidents, and absenteeism and less productivity than employees with less noise exposure. Noise appeared to affect the quality of work, as reflected by disciplinary actions for material damage, and was particularly evident for spinning operations involving vigilance. Sundstrom, Town, Rice, and Osborn (1994) reported in a field study of office workers that 54% said they were bothered by noise, especially by people talking and telephones ringing. Increasing dissatisfaction with the work environment was directly related to increasing noise.

There are no simple relationships between noise and human performance. Noise adversely affects performance on some tasks but not on others. Additionally, some people are more sensitive than others to noise. To the extent that I/O psychologists can (1) identify tasks whose performance will be impaired by noise and (2) identify people sensitive to noise, steps can be taken to improve the worker/workplace fit. Headphones and sound-proofed construction materials can be used in jobs prone to interference from noise. People can be hired based on their sensitivity to noise. As stated, with differences in both jobs and people, the I/O psychologist's job is to get as good a match as possible between abilities and work requirements.

Hearing Loss from Work. Employees exposed to intense noise over long periods usually lose a portion of their hearing. If the noise is of a particular frequency, partial or complete hearing loss to tones of that frequency is quite possible. Em-

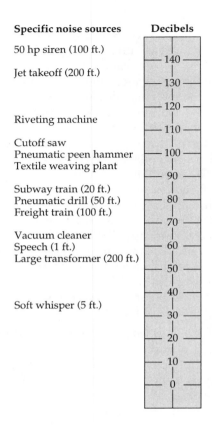

Specific noise sources	Decibels
50 hp siren (100 ft.)	
	140
Jet takeoff (200 ft.)	
	130
	120
Riveting machine	
	110
Cutoff saw	
Pneumatic peen hammer	100
Textile weaving plant	
	90
Subway train (20 ft.)	
Pneumatic drill (50 ft.)	80
Freight train (100 ft.)	
	70
Vacuum cleaner	
Speech (1 ft.)	60
Large transformer (200 ft.)	
	50
	40
Soft whisper (5 ft.)	
	30
	20
	10
	0

Figure 15–6   *Decibel levels for various sounds*

SOURCE: From *Handbook of Noise Measurement,* 8th ed. by A. P. Petersen and F. E. Gross, 1978, New Concord, MA: GenRad.

ployees exposed to intense noise over the full spectrum of frequencies may suffer a general hearing decrease.

To protect workers from hearing loss in noisy jobs (like airline ground employees, construction workers, and data processors), companies provide headphones or earplugs. Many labor contracts specify that not wearing such safety equipment is grounds for dismissal. Some companies also approach the problem of noise stress by means of personnel selection, hiring partially or totally deaf people for noisy jobs.

Noise stress is a major concern for some companies. Noisy equipment may have to be reengineered or housed in certain areas to lessen disruptive influences. Special ear protection has been devised, eliminating the intensity of unwanted noise while still permitting communication among workers. Employees suffering from work-related hearing impairment are eligible for special compensation from employers; some victims of hearing loss have sued employers for not providing safe working conditions. Fortunately, risk of hearing impairment is slight in most jobs, but in those where it is a problem, corrective measures are necessary.

Heat

Discomfort from heat is not only due to high temperatures. Adjustment to heat is a function of three variables: air temperature, humidity, and airflow. High temperatures, high humidity, and a lack of airflow are most uncomfortable. Some research indicated that humidity may be the most important variable in determining discomfort. With high temperature and humidity, rapid air movement can make the situation tolerable. Because the sensation of heat cannot be adequately measured by simply recording air temperature, other indexes have been developed. One index used in enclosed environments is the wet-bulb globe temperature (WBGT), which takes into account the effects of humidity in combination with air temperature. The WBGT is a more sensitive index of discomfort than simple air temperature.

Heat stress is a problem not only for those who work outdoors but also for people working around furnaces, boilers, dryers, and other heat-producing equipment. Heat stress can greatly impair productivity of those doing strenuous work. Workers lose stamina because their bodies are taxed by the combination of heat and physical exertion. However, heat stress can also impair performance in tasks requiring little physical effort, even those limited to mental skills. For example, Fine and Kobrick (1978) compared performance of individuals working on problem-solving tasks under different heat-stress conditions. The treatment group worked under 95° F and 88% humidity; the control group worked under 70° F and 25% humidity. Performance was monitored for seven hours. Results are shown in Figure 15–7. The number of errors made by the treatment group was considerably greater, and the extent of the difference became greater over time.

Organizations are aware of the effects of heat and expend a lot of money to cope with the problem. Central air-conditioning is a standard feature of most new office buildings. Dehumidifiers are installed where humidity may affect performance or damage sensitive equipment (like computers). Industrial fans are often installed to draw off the heat (and noxious fumes) associated with some types of manufacturing. However, in many cases the climate cannot be controlled or modified, as in outdoor work. In such cases workers may be allowed more rest breaks or may be relieved by other crews. Given rising energy costs, it is increasingly expensive to maintain ideal climates. Federal rulings specify thermostat levels (65° F in the winter, 78° F in the summer) for office buildings as a means of limiting energy consumption. How do people react to these temperature conditions? Vickroy, Shaw, and Fisher (1982) studied the effect of employees' clothing (suit, long-sleeved or short-sleeved shirts) on performance and satisfaction at the two temperature levels. They found that employees who wore appropriate clothing for the temperature showed higher levels of performance and satisfaction with the working conditions than did those who wore inappropriate clothing.

Cold

Both mental and physical tasks are affected by cold; however, there is evidence that people can adapt to cold over time. Prolonged exposure constricts blood

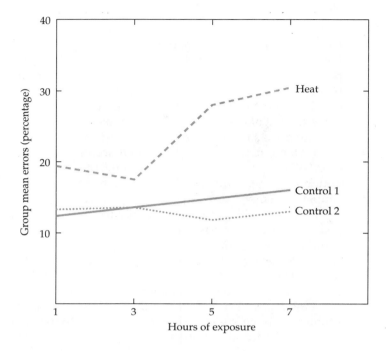

Figure 15-7   *Mean percentage of errors in cognitive tasks for a group working under heat and for two control groups*

SOURCE: From "Effects of Altitude and Heat on Complex Cognitive Tasks" by B. J. Fine and J. L. Kobrick, 1978, *Human Factors*, 20, pp. 115–122. Copyright 1978 by The Human Factors Society, Inc., and reproduced by permission.

vessels, which reduces blood flow to the skin surface and reduces skin temperature. Under such conditions, exposed skin and extremities (fingers and toes) become numb. Under more extreme conditions, total body temperature will be lowered. Manual performance is adversely affected by lowered body temperature, even when hands are kept warm. Similar results have been reported for tasks requiring concentration. In attempting to explain this, Fox (1967) suggested that cold causes other stimuli to compete for the individual's attention. Cooling of the extremities, with the resulting threat of injury, distracts the worker from the task at hand, thus lowering performance. In particular, tasks requiring fine finger dexterity are more susceptible to impairment from the cold than grosser types of manual activity. Enander (1987) found exposure to moderate cold produced decrements in manual dexterity, but no effects on simple reaction time were observed.

With outdoor activities, wind chill can be a major factor affecting workers. The wind chill index provides a means for making a quantitative comparison of combinations of temperature and wind speed. Table 15-2 shows the cooling effects of combinations of certain temperatures and wind speeds derived from the index, these being expressed as equivalent temperatures. An equivalent tempera-

Table 15-2 *Cooling effects of temperature and wind speed*

Wind Speed (mph)	Air Temperature (°F)					
	40	*20*	*10*	*0*	*−10*	*−30*
Calm	40	20	10	0	−10	−30
5	37	16	6	−5	−15	−36
10	28	4	−9	−21	−33	−46
20	18	−10	−25	−39	−53	−67
30	13	−18	−33	−48	−63	−79
40	10	−21	−37	−53	−69	−85

ture refers to the sensation of cold and wind. For example, an air temperature of 10° F with a 20-mph wind produces the same cooling sensation as a temperature of −25° F under calm wind conditions. Extreme cold produced by a wind chill increases numbness and reaction time (Ellis, 1982). However, visual performance (as measured by speed or precision in responding) is generally not impaired by exposure to cold. Continued exposure to extremely cold temperatures produces frostbite, a danger encountered by outdoor workers, especially in the Midwest. In Midwestern states the temperature gets down to −20° F, and with the strong 30–40 mph wind that blows across the plains, the wind chill temperature can reach −70° F. Special clothing and footwear have been designed for the workers' protection. Additionally, some workers receive extra compensation for working in the cold. Fortunately, few indoor jobs involve exposure to extremely cold temperatures.

Multiple Stressors

Stressors do not always exist in isolation. If they exist jointly, a worker must contend with their additive or interactive effects. For example, if the noise level and the heat level each decrease performance by 10%, the combined effect of a hot, noisy workplace may reduce performance by 20%. These two stressors have an additive effect. However, in some cases, stressors have an interactive effect; their combined effect may exceed the sum of the independent effects.

I recall an episode from a job analysis that illustrates the effect of multiple stressors. A construction worker described his job in the summer as being "hot and noisy." I wanted to observe him at work. He was using a pneumatic air drill to remove street pavement, and the temperature was 90° F. However, the heat radiating off the pavement made the temperature at street level over 110° F. The noise from a pneumatic drill (at a range of about 15 feet) was over 100 dB. After observing this worker for about five minutes and taking notes on his job duties, the effect of the heat and noise made me feel faint and nauseated. While the construction worker could perform under those conditions, I could not. I found the noise worse than the heat, but the combined effect made me abandon my efforts. I also learned that simple descriptive phrases like "hot and noisy" mean different things to different people.

From a practical standpoint, stressors occurring in combination create a far more dangerous work environment than stressors occurring in isolation. Attempts to minimize the effects of one stressor may compound the effects of the other. While protective headgear may reduce noise, the extra covering can increase the effects of heat. Headgear for protecting a worker from cold may also impair hearing and cause accidents. Action taken to minimize stressor effects must not make the worker vulnerable to other potential hazards.

Fatigue

Fatigue is quite elusive, yet it is a major symptom associated with poor worker/workplace fit. There are several kinds of fatigue, and they all have physiological and psychological characteristics. The I/O psychologist studies fatigue in order to eliminate as many of its effects, particularly on performance and satisfaction, as possible.

The symptoms of fatigue include tiredness, diminished willingness to work, and boredom. Fatigue is a physiological phenomenon meaning a reduction in performance capability that can be restored by rest. In contrast, boredom is a psychological phenomenon meaning a reduction in mental performance capability, which is the result of monotony. However, fatigue is not synonymous with being bored or tired; such feelings may be short-lived and can be "cured" by a diversion or a night's sleep. Fatigue is more generalized and enduring. Also, distinguishing various kinds of fatigue is difficult because of interrelated effects.

Several authors (for example, Grandjean, 1968) have attempted to isolate different kinds of fatigue; there seem to be four major varieties. The most distinct type is *muscular fatigue,* caused by prolonged and demanding physical activity. This is associated with biochemical changes and is an acute pain in the muscles. *Mental fatigue* is more closely aligned with feelings of boredom associated with monotonous work. *Emotional fatigue* results from intense stress and is generally characterized by a dulling of emotional responses. Finally, *skills fatigue* is associated with a decline in attention to certain tasks. With skills fatigue, standards of accuracy and performance become progressively lower. This decline is thought to be a major cause of accidents, particularly those involving automobiles and airplanes.

All four kinds of fatigue are associated with neurochemical changes in the blood. They serve to create an inhibiting system in the body that operates in contrast to our arousal system. The inhibiting system tends to retard our normal functioning, so that mentally, physically, and emotionally we operate in a more subdued fashion. That is, our physiological mechanisms protect us in response to some previous form of overstimulation that precipitated the fatigue. Our ability to react normally to job contexts becomes retarded when we suffer from fatigue. In particular, both our sense of timing and vigilance are often impaired. *Timing* involves the precise coordination of integrated behaviors into a pattern or sequence. Typing on a typewriter or driving a car would be two examples. *Vigilance* refers to alertness in monitoring and responding to critical stimuli in the environment. Reading the text material to be typed and paying attention to traffic, road conditions, and pedestrians would be examples of vigilance. Fatigue has been found to impede our sense of timing and our capacity to be vigilant. Individuals can more readily endure the effects of fatigue in jobs that require little timing or vigilance, but these components are critical to the conduct of many jobs.

I/O psychologists are concerned with all four types of fatigue, but their response to each is different. Muscular fatigue is best dealt with through new work procedures so people will not overexert themselves. It may involve redesigning a piece of equipment or finding other, less strenuous ways to perform the task. Mental fatigue is addressed through job redesign that attempts to make work more stimulating and challenging. However, as we saw in Chapter 13, individuals differ in what they think is boring. Emotional fatigue is usually caused by factors external to the workplace. However, an increasing number of organizations are providing counseling services for employees because performance can be affected by problems either within or outside the workplace. Skills fatigue is a major concern for those in jobs with a small margin for error. For a pilot or air-traffic controller, the consequences of lower standards can be severe and tragic. Such employees are continually monitored for skills fatigue and given time off when necessary.

People differ in susceptibility to fatigue, and jobs differ in inducing fatigue. I/O psychologists still have much to learn about fatigue, particularly its treatment and prediction. Kumar (1994) has proposed a conceptual model of muscle fatigue based on four job demands: strength required, frequency-duration of exposure, recovery time from exposure, and range of required motion. Kumar believes that this model will be useful in explaining work-related injuries caused by overexertion.

Work Schedules

Shift Work

Not all employees work 8:00 A.M. to 5:00 P.M., Monday through Friday. The nature of the services performed may necessitate other schedules. Police officers, firefighters, and telephone operators provide 24-hour-a-day service. In industrial manufacturing some technology requires constant monitoring and operation. It isn't practical to shut off furnaces, boilers, and chemical process operations at 5:00 P.M. just because the workers went home. In those cases it is advantageous to run continually by having different shifts work around the clock. About 25% of all working hours in the United States are estimated as "nontraditional." Psychologists have become interested in how different hours (or shift work) affect employee attitudes and behavior.

There are no uniform shift work hours; various companies use different shifts. Usually, a 24-hour day is broken into three 8-hour work shifts: 7:00 A.M.–3:00 P.M. (day shift), 3:00 P.M.–11:00 P.M. (swing or afternoon shift), and 11:00 P.M.–7:00 A.M. (night shift). Some companies have employees work just one shift; but workers generally don't like the swing and night shifts, so many firms rotate the shifts. Employees may work two weeks on the day shift, two weeks on the swing shift, and then two weeks on the night shift. A shift workweek need not be Monday to

Friday. Also, there may be an uneven number of days off between shifts, for example, two days off after the swing shift and three after the night shift.

Psychologists have investigated to what degree workers cope with changes in work time. Research has focused on satisfaction with shift work, physiological adjustments to shift work, and social and cultural adjustment. I will briefly examine some of the findings.

Satisfaction.   Many people prefer traditional hours, but some are quite satisfied with aspects of shift work. De la Mare and Walker (1968) reported the following data on preferences in work schedules:

Preference	Percentage
Permanent day work	61
Rotating shift work	12
Permanent night work	27

In de la Mare and Walker's study, workers favored permanent day work; other researchers report positive preferences for shift work. For example, Wedderburn (1978) reported the following responses from British steelworkers to the question "On the whole, how do you feel about working shifts?"

Responses	Percentage
I like it very much	18
I like it more than I dislike it	29
I neither like it nor dislike it	22
I dislike it more than I like it	23
I dislike it very much	8

There was large variability in individual worker attitudes. In the same study, Wedderburn obtained responses about perceived advantages and disadvantages of shift work in a number of specific areas. These are reported in Table 15–3. Though advantages and disadvantages are seen with each shift, on par, it seems that more disadvantages are associated with the night shift. Wedderburn's findings are representative of other such studies. Zedeck, Jackson, and Summers (1983) concluded that shift work is not inherently bad for the health of all workers. Some workers adapt and do not allow shift work to lead to medical problems and family disturbances.

Adjustment Problems.   Thierry and Meijman (1994) identified 11 characteristics of adjustment problems that are aversely affected by shift work. These characteristics are shown in Table 15–4. Their effects are more strongly aversive in some patterns of shift work than in others. Shift workers experience many problems in physiological and social adjustment. Most physiological problems are associated with interruptions of the circadian rhythm; that is, our bodies are "programmed" for a certain time cycle (Aschoff, 1978). Because shift work interrupts the cycle of

Table 15–3   *Reported perceptions of steel mill workers regarding shift work*

Descriptive Item	Percentage of "Yes" Responses*		
	Day Shift	Afternoon Shift	Night Shift
Quickly over	84	38	29
Seems a longer shift	12	40	64
Gives me indigestion	7	4	21
Tiring	58	15	80
Disturbs my sleep	36	2	52
More friendly atmosphere	48	51	21
Makes me irritable	25	18	48
Peaceful	49	62	58
More responsibility at work	28	16	24
More independent	35	26	42
Good for family life	73	19	17
Gives me more spare time	88	15	49
Wastes the day	10	68	55
Starts too early	53	7	20
Restricts my social life	17	79	77
Sexless	13	11	44

*Responses were to the question: "Think of work on _____ shift. How well does each of the above words describe what it is like for you on _____ shift?"

SOURCE: From "Some Suggestions for Increasing the Usefulness of Psychological and Sociological Studies of Shiftwork" by A. A. Wedderburn, 1978, *Ergonomics, 21*, p. 830.

eating, sleeping, and working, workers often experience physiological problems. They complain of lack of sleep, fatigue, constipation, irritability, and appetite loss. Meers, Maasen, and Verhaagen (1978) reported that the health of a sample of shift workers declined during the first six months of shift work; the decline became more pronounced after four years.

Because most people work during the day and sleep at night, shift workers also have social problems. They often experience difficulties with children, marital relationships, and recreation. Frost and Jamal (1979) reported that shift workers experienced less need fulfillment, were more likely to quit their jobs, and participated in fewer voluntary organizations. Jamal (1981) reported similar findings; workers on fixed work schedules were better off than workers on rotating schedules in terms of mental health, job satisfaction, and social participation.

Shift workers are a relatively small proportion of the population; they are thus forced to fit their schedules around the rest of society. Dunham (1977) makes the interesting point that many social problems would be alleviated by increasing shift work. Society would then make more concessions to the needs of shift workers. Changes might be made in such things as hours of television broadcasting, restaurant service, recreational services, and hours of business operation (banks, supermarkets, gas stations, and the like). In fact, convenience food stores and automated bank machines derive much of their business from employees who work nontraditional hours.

Research indicates that shift work has a strong influence on the lives of people who perform it. As long as certain industries require 24-hour-a-day operations,

Table 15–4   *Aversive characteristics of shift work*

Characteristic	Definition	Inconveniences
Regularity	Mean number of changes in the starting times of working periods during the week	Unrest, nervous complaints, constipation
Periodicity	Weekly mean of the sum of the accumulated number of successive night shifts plus half of the number of accumulated successive afternoon shifts	Sleeping problems, fatigue, stomach and intestinal complaints
Load per shift	Mean shift length in hours	Fatigue, feelings of overload
Load per week	Mean weekly working time in hours	Fatigue, feelings of overload
Opportunity to rest at night	Mean weekly number of hours off work between 11:00 P.M. and 7:00 A.M.	Sleeping problems, insomnia, fatigue, nervous complaints
Predictability	Cycle time in weeks	Planning/coordination problems
Opportunity for household and family tasks	Weekly mean number of hours off work from Monday through Friday between 7:00 A.M. and 7:00 P.M.	Frustration of partner/ parental role, complaints on limitation of household tasks
Constancy of opportunity for household and family tasks	Variation coefficient of weekly opportunity for household and family tasks	Lack of continuity in partner/ parental role and in household tasks
Opportunity for evening recreation	Mean weekly number of hours off work from Monday through Fridays between 7:00 P.M. and 11:00 P.M.	Lack of continuity in partner role, limitation of social and recreational activities
Opportunity for weekend recreation	Half of the number of days off work during the weekend per week	Limitation of social and recreational activities
Constancy of opportunity for weekend recreation	Variation coefficient of the number of days off during the weekend per week	Lack of continuity in social and recreational activities

SOURCE: From "Time and Behavior at Work" (p. 360) by H. Thierry and T. Meijman, 1994, in H. C. Triandis, M. D. Dunnette, and L. M. Hough (Eds.), *Handbook of Industrial and Organizational Psychology* (Vol. 4), Palo Alto, CA: Consulting Psychologists Press.

psychologists will continue searching for ways to improve this particularly difficult person/environment fit. Social problems may be lessened by changing some existing patterns in the community. However, physiological problems will be more difficult to overcome.

At least one major source of physiological difficulty is the rotation of workers across shifts. If workers were assigned to a fixed shift (day, swing, or night), their behavior would be consistent, which would help in adjusting to the circadian rhythm. Some people prefer to work afternoons or nights; part of the solution may be personnel selection. Workers could choose a shift; if enough workers of the appropriate skill level were placed in the shift of their choice, both individual and organizational needs would be met. Barton (1994) found that the physical and psychological health of nurses was better if they worked a fixed night shift than if they engaged in night work as part of a rotating-shift schedule. Smith, Reilly, and Midkiff (1989) developed a scale to predict morningness based on circadian rhythms. The authors concluded that the scale could be used to select workers for the night shift based on their preference for evening activities. Indeed, Jamal and Jamal (1982) found that employees who worked a fixed shift experienced better mental and physical health than employees on a rotating shift. Rotating shift work seems particularly difficult to adjust to. There is also evidence that backward rotation (from day to night to afternoon shifts) is more difficult to adjust to than forward rotation (from day to afternoon to night). Totterdell, Spelten, Smith, Barton, and Folkard (1995) reported that nurses felt worse (on such measures as alertness, calmness, moodiness, and so forth) on a rest day following a night shift rather than a day shift. The findings attest to the costs of fatigue and adjustment to and from a nocturnal work routine. In fact, Freese and Okonek (1984) report that some people who have reached the emotional, mental, and physical breaking point because of rotating shift work are told by their physicians to find jobs with traditional work hours. Tepas (1993) concluded that organizations should design educational programs for shift workers and their families to better prepare them for the demands imposed by this work schedule.

Compressed Workweek

Employees traditionally have worked 8 hours a day, five days a week, for a 40-hour workweek. However, in the past 20 years, many organizations have adopted a different schedule. Some employees work 10 hours a day for four days, popularly known as the "4/40."

There are several obvious advantages to a compressed workweek for both the individual and the organization. Individuals have a three-day weekend, which gives them more recreation time, the chance to work a second job, more time for family life, and so on. Organizations have fewer overhead costs because they are open one day less per week. However, there are also possible drawbacks, including fatigue, fewer productive hours, and more accidents.

In a major review of 4/40, Ronen and Primps (1981) reached these conclusions based on many studies. It has a positive effect on home and family life as well as on leisure and recreation. There appears to be no change in employee job performance with 4/40. Finally, there are mixed results with regard to absenteeism, but worker fatigue definitely increases. A few studies have been reported on reactions to a 12-hour shift, typically noon to midnight and then midnight to noon. The results are mixed. Breaugh (1983b) reported nurses on 12-hour shifts incurred substantial fatigue associated with the longer hours. However, the midnight-to-noon shift felt more out of phase with physiological and social rhythms than did the noon-to-midnight shift. Pierce and Dunham (1992) reported significant improvements in work-schedule attitudes, general affect, and fatigue in a sample of police officers who switched from a rotating 8-hour shiftwork schedule to a fixed 12-hour schedule. Duchon, Keran, and Smith (1994) examined underground miners who switched from an 8-hour to a 12-hour schedule. The miners reported improved sleep quality with the new schedule, while their levels of fatigue showed either no change or slight improvement. The findings from such studies may be influenced by the variety of jobs examined in the research.

Conversion to a compressed workweek is not simply a matter of worker preference. Organizations are limited in altering their work schedules by the services they provide and other factors. For example, Goodale and Aagaard (1975) believe that a compressed workweek is not viable if customer service must be provided five days a week. The success of organizations providing services depends partially on accessibility. Dunham, Pierce, and Castaneda (1987) cautioned against blanket support for the 4/40; its success depends on the type of organization and the people in it.

Flexible Working Hours

Another variation in work schedules is flexible working hours, popularly known as flextime. Approximately 25% of private-sector organizations have adopted a form of flextime since it was introduced in the early 1970s. According to Ronen (1981), the main objective of flextime is to create an alternative to the traditional, fixed working schedule by giving workers some choice in arrival and departure times. The system is usually arranged so that everyone must be present during certain designated hours ("coretime"), but there is latitude in other hours ("flexband"). For example, coretime may be 9:00 A.M. to 3:00 P.M. However, flexband may range from 6:00 A.M. to 6:00 P.M. Some employees may start working at 9:00 A.M. and work until 6:00 P.M., some may end at 3:00 P.M. by starting at 6:00 A.M., or any combination in between. Problems with family commitments, recreation, second jobs, commuting, and stress may be alleviated by flexible working hours. Lateness is virtually eliminated since the workday begins with arrival. Workers can be late only if they arrive after coretime has begun.

In general, the findings on flextime appear quite positive—at least no very adverse effects have yet been reported. The variables examined include satisfaction, productivity, absence, and turnover. Some studies reported more positive results than others. Golembiewski and Proehl (1978) summarized findings of several studies on flextime; they reported that worker support for adoption or continuation of flextime across nine samples of workers ranged from 80% to 100%. Thus, it appears that many employees are highly receptive to the idea.

Hicks and Klimoski (1981) found that employees did not become more satisfied with their work after flextime was adopted. Nevertheless, they reported other benefits like easier travel and parking, less interrole conflict, more feelings of control in the work setting, and more time for leisure activities.

Narayanan and Nath (1982) examined the impact of flextime at two organizational levels: lower-level and professional employees. They concluded that flextime primarily benefitted lower-level employees by giving them more flexibility in their schedules. For professional employees, the flextime system merely formalized the already existing informal system they had with the company. Ralston (1989) found flextime especially helpful for working mothers and dual-career couples, two growing segments of the work force. In a six-year study of flextime, Dalton and Mesch (1990) reported large reductions in the amount of employee absenteeism compared to a control group on regular hours. However, the rate of turnover in the two groups was equivalent.

While there is ample evidence that flextime benefits individuals, it is quite possible it could be detrimental to the functioning of teams (see Field Note 3). If employees must work as a team, the individualized schedules flextime permits would limit the continuity of the team. However, we need additional research to address this issue. For the present, flextime appears to be highly beneficial in accommodating the scheduling needs of individual employees.

Alcoholism and Drug Abuse in the Workplace

Alcoholism and drug abuse are international problems affecting all arenas of life. While we have long been aware of issues pertaining to their treatment, only recently have we begun to examine their impact in the workplace. Due to the sensi-

FIELD NOTE 3

Flextime is certainly a popular alternative to traditional hours of work and is favored by large numbers of employees. Indeed, it should be, for it was designed to accommodate their needs. However, flextime can produce a particular problem that is not encountered with traditional work hours.

Let us say coretime is 9:00 A.M. to 3:00 P.M., and the flexband is from 6:00 A.M. to 6:00 P.M. Employees are free to come and go within this 12-hour period. In all likelihood, some employees will arrive early and leave early (6:00 A.M. to 3:00 P.M.); others will arrive late and leave late (9:00 A.M. to 6:00 P.M.).

The problem relates to supervision. Because supervisors cannot work 12-hour days, there will be times when the employees are unsupervised. Let us assume the normal hours for a supervisor are 8:00 A.M. to 5:00 P.M., the typical 8-hour day. This means that from 6:00 to 8:00 A.M. and from 5:00 to 6:00 P.M., the work force will be unsupervised. As was discussed in Chapter 12, sometimes the job itself provides direction for employees so that they do not need a boss present. However, in many cases there are no substitutes for leadership, and employees simply need some guidance. In this case the unsupervised hours may be very unproductive from the organization's standpoint. Without a supervisor, employees may also become lax in performing their duties during these hours because they are not being monitored. Finally, flextime may weaken supervisor/subordinate relations in general, as they will not see each other as often (that is, their two 8-hour days do not overlap completely). The organization would either have to have supervisors work longer hours, have more supervisors to "cover" the 12-hour day, or accept having an unsupervised work force for a portion of the day. While flextime solves a lot of problems, it can create a few as well.

tivity and confidentiality of substance abuse, we do not have a very strong research foundation on which to base our knowledge. That is, it is difficult to collect reliable and valid data on substance abuse given the delicacy of the issue. What follows is a brief overview of some of the major dimensions of this complex social problem.

The term *substance abuse* covers a broad array of substances but usually includes alcohol, prescription drugs, and illegal drugs. Some people include tobacco (both smoking and chewing) within the domain of substance abuse. Most of our knowledge is limited to alcoholism and illegal drugs. It has been estimated that there are more than 10 million alcoholic American workers. Tyson and Vaughn (1987) report that approximately two-thirds of the people entering the work force have used illegal drugs. Four to 5 million people in the United States use cocaine monthly. The frequency of use of marijuana is much higher. Every year $50 billion is spent on cocaine in the United States—the same amount that companies spend annually on substance abuse programs for their employees. By any reasonable standard, substance abuse is a major problem in industry today.

Although I/O psychologists may approach the area of substance abuse from several perspectives, a primary area of concern is performance impairment—that is, the extent to which substance abuse contributes to lower job performance. Experts in the area of employee assistance programs estimate that as much as 50% of absenteeism and on-the-job accidents are related to drugs and alcohol. Drug addiction has also contributed to employee theft to support a habit. Thus, we have some knowledge about how substance abuse affects the more global performance criteria of absence, accidents, and theft. Our knowledge of the effects of substance abuse on skill decay is more tentative. Much of our knowledge is based on industrial accidents in which alcohol or drug usage was confirmed. It is also very difficult to make categorical statements about "drugs" in general because of their variety, duration of effects, and interactive properties with other substances. We do know that cognitively related skills such as vigilance, monitoring, reaction time, and decision making are adversely affected by many kinds of drugs. We do not know if these drugs simply lengthen the amount of time needed to perform these cognitive functions, or whether they cause attention to be focused on irrelevant or competing stimuli. Jobs involving the use of these skills in areas like the transportation industry (for example, pilots and railroad engineers) have regrettably contributed to our knowledge through tragic accidents. Some drugs (such as anabolic steroids) have been found to enhance aspects of physical performance (most notably, strength and speed), but their long-term effects can be very harmful to the individual.

Hollinger (1988) concluded that the employees most likely to work under the influence of alcohol or other drugs were men younger than 30, and that the likelihood of their (or other employees') doing so increased when they felt unhappy about their jobs and socialized frequently with co-workers off the job. Trice and Sonnenstuhl (1988) found not only do employees seek relief from the effects of job stress with alcohol but some organizational subcultures establish norms for alcohol use. That is, employees may be expected to consume alcohol after work with their co-workers if there is a norm that encourages such behavior. Stein, Newcomb, and Bentler (1988) believe that drug involvement and the resulting adverse consequences are facets of a lifestyle that may be more than drug use only. They feel that we must appreciate the diverse range of life areas affected by drug use and not treat drug use as an isolated or singular problem in the individual.

Bruno (1994) reports that in Italy drug dependence does not limit a person's right to keep a job, even if employees carry out tasks dangerous to their own or others' safety. To safeguard others, federal laws require employers to reassign such employees to other tasks. The introduction of drug testing in the workplace in Italy has been delayed because it appears to imply a conflict between the organization's right to safeguard its interest and the individual's right to privacy. Furthermore, economic issues are also salient. Bennett, Blum, and Roman (1994) noted that organizations typically address the problem of drug usage at work in two ways. The first is drug testing, whose purpose is designed to exclude drug users from the workplace. The second is Employee Assistance Programs (EAPs), whose purpose is to rehabilitate current employees who abuse drugs. Bennett et al. found that organizations situated in geographic areas with high unemployment rates are more likely to engage in pre-employment drug testing, while worksites with low turnover more often provided an EAP.

Finally, Normand, Lempert, and O'Brien (1994) offered some staggering estimates of the yearly financial costs of alcohol and drug abuse to society. Estimates were based on four factors: the costs of treatment, lowered work productivity, the lost income that would have been earned by individuals who die prematurely from substance abuse, and crime-related costs. The total estimated cost of alcohol abuse was $70 billion, while the total estimated cost of drug abuse was $44 billion.

It is very difficult for I/O psychologists to conduct high-quality research on substance abuse. Administration of alcohol or drugs in an experimental setting can be conducted only under the most restrictive conditions, given ethical concerns. Reliance on self-report measures are problematic, given issues associated with social desirability and accuracy. There are also civil and legal issues associated with drug testing, both in this country and internationally, particularly pertaining to the constitutional rights of individuals to submit to drug testing. As with most complex social problems, researchers and scholars from many professions (such as pharmacology, toxicology, law, and genetics) must take an interdisciplinary approach to addressing these issues. While I/O psychologists will contribute only a small piece of the total picture, I envision our efforts as concentrated in two traditional areas: issues relating to individual assessment and to performance measurement. Perhaps in 20 years an evaluation of working conditions may also include the propensity of certain jobs to induce substance abuse and the likelihood your co-worker is under the influence of drugs or alcohol. Whether we are ready for it or not, I believe society will expect I/O psychologists to help provide information on problems our predecessors could scarcely have imagined.

CASE STUDY   *Will Life Ever Get Back to Normal?*

Janet Ryder sat at her kitchen table reading the entertainment section of the local newspaper. A movie was playing that she had heard a lot about, and she was hoping it would stay in town for at least two weeks. Her husband, Mark, had recently changed jobs and was now working for St. Regis Aluminum, a large manufacturer of lightweight metal products. The company worked shifts, and Mark was starting a two-week stint on the night shift. Neither Janet nor Mark had any previous experience with shift work, and the switch from conventional hours was difficult for both of them.

Janet tried to plan their family life around Mark's changing hours, but she couldn't get the hang of it. Little things kept cropping up that had never been a problem before. For example, the boy next door had been taking trumpet lessons for about two months. He would practice after school. Janet heard the notes straining from the trumpet, but after a while the sounds seemed to blend in with the rest of the neighborhood noise, and she could ignore them. When Mark was sleeping in the afternoon, the noise of the trumpet often woke him up. They had two arguments about whether they should call the boy's mother and ask that he practice at another time.

Yesterday there had been a sale on roast beef, which was one of their favorite dinners. Janet liked to fix a fancy dinner when there was something special to eat. However, with Mark's schedule, she had to "time" special meals when he worked the night shift. While Mark might be ready to sit down to a full meal at 7:00 A.M. after working the night shift, Janet couldn't quite handle either fixing it or eating it after just getting up. The roast beef would sit in the freezer, waiting for a time when they both could enjoy it.

It was also awkward for their friends. They had been in a biweekly poker club that met on Friday nights. They got together with some other couples at 8 o'clock, and the party would break up around midnight. When Mark worked afternoons, there was no way they could play. When he worked the night shift, they would have to leave at 10 o'clock, just when things were going great. Only when he worked the day shift could they make it. Now they played in the poker club about once every two months, and their friends got another couple to sub for them.

Janet started to feel guilty about feeling sorry for herself. It had been no bargain for Mark either. The weekend the long-awaited Custom Boat and Trailer Show arrived in town, Mark was working the swing shift. He got to visit the show for about a half hour before he had to leave for work. It seemed that on Saturdays and Sundays just when he found something he liked to do, it was time to go to the plant.

Their 10-year-old son Billie wandered into the kitchen. Billie was holding a Little League schedule in his hand. "Mom," he said, "in three weeks there's the regional tournament in Union City. Will you and Dad make it to my game?"

Janet got up and checked Mark's work schedule, which was posted on the cupboard. "I can make it, Billie, but Dad will be working the afternoon shift that week," Janet said.

Billie looked downcast. "I never get to see Dad very much any more," he said, as he slowly walked out of the kitchen.

Questions
1. Think of Chapter 10 on work stress. Do you see any relationship between work and nonwork satisfaction for shift workers?
2. What other disruptions in family life might you predict for the Ryder family as a result of shift work?

3. Are there things the St. Regis Aluminum Company could do to alleviate some of the problems of shift workers? What might they be?
4. Are there things the community might do to make life easier for shift workers? What might they be?
5. How long would you guess it takes for a family to get into the "rhythm" of shift work?

The Changing Nature of Work

Major Chapter Objectives

- *Be able to identify the types of individuals likely to be successful in our changing work environments.*

- *Understand the profound changes taking place in how we work.*

- *Understand how global competition in the marketplace will affect traditional social values and priorities.*

This final chapter of the book is intended to provide a glimpse into the future rather than a capstone summary of the past. I will examine ways in which the nature of work is changing, and how these changes are influencing I/O psychology.

Change is inevitable and unavoidable. However, the rate of change can vary from slow to fast, and the nature of change can exhibit continuity or discontinuity. As a society we are currently in the midst of a period of rapid change of a highly discontinuous nature. As Havel (1994) expressed it, "Many things indicate we are going through a transitional period, when it seems that something is on the way out and something else is painfully being born. It is as if something were crumbling, decaying and exhausting itself, while something else, still indistinct, were arising from the rubble" (p. 27). Discontinuous change implies that the past is no longer a guide to the future. According to Drucker (1993), every few hundred years in Western civilization a sharp transformation creates a very different world. We are in the middle of a transformation that is not yet complete. A primary cause of the discontinuous change is the tremendous growth in knowledge, produced by higher levels of education, new technologies, and increased research. This burst of knowledge causes social systems to adapt in fits and starts, as opposed to adapting through a steady stream of continuous change.

Three major dimensions of change affecting I/O psychology will be examined—changes pertaining to individuals, to work, and to society. In turn, each dimension will be represented by three illustrative exemplars. In particular, I will consider how these dimensions of change influence the conduct of I/O psychology, as described in the preceding chapters of this book.

Individual Dimensions

If the world of work is going through tumultuous change, it most certainly will influence the type of individuals who will prosper in this new environment. It will also influence the attributes of individuals organizations find desirable and how job applicants will be assessed.

Employees Who Are Smart. As Howard (1995) observed, complex work requires smart people. Employees must be able to acquire and apply knowledge and do so continuously. One conclusion is that most work in changing organizations will require higher levels of general mental ability (g). Landy, Shankster-Cawley, and Moran (1995) propose that in a constantly changing technical environment high levels of g will be necessary to acquire specific knowledge, but special abilities will permit application of that knowledge.

However, viewing intelligence from the perspective of g may no longer be sufficient. Sternberg, Wagner, Williams, and Horvath (1995) noted that predictors of success in school (such as tests that measure g) are less predictive of success out of school. Even our best tests of traditional intelligence fail to predict 75% of the variance in real-world job performance. Sternberg et al. have begun to explore new constructs as predictors of real-world performance. Among the most promising is what they call practical intelligence or common sense. Practical intelligence refers to action-oriented knowledge that allows individuals to achieve goals they personally value. The assessment of practical knowledge involves measuring the capacity to reason a problem through to a successful outcome, as opposed to measuring knowledge of a concept that has a single correct answer. The authors found that measures of practical intelligence predicted job performance criteria but were relatively unrelated to performance on traditional intelligence tests. An emphasis on cultivating practical intelligence through education will also necessitate changing the conventional process of teachers focusing on students giving right answers rather than understanding processes.

A similar trend toward assessing patterns of reasoning emerges in the situational interview. As Cascio (1995b) notes, in a traditional interview the following question might be posed: "How would you reprimand an employee?" In a situational interview the emphasis is more on the process by which the candidate handled a situation, such as "Give me a specific example of a time you had to reprimand an employee. What action did you take, and what was the result?" In the future there will be increased reliance on assessment methods that evaluate a candidate's capacity to reason and adapt to environments that continue to grow in complexity.

Employees Who Are Adaptable.   If intelligence reflects whether a person *can* learn, it does not reflect whether a person wants to learn. Adaptability is a personality construct that relates to a willingness to experience new situations, one of the Big 5 personality factors. Reliance on personality assessment is experiencing renewed vigor in I/O psychology because of its capacity to predict the "will do" component of behavior, while ability tests assess the "can do" component (Katzell, 1994).

Associated with the capacity to adapt to new situations is the capacity to adapt to, and relate to, other people. With a growing shift to the use of teams, it is becoming increasingly important to staff organizations with employees who have effective relational skills. Relational skills include communication, interpersonal, conflict resolution, and influencing capabilities. Quite apart from team-based work, organizations want employees who are responsible, conscientious, and can get along with their co-workers. Dunn, Mount, Barrick, and Ones (1995) found that managers considered general mental ability and conscientiousness to be the most important attributes related to applicants' hirability. Furthermore, emotional stability, conscientiousness, and agreeableness were the most important attributes relating to insubordination, rule infractions, and theft. It will be recalled that integrity tests primarily measure these attributes. It is therefore reasonable to conclude that the foundation of a selection test battery would include an assessment of the "can do" (intelligence) and "will do" (personality) constructs. It is a matter of debate among I/O psychologists as to whether the selection test battery should consist of an assessment of just these two constructs or whether additional constructs should be assessed as well. What is agreed upon is that an employee's capacity to adapt to change and to relate well to others is becoming as critical to successful job performance as possessing the needed cognitive ability.

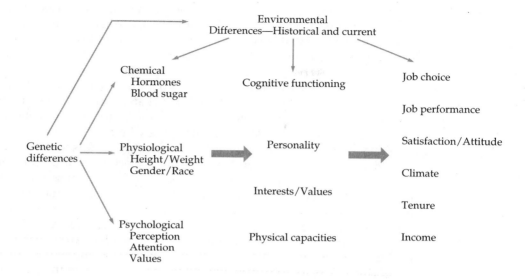

Figure 16–1   *Model of genetic and environmental variables and their influence on traditional I/O psychology constructs*

SOURCE: From "Genetics, Twins, and Organizational Behavior" by R. D. Arvey and T. J. Bouchard, Jr., 1994, *Research in Organizational Behavior, 16,* p. 55.

Genetic Influences on Work Behavior.   Psychology has long been captivated by the nature/nurture debate—the degree to which heredity and the environment influence behavior. For at least the past 40 years the nurture or environmental perspective dominated thinking in psychology. That is, by carefully crafting our environment (as by providing certain types of educational experiences for children), we could fashion a society where all people could have a high likelihood of attaining selected outcomes, such as maintaining good health or achieving satisfying employment. However, the pendulum is starting to swing back toward the importance of genetic or heredity influences on behavior. That is, because of our individual genetic compositions, we are *not* all equally likely to attain selected outcomes. As Arvey and Bouchard (1994) stated, "biology is back" as an explanation for behavior. Recently, researchers have identified genetic structures that account for a wide range of conditions, including obesity and alcoholism.

Arvey and Bouchard (1994) described genetic influences on work behavior and the extent to which genetics will play a role in I/O psychology. They presented a descriptive model of how genetic and environmental factors influence concepts important to I/O psychology; this is shown in Figure 16–1. As can be seen in the model, genetic differences across individuals are hypothesized to influence such factors as job choice, job performance, how we feel about our work, how we perceive our work environment, our length of service on a job, and our level of income. Research has identified work situations where individuals with certain genetic makeups are at risk when exposed to radiation or certain chemicals. Commercially available tests exist for detection of genetic conditions such as sickle-cell anemia, cystic fibrosis, and polycystic kidney disease. Future tests for cancer and hypertension are likely. In addition, methods have been developed for detecting the potential susceptibility to environmental work hazards, as well as methods to determine if there has been any modification in chromosomes due to workplace conditions.

Genetics offers opportunities for us to gain new insights into serious work problems, such as stress. Research indicates that life stress can be divided into two types of causing factors—controllable and uncontrollable. Genetic research has shown that controllable stress exhibits high heritability while uncontrollable stress has low heritability. However, a critical question is whether organizations should use such information for screening, selection, and placement purposes. Ethical issues that have yet to be resolved from a practical standpoint abound in this area. Among them is the precision of measurement of genetic factors, and the likelihood of misclassification of individuals. This is the same issue that applies to the use of psychological tests in making selection decisions. Are the consequences of making true and false positive and negative decisions any different when using genetic tests versus psychological tests? A more extreme ethical concern applies to altering a person's genetic structure through such procedures as gene splicing, gene transfer, and gene replacement. Such interventions are currently being discussed and implemented in medical settings.

We are entering an era where there is growing recognition of the importance of genetic factors in influencing behavior, including behavior in the workplace. The degree of impact this will have across the full spectrum of concepts studied by I/O psychologists remains to be seen. However, if indeed "biology is back" as an explanation of work behavior, I/O psychologists will have to adjust to the discontinuous change in our own thinking caused by this perspective.

Work Dimensions

Perhaps more than any other dimension, change is affecting the very nature of how work is performed. These changes in work are profound and reverberate throughout the complete domain of I/O psychology.

Technology.   Van der Spiegel (1995) asserts that advances in information technologies (computers and communication systems) are the driving forces behind major changes in how we work. Only a few decades ago computers were accessible only to a privileged few, mainly engineers and scientists. The advent of the microprocessor and the personal computer has now given a large proportion of the population access to new information technologies. As we move into the next century, the emergence of portable systems, such as cellular phones, faxes, notebook computers, personal digital assistants, and pen-based computers, will provide multimedia capabilities to the user independent of space or time. Van der Spiegel believes that in the not-too-distant future we will see emergence of instruments with learning capabilities that can understand natural language instructions and make intelligent decisions. The information technologies will have an impact on office space and facility usage. It may become more efficient to work at home for several days where the worker can work uninterrupted using a personal desktop that provides the worker with access to the same resources available in the office.

These new technologies are posited to change not only the knowledge, skills, and abilities (KSAs) of individual workers but also the manner in which we think of KSAs. Davis (1995) posits that organizations develop differences in their competencies—that is, organizations have their own unique KSAs. Organizational competencies include the sum of knowledge possessed collectively by all employees in the organization. These competencies, particularly core competencies used to coordinate diverse production skills and integrate multiple technologies, have a strategic advantage. Unlike physical assets that deteriorate over time, knowledge grows with use. Hesketh and Bochner (1994) believe that massive technological changes are compelling individuals and organizations to become *multiskilled*, increasing their flexibility to adapt to their dynamic environments. The new information technologies are the driving mechanisms behind changes in the way work is conducted, and the corresponding talents of individuals and organizations needed to adapt to these changes.

Groups at Work. Katzell (1994) regards the use of groups or teams as a primary vehicle for conducting work as one of the major "meta-trends" in contemporary I/O psychology. While interest in groups first manifested itself in the Hawthorne studies, there has been an explosion of interest in work groups that will undoubtedly continue. Two targets of interest in work groups identified by Katzell are the effect of the group on its individual members, and the work group as a productive entity.

Although the performance of groups is generally superior to that of the average of its individual members, it is often less than that of the best individual performer in tasks that can be performed by individuals. This is partly a consequence of the loss of motivation among individual members. The loss of motivation among some group members has been attributed to "social loafing," a phenomenon where some individuals in a work group slacken their performance in the belief that other group members will accelerate their own performance. However, the group's influence on the individual can also be positive. Groups can help members learn effective skills and behaviors by providing role models. Katzell believes that I/O psychology is in a position to create conditions that generate positive and avoid negative consequences of group membership.

The issue of determining the ideal mix of individuals in a work group has been approached from selection based on ability, personality, or attitude. However, successful group composition appears to be influenced by the kind of tasks the group performs. For example, heterogeneity in members' personalities typically facilitate performance in tasks emphasizing group problem solving and creativity, but not when the task mainly involves performance using available knowledge and skills. Likewise, the degree of autonomy accorded the team has attracted much interest. The allocation of greater control and self-regulation to work groups is increasingly popular and is referred to as "team empowerment."

However, we do not yet know the boundaries of its effectiveness, and whether there are cross-cultural differences in its acceptability. The issue of team development embraces enhancing the collective skills of the team as a team rather than focusing on the skills of individual members. Most of our knowledge from training and development applies to individuals, not groups. This issue pertains to what researchers refer to as the "unit of analysis" and reminds us that findings derived from one unit (the individual) do not necessarily generalize to another unit (the group).

Katzell (1994) believes that I/O psychology will be heavily influenced by the movement toward team-based work operations. We have much to learn about the degree to which our knowledge base developed on individuals concerning such matters as recruitment, selection, placement, training, performance appraisal, motivation, and leadership extends to work groups.

Lifelong Learning.   The conventional view of learning is that learning attained by formal education transpires during the years through college, followed by a relatively brief period of on-the-job learning. Following this phase of knowledge and skill acquisition, you set about "doing" your job, and for the most part your learning days are over. This model of learning (and living) is being replaced by an ethic that emphasizes learning throughout the individual's lifetime. Failure to follow this model will render individuals more susceptible to job loss and increase the likelihood that they will have difficulty gaining re-employment. The changing nature of the psychological contract between employer and employee makes it necessary for the individual to assume greater responsibility for career development. Organizations are now far less likely to offer the implicit promise that they will provide career advancing opportunities. Organizations are increasingly becoming "vendors of employment" as opposed to being incubators of individual professional growth. Consider the following message found posted on the bulletin board of a plant experiencing widespread layoffs (as reported by Hall & Mirvis, 1995).

- We can't promise you how long we'll be in business.
- We can't promise you that we won't be bought by another company.
- We can't promise that there'll be room for promotion.
- We can't promise that your job will exist until you reach retirement age.
- We can't promise that the money will be available for your pension.
- We can't expect your undying loyalty, and we aren't sure we want it. (p. 326)

Hall and Mirvis believe that workers will have to change jobs, companies, and even careers over their life course in the years ahead. Workers who cannot adapt to this kind of change will likely find themselves plateaued in their work lives or simply ushered out of the organization. This shift puts a premium on learning how to adapt to new situations. It will become increasingly important for workers to be immersed in a wide variety of professional experiences. The authors assert that it is fruitless to try to predict exactly which kinds of skills will be required in a given organization in the future. Rather, organizations should facilitate employees learning how to learn so they are capable of learning job-specific skills for themselves as the need becomes apparent. Hall and Mirvis refer to the process of continuous development as "learning a living."

While the general blueprint for such a new system is evident for both individuals and organizations, it is not clear whether both parties have the capability to deliver what is needed. At the individual level, we do not know if people can learn to be adaptable. Is adaptability a characteristic of the individual that is relatively fixed, or can it be developed? Can we measure the capacity to be adaptable, and would it predict how people cope with organizations restructuring and rapid job movement? At the organizational level, we need to identify what company practices really help people adapt and learn to learn. To become proficient learning centers, companies would have to tailor training and work assignments to people's learning styles and set up systems of advanced skill certification, mentoring, and so forth. These are daunting assignments for organizations not accustomed to functioning as learning centers. Despite these issues, it is clear that one consequence of continuous change is the need to enhance our capability to respond to it. For that reason, lifelong learning is posited as a critical adaptive mechanism for both individuals and organizations.

Societal Dimensions

Societal dimensions of change are broad-based forces that shape both individuals and organizations. While they are abstract in nature, their influence can be direct and potent.

Economic Competition.   Cascio (1995b) states that wars—two World Wars, Korea, Vietnam, and the Persian Gulf—were the driving forces behind geopolitical development in the 20th century. However, in the 21st century economic forces will rule. The competition that is normal and inevitable among nations will be acted out not in war but in commerce. The weapons will be growth rates, investments, trade blocs, and imports and exports.

These changes reflect the impact of globalized product and service markets. In the 1960s only 7% of the U.S. economy was exposed to international competition. By the 1980s that number exceeded 70%. Merchandise exports have risen by 50% since 1986, and every $1 billion in U.S. merchandise exported generates approximately 20,000 new jobs. Free market enterprise in the former Soviet Union will further intensify economic competition. The competition for business has resulted in a worldwide need for a highly skilled work force. Nations are judged in economic surveys based on the quality of public education, secondary schooling, on-the-job training, and computer literacy. There is a global need to create a broad, technically literate labor pool.

Changes in the global economy have had profound impacts on jobs in the United States. More than 7 million jobs have been lost permanently since 1987. As a rule, companies do not downsize because they are losing money but rather to strategically improve themselves. Cascio states that we are moving from an economy where there are a lot of hard-working people to one where there are fewer, smarter-working people. Jobs aren't being lost temporarily because of an economic recession; rather, they are being eliminated permanently as a result of new technology, improved machinery, and new ways of organizing work.

Carnevale (1995) aptly summarized how economic issues have transformed the work world:

> Something happened on the way to the second century of American economic dominance. The globalization of wealth and technology created a whole new economic ball game with new rules and an expanded set of competitive standards. . . . In addition, the globalization of competition assures that if Americans don't deliver on the new competitive standards, someone else will, and that someone else is likely to be a foreign worker in Europe or Asia. The new economy requires profound changes in American institutions. (pp. 238–239)

While economic issues have always been a driving influence in our society, they have never attained the level of potency they now possess. Increased globalization of society has ensured that no country is immune from its effects.

Values. The issue of values, particularly values that guide our society, have been hotly debated over the past decade. Furthermore, values become the basis of legislation and judicial decisions that have profound effects on our lives. Conflicting values in society regarding such issues as abortion and the separation of church and state generate intense reactions among partisan supporters. Values also pervade employment matters, especially in regard to what is meant by "fairness." There are conflicting standards of fairness in employment, standards that seemingly do not lend themselves to a widely endorsed middle ground or compromise position. It has been argued that as a society we do *not* necessarily need a singular conception of fairness and thus a reduction in conflict. That is, open discourse on strongly held differing viewpoints is one of the hallmarks of a vibrant and healthy society. However, an alternative view is that if there is not some fusion or coalescence between differing societal values, we will be continuously embroiled in the conflict such divergent values produce.

Although there are many ways to conceptualize the conflict about values in employment, a useful framework is the distinction between the standards of equity and equality in social justice. The equity standard stems from the position that individuals differ in a wide variety of attributes, such as intelligence or physical strength. When these attributes are judged critical for performance in societal roles, it is acceptable to base membership in these roles on the basis of these attributes. Thus, one role in society is to maintain the security and welfare of its members, as witnessed by police and firefighter jobs. If the attribute of strength is judged critical to performance in this role, it is acceptable to select members of police and fire departments, in part, on the basis of physical strength. Because not all individuals are equally strong physically, some individuals will be judged to be more suitable than others for police and firefighter jobs.

The equality standard of fairness is predicated on minimizing differences in individuals, thus ensuring that all individuals in society are treated the same, or equally. Thus, we all have the same opportunity to vote in an election, and each person's vote counts the same as any other person's vote. Voting is an institution whereby individuals can have a voice in matters affecting their welfare. Another institution affecting individual welfare is employment. It is through employment that we earn a living, as well as having the opportunity to better ourselves in life. Accordingly, the opportunity for employment should be extended equally to all members of society.

It is at this point where the two standards of social fairness, equity and equality, frequently clash. The basis for the clash is that the attributes that differentiate individuals (such as strength) are not equally distributed across all groups comprising society. That is, there are *group* differences in the attributes used to determine individual membership in employment. Members of society can be grouped in several ways; one major grouping factor is by gender. In the case of physical strength, there is a pronounced difference between males and females, with males (as a group) being physically stronger than females (as a group). Thus, it might be reasonable to conclude that if males are physically stronger than females, and if physical strength is a requisite attribute needed to be a firefighter, males are more suited to be firefighters than females. Thus, because of a difference between the two genders with regard to an attribute, males and females have an *unequal* opportunity to assume membership in the role of firefighter in our society.

Proponents of the equity standard of fairness argue that male-populated fire departments merely reflect the reality that males are stronger than females. Proponents of the equality standard of fairness argue that it is not fair, for a variety of reasons. One is that while males are stronger than females, the strongest males are not necessarily the best firefighters. A certain amount of strength may be required, but greater amounts of strength beyond that threshold are unrelated to job performance. Even though females are not as strong as males, they may be "strong enough" to perform the job of firefighter. Also, while strength is important to being a firefighter, many other attributes, such as judgment, which females possess to the same degree as males, are also important. Therefore females shouldn't be disproportionately excluded from the job of firefighter because of one attribute. Third, it can be argued that with the advent of technical advances in firefighting equipment, the equipment exerts the force needed on the job, not the human body. Thus, the manual aspects of firefighting that require physical strength are being replaced through technological advances in equipment design, which females can operate as proficiently as males. And fourth, not all jobs in the fire department require the same degree of physical strength. Jobs such as radio dispatcher, fire truck driver, and paramedic within the fire department are less physically demanding than other jobs. Females would be as proficient as males in meeting the demands of these types of jobs in the fire department.

While counterarguments can be raised for each of these issues, the clash between the equity and equality standards of fairness with regard to gender and physical strength are evident. The same type of argument can be extended to other classifications of societal groups, such as by race and age, and the attendant unequal distribution of attributes across these groups. The dilemma is how to be fair to groups that are unequal in selected attributes yet equally deserving of participating in the societal benefits of employment.

Throughout the past 30 years the pendulum has swung between the equity and equality perspectives. Despite strident claims by proponents of each perspective regarding the "correctness" of their position, the reality is that both perspectives are manifestations of social justice. Whatever the next iteration in societal preference for these two positions will be, it will continue to have a major impact on I/O psychology. As a scientific discipline psychology focuses on how we differ as individuals, which has the effect of gravitating us more toward the equity perspective of justice. However, the philosophic underpinnings of law are seemingly more directed toward the equality perspective of justice. I/O psychology will continue to operate at the cusp of the interplay between these two standards of justice. We will also be compelled to be responsive to the implications of their dictates in the workplace.

Time.   A resource possessed by all is time. Each of us has 24 hours in a day, each day, to live our lives. While many resources (both financial and natural) have been the object of inquiry, we are about to enter an era where time will be a focal point of our attention.

There are many manifestations of our interest in time, both scientific and practical. Katzell (1994) asserts that time is one of the major meta-trends in I/O psychology. He points to research findings that indicate that the accuracy of predictive relationships change over time. Some aspects of behavior are more predictable in the immediate future than in the distant future. Other aspects of behavior may not be immediately evident but will begin to manifest themselves over time. These relationships can be viewed in terms of the specific constructs being measured or by examining the temporal-based developmental process. Other examples include issues pertaining to career development and motivation. In particular, researchers examine the stages of a career that evolve over time and question how the new economic order will affect these stages. While most theories of motivation have typically addressed "how much" motivation a person will exhibit in pursuit of a goal, more recent research is addressing "how long" a person will persevere in pursuit of a goal. Also of interest is how time affects group formation. I/O psychologists are becoming more attuned to time as a prominent issue that affects many other constructs. As Katzell (1994) noted, "Paying more attention to consistencies and changes over time contributes to a better understanding of various subjects of interest, and thereby to more effective ways of dealing with them" (p. 8).

Another manifestation of an interest in time pertains to the identification of a personality construct that reflects our preferred use of time. Serial monochronicity refers to the pattern of preferring to start and complete one major task before moving on to another. Polychronicity is the pattern of preferring to attend to multiple tasks simultaneously. Preferred patterns of time utilization are posited to be predictive of performance in jobs that demand the individual be responsive to overlaying waves of stimuli from divergent sources.

Time and time management have also attracted growing interest among individuals as a factor affecting the quality of life. Among the memorable statements expressed about the importance of time in our lives are the following:

How many people on their deathbed wish they'd spent more time at the office?

Time is gone forever, once spent, and is the ultimate equal opportunity employer.

Covey, Merrill, and Merrill (1994) assert that time-based issues are the leading causes of stress in life. As a way to reduce stress, they advocate partitioning issues in terms of importance and urgency. They recommend that we do not confuse the two, because important but nonurgent issues do not require the same type or speed of response as do important and urgent issues. Covey et al. believe that stress reduction through time management does not involve "working harder" or "working smarter" but being cognizant of the principles that serve to guide our behavior. While we cannot control events in our lives, we can control how we appraise them and respond to them.

The foregoing discussion is not meant to imply that I/O psychologists have been oblivious to time as an issue in our lives. Rather, it reflects an expanding focus from the particular substantive concepts of interest to include the temporal framework in which they are evidenced. It is also likely that the perspective of time as a precious resource will grow among researchers as we seek ways to cultivate this universal resource. Time is not a *fungible* resource, a resource that can readily be traded or exchanged for another. While we can trade money for goods, we cannot trade money for time. It is anticipated that time will be a critical variable on the research agenda of many scientific disciplines in the 21st century.

Concluding Comments

The axiom that "the best predictor of the future is the past" may have to be modified in the next century, at least as it applies to I/O psychology. A few modifiers may be in order, such as "the best predictor of the future is the *very recent* past." Also, we would be advised to pay close attention to emerging trends. Finally, the concept of discontinuous change indicates that the future may look very little like the past. Forces of change are operating with such intensity and velocity that it is indeed very difficult to predict the future, more so now than ever before. This chapter outlines some of the major dimensions of change in individuals, work, and society. I/O psychology will continue to address itself to human behavior in the work world, and in that sense our mission and purpose as a discipline will not waver. We also have much to gain by all that we have learned in the past. However, it seems that we will no longer be allowed the luxury of prolonged deliberation over relatively static events and conditions. The pace of change in employment issues will require adaptive responses to mixes of individual, work, and societal factors that are cascading at accelerated speed.

References

Ackerman, P. L. (1987). Individual differences in skill learning: An integration of psychometric and information processing perspectives. *Psychological Bulletin, 102,* 3–27.

Ackerman, P. L. (1992). Predicting individual differences in complex skill acquisition: Dynamics of ability determinants. *Journal of Applied Psychology, 77,* 598–614.

Ackerman, P. L., & Kanfer, R. (1993). Integrating laboratory and field study for improving selection: Development of a battery for predicting air traffic controller success. *Journal of Applied Psychology, 78,* 413–432.

Adair, J. G. (1984). The Hawthorne effect: A reconsideration of the methodological artifact. *Journal of Applied Psychology, 69,* 334–345.

Adams, J. S. (1965). Inequity in social exchange. In L. Berkowitz (Ed.), *Advances in experimental social psychology* (Vol. 2, pp. 267–299). New York: Academic Press.

Adler, N. J., Doktor, R., & Redding, S. G. (1986). From the Atlantic to the Pacific Century: Cross-cultural management reviewed. *Journal of Management, 12,* 295–318.

Aldag, R. J., & Brief, A. P. (1979). *Task design and employee motivation.* Glenview IL: Scott, Foresman.

Alfredsson, L., & Theorell, T. (1983). Job characteristics of occupations and myocardial infarction risk: Effect of possible confounding factors. *Social Science and Medicine, 17,* 1497–1503.

Alley, W. E. (1994). Recent advances in classification theory and practice. In M. G. Rumsey, C. B. Walker, & J. H. Harris (Eds.), *Personnel selection and classification* (pp. 431–442). Hillsdale, NJ: Erlbaum.

Alliger, G. M., & Janak, E. A. (1989). Kirkpatrick's levels of training criteria: Thirty years later. *Personnel Psychology, 42,* 331–342.

American Psychological Association. (1985). *Standards for educational and psychological testing.* Washington, DC: Author.

American Psychological Association. (1992). Ethical principles of psychologists and code of conduct. *American Psychologist, 47,* 1597–1611.

American Psychological Association. (1993). *Profile of Division 14 members: 1993.* Report prepared by the Office of Demographic, Employment, and Educational Research, American Psychological Association, Washington, DC.

Americans with Disabilities Act of 1990. P.L. 101–336, 104 Stat. 327, 26 July (1990).

Anderson, C. C., Warner, J. L., & Spencer, C. C. (1984). Inflation bias in self-assessment examinations: Implications for valid employee selection. *Journal of Applied Psychology, 69,* 574–580.

Anderson, J. R. (1985). *Cognitive psychology and its implications* (2nd ed.). New York: Freeman.

Annett, J. (1994). The learning of motor skills: Sports science and ergonomic perspectives. *Ergonomics, 37,* 5–16.

Appelbaum, E., & Batt, R. (1993). *High-performance work systems.* Washington, DC: Economic Policy Institute.

Argyris, C. (1968). Some unintended consequences of rigorous research. *Psychological Bulletin, 70,* 185–197.

Arthur, W., & Bennett, W. (1995). The international assignee: The relative importance of factors perceived to contribute to success. *Personnel Psychology, 48,* 99–114.

Arvey, R. D. (1986). Sex bias in job evaluation procedures. *Personnel Psychology, 39,* 315–335.

Arvey, R. D., & Begalla, M. E. (1975). Analyzing the homemaker job using the PAQ. *Journal of Applied Psychology, 60,* 513–517.

Arvey, R. D., & Bouchard, T. J., Jr. (1994). Genetics, twins, and organizational behavior. *Research in Organizational Behavior, 16,* 47–82.

Arvey, R. D., Bouchard, T. J., Jr., Segal, N. L., & Abraham, L. M. (1989). Job satisfaction: Environmental and genetic components. *Journal of Applied Psychology, 74,* 187–192.

Arvey, R. D., & Campion, J. E. (1982). The employment interview: A summary and review of recent research. *Personnel Psychology, 35,* 281–322.

Arvey, R. D., & Cole, D. A. (1989). Evaluating change due to training. In I. L. Goldstein (Ed.), *Training and development in organizations.* (pp. 89–118). San Francisco, CA: Jossey-Bass.

Arvey, R. D., Landon, T. E., Nutting, S. M., & Maxwell, S. E. (1992). Development of physical ability tests for police officers: A construct validation approach. *Journal of Applied Psychology, 77,* 996–1009.

Arvey, R. D., Passino, E. M., & Lounsbury, J. W. (1977). Job analysis results as influenced by sex of incumbent and sex of analyst. *Journal of Applied Psychology, 62,* 411–416.

Aschoff, J. (1978). Features of circadian rhythms relevant to the design of shift schedules. *Ergonomics, 21,* 739–754.

Ash, P. (1970). The parties to the grievance. *Personnel Psychology, 23,* 13–37.

Ash, R. A., & Edgell, S. L. (1975). A note on the readability of the PAQ. *Journal of Applied Psychology, 60,* 765–766.

Austin, J. T., & Villanova, P. (1992). The criterion problem: 1917–1992. *Journal of Applied Psychology, 77,* 836–874.

Bakke, E. W. (1945). Why workers join unions. *Personnel, 22,* 37–46.

Baldwin, T. T., & Ford, J. K. (1988). Transfer of training: A review and directions for future research. *Personnel Psychology, 41,* 63–105.

Baldwin, T. T., & Magjuka, R. J. (1991). Organizational training and signals of importance: Effects of pre-training perceptions on intentions to transfer. *Human Resource Development, 2*(1), 25–36.

Baldwin, T. T., Magjuka, R. J., & Loher, B. T. (1991). The perils of participation: Effects of choice of training on trainee motivation and learning. *Personnel Psychology, 44,* 51–66.

Baldwin, T. T., & Padgett, M. Y. (1993). Management development: A review and commentary. In C. L. Cooper & I. T. Robertson (Eds.), *International review of industrial and organizational psychology* (pp. 35–85). London: Wiley.

Balzer, W. K., & Sulsky, L. M. (1992). Halo and performance appraisal research. *Journal of Applied Psychology, 77,* 975–985.

Barling, J. (1990). *Employment, stress and family functioning.* Chicester: Wiley.

Barnett, G. A. (1988). Communication and organizational culture. In G. M. Goldhaber & G. A. Barnett (Eds.), *Handbook of Organizational Communication.* Norwood, NJ: Ablex.

Barrett, G. V., Alexander, R. A., & Doverspike, D. (1992). The implications for personnel selection of apparent declines in predictive validities over time: A critique of Hulin, Henry, and Noon. *Personnel Psychology, 45,* 601–617.

Barrett, G. V., Caldwell, M. S., & Alexander, R. A. (1985). The concept of dynamic criteria: A critical reanalysis. *Personnel Psychology, 38,* 41–56.

Barrett, G. V., & Kernan, M. C. (1987). Performance appraisal and terminations: A review of court decisions since Brito v. Zia with implications for personnel practices. *Personnel Psychology, 40,* 489–503.

Barrett, G. V., Phillips, J. S., & Alexander, R. A. (1981). Concurrent and predictive validity designs: A critical reanalysis. *Journal of Applied Psychology, 66,* 1–6.

Barrick, M. R., & Mount, M. K. (1991). The big five personality dimensions and job performance: A meta-analysis. *Personnel Psychology, 44,* 1–26.

Bartlett, C. J. (1978). Equal employment opportunity issues in training. *Human Factors, 20,* 179–188.

Bartlett, C. J. (1983). What's the difference between valid and invalid halo? Forced-choice measurement without forcing a choice. *Journal of Applied Psychology, 68,* 218–226.

Barton, J. (1994). Choosing to work at night: A moderating influence on individual tolerance to shiftwork. *Journal of Applied Psychology, 79,* 449–454.

Bartram, D. (1993). Emerging trends in computer-assisted assessment. In H. Schuler, J. L. Farr, & M. Smith (Eds.) *Personnel selection and assessment* (pp. 267–288). Hillsdale, NJ: Erlbaum.

Bashore, T. R., & Rapp, P. E. (1993). Are there alternatives to traditional polygraph procedures? *Psychological Bulletin, 113,* 3–22.

Bass, B. M. (1985). *Leadership and performance beyond expectations.* New York: Free Press.

Baumgartel, H., & Jeanpierre, F. (1972). Applying new knowledge in the back-home setting: A study of Indian managers' adaptive efforts. *Journal of Applied Behavioral Science, 8,* 674–694.

Baytos, L. (1986). The human resource side of acquisitions and divestitures. *Human Resource Planning, 9,* 167–175.

Bazerman, M. H., & Neale, M. A. (1982). Improving negotiation effectiveness under final offer arbitration: The role of selection and training. *Journal of Applied Psychology, 67,* 543–548.

Becker, F., & Steele, F. (1995). *Workplace by design: Managing the high-performance workscape.* San Francisco, CA: Jossey-Bass.

Becker, T. E., & Colquitt, A. L. (1992). Potential versus actual faking of a biodata form: An analysis along several dimensions of item type. *Personnel Psychology, 45,* 389–406.

Beirness, D. J. (1993). Do we really drive as we live? The role of personality factors in road crashes. *Alcohol, Drugs, and Driving, 9,* 129–143.

Ben-Shakhar, G., Bar-Hillel, M., Bilu, Y., Ben-Abba, E., & Flug, A. (1986). Can graphology predict occupational success? Two empirical studies and some methodological ruminations. *Journal of Applied Psychology, 71,* 645–653.

Bennett, G. K. (1980). *Test of mechanical comprehension.* New York: Psychological Corporation.

Bennett, N., Blum, T. C., & Roman, P. M. (1994). Pressure of drug screening and employee assistance programs: Exclusive and inclusive human resource management practices. *Journal of Organizational Behavior, 15,* 549–560.

Berman, F. E., & Miner, J. B. (1985). Motivation to manage at the top executive level: A test of the hierarchic role-motivation theory. *Personnel Psychology, 38,* 377–391.

Bernardin, H. J., & Cooke, D. K. (1993). Validity of an honesty test in predicting theft among convenience store employees. *Academy of Management Journal, 36,* 1097–1108.

Bernardin, H. J., & Pence, E. C. (1980). Effects of rater training: Creating new response sets and decreasing accuracy. *Journal of Applied Psychology, 65,* 60–66.

Betz, E. L. (1984). Two tests of Maslow's theory of need fulfillment. *Journal of Vocational Behavior, 24,* 204–220.

Beyer, J. M., & Trice, H. M. (1987). How an organization's rites reveal its culture. *Organizational Dynamics, 15,* 5–24.

Bigoness, W. J. (1978). Correlates of faculty attitudes toward collective bargaining. *Journal of Applied Psychology, 63,* 228–233.

Bingham, W. V. (1917). Mentality testing of college students. *Journal of Applied Psychology, 1,* 38–45.

Bingham, W. V., & Moore, B. V. (1941). *How to interview* (3rd ed.). New York: Harper & Row.

Binning, J. F., & Barrett, G. V. (1989). Validity of personnel decisions: A conceptual analysis of the inferential and evidential bases. *Journal of Applied Psychology, 74,* 478–494.

Birdwhistell, R. L. (1970). *Kinesics and context.* Philadelphia, PA: University of Pennsylvania Press.

Black, J. S., & Mendenhall, M. (1990). Cross-cultural training effectiveness: A review and theoretical framework for future research. *Academy of Management Review, 15,* 113–136.

Blum, M. L., & Naylor, J. C. (1968). *Industrial psychology: Its theoretical and social foundations.* New York: Harper & Row.

Bobko, P. (1994). Issues in operational selection and classification systems: Comments and commonalities. In M. G. Rumsey, C. B. Walker, & J. H. Harris (Eds.), *Personnel selection and classification* (pp. 443–456). Hillsdale, NJ: Erlbaum.

Bobko, P., & Karren, R. (1979). The perception of Pearson product moment correlations from bivariate scatterplots. *Personnel Psychology, 32,* 313–326.

Boehm, V. R. (1980). Research in the "real world"—A conceptual model. *Personnel Psychology, 33,* 495–504.

Bok, D., & Dunlop, J. (1970). *Labor and the American community.* New York: Simon & Schuster.

Borman, W. C. (1974). The rating of individuals in organizations: An alternative approach. *Organizational Behavior and Human Performance, 12,* 105–124.

Borman, W. C. (1978). Exploring upper limits of reliability and validity in performance ratings. *Journal of Applied Psychology, 63,* 135–144.

Borman, W. C. (1982). Validity of behavioral assessment for predicting military recruiter performance. *Journal of Applied Psychology, 67,* 3–9.

Borman, W. C., & Motowidlo, S. J. (1993). Expanding the criterion domain to include elements of contextual performance. In N. Schmitt & W. C. Borman (Eds.), *Personnel selection in organizations* (pp. 71–98). San Francisco, CA: Jossey-Bass.

Borman, W. C., White, L. A., & Dorsey, D. W. (1995). Effects of ratee task performance and interpersonal factors on supervisor and peer performance in ratings. *Journal of Applied Psychology, 80,* 168–177.

Bouchard, T. J., Jr., Arvey, R. D., Keller, L. M., & Segal, N. L. (1992). Genetic influences on job satisfaction: A reply to Cropanzano and James. *Journal of Applied Psychology, 77,* 89–93.

Boudreau, J. W. (1991). Utility analysis for decisions in human resource management. In M. D. Dunnette & L. M. Hough (Eds.), *Handbook of industrial and organizational psychology* (Vol. 2, pp. 621–745). Palo Alto, CA: Consulting Psychologists Press.

Bramel, D., & Friend, R. (1981). Hawthorne, the myth of the docile worker, and class bias in psychology. *American Psychologist, 36,* 867–878.

Bramwell, R., & Cooper, C. L. (1995). VDTs in the workplace: Psychological and health implications. In C. L. Cooper & I. T. Robertson (Eds.), *International review of industrial and organizational psychology* (Vol. 10, pp. 213–228). Chichester: Wiley.

Brand, C. (1987). The importance of general intelligence. In S. Modgil & C. Modgil (Eds.), *Arthur Jensen: Consensus and controversy.* New York: Falmer.

Bray, D. W. (1982). The assessment center and the study of lives. *American Psychologist, 37,* 180–189.

Bray, D. W., Campbell, R. J., & Grant, D. L. (1974). *Formative years in business.* New York: Wiley.

Breaugh, J. A. (1983a). Realistic job previews: A critical appraisal and future research directions. *Academy of Management Review, 8,* 612–619.

Breaugh, J. A. (1983b). The 12-hour work day: Differing employee reactions. *Personnel Psychology, 36,* 277–288.

Brenner, M. H., & Mooney, A. (1983). Unemployment and health in the context of economic change. *Social Science and Medicine, 17*, 1125–1138.

Brethower, K. S. (1976). Programmed instruction. In R. L. Craig (Ed.), *Training and development handbook* (2nd ed.). New York: McGraw-Hill.

Brett, J. M. (1980). Behavioral research on unions and union management systems. In B. M. Staw & L. L. Cummings (Eds.), *Research in organizational behavior*, Greenwich, CT: JAI Press.

Brett, J. M., Goldberg, S. B., & Ury, W. L. (1990). Designing systems for resolving disputes in organizations. *American Psychologist, 45*, 162–170.

Brief, A. P., & Rude, D. E. (1981). Voting in a union certification election: A conceptual analysis. *Academy of Management Review, 6*, 261–267.

Brockner, J., Davy, J., & Carter, C. (1985). Layoffs, self-esteem, and survivor guilt: Motivational, affective, and attitudinal consequences. *Organizational Behavior and Human Decision Processes, 36*, 229–244.

Brockner, J., & Greenberg, J. (1990). The impact of layoffs on survivors: An occupational justice perspective. In J. Carroll (Ed.), *Applied social psychology and organizational settings* (pp. 45–75). Hillsdale, NJ: Erlbaum.

Brogden, H. E. (1951). Increased efficiency of selection resulting from replacement of a single predictor with several differential predictors. *Educational and Psychological Measurement, 11*, 173–195.

Brogden, H. E., & Taylor, E. K. (1950). The theory and classification of criterion bias. *Educational and Psychological Measurement, 10*, 159–186.

Brown, B. K., & Campion, M. A. (1994). Biodata phenomenology: Recruiters' perceptions and use of biographical information in resume screening. *Journal of Applied Psychology, 79*, 897–908.

Bruno, F. (1994). Drug and alcohol problems in the workplace in Italy. *Journal of Drug Issues, 24*, 697–713.

Bryan, W. L. (1904). Theory and practice. *Psychological Review, 11*, 71–82.

Bryan, W. L., & Harter, N. (1897). Studies in the physiology and psychology of the telegraphic language. *Psychological Review, 4*, 27–53.

Bryan, W. L., & Harter, N. (1899). Studies in the telegraphic language. *Psychological Review, 6*, 345–375.

Buono, A. F., & Bowditch, J. L. (1989). *The human side of mergers and acquisitions: Managing collision between people, cultures, and organizations*. San Francisco, CA: Jossey-Bass.

Burke, M. J. (1984). Validity generalization: A review and critique of the correlational model. *Personnel Psychology, 37*, 93–116.

Burke, M. J., & Day, R. R. (1986). A cumulative study of the effectiveness of managerial training. *Journal of Applied Psychology, 71*, 232–246.

Buss, T. F., & Redburn, F. S. (1987). Plant closings: Impacts and responses. *Economic Development Quarterly, 1*, 170–177.

Byham, W. C. (1970). Assessment centers for spotting future managers. *Harvard Business Review, 48*, 150–167.

Cain, P. S., & Green, B. F. (1983). Reliabilities of selected ratings available from the Dictionary of Occupational Titles. *Journal of Applied Psychology, 68*, 155–165.

Camara, W. J., & Schneider, D. L. (1994). Integrity tests: Facts and unresolved issues. *American Psychologist, 49*, 112–119.

Cameron, K. (1982). The relationship between faculty unionism and organizational effectiveness. *Academy of Management Journal, 25*, 6–24.

Campbell, D. J., & Lee C. (1988). Self-appraisal in performance evaluation: Development versus evaluation. *Academy of Management Review, 13*, 302–314.

Campbell, J. P. (1990). An overview of the Army selection and classification project. *Personnel Psychology, 43*, 231–240.

Campion, J. E. (1972). Work sampling for personnel selection. *Journal of Applied Psychology, 56*, 40–44.

Campion, M. A. (1988). Interdisciplinary approaches to job design: A constructive replication with extensions. *Journal of Applied Psychology, 73*, 467–481.

Campion, M. A. (1989). Ability requirement implications of job design: An interdisciplinary perspective. *Personnel Psychology, 42*, 1–24.

Campion, M. A. (1991). Meaning and measurement of turnover: Comparison of alternative measures and recommendations for research. *Journal of Applied Psychology, 76*, 199–212.

Campion, M. A., & Berger, C. J. (1990). Conceptual integration and empirical test of job design and compensation relationships. *Personnel Psychology, 43*, 525–554.

Campion, M. A., & Campion, J. E. (1987). Evaluation of an interviewee skills training program in a natural field experiment. *Personnel Psychology, 40*, 675–691.

Campion, M. A., Cheraskin, L., & Stevens, M. J. (1994). Career-related antecedents and outcomes of job rotation. *Academy of Management Journal, 37*, 1518–1542.

Campion, M. A., & McClelland, C. L. (1991). Interdisciplinary examination of the costs and benefits of enlarged jobs: A job design quasi-experiment. *Journal of Applied Psychology, 76*, 186–198.

Campion, M. A., & McClelland, C. L. (1993). Follow-up and extension of the interdisciplinary costs and benefits of enlarged jobs. *Journal of Applied Psychology, 78*, 339–351.

Campion, M. A., Medsker, G. J., & Higgs, A. C. (1993). Relations between work group characteristics and effectiveness: Implications for designing effective work groups. *Personnel Psychology, 46*, 823–850.

Campion, M. A., & Thayer, P. W. (1985). Development and field evaluation of an interdisciplinary measure of job design. *Journal of Applied Psychology, 70*, 29–43.

Carillon, J. W., & Sutton, R. I. (1982). The relationship between union effectiveness and the quality of members' worklife. *Journal of Occupational Behavior, 3,* 171–179.

Carling, P. (1994). Reasonable accommodations in the workplace for persons with psychiatric disabilities. In S. M. Bruyere & J. O'Keeffe (Eds.), *Implications of the Americans with Disabilities Act for psychology* (pp. 103–136). New York: Springer.

Carlson, R. E. (1968). Employment decisions: Effect of mode of applicant presentation on some outcome measures. *Personnel Psychology, 21,* 193–207.

Carlson, R. E. (1972). *The current status of judgmental techniques in industry.* Paper presented at the symposium, Alternatives to Paper and Pencil Personnel Testing, University of Pittsburgh.

Carnevale, A. P. (1995). Enhancing skills in the new economy. In A. Howard (Ed.), *The changing nature of work* (pp. 238–251). San Francisco, CA: Jossey-Bass.

Cartwright, S., & Cooper, C. L. (1994). The human effect of mergers and acquisitions. In C. L. Cooper & D. M. Rousseau (Eds.), *Trends in organizational behavior* (pp. 47–62). New York: Wiley.

Cascio, W. F. (1976). Turnover, biographical data, and fair employment practice. *Journal of Applied Psychology, 61,* 576–580.

Cascio, W. F. (1982). *Applied psychology in personnel management* (2nd ed.). Reston, VA: Reston.

Cascio, W. F. (1989). Using utility analyses to assess training outcomes. In I. L. Goldstein (Ed.), *Training and development in organizations* (pp. 63–88). San Francisco, CA: Jossey-Bass.

Cascio, W. F. (1991). *Costing human resources: The financial impact of behavior in organizations* (3rd ed.). Boston, MA: PWS-Kent.

Cascio, W. F. (1993). Assessing the utility of selection decisions: Theoretical and practical considerations. In N. Schmitt & W. C. Borman (Eds.), *Personnel selection in organizations* (pp. 310–340). San Francisco, CA: Jossey-Bass.

Cascio, W. F. (1995a). *Managing human resources* (4th ed.). New York: McGraw-Hill.

Cascio, W. F. (1995b). Whither industrial and organizational psychology in a changing world of work? *American Psychologist, 50,* 928–939.

Cascio, W. F., Alexander, R. A., & Barrett, G. V. (1988). Setting cutoff scores: Legal, psychometric, and professional issues and guidelines. *Personnel Psychology, 41,* 1–24.

Cascio, W. F., & Phillips, N. F. (1979). Performance testing: A rose among thorns? *Personnel Psychology, 32,* 751–766.

Castellow, W. A., Wuensch, K. L., & Moore, C. H. (1990). Effects of physical attractiveness of the plaintiff and defendant in sexual harassment judgments. *Journal of Social Behavior and Personality, 15,* 547–562.

Catalanello, R. E., & Kirkpatrick, D. L. (1968). Evaluating training programs: The state of the art. *Training and Development Journal, 22,* 2–9.

Cederblom, D. (1982). The performance appraisal interview: A review, implications and suggestions. *Academy of Management Review, 7,* 219–227.

Cederblom, D., & Lounsbury, J. W. (1980). An investigation of user acceptance of peer evaluations. *Personnel Psychology, 33,* 567–580.

Chalykoff, J., & Kochan, T. A. (1989). Computer-aided monitoring: Its influence on employee job satisfaction and turnover. *Personnel Psychology, 42,* 807–834.

Chao, G. T., & Kozlowski, S. W. (1986). Employee perceptions on the implementation of robotic manufacturing technology. *Journal of Applied Psychology, 71,* 70–76.

Chao, G. T., Walz, P. M., & Gardner, P. D. (1992). Formal and informal mentorships: A comparison on mentoring functions and contrast with nonmentored counterparts. *Personnel Psychology, 45,* 619–636.

Chapanis, A., Garner, W. R., & Morgan, C. T. (1949). *Applied experimental psychology.* New York: Wiley.

Chemers, M. M., & Murphy, S. E. (1995). Leadership and diversity in groups and organizations. In M. M. Chemers, S. Oskamp, & M. A. Costanzo (Eds.), *Diversity in organizations: New perspectives for a changing workforce* (pp. 157–188). Thousand Oaks, CA: Sage.

Childs, A., & Klimoski, R. J. (1986). Successfully predicting career success: An application of the biographical inventory. *Journal of Applied Psychology, 71,* 3–8.

Civil Rights Act of 1991. P. L. 102–166.105, Stat. 1071, 21 Nov. (1991).

Clegg, C., & Wall, T. (1990). The relationship between simplified jobs and mental health: A replication study. *Journal of Occupational Psychology, 63,* 289–296.

Cleveland, J. N., & Kerst, M. E. (1993). Sexual harassment and perceptions of power: An under-articulated relationship. *Journal of Vocational Behavior, 42,* 49–67.

Cobb, S., & Kasl, S. V. (1977). *Termination: The consequence of job loss.* U.S. Department of Health, Education and Welfare. Washington, DC: U.S. Government Printing Office.

Cohen, A. (1977). Factors in successful occupational safety programs. *Journal of Safety Research, 9,* 168–178.

Cohen, D. J. (1990, November). What motivates trainees. *Training and Development Journal,* 91–93.

Collins, J. M., & Muchinsky, P. M. (1993). An assessment of the construct validity of three job evaluation methods: A field experiment. *Academy of Management Journal, 36,* 895–904.

Collins, J. M., & Schmidt, F. L. (1993). Personality, integrity, and white collar crime: A construct validity study. *Personnel Psychology, 46,* 295–311.

Conger, J. A. (1989). *The charismatic leader: Behind the mystique of exceptional leadership.* San Francisco: Jossey-Bass.

Conger, J. A., & Kanungo, R. N. (1987). Toward a behavioral theory of charismatic leadership in organizational settings. *Academy of Management Review, 12,* 637–647.

Conley, P. R., & Sackett, P. R. (1987). Effects of using high- versus low-performing job incumbents as sources of job analysis information. *Journal of Applied Psychology, 72,* 434–437.

Conoley, J. C., & Impara, J. C. (1995). *The twelfth mental measurements yearbook.* Lincoln, NE: Buros Institute of Mental Measurements.

Cooke, P. (1987). Role playing. In R. L. Craig (Ed.), *Training and development handbook* (3rd ed.). New York: McGraw-Hill.

Cooper, W. H. (1981). Ubiquitous halo. *Psychological Bulletin, 90,* 218–244.

Cornelius, E. T., DeNisi, A. S., & Blencoe, A. G. (1984). Expert and naive raters using the PAQ: Does it matter? *Personnel Psychology, 37,* 453–464.

Covey, S. R., Merrill, A. R., & Merrill, R. R. (1994). *First things first.* New York: Simon & Schuster.

Cox, T., & Leather, P. (1994). The prevention of violence at work: Application of a cognitive behavioral theory. In C. L. Cooper & I. T. Robertson (Eds.), *International review of industrial and organizational psychology* (pp. 213–245). London: Wiley.

Cronbach, L. J., & Gleser, G. C. (1965). *Psychological tests and personnel decisions* (2nd ed.). Urbana: University of Illinois Press.

Cunningham, M. R., Wong, D. T., & Barbee, A. P. (1994). Self-presentation dynamics on overt integrity tests: Experimental studies of the Reid Report. *Journal of Applied Psychology, 79,* 643–658.

Daft, R. L. (1983). Learning the craft of organizational research. *Academy of Management Review, 8,* 539–546.

Dalton, D. R., & Mesch, D. J. (1990). The impact of flexible scheduling on employee attendance and turnover. *Administrative Science Quarterly, 35,* 370–387.

Dalton, D. R., & Todor, W. D. (1982). Antecedents of grievance filing behavior: Attitude/behavioral consistency and the union steward. *Academy of Management Journal, 25,* 158–169.

Dansereau, F., Graen, G., & Haga, W. (1975). A vertical dyad linkage approach to leadership in formal organizations. *Organizational Behavior and Human Performance, 13,* 46–78.

Davis, D. D. (1995). Form, function, and strategy in boundaryless organizations. In A. Howard (Ed.), *The changing nature of work* (pp. 112–138). San Francisco, CA: Jossey-Bass.

Davis, G. F., & Powell, W. W. (1992). Organization-environment relations. In M. D. Dunnette & L. M. Hough (Eds.), *Handbook of industrial and organizational psychology* (Vol. 3, pp. 315–375). Palo Alto, CA: Consulting Psychologists Press.

Day, D. V., & Sulsky, L. M. (1995). Effects of frame-of-reference training and information configuration on memory organization and rater accuracy. *Journal of Applied Psychology, 80,* 158–167.

Deadrick, D. L., & Madigan, R. M. (1990). Dynamic criteria revisited: A longitudinal study of performance stability and predictive validity. *Personnel Psychology, 43,* 717–744.

Deal, T., & Kennedy, A. (1982). *Corporate cultures.* Reading, MA: Addison-Wesley.

Dean, R. A., & Wanous, J. P. (1984). Effects of realistic job previews on hiring bank tellers. *Journal of Applied Psychology, 69,* 61–68.

DeCotiis, T. A., & LeLouarn, J. Y. (1981). A predictive study of voting behavior in a representation election using union instrumentality and work perceptions. *Organizational Behavior and Human Performance, 27,* 103–118.

Dedobbeleer, N., & Beland, F. (1991). A safety climate measure for construction sites. *Journal of Safety Research, 22,* 97–103.

De la Mare, G., & Walker, J. (1968). Factors influencing the choice of shift rotation. *Occupational Psychology, 42,* 1–21.

DeMeuse, K. P. (1987). Employee nonverbal cues: Their effects on the performance appraisal process. *Journal of Occupational Psychology, 60,* 207–226.

DeReamer, R. (1980). *Modern safety and health technology.* New York: Wiley.

Dickinson, T. L. (1993). Attitudes about performance appraisal. In H. Schuler, J. L. Farr, & M. Smith (Eds.), *Personnel selection and assessment* (pp. 141–162). Hillsdale, NJ: Erlbaum.

Dienesch, R. M., & Liden, R. C. (1986). Leader-member exchange model of leadership: A critique and further development. *Academy of Management Review, 11,* 618–634.

Digman, J. M., & Takemoto-Chock, N. K. (1981). Factors in the natural language of personality: Re-analysis and comparison of six major studies. *Multivariate Behavioral Research, 16,* 149–170.

Dipboye, R. L. (1990). Laboratory vs. field research in industrial and organizational psychology. In C. L. Cooper & I. T. Robertson (Eds.), *International review of industrial and organizational psychology* (pp. 1–34). London: Wiley.

Dompierre, J., & Lavoie, F. (1994). Subjective work stress and family violence. In G. P. Keita & J. J. Hurrell (Eds.), *Job stress in a changing workforce* (pp. 213–228). Washington, DC: American Psychological Association.

Dossett, D. L., & Hulvershorn, P. (1983). Increasing technical training efficiency: Peer training via computer-assisted instruction. *Journal of Applied Psychology, 68,* 552–558.

Dotlich, D. L. (1982, October). International and intracultural management development. *Training and Development Journal, 36,* 26–31.

Dougherty, T. W., Turban, D. B., & Callender, J. C. (1994). Confirming first impressions in the employment interview: A field study of interviewer behaviors. *Journal of Applied Psychology, 79,* 659–665.

Drakeley, R. J., Herriot, P., & Jones, A. (1988). Biographical data, training success, and turnover. *Journal of Occupational Psychology, 61,* 145–152.

Dreher, G. F., & Ash, R. A. (1990). A comparative study of mentoring among men and women in managerial, professional, and technical positions. *Journal of Applied Psychology, 75,* 539–546.

Dreher, G. F., Ash, R. A., & Hancock, P. (1988). The role of the traditional research design in underestimating the validity of the employment interview. *Personnel Psychology, 41,* 315–328.

Drucker, P. F. (1993). *Post-capitalist society.* New York: Harper.

Duchon, J. C., Keran, C. M., & Smith, T. J. (1994). Extended workdays in an underground mine: A work performance analysis. *Human Factors, 36,* 258–268.

Dudycha, A. L., Dudycha, L. W., & Schmitt, N. W. (1974). Cue redundancy: Some overlooked analytical relationships in MCPL. *Organizational Behavior and Human Performance, 11,* 222–234.

Dugoni, B. L., & Ilgen, D. R. (1981). Realistic job previews and the adjustment of new employees. *Academy of Management Journal, 24,* 579–591.

Dunham, R. B. (1976). The measurement and dimensionality of job characteristics. *Journal of Applied Psychology, 61,* 404–409.

Dunham, R. B. (1977). Shift work: A review and theoretical analysis. *Academy of Management Review, 2,* 626–634.

Dunham, R. B., Pierce, J. L., & Castaneda, M. B. (1987). Alternative work schedules: Two field quasi-experiments. *Personnel Psychology, 40,* 215–242.

Dunn, W. S., Mount, M. K., Barrick, M. R., & Ones, D. S. (1995). Relative importance of personality and general mental ability in managers' judgments of applicant qualifications. *Journal of Applied Psychology, 80,* 500–509.

Dunnette, M. D. (1993). My hammer or your hammer? *Human Resource Management, 32,* 373–384.

Dunnette, M. D., & Hough, L. M. (Eds.) (1990). *Handbook of industrial and organizational psychology* (2nd ed.), Vol. 1. Palo Alto, CA: Consulting Psychologists Press.

Dyer, L., Schwab, D. P., & Theriault, R. D. (1976). Managerial perceptions regarding salary increase criteria. *Personnel Psychology, 29,* 233–242.

Eagly, A. H., Karau, S. J., & Makhijani, M. G. (1995). Gender and the effectiveness of leaders: A meta-analysis. *Psychological Bulletin, 117,* 125–145.

Eagly, A. H., Makhijani, M. G., & Klonsky, B. G. (1992). Gender and the evaluation of leaders: A meta-analysis. *Psychological Bulletin, 111,* 3–22.

Ebel, R. L. (1972). *Essentials of educational measurement.* Englewood Cliffs, NJ: Prentice-Hall.

Ellis, H. D. (1982). The effect of cold on the performance of serial choice reaction time and various discrete tasks. *Human Factors, 24,* 589–598.

Enander, A. (1987). Effects of moderate cold on performance of psychomotor and cognitive tasks. *Ergonomics, 30,* 1431–1445.

England, P. (1992). *Comparable worth: Theories and evidence.* Hawthorne, NY: Aldine de Gruyter.

Equal Employment Opportunities Commission. (1980). Discrimination because of sex under Title VII of the Civil Rights Act of 1964, as amended; adoption of interim interpretive guidelines. *Federal Register, 45,* 25024–25025.

Erez, M. (1994). Toward a model of cross-cultural industrial and organizational psychology. In H. C. Triandis, M. D. Dunnette, & L. M. Hough (Eds.), *Handbook of industrial and organizational psychology,* (Vol. 4, pp. 559–608). Palo Alto, CA: Consulting Psychologists Press.

Erikson, E. H. (1963). *Childhood and society* (2nd ed.). New York: Norton.

Estey, M. (1981). *The unions: Structure, development, and management* (3rd ed.). New York: Harcourt Brace Jovanovich.

Fagenson, E. A. (1989). The mentor advantage: Perceived career/job experiences of protégés versus non-protégés. *Journal of Organizational Behavior, 10,* 309–320.

Feild, H. S., & Holley, W. H. (1982). The relationship of performance appraisal system characteristics to verdicts in selected employment discrimination cases. *Academy of Management Journal, 25,* 392–406.

Ferdman, B. M. (1992). The dynamics of ethnic diversity in organizations: Toward integrative models. In K. Kelly (Ed.), *Issues, theory, and research in industrial/organization psychology* (pp. 339–384). Amsterdam: North Holland.

Ferguson, L. W. (1962). *The heritage of industrial psychology.* Hartford, CT: Finlay.

Feuille, P., & Blandin, J. (1974). Faculty job satisfaction and bargaining sentiment: A case study. *Academy of Management Journal, 17,* 678–692.

Fiedler, F. E., & Garcia, J. E. (1987). *New approaches to leadership: Cognitive resources and organizational performance.* New York: Wiley.

Fields, M. W., & Thacker, J. W. (1992). Influence of quality of work life on company and union commitment. *Academy of Management Journal, 35,* 439–450.

Fine, B. J., & Kobrick, J. L. (1978). Effects of altitude and heat on complex cognitive tasks. *Human Factors, 20,* 115–122.

Flanagan, J. C. (1954). The critical incident technique. *Psychological Bulletin, 51,* 327–358.

Flanagan, M. F., & Dipboye, R. L. (1981). Research settings in industrial and organizational psychology: Facts, fallacies, and the future. *Personnel Psychology, 34,* 37–47.

Fleishman, E. A., & Quaintance, M. K. (1984). *Taxonomies of human performance.* New York: Academic Press.

Folger, R., & Greenberg, J. (1985). Procedural justice: An interpretive analysis of personnel systems. In K. Rowland & G. Ferris (Eds.), *Research in personnel and human resources management* (Vol. 3, pp. 141–183). Greenwich, CT: JAI Press.

Ford, J. K., Quinones, M., Sego, D., & Speer, J. (1991). *Factors affecting the opportunity to use trained skills on the job.* Paper presented at the 6th annual conference of the Society for Industrial and Organizational Psychology, St. Louis.

Foti, R. J., & Lord, R. G. (1987). Prototypes and scripts: The effects of alternative methods of processing information on rating accuracy. *Organizational Behavior and Human Decision Processes, 39,* 318–340.

Fox, W. F. (1967). Human performance in the cold. *Human Factors, 9,* 203–220.

Frankenhaeuser, M. (1988). Stress and reactivity patterns at different stages of the life cycle. In P. Pancheri & L. Zichella (Eds.), *Biorythms and stress in physiopathology of reproduction.* Washington, DC: Hemisphere.

Franklin, W. S. (1976). Are construction apprenticeships too long? *Labor Law Journal, 27,* 99–106.

Freeberg, N. E. (1976). Criterion measures for youth-work training programs: The development of relevant performance dimensions. *Journal of Applied Psychology, 61,* 537–545.

Freeman, R. E. (1990). Ethics in the workplace: Recent scholarships. In C. L. Cooper & I. T. Robertson (Eds.), *International review of industrial and organizational psychology* (pp. 149–168). London: Wiley.

Freese, M. (1987). Human-computer interaction in the office. In C. L. Cooper & I. T. Robertson (Eds.), *International review of industrial and organizational psychology* (pp. 117–165). London: Wiley.

Freese, M., & Okonek, K. (1984). Reasons to leave shiftwork and psychological and psychosomatic complaints of former shiftworkers. *Journal of Applied Psychology, 69,* 509–514.

French, J. R. P., & Raven, B. (1960). The basis of social power. In D. Cartwright & A. F. Zander (Eds.), *Group dynamics* (2nd ed.). Evanston, IL: Row & Peterson.

Fretz, B. R., & Mills, D. H. (1980). *Licensing and certification of psychologists and counselors.* San Francisco: Jossey-Bass.

Fried, Y., & Ferris, G. R. (1987). The validity of the job characteristics model: A review and meta-analysis. *Personnel Psychology, 40,* 287–322.

Friedman, D. E., & Galinsky, E. (1992). Work and family issues: A legitimate business concern. In S. Zedeck (Ed.), *Work, families, and organizations* (pp. 168–207). San Francisco: Jossey-Bass.

Friedman, L., & Harvey, R. J. (1986). Factors of union commitment: The case for a lower dimensionality. *Journal of Applied Psychology, 71,* 371–376.

Fromkin, H. L., & Streufert, S. (1976). Laboratory experimentation. In M. D. Dunnette (Ed.), *Handbook of industrial and organizational psychology* (pp. 415–465). Skokie, IL: Rand McNally.

Frone, M. R., Russell, M., & Cooper, M. L. (1992a). Antecedents and outcomes of work-family conflict: Testing a model of the work-family interface. *Journal of Applied Psychology, 77,* 65–78.

Frone, M. R., Russell, M., & Cooper, M. L. (1992b). Prevalence of work-family conflict: Are work and family boundaries asymmetrically permeable? *Journal of Organizational Behavior, 13,* 723–729.

Frost, P. J., & Jamal, M. (1979). Shift work, attitudes and reported behaviors: Some association between individual characteristics and hours of work and leisure. *Journal of Applied Psychology, 64,* 77–81.

Fryer, D., & Payne, R. (1986). Being unemployed: A review of the literature on the psychological experience of unemployment. In C. L. Cooper & I. Robertson (Eds.), *International review of industrial and organizational psychology* (pp. 235–278). London: Wiley.

Fryxell, G. E., & Gordon, M. E. (1989). Workplace justice and job satisfaction as predictors of satisfaction with union and management. *Academy of Management Journal, 32,* 851–866.

Fukami, C. V., & Larson, E. W. (1984). Commitment to company and union: Parallel models. *Journal of Applied Psychology, 69,* 367–371.

Fullagar, C., & Barling, J. (1989). A longitudinal test of a model of the antecedents and consequences of union loyalty. *Journal of Applied Psychology, 74,* 213–227.

Fullagar, C., Clark, P. F., Gallagher, D. G., & Gordon, M. E. (1994). A model of the antecedents of early union commitment: The role of socialization experiences and steward characteristics. *Journal of Organizational Behavior, 15,* 517–533.

Fullager, C., Gallagher, D. G., Gordon, M. E., & Clark, P. F. (1995). Impact of early socialization on union commitment and participation: A longitudinal study. *Journal of Applied Psychology, 80,* 147–157.

Fulmer, R. (1986). Meeting the merger integration challenge with management development. *Journal of Management Development, 5,* 7–16.

Furnham, A., & Gunter, B. (1993). Corporate culture: Definition, diagnosis and change. In C. L. Cooper & I. T. Robertson (Eds.), *International review of industrial and organizational psychology* (pp. 234–261). London: Wiley.

Garvin, D. A. (1986). Quality problems, policies, and attitudes in the United States and Japan: An exploratory study. *Academy of Management Journal, 29,* 653–673.

Geen, R. G. (1990). *Human aggression.* London: Open University Press.

Gerhart, B., & Milkovich, G. T. (1992). Employee compensation: Research and practice. In M. D. Dunnette & L. M. Hough (Eds.), *Handbook of industrial and organizational psychology* (Vol. 3, pp. 481–569). Palo Alto, CA: Consulting Psychologists Press.

Ghiselli, E. E., & Brown, C. W. (1955). *Personnel and industrial psychology.* New York: McGraw-Hill.

Gifford, R., Ng, C. F., & Wilkinson, M. (1985). Nonverbal cues in the employment interview: Links between applicant qualities and interviewer judgments. *Journal of Applied Psychology, 70,* 729–736.

Gilliland, S. W. (1993). The perceived fairness of selection systems: An organizational justice perspective. *Academy of Management Review, 18,* 694–734.

Goktepe, J. R., & Schneier, C. E. (1989). Role of sex, gender roles, and attraction in predicting emergent leaders. *Journal of Applied Psychology, 74,* 165–167.

Goldberg, S. L., Mastaglio, T. W., & Johnson, W. R. (1995). Training in the close combat tactical trainer. In R. J. Seidel & P. R. Chatelier (Eds.), *Learning without boundaries: Technology to support distance/distributed learning* (pp. 119–133). New York: Plenum.

Goldstein, I. L. (1978). The pursuit of validity in the evaluation of training programs. *Human Factors, 20,* 131–144.

Goldstein, I. L. (1980). Training in work organizations. *Annual Review of Psychology, 31,* 229–272.

Goldstein, I. L. (1986). *Training in organizations: Needs assessment, development and evaluation* (2nd ed.). Pacific Grove, CA: Brooks/Cole.

Goldstein, I. L. (1991). Training in work organizations. In M. D. Dunnette & L. M. Hough (Eds.), *Handbook of industrial and organizational psychology* (2nd ed.), (Vol. 2, pp. 507–619). Palo Alto, CA: Consulting Psychologists Press.

Goldstein, I. L. (1993). *Training in organizations: Needs assessment, development and evaluation* (3rd ed.). Pacific Grove, CA: Brooks/Cole.

Goldstein, I. L., & Gilliam, P. (1990). Training system issues in the year 2000. *American Psychologist, 45,* 134–143.

Goldstein, I. L., Zedeck, S., & Schneider, B. (1993). An exploration of the job analysis-content validity process. In N. Schmitt & W. C. Borman (Eds.), *Personnel selection in organizations* (pp. 3–34). San Francisco, CA: Jossey-Bass.

Golembiewski, R. T., & Proehl, C. W. (1978). A survey of the empirical literature on flexible workhours: Character and consequences of a major innovation. *Academy of Management Review, 3,* 837–853.

Gomez-Mejia, L. R., & Balkin, D. B. (1984). Faculty satisfaction with pay and other job dimensions under union and nonunion conditions. *Academy of Management Journal, 27,* 591–602.

Gomez-Mejia, L. R., Page, R. C., & Tornow, W. W. (1982). A comparison of the practical utility of traditional, statistical, and hybrid job evaluation approaches. *Academy of Management Journal, 25,* 790–809.

Goodale, J. G., & Aagaard, A. K. (1975). Factors relating to varying reactions to the 4-day workweek. *Journal of Applied Psychology, 60,* 33–38.

Gordon, M. E., & Bowlby, R. L. (1988). Propositions about grievance settlements: Finally, consultation with grievants. *Personnel Psychology, 41,* 107–124.

Gordon, M. E., & Bowlby, R. L. (1989). Reactance and intentionality attributions as determinants of the intent to file a grievance. *Personnel Psychology, 42,* 309–330.

Gordon, M. E., & Ladd, R. T. (1990). Dual allegiance: Renewal, reconsideration, and recantation. *Personnel Psychology, 43,* 37–69.

Gordon, M. E., & Miller, S. J. (1984). Grievances: A review of research and practice. *Personnel Psychology, 37,* 117–146.

Gordon, M. E., & Nurick, A. J. (1981). Psychological approaches to the study of unions and union-management relations. *Psychological Bulletin, 90,* 293–306.

Gordon, M. E., Philpot, J. W., Burt, R. E., Thompson, C. A., & Spiller, W. E. (1980). Commitment to the union: Development of a measure and an examination of its correlates. *Journal of Applied Psychology, 65,* 479–499.

Gordon, M. E., Schmitt, N., & Schneider, W. G. (1984). Laboratory research on bargaining and negotiations: An evaluation. *Industrial Relations, 23,* 218–233.

Gottfredson, L. S. (1994). The science and politics of race norming. *American Psychologist, 49,* 955–963.

Gough, H. G. (1984). A managerial potential scale for the California Psychological Inventory. *Journal of Applied Psychology, 69,* 233–240.

Graen, G. B., & Scandura, T. A. (1987). Toward a psychology of dyadic organizing. *Research in Organizational Behavior, 9,* 175–208.

Graen, G. B., & Wakabayashi, M. (1994). Cross-cultural leadership making: Bridging American and Japanese diversity for team advantage. In H. C. Triandis, M. D. Dunnette, & L. M. Hough (Eds.), *Handbook of industrial and organizational psychology* (Vol. 4, pp. 415–446). Palo Alto, CA: Consulting Psychologists Press.

Grandjean, E. (1968). Fatigue: Its physiological and psychological significance. *Ergonomics, 11,* 427–436.

Grandjean, E. (1986). *Fitting the task to the man: An ergonomic approach.* London: Taylor & Frances.

Grandjean, E. (1987). *Ergonomics in computerized offices.* London: Taylor & Frances.

Green, S. G., & Nebeker, D. M. (1977). The effects of situational factors and leadership style on leader behavior. *Organizational Behavior and Human Performance, 19,* 368–377.

Greenberg, J. (1986). Determinants of perceived fairness of performance evaluations. *Journal of Applied Psychology, 71,* 340–342.

Greenberg, J. (1988). Equity and workplace status: A field experiment. *Journal of Applied Psychology, 73,* 606–613.

Greenberg, J. (1990). Employee theft as a reaction to underpayment inequity: The hidden cost of pay cuts. *Journal of Applied Psychology, 75,* 561–568.

Greenberg, J. (1993). The social side of fairness: Interpersonal and informational classes of organizational justice. In R. Cropanzano (Ed.), *Justice in the workplace: Approaching fairness in human resource management* (pp. 79–103). Hillsdale, NJ: Erlbaum.

Greenberg, J. (1994). Using socially fair treatment to promote acceptance of a work site smoking ban. *Journal of Applied Psychology, 79*, 288–297.

Greene, C. N., & Schriesheim, C. A. (1980). Leader-group interactions: A longitudinal field investigation. *Journal of Applied Psychology, 65*, 50–59.

Grether, W. F. (1968). Engineering psychology in the United States. *American Psychologist, 23*, 743–751.

Griffin, R. W., Welsh, A., & Moorhead, G. (1981). Perceived task characteristics and employee performance: A literature review. *Academy of Management Review, 6*, 655–664.

Grigsby, D. M., & Bigoness, W. J. (1982). Effects of mediation and alternative forms of arbitration on bargaining behavior: A laboratory study. *Journal of Applied Psychology, 67*, 549–554.

Grover, S. L., & Crooker, K. J. (1995). Who appreciates family-responsive human resource policies: The impact of family-friendly policies on the organizational attachment of parents and non-parents. *Personnel Psychology, 48*, 271–288.

Guion, R. M. (1965). Industrial psychology as an academic discipline. *American Psychologist, 20*, 815–821.

Guion, R. M. (1991). Personnel assessment, selection, and placement. In M. D. Dunnette & L. M. Hough (Eds.), *Handbook of industrial and organizational psychology* (Vol. 2, pp. 327–398). Palo Alto, CA: Consulting Psychologists Press.

Guion, R. M., & Gottier, R. F. (1965). Validity of personality measures in personnel selection. *Personnel Psychology, 18*, 135–164.

Gunter, B., Furnham, A., & Drakeley, R. (1993). *Biodata: Biographical indicators of business performance.* London: Routledge.

Gutek, B. A. (1985). *Sex and the workplace.* San Francisco, CA: Jossey-Bass.

Gutek, B. A., Cohen, A. G., & Konrad, A. M. (1990). Predicting social-sexual behavior at work: A contact hypothesis. *Academy of Management Journal, 33*, 560–577.

Guzzo, R. A. (1995). Introduction: At the intersection of team effectiveness and decision making. In R. A. Guzzo & E. Salas (Eds.), *Team effectiveness and decision making in organizations* (pp. 1–8). San Francisco, CA: Jossey-Bass.

Guzzo, R. A., Jette, R. D., & Katzell, R. A. (1985). The effects of psychologically based intervention programs on worker productivity: A meta-analysis. *Personnel Psychology, 38*, 275–291.

Guzzo, R. A., & Shea, G. P. (1992). Group performance and intergroup relations in organizations. In M. D. Dunnette & L. M. Hough (Eds.), *Handbook of industrial and organizational psychology* (Vol. 3, pp. 269–313). Palo Alto, CA: Consulting Psychologists Press.

Hackman, J. R., & Lawler, E. E. (1971). Employee reactions to job characteristics. *Journal of Applied Psychology, 55*, 259–286.

Hackman, J. R., & Oldham, G. R. (1975). Development of the Job Diagnostic Survey. *Journal of Applied Psychology, 60*, 159–170.

Hackman, J. R., & Oldham, G. R. (1976). Motivation through the design of work: Test of a theory. *Organizational Behavior and Human Performance, 16*, 250–279.

Hahn, D. C., & Dipboye, R. L. (1988). Effects of training and information on the accuracy and reliability of job evaluations. *Journal of Applied Psychology, 73*, 146–153.

Haigh, R. (1993). The aging process: A challenge for design. *Applied Ergonomics, 24*, 9–14.

Hall, D. T., & Mirvis, P. H. (1995). Careers as lifelong learning. In A. Howard (Ed.), *The changing nature of work* (pp. 323–381). San Francisco, CA: Jossey-Bass.

Hall, G. S. (1917). Practical relations between psychology and the war. *Journal of Applied Psychology, 1*, 9–16.

Hall, G. S., Baird, J. W., & Geissler, L. R. (1917). Foreword. *Journal of Applied Psychology, 1*, 5–7.

Hammer, T. H., & Berman, M. (1981). The role of noneconomic factors in faculty union voting. *Journal of Applied Psychology, 66*, 415–421.

Hammer, W. C., & Smith, F. J. (1978). Work attitudes as predictors of unionization activity. *Journal of Applied Psychology, 63*, 415–421.

Hand, H. H., & Slocum, J. W., Jr. (1972). A longitudinal study of the effects of a human relation training program on management effectiveness. *Journal of Applied Psychology, 56*, 412–417.

Handbook of human engineering data. (1949). Medford, MA: Tufts College and United States Naval Training Devices Center.

Haney, W. (1981). Validity, vaudeville, and values: A short history of social concerns over standardized testing. *American Psychologist, 36*, 1021–1034.

Hansen, C. P. (1989). A causal model of the relationship among accidents, biodata, personality, and cognitive factors. *Journal of Applied Psychology, 74*, 81–90.

Harmon, L. W. (1991). Twenty years of the Journal of Vocational Behavior. *Journal of Vocational Behavior, 39*, 297–304.

Harrell, T. W. (1992). Some history of the Army General Classification Test. *Journal of Applied Psychology, 77*, 875–878.

Harris, M. M. (1989). Reconsidering the employment interview: A review of recent literature and suggestions for future research. *Personnel Psychology, 42*, 691–726.

Harris, M. M., Smith, D. E., & Champagne, D. (1995). A field study of performance appraisal purpose: Research- versus administrative-based ratings. *Personnel Psychology, 48*, 151–160.

Hart, F. A. (1987). Computer-based training. In R. L. Craig (Ed.), *Training and development handbook* (3rd ed.). New York: McGraw-Hill.

Hartley, J. F. (1992). The psychology of industrial relations. In C. L. Cooper & I. T. Robertson (Eds.), *Inter-*

national review of industrial and organizational psychology (pp. 201–243). London: Wiley.

Harvey, R. J. (1991). Job analysis. In M. D. Dunnette & L. M. Hough (Eds.), *Handbook of industrial and organizational psychology* (Vol. 2, pp. 71–163). Palo Alto, CA: Consulting Psychologists Press.

Harvey, R. J., Friedman, L., Hakel, M. D., & Cornelius, E. T. (1988). Dimensionality of the Job Element Inventory, a simplified worker-oriented job analysis questionnaire. *Journal of Applied Psychology, 73,* 639–646.

Harvey, R. J., & Lozada-Larsen, S. R. (1988). Influence of amount of job descriptive information on job analysis rating accuracy. *Journal of Applied Psychology, 73,* 457–461.

Havel, V. (1994, July 8). The new measure of man. *The New York Times,* p. A27.

Hawk, R. H. (1967). *The recruitment function.* New York: American Management Association.

Hedge, A., Erickson, W. A., & Rubin, G. (1992). Effects of personal and organizational factors on sick building syndrome in air-conditioned offices. In J. C. Quick, L. R. Murphy, & J. J. Hurrell (Eds.), *Stress and well-being at work* (pp. 286–298). Washington, DC: American Psychological Association.

Hedge, J. W., & Kavanagh, M. J. (1988). Improving the accuracy of performance evaluations: Comparison of three methods of performance appraisal training. *Journal of Applied Psychology, 73,* 68–73.

Heilman, M. E., Block, C. J., & Lucas, J. A. (1992). Presumed incompetent? Stigmatization and affirmative action efforts. *Journal of Applied Psychology, 77,* 536–544.

Heilman, M. E., & Herlihy, J. M. (1984). Affirmative action, negative reaction? Some moderating considerations. *Organizational Behavior and Human Performance, 33,* 204–213.

Heilman, M. E., Simon, M. C., & Repper, D. P. (1987). Intentionally favored, unintentionally harmed? Impact of sex-based preferential selection in self-perceptions and self-evaluations. *Journal of Applied Psychology, 72,* 62–68.

Heneman, R. L. (1986). The relationship between supervisory ratings and results-oriented measures of performance: A meta-analysis. *Personnel Psychology, 39,* 811–826.

Hesketh, B., & Bochner, S. (1994). Technological change in a multicultural context: Implications for training and career planning. In H. C. Triandis, M. D. Dunnette, & L. M. Hough (Eds.), *Handbook of industrial and organizational psychology* (Vol. 4, pp. 191–240). Palo Alto, CA: Consulting Psychologists Press.

Hess, H. F. (1977). Entry requirements for professional practice of psychology. *American Psychologist, 32,* 365–368.

Hicks, W. D., & Klimoski, R. J. (1981). The impact of flexitime on employee attitudes. *Academy of Management Journal, 24,* 333–341.

Hilakivi, I., Veilahti, J., Asplund, P., & Sinivuo, J. (1989). A sixteen-factor personality test for predicting automobile accidents of young drivers. *Accident Analysis and Prevention, 21,* 413–418.

Hoffman, P. J. (1980). On the establishment of an appropriate length for the EPPP. *Professional Psychology, 11,* 784–791.

Hofmann, D. A., Jacobs, R., & Baratta, J. E. (1993). Dynamic criteria and the measurement of change. *Journal of Applied Psychology, 78,* 194–204.

Hogan, E. A., & Overmyer-Day, L. (1994). The psychology of mergers and acquisitions. In C. L. Cooper & I. T. Robertson (Eds.), *International review of industrial and organizational psychology* (pp. 247–281). London: Wiley.

Hogan, J. (1991a). Physical abilities. In M. D. Dunnette & L. M. Hough (Eds.), *Handbook of industrial and organizational psychology* (Vol. 2, pp. 753–831). Palo Alto, CA: Consulting Psychologists Press.

Hogan, J. (1991b). Structure of physical performance in organizational tasks. *Journal of Applied Psychology, 76,* 495–507.

Hogan, J., & Hogan, R. (Eds.) (1990). *Business and industry testing: Current practices and reviews.* Austin, TX: Pro-Ed.

Hogan, J., Hogan, R., & Busch, C. M. (1984). How to measure service orientation. *Journal of Applied Psychology, 69,* 167–173.

Hogan, R. T. (1991). Personality and personality measurement. In M. D. Dunnette & L. M. Hough (Eds.), *Handbook of industrial and organizational psychology* (Vol. 2, pp. 873–919). Palo Alto, CA: Consulting Psychologists Press.

Hogan, R., Curphy, G. J., & Hogan, J. (1994). What we know about leadership: Effectiveness and personality. *American Psychologist, 49,* 493–504.

Hogan, R. T., & Hogan, J. (1992). *Hogan Personality Inventory.* Tulsa, OK: Hogan Assessment Systems.

Hogan, R., Raskin, R., & Fazzini, D. (1990). The dark side of charisma. In K. E. Clark & M. B. Clark (Eds.), *Measures of leadership* (pp. 343–354). West Orange, NJ: Leadership Library of America.

Hollander, E. P. (1965). Validity of peer nominations in predicting a distant performance criterion. *Journal of Applied Psychology, 49,* 434–438.

Hollenbeck, J. R., Ilgen, D. R., & Crampton, S. M. (1992). Lower back disability in organizational settings: A review of the literature from a human resource management view. *Personnel Psychology, 45,* 247–278.

Hollenbeck, J. R., Ilgen, D. R., Tuttle, D. B., & Sego, D. J. (1995). Team performance on monitoring tasks: An examination of decision errors in contexts requiring sustained attention. *Journal of Applied Psychology, 80,* 685–696.

Hollenbeck, J. R., & Klein, H. J. (1987). Goal commitment and the goal-setting process: Problems, prospects, and proposals for future research. *Journal of Applied Psychology, 72,* 212–220.

Hollenbeck, J. R., Williams, C. R., & Klein, H. J. (1989). An empirical examination of the antecedents of commitment to difficult goals. *Journal of Applied Psychology, 74,* 18–23.

Holley, W. H., & Feild, H. S. (1975). Performance appraisal and the law. *Labor Law Journal, 26,* 423–430.

Hollinger, R. C. (1988). Working under the influence (WUI): Correlates of employees' use of alcohol and other drugs. *Journal of Applied Behavioral Science, 24,* 439–454.

Hollinger, R., & Clark, J. (1983). *Theft by employees.* Lexington, MA: Lexington Books.

Holzbach, R. L. (1978). Rater bias in performance ratings: Superior, self-, and peer assessments. *Journal of Applied Psychology, 63,* 579–588.

Hom, P. W., & Griffeth, R. W. (1995). *Employee turnover.* Cincinnati, OH: South-Western.

Honts, C. R. (1991). The emperor's new clothes: Application of polygraph tests in the American workplace. *Forensic Reports, 4,* 91–116.

House, R. J. (1971). A path-goal theory of leader effectiveness. *Administrative Science Quarterly, 16,* 321–338.

House, R. J. (1977). A 1976 theory of charismatic leadership. In J. G. Hunt & L. L. Larson (Eds.), *Leadership: The cutting edge.* Carbondale, IL: Southern Illinois University Press.

House, R. J., Spangler, W. D., & Woycke, J. (1991). Personality and charisma in the U.S. presidency: A psychological theory of leader effectiveness. *Administrative Science Quarterly, 36,* 364–396.

Howard, A. (1990). *The multiple facets of industrial-organizational psychology.* Arlington Heights, IL: Society for Industrial and Organizational Psychology, Inc.

Howard, A. (1992). Work and family crossroads spanning the career. In S. Zedeck (Ed.), *Work, families, and organizations* (pp. 70–137). San Francisco: Jossey-Bass.

Howard, A. (1995). Rethinking the psychology of work. In A. Howard (Ed.), *The changing nature of work* (pp. 513–555). San Francisco, CA: Jossey-Bass.

Howard, A., & Lowman, R. L. (1985). Should industrial/organizational psychologists be licensed? *American Psychologist, 40,* 40–47.

Howell, J. P., & Dorfman, P. W. (1981). Substitutes for leadership: Test of a construct. *Academy of Management Journal, 24,* 714–728.

Howell, W. C. (1993). Engineering psychology in a changing world. *Annual Review of Psychology, 44,* 231–263.

Howell, W. C., & Cooke, N. J. (1989). Training the human information processor: A review of cognitive models. In I. L. Goldstein (Ed.), *Training and development in organizations* (pp. 121–182). San Francisco, CA: Jossey-Bass.

Huck, J. R. (1973). Assessment centers: A review of their external and internal validities. *Personnel Psychology, 26,* 191–212.

Huck, J. R., & Bray, D. W. (1976). Management assessment center evaluations and subsequent job performance of white and black females. *Personnel Psychology, 29,* 13–31.

Hulin, C. L., Henry, R. A., & Noon, S. L. (1990). Adding a dimension: Time as a factor in the generalizability of predictive relationships. *Psychological Bulletin, 107,* 328–340.

Hunt, D. M., & Michael, C. (1983). Mentorship: A career training and development tool. *Academy of Management Review, 8,* 475–485.

Hunter, J. E., & Hunter, R. F. (1984). Validity and utility of alternative predictors of job performance. *Psychological Bulletin, 96,* 72–98.

Hunter, J. E., & Schmidt, F. L. (1990). *Method of meta-analysis: Correcting error and bias in research findings.* Newbury Park, CA: Sage.

Huse, E. F., & Cummings, T. G. (1985). *Organizational development and change* (3rd ed.). St. Paul, MN: West.

Huseman, R. C., Hatfield, J. D., & Miles, E. W. (1987). A new perspective on equity theory: The equity sensitivity construct. *Academy of Management Review, 12,* 222–234.

Huszczo, G. E., Wiggins, J. G., & Currie, J. S. (1984). The relationship between psychology and organized labor. Past, present and future. *American Psychologist, 39,* 432–440.

Ilgen, D. R. (1990). Health issues at work: Opportunities for industrial/organizational psychology. *American Psychologist, 45,* 273–283.

Ilgen, D. R., Barnes-Farrell, J. L., & McKellin, D. B. (1993). Performance appraisal process research in the 1980s: What has it contributed to appraisals in use? *Organizational Behavior and Human Decision Processes, 54,* 321–368.

Ilgen, D. R., Fisher, C. D., & Taylor, M. S. (1979). Motivational consequences of individual feedback on behavior in organizations. *Journal of Applied Psychology, 64,* 349–371.

Ilgen, D. R., Peterson, R. B., Martin, B. A., & Boeschen, D. A. (1981). Supervisor and subordinate reactions to performance appraisal sessions. *Organizational Behavior and Human Performance, 28,* 311–330.

Imada, A. S. (1990). Ergonomics: Influencing management behavior. *Ergonomics, 33,* 621–628.

Jackson, S. E., & Schuler, R. S. (1990). Human resource planning. *American Psychologist, 45,* 223–239.

Jackson, P. R., & Warr, P. B. (1984). Unemployment and psychological ill-health: The moderating role of duration and age. *Psychological Medicine, 14,* 605–614.

Jahoda, M. (1981). Work, employment, and unemployment: Values, theories and approaches in social research. *American Psychologist, 36,* 184–191.

Jamal, M. (1981). Shift work related to job attitudes, social participation, and withdrawal behavior. A study of nurses and industrial workers. *Personnel Psychology, 34,* 535–548.

Jamal, M., & Jamal, S. M. (1982). Work and nonwork experiences of employees on fixed and rotating shifts: An empirical assessment. *Journal of Vocational Behavior, 20,* 282–293.

Janssens, M., Brett, J. M., & Smith, F. J. (1995). Confirmatory cross-cultural research: Testing the viability of a corporation-wide safety policy. *Academy of Management Journal, 38,* 364–382.

Jarrell, S. B., & Stanley, T. D. (1990). A meta-analysis of the union-nonunion wage gap. *Industrial and Labor Relations Review, 44,* 54–67.

Jemison, D. B., & Sitkin, S. B. (1986). Corporate acquisitions: A process perspective. *Academy of Management Review, 11,* 145–163.

Jenkins, J. G. (1946). Validity for what? *Journal of Consulting Psychology, 10,* 93–98.

Johns, G. (1993). Constraints on the adoption of psychology-based personnel practices: Lessons from organizational innovation. *Personnel Psychology, 46,* 569–592.

Johns, G. (1994). How often were you absent? A review of the use of self-reported absence data. *Journal of Applied Psychology, 79,* 574–591.

Johnson, P. R., & Indvik, J. (1994). Workplace violence: An issue of the nineties. *Public Personnel Management, 23,* 515–523.

Jones, A. P., & Butler, M. C. (1980). A role transition approach to stresses of organizationally induced family role disruption. *Journal of Marriage and the Family, 42,* 367–376.

Jones, N. (1994). The alcohol and drug provisions of the ADA: Implications for employers and employees. In S. M. Bruyere & J. O'Keeffe (Eds.), *Implications of the Americans with Disabilities Act for Psychology* (pp. 151–168). New York: Springer.

Joure, S. A., Leon, J. S., Simpson, D. B., Holley, G. H., & Frye, R. L. (1989, March). Stress: The pressure cooker of work. *The Personnel Administrator, 34,* 92–95.

Kagiticibasi, C., & Berry, J. W. (1989). Cross-cultural psychology: Current research and trends. *Annual Review of Psychology, 40,* 493–531.

Kahn, R. L., & Byosiere, P. B. (1992). Stress in organizations. In M. D. Dunnette & L. M. Hough (Eds.), *Handbook of industrial and organizational psychology* (Vol. 3, pp. 571–650). Palo Alto, CA: Consulting Psychologists Press.

Kane, J. S., & Lawler, E. E., III. (1978). Methods of peer assessment. *Psychological Bulletin, 85,* 555–586.

Kanfer, R. (1990). Motivation theory and industrial and organizational psychology. In M. D. Dunnette & L. M. Hough (Eds.), *Handbook of industrial and organizational psychology* (Vol. 1, pp. 75–170). Palo Alto, CA: Consulting Psychologists Press.

Kanfer, R. (1992). Work motivation: New directions in theory and research. In C. L. Cooper & I. T. Robertson (Eds.), *International review of industrial and organizational psychology* (pp. 1–53). London: Wiley.

Kanfer, R., & Ackerman, P. L. (1989). Motivation and cognitive abilities: An integrative/aptitude–treatment interaction approach to skill acquisition. *Journal of Applied Psychology, 74,* 657–690.

Kanter, R. M. (1977). *Work and family in the United States: A critical review and agenda for research and policy.* New York: Russell Sage Foundation.

Kaplan, A. (1964). *The conduct of inquiry.* New York: Harper & Row.

Karambayya, R., & Reilly, A. H. (1992). Dual earner couples: Attitudes and actions restructuring work for family. *Journal of Organizational Behavior, 13,* 585–601.

Kast, F. E., & Rosenzweig, J. E. (1972). General systems theory: Applications for organization and management. *Academy of Management Journal, 15,* 444–465.

Katz, D., & Kahn, R. L. (1978). *The social psychology of organizations* (2nd ed.). New York: Wiley.

Katzell, R. A. (1994). Contemporary meta-trends in industrial and organizational psychology. In H. C. Triandis, M. D. Dunnette, & L. M. Hough (Eds.), *Handbook of industrial and organizational psychology* (Vol. 4, pp. 1–89). Palo Alto, CA: Consulting Psychologists Press.

Katzell, R. A., & Austin, J. T. (1992). From then to now: The development of industrial-organizational psychology in the United States. *Journal of Applied Psychology, 77,* 803–835.

Katzell, R. A., & Guzzo, R. A. (1983). Psychological approaches to productivity improvement. *American Psychologist, 38,* 468–472.

Katzell, R. A., & Thompson, D. E. (1990). Work motivation: Theory and practice. *American Psychologist, 45,* 144–153

Kay, E., Meyer, H. H., & French, J. R. P., Jr. (1965). Effects of threat in a performance appraisal interview. *Journal of Applied Psychology, 49,* 311–317.

Keinan, G., & Eilat-Greenberg, S. (1993). Can stress be measured by handwriting analysis? The effectiveness of the analytic method. *Applied Psychology: An International Review, 42,* 153–170.

Keller, L. M., Bouchard, T. J., Jr., Arvey, R. D., Segal, N. L., & Dawis, R. V. (1992). Work values: Genetic and environmental influences. *Journal of Applied Psychology, 77,* 79–88.

Kelly, J. E., & Kelly, C. (1991). "Them and us": Social psychology and "The new industrial relations." *British Journal of Industrial Relations, 29,* 25–48.

Kelman, H. C. (1972). The rights of the subject in social research: An analysis in terms of relative power and legitimacy. *American Psychologist, 27,* 989–1016.

Kennedy, C. W., Fossum, J. A., & White, B. J. (1983). An empirical comparison of within-subjects and between-subjects expectancy theory models. *Organizational Behavior and Human Performance, 32,* 124–143.

Kernan, M. C., & Lord, R. G. (1990). Effects of valence, expectancies, and goal-performance discrepancies in single and multiple goal environments. *Journal of Applied Psychology, 75,* 194–203.

Kerr, S. (1995). On the folly of rewarding A, while hoping for B. *Academy of Management Executive, 9*(1), 7–14.

Kerr, S., & Jermier, J. M. (1978). Substitutes for leadership: Their meaning and measurement. *Organizational Behavior and Human Performance, 22,* 375–403.

Kidd, J. S. (1961). A comparison of two methods of training in a complex task by means of a task simulation. *Journal of Applied Psychology, 45,* 165–169.

Kirkpatrick, D. L. (1976). Evaluation of training. In R. L. Craig (Ed.), *Training and development handbook* (2nd ed.) (pp. 301–319). New York: McGraw-Hill.

Kirkpatrick, S. A., & Locke, E. A. (1991). Leadership: Do traits matter? *Academy of Management Executive, 5*(2), 48–60.

Klaas, B. S. (1989). Managerial decision making about employee grievances: The impact of the grievant's work history. *Personnel Psychology, 42,* 53–68.

Klandermans, B. (1989). Union commitment. Replications and tests in the Dutch context. *Journal of Applied Psychology, 74,* 869–875.

Kleiman, L. S., & Durham, R. L. (1981). Performance appraisal, promotion and the courts: A critical review. *Personnel Psychology, 34,* 103–121.

Kleiman, L. S., & Faley, R. H. (1988). Voluntary affirmative action and preferential treatment: Legal and research implications. *Personnel Psychology, 41,* 481–496.

Klein, H. J. (1991). Further evidence on the relationship between goal setting and expectancy theories. *Organizational Behavior and Human Decision Processes, 49,* 230–257.

Kleinmann, M. (1993). Are rating dimensions in assessment centers transparent for participants? Consequences for criterion and construct validity. *Journal of Applied Psychology, 78,* 988–993.

Klimoski, R. J., & Brickner, M. (1987). Why do assessment centers work? The puzzle of assessment center validity. *Personnel Psychology, 40,* 243–260.

Klimoski, R. J., & Inks, L. (1990). Accountability forces in performance appraisal. *Organizational Behavior and Human Decision Processes, 45,* 194–208.

Klimoski, R. J., & Jones, R. G. (1995). Staffing for effective group decision making: Key issues in marketing people and teams. In R. A. Guzzo & E. Salas (Eds.), *Team effectiveness and decision making in organizations* (pp. 291–332). San Francisco, CA: Jossey-Bass.

Klimoski, R. J., & Palmer, S. N. (1994). The ADA and the hiring process in organizations. In S. M. Bruyere & J. O'Keeffe (Eds.), *Implications of the Americans with Disabilities Act for Psychology* (pp. 37–84). New York: Springer.

Klimoski, R. J., & Strickland, W. J. (1977). Assessment centers—Valid or merely prescient? *Personnel Psychology, 30,* 353–361.

Kluger, A. N., Reilly, R. R., & Russell, C. J. (1991). Faking biodata tests: Are option-keyed instruments more resistant? *Journal of Applied Psychology, 76,* 889–896.

Komaki, J. L. (1986). Toward effective supervision: An operant analysis and comparison of managers at work. *Journal of Applied Psychology, 71,* 270–279.

Komaki, J. L., Barwick, K. D., & Scott, L. R. (1978). A behavioral approach to occupational safety: Pinpointing and reinforcing safe performance in a food manufacturing plant. *Journal of Applied Psychology, 63,* 434–445.

Konz, S. A., & Dickey, G. L. (1969). Manufacturing assembly instructions: A summary. *Ergonomics, 12,* 369–382.

Kotter, J. P. (1988). *The leadership factor.* New York: Free Press.

Kotter, J. P., & Heskett, J. L. (1992). *Corporate culture and performance.* New York: Free Press.

Kouzes, J. M., & Posner, B. Z. (1995). *The leadership challenge.* San Francisco: Jossey-Bass.

Kozlowski, S. W., Chao, G. T., Smith, E. M., & Hedlund, J. (1993). Organizational downsizing: Strategies, interventions, and research implications. In C. L. Cooper & I. T. Robertson (Eds.), *International review of industrial and organizational psychology* (pp. 263–331). London: Wiley.

Kram, K. E., & Isabella, L. A. (1985). Alternatives to mentoring: The role of peer relationships in career development. *Academy of Management Journal, 28,* 110–132.

Krantz, J. (1985). Group processes under conditions of organizational decline. *Journal of Applied Behavioral Science, 21,* 1–17.

Kroemer, K. H., Kroemer, H. J., & Kroemer-Elbert, K. E. (1986). *Engineering physiology: Physiologic bases of human factors/ergonomics.* New York: Elsevier.

Kuhl, J., & Beckmann, J. (Eds.) (1994). *Volition and personality: Action- and state-oriented modes of control.* Gottingen, Germany: Hogrefe.

Kulik, C. T., Oldham, G. R., & Langner, P. H. (1988). Measurement of job characteristics: Comparison of the original and the revised Job Diagnostic Survey. *Journal of Applied Psychology, 73,* 462–466.

Kumar, S. (1994). A conceptual model of overexertion, safety, and risk of injury in organizational settings. *Human Factors, 36,* 197–209.

Ladd, R. T., Gordon, M. E., Beauvais, L. L., & Morgan, R. L. (1982). Union commitment: Replication and extension. *Journal of Applied Psychology, 67,* 640–644.

Lance, C. E., LaPointe, J. A., & Fisicaro, S. A. (1994). Tests of three causal models of halo rater error. *Organizational Behavior and Human Decision Processes, 57,* 83–96.

Landy, F. J. (1992). Hugo Münsterberg: Victim or visionary? *Journal of Applied Psychology, 77,* 787–802.

Landy, F. J., & Shankster, L. J. (1994). Personnel selection and employment. *Annual Review of Psychology, 45,* 261–296.

Landy, F. J., Shankster-Cawley, L., & Moran, S. K. (1995). Advancing personnel selection and placement methods. In A. Howard (Ed.), *The changing nature of work* (pp. 252–289). San Francisco, CA: Jossey-Bass.

Landy, F. J., & Trumbo, D. A. (1980). *Psychology of work behavior* (rev. ed.). Pacific Grove, CA: Brooks/Cole.

Landy, F. J., & Vasey, J. (1991). Job analysis: The composition of SME samples. *Personnel Psychology, 44,* 27–50.

Larson, C. E., & La Fasto, F. M. (1989). *Teamwork.* Newbury Park, CA: Sage.

Larson, J. R., Jr., & Callahan, C. (1990). Performance monitoring: How it affects work productivity. *Journal of Applied Psychology, 75,* 530–538.

Latham, G. P. (1986). Job performance and appraisal. In C. L. Cooper & I. T. Robertson (Eds.), *International review of industrial and organizational psychology.* London: Wiley.

Latham, G. P., & Baldes, J. J. (1975). The practical significance of Locke's theory of goal setting. *Journal of Applied Psychology, 60,* 122–124.

Latham, G. P., Fay, C. H., & Saari, L. M. (1979). The development of behavioral observation scales for appraising the performance of foremen. *Personnel Psychology, 32,* 299–311.

Latham, G. P., & Finnegan, B. J. (1993). Perceived practicality of instructional, patterned, and situational interviews. In H. Schuler, J. L. Farr, & M. Smith (Eds.), *Personnel selection and assessment* (pp. 41–56). Hillsdale, NJ: Erlbaum.

Latham, G. P., & Kinne, S. B. (1974). Improving job performance through training in goal setting. *Journal of Applied Psychology, 59,* 187–191.

Latham, G. P., & Locke, E. A. (1991). Self-regulation through goal-setting. *Organizational Behavior and Human Decision Processes, 50,* 212–247.

Latham, G. P., & Marshall, H. A. (1982). The effects of self-set, participatively set, and assigned goals on the performance of government employees. *Personnel Psychology, 35,* 399–404.

Latham, G. P., & Saari, L. M. (1979). The application of social learning theory to training supervisors through behavioral modeling. *Journal of Applied Psychology, 64,* 239–246.

Latham, G. P., Skarlicki, D., Irvine, D., & Siegel, J. P. (1993). The increasing importance of performance appraisals to employee effectiveness in organizational settings in North America. In C. L. Cooper & I. T. Robertson (Eds.), *International review of industrial and organizational psychology* (Vol. 8, pp. 87–132). London: Wiley.

Latham, G. P., & Wexley, K. N. (1977). Behavioral observation scales for performance appraisal purposes. *Personnel Psychology, 30,* 255–268.

Latham, G. P., & Wexley, K. N. (1981). *Increasing productivity through performance appraisal.* Reading, MA: Addison-Wesley.

Latham, G. P., Wexley, K. N., & Pursell, E. D. (1975). Training managers to minimize rating errors in the observation of behavior. *Journal of Applied Psychology, 60,* 550–555.

Latham, G. P., & Whyte, G. (1994). The futility of utility analysis. *Personnel Psychology, 47,* 31–46.

Lawler, E. E., III. (1967). The multitrait-multirater approach to measuring managerial job performance. *Journal of Applied Psychology, 51,* 369–381.

Lawler, E. E. (1982). Strategies for improving the quality of work life. *American Psychologist, 37,* 486–493.

Lawler, E. E., Mohrman, S. A., & Ledford, G. E. (1995). *Creating high performance organizations.* San Francisco, CA: Jossey-Bass.

Lawler, E. E., & Suttle, J. L. (1972). A causal correlational test of the need hierarchy concept. *Organizational Behavior and Human Behavior, 7,* 265–287.

Lazarus, R. S., & Folkman, S. (1984). *Stress, appraisal, and coping.* New York: Springer.

Leana, C. R., & Feldman, D. C. (1991). Gender differences in responses to unemployment. *Journal of Vocational Behavior, 38,* 65–77.

Lefkowitz, J. (1970). Effect of training on the productivity and tenure of sewing machine operators. *Journal of Applied Psychology, 54,* 81–86.

Lent, R. H., Aurbach, H. A., & Levin, L. S. (1971). Predictors, criteria, and significant results. *Personnel Psychology, 24,* 519–533.

Levine, E. L., Ash, R. A., Hall, H., & Sistrunk, F. (1983). Evaluation of job analysis methods by experienced job analysts. *Academy of Management Journal, 26,* 339–347.

Levinson, H. (1994). Why the behemoths fell: Psychological roots of corporate failure. *American Psychologist, 49,* 428–436.

Lewandowsky, S. (1993). The rewards and hazards of computer simulations. *Psychological Science, 4,* 236–243.

Lim, C. S., Ong, C. N., & Phoon, W. O. (1987). Work stress of firemen as measured by heart rate and catecholamine. *Journal of Human Ergology, 16,* 209–218.

Lippitt, G. L. (1982). *Organizational renewal: A holistic approach to organizational development* (2nd ed.). Englewood Cliffs, NJ: Prentice-Hall.

Lobel, S. A. (1993). Sexuality at work: Where do we go from here? *Journal of Vocational Behavior, 42,* 136–152.

Locke, E. A. (Ed.). (1985). *The generalizability of laboratory experiments: An inductive study.* Lexington, MA: D.C. Heath.

Locke, E. A. (1991). The motivation sequence, the motivation hub, and the motivation core. *Organizational Behavior and Human Decision Processes, 50,* 288–299.

Locke, E. A., Feren, D. B., McCaleb, V. M., Shaw, K. N., & Denny, A. T. (1980). The relative effectiveness of four methods of motivating employee performance. In

K. Duncan, M. Gruneberg, & D. Wallis (Eds.), *Changes in working life*. New York: Wiley.

Locke, E. A., & Latham, G. P. (1990). *A theory of goal setting and task performance*. Englewood Cliffs, NJ: Prentice-Hall.

Locke, E. A., Shaw, K. N., Saari, L. M., & Latham, G. P. (1981). Goal setting and task performance: 1969–1980. *Psychological Bulletin, 90*, 125–152.

Loher, B. T., Noe, R. A., Moeller, N. L., & Fitzgerald, M. P. (1985). A meta-analysis of the relation of job characteristics to job satisfaction. *Journal of Applied Psychology, 70*, 280–289.

Lombardo, M. M., & McCauley, C. D. (1988). *The dynamics of management derailment*. (Tech. Report No. 134). Greensboro, NC: Center for Creative Leadership.

London, M., & Bray, D. W. (1980). Ethical issues in testing and evaluation for personnel decisions. *American Psychologist, 35*, 890–901.

Lopez, F. M., Kesselman, G. A., & Lopez, F. E. (1981). An empirical test of a trait-oriented job analysis technique. *Personnel Psychology, 34*, 479–502.

Lord, R. G. (1985). An information processing approach to social perceptions, leadership, and behavioral measurement in organizations. *Research in Organizational Behavior, 7*, 87–128.

Lord, R. G., Foti, R. J., & Phillips, J. S. (1982). A theory of leadership organization. In J. G. Hunt, U. Sekaran, & C. Schriesheim (Eds.), *Leadership: Beyond establishment views*. Carbondale: Southern Illinois University.

Lord, R. G., & Hohenfeld, J. A. (1979). Longitudinal field assessment of equity effects in the performance of major league baseball players. *Journal of Applied Psychology, 64*, 19–26.

Lord, R. G., & Kernan, M. C. (1989). Application of control theory to work settings. In W. A. Herschberger (Ed.), *Volitional action* (pp. 493–514). Amsterdam: Elsevier.

Lowman, R. L. (Ed.). (1985). *Casebook on ethics and standards for the practice of psychology in organizations*. College Park, MD: Society for Industrial and Organizational Psychology, Inc., Division 14 of the American Psychological Association.

Lund, J. (1992). Electronic performance monitoring: A review of research issues. *Applied Ergonomics, 23*, 54–58.

Mabe, P. A., & West, S. G. (1982). Validity of self-evaluation of ability: A review and meta-analysis. *Journal of Applied Psychology, 67*, 280–296.

MacKenzie, S. B., Podsakoff, P. M., & Fetter, R. (1991). Organizational citizenship behavior and objective productivity as determinants of managerial evaluations of salespersons' performance. *Organizational Behavior and Human Decision Processes, 50*, 123–150.

Macy, B. A., & Izumi, H. (1993). Organizational change, design and work innovation: A meta-analysis of 131 North American field studies—1961–1991. In W. A. Pasmore & R. W. Woodman (Eds.), *Research in organizational change and development* (Vol. 7, pp. 235–313). Greenwich, CT: JAI.

Mael, F. A. (1991). A conceptual rationale for the domain and attributes of biodata items. *Personnel Psychology, 44*, 763–792.

Mahoney, T. A. (1983). Approaches to the definition of comparable worth. *Academy of Management Review, 8*, 14–22.

Malhotra, M. S., & Sengupta, J. (1965). Carrying of school bags by children. *Ergonomics, 8*, 55–60.

Mantell, M. (1994). *Ticking bombs: Defusing violence in the workplace*. Burr Ridge, IL: Irwin.

Manz, C. C. (1986). Self-leadership: Toward an expanded theory of self-influence. *Academy of Management Review, 11*, 585–600.

Manz, C. C., & Sims, H. P. (1991). Superleadership: Beyond the myth of heroic leadership. *Organizational Dynamics, 19*(4), 18–35.

Margenau, J. M., Martin, J. E., & Peterson, M. M. (1988). Dual and unilateral commitment among stewards and rank-and-file union members. *Academy of Management Journal, 31*, 359–376.

Markowitz, J. S. (1989). Long-term psychological distress among chemically exposed firefighters. *Behavioral Medicine, 15*, 75–83.

Martin, J. E., & Berthiaume, R. D. (1995). Predicting the outcome of a contract ratification vote. *Academy of Management Journal, 38*, 916–928.

Martin, S. L., & Terris, W. (1991). Predicting infrequent behavior: Clarifying the impact on false-positive rates. *Journal of Applied Psychology, 76*, 484–487.

Martocchio, J. J., & Harrison, D. A. (1993). To be there or not to be there: Questions, theories, and methods in absenteeism research. *Research in Personnel and Human Resources Management, 11*, 259–329.

Marx, R. D. (1982). Relapse prevention for managerial training: A model for maintenance of behavior change. *Academy of Management Review, 7*, 433–441.

Marx, R. D., & Karren, R. K. (1988). *The effects of relapse prevention training and interactive followup on positive transfer of training*. Paper presented at the National Academy of Management Meeting, Anaheim.

Maslow, A. H. (1970). *Motivation and personality* (2nd ed.). New York: Harper & Row.

Maslow, A. H. (1987). *Motivation and personality* (3rd ed.). New York: Harper & Row.

Matarazzo, J. D. (1987). There is only one psychology, no specialties, but many applications. *American Psychologist, 42*, 893–903.

Mateer, F. (1917). The moron as a war problem. *Journal of Applied Psychology, 1*, 317–320.

Mathieu, J. E., Tannenbaum, S. I., & Salas, E. (1990). *A causal model of individual and situational influences on training effectiveness measures*. Paper presented at the 5th annual conference of the Society for Industrial and Organizational Psychology, Miami.

Maurer, S. D., & Fay, C. (1988). Effect of situational interviews, conventional structured interviews, and training on interview rating agreement: An empirical analysis. *Personnel Psychology, 41,* 329–344.

Mawhinney, T. C. (1975). Operant terms and concepts in the description of individual work behavior: Some problems of interpretation, application, and evaluation. *Journal of Applied Psychology, 60,* 704–712.

Mayfield, E. C. (1972). Value of peer nominations in predicting life insurance sales performance. *Journal of Applied Psychology, 56,* 319–323.

Mayfield, E. C. (1975). *Preparation for work in business and industry: results of a survey of recent graduates.* Unpublished manuscript.

McAfee, R. B., & Winn, A. R. (1989). The use of incentives/feedback to enhance workplace safety: A critique of the literature. *Journal of Safety Research, 20,* 7–19.

McCall, M. W., & Bobko, P. (1990). Research methods in the service of discovery. In M. D. Dunnette & L. M. Hough (Eds.), *Handbook of industrial and organizational psychology* (Vol. 1, pp. 381–418). Palo Alto, CA: Consulting Psychologists Press.

McClelland, D. C., & Boyatzis, R. E. (1982). Leadership motive pattern and long term success in management. *Journal of Applied Psychology, 67,* 737–743.

McCormick, E. J. (1976). Job and task analysis. In M. D. Dunnette (Ed.), *Handbook of industrial and organizational psychology* (pp. 657–696). Skokie, IL: Rand McNally.

McCormick, E. J., Jeanneret, P. R., & Mecham, R. C. (1972). A study of job characteristics and job dimensions as based on the Position Analysis Questionnaire (PAQ). *Journal of Applied Psychology, 56,* 347–368.

McCrae, R. R. (1989). Why I advocate the five-factor model: Joint factor analyses of the NEO-PI with other instruments. In D. M. Buss & N. Cantor (Eds.), *Personality psychology: Recent trends and emerging directions.* New York: Springer-Verlag.

McCrae, R. R., & Costa, P. T. (1987). Validation of the five-factor model of personality across instruments and observers. *Journal of Personality & Social Psychology, 56,* 586–595.

McDaniel, M. A., Whetzel, D. L., Schmidt, F. L., & Maurer, S. D. (1994). The validity of employment interviews: A comprehensive review and meta-analysis. *Journal of Applied Psychology, 79,* 599–616.

McIntyre, R. M., & Salas, E. (1995). Measuring and managing for team performance: Lessons from complex environments. In R. A. Guzzo & E. Salas (Eds.), *Team effectiveness and decision making in organizations* (pp. 9–45). San Francisco, CA: Jossey-Bass.

McNeely, B. L., & Meglino, B. M. (1994). The role of dispositional and situational antecedents in prosocial organizational behavior: An examination of the intended beneficiaries of prosocial behavior. *Journal of Applied Psychology, 79,* 836–844.

Meers, A., Maasen, A., & Verhaagen, P. (1978). Subjective health after six months and after four years of shift work. *Ergonomics, 21,* 857–859.

Meindl, J. R., & Ehrlich, S. B. (1987). The romance of leadership and the evaluation of organizational performance. *Academy of Management Journal, 30,* 91–109.

Melamed, S., Ben-Avi, I., Luz, J., & Green, M. (1995). Objective and subjective work monitoring: Effects on job satisfaction, psychological distress, and absenteeism in blue-collar workers. *Journal of Applied Psychology, 80,* 29–42.

Mellor, S. (1990). The relationship between membership decline and union commitment: A field study of local unions in crisis. *Journal of Applied Psychology, 75,* 258–267.

Mellor, S. (1995). Gender composition and gender representation in local unions: Relationships between union's participation in local office and women's participation in local activities. *Journal of Applied Psychology, 80,* 706–720.

Mento, A. J., Steel, R. P., & Karren, R. J. (1987). A meta-analytic study of the effects of goal setting on task performance: 1966–1984. *Organizational Behavior and Human Decision Processes, 39,* 52–83.

Mero, N. P., & Motowidlo, S. J. (1995). Effects of rater accountability on the accuracy and the favorability of performance ratings. *Journal of Applied Psychology, 80,* 517–524.

Messick, S. (1995). Validity of psychological assessment: Validation of inferences from persons' responses and performances as scientific inquiry into score meaning. *American Psychologist, 50,* 741–749.

Meyer, H. H. (1972). The future for industrial and organizational psychology: Oblivion or millennium? *American Psychologist, 27,* 608–614.

Meyer, H. H. (1980). Self-appraisal of job performance. *Personnel Psychology, 33,* 291–296.

Meyer, H. H., Kay, E., & French, J. R. P., Jr. (1965). Split roles in performance appraisal. *Harvard Business Review, 43,* 123–129.

Michalak, D. F. (1981). The neglected half of training. *Training and Development Journal, 35,* 22–28.

Mintzberg, H. (1993). *Structure in fives: Designing effective organizations.* Englewood Cliffs, NJ: Prentice-Hall.

Mirvis, P. H. (1985). Negotiations after the sale: The roots and ramifications of conflict in an acquisition. *Journal of Organizational Behavior, 6,* 65–84.

Mirvis, P. H. (1988). Organization development: Part I— An evolutionary perspective. In W. A. Pasmore & R. W. Woodman (Eds.), *Research in organizational change and development* (Vol. 2, pp. 1–57). Greenwich, CT: JAI.

Mirvis, P. H. (1990). Organizational development: Part II—A revolutionary perspective. In W. A. Pasmore & R. W. Woodman (Eds.), *Research in organizational change and development* (Vol. 4, pp. 1–66). Greenwich, CT: JAI.

Mirvis, P. H., & Seashore, S. E. (1979). Being ethical in organizational research. *American Psychologist, 34,* 766–780.

Mischel, W. (1968). *Personality and assessment*. New York: Wiley.

Mitchell, T. R. (1985). An evaluation of the validity of correlation research conducted in organizations. *Academy of Management Review, 10*, 192–205.

Monahan, C. J., & Muchinsky, P. M. (1983). Three decades of personnel selection research: A state-of-the-art analysis and evaluation. *Journal of Occupational Psychology, 56*, 215–225.

Mook, D. G. (1983). In defense of external invalidity. *American Psychologist, 38*, 379–387.

Moorman, R. H. (1991). Relationship between organizational justice and organizational citizenship behaviors: Do fairness perceptions influence employee citizenship? *Journal of Applied Psychology, 76*, 845–855.

Moreland, J. L., Eyde, L. D., Robertson, G. J., Primoff, E. S., & Most, R. B. (1995). Assessment of test user qualifications. *American Psychologist, 50*, 14–23.

Morgan, B. B., Jr., & Bowers, C. A. (1995). Teamwork stress: Implications for team decision making. In R. A. Guzzo & E. Salas (Eds.), *Team effectiveness and decision making in organizations* (pp. 262–290). San Francisco, CA: Jossey-Bass.

Morrison, R. F., & Brantner, T. M. (1992). What enhances or inhibits learning a new job? A basic career issue. *Journal of Applied Psychology, 77*, 926–940.

Morsh, J. E., & Archer, W. B. (1967). *Procedural guide for conducting occupational surveys in the United States Air Force*. Lackland Air Force Base, TX: Personnel Research Laboratory, Aerospace Medical Division, PRL-TR-67–11.

Moses, J. L., & Boehm, V. R. (1975). Relationship of assessment center performance to management progress of women. *Journal of Applied Psychology, 60*, 527–529.

Moses, J., Hollenbeck, G. P., & Sorcher, M. (1993). Other people's expectations. *Human Resource Management, 32*, 283–298.

Motowidlo, S. J., & Van Scotter, J. R. (1994). Evidence that task performance should be distinguished from contextual performance. *Journal of Applied Psychology, 79*, 475–480.

Mount, M. K. (1984). Psychometric properties of subordinate ratings of managerial performance. *Personnel Psychology, 37*, 687–702.

Mowday, R. T., & Sutton, R. I. (1993). Organizational behavior: Linking individuals and groups to organizational contexts. *Annual Review of Psychology, 44*, 195–229.

Muchinsky, P. M. (1973). Graduate training in industrial psychology: One more time. *Professional Psychology, 4*, 286–295.

Muchinsky, P. M. (1975a). A comparison of three analytic techniques in predicting consumer installment credit risk: Toward understanding a construct. *Personnel Psychology, 28*, 511–524.

Muchinsky, P. M. (1975b). Consumer installment credit risk: A need for criterion refinement and validation. *Journal of Applied Psychology, 60*, 87–93.

Muchinsky, P. M. (1976). Graduate internships in industrial psychology: A success story. *Professional Psychology, 7*, 664–670.

Muchinsky, P. M. (1977a). A comparison of within- and across-subjects analyses of the expectancy-valence model for predicting effort. *Academy of Management Journal, 20*, 154–158.

Muchinsky, P. M. (1977b). Employee absenteeism: A review of the literature. *Journal of Vocational Behavior, 10*, 316–340.

Muchinsky, P. M. (1979). The use of reference reports in personnel selection: A review and evaluation. *Journal of Occupational Psychology, 52*, 287–297.

Muchinsky, P. M. (1993). Validation of intelligence and mechanical aptitude tests in selecting employees for manufacturing jobs. *Journal of Business and Psychology, 7*, 373–382.

Muchinsky, P. M. (1994). What is the shape of the distribution of job performance (and what difference does it make)? *International Journal of Selection and Assessment, 2*, 255–258.

Muchinsky, P. M., & Maassarani, M. A. (1980). Work environment effects on public sector grievances. *Personnel Psychology, 33*, 403–414.

Muchinsky, P. M., & Maassarani, M. A. (1981). Public sector grievances in Iowa. *Journal of Collective Negotiations, 10*, 55–62.

Mumford, M. D., & Stokes, G. S. (1992). Developmental determinants of individual action: Theory and practice in applying background measures. In M. D. Dunnette & L. M. Hough (Eds.), *Handbook of industrial and organizational psychology* (Vol. 3, pp. 61–138). Palo Alto, CA: Consulting Psychologists Press.

Münsterberg, H. (1913). *Psychology and industrial efficiency*. Boston: Houghton Mifflin.

Murphy, K. R., & Anhalt, R. L. (1992). Is halo error a property of the rater, ratees, or the specific behaviors observed? *Journal of Applied Psychology, 77*, 494–500.

Murphy, K. R., & Cleveland, J. N. (1995). *Understanding performance appraisal: Social, organizational, and goal-based perspectives*. Thousand Oaks, CA: Sage.

Murphy, K. R., Jako, R. A., & Anhalt, R. L. (1993). Nature and consequences of halo error: A critical analysis. *Journal of Applied Psychology, 78*, 218–225.

Murphy, K. R., Osten, K., & Myors, B. (1995). Modeling the effects of banding in personnel selection. *Personnel Psychology, 48*, 61–84.

Murphy, K. R., & Reynolds, D. H. (1988). Does true halo affect observed halo? *Journal of Applied Psychology, 73*, 235–238.

Murphy, K. R., Thornton, G. C., III, & Prue, K. (1991). Influence of job characteristics on the acceptability of employee drug testing. *Journal of Applied Psychology, 76,* 447–453.

Murphy, L. L., Conoley, J. C., & Impara, J. C. (1994). *Tests in print IV.* Lincoln, NE: Buros Institute of Mental Measurements.

Murphy, L. R., Hurrell, J. J., & Quick, J. C. (1992). Work and well-being: Where do we go from here? In J. C. Quick, L. R. Murphy, & J. J. Hurrell (Eds.), *Stress and well-being at work* (pp. 331–347). Washington, DC: American Psychological Association.

Murray, H. A., & MacKinnon, D. W. (1946). Assessment of OSS personnel. *Journal of Consulting Psychology, 10,* 76–80.

Musser, S. J. (1987). *The determination of positive and negative charismatic leadership.* Unpublished manuscript, Messiah College, Grantham, PA.

Nagle, B. F. (1953). Criterion development. *Personnel Psychology, 6,* 271–289.

Napoli, D. S. (1981). *The architects of adjustment: The history of the psychological profession in the United States.* Port Washington, NY: Kennikat.

Narayanan, V. K., & Nath, R. (1982). Hierarchical level and the impact of flextime. *Industrial Relations, 21,* 216–230.

National Institute for Occupational Safety and Health. (1988). *Proposed national strategies for the prevention of leading work-related diseases and injuries—Psychological disorders.* Washington, DC: U.S. Department of Health and Human Services.

Naylor, J. C. (1970). Training patterns in industrial psychology. *Personnel Psychology, 23,* 192–198.

Neale, M. A. (1984). The effects of negotiation and arbitration cost salience on bargainer behavior. The role of the arbitrator and constituency in negotiator judgment. *Organizational Behavior and Human Performance, 34,* 97–111.

Nickels, B. J. (1994). The nature of biodata. In G. S. Stokes, M. D. Mumford, & W. A. Owens (Eds.), *Biodata handbook: Theory, research, and use of biographical information in selection and performance prediction* (pp. 1–16). Palo Alto, CA: Consulting Psychologists Press.

Nilsen, D., & Campbell, D. P. (1993). Self-observer rating discrepancies: Once an overrater, always an overrater? *Human Resource Management, 32,* 265–282.

Noe, R. A. (1988). An investigation of the determinants of successful assigned mentoring relationships. *Personnel Psychology, 41,* 457–480.

Noe, R., & Ford, J. K. (1992). Emerging issues and new directions for training research. In K. Rowland & G. Ferris (Eds.), *Research in personnel and human resource management* (pp. 345–384). Greenwich, CT: JAI.

Normand, J., Lempert, R. O., & O'Brien, C. P. (1994). *Under the influence?: Drugs and the American workforce.* Washington, DC: National Academy Press.

Normand, J., Salyards, S. D., & Mahoney, J. J. (1990). An evaluation of preemployment drug testing. *Journal of Applied Psychology, 75,* 629–639.

Northwestern National Life Insurance Company. (1991). *Employee burnout: American's newest epidemic.* Minneapolis: Author.

Noweir, M. H. (1984). Noise exposure as related to productivity, disciplinary actions, absenteeism, and accidents among textile workers. *Journal of Safety Research, 15,* 163–174.

O'Keeffe, J. (1994). Disability, discrimination, and the Americans with Disabilities Act. In S. M. Bruyere & J. O'Keeffe (Eds.), *Implications of the Americans with Disabilities Act for psychology* (pp. 1–14). New York: Springer.

Oakley, A. (1974). *The sociology of housework.* New York: Pantheon.

Offerman, L. R., & Gowing, M. K. (1990). Organizations of the future. *American Psychologist, 45,* 95–108.

Olian, J. D. (1984). Genetic screening for employment purposes. *Personnel Psychology, 37,* 423–438.

Ones, D. S., Viswesvaran, C., & Schmidt, F. L. (1993). Comprehensive meta-analysis of integrity test validities: Findings and implications for personnel selection and theories of job performance. *Journal of Applied Psychology, 78,* 679–703.

Organ, D. W. (1988). *Organizational citizenship behavior: The good soldier syndrome.* Lexington, MA: Lexington.

Organ, D. W. (1994). Organizational citizenship behavior and the good soldier. In M. G. Rumsey, C. B. Walker, & J. H. Harris (Eds.), *Personnel selection and classification* (pp. 53–68). Hillsdale, NJ: Erlbaum.

Organ, D. W., & Ryan, K. (1995). A meta-analytic review of attitudinal and dispositional predictors of organizational citizenship behavior. *Personnel Psychology, 48,* 775–802.

Ostroff, C., & Ford, J. K. (1989). Assessing training needs: Critical levels of analysis. In I. L. Goldstein (Ed.), *Training and development in organizations* (pp. 25–62). San Francisco, CA: Jossey-Bass.

Parks, J. M., & Kidder, D. L. (1994). "Till death do us part . . .": Changing work relationships in the 1990s. In C. L. Cooper & D. M. Rousseau (Eds.), *Trends in organizational behavior* (pp. 111–136). New York: Wiley.

Parsons, H. M., & Kearsley, G. P. (1982). Robotics and human factors: Current status and future prospects. *Human Factors, 24,* 535–552.

Pedalino, E., & Gamboa, V. U. (1974). Behavior modification and absenteeism. *Journal of Applied Psychology, 59,* 694–698.

Pelletier, K. (1977). *Mind as healer, mind as slayer: A holistic approach to preventing stress disorders.* New York: Delcorte.

Pernanen, K. (1991). *Alcohol in human violence.* London: Guilford Press.

Peters, R. H. (1991). Strategies for encouraging self-protective employee behavior. *Journal of Safety Research, 22,* 53–70.

Petersen, A. P., & Gross, F. E. (1978). *Handbook of noise measurement* (8th ed.). New Concord, MA: GenRad.

Pfeffer, J. (1991). Organization theory and structural perspectives on management. *Journal of Management, 17,* 789–803.

Phillips, J. S., & Lord, R. G. (1981). Causal attribution and prescriptions of leadership. *Organizational Behavior and Human Performance, 28,* 143–163.

Pickard, C. O. (1945). Absentee control plans. *Personnel Journal, 23,* 271–276.

Pierce, J. L., & Dunham, R. B. (1992). The 12-hour work day: A 48 hour, four day week. *Academy of Management Journal, 35,* 1086–1098.

Pierce, J. L., Dunham, R. B., & Cummings, L. L. (1984). Sources of environmental structuring and participant responses. *Organizational Behavior and Human Performance, 33,* 214–242.

Podlesny, J. A., & Truslow, C. M. (1993). Validity of an expanded-issue (Modified General Question) polygraph technique in a simulated distributed-crime-roles context. *Journal of Applied Psychology, 78,* 788–797.

Porras, J. I., & Robertson, P. J. (1992). Organizational development: Theory, practice, and research. In M. D. Dunnette & L. M. Hough (Eds.), *Handbook of industrial and organizational psychology* (Vol. 3, pp. 719–822). Palo Alto, CA: Consulting Psychologists Press.

Premack, S. L., & Hunter, J. E. (1988). Individual unionization decisions. *Psychological Bulletin, 103,* 223–234.

Prieto, J. M. (1993). The team perspective in selection and assessment. In H. Schuler, J. L. Farr, & M. Smith (Eds.), *Personnel selection and assessment* (pp. 221–234). Hillsdale, NJ: Erlbaum.

Prince, J. B., & Lawler, E. E. (1986). Does salary discussion hurt the developmental performance appraisal. *Organizational Behavior and Human Decision Processes, 37,* 357–375.

Pritchard, R. D., DeLeo, P. J., & Von Bergen, C. W. (1976). A field experimental test of expectancy-valence incentive motivation techniques. *Organizational Behavior and Human Performance, 15,* 355–406.

Pritchard, R. D., Jones, S. D., Roth, P. L., Stuebing, K. K., & Ekeberg, S. E. (1988). Effects of group feedback, goal setting, and incentives on organizational productivity. *Journal of Applied Psychology, 73,* 337–358.

Pritchard, R. D., Leonard, D. W., Von Bergen, C. W., & Kirk, R. J. (1976). The effect of varying schedules of reinforcement on human task performance. *Organizational Behavior and Human Performance, 16,* 205–230.

Pruitt, D. G. (1993). *Negotiation in social conflict.* Pacific Grove, CA: Brooks/Cole.

Pulakos, E. D., Borman, W. C., & Hough, L. M. (1988). Test validation for scientific understanding: Two demonstrations of an approach to studying predictor-criterion linkages. *Personnel Psychology, 41,* 703–716.

Pursell, E. D., Dossett, D. L., & Latham, G. P. (1980). Obtaining valid predictors by minimizing rating errors in the criterion. *Personnel Psychology, 33,* 91–96.

Pynes, J. E., & Bernardin, H. J. (1989). Predictive validity of an entry-level police officer assessment center. *Journal of Applied Psychology, 74,* 831–833.

Quick, J. C., Murphy, L. R., Hurrell, J. J., & Orman, D. (1992). The value of work in the risk of distress and the power of prevention. In J. C. Quick, L. R. Murphy, & J. J. Hurrell (Eds.), *Stress and well-being at work* (pp. 3–13). Washington, DC: American Psychological Association.

Quinn, R. E., & Lees, P. L. (1984). Attraction and harassment: Dynamics of sexual politics in the workplace. *Organizational Dynamics, 13*(2), 36–46.

Quinones, M. A. (1995). Pretraining context effects: Training assignment as feedback. *Journal of Applied Psychology, 80,* 226–238.

Raelin, J. A. (1989). Unionization and deprofessionalization: Which comes first? *Journal of Organizational Behavior, 10,* 101–115.

Rafaeli, A., & Klimoski, R. J. (1983). Predicting sales success through handwriting analysis: An evaluation of the effects of training and handwriting sample content. *Journal of Applied Psychology, 68,* 212–217.

Ragins, B. R., & Cotton, J. L. (1991). Easier said than done: Gender differences in perceived barriers to gaining a mentor. *Academy of Management Journal, 34,* 939–951.

Ragins, B. R., & McFarlin, D. B. (1990). Perceptions of mentor roles in cross-gender mentoring relationships. *Journal of Vocational Behavior, 37,* 321–339.

Ragins, B. R., & Sundstrom, E. (1989). Gender and power in organizations. A longitudinal perspective. *Psychological Bulletin, 105,* 51–88.

Raju, N. S., Burke, M. J., Normand, J., & Langlois, G. M. (1991). A new meta-analytic approach. *Journal of Applied Psychology, 76,* 432–446.

Ralston, D. A. (1989). The benefits of flextime: Real or imagined? *Journal of Organizational Behavior, 10,* 369–374.

Rawls, J. (1971). *A theory of justice.* Cambridge, MA: Harvard University Press.

Reason, J. T. (1994). Foreword. In M. S. Bogner (Ed.), *Human error in medicine* (pp. vii–xv). Hillsdale, NJ: Erlbaum.

Reber, R. A., Wallin, J. A., & Chhokar, J. S. (1984). Reducing industrial accidents: A behavioral experiment. *Industrial Relations, 23,* 119–125.

Ree, M. J., & Earles, J. A. (1991). Predicting training success: Not much more than *g. Personnel Psychology, 44,* 321–332.

Ree, M. J., Earles, J. A., & Teachout, M. S. (1994). Predicting job performance: Not much more than *g. Journal of Applied Psychology, 79,* 518–524.

Reeves, C. A., & Bednar, D. A. (1994). Defining quality: Alternatives and implications. *Academy of Management Review, 19,* 419–445.

Reilly, R. R., Brown, B., Blood, M. R., & Malatesta, C. Z. (1981). The effects of realistic previews: A study and discussion of the literature. *Personnel Psychology, 34,* 823–834.

Repetti, R. L. (1987). Linkages between work and family roles. *Applied Social Psychology Annual, 7,* 98–127.

Reschetyuk, A. L. (1992). The working ability of aging workers. *Gerontology & Geriatrics Education, 13,* 91–102.

Rhodes, S. R., & Steers, R. M. (1990). *Managing employee absenteeism.* Reading, MA: Addison-Wesley.

Ritchie, R. J., & Moses, J. L. (1983). Assessment center correlates of women's advancement into middle management: A 7-year longitudinal analysis. *Journal of Applied Psychology, 68,* 227–231.

Robertson, I. T., Gratton, L., & Rout, U. (1990). The validity of situational interviews for administrative jobs. *Journal of Organizational Behavior, 11,* 69–76.

Robertson, I. T., & Kandola, R. S. (1982). Work sample tests: Validity, adverse impact and applicant reaction. *Journal of Occupational Psychology, 55,* 171–183.

Robertson, P. J., Roberts, D. R., & Porras, J. I. (1993). Dynamics of planned organizational change: Assessing empirical support for a theoretical model. *Academy of Management Journal, 36,* 619–634.

Robinson, S. L., Kraatz, M. S., & Rousseau, D. M. (1994). Changing obligations and the psychology contract: A longitudinal study. *Academy of Management Journal, 37,* 137–152.

Robinson, S. L., & Rousseau, D. M. (1994). Violating the psychological contract: Not the exception but the norm. *Journal of Organizational Behavior, 15,* 245–259.

Roe, R. A. (1995). Development in Eastern Europe and work and organizational psychology. In C. L. Cooper & I. T. Robertson (Eds.), *International review of industrial and organizational psychology* (pp. 275–349). Chichester: Wiley.

Roebuck, J. A. (1995). *Anthropometric methods: Designing to fit the human body.* Santa Monica, CA: Human Factors and Ergonomics Society.

Roethlisberger, F. J., & Dickson, W. J. (1939). *Management and the worker.* Cambridge, MA: Harvard University Press.

Ronan, W. W. (1963). Work group attributes and grievance activity. *Journal of Applied Psychology, 47,* 38–41.

Ronen, S. (1981). *Flexible working hours: An innovation in the quality of working life.* New York: McGraw-Hill.

Ronen, S. (1989). Training the international assignee. In I. L. Goldstein (Ed.), *Training and development in organizations* (pp. 417–454). San Francisco, CA: Jossey-Bass.

Ronen, S., & Primps, S. B. (1981). The compressed work week as organizational change: Behavioral and attitudinal outcomes. *Academy of Management Review, 6,* 61–74.

Rosen, H., & Stagner, R. (1980). Industrial/organizational psychology and unions: A viable relationship? *Professional Psychology, 11,* 477–483.

Rosenthal, R. (1991). *Meta-analytic procedures for social research* (2nd ed.). Newbury Park, CA: Sage.

Ross, R. R., & Altmaier, E. M. (1994). *Intervention in occupational stress.* London: Sage.

Rouillier, J. Z., & Goldstein, I. L. (1990). *The determination of positive transfer of training climate through organizational analysis.* Unpublished manuscript.

Rousseau, D. M. (1989). Psychological and implied contracts in organizations. *Employee Responsibilities and Rights Journal, 2,* 121–139.

Rousseau, D. M. (1995). *Psychological contracts in organizations.* Thousand Oaks, CA: Sage.

Rousseau, D. M., & Parks, J. M. (1993). The contracts of individuals and organizations. *Research in Organizational Behavior, 15,* 1–43.

Ruback, R. B., & Innes, C. A. (1988). The relevance and irrelevance of psychological research. *American Psychologist, 43,* 683–693.

Rumsey, M. G., Walker, C. B., & Harris, J. H. (Eds.) (1994). *Personnel selection and classification.* Hillsdale, NJ: Erlbaum.

Russell, C. J., Colella, A., & Bobko, P. (1993). Expanding the context of utility: The strategic impact of personnel selection. *Personnel Psychology, 46,* 781–801.

Russell, J. S. (1984). A review of fair employment cases in the field of training. *Personnel Psychology, 37,* 261–276.

Russell, J. S., & Goode, D. L. (1988). An analysis of managers' reactions to their own performance appraisal feedback. *Journal of Applied Psychology, 73,* 63–67.

Rynes, S. L., (1993). Who's selecting whom? Effects of selection practices on applicant attitudes and behavior. In N. Schmitt & W. C. Borman (Eds.), *Personnel selection in organizations* (pp. 240–274). San Francisco, CA: Jossey-Bass.

Rynes, S. L., & Milkovich, G. T. (1986). Wage surveys: Dispelling some myths about the "market wage." *Personnel Psychology, 39,* 71–90.

Rynes, S., & Rosen, B. (1995). A field survey of factors affecting the adoption and perceived success of diversity training. *Personnel Psychology, 48,* 247–270.

Saal, F. E., Downey, R. G., & Lahey, M. A. (1980). Rating the ratings: Assessing the psychometric quality of rating data. *Psychological Bulletin, 88,* 413–428.

Saari, L. M., Johnson, T. R., McLaughlin, S. D., & Zimmerle, D. M. (1988). A survey of management training and education practices in U.S. companies. *Personnel Psychology, 41,* 731–744.

Sackett, P. R., Burris, L. R., & Callahan, C. (1989). Integrity testing for personnel selection: An update. *Personnel Psychology, 42,* 491–530.

Sackett, P. R., & Harris, M. M. (1984). Honesty testing for personnel selection: A review and critique. *Personnel Psychology, 37,* 221–245.

Sackett, P. R., & Harris, M. M. (1985). Honesty testing for personnel selection: A review and critique. In H. J. Bernardin & D. A. Bownas (Eds.), *Personality assessment in organizations*. New York: Praeger.

Sackett, P. R., & Larson, J. R., Jr. (1990). Research strategies and tactics in industrial and organizational psychology. In M. D. Dunnette & L. M. Hough (Eds.), *Handbook of industrial and organizational psychology* (Vol. 1, pp. 419–489). Palo Alto, CA: Consulting Psychologists Press.

Sackett, P. R., & Mullen, E. J. (1993). Beyond formal experimental design: Towards an expanded view of the training evaluation process. *Personnel Psychology, 46,* 613–627.

Sackett, P. R., & Wilk, S. L. (1994). Within-group norming and other forms of score adjustment in pre-employment testing. *American Psychologist, 49,* 929–954.

Schaufeli, W. B., & Van Yperen, N. W. (1992). Unemployment and psychological distress among graduates: A longitudinal study. *Journal of Occupational and Organizational Psychology, 65,* 291–305.

Schippman, J. S., Prien, E. P., & Katz, J. A. (1990). Reliability and validity of in-basket performance measures. *Personnel Psychology, 43,* 837–859.

Schmidt, F. L. (1991). Why all banding procedures in personnel selection are logically flawed. *Human Performance, 4,* 265–278.

Schmidt, F. L. (1992). What do data really mean?: Research findings, meta-analysis, and cumulative knowledge in psychology. *American Psychologist, 47,* 1173–1181.

Schmidt, F. L., & Hunter, J. E. (1978). Moderator research and the law of small numbers. *Personnel Psychology, 31,* 215–232.

Schmidt, F. L., & Hunter, J. E. (1980). The future of criterion-related validity. *Personnel Psychology, 33,* 41–60.

Schmidt, F. L., & Hunter, J. E. (1995). The fatal internal contradiction in banding: Its statistical rationale is logically inconsistent with its operational procedures. *Human Performance, 8,* 203–214.

Schmidt, F. L., Hunter, J. E., McKenzie, R. C., & Muldrow, T. W. (1979). Impact of valid selection procedures on work-force productivity. *Journal of Applied Psychology, 64,* 609–626.

Schmidt, F. L., Pearlman, K., Hunter, J. E., & Hirsh, H. R. (1985). Forty questions about validity generalization and meta-analysis. *Personnel Psychology, 38,* 697–798.

Schmit, M. J., & Ryan, A. M. (1993). The big five in personnel selection: Factor structure in applicant and nonapplicant populations. *Journal of Applied Psychology, 78,* 966–974.

Schmitt, N. (1976). Social and situational determinants of interview decisions: Implications for the employment interview. *Personnel Psychology, 29,* 79–101.

Schmitt, N., Gooding, R. Z., Noe, R. D., & Kirsch, M. (1984). Meta-analyses of validity studies published between 1964 and 1982 and the investigation of study characteristics. *Personnel Psychology, 37,* 407–422.

Schmitt, N., & Landy, F. J. (1993). The concept of validity. In N. Schmitt & W. C. Borman (Eds.), *Personnel selection in organizations* (pp. 275–309). San Francisco, CA: Jossey-Bass.

Schmitt, N., & Lappin, M. (1980). Race and sex as determinants of the mean and variance of performance ratings. *Journal of Applied Psychology, 65,* 428–435.

Schneider, B., Reichers, A. E., & Mitchell, T. M. (1982). A note on some relationships between the aptitude requirements and reward attributes of tasks. *Academy of Management Journal, 25,* 567–574.

Schor, J. (1992). *The overworked American*. New York: Basic Books.

Schriesheim, C. A. (1978). Job satisfaction, attitudes toward unions, and voting in a union representation election. *Journal of Applied Psychology, 63,* 548–552.

Schuler, H. (1993). Social validity of selection situations: A concept and some empirical results. In H. Schuler, J. L. Farr, & M. Smith (Eds.), *Personnel selection and assessment* (pp. 11–26). Hillsdale, NJ: Erlbaum.

Schwab, D. P., & Wichern, D. W. (1983). Systematic bias in job evaluation and market wages: Implications for the comparable worth debate. *Journal of Applied Psychology, 68,* 60–69.

Scott, W. D. (1903). *The theory of advertising*. Boston: Small, Maynard.

Scott, W. D. (1908). *The psychology of advertising*. New York: Arno Press.

Scott, W. D. (1911a). *Increasing human efficiency in business*. New York: Macmillan.

Scott, W. D. (1911b). *Influencing men in business*. New York: Ronald Press.

Scott, W. G., Mitchell, T. R., & Birnbaum, P. H. (1981). *Organization theory: A structural and behavioral analysis*. Homewood, IL: Richard D. Irwin.

Scott, W. R. (1992). *Organizations: Rational, natural, and open systems* (3rd ed.). Englewood Cliffs, NJ: Prentice-Hall.

Seashore, S. E., Indik, B. P., & Georgopoulos, B. S. (1960). Relationships among criteria of job performance. *Journal of Applied Psychology, 44,* 195–202.

Selye, H. (1982). History and present status of the stress concept. In L. Goldberger & S. Breznitz (Eds.), *Handbook of stress* (pp. 7–17). New York: Free Press.

Senders, J. W., & Moray, N. P. (1991). *Human error: Cause, prediction, and reduction*. Hillsdale, NJ: Erlbaum.

Senge, P. (1990). *The fifth discipline: The art and practice of the learning organization*. New York: Doubleday/Currency.

Seymour, G. O., Stahl, J. M., Levine, S. L., Ingram, J. L., & Smith, R. F. (1994). Modifying law enforcement training simulators for use in basic research. *Behavior Research Methods, Instruments, & Computers, 26,* 266–268.

Sheehy, N. P., & Chapman, A. J. (1987). Industrial accidents. In C. L. Cooper & I. T. Robertson (Eds.), *Interna-*

tional review of industrial and organizational psychology (pp. 201–227). London: Wiley.

Shenkar, O. (1988). Robotics: A challenge for occupational psychology. *Journal of Occupational Psychology, 61,* 103–112.

Shore, L. M., & Tetrick, L. E. (1994). The psychological contract as an explanatory framework in the employment relationship. In C. L. Cooper & D. M. Rousseau (Eds.), *Trends in organizational behavior* (pp. 91–110). New York: Wiley.

Shore, T. H., Shore, L. M., & Thornton, G. C. (1992). Construct validity of self- and peer evaluations of performance dimensions in an assessment center. *Journal of Applied Psychology, 77,* 42–54.

Shostak, A. B. (1964). Industrial psychology and the trade unions: A matter of mutual indifference. In G. Fisk (Ed.), *The frontiers of management psychology.* New York: Harper & Row.

Silberstein, L. R. (1992). *Dual-career marriage: A system in transition.* Hillsdale, NJ: Erlbaum.

Sims, H. P., Szilagyi, A. D., & Keller, R. T. (1976). The measurement of job characteristics. *Academy of Management Journal, 19,* 195–212.

Siskin, B. R. (1995). Relation between performance and banding. *Human Performance, 8,* 215–226.

Smith, C. S., Reilly, C., & Midkiff, K. (1989). Evaluation of three circadian rhythm questionnaires with suggestions for an improved measure of morningness. *Journal of Applied Psychology, 74,* 728–738.

Smith, M. J., Cohen, H. H., Cohen, A., & Cleveland, R. J. (1978). Characteristics of successful safety programs. *Journal of Safety Research, 10,* 5–15.

Smith, M., Farr, J. L., & Schuler, H. (1993). Individual and organizational perspectives on personnel procedures: Conclusions and horizons for future research. In H. Schuler, J. L. Farr, & M. Smith (Eds.), *Personnel selection and assessment* (pp. 333–351). Hillsdale, NJ: Erlbaum.

Smith, P. C., & Kendall, L. M. (1963). Retranslation of expectations: An approach to the construction of unambiguous anchors for rating scales. *Journal of Applied Psychology, 47,* 149–155.

Smither, J. W. (1995). Creating an internal contingent workforce: Managing the resource link. In M. London (Ed.), *Employees, careers, and job creation* (pp. 142–164). San Francisco: Jossey-Bass.

Smither, J. W., Reilly, R. R., Millsap, R. E., & Pearlman, K. (1993). Applicant reactions to selection procedures. *Personnel Psychology, 46,* 49–76.

Society for Industrial and Organizational Psychology, Inc. (1987). *Principles for the validation and use of personnel selection procedures* (3rd ed.). College Park, MD: Author.

Soine, L. (1995). Sick building syndrome and gender bias: Imperiling women's health. *Social Work in Health Care, 20,* 51–65.

Spector, P. E. (1992). A consideration of the validity and meaning of self-report measures of job conditions. In C. L. Cooper & I. T. Robertson (Eds.), *International review of industrial and organizational psychology* (pp. 123–151). London: Wiley.

Spector, P. E., Brannick, M. T., & Coovert, M. D. (1989). Job analysis. In C. L. Cooper & I. T. Robertson (Eds.), *International review of industrial and organizational psychology* (pp. 281–328). London: Wiley.

Spector, P. E., & Jex, S. M. (1991). Relations of job characteristics from multiple data sources with employee affect, absence, turnover interventions, and health. *Journal of Applied Psychology, 76,* 46–53.

Spettell, C. M., & Liebert, R. M. (1986). Training for safety in automated person-machine systems. *American Psychologist, 41,* 545–550.

Spool, M. D. (1978). Training programs for observers of behavior: A review. *Personnel Psychology, 31,* 853–888.

Stagner, R. (1981). Training and experiences of some distinguished industrial psychologists. *American Psychologist, 36,* 497–505.

Stagner, R. (1982). Past and future of industrial/organizational psychology. *Professional Psychology, 13,* 892–903.

Stagner, R., & Effal, B. (1982). Internal union dynamics during a strike: A quasi-experimental study. *Journal of Applied Psychology, 67,* 37–44.

Stagner, R., & Rosen, H. (1965). *Psychology of union-management relations.* Belmont, CA: Wadsworth.

Stahelski, A. J., Frost, D. E., & Patch, M. E. (1989). Use of socially dependent bases of power: French and Raven's theory applied to workgroup leadership. *Journal of Applied Psychology, 19,* 283–297.

Stahl, M. J., & Harrell, A. M. (1981). Modeling effort decisions with behavioral decision theory: Toward an individual differences model of expectancy theory. *Organizational Behavior and Human Performance, 27,* 303–325.

Starke, F. A., & Notz, W. W. (1981). Pre- and post-intervention effects of conventional versus final offer arbitration. *Academy of Management Journal, 24,* 832–850.

Steel, R. P., & Ovalle, N. K. (1984). Self-appraisal based upon supervisory feedback. *Personnel Psychology, 37,* 667–686.

Stein, J. A., Newcomb, M. D., & Bentler, P. M. (1988). Structure of drug use behaviors and consequences among young adults: Multitrait-multimethod assessment of frequency, quantity, work site, and problem substance abuse. *Journal of Applied Psychology, 73,* 595–605.

Stellman, J. M., Klitzman, S., Gordon, G. C., & Snow, B. R. (1987). Work environment and the well-being of clerical and VDT workers. *Journal of Occupational Behavior, 8,* 95–114.

Stenberg, B., & Wall, S. (1995). Why do women report "sick building symptoms" more often than men? *Social Science and Medicine, 40,* 491–502.

Sternberg, R. J. (1995). A triarchic view of cognitive resources and leadership performance. *Applied Psychology: An International Review, 44,* 29–32.

Sternberg, R. J., Wagner, R. K., Williams, W. W., & Horvath, J. A. (1995). Testing common sense. *American Psychologist, 50,* 912–927.

Stevens, S. (1958). Problems and methods of psychophysics. *Psychological Bulletin, 55,* 177–196.

Stokes, G. S., Mumford, M. D., & Owens, W. A. (Eds.) (1994). *Biodata handbook: Theory, research, and use of biographical information in selection and performance prediction.* Palo Alto, CA: Consulting Psychologists Press.

Stone, D. L., & Kotch, D. A. (1989). Individuals' attitudes toward organizational drug testing policies and practices. *Journal of Applied Psychology, 74,* 518–521.

Strasser, S., & Bateman, T. S. (1984). What we should study, problems we should solve: Perspectives of two constituencies. *Personnel Psychology, 37,* 77–92.

Streufert, S., Pogash, R. M., Roache, J., Gingrich, D., Landis, R., Severs, W., Lonardi, L., & Kantner, A. (1992). Effects of alcohol intoxication on risk taking, strategy, and error rate in visuomotor performance. *Journal of Applied Psychology, 77,* 515–524.

Sulsky, L. M., & Balzer, W. K. (1988). Meaning and measurement of performance rating accuracy: Some methodological and theoretical concerns. *Journal of Applied Psychology, 73,* 497–506.

Sulsky, L. M., & Day, D. V. (1992). Frame-of-reference training and cognitive categorization: An empirical investigation of rater memory issues. *Journal of Applied Psychology, 77,* 501–510.

Summers, T. P., Betton, J. H., & DeCotiis, T. A. (1986). Voting for and against unions: A decision model. *Academy of Management Review, 11,* 643–655.

Sundstrom, E., Town, J. P., Rice, R. W., & Osborn, D. P. (1994). Office noise, satisfaction, and performance. *Environment & Behavior, 26,* 195–222.

Sussman, M., & Robertson, D. U. (1986). The validity of validity: An analysis of validation study designs. *Journal of Applied Psychology, 71,* 461–468.

Sutton, R. I., & Kahn, R. L. (1987). Prediction, understanding, and control as antidotes to organizational stress. In J. W. Lorsch (Ed.), *Handbook of organizational behavior.* Englewood Cliffs, NJ: Prentice-Hall.

Sweetland, R. C., & Keyser, D. J. (Eds.) (1991). *Tests: A comprehensive reference for assessments in psychology, education, and business* (3rd ed.). Kansas City, MO: Test Corporation of America.

Taber, T. D., & Taylor, E. (1990). A review and evaluation of the psychometric properties of the Job Diagnostic Survey. *Personnel Psychology, 43,* 467–500.

Tangri, S. S., Burt, M. R., & Johnson, L. B. (1982). Sexual harassment at work: Three explanatory models. *Journal of Social Issues, 38*(4), 33–54.

Tannenbaum, S. I., & Yukl, G. (1992). Training and development in work organizations. *Annual Review of Psychology, 43,* 399–441.

Task Force on the Practice of Psychology in Industry. (1971). Effective practice of psychology in industry. *American Psychologist, 26,* 974–991.

Taylor, C. W., Price, P. B., Richards, J. M., & Jacobsen, T. L. (1964). An investigation of the criterion problem for a medical school faculty. *Journal of Applied Psychology, 48,* 294–301.

Taylor, C. W., Price, P. B., Richards, J. M., & Jacobsen, T. L. (1965). An investigation of the criterion problem for a group of medical general practitioners. *Journal of Applied Psychology, 49,* 339–406.

Taylor, F. W. (1911). *The principles of scientific management.* New York: Harper.

Taylor, L. R. (1978). Empirically derived job families as a foundation for the study of validity generalization: The construction of job families based on the component and overall dimensions of the PAQ. *Personnel Psychology, 31,* 325–340.

Taylor, T. O., Friedman, D. J., & Couture, D. (1987). Operating without supervisors: An experiment. *Organizational Dynamics, 15*(3), 26–38.

Tenopyr, M. L. (1981). The realities of employment testing. *American Psychologist, 36,* 1120–1127.

Tepas, D. I. (1993). Educational programmes for shiftworkers, their families, and prospective shiftworkers. *Ergonomics, 36,* 199–209.

Tetrick, L. E. (1995). Developing and maintaining union commitment: A theoretical framework. *Journal of Organizational Behavior, 16,* 583–595.

Tett, R. P., Jackson, D. N., & Rothstein, M. (1991). Personality measures as predictors of job performance: A meta-analytic review. *Personnel Psychology, 44,* 703–742.

Thacker, J. W., Fields, M. W., & Barclay, L. A. (1990). Union commitment: An examination of antecedent and outcome factors. *Journal of Occupational Psychology, 63,* 33–48.

Thacker, J. W., Fields, M. W., & Tetrick, L. E. (1989). The factor structure of union commitment. An application of confirmatory factor analysis. *Journal of Applied Psychology, 74,* 228–232.

Tharenou, P., Latimer, S., & Conroy, D. (1994). How do you make it to the top? An examination of influences on women's and men's managerial advancement. *Academy of Management Journal, 37,* 899–931.

Thierry, H., & Meijman, T. (1994). Time and behavior at work. In H. C. Triandis, M. D. Dunnette, & L. M. Hough (Eds.), *Handbook of industrial and organizational psychology* (Vol. 4, pp. 341–413). Palo Alto, CA: Consulting Psychologists Press.

Thomas, D. A. (1990). The impact of race on managers' experiences of developmental relationships (mentorship and sponsorship): An intra-organizational study. *Journal of Organizational Behavior, 11,* 479–492.

Thomas, D. A. (1993). Racial dynamics in cross-race developmental relationships. *Administrative Science Quarterly, 38,* 169–194.

Thomas, J. L. (1992). Occupational violent crime: Research on an emerging issue. *Journal of Safety Research, 23,* 55–62.

Thomas, K. W., & Tymon, W. G., Jr. (1982). Necessary properties of relevant research: Lessons from recent criticisms of the organizational sciences. *Academy of Management Review, 7,* 345–352.

Thomas, L. T., & Ganster, D. C. (1995). Impact of family-supportive work variables on work-family conflict and strain: A control perspective. *Journal of Applied Psychology, 80,* 6–15.

Thompson, D. E., & Thompson, T. A. (1982). Court standards for job analysis in test validation. *Personnel Psychology, 35,* 865–874.

Thornton, G. C., III. (1980). Psychometric properties of self-appraisals of job performance. *Personnel Psychology, 33,* 263–272.

Tornow, W. W. (1993). Perceptions or reality: Is multiperspective measurement a means or an end? *Human Resource Management, 32,* 221–230.

Totterdell, P., Spelten, E., Smith, L., Barton, J., & Folkard, S. (1995). Recovering from work shifts: How long does it take? *Journal of Applied Psychology, 80,* 43–57.

Tracey, J. B., Tannenbaum, S. I., & Kavanagh, M. J. (1995). Applying trained skills on the job: The importance of the work environment. *Journal of Applied Psychology, 80,* 239–252.

Triandis, H. C. (1975). Culture training, cognitive complexity, and interpersonal attitudes. In R. Brislin, S. Bochner, & W. Lonner (Eds.), *Cross-cultural perspectives on learning* (pp. 39–77). Beverly Hills, CA: Sage.

Triandis, H. C. (1994). Cross-cultural industrial and organizational psychology. In H. C. Triandis, M. D. Dunnette, & L. M. Hough (Eds.), *Handbook of industrial and organizational psychology* (Vol. 4, pp. 103–172). Palo Alto, CA: Consulting Psychologists Press.

Triandis, H. C., Kurowski, L. L., & Gelfand, M. J. (1994). Workplace diversity. In H. C. Triandis, M. D. Dunnette, & L. M. Hough (Eds.), *Handbook of industrial and organizational psychology* (Vol. 4, pp. 769–827). Palo Alto, CA: Consulting Psychologists Press.

Trice, H. M., & Sonnenstuhl, W. J. (1988). Drinking behavior and risk factors related to the work place: Implications for research and practice. *Journal of Applied Behavioral Science, 24,* 327–346.

Tubbs, M. E. (1986). Goal setting: A meta-analytic examination of the empirical evidence. *Journal of Applied Psychology, 71,* 474–483.

Turnage, J. J. (1990). The challenge of new workplace technology for psychology. *American Psychologist, 45,* 171–178.

Turnage, J. J., & Muchinsky, P. M. (1984). A comparison of the predictive validity of assessment center evaluations versus traditional measures in forecasting supervisory job performance: Interpretive implications of criterion distortion for the assessment paradigm. *Journal of Applied Psychology, 69,* 595–602.

Turner, A. N., & Lawrence, P. R. (1965). *Industrial jobs and the worker: An investigation of response to task attributes.* Cambridge, MA: Harvard University Press.

Tyson, P. R., & Vaughn, R. A. (1987, April). Drug testing in the work place: Legal responsibilities. *Occupational Health and Safety,* 24–36.

Tziner, A., & Dolan, S. (1982). Validity of an assessment center for identifying future female officers in the military. *Journal of Applied Psychology, 67,* 728–736.

U.S. Department of Labor. (1994). *Apprenticeship: Past and present.* Washington, DC: Government Printing Office.

U.S. Department of Labor, Employment, and Training Administration. (1991). *Dictionary of occupational titles* (4th ed.). Washington, DC: Government Printing Office.

Vaill, P. (1982). The purposing of high-performing systems. *Organizational Dynamics, 2*(2), 23–39.

Vandenberg, R. J., & Scarpello, V. (1990). The matching model: An examination of the processes underlying realistic job previews. *Journal of Applied Psychology, 75,* 60–67.

Van der Spiegel, J. (1995). New information technologies and changes in work. In A. Howard (Ed.), *The changing nature of work* (pp. 97–111). San Francisco, CA: Jossey-Bass.

Van der Veen, G., & Klandermans, B. (1995). Introduction to special issue on union commitment. *Journal of Organizational Behavior, 16,* 503–504.

Van Dyne, L., Graham, J. W., & Dienesch, R. M. (1994). Organizational citizenship behavior: Construct redefinition, measurement, and validation. *Academy of Management Journal, 37,* 765–802.

Van Velsor, E., Ruderman, M. N., & Young, D. P. (1991). *Enhancing self objectivity and performance on the job: The role of upward feedback.* Paper presented at Sixth Annual Conference of the Society of Industrial and Organizational Psychology, St. Louis, MO.

Varca, P. E., & Pattison, P. (1993). Evidentiary standards in employment discrimination: A view toward the future. *Personnel Psychology, 46,* 239–258.

Vecchio, R. P. (1990). Theoretical and empirical examination of cognitive resource theory. *Journal of Applied Psychology, 75,* 141–147.

Vetter, H. J. (1969). *Language behavior and communication.* Itasca, IL: F. E. Peacock.

Viano, D. C., Lau, I. V., Asbury, C., & King, A. I. (1989). Biomechanics of the human chest, abdomen, and pelvis in lateral impact. *Accident Analysis and Prevention, 21,* 553–574.

Vickroy, S. C., Shaw, J. B., & Fisher, C. D. (1982). Effects of temperature, clothing, and task complexity on task performance and satisfaction. *Journal of Applied Psychology, 67,* 97–102.

Vinokur, A. D., Threatt, B. A., Vinokur-Caplan, D., & Satariano, W. A. (1990). The process of recovering from breast cancer in younger and older patients. *Cancer, 65,* 1242–1254.

Visweswaran, C. & Schmidt, F. L. (1992). A meta-analytic comparison of the effectiveness of smoking cessation methods. *Journal of Applied Psychology, 77,* 554–566.

Viteles, M. S. (1932). *Industrial psychology.* New York: W. W. Norton.

Voevodsky, J. (1974). Evaluation of a deceleration warning light for reducing rear end automobile collisions. *Journal of Applied Psychology, 59,* 270–273.

Vroom, V. H. (1964). *Work and motivation.* New York: Wiley.

Wagner, R. K., & Sternberg, R. J. (1990). Street smarts. In K. E. Clark & M. B. Clark (Eds.), *Measures of leadership* (pp. 493–504). West Orange, NJ: Leadership Library of America.

Wahba, M. A., & Bridwell, L. T. (1976). Maslow reconsidered. A review of research on the need hierarchy theory. *Organizational Behavior and Human Performance, 15,* 212–240.

Wallace, S. R. (1965). Criteria for what? *American Psychologist, 20,* 411–417.

Wang, Z. (1993). Editorial: Strategies for ergonomics in developing countries. *Ergonomics, 36,* 597–599.

Wanous, J. P. (1989). Installing a realistic job preview: Ten tough choices. *Personnel Psychology, 42,* 117–134.

Wanous, J. P., Sullivan, S. E., & Malinak, J. (1989). The role of judgment calls in meta-analysis. *Journal of Applied Psychology, 74,* 259–264.

Warr, P. B. (1987). *Work, unemployment, and mental health.* Oxford: Clarendon.

Warr, P. B., & Jackson, P. R. (1985). Factors influencing the psychological impact of prolonged unemployment and of re-employment. *Psychological Medicine, 15,* 795–807.

Warr, P. B., & Payne, R. L. (1983). Social class and reported changes in behavior after job loss. *Journal of Applied Social Psychology, 13,* 206–222.

Webster, J., & Starbuck, W. H. (1988). Theory building in industrial and organizational psychology. In C. L. Cooper & I. T. Robertson (Eds.), *International review of industrial and organizational psychology* (pp. 93–138). London: Wiley.

Wedderburn, A. A. (1978). Some suggestions for increasing the usefulness of psychological and sociological studies of shiftwork. *Ergonomics, 21,* 827–833.

Weekley, J. A., & Gier, J. A. (1989). Ceilings in the reliability and validity of performance ratings: The case of expert raters. *Academy of Management Journal, 32,* 213–222.

Weiss, D. J., & Vale, C. D. (1987). Adaptive testing. *Applied Psychology: An International Review, 36,* 249–262.

Weiss, H. M. (1990). Learning theory and industrial and organizational psychology. In M. D. Dunnette, & L. M. Hough (Eds.), *Handbook of industrial and organizational psychology* (Vol. 1, pp. 171–221). Palo Alto, CA: Consulting Psychologists Press.

Weitz, J. (1961). Critria for criteria. *American Psychologist, 16,* 228–231.

Wernimont, P. F., & Campbell, J. P. (1968). Signs, samples, and criteria. *Journal of Applied Psychology, 52,* 372–376.

Westin, A. F. (1992). Two key factors that belong in a macroergonomic analysis of electronic monitoring: Employee perceptions of fairness and the climate of organizational trust or distrust. *Applied Ergonomics, 23,* 35–42.

Wherry, R. J. (1957). The past and future of criterion evaluation. *Personnel Psychology, 10,* 1–5.

Whetten, D. A., & Cameron, K. S. (1991). *Developing management skills* (2nd ed.). New York: Harper Collins.

White, L. P., & Wooten, K. C. (1983). Ethical dilemmas in various stages of organizational development. *Academy of Management Review, 8,* 690–697.

White, L. P., & Wooten, K. C. (1986). *Professional ethics and practice in organizational development.* New York: Praeger.

Wigdor, A. K., & Sackett, P. R. (1993). Employment testing and public policy: The case of the General Aptitude Test Battery. In H. Schuler, J. L. Farr, & M. Smith (Eds.), *Personnel selection and assessment* (pp. 183–204). Hillsdale, NJ: Erlbaum.

Williams, C. R., & Livingstone, L. P. (1994). Another look at the relationship between performance and voluntary turnover. *Academy of Management Journal, 37,* 269–298.

Williams, L. K., Seybolt, J. W., & Pinder, C. C. (1975). On administering questionnaires in organizational settings. *Personnel Psychology, 28,* 93–103.

Wilpert, B. (1995). Organizational behavior. *Annual Review of Psychology, 46,* 59–90.

Winefield, A. H. (1995). Unemployment: Its psychological costs. In C. L. Cooper & I. T. Robertson (Eds.), *International review of industrial and organizational psychology* (Vol. 10, pp. 169–212). Chichester: Wiley.

Winefield, A. H., & Tiggemann, M. (1990). Employment status and psychological well-being: A longitudinal study. *Journal of Applied Psychology, 75,* 455–459.

Winefield, A. H., Tiggemann, M., & Winefield, H. R. (1992). Unemployment distress, reasons for job loss and causal attributions for unemployment in young people. *Journal of Occupational and Organizational Psychology, 65,* 213–218.

Woehr, D. J. (1994). Understanding frame-of-reference training: The impact of training on the recall of performance information. *Journal of Applied Psychology, 79,* 524–534.

Woehr, D. J., & Huffcutt, A. I. (1994). Rater training for performance appraisal: A quantitative review. *Journal of Occupational and Organizational Psychology, 67,* 189–205.

Wong, C., & Campion, M. A. (1991). Development and test of a task level model of motivational job design. *Journal of Applied Psychology, 76*, 825–837.

Wright, L. (1988). The Type A behavior pattern and coronary artery disease: Quest for the active ingredients and the elusive mechanism. *American Psychologist, 43*, 2–14.

Wright, P. M. (1990). Operationalization of goal difficulty as a moderator of the goal difficulty–performance relationship. *Journal of Applied Psychology, 75*, 227–234.

Youngblood, S. A., DeNisi, A. S., Molleston, J. L., & Mobley, W. H. (1984). The impact of work environment, instrumentality beliefs, perceived labor union image, and subjective norms on union voting intentions. *Academy of Management Journal, 17*, 576–590.

Yukl, G. (1989a). *Leadership in organizations* (2nd ed.). Englewood Cliffs, NJ: Prentice-Hall.

Yukl, G. (1989b). Managerial leadership: A review of theory and research. *Journal of Management, 15*, 251–289.

Yukl, G. (1994). *Leadership in organizations* (3rd ed.). Englewood Cliffs, NJ: Prentice-Hall.

Yukl, G., & Falbe, C. M. (1991). The importance of different power sources in downward and lateral relations. *Journal of Applied Psychology, 76*, 416–423.

Yukl, G. A., & Latham, G. P. (1975). Consequences of reinforcement schedules and incentive magnitudes for employee performance: Problems encountered in an industrial setting. *Journal of Applied Psychology, 60*, 294–298.

Yukl, G. A., Latham, G. P., & Pursell, E. D. (1976). The effectiveness of performance incentives under continuous and variable ratio schedules of reinforcement. *Personnel Psychology, 29*, 221–232.

Yukl, G., & Tracey, J. B. (1992). Consequences of influence tactics used with subordinates, peers, and bosses. *Journal of Applied Psychology, 77*, 525–535.

Yukl, G., & Van Fleet, D. D. (1992). Theory and research on leadership in organizations. In M. D. Dunnette & L. M. Hough (Eds.), *Handbook of industrial and organizational psychology* (Vol. 3, pp. 147–197). Palo Alto, CA: Consulting Psychologists Press.

Yukl, G., Wall, S., & Lepsinger, R. (1990). Preliminary report on validation of the management practices survey. In K. E. Clark & M. B. Clark (Eds.), *Measures of leadership* (pp. 223–238). West Orange, NJ: Leadership Library of America.

Zaharia, E. S., & Baumeister, A. A. (1981). Job preview effects during the critical initial employment period. *Journal of Applied Psychology, 66*, 19–22.

Zalesny, M. D. (1985). Comparison of economic and noneconomic factors in predicting faculty vote preference in a union representation election. *Journal of Applied Psychology, 70*, 243–256.

Zedeck, S. (1992). Introduction: Exploring the domain of work and family careers. In S. Zedeck (Ed.), *Work, families, and organizations* (pp. 1–32). San Francisco: Jossey-Bass.

Zedeck, S., & Cascio, W. F. (1982). Performance appraisal decisions as a function of rater training and purpose of the appraisal. *Journal of Applied Psychology, 67*, 752–758.

Zedeck, S., Jackson, S. E., & Summers, E. (1983). Shift work schedules and their relationship to health, adaptation, satisfaction, and turnover intention. *Academy of Management Journal, 26*, 297–310.

Zedeck, S., Outtz, J., Cascio, W. F., & Goldstein, I. L. (1995). Why do "testing experts" have such limited vision? *Human Performance, 8*, 179–190.

Zedeck, S., Tziner, A., & Middlestadt, S. E. (1983). Interviewer validity and reliability: An individual analysis approach. *Personnel Psychology, 36*, 355–370.

Zeidner, J., & Johnson, C. D. (1994). Is personnel classification a concept whose time has passed? In M. G. Rumsey, C. B. Walker, & J. H. Harris (Eds.), *Personnel selection and classification* (pp. 377–410). Hillsdale, NJ: Erlbaum.

Zohar, D. (1980). Safety climate in industrial organizations. Theoretical and applied implications. *Journal of Applied Psychology, 65*, 96–102.

Name
Index

Subject Index

Ability, 328. *See also* Testing; Work motivation
Absenteeism, 83–84, 219–220
Accidents, 84, 220
Achievement, 362, 371
Across-subjects design, 341
Action control, 351–352
Actual criteria, 63–66
Actuarial prediction, 460
ADA (Americans with Disabilities Act), 20, 136, 194
Adaptability, 486
Adverse impact, 134–135, 163–164
Affect, 368
Affective well-being, 302
Affiliation, need for, 362
Affirmative action, 151–153
Agreeableness, 281
Albemarle v. Moody, 135
Alcoholism. *See* Substance abuse
Alienation, 249
Altruism, 281
American Arbitration Association (AAA), 430
American Psychological Association (APA), 4–5, 10, 13
American Psychological Society (APS), 4–5
Americans with Disabilities Act (ADA), 20, 136, 194
Anthropometric approach, 451–452
APA (American Psychological Association), 4–5, 10, 13
Applicability, 129
Apprenticeship, 185, 444
Arbitration, 429–430

Armed Services Vocational Aptitude Battery (ASVAB), 20–21, 110
Army Alpha test, 14, 100
Army Beta test, 14, 100
Army General Classification Test (AGCT), 17–18
Aspiration, 302–303
Assessment. *See* Predictors
Assessment center evaluations, 116–119
Attitude change programs, 194–195
Audiovisual training materials, 186–187
Authority, 358
Autonomy, 302, 392

Bakke v. University of California, 135–136
Banding, 162–163
BARS (Behaviorally anchored rating scales), 229–230
Base rate, 157–158
Behavior, 327. *See also* Organizational behavior; Work motivation
Behavioral approach to leadership, 357, 363–365
Behavioral change approach to diversity training, 195
Behavioral checklists and scales, 227–232
Behaviorally anchored rating scales (BARS), 229–230
Behavioral-observation scales (BOS), 230–232
Bell-shaped distribution, 38, 40

Bennett Test of Mechanical Comprehension, 103–104, 105
Bias, 65, 80–81
Big 5 personality theory, 107, 281, 349
Biographical information, 121–122, 123
Biomechanical approach, 452–454
BOS (Behavioral-observation scales), 230–232
Bureau of Salesmanship Research, 15
Bush, George, 20, 137

CAI (Computer-assisted instruction), 188–190
Career counseling. *See* Vocational/ career counseling
Case studies
  criteria, 89–90
  leadership, 383–384
  mental health, 324–325
  organizational behavior, 297–298
  organization development, 417–418
  performance appraisal, 240–241
  personnel decisions, 172–173
  predictors, 131–132
  research methods, 56–57
  training/development, 210–211
  unions, 446–447
  working conditions, 481–482
  work motivation, 353–354
  work teams, 271–272
Central-tendency errors, 224–225
Central-tendency measures, 39–41
Certification laws, 9

Training validity, 207
Trait approach to leadership, 361–362
Transfer of training, 184
Transfer validity, 207
Transformational leadership, 373–374, 375
Turnover, 83, 220, 292–294
Type A behavior, 310

Underload, 390
Unemployment, 319–323. *See also* Downsizing
Unions, 8, 421–447
    case study, 446–447
    collective bargaining, 426–437
    definitions, 422–423
    dispute settlement research, 441–442
    and employee involvement, 444–445
    employee support for, 438–439, 442–443
    formation, 424–426
    influence of, 439–441
    and nonunionized companies, 437–438
    as organizations, 423–424
    and personnel selection, 443–444
    and training/development, 444

Valences, 338
Validity, 94–98, 129. *See also specific measures and topics*

interviews, 114–115
personnel decisions, 137–138, 145–148
Validity coefficient, 95
Validity generalization, 146–148
Values, 415, 492–494. *See also* Ethical issues
Variability, 42–44
Variables, 34–37. *See also* Predictors
Vestibule training, 184
Video display terminals (VDTs), 455–456
Videotape, 186–187
Vigilance, 472
Violence, 294–296
Vision, 409–410
Vocational/career counseling, 8
Vocational guidance placement strategy, 171
Voluntary arbitration, 430

Wages. *See* Compensation
Wards Cove Packing Company v. Atonio, 137
Weighted checklists, 228–229
Well-being. *See* Mental health
Wet-bulb globe temperature (WBGT), 469
Will to achieve, 350
Wind chill, 470–471
Within-subjects design, 341
Women. *See* Gender
Work diaries, 71

Work/family interaction, 23, 312–319
    dual-career families, 318–319
    and flextime, 478–479
Working conditions
    case study, 481–482
    changes in, 488–491
    computer use, 455–457
    ergonomics, 8, 449–456
    safety issues, 457–466
    schedules, 473–479
    and stress, 305–312, 466–473
    substance abuse, 479–481
Work motivation, 327–354. *See also* Job design
    case study, 353–354
    definitions, 327–328
    equity theory, 332–337, 350–351
    expectancy theory, 338–342, 351
    genetics-based theories, 349–350
    goal-setting theory, 345–349, 351
    and leadership, 379
    need hierarchy theory, 329–332, 350
    reinforcement theory, 343–345, 346, 351
    theory synthesis, 349–353
Work samples, 119–120
Work slowdowns, 432
Work teams, 266–272, 412, 489–490
World War I, 13–15
World War II, 17–18, 172

Optional:

Your name: _____ Date: _____

May Brooks/Cole quote you, either in promotion for *Psychology Applied to Work: An Introduction to Industrial and Organizational Psychology,* Fifth Edition, or in future publishing ventures?

Yes: _____ No: _____

Sincerely,

Paul Muchinsky

FOLD HERE

FOLD HERE

TO THE OWNER OF THIS BOOK:

I hope that you have found *Psychology Applied to Work: An Introduction to Industrial and Organizational Psychology,* Fifth Edition, useful. So that this book can be improved in a future edition, would you take the time to complete this sheet and return it? Thank you.

School and address: _____

Department: _____

Instructor's name: _____

1. What I like most about this book is: _____

_____

_____

2. What I like least about this book is: _____

_____

_____

3. My general reaction to this book is: _____

_____

4. The name of the course in which I used this book is: _____

_____

5. Were all of the chapters of the book assigned for you to read? _____

   If not, which ones weren't? _____

6. In the space below, or on a separate sheet of paper, please write specific suggestions for improving this book and anything else you'd care to share about your experience in using the book.

_____

_____

_____

_____

_____